The Cash Nexus

ALSO BY NIALL FERGUSON

The Pity of War

Virtual History: Alternatives and Counterfactuals (editor)

The House of Rothschild

Paper and Iron: Hamburg Business and German Politics in the Era of Inflation, 1897–1927

NIALL FERGUSON

The Cash Nexus

MONEY AND POWER IN THE
MODERN WORLD, 1700-2000

Member of the Perseus Books Group
New York

Published by Basic Books
A Member of the Perseus Books Group

A Cataloging-in-Publication record for this book is available from the Library of Congress.

ISBN 0-465-02325-8 (cloth); ISBN 0-465-02326-6 (pbk.)
ISBN 978-0-795-02326-4
EBA   10 9 8 7

For Mary and May

In these complicated times . . . Cash Payment is the sole nexus between man and man . . . Cash Payment the sole nexus; and there are so many things which cash will not pay! Cash is a great miracle; yet it has not all power in Heaven, nor even on Earth. . . .

THOMAS CARLYLE, *Chartism* (1840)

The Gospel of Mammonism . . . has also its corresponding heaven. For there *is* one Reality among so many Phantasms; about one thing we are entirely in earnest: The making of money. . . . We have profoundly forgotten everywhere that *Cash-payment* is not the sole relation of human beings.

THOMAS CARLYLE, *Past and Present* (1843)

The bourgeoisie . . . has left remaining no other nexus between man and man than naked self-interest, than callous 'cash payment'.

MARX AND ENGELS, *The Communist Manifesto* (1848)

We are told by men of science that all the venture of mariners on the sea, all that counter-marching tribes and races that confounds all history with its dust and rumour, sprang from nothing more abstruse than the laws of supply and demand, and a certain natural instinct for cheap rations. To any one thinking deeply, this will seem a dull and pitiful explanation.

ROBERT LOUIS STEVENSON, *"Will o' the Mill"* (1978)

Contents

List of Tables

Appendices

List of Figures

List of Illustrations

Photographic acknowledgments, where applicable: Andrew Edmunds: 1, 2; Bridgeman Art Library: 6; Fotomas Index: 3, 4, 7, 8, 10, 14; Mary Evans Picture Library: 9, 11, 12.

Acknowledgments

This book would not have come into existence without the generosity of the Trustees of the Houblon-Norman Fund at the Bank of England, whose financial support allowed me to spend a year of full-time research at the Bank.

As an historian venturing into economists' territory, I was especially grateful to Mervyn King, Charles Goodhart and John Vickers for their encouragement and advice throughout my times in Threadneedle Street. I should also like to thank Bill Allen, Spencer Dale, Stephen Millard, Katherine Neiss, Nick Oulton, Andrew Scott, Paul Tucker and Tony Yates. In the Information Centre, I was greatly assisted by Howard Picton and Kath Begley; and in the Archive Henry Gillett and Sarah Millard were always ready to answer my questions, no matter how obscure. Last, but most certainly not least, Hilary Clark, Sandra Dufuss, Chris Jewson and Margot Wilson provided first-class secretarial support.

The corollary of my year at the Bank was my absence from Jesus College, Oxford. I am particularly grateful to Dr. Jan Palmowski for so ably taking over my tutorial and other responsibilities; as well as to my colleague Dr. Felicity Heal, whose life was not made easier by my absence. I would also like to thank the Principal and Fellows of Jesus for granting me special leave, not least Peter Clarke and Peter Mirfield, who punctiliously dealt with the financial arrangements. The book was largely written after I returned to Jesus, and I should like to express my gratitude to all the staff at the College who in their various ways made the task easier, especially Vivien Bowyer and Robert Haynes.

Some parts of this book originated in collaborative work. I am especially indebted to Glen O'Hara, who provided substantial assistance with Chapter 8. My roommate at the Bank, Laurence Kotlikoff, introduced me to generational accounting and tried to improve my economics; his influence is most apparent in Chapters 7 and 11. I would also like to thank Brigitte Granville and Richard Batley, with whom I co-wrote academic articles on related subjects while I was working on the book, and whose influence is discernible here too. Daniel Fattal was indefatigable in gathering statistics and quotations from *The Economist,* while Thomas Fleuriot hunted down elusive references with equal zeal.

Special thanks are due to Mike Bordo, Forrest Capie, Charles Goodhart and Harold James, all of whom generously took time to look at the entire manuscript in draft, and saved me from numerous errors. Benjamin Friedman and Barry Weingast also read sections of the manuscript and offered penetrating criticism.

My first stab at the history of the bond market was given an airing at the opening conference of the Yale School of Management's International Center for Finance; thanks are due to William Goetzmann and Geert Rouwenhorst for inviting me to participate, as well as to those who offered comments and suggestions. A part of Chapter 11 was presented at N. M. Rothschild & Sons during the June 1999 FT Gold Conference; I am grateful to Sir Evelyn de Rothschild and Sir Derek Taylor for their invitation to speak. Fareed Zakaria encouraged me to put EMU into historical perspective for *Foreign Affairs;* he will see how that argument developed in the later sections of Chapter 11. Some of Chapter 12 originated in a paper given at the conference on social science and the future held in Oxford in July 1999; I should like to thank Richard Cooper, Graham Ingham and Richard Layard for their invitation to participate in the conference, and all those present for their comments, particularly Lord Lipsey. Chapter 13 made an appearance in draft at a Stanford History Department seminar; I am grateful to Norman Naimark and his colleagues for their hospitality.

I would also like to thank for miscellaneous comments and information: Lord Baker, Sir Samuel Brittan, Phil Cottrell, Eugene Dattel, Lance Davis, Luca Einaudi, Walter Eltis, Campbell and Molly Ferguson, Marc Flandreau, John Flemming, Christian Gleditsch, Michael Hughes, Paul Kennedy, Jan Tore Klovland, David Landes, Ronald McKinnon, Ranald Michie, Paul Mills, Larry Neal, Patrick O'Brien, Avner Offer, Richard Roberts, Hugh Rockoff, Emma Rothschild, Lord Saatchi, Norman Stone, Martin Thomas, François Velde, Joachim Voth, Digby Waller, Michael Ward, Eugene White, David Womersley, Geoffrey Wood and J. F. Wright.

I owe a huge debt to Simon Winder and Don Fehr, my editors, who labored long and hard to improve the original manuscript. Thanks are also due to Clare Alexander, my agent, and Elizabeth Stratford, my copy-editor.

Most of my references are to published articles and books, rather than to original documents, with a very few exceptions. Leopold I's letter to Queen Victoria of 19 September 1840 is quoted with the gracious permission of Her Majesty the Queen. I would also like to thank Sir Evelyn de Rothschild for permission to quote from documents in the Rothschild Archive.

Finally, to Susan, Felix, Freya and Lachlan I can offer only an apology for all the sins of omission and commission perpetrated by the author during the writing of this book.

Abbreviations

ECB	European Central Bank
GDP	Gross Domestic Product
GNP	Gross National Product
HMSO	Her Majesty's Stationery Office
IISS	International Institute for Strategic Studies
IMF	International Monetary Fund
INSEE	Institut National de la Statistique et des Études Économiques
NBER	National Bureau of Economic Research
NIC	National Insurance Contributions
NNP	Net National Product
OECD	Organisation of Economic Cooperation and Development
ONS	Office of National Statistics
OPEC	Organization of Petroleum Exporting Countries
PSBR	Public Sector Borrowing Requirement
SIPRI	Stockholm International Peace Research Institute
SPD	Social Democratic Party of Germany

Introduction:
The Old Economic Determinism and the New

Money makes the world go round, of that we all are sure—On being poor.

Cabaret (1972)

The idea that money makes the world go round—as the Master of Ceremonies sang in the musical *Cabaret*—is an old one, yet remarkably resilient. It is there in the Bible, in both the Old and the New Testaments: compare "Money answereth all things" (Ecclesiastes 10: 19) with "The love of money is the root of all evil" (1 Timothy, 6: 10). The sin of avarice was, of course, condemned by Mosaic law. But in Christian doctrine, as the second aphorism suggests, even the normal pecuniary motive was condemned. Part of the revolutionary appeal of Christ's teaching was the prospect that the rich would be excluded from the Kingdom of God: it was easier "for a camel to go through the eye of needle, than for a rich man to enter into the kingdom of God" (Matthew 19: 24).

Plainly, Western Europe would not have progressed so successfully from feudalism to capitalism had this dogma deterred people from making money. The point, of course, was that it did nothing of the sort. Rather, it consoled those (the majority) who had no money and instilled a sense of guilt in those who had much: an optimal strategy for an organization seeking both mass membership and substantial private donations from the élite.

The notion of a fundamental conflict between morality and Mammon also informed the most successful "secular religion" of modern times. To Karl Marx and Friedrich Engels, what was odious about their own class, the bourgeoisie, was its ethos of "naked self interest" and "callous 'cash payment.'"[1] Of course, Marx's claim that the internal contradictions of capitalism would precipitate its own downfall was supposed to be "scientific" and "objective." It was the inexorable rise of capitalism and the bourgeoisie that had overthrown the feudal aristocratic order; in turn, the formation in the factories of an impoverished but immense proletariat would inevitably destroy capitalism and the bourgeoisie. Marx was contemptuous of the faith of his ancestors, and indifferent to the Lutheranism his father had adopted. Yet Marxism would not have won so many adherents if it had not offered the prospect of a secular Day of Judgement in the form of the promised revolution in which, once again, the rich would get their deserts. As Isaiah Berlin observed, the more thunderous passages in *Capital* are the work of a man who "in the manner of an ancient Hebrew prophet . . . speaks the name of the elect, pronouncing the burden of capitalism, the doom of the accursed system, the punishment that is in store for those who are blind to the course and goal of history and therefore self-destructive and condemned to liquidation."[2] Marx's debts to Hegel, Ricardo and the French Radicals are well known. But it is worth recalling that the *Communist Manifesto* also owed a debt to a more overtly religious and indeed conservative critique of capitalism. It was in fact Thomas Carlyle who coined the phrase "cash nexus" in his *Chartism* (1840),[3] though where Marx looked forward to a proletarian utopia, Carlyle regretted the passing of a romanticized medieval England.[4]

Though it is no longer fashionable to do so, it is possible to interpret Richard Wagner's *The Ring of the Nibelung* as another romantic critique of capitalism. Its central argument, as one of the Rhine maidens tells the dwarf Alberich in the very first scene, is that money—to be precise, gold which has been mined and worked—is power: "He that would fashion from the Rhinegold the ring / that would confer on him immeasurable might / could win the world's wealth for his own." But there is a catch: "Only he who forswears love's power, / only he who forfeits love's delight, / only he can attain the magic / to fashion the gold into a ring." In other words, the acquisition of wealth and emotional fulfilment are mutually exclusive. His lecherous advances having been mockingly rebuffed by the Rhine maidens, Alberich has little difficulty in opting for the former: significantly, the first act of capital accumulation in *The Ring* is his theft of the gold.

This is not the only economic symbolism in *The Rhinegold*. The next scene is dominated by a contractual dispute between the god Wotan and the giants Fafner and Fasolt, who have just completed the construction of a new fortress, Valhalla. It is the third scene, however, which contains the most explicit economics. Here we see Alberich in his new incarnation as the heartless master of Nibelheim, mercilessly sweating his fellow dwarfs, the Nibelungs, in an immense gold factory. As his wretched brother Mime explains, his people were once "carefree smiths" who "created / ornaments for our women, wondrous trinkets, / dainty trifles for Nibelungs, / and lightly laughed out our work." But "now this villain compels us / to creep into our caverns / and ever toil for him alone . . . without pause or peace." The relentless pace of work demanded by Alberich is memorably evoked by the sound of hammers rhythmically striking anvils. It is a sound we hear again later in the cycle when Siegfried reforges his father's shattered sword Notung: perhaps the only example of a breakthrough in arms manufacturing set to music.

Of course, few serious Wagnerians nowadays would wish to overplay the economic theme in *The Ring*.[5] What still seemed fresh in the 1976 production at Bayreuth was tired by 1991, when a Covent Garden production dressed Alberich in a top hat and Siegfried in a worker's blue overalls. On the other hand, it was Wagner himself who compared the smog-filled London of his day with Nibelheim. Nor is it without significance that he first conceived the cycle in the revolutionary year 1848, shortly before taking to the barricades of Dresden alongside the anarchist Mikhail Bakunin (where the two passed the time by sketching out a blasphemous crucifixion scene for a projected opera entitled "Jesus of Nazareth"). By the time the completed *Ring* was given its first performance in August 1876 Wagner had certainly moved away from the radical politics of his youth. But to the young Irish writer George Bernard Shaw, who turned 20 that same year, the economic subtext of Wagner's work was still discernible: he was even seen in the Reading Room of the British Museum studying the orchestral score of *Tristan und Isolde* alongside a French translation of Marx's *Capital*. For Shaw, *The Ring* was an allegory of the class system: Alberich was a "poor, rough, vulgar, coarse fellow" who sought "to take his part in aristocratic society" but was "snubbed into the knowledge that only as a millionaire could he ever hope to bring that society to his feet and buy himself a beautiful and refined wife. His choice is forced upon him. He forswears love as thousands forswear it every day; and in a moment the gold is in his grasp."[6]

The crux of Wagner's *Gesamtkunstwerk* is the curse Alberich places on the ring at the moment it is stolen from him by the gods:

> Since its gold gave me measureless might,
> now may its magic bring death to whoever wears it!
> . . . Whoever possesses it shall be consumed with care,
> and whoever has it not be gnawed with envy!
> Each shall itch to possess it,
> but none shall in it find pleasure!
> Its owner shall guard it profitlessly,
> for through it he shall meet his executioner!

That curse is ultimately fulfilled with Siegfried's murder in *Twilight of the Gods*, at the end of which Brünnhilde flings herself on to his funeral pyre, hurls the ring back into the Rhine and sets "Valhalla's vaulting towers" ablaze in an almost unstageable conflagration.

It is no coincidence that Marx foresaw a similar end for capitalism in the first volume of his *Capital*—a work comparable with *The Ring* in scale if not in aesthetic beauty. In chapter 32, Marx gives a memorable sketch of capitalist economic development:

The transformation of the individualized and scattered means of production into socially concentrated means of production, the transformation, therefore, of the dwarf-like property of the many into the giant property of the few and the expropriation of the great mass of the people from the soil, from the means of subsistence and from the instruments of labour . . . forms the pre-history of capital . . . Private property which is personally earned . . . is supplanted by capitalist private property, which rests on the exploitation of alien, but formally free labour.[7]

The imagery of dwarves and giants is at least suggestive. Moreover, like Wagner, Marx foresees a day of reckoning:

Along with the constant decrease of the number of capitalist magnates, who usurp and monopolize all the advantages of this process of transformation, the mass of misery, oppression, slavery, degradation and exploitation grows; but with this there also grows the revolt of the working class, a class constantly increasing in numbers, and trained, united and organized by the very mechanism of the capitalist mode of production. The monopoly of capital becomes a fetter upon the mode of production . . . The centralization of the means of production and the socialization of labour reach a point at which they become incompatible with their capitalist integument. This integument is burst asunder. The knell of capitalist private property sounds. The expropriators are expropriated.[8]

A later German Marxist, August Bebel, made the parallel explicit when he prophesied "the twilight of the gods of the bourgeois world."

The least original thing about *Capital* was its prediction that capitalism would go the way of Valhalla. The idea of an approaching cataclysm was, to use another Wagnerian term, one of the great leitmotifs of nineteenth-century culture, and was far from being the sole property of the political Left. On a smaller scale, the topos of dissolution as a consequence of economic modernization recurs throughout nineteenth-century literature. In Theodor

Fontane's nostalgic novel *Der Stechlin*, published in 1899, the local glass factory at Globsow symbolizes the impending collapse of the old rural order in the Mark of Brandenburg. As the old Junker Dubslav von Stechlin laments:

They . . . send [the stills which they manufacture] to other factories and right away they start distilling all kinds of dreadful things in these green balloons: hydrochloric acid; sulphuric acid; smoking nitric acid . . . And each drop burns a hole, whether in linen, or in cloth, or in leather; in everything; everything is burnt and scorched. And when I think that my Globsowers are playing a part, and quite happily supplying the tools for the great general world conflagration [*Generalweltanbrennung*]—ah, *meine Herren*, that gives me pain.[9]

Nor was this association of capitalism with dissolution a German peculiarity. In Dickens's *Dombey and Son*, the railways which carve their way through London are sinister agents of destruction and death. In Zola's *L'Argent*, the rise and fall of a bank provides a metaphor for the rottenness of Louis Napoleon's Second Empire. In a not dissimilar vein, Maupassant's *Bel-Ami* portrays the corruption of a presentable young man in the Third Republic: here all human relationships are subordinated to the manipulation of the stock exchange.[10]

Perhaps this outlook is not wholly surprising. As an occupational group, professional writers have always been conspicuously ungrateful for the benefits conferred by economic progress, not the least of which has been a huge expansion in the market for printed words. Fontane, Dickens, Zola and Maupassant were all beneficiaries of that expansion, though Wagner had to rely on the artist's traditional prop of royal patronage. As for Marx, he depended on handouts from the factory-owning, fox-hunting Engels, bequests from his wife's wealthy Rhineland relatives or—richest of ironies— his own occasional stock market speculations. Like most unsuccessful "day-traders", however, Marx never had enough money in hand to make his longed-for "killing on the Stock Exchange."[11]

The reality was, of course, that the second half of the nineteenth century witnessed unprecedented economic growth in most of the world, and not even Marx could resist the lure of the mid-Victorian boom. Moreover, when the socialist revolution finally came, it afflicted not the most advanced industrial societies but mainly agrarian ones like Russia and China. Yet the romantic notion, which Marx shared with Carlyle, Wagner and so many others of the Victorian generation, that the world had entered into a kind of Faustian pact—

that industrialization would be bought at the price of human degradation and ultimately a "general world conflagration"—outlived the generation of 1848. At once materialist in conception and romantic at heart, an entire library of history has been based on the assumption that there was something fundamentally amiss with the capitalist economy; that the conflict of interest between the propertied few and the impoverished many was irreconcilable; and that some kind of revolutionary crisis would bring about a new socialist order.

Consider just two examples. A central question which historians still address today is the one posed by many radicals following the failure of the 1848 revolutions: why did the bourgeoisie prefer authoritarian, aristocratic regimes to workers and artisans movements with which they could (in theory) have made common cause? The answer offered by Marx in *The Eighteenth Brumaire of Louis Bonaparte* was that, so long as their economic aspirations were not obstructed, the middle classes were willing to relinquish their political aspirations and to leave the old regime substantially in charge, in return for protection from an increasingly threatening proletariat. The influence of this model would be hard to exaggerate. Typical of the way historians have continued to work with Marxist concepts (even when not themselves overtly Marxist) has been the link often posited between the "Great Depression" of the 1870s and 1880s and the contemporaneous shift away from liberalism towards protectionism in most European countries, notably Germany.[12] The First World War too has frequently been interpreted as a kind of capitalist *Generalweltanbrennung*, the inevitable consequence of imperialist rivalries. According to the posthumously influential German historian Eckart Kehr, the explanation for Wilhelmine Germany's commitment to a two-front war lay in the Prussian agrarians' desire for tariffs, which antagonized Russia; the heavy industrialists' desire for naval orders, which antagonized Britain; and their combined desire to combat the advance of Social Democracy by a strategy of "social imperialism", which antagonized both.[13] Despite much tinkering at the margins, the influence of this approach is still discernible today.

The greatest advantage of Marx's model is its simplicity. Armed with dialectical materialism, the historian can grapple with bigger subjects and longer periods than the historicist who struggles, as Ranke exhorted, to understand each epoch in its own terms. It is not without significance that two of the most ambitious works of historical writing of the past half-century have been by Marxists: Immanuel Wallerstein's *Modern World System* and Eric Hobsbawm's four-volume history of the modern world, completed as late as 1994. In the final *Age of Extremes*, Hobsbawm sought to salvage some consolation for his generation of Communist intellectuals by arguing that capitalism had been rescued from its own collapse in the 1930s and 1940s only by the economic and military might of Stalin's Soviet Union; and that the collapse of the latter in the 1990s was no more than a temporary setback for the socialist critique of capitalism. State ownership and central planning might have failed in Russia, Hobsbawm conceded; but it "could hardly be doubted" that "Marx would live on as a major thinker"; whereas the doctrine of the "unrestricted free market" had been just as discredited by the "generally admitted . . . economic failure" of Thatcherism. Moreover, demographic and economic pressures on the global environment were already paving the way for an "irreversible crisis." Sustainable development was "incompatible with a world economy based on the unlimited pursuit of profit by economic enterprises dedicated, by definition, to this object and competing with each other in a global free market." The widening gap between rich and poor nations was also "accumulating future troubles," as was the widening gap between rich and poor individuals within developed economies, which would sooner or later necessitate a restoration of state control over the economy: "Non-market allocation of resources, or, at least [*sic*], ruthless limitation of market allocation, was essential to head off the impending ecological crisis. . . . The fate of humanity . . . would depend on the restoration of public authorities."

Nor could Hobsbawm resist concluding in the familiar apocalyptic language of the 1840s:

The historic forces that shaped the century, are continuing to operate. We live in a world captured, uprooted and transformed by the titanic economic and techno-scientific process of the development of capitalism . . . We know, or at least it is reasonable to suppose, that it cannot go on *ad infinitum*. . . . There are signs . . . that we have reached a point of historic crisis. The forces generated by the techno-scientific economy are now great enough to destroy . . . the material foundations of human life. The structures of human societies themselves . . . are on the point of being destroyed . . . Our world risks both explosion and implosion. . . . The alternative to a changed society is darkness.[14]

It is hard not to be reminded of the *Beyond the Fringe* sketch in which Peter Cooke and his followers vainly brace themselves for the end of the world, week after week.

THE NEW DETERMINISM

Yet the conspicuous failure of Marx's prophecies to come true need not discredit the fundamental notion that it is money—economics—that makes the world go round. All that is needed is to jettison the biblical assumption of an impending apocalypse, and to recast modern economic history as a tale of capitalist triumph.

In his forthcoming history of the twentieth century, the eminent American economist Bradford DeLong is writing what may prove to be a defining text of the new economic determinism. It is certainly an antidote to the *Age of Extremes*. DeLong's twentieth century is fundamentally "the story of liberty and prosperity," in which the extremes of totalitarianism appear as a massive historical wrong-turning between two eras of benign global growth.[15] Yet the fundamental assumption—that economic change is the motor of history—is not so different from Hobsbawm's. According to DeLong:

the history of the twentieth century was overwhelmingly *economic* history: the economy was the dominant arena of events and change, and economic changes were the driving force behind changes in other areas of life . . . The pace of economic change was so great as to the shake the rest of history to its foundation. For perhaps the first time, the making and using the necessities of and conveniences of daily life—and how production, consumption and distribution changed—was the driving force behind a single century's history.[16]

Even the mid-century dictatorships "had their origins in *economic* discontents and found their expressions in *economic* ideologies. People killed each other in their millions over how economic life should be organised."[17] DeLong goes so far as to explain even the Second World War in economic terms: "It is hard to see World War II in the absence of Adolf Hitler's insane *idée fixe* that the Germans needed a better land-labour ratio—more living space—if they were to be a strong nation."[18] However, these were erroneous ideologies, the malformed offspring of the catastrophic mismanagement of economic policy during the Great Depression. Only in the final decade of the twentieth century, with the collapse of Communism and the global acceptance of liberalized markets, could history resume the upward trajectory of the pre-1914 period.

DeLong's claim that the principal political events of modern history can be explained in economic terms has a distinguished pedigree. It will also find widespread public assent, particularly in the United States, where this kind of economic determinism is close to being conventional wisdom. In what follows, I will deal in detail with a number of different versions of this idea; at this stage it will suffice to sketch three typical hypotheses:

1. *Economic growth promotes democratization (and economic crises have the opposite effect).* This idea can be traced back to the work of the social scientist Seymour Martin Lipset since the late 1950s,[19] and has found widespread endorsement in numerous recent studies by political scientists and economists such as Robert Barro, who detects "a strong positive linkage from prosperity to the propensity to experience democracy."[20] In the words of another eminent American economist, Benjamin Friedman, "a society is more likely to become more open and tolerant and democratic when its citizens standard of living is rising, and to move in the opposite direction when living standards stagnate."[21] The most obvious example which most readers will think of is a negative one: the causal link—which can be found in innumerable textbooks—between the Great Depression, the rise of Hitler and fascism generally and the origins of the Second World War. Here is a classic example of the argument:

   The immediate effect of the economic crisis in Europe was to increase domestic political and social tensions, to bring Hitler to power in Germany and to encourage the development of fascist movements elsewhere. . . . But the economic crisis was also a world crisis . . . In particular the disastrous results for the Japanese economy of the loss of her silk exports, and the undoubted hardship caused to Japanese peasants and small farmers, contributed to a new expansionist policy on the part of the Japanese army.[22]

2. *Economic success ensures re-election (and poor economic performance leads to election defeat).* According to one school of political science, voters are primarily motivated by their economic experience or prospects in making their choices at elections. In the words of Helmut Norpoth, "Economic voting . . . is hard-wired into the brain of citizens in democracies."[23] This has encouraged many politicians to pin their hopes of re-election on the 'feelgood factor': the belief that the popularity of a government is a function of the performance of the economy. A widely held version of this theory explained President Clinton's survival of the 1999 impeachment process with reference to the sustained

rise of the US stock market. The 1992 Clinton campaign watchword—
"It's the Economy, Stupid"—has become a kind of shorthand for this
theory.

3. *Economic growth is the key to international power (but too much
power can lead to economic decline)*. In *The Rise and Fall of the Great
Powers*, Paul Kennedy argued that economics provided the key to the
history of international relations: "all of the major shifts in the world's
military-power balance have followed alterations in the *productive* balances . . . where victory has always gone to the side with the greatest
material resources."[24] Given the overwhelming superiority of the victorious coalitions in both world wars, this is at first sight a persuasive
hypothesis. Even Kennedy's rider—that all great powers eventually succumb to "overstretch" because their growing military commitments
start to undermine their economic strength—is less easily challenged
than is sometimes assumed.[25] While it has been tempting to deride his
warning about American overstretch in the wake of the collapse of the
Soviet Union and the acceleration of American economic growth,
Kennedy could legitimately argue that the United States has followed
his advice by making deep cuts in defence expenditure since the mid-
1980s. Nor did his analysis ever rule out the possibility that the USSR
might succumb to overstretch first; on the contrary, a careful reader of
The Great Powers when it first appeared would have inferred that it
was the Soviets who were closer to decline. In other words, while Marxism may have suffered a setback in 1989, economic determinism did
not. All that has happened is that the signs have been reversed: it was
the stagnation of the planned economy that doomed the Soviet system,
whereas the success of the capitalist economy ensured the triumph of
democracy.[26] For Gorbachev's failure, as for Clinton's success, it was
the economy, stupid.

THE CASH NEXUS UNTIED

But *was* it the economy? In the chapters that follow, I have set out to re-
examine the link—the nexus, in Carlyle's phrase—between economics and
politics, in the aftermath not only of the failure of socialism but also the
apparent triumph of the Anglo-American model of capitalism. In his latest
book, Francis Fukuyama confidently declares that "in the political and economic sphere" history has turned out to be "progressive and directional";

what he calls "liberal democracy" has emerged as "the only viable alternative for technologically advanced societies."[27] Are capitalism and democracy—to borrow an analogy from the field of genetics—the "double helix" of the modern world? Or might there be sources of friction between the two which we ignore at our peril?

But first a caveat. The allusion to DNA prompts a simple but important reminder about human nature. As evolutionary biologists have demonstrated, *homo sapiens* is not *homo economicus*. Human beings—as Carlyle knew—are motivated by much more than profit maximization: "Cash is a great miracle; yet it has not all power in Heaven, nor even on Earth . . . *Cash-payment* is not the sole relation of human beings."

Within economic theory, there are in any case quite different assumptions about individual behaviour. Some neo-classical models assume that individuals expectations are rational, that is, they draw economically optimal conclusions from available information. In other models, expectations are more slowly "adaptive," or there is uncertainty about the future. Yet experimental research shows that most people are remarkably bad at assessing their own economic best interest, even when they are given clear information and time to learn. Faced with a simple economic dilemma, people are quite likely to make the wrong decision because of "bounded rationality" (the effect of misleading preconceptions or emotions) or basic computational mistakes (the inability to calculate probabilities and discount rates).[28] Psychologists have also identified the phenomenon of "myopic discounting:" our tendency to prefer a large reward later to a small reward soon—a preference we then switch as the small reward becomes irresistibly imminent.[29] Prospect theorists have shown that people are risk-averse when choosing between a certain gain and a possible bigger gain—they will choose the certain but smaller gain—but not when offered a choice between a certain loss and a possible bigger loss.[30]

Most economic institutions, if they depend on credit, also depend in some measure on credibility. But credibility can be based on credulity. In late nineteenth-century France, Thérèse Humbert enjoyed a glittering career on the basis of a chest supposedly containing a hundred million francs in bearer bonds, which it was claimed she had inherited from her natural father, a mysterious Portuguese (later American) millionaire named Crawford. Borrowing against these securities, she and her husband were able to buy a luxurious *hôtel* in the avenue de la Grande Armée, to gain a controlling interest in a Parisian newspaper and to engineer his election as a socialist deputy. Ten thousand people gathered outside the house when the box was finally opened in May 1902. It was found to contain "nothing but an old newspaper, an Italian coin and a trouser button."[31]

Even when we are not miscalculating—as the Humberts' creditors plainly did—our economic calculations are often subordinated to our biological impulses: the desire to reproduce, rooted (according to neo-Darwinian theories) in our "selfish genes,"[32] the capacity for violence against rivals for mates and sustenance—to say nothing of the erotic or morbid forms of behavior analysed by Freud, which cannot always by explained by evolutionary biology.[33] Man is a social animal whose motivations are inseparable from his cultural milieu. As Max Weber argued, even the profit motive has its roots in a not wholly rational asceticism, a desire to work for its own sake which is as much religious as economic.[34] Under different cultural conditions, human beings may prefer leisure to toil. Or they may win the esteem of their fellows by economically "irrational" behaviour; for social status is seldom the same as mere purchasing power.[35]

And man is also a political animal. The groups into which human beings divide themselves—kinship groups, tribes, faiths, nations, classes and parties (not forgetting firms)—satisfy two fundamental needs: the desire for security (safety, both physical and psychological, in numbers) and what Nietzsche called the will to power: the satisfaction that comes from dominating other weaker groups. No theory has adequately described this phenomenon, not least because individuals are plainly capable of sustaining multiple, overlapping identities; and of tolerating the proximity of quite different groups, and indeed co-operating with them. Only occasionally, and for reasons that seem historically specific, are people willing to accept an exclusive group identity. Only sometimes—but often enough—does the competition between groups descend into violence.

The guiding assumption of *The Cash Nexus* is that these conflicting impulses—call them, for the sake of simplicity, sex, violence and power—are individually or together capable of over-riding money, the economic motive. In particular, political events and institutions have often dominated economic development—and indeed explain its far from even trend. (Note that I say "often": sometimes the economic motive *does* prevail, or complements rather than contradicts the other motives.) Economists know this, but naturally shy away from it. Often they use the generic term "shock" to describe events that are "exogenous" to their carefully constructed models. Yet the notion that a war is comparable with a meteorological disaster is hardly satisfactory to the historian, who has the daunting task of trying to explain shocks as well as market equilibria.[36]

Political scientists, it is true, have sought to construct models of political change. And this book owes almost as much to their work as to the work of economists. In the historian's mind, however, the attempt to construct and test equations to explain (for example) the incidence of war, the spread of democracy or the outcomes of elections inspires almost as much scepticism as admiration. Nothing can be said against the method which constructs formal hypotheses and then tests them against empirical evidence; it is the best way of debunking would-be "laws" of human behaviour. But we must be deeply suspicious of any equation that seems to *pass* the empirical test. For human beings are not atoms. They have consciousness, and that consciousness is not always rational. In his *Notes from Underground*, Dostoevsky derides the economists' assumption that man acts out of self-interest, and satiries the notion of a deterministic theory of human behaviour:

You seem certain that man himself will give up erring *of his own free will . . .,* that . . . there are natural laws in the universe, and whatever happens to him happens outside his will . . . All human acts will be listed in something like logarithm tables, say up to the number 108,000, and transferred to a timetable . . . They will carry detailed calculations and exact forecasts of everything to come . . . But then, one might do anything out of boredom . . . because man . . . prefers to act in the way he feels like acting and not in the way his reason and interest tell him . . . One's own free, unrestrained choice, one's own whim, be it the wildest, one's own fancy, sometimes worked up to a frenzy—that is the most advantageous advantage that cannot be fitted into any table . . . A man can wish upon himself, in full awareness, something harmful, stupid and even completely idiotic . . . in order to *establish his right* to wish for the most idiotic things.

History may be "grand" and "colourful," but for Dostoevsky its defining characteristic is irrational violence: "They fight and fight and fight; they are fighting now, they fought before, and they'll fight in the future. . . . So you see, you can say anything about world history. . . . Except one thing, that is. It cannot be said that world history is reasonable."[37]

This book's central conclusion is that money does not make the world go round, any more than the characters in *Crime and Punishment* act according to logarithm tables. Rather, it has been political events—above all, wars—that have shaped the institutions of modern economic life: tax-collecting bureaucracies, central banks, bond markets, stock exchanges. Moreover, it has been domestic political conflicts—not only over expenditure, taxation and borrowing, but also over non-economic issues like religion and national identity—that have driven the evolution of modern political institutions: above all, parliaments and parties. Though economic growth may promote the spread of democratic institutions, there is ample historical evidence that democracy is capable of generating economically perverse policies; and that times of economic crisis (such as those caused by war) may be equally conducive to democratization.

The book is divided into fourteen chapters, each of which deals with a specific aspect of the relationship between economics and politics. It falls into four sections: "Spending and Taxing," "Promises to Pay," "Economic Politics" and "Global Power." The first three chapters are concerned with the political origins of the basic fiscal institutions associated with expenditure and revenue. Chapter 1 shows how the main impetus for the development of the state as a fiscal institution has come—until very recently—from war. Though the chapter challenges the widely held notion that the cost of war has tended to rise over the long run, it emphasizes that military expenditures have been the principal cause of fiscal innovation for most of history. Chapter 2 traces the development of taxation and other forms of revenue in response to the costs of warfare, showing how the proportions of indirect and direct taxation have varied over time and from country to country. The third chapter explores the relationship between direct taxation and political representation. Although rising taxation has been associated in some contexts with parliamentarization and democratization, the exigencies of revenue-raising have also tended to increase the scale of bureaucracy. The first section concludes with an explanatory sketch of the evolution of the welfare state—in which redistribution rather than defence becomes the prime function of government.

The second section is concerned with the evolution of the institution of the public debt. Chapter 4 considers the theoretical and empirical significance of national debts. The next chapter then considers the various ways in which crises of excessive indebtedness have been dealt with, concentrating principally on default and inflation, and describing the evolution of the central bank as an institution of debt and monetary management. Chapter 6 brings interest rates—and particularly bond yields—into the argument, and offers an explanation for the fluctuations and differentials between the interest rates paid by states on their debts.

My intellectual debt to the theoretical work of Douglass North and others on the relationship between institutions and economics will by now be obvious to students of economics.[38] The basic institutional framework I have

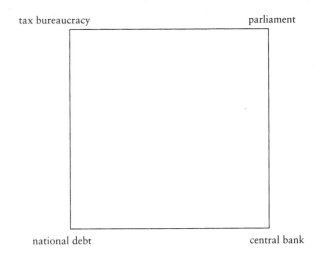

tax bureaucracy   parliament

national debt   central bank

Figure 1. The square of power

in mind may be thought of as a square. To put it simply, the exigencies of war finance had led by the eighteenth century to the evolution of an optimal combination of four institutions. First, as illustrated in the top left-hand corner of Figure 1, there was a professional tax-gathering bureaucracy. Salaried officials proved to be better at revenue raising than local property owners or private tax "farmers," who tended to retain a larger proportion of tax revenue for themselves. Second, parliamentary institutions in which taxpayers were granted a measure of political representation tended to enhance the amount of revenue a state could raise, in that taxation could be "traded" for other legislation and the entire budgetary process legitimated. Third, a system of national debt allowed a state to anticipate tax revenues in the event of a sudden increase in expenditure, such as that caused by a war. The benefit of borrowing was that it allowed the costs of wars to be spread over time, thus "smoothing" the necessary taxation. Finally, a central bank was required not only to manage debt issuance but also to exact seigniorage from the issuance of paper money, which the bank monopolized.

Though each of these four institutions had deep historical roots, it was in Britain after the Glorious Revolution that their potential in combination was realized—though it should be made clear at once that Hanoverian reality fell some way short of the ideal type I have just described. The Excise, Parliament, the National Debt and the Bank of England nevertheless formed a kind of institutional "square of power" which was superior to any alternative arrangement—notably the French system of privatized tax collection based on sales of office and tax "farming," minimal representation in the form of the *parlements*, a fragmented and expensive system of borrowing and no central monetary authority.

It was not just its revenue-raising property that made the British "square" superior to rival systems. It was also the more or less unintended side-effects it had on the private sector of the economy. To speak in general terms, the need for an efficient tax-gathering bureaucracy implied a need for a system of formal education, to ensure an adequate supply of civil servants who were both literate and numerate. Secondly, the existence of a parliament almost certainly enhanced the quality of legislation in the sphere of private property rights. Thirdly, the development of a sophisticated system of government borrowing through a funded national debt encouraged financial innovation in the private sector. Far from "crowding out" private investment, high levels of government bond issuance widened and deepened the capital market, creating new opportunities for the issuance and trading of corporate bonds and equities, especially in peacetime when the state no longer needed to borrow. Finally, a central bank with a monopoly over note-issue and the government's current account was also capable of developing functions—such as manager of the exchange rate or lender of last resort—which tended to stabilize the credit system as a whole by reducing the risk of financial crises or banking panics. In these ways, institutions that initially existed to serve the state by financing war also fostered the development of the economy as a whole. Better secondary and higher education, the rule of law (especially with respect to property), the expansion of financial markets and the stabilization of the credit system: these were vital institutional preconditions for the industrial revolution.

The third section of the book explores three hypotheses which relate the fiscal institutions already described in the previous sections to politics. The first is the argument of the early classical economists and the Marxists that the fundamental social conflict within modern societies was between landowners, capitalists and workers (the earners respectively of rents, profits and wages). Chapter 7 suggests two alternative models of social conflict, one based on strictly fiscal categories (state employees, tax-payers, bondholders and welfare-recipients), the other based on generations. An obvious source of weakness for the ideal state depicted above arises from conflicts between such groups. A state which accumulates a large national debt and then services that debt out of revenue derived mainly from indirect taxation may face political opposition from poorer consumers because of the regressive distributional consequences of its fiscal policy. On the other hand, a state which effectively defaults on its debt or inflates it away may precipitate an equally formidable reaction if the bondholders are numerous enough.

Chapter 8 begins by looking at a second source of weakness: the temptation all governments feel to manipulate fiscal and (if they control it) monetary policy to enhance their own power. How far does the popularity of democratic governments depend on economic success; and can governments really manipulate the business cycle to promote their own chances of re-election? Here it is possible to show with much more precision the relationship between political popularity and the management of fiscal and monetary policy, and to question the simplistic notion that re-election is a function of economic success. It is equally obvious, however, that politicians continue to believe in this notion.

Turning from public finance to the finances of political parties themselves, the chapter then considers the consequences of the rising cost of election campaigns. Does it matter that the key institutions of the democratic process can no longer rely on the revenue generated by mass memberships, and are therefore increasingly dependent on donations from wealthy individuals or taxpayers? And is the phenomenon of corruption—"sleaze"—explicable in economic rather than moral terms? Here again I am concerned to show how the "square of power" can be undermined from within—in this case by the decrepitude of those peripheral but still vital institutions, the political parties, which compete for control of the legislature and thereby make democratic choice a reality.

Thus far the argument has largely been confined to the development of institutions within states. The fourth and final section of the book extends the analysis to the international level. Chapter 9 considers the extent of financial globalization in historical perspective, and in particular asks how the development of an international bond market served to export the "square of power" model to other countries. In theory, the liberalization of the capital market, if it is accompanied by a comparable liberalization of the international markets for goods and labour, should increase aggregate growth. However, past experience of globalization suggests that free flows of capital are liable to substantial fluctuations in response to international political events, while free flows of goods and people can generate domestic political reactions.

Chapter 10 examines the impact of free capital movements and political events on stock markets, drawing some comparisons between stock market "bubbles," past and present.

Chapter 11 considers two ways of limiting the volatility of international financial markets: through systems of fixed exchange rates or international monetary unions. In particular, the chapter asks how long such "financial architecture" can endure when nation states remain more or less free to determine their own fiscal policies.

Chapter 12 then turns to consider the globalization of democracy: specifically, the relationship between economic growth and the spread of democratic institutions. As we have seen, it is often assumed that growth and democratization are mutually reinforcing. But is their relationship more tangential than the "double helix" model implies? Or to put it in institutional terms: how far does the democratization of the parliamentary corner of the "square of power" create problems for the other institutions and the model as a whole?

Chapter 13 explores the relationship between ethnicity and economics, and asks whether the world is destined to be "united" by supra-national institutions or "untied" by national self-determination.

The last chapter in the book brings the argument back to where it began—with war—by relating military power to financial power. Here a distinction is drawn between economic resources and the fiscal institutions needed to harness those resources for political ends. Their more sophisticated financial institutions—particularly the four corners of the square—do appear to give parliamentary regimes greater potential strength than dictatorships. However, *democratic* states have generally tended to lack the political will to make full use of their strength. In the absence of an urgent external threat, democratic regimes prefer to shift their resources away from their military forces, increasingly using the fiscal system to achieve domestic redistribution (the welfare state, rather than the warfare state). This tendency of democracies to demilitarize lays them open to challenges from productively inferior but, in the short run, destructively superior autocracies. In this sense, the decline of British power—and the present fragility of American power—may have more to do with "understretch" than "overstretch."

Let me try to simplify my argument by suggesting that each of the chapters offers an answer to an examination-style question:

1. How far are modern states the products of war?
2. Is there an optimal "mix" of taxation?

18

3. What is the relationship between parliamentarization and bureaucratization?
4. Are government debts a source of weakness or strength?
5. Why have large government debts so often led to defaults and inflations?
6. What determines the interest rates governments pay when they borrow?
7. Are distributional conflicts best understood in terms of class or generations?
8. Does economic prosperity (or lavish campaign expenditure) lead to government popularity?
9. What are the implications of the globalization of finance?
10. What causes stock market bubbles?
11. How far can exchange rate systems or monetary unions increase international financial stability?
12. Does economic growth lead to democratization and/or *vice versa*?
13. Is the world becoming more politically fragmented or more integrated?
14. Are democratic powers vulnerable to military understretch?

Another way of putting this last question might be: Why can't the United States today be more like the United Kingdom a hundred years ago? For one of the central conclusions of the book is that allowing economic globalization to proceed in the absence of a guiding imperial hand is risky, and may one day be judged a foolish abdication of responsibility.

In answering all these questions, *The Cash Nexus* seeks to challenge the economic determinist models of history, both old and new. The nexus between economics and politics *is* the key to understanding the modern world. But the idea that there is a simple causal link from one to the other—in particular, from capitalism to democracy—is mistaken. One version of the relationship does indeed produce the happy outcome of the capitalist democracy: the double helix of Western development. But like DNA, the cash nexus is capable of mutation. Sometimes democracy can stifle economic growth. Sometimes an economic crisis can undermine a dictatorship. Sometimes democracy can prosper even as the economy flounders. Sometimes growth can strengthen an authoritarian ruler.

The biological analogy should not be pursued too far. Unlike the natural world—because of the complication of human consciousness—the human world we know as history has hardly any linear causal relationships. As Carlyle said: "Acted history . . . is an ever-living, ever-working Chaos of Being, wherein shape after shape bodies itself forth from innumerable elements. And this Chaos . . . is what the historian will depict, and scientifically gauge!"[39] I remain persuaded that history is a chaotic process, in the scientists' sense of "stochastic behaviour in a deterministic system."[40] The causal connections between the economic and political world do exist; but they are so complex and so numerous that any attempt to reduce them to a model with reliable predictive power seems doomed to fail. I should emphasize that the "square of power" introduced in Figure 1 is not a model in this sense. It offers no predictions, merely a simplified version of the institutional structures described in the book, within which all modern history has been made, but made by individuals with free will and bloody-mindedness. It was in the eighteenth century that the British state developed the peculiar institutional combination of bureaucracy, parliament, debt and bank that enabled Britain at once to empire-build and to industrialize. But the extent and duration of British power depended on how these institutions were used or abused by fallible men and, latterly, women. As so often, Samuel Johnson put it nicely when he warned against the

almost . . . universal error of historians to suppose it politically, as it is physically true, that every effect has a proportionate cause. In the inanimate action of matter upon matter, the motion produced can be but equal to the force of the moving power; but the operations of life, whether private or publick admit no such laws. The caprices of voluntary agents laugh at calculation.[41]

The word "nexus" derives from the Latin *nectere*, to bind. It seemed an ideal title for this book, which originated, strange to say, as a study of the history of the international bond market. I came to realize in the course of my research, however, that the bond between creditor and debtor was only one of many bonds I needed to consider; and that in many ways the bond market was interesting precisely because it concerned itself with these other bonds as well: above all, the usually implicit contractual bonds between ruler and ruled, the elected and the electors, but also the bonds—more often (though not always) contractual—between states. A weakening of those bonds has almost always manifested itself in a weakening of the bond market, because political uncertainty loosens the bond of confidence between creditor and debtor.

If the reader takes only one thing from this book, then I hope it is the realization that, even in such dry-as-dust entities as bond yields, Carlyle's "ever-working Chaos of Being" may be discerned.

SECTION ONE
SPENDING AND TAXING

I

The Rise and Fall of the Warfare State

Ring out the narrowing lust of gold;
Ring out the thousand wars of old.
Tennyson, In Memoriam A.H.H.

In the beginning was war. From the very earliest days of recorded history until the very recent past, war has been the motor of financial change.[1] "War is the father of all things," as Herodotus said; and among those things during the Pelopponesian War was an increase in Athenian expenditure, and consequently a need for higher taxes and other sources of revenue. It was war which, with a powerful symbolism, caused the golden statue of Athena to be melted down and coined.[2]

It is a truth—almost—universally acknowledged. *Nervos belli, pecuniam infinitam*: "The sinews of war [are] unlimited money," declared Cicero in his Fifth Philippic, a view echoed by Rabelais in *Gargantua*: "The strength of a war waged without monetary reserves is as fleeting as a breath." "What Your Majesty needs," Marshal Tribulzio told Louis XII before his invasion of Italy in 1499, "is money, more money, money all the time."[3] The early sixteenth-century writer Robert de Balsac agreed: "Most important of all, success in war depends on having enough money to provide whatever the enterprise needs."[4] "Your majesty is the greatest prince in Christendom," the Emperor Charles V was told by his sister Mary, "but you cannot undertake a war in the name of all Christendom until you have the means to carry it through to certain victory."[5] Writing a century later, Cardinal Richelieu echoed her words: "Gold and money are among the chief and most necessary sources of the state's power . . . a poor prince would not be able to undertake glorious action."[6]

It goes without saying that money at the immediate disposal of the state treasury is usually more limited than the costs of war; and the history of finance is largely the history of attempts to close that gap. Only in the recent

24

past has this relationship between war and finance grown weak. After many centuries during which the cost of warfare was the biggest influence on state budgets, that role was usurped in the second half of the twentieth century by the cost of welfare. No doubt this is a great change for the better: though idleness is no virtue, it is morally preferable to pay men for doing nothing than to pay them for killing one another. But the remarkable extent and novelty of this change are not well understood. It is no exaggeration to speak today of the demilitarization of the West—and, indeed, of large areas of the rest of the world.

A common error is to suppose that, over the long run, there has been a linear or exponential upward trend in the cost of war.[7] In absolute terms, of course, the price of military hardware and the level of defence budgets have risen more or less inexorably since the beginning of written records. In relative terms, however, the patterns are more complicated. We need to relate military expenditure to the scale and frequency of war; to the size of armies in relation to total populations; to the destructiveness of military technology ("bangs per buck"); and above all to total economic output. Allowing for changes in population, technology, prices and output, the costs of war have in fact fluctuated quite widely throughout history. These fluctuations have been the driving force of financial innovation.

THE INTENSITY OF WAR

It is no part of this chapter to explain why wars happen, though the question will be returned to later. Let us for the moment simply acknowledge that they do, and often. How often is a matter for debate.

There have been several attempts to quantify the frequency of military conflict, each based on a somewhat different definition of war and covering periods of varying lengths. P. A. Sorokin counted 97 wars in the period 1819–1925,[8] compared with Quincy Wright's total of 112 between 1800 and 1945.[9] Wright confined himself to what he called "wars of modern civilization . . . involving members of the family of nations . . . which were recognized as states of war in the legal sense or which involved over 50,000 troops;" whereas L. F. Richardson, counting all the "deadly quarrels" he could find, arrived at the much higher figure of 289 for the period 1819–1949.[10] Luard's survey of all "organized large-scale fighting sustained over a significant period and involving at least one sovereign state" arrives at an even higher total of 410 for the period 1815–1984.[11] However, the

"Correlates of War" project based at the University of Michigan adopts a narrower definition which excludes most minor colonial wars, as well as wars involving countries with populations of less than 500,000, and wars in which total battle-deaths were less than a thousand per annum. For the period 1816 to 1992, their database lists 210 interstate wars and 151 civil wars.[12] The lowest figure of all for the modern period is Levy's—31—but his survey considers only wars that involved one or more of the great powers.[13]

It is possible to take an even longer view, though for extra-European conflicts the evidence becomes more patchy the further back one goes, and even the most ambitious attempts avoid the ancient and medieval periods. On the basis of his relatively broad definition of what constitutes a war, Luard arrives at a total of over a thousand for the period 1400 to 1984.[14] Levy, by contrast, counts just 119 great-power wars in the period 1495 to 1975. Even on the basis of the latter's narrower definition, the perennial nature of war is striking:

The Great Powers have been involved in interstate wars for nearly 75 per cent of the 481 years [from 1495 to 1975] . . . On average a new war begins every four years and a Great Power war [i.e. a war involving more than one great power] every seven or eight years. . . . In the typical [median] year . . . slightly over one war involving the Great Powers . . . is under way . . .[15]

No twenty-five year period since 1495 has been entirely without war.

It is possible to bring this audit of war up to the present. The Stockholm International Peace Research Institute (SIPRI) estimates that there were 103 "armed conflicts" between 1989 and 1997, of which six were inter-state conflicts.[16] In 1999 there were some 27 major armed conflicts in progress, though only two were between sovereign states (between India and Pakistan and between Eritrea and Ethiopia).[17] Adopting Levy's criteria for wars involving at least one great power, there have been six since Vietnam (the last war considered in his survey): the Sino-Russian War (1969), the Sino-Vietnamese War (1979), the Soviet-Afghan War (1979–89), the Falklands War (1982), the Gulf War (1990–91) and the Kosovo War (1999).[18]

Has war grown more or less frequent over time? Some would say less so.[19] Counting only wars involving one or more great powers, there was at least one war underway in ninety-five of the years of the sixteenth century and in ninety-four of the years in the seventeenth; but that the figure falls to seventy-eight for the eighteenth and forty for the nineteenth, and rises to barely more than fifty for the twentieth. Put differently, the "average yearly amount of war" was highest in the sixteenth century and lowest in the nineteenth and twentieth centuries.[20] However, using a broader definition of war, Luard lists 281 wars for the period 1400–1559, falling to 162 (1559–1648) and 145 (1648–1789), but then rising to 270 (1789–1917) before returning to 163 between 1917 and 1984. Adding together all the wars covered by the Correlates of War database—including wars that did not involve a major power, as well as civil wars—provides further evidence of modern bellocosity. It is striking that there has not been a single year since 1816 without at least one war going on in the world. Only in Europe has war has grown less frequent since 1945. The percentage of wars that took place in Europe falls steadily from more than 80 per cent in Luard's first sub-period (1400–1559) to just 9 per cent in his last (1917–1984).[21]

Which of the great powers has been the most belligerent? On the basis of a slightly modified and extended version of Levy's dataset, the answer would appear to be France, which has participated in some 50 of 125 major wars since 1495. Austria is not far behind (47), followed by another former Habsburg realm, Spain (44) and, in fourth place, England (43).[22] According to Luard's larger list of wars, however, the most warlike states in the years 1400 to 1559 were the Habsburg and Ottoman Empires. Between 1559 and 1648 Spain and Sweden led the field, waging war in 83 of those years. France was certainly the prime warmonger from 1648 until 1789 (80 out of 141 years) and again, with respect to European wars, from 1789 until 1917 (32 out of 128 years). However, Britain was more often involved in wars outside Europe between 1815 and 1914 (71 out of 99 years). There were 72 separate British military campaigns in the course of Queen Victoria's reign—more than one for every year of the so-called *pax britannica*.[23]

Simply counting raw numbers of wars can only tell us so much, of course. For example, eighteenth-century wars lasted longer[24] and involved more powers than wars in previous or subsequent centuries: in that sense, the average war was, perhaps surprisingly, a bigger affair in the Age of Enlightenment than the average war before or since. Even in terms of "severity" (total battle deaths), the average eighteenth-century war ranks above the average twentieth-century war, to say nothing of the wars of all other centuries. Only in terms of "concentration" (battle deaths per nation-year) was the average twentieth-century war bigger. This reflects the fact that the great-power wars of the twentieth century were more compressed than those of the period before 1815; whereas the periods of peace between the great powers were significantly longer. While the average length of war declined from eight years in the eighteenth century to four and a half in the twentieth, the number of battles in each year of war rose steeply.[25]

Almost as remarkable in this long-term perspective was the comparative peacefulness of the century between 1816 and 1913. Although there were around a hundred colonial wars in the period—the majority fought by Britain, France or Russia—the scale of these wars tended to be small because of the technological superiority of the imperial powers. Also on a relatively small scale were the numerous wars of national independence.[26] At the same time, the great powers kept war between themselves to an historical minimum.[27] Apart from the Crimean War, the great power clashes of the period 1854–71 seldom lasted longer than a few weeks. The late twentieth century saw a return to this pattern: the war against Iraq in the Gulf lasted eighty-five days; the war against Serbia over Kosovo a mere seventy-eight. If there has been a discernible trend over the past two or three centuries, then, it has been the increasing *concentration* or intensity of war.

MEN OF WAR

The dramatic difference between the world wars and the rest of modern history is immediately apparent when we turn to the extent of military *mobilization*: that is to the say, the proportion of the population employed in the armed forces. In absolute terms, armies reached historically unprecedented sizes in the twentieth century: probably the largest military force in history was that of the Soviet Union in 1945, which numbered around 12.5 million. By comparison, the armies that fought the Hundred Years War seldom exceeded twelve *thousand* in size. Even today, after some fifteen years of troop reductions, the American services still employ 1.4 million people.

But such figures tell us little about the relative degrees of mobilization involved. In the eighteenth century the highest recorded percentage of the British population under arms was 2.8 per cent in 1780, when Britain was at war not only with her American colonists, but also with France, Spain and Holland. But in more peaceful years the figure fell below 1 per cent. For France, the proportion of men in the armed forces tended to decline in the eighteenth century, from 1.8 per cent in 1710 to 0.8 per cent in 1790. Austria consistently kept between 1 and 2 per cent of her population under arms throughout the century; but this was a much lower proportion than that of Prussia, which in 1760 had as many as 4.1 per cent of her people in the army.

For all countries, the Napoleonic "revolution in war" meant an increase in the proportion of the population that had to be mobilized. In 1810 Britain had more than 5 per cent of her people under arms, Prussia 3.9 per cent, France 3.7 per cent and Austria 2.4 per cent.[28]

By comparison, the nineteenth century saw relatively low rates of military participation. With the exceptions of Russia during the Crimean War, the United States during the Civil War and France and Prussia during the war of 1870–1, none of the major powers mobilized more than 2 per cent of the population between 1816 and 1913. Apart from the years 1855–6, 1858–63 and 1900–1902, the figure in Britain remained less than 1 per cent until 1912, reaching a low point of 0.5 per cent in 1835. On average, Austria and Piedmont/Italy also had armed forces of less than 1 per cent of the population between 1816 and 1913; and for Prussia, Russia and France, the average proportions were all below 1.3 per cent. Just 0.2 per cent of the population of the United States was in the armed forces during the nineteenth century as a whole. Even in 1913, despite contemporary and historical perceptions of an arms race, only Britain, France and Germany had more than 1 per cent of their populations under arms.

The First World War saw the highest rates of military participation in all history. At their peaks of wartime mobilization, France and Germany had more than 13 per cent of their populations in the services, Britain more than 9 per cent, Italy more than 8 per cent, Austria-Hungary just over 7 and Russia only slightly less. But immediately after the war, as if in reaction, all the major powers substantially reduced their military participation ratios. On average, only France mobilized more than 1 per cent of her population. In Britain the figure touched a nadir of 0.7 per cent in the mid-1930s; while in the Soviet Union in 1932 it was less than a third of 1 per cent. The United States also reverted to its nineteenth-century level of military unreadiness. Even Nazi Germany took time to raise the share of the population in the army, navy and air force after the enforced reduction that had been a part of the Versailles Treaty of 1919. Not until 1938 did the German armed services exceed 1 per cent of the population. Italy's Abyssinian adventure pushed its armed forces up to above 3 per cent in 1935, but by the eve of the Second World War the figure had sunk back to just over 1 per cent.

Surprisingly, no country mobilized as large a percentage of the population into its armed forces between 1939 and 1945 as France managed in 1940 (just short of 12 per cent). The peak figure for Germany was 8.3 per cent in 1941, rather less than Britain managed in 1945 (10.4 per cent). It is also noteworthy that the Soviet proportion in that year (7.4 per cent) was less than the

American (8.6 per cent). In the First World War, Germany had almost certainly committed too many men to the army at the expense of the industrial workforce. The Second World War apparently saw a more balanced allocation of labour.

By comparison with the previous two post-war eras after 1815 and 1918, the years after 1945 did not witness such a rapid and sustained demobilization. In the Soviet case, the armed forces jumped back up from 1.5 per cent of the population in 1946 to 3.1 per cent in 1952; while American military participation rose from 0.9 per cent in 1948 to a post-war high of 2.2 per cent in 1952. Britain too experienced a slight rise associated with the Korean War. The French figure rose to a peak of 2.2 per cent in 1960 as a result of conflicts associated with decolonization.

Nevertheless, during the Cold War period as a whole there was a steady fall in military participation ratios in many major countries. The average rate of mobilization in Germany, Italy and Austria was lower in the period 1947–85 than it had been between 1816 and 1913. Even for Russia the figure was below 2 per cent. Moreover, the break-up of the Warsaw Pact and the collapse of the Soviet Union has allowed military participation to fall back to inter-war levels and in some cases even lower. In 1997 just 0.37 per cent of the British population was serving in the armed forces: the lowest figure since 1816. The present French proportion (0.65 per cent) is the lowest since 1821.

Rates of military mobilization, then, have been subject to sharp fluctuations above a relatively stable (and perhaps over the very long run even declining) base line. The major wars of the modern period, and particularly the world wars, have necessitated large but not sustained increases in military participation. Indeed, it is precisely because of its discontinuous, non-cyclical character that warfare has exerted such a decisive influence over the development of financial and political institutions.

BANGS PER BUCK

Sudden increases in the proportion of men under arms are not the principal source of pressure on military budgets, however. Changes in military technology matter more. From the fourteenth-century gunpowder revolution onwards, artillery has periodically increased its range, accuracy and destructive power. The development of the cast-iron cannon, with its iron ball, "corns" of powder and wheel base, necessitated a parallel improvement in fortifications like

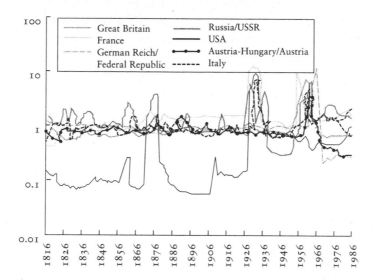

Figure 2. Military personnel as a percentage of population, 1816–1986 (log. scale)

Sources: Correlates of War data base; IISS, Military Balance database; OECD.

the *trace italienne*.[29] Indeed, it was partly the rising cost of fortifications that put the finances of continental powers under strain in the sixteenth century.[30] Likewise, the standardization and improvement of handguns in the early eighteenth century enhanced the firepower and raised the cost of equipping the individual infantry man.[31] The eighteenth century saw further improvements in the manufacture of artillery, notably the bored barrel introduced to France by the Swiss engineer Jean Maritz, which set the standard until the advent of the breech-loading gun in the 1850s.[32] The parallel development in Britain was in maritime technology: copper-sheathed bottoms for ships, short-barrelled, large-calibre carronades and steering wheels for ships.[33]

Moreover, the pace of technological advance quickened in the course of the nineteenth century: at sea, the application of steam power, Henri Paxihans' large-calibre shell-firing gun and iron cladding, followed by the torpedo, the submarine, Nordenfeldt's and Vavasseur's naval guns, the tube-boiler and the turbine; on land, the new rifles of Minié, Dreyse and Colt and the improved breech-loading artillery pieces of Krupp, Armstrong and Whitworth—to say nothing of brass cartridges (1867), steel artillery (1883), the Maxim Gun (1884), magazine rifles (1888) and the Schneider-Creusot quick-firing field gun (1893).[34] The cauldron of the First World War brought forth new instruments of destruction, barely imagined before 1914: among them the tank, the aerial bomber and the fighter plane, as well as the hand grenade, the trench mortar and poison gas. Despite all talk of war-weariness, the process did not halt in the 1920s and 1930s: one need only compare the aircraft and tanks of 1938 with those of 1918 to see that. But the pace of change accelerated dramatically during the Second World War as the major combatants sought to out-innovate as well as out-produce one another, increasing the speed, range, accuracy and armour-plating of nearly all the machines of mid-century warfare. The British Spitfire—to give one example—was modified 1,000 times between 1938 and 1945, adding 100 mph to its top speed.[35] At the same time, advances in radio technology ushered in a revolution in battlefield communications (wireless communication, radar detection), while a host of new inventions arrived in time for use in the final phase of the conflict: jet engines, amphibious vehicles, guided missiles, rockets and, of course, atomic bombs.[36] This technological race continued in the Cold War, as A-bombs gave way to hydrogen and neutron bombs and the arms race became simultaneously a space race between rockets and satellites (with astronauts and cosmonauts thrown in to sustain public interest).[37]

In absolute terms, expenditure on military hardware has therefore risen inexorably in the long run. By 1982 a critic of the arms race could lament: "Bombers cost two hundred times as much as they did in World War II. Fighters cost one hundred times or more than they did in World War II. Aircraft carriers are twenty times as expensive and battle tanks are fifteen times as expensive as in World War II."[38] Writing four years later, Paul Kennedy enlarged on this point:

Edwardian statesmen, appalled that a pre-1914 battleship cost £2.5 million, would be staggered that it now costs the British Admiralty £120 million and more for a replacement *frigate*! . . . The new [American] B-1 bomber . . . will cost over $200 billion for a mere one hundred planes . . . Cynics [forecast] that the entire Pentagon budget may be swallowed up by *one* aircraft by the year 2020.[39]

According to Kennedy, weapon prices in the 1980s were "rising 6 to 10 per cent faster than inflation, and . . . every new weapon system is three to five times costlier than that which it is intended to replace."[40] Despite a "near trebling of the American defence budget since the late 1970s," there had occurred by the late 1980s "a mere 5 per cent increase in the numerical size of the armed forces on active duty."[41] To Kennedy, warnings were not misplaced of an impending "militarization of the world economy."[42]

Even allowing for inflation and relating expenditure to the size of armed forces, military expenditure has tended to rise. In 1850 Britain spent just under £2,700 per man on her armed forces (in 1998 prices); by 1900 the figure had risen to £12,900, and by 1950 £22,000. In 1998 the figure was close to £105,500. The United States spent $30,000 per serviceman in 1900 (again in 1998 prices); $71,900 in 1950; and $192,5000 in 1998 (see Figure 3).[43] Nearly all the increase has been due to increased quantity and quality of military hardware (as opposed to improvements in soldiers' pay and living conditions). It is not too much to say that the increase in the military capital/labour ratio in the course of the twentieth century has been exponential.

Yet in assessing the growing sophistication of military technology there are a number of things we should not lose sight of: in particular, its increasing destructiveness. For in the purchase of a new weapon, it is not only the price that matters; it is also its capacity, compared with the weapon it is intended to replace, to mete out murder.

The death toll of the War of the Spanish Succession (1701–13) was 1.2 million. A century later, the Napoleonic Wars killed 1.9 million men. And a century after that, the First World War cost more than 9 million servicemen their lives. Perhaps as many as 8 million people died in the maelstrom of the Russian Civil War of 1918–21 (though most of these were the victims of the famine and pestilence unleashed by the conflict). But even this figure pales into insignificance alongside the total mortality caused by the Second World War. For military personnel, the total body count was roughly twice the figure for the First World War. But this figure excludes civilian casualties. According to the best available estimates, total civilian deaths in the Second World War amounted to 37.8 million, bringing the total death toll to nearly 57 million people.[44] In other words, the majority of deaths in the Second World War were due to deliberate targeting—by all sides—of civilians on land and sea and from the air. Including all the minor colonial wars like the Boer War and all the civil wars like the one that raged in India after independence, the total figure for war deaths between 1900 and 1950 approaches 80 million.

The increase in the destructiveness of war becomes even more striking when the relative brevity of the world wars is taken into account. Though it lasted five times as long, the Thirty Years War caused only a ninth of the battlefield mortality inflicted during the Second World War, and an even smaller fraction of the civilian mortality. The First World War caused five times as many deaths in four and a quarter years as the entire Napoleonic Wars in the space of twelve. Another way of expressing this is to calculate the approximate annual death rate during the various wars. This rose from

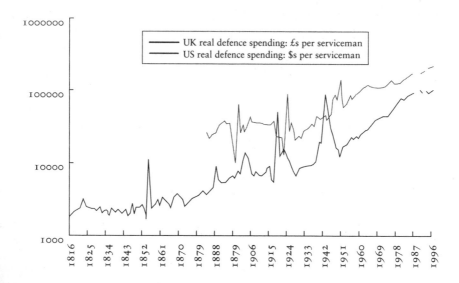

Figure 3. Defense spending per serviceman in Britain and the United States, 1816–1998 (log. scale)

Sources: Defense spending: UK: 1850–1914: Singer and Small, Correlates database; 1914–1988: Butler and Butler, *British Political Facts,* pp. 393 f.; 1989–98: SIPRI. US: 1870–1913: Hobson, "Military-extraction Gap and the Wary Titan," p. 501; 1914–85: Correlates database; 1986–98 SIPRI. CPI: UK: Goodhart, "Monetary Policy," appendix; US: Economist, *Economic Statistics,* pp. 108 f.; Federal Reserve Bank of St. Louis. Armed forces: Correlates of War database.

above 69,000 in the Thirty Years War to some 104,000 in the War of the Spanish Succession, 124,000 in the Seven Years War, 155,000 in the Napoleonic Wars and for the world wars, respectively, 2.2 and 3.2 million— or 9.5 million if civilian deaths in the Second World War are included. In short, between the seventeenth and the twentieth century, the capacity of war to kill rose by a factor of roughly 140. From the time of Napoleon to the time of Hitler—born a mere 120 years apart—the increase was more than sixty-fold (see Appendix, table A).

Even allowing for the accelerating growth in the world's population, then, the world wars were the most destructive in history. Somewhere in the region of 2.4 per cent of the world's entire population was killed in the Second World War and 0.5 per cent in the First, compared with roughly 0.4 per cent in the Thirty Years War and 0.2 per cent in the Napoleonic Wars and the

War of the Spanish Succession. The total death toll in the First World War amounted to something like 1 per cent of the pre-war population of all fourteen combatant countries, 4 per cent of all males between 15 and 49 and 13 per cent of all those mobilized. For Turkey the equivalent figures were 4 per cent of the population, 15 per cent of males between 15 and 49 and almost 27 per cent of all those mobilized. Even worse affected was Serbia, which lost 6 per cent of the population, nearly a quarter of all men of fighting age and over a third of all those mobilized.[45] In the Second World War roughly 3 per cent of the entire pre-war population of all combatant countries died as a result of the war. For Germany, Austria and Hungary the figure was around 8 per cent, for Yugoslavia and the Soviet Union 11 per cent and for Poland—of all countries the worst affected by the war—nearly 19 per cent: almost a fifth of the entire pre-war population. The armies of some countries were almost wholly annihilated. Military deaths as a proportion of all troops mobilized were in the region of 85 per cent for both Poland and Romania. Forty-five per cent of the troops mobilized in Yugoslavia were killed. For the Soviet Union and Germany, locked for four years in the most bloody conflict of all time, the equivalent figures were, respectively, 25 and 29 per cent. Around a quarter of Japanese and Chinese troops were killed in the war in Asia and the Pacific.

To be sure, casualties as a proportion of troops engaged were sometimes very high in previous wars. Though the statistics are far from reliable for medieval battles, it is nevertheless plausible that the proportions (including wounded and prisoners) were between a quarter and a third of combatants at the battles of Hastings (1066), Crécy (1346), Agincourt (1415), Breitenfeld (1631), Lützen (1632), Naseby (1645), Austerlitz (1805), Waterloo (1815) and Gettysburg (1863). At Blenheim (1704) the figure may have been as high as 43 per cent.[46] These figures bear comparison with some First and Second World War battles: for instance, El Alamein (c.14 per cent), though not Stalingrad, where, in the space of six and a half months, the Red Army alone suffered 1.1 million casualties and the Wehrmacht as many, if not more.[47] Yet these proportions need to be seen in the context of substantial increases in the numbers of troops committed to battle. Perhaps 14,000 men fought at Hastings; perhaps 39,000 at Crécy. But 68,000 fought at Breitenfeld and 108,000 at Blenheim, while more than double the number who fought at Breitenfeld were deployed at Austerlitz. The Battle of Waterloo saw 218,000 men in the field; but even it was dwarfed by El Alamein (300,000) and Stalingrad, where millions fought. Just as military technology had magnified the destructive power of the individual, innovations in drill, discipline, communications and logistics had allowed armies to get ever larger, battles longer.

Why then have the casualties suffered by Western forces in wars since 1945 tended to fall? The number of US servicemen who died in the Vietnam War was "only" 57,939; the number killed in Korea 37,904. And the death toll has continued to decline. In the Gulf War there were 148 American combat deaths, excluding victims of accidents and "friendly fire": a tiny proportion of a total force numbering 665,000. In the 1999 war against Serbia the figure was precisely zero. Compare those figures with the body counts in the two world wars: 114,000 American servicemen in the First World War and 292,100 in the Second. The drop in military casualties is even more marked in the case of Britain: 720,000 Britons lost their lives in the First World War; over 270,000 in the Second; yet in the Korean War just 537 British soldiers were killed. All told, 719 British soldiers have been killed in Northern Ireland since "the Troubles" began in 1969, along with 302 members of the Royal Ulster Constabulary.[48] Just 24 UK servicemen were killed in the Gulf War, not including 9 killed accidentally by their own side.

The answer lies in the nature of the wars fought since 1945—which have invariably been against far less well-equipped opposition. These death rates do not, however, signify a decline in the destructiveness of modern weaponry. As we have already seen, there was no shortage of wars in the rest of the world in the second half of the twentieth century. Indeed, according to one estimate, the total war-induced death toll for 1945–99 lies somewhere between 15 and 20 million. The world has not become that much more peaceful. It is just that the overwhelming majority of the victims of war have been Asians and Africans.

Moreover, the wars that have been fought since 1945 have given barely a glimpse of the colossal increase in destructiveness achieved in the past half-century. A simple calculation suffices to give an illustration of the potential for military catastrophe that still existed shortly after the end of the Cold War. In January 1992 the deployed strategic nuclear forces of the two superpowers had a combined "yield" of at least 5,229 megatons; and this was *after* a 22 per cent reduction in the total number of superpower warheads since the peak in 1987, and excludes non-strategic nuclear warheads. Since the 12–15 kiloton bomb dropped on Hiroshima in 1945 killed around 100,000 people instantly and a further 100,000 subsequently through radiation sickness, the superpowers in 1992 had the notional capacity to destroy (with their strategic forces alone) 387,302 Hiroshimas or 77.5 billion people. To put it another way, given that the Hiroshima bomb destroyed around

4.7 square miles, the superpowers had the capability to lay waste to 1.8 million square miles, an area rather larger than the state of India. It is scant consolation to reflect that this amounts to just 3 per cent of the planet's land surface, since the contamination after such a conflagration would spread much further. Given that the population of the world in 1992 was approximately 5 billion, nuclear weapons gave the superpowers the notional ability to destroy the entire human race fifteen times over.[49] Any assessment of the changing cost of defence needs to take account of this astonishing increase in the destructiveness of weaponry.

Also relevant to such an assessment is the way techniques of mass production have tended to lower the unit cost of almost any new piece of hardware. Because of the relative lack of competition in the arms market—with governments the biggest buyers and a small number of huge producers enjoying more or less privileged positions in their home markets—the defence industry has acquired a reputation for excessive pricing. This reputation was certainly merited in the United States and Britain in the 1980s, when public attention was drawn to such puzzling phenomena as "cost-plus contracts" and gold-plated taps in admirals" baths. But over the long run, and considering all levels of armament, the theory that the price of arms tends to rise above the price of consumer goods looks unsustainable. The Second World War in particular showed how techniques of mass production could dramatically reduce the unit-cost of guns, tanks, planes and even naval vessels. High prices for new aircraft and submarines in the late Cold War period merely reflected the very low quantities being ordered; where there has continued to be a significant demand for defence industry wares, prices do not seem to have been subject to above-average inflation.

Moreover, the Soviet practice of systematically under-pricing defence goods has left an enduring legacy of cheap weaponry, the main beneficiaries of which have been and remain the guerrilla armies of sub-Saharan Africa, the terrorist groups of Western Europe and the drug gangs of the Americas. At the time of writing, a used AK-47 assault rifle could be purchased in the United States for $700; a new one for $1,395: almost exactly as much as the cost of the portable computer on which this book was written. For around $160 billion—just over half the current US defence budget—every American male between the ages of 15 and 65 could be issued with a new Kalashnikov (or, for that matter, two second-hand ones). And of course the prices for such weapons are substantially lower in the developing world. In the same way, the real cost of a nuclear warhead—and certainly the real cost of a kiloton of nuclear yield—is almost certainly lower today than at any time since the

Manhattan Project achieved its goal at a cost of $2 billion 1945 dollars. Converted into prices of 1993, that figure rises tenfold: enough to buy 400 Trident II missiles.[50] The fact that France could almost double its nuclear arsenal from 222 warheads in 1985 to 436 in 1991 while increasing its defence budget by less than 7 per cent in real terms speaks for itself.[51] In terms of "bangs per buck"—destructive capability in relation to expenditure—military technology has never been cheaper.

THE ABOLITION OF DISTANCE

A final factor to be taken into account when assessing military burdens is the geographical extent of a state's military commitments relative to the mobility of its military forces, including their supplies. In his classic study of military logistics, Martin van Creveld has shown that there was no real breakthrough in the way armies were supplied between the seventeenth century and the early twentieth. From the Battle of Mons in 1692 to the Battle of Mons in 1914, "armies could only be fed as long as they kept moving": they had to live off the country by buying—or more commonly stealing—local produce. In this respect, railways had a much smaller impact on nineteenth-century warfare than was believed by many contemporaries, not least the Prussian General Staff. However, after 1914 "the products of the machine . . . finally superseded those of the field as the main items consumed by armies, with the result that warfare . . . shackled by immense networks of tangled umbilical cords, froze and turned into a process of slaughter on a [vast] scale."[52] The *reductio ad absurdum* of this kind of static industrial warfare was the Battle of Passchendaele, during which 120,000 British gunners fired off 4.3 million shells or 107,000 tons of explosives in a preliminary bombardment that lasted for nineteen days. The subsequent infantry offensives gained forty-five square miles at a cost per square mile (according to J. F. C. Fuller's macabre calculation) of 8,222 casualties.[53]

Despite the motorization of armies in the Second World War, the growing burden of ammunition and equipment prevented even the best armies from exploiting the maximum speed of their means of transportation. As Rommel came to realize in North Africa in 1942:

The first essential condition for an army to be able to stand the strain of battle is an adequate stock of weapons, petrol and ammunition. In fact, the battle is fought and decided by the quartermasters before the shooting begins. The bravest men can do nothing without guns, the guns nothing without plenty of ammunition; and neither guns nor ammunition are of much use in mobile warfare unless there are vehicles with sufficient petrol to haul them around.[54]

It was unforeseen "frictional" problems of supply that ultimately halted the German push into the Soviet Union in 1941–2 and, despite far better weather conditions and infrastructure, they also hindered the Anglo-American advance towards Germany in August and early September 1944. By that stage in the war, an active US army division was consuming around 650 tons of supplies a day. In all, there were twenty-two American divisions in France, requiring 14,300 tons a day. Yet a single army truck could carry just five tons. As supply lines were stretched from 200 to 400 miles, deliveries to the advancing armies slumped from 19,000 tons a day to 7,000 tons.[55] The resulting slow-down prevented the Americans from fully exploiting their massive superiority in terms of manpower, firepower and air power.

The last phase of the war revealed the importance (consistently underrated by both the Germans and the Japanese) of assigning ample numbers of men to the task of supply rather than combat. The ratio of combatants to non-combatants in the German army was two to one; but the equivalent American ratio in the European theatre was one to two. In the Pacific, the Japanese ratio was one to one; the Americans had eighteen non-combatants for every man at the front.[56] (The high British and American military participation ratios in the closing years of the war seen in Figure 2 included large numbers of men and women who were in uniform but far from the action.)

Nevertheless, advances in sea and air transport have done much to mitigate the apparently perennial problems of overland supply. Far from "striking a fatal blow at the naval supremacy of the Empire," as some feared, the introduction of steam power allowed Britain to exercise power effectively at unprecedented distances.[57] Between 1815 and 1865 the Empire expanded at an average annual rate of 100,000 square miles; between 1860 and 1909 it increased in size from 9.5 to 12.7 million square miles, a fifth of the world's land surface. Exerting even minimal control over such a vast imperium with a relatively small army thinly spread over just twenty major garrisons would have been impossible without the rapid increase in the number, speed, range and firepower of British naval vessels. Between 1857 and 1893 the journey time from England to Cape Town was cut from forty-two to nineteen days, while the gross tonnage of steamships roughly doubled.[58] Almost as important in accelerating information flows to and from the "periphery" was the spread of the telegraph. In the space of ten years after a telegraph link had been established between London and Lagos, the number of cables sent there from the Foreign Office quintupled.[59] As the historian J. R. Seeley wonderingly exclaimed: "Distance has been almost abolished by steam and electricity."[60]

By analogy, the extent of American power in the second half of the twentieth century was in large part dependent on the even greater capability of the United States navy and air force, not to mention her intercontinental missiles. True, the United States maintained a rather larger standing army relative to its population during the Cold War than did Victorian Britain in her heyday; and the British army never suffered a colonial humiliation as protracted as Vietnam (though the Boer War briefly threatened to become one). But in the 1990s the US army was increasingly used in the manner of its Victorian counterpart—sparingly, against much weaker foes—with Operation "Desert Storm" as a latter-day Omdurman.[61] It is ships and planes that do the lion's share of American overseas enforcement. One of the most potent symbols of the American war against Serbia in 1999 was the report that "Stealth" bomber pilots were able to fly from their bases in Knob Noster, Missouri, rain down destruction on Belgrade, and return home in time for pizza and the ball game.[62] At $2.2 billion each, these planes look hugely expensive: but in relation to American gross national product, they are substantially less expensive than the Dreadnought (at £2.5 million) was in its day, and perform a very similar function.[63] When one reflects on how difficult it was for Spain to sustain its control over South America in the age of the wooden galleon, it seems at least arguable that here, once again, technology has lowered rather than raised the costs of war.

COSTING WAR

It is now possible to set the changing financial burden of war into some kind of meaningful long-term perspective. It is, of course, far from easy to distinguish between military and civilian expenditures in most state budgets. Should we include in the total for military spending expenditures on strategically useful infrastructure such as roads or railways? What about veterans' pensions or payments to the widows and orphans of men killed in action? Such questions arise whether one is considering Augustan Rome or Nazi Germany, and there is no consensus as to the correct definition.

What is nevertheless clear is that the share of military expenditure in state finances has varied enormously from place to place and time to time. It can be inferred from Xenophon, for example, that rather more than a third of the expenditure of Athenian state in the time of Pericles went on military ends, a proportion which certainly rose during the Pelopponesian War.[64] A comparable estimate for the Roman Empire around the year AD 14 would lie between 45 and 58 per cent.[65] The early Abbasid caliphate spent around a third of total government receipts on the army.[66]

Calculations for the early modern period show a remarkable range of fiscal militarism in Europe. The share of military expenditure in total spending ranged from as little as 2 per cent in fifteenth-century Burgundy to as much as 93 per cent in late-seventeenth-century Austria.[67] Averaging the available figures for the European monarchies, military spending fell from 40 per cent of the total in the fifteenth century to just 27 per cent in the sixteenth, but then rose to 46 per cent in the seventeenth century and 54 per cent in the eighteenth. The percentages spent by city-states tended to be lower than Hamburg's in the seventeenth century (which was around 50 per cent), but that was because Hamburg had opted for self-defence, whereas other cities paid for security in the form of tributes to imperial protectors. A comparative analysis of the expenditures of a sample of early modern states (in terms of tons of silver) confirms, unsurprisingly, that the peaks of total state spending almost always coincided with wars.[68] In the case of Elizabethan England, for example, military expenditures rose from just 20 per cent of total expenditures between 1560 and 1585 to 79 per cent (1585–1600) as a result of the conflict with Spain after 1585.[69] Around 90 per cent of the budget of the Dutch Republic in the seventeenth century went to pay for the Eighty Years War with Spain, the Anglo-Dutch Wars and the Nine Years War. Austria's wars with the Ottoman Empire pushed the proportion up to 98 per cent for the Habsburg Empire in the same period, though this had fallen back to 43 per cent by 1716.[70]

For the great powers, this pattern of frequent war and fiscal militarism continued into the early nineteenth century. In the British case, military expenditure fluctuated between 55 and 90 per cent of total central government expenditure between 1685 and 1813.[71] For Prussia the proportion varied between 74 and 90 per cent in the period 1760–1800. After dipping in the period before and after the Revolution, the French proportion rose to a peak of 75 per cent in 1810. Even the central government of the United States was spending close to half its total budget on military ends in 1810.[72] As we shall see, the ability to raise such large sums of money at short notice and at minimum economic cost was the key to combining military success and internal stability.

In the course of the nineteenth century, however, military spending declined in its relative importance. End-of-decade figures for the period 1820 to 1910 show that military expenditure averaged roughly 54 per cent of central government spending in the United States, 49 per cent in Prussia/ Germany, 34 per cent in Britain, 33 per cent in France and 29 per cent in Austria.[73] This was of course mainly because, as we have seen, nineteenth-century wars tended to be shorter and cheaper than those of the previous century. However, the falling percentages for Austria and Germany between 1880 and 1910—from 82 per cent to just 52 per cent in the German case— should not be mistaken for defence cuts. In both cases, the declines were mainly due to rising state expenditures on non-military functions (about which more later).[74] And a closer look at the British figures, including colonial expenditures officially classified as "civil," suggests a long-term rise in the share of military and imperial spending as a proportion of the budget from the nadir of 19 per cent in 1836. Despite the Gladstonian mantra of "retrenchment," the proportion never fell below 30 per cent after the Crimean War and showed a sustained upward trend from 1883 onwards. Between the Boer War and the First World War, the figure was consistently above 40 per cent.[75]

In the twentieth century the military role of government waxed then waned. Indeed, the extent of economic mobilization in the two world wars was so great that the distinction between military and non-military expenditure became increasingly artificial: that, indeed, was the essence of "total war." The available figures for the First World War suggest a return to levels of fiscal militarism not seen since early modern times. At its wartime peak in 1917 military expenditure represented 96 per cent of the Russian central government budget. For Britain the figure was 90 per cent, for Germany 86 per cent, for Italy 83 per cent and for France 71 per cent. Even the United States saw an unprecedented rise in military spending, which peaked in 1919 at 62 per cent of central government spending.[76] Yet in the inter-war period, defence budgets were slashed both absolutely and relatively. From 1923 until 1934 the British defence budget was consistently less than a fifth of central government spending, falling to a nadir of 15 per cent in 1932. In Germany the military proportion of the Reich budget sank to less than a tenth in the years 1928 to 1931. Even fascist Italy devoted less than a fifth of the central budget to the military until Mussolini's adventure in Abyssinia. Ironically, it was the French who maintained the highest level of military expenditure in Europe between 1920 and 1935 (30 per cent per year on average).[77] Unfortunately, not enough of that money was going into new planes and tanks:[78] a big army with elaborate forts but without adequate air power and armour could not withstand the German *Blitzkrieg* in 1940.

The blurring of the distinction between military and civilian expenditures makes it almost impossible to quantify what were certainly very large increases in the period before and during the Second World War. According to the somewhat archaic conventions of British budgets, the defence "quota" rose rapidly from its low of 15 per cent of total expenditure in 1932 to 44 per cent in 1938; at its peak in 1944 it exceeded 84 per cent.[79] The Third Reich inherited a military budget of less than 10 per cent of Reich expenditure; but ever since the 1930s there has been uncertainty about how much was subsequently spent by the Nazis on rearmament. Estimates of the total amount spent on the military between 1933 and 1938 range from 34.5 billion reichsmarks—the figure proposed by the former Reichsbank president Hjalmar Schacht—to the East German historian Kuczynski's estimate of more than twice that sum. To intimidate his enemies at the outbreak of war, Hitler himself claimed that 90 billion had been spent. However, the most plausible estimates—excluding, for example, investments in industry which might have enhanced the Reich's military capability at some future date— are based on the testimony of the former Finance Minister Count Schwerin von Krosigk and put the pre-war total somewhere between 48 and 49 billion.[80] As a percentage of the Reich budget, that meant an increase from less than a tenth to more than half. Wartime figures are also problematic, but it seems likely that the proportion rose to three-quarters between 1940 and 1944.[81] In Japan, military spending started at a higher level (31 per cent in 1931–2) and reached 70 per cent as early as 1937–8.[82]

Because of the Cold War, the sharp reductions in military budgets that followed the defeat of the Axis powers were short-lived. Having fallen to just 21 per cent of the central government budget in 1949, British defence spending rose to a post-war peak of 38 per cent in 1954, which was also the peak year for France. The "shrinking pains" of decolonization faded thereafter: the British defence budget was already in relative decline by the time of Suez, while the French fell rapidly after Dien Bien Phu. By 1968 defence accounted for just a fifth of spending in both countries.[83] Nor was the downward trend of British defence spending more than slowed by the Thatcher government. As a share of expenditure it rose only slightly from 10 per cent in 1975 to 11.8 per cent in 1986; but in 1990 it was back down to 10.7 per cent.[84] In 1997–8 it accounted for less than 7 per cent of the general government spending "control total." This is a figure lower than at any time in British history since the Wars of the Roses.

None of the above figures, however, tells us the relative *economic* importance of military expenditure. Indeed, given the profound changes in the nature of total state expenditure, not only at the central but also at the local level, it may be that they tell us hardly anything meaningful at all. For example, in order to make German and British figures comparable after 1870, the spending of the German states of *Länder* need to be added to the federal government's expenditure total; or alternatively, the defence budget should be calculated as a proportion of total public sector spending, including all tiers of government. Table 1 gives a rather better indication of the remarkable decline of military expenditure in relation to public spending by all levels of government in the past hundred years. In Britain, France and Germany alike, the share of defence spending in the total public sector budget has declined from around a quarter to barely twentieth.

More important than calculations of that sort, are those which express the "military burden" of expenditure as a proportion of total economic output. To give a classical example: Goldsmith estimates total Athenian public expenditure at around 20 per cent of national product—necessarily a very approximate calculation—compared with an equivalent figure for Augustan Rome of no more than 5 per cent. In relative economic terms, therefore, the Greek military burden was probably higher than the Roman: perhaps around 7 per cent of national product, compared with a Roman figure of just 2 or 3 per cent. This kind of calculation—the cost of military expenditure in

Table 1. *Defense expenditure as a percentage of total public spending, 1891–1997*

	France	UK	Germany
1891	24.9	26.7	26.3
1900	27.2	48.0	25.2
1913	28.8	29.9	26.6
1925	21.4	12.5	4.4
1935	20.5	12.6	24.8
1953	25.9	28.5	12.5
1962	15.3	16.7	15.9
1971	11.9	11.4	9.7
1997	5.5	6.6	3.3

Sources: 1872–1971: Flora et al., *State, Economy and Society*, vol. i, pp. 345–449; 1997: SIPRI and OECD.

relation to gross national or domestic product—is not without its technical difficulties even in the present day, when estimates of national product are relatively reliable, though still far from perfect. Nevertheless, there is no better way of estimating relative military spending that allows comparisons between countries and over time.

The proportion of military spending in relation to national product naturally fluctuates quite substantially according to whether or not a state is at war; and this is the crucial point. In the case of Medici Florence in the 1420s, for example, the ratio of military spending to "national" product varied between 3 per cent in peacetime and 20 per cent during wars.[85] As a proportion of national income, British defence spending in the eighteenth century varied between 4 and 18 per cent depending on whether or not the country was at war, reaching a peak between 1778 and 1782.[86] This was a significantly larger proportion than the French state spent in the same period. According to one calculation, total British war expenditure between 1776 and 1782 was nearly two and a half times the equivalent French figure in absolute terms. However, this differential does not take into account the relative size of the rival states' economies. In fact, the cost in relation to a year's GNP was even higher for Britain than the absolute numbers suggest: 75 per cent compared with just 15 per cent for France.[87] In relative terms, war was far more burdensome for Britain than for France; or, to put it differently, Britain was able to mobilize a larger share of national product at times of military crisis.

As Figure 4 shows, such levels were rarely attained in the nineteenth century. Between 1850 and 1914 the highest proportion of GDP consumed by the British armed services was just 11 per cent in the first year of the Crimean War; even during the Boer War the figure did not rise above 6 per cent. None of the other European powers ever spent more than 5 per cent of national output on defence, with the exception of Italy in 1866 (though if GDP figures were available for Prussia before German unification, the military quota would almost certainly exceed 5 per cent in the period 1866–71). Average defence expenditure as a percentage of net national product between 1870 and 1913 amounted to just 3.1 per cent for Britain and Austria, 3.2 per cent for Germany, 3.3 per cent for Italy and 4 per cent for France.

Considering how much has been written on the subject of the pre-First World War arms race—not to mention the scramble for overseas empires— these numbers are surprisingly low. It is especially striking that Germany, the state most notorious for its "militarism" in this period, was by this measure somewhat less militaristic than her two neighbours and rivals, France and

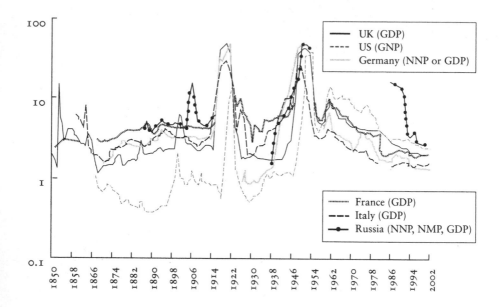

Figure 4. Defense spending as a percentage of national product, 1850–1998 (log. scale)

Sources: Defense spending: UK: 1850–1914: Correlates of War database; 1914–1988: Butler and Butler, British Political Facts, pp. 393 f.; 1989–98: SIPRI. US: 1870–1913: Hobson, 'Wary Titan', p. 501; 1914–1985: Correlates of War database; 1986–98: SIPRI. Germany: 1872–1913, 1925–32: Andic and Veverka, "Growth of Government Expenditure", p. 262; 1933–38: Overy, *War and Economy*, p. 203; 1938–44: Petzina et al. (eds.), *Sozialgeschichtliches Arbeitsbuch*, vol. iii. p. 149 (however, 1933–43 percentages are from Abelshauser, "Germany", p. 138); 1950–80: Rytlewsi (ed.), *Bundesrepublik in Zahlen*, pp. 183 f.; 1982–98: SIPRI. France: 1820–70: Flora *et al.*, *State, Economy and Society*, vol. i, pp. 380–2; 1870–1913: Hobson, "Wary Titan", p. 501; 1920–1975: Flora et al., op. cit.; 1981–97: SIPRI. Italy : 1862–1973: Flora et al., op. cit., pp. 402ff.; 1981–97: SIPRI. Russia: 1885–1913: Hobson, "Wary Titan", p. 501; 1933–38: Nove, *Economic History*, p. 230; 1940–45: Harrison, "Overview", p. 21; 1985–91: IISS, *Military Balance*; 1992–97: SIPRI. GDP/GNP/ NNP/: UK: 1850–70: Mitchell, *European Historical Statistics*, p. 408; 1870–1948: Feinstein, *National Income, Expenditure and Output*, Statistical Tables, table 3; 1948–1998: ONS. US: 1850–1958: Mitchell, *International Historical Statistics: The Americas*, pp. 761–74; 1959–98: Federal Reserve Bank of St. Louis. Germany: 1870–1938: Hoffman, Grumbach and Hesse, *Wachstum*; 1950–60: Rytlewsi (ed.), *Bundersrepublik in Zahlen*. p. 188; 1960–99: OECD. France: 1820–1913: Lévy-Leboyer and

Russia.[88] However, the idea of "militarism run mad" as a general *European* phenomenon seems more intelligible when these figures are compared with those for the United States. On average, Americans spent less than 1 per cent of net national income on the military between 1870 and 1913. Nor was this significantly altered by the First World War. Only in the last year of the Great War did defence spending rise above 5 per cent of GNP and, after peaking at 13 per cent in 1919, it rapidly fell back down below 1 per cent for most of the 1920s. Again, the contrast with the European powers is very marked. At their respective peaks in the First World War, both Britain and Germany spent more than 50 per cent of GDP on the military; Italy was not far behind with 35 per cent.

The inter-war period saw a vain attempt by Britain to return to the pre-war pattern of expenditure; no other power attempted to do so. From the mid-1920s onwards both Italy and France increased military expenditure ahead of the growth rate: the French defence burden exceeded 5 per cent of GDP in 1930, the Italian in 1935. Germany, of course, had its military budget slashed almost to American levels by the Versailles Treaty; but after Hitler came to power an immense shift of resources took place, increasing the military quota from less than 2 per cent in 1933 to 23 per cent in 1939.

To the European powers, the relative cost of the Second World War was in fact not much greater than had been the First. The most striking difference, however, was that from 1943 onwards the United States for the first time began to divert resources to warfare on a scale comparable with the European states. Nor, since this "rise to globalism," has it been possible for Americans to revert to their earlier level of military parsimony. On the contrary: since the time of the Korean War the United States has consistently spent a higher proportion of GDP on defence than her principal allies. Needless to say, this reflected the high level of military expenditure necessitated by the Cold War.

The greatest difficulties arise in the case of Russia and the Soviet Union: hence the many gaps in the series in Figure 4. This is because of the patchiness of Tsarist data and, more seriously, the idiosyncrasies of Soviet accounting conventions—notably the concept of "net material product," which

Sources (cont.)

Bourgignon, *L'Économie française*, pp. 318–22; 1960–99: OECD. Notes: UK: GDP figures after 1920 excluding Southern Ireland. Germany: GDP 1950–60: West Germany, excluding Saarland and W. Berlin; 1960–90: West Germany; 1991–99: reunified Germany.

effectively excluded services from the national accounts—as well as the policy of under-pricing armaments mentioned above. Before the First World War, Tsarist Russia was certainly the most economically militaristic of the great powers, spending more than 5 per cent of net national product on defence between 1885 and 1913—though this average was undoubtedly inflated by the relatively high cost of the 1904–5 war with Japan. Between 1915 and 1917 the military burden also probably rose slightly higher than those of the other combatants. The picture, however, becomes obscure in the Soviet period. If defence expenditure appears to have been relatively low in the period of the New Economic Policy and Stalin's collectivization, it rose quite rapidly after 1935: ahead of Britain's, though behind Germany's. At the height of the Second World War the relative military burden exceeded 60 per cent, still slightly less than the same figure for Germany. It is much harder to be sure how much of Soviet output went on defence after 1945, however. Official Soviet figures were certainly too low. In 1975 the Central Intelligence Agency doubled its estimate of Soviet military spending from 6–8 per cent of GNP to 11–13 per cent on the basis of new price data.[89] Ten years later the International Institute for Strategic Studies put the figure at 16 per cent.[90] The equivalent figure for the United States at this time was 6 per cent. Even at the height of the Korean War, American defence spending as a proportion of output was below the Soviet level of the 1980s.

Finally, Figure 4 shows how sharply defence expenditure has fallen in relative terms since the end of the Cold War. The latest estimates from the Stockholm International Peace Research Institute (for 1999) suggest expenditure to GDP ratios of around 4 per cent for Russia, 3.2 per cent for the United States, 2.8 per cent for France, 2.6 per cent for Britain, 2 per cent for Italy and just 1.5 per cent for Germany.[91] These are figures reminiscent of the 1920s, if not the nineteenth century. The United States, Russia, Germany and Britain have not spent so little on defence since the 1920s, though in the German case this was under duress. French and Italian defence spending has not been so low in relative terms since the early 1870s.

THE "DEMILITARIZATION" OF THE WEST

The demilitarization of the West in the late twentieth century seems remarkable when compared with the era of the world wars. The average Western man now has every chance of avoiding war altogether. Indeed, the most violent experience he is ever likely to have is a Saturday night brawl or a mugging. If he has an appetite for war, he must rest content with electronically generated visions: occasional television bulletins from far-off places or, more often, cinematic re-enactments of past wars or fictional future wars. In the first half of the twentieth century, men saw action: their grandsons and great-grandsons see acting. In 1999 many thousands of American actors feigned death in harrowing but hugely popular war films like *Saving Private Ryan*. Only a handful of American soldiers died as a result of real military operations, and all were the victims of accidents rather than enemy action.

Yet it would be wrong to attribute demilitarization to that revulsion against war which characterized both elite and "pop" culture during and after the Vietnam War. Demilitarization has been the norm in times of peace, as Figures 2 and 4 make clear. In addition, there has been a long-run tendency in Britain and the United States to reduce military participation by substituting capital for labour.

Historically, the two most appealing things about war have been the pleasure of comradeship and the excitement of combat. But with the advance of military technology in the twentieth century, both experiences became more elusive. The nadir of conventional warfare was reached on the Eastern Front in the Second World War. With the death toll averaging nearly one in three, there could be no enduring bonds and no thrill, simply a desperate struggle for survival:

Man becomes an animal. One must destroy in order to live. There is nothing heroic on this battlefield . . . The battle returns here to its most primeval, animal-like form; whoever does not see well, fires too slowly, fails to hear the crawling on the ground in front of him as the enemy approaches, he will be sent under . . . The battle here is no assault with "hurrah cries" over a field of flowers.[92]

In this war, female medics used their teeth to amputate smashed limbs.[93] Starving prisoners of war were reduced to cannibalism. This was not just total war but totalitarian war, in which the value of human life sank close to zero on the battlefield, and to precisely zero in the slave labour camps which were an integral part of the war effort on both sides.[94]

The alternative route, taken by the United States and Britain precisely in order to economize on lives, was to industrialize war—shifting resources into artillery, tanks, warships and, above all, aircraft. In many ways, the turning point was 1940, when Britain evacuated her army from Dunkirk and then relied on a force of just 1,400 fighter pilots to deter a German invasion and keep Britain in the war.[95] But it was the bomber rather than the fighter that became the key to subsequent British (and American) strategy. In effect, investment in bombers reduced casualties among Allied servicemen and greatly increased casualties among Axis civilians, a process that culminated at Hiroshima. Once dominance of the skies had been established, ground forces could be used at a far lower cost to life and limb.

The present "Revolution in Military Affairs" made possible by improvements in electronic communications is therefore part of a prolonged and far from revolutionary process. What does not change over the long run is that money must be found—whether it is for the mass armies of the age of total war, or the "smart weapons" that account for a rising share of modern military budgets. And often, as this chapter has made clear, the money needs to be found at very short notice. The sums involved have varied greatly in relation to economic growth, as well as in relation to the destructive efficiency of weaponry. But this basic need to finance war has been—until the relatively recent past—the prime mover in the process of state formation; the father, indeed, of what follows.

2

"Hateful Taxes"

And it came to pass in those days, that there went out a decree from Caesar Augustus, that all the world should be taxed.

Luke, 2:1

"In this world," as one revolutionary wrote to another in the fateful year 1789, "nothing can be said to be certain except death and taxes."[1] Even in the New Testament, tax plays its part: it was to render what was due to Caesar that Mary and Joseph went to Bethlehem. Without tax, Christ would not have been born in a manger.

The quest for increased revenues—usually, as we have seen, to pay for war or preparation for war—has led in more than one direction. In some systems, including feudal monarchies and socialist republics, a substantial portion of revenue has come from state-owned assets, whether royal domains or "nationalized" monopolies. In theory, then, taxes in the conventional sense are not quite inevitable: a state could notionally rely exclusively on public assets to generate revenue. But the profits from those assets would be generated by taxes of a sort, whether in the form of additional labor by royal serfs or above-cost charges by state industries. In any case, the temptation to sell state assets to meet sudden increases in expenditure has tended to mean that such assets dwindle over time: the sale of crown lands in the medieval period has its modern counterpart in the "privatization" of publicly-owned utilities. Taxes are therefore inevitable—though not unavoidable.

In systems with limited representation confined to wealthy élites, there is a tendency to rely heavily on indirect taxation—principally customs levied on imports and excise duties on consumption—for revenue. The taxation of consumption may, within certain limits, be economically preferable to the alternative, namely taxation of wealth and incomes. But indirect tax rarely suffices for long because, first, in times of crisis trade and consumption tend to be reduced, and with them also tax revenues; secondly, because indirect

51

taxation is usually regressive, and over-reliance on it can lead to political unrest. Sooner or later most states have therefore been obliged to raise direct taxes, such as levies on property or deductions from income.

As the eighteenth-century Austrian Chancellor Wenzel Anton von Kaunitz-Rittberg observed:

It does not require much reflection or any profound insight to invent all kinds of ways and means of squeezing money out of our subjects. He who wishes to do so in a manner both reasonable and beneficial to the monarch and the state, however, must first, or at least at the same time, devote an equal measure of zeal to increasing his subjects wealth so that they might bear this additional burden.[2]

The history of taxation is best understood as a quest for an elusive *juste milieu*: a system that extracts the maximum revenue while at the same time imposing the minimum constraint on the growth of the economy, for that is the proverbial goose which lays the golden eggs.

FAMILY SILVER

State assets have long been a source of government revenue. Ancient Athens had silver mines of Laureion.[3] Rome derived around a sixth of its income from state-owned land.[4] Renaissance Genoa had its alum mine at Phocea.[5]

The great European monarchies started life with large royal domains which were for a time their principal source of revenue. In England the parliamentary catch-phrase of the fourteenth century—a reaction to royal requisitions known as "purveyances"—was that "the king should live of his own." This was in fact an almost universal European notion: in France the king was exhorted to "vivre du sien," in Spain to "conformare con lo suyo." Few kings could. The temptation to sell assets for the sake of ready cash— or to use grants of land as a form of payment in kind for loyal servants— was too powerful.

This was especially true in France. By 1460 the French royal domain accounted for less than 3 per cent of total royal revenues;[6] and though it rose to around a tenth in the 1520s, within fifty years it was back to around 4 per cent.[7] By 1773 the royal lands brought in less than 2 per cent of total revenue.[8] Not even the revolutionary confiscation of aristocratic estates and church lands did much to replenish the assets of the state, as they were soon sold off to raise cash: the sale of church lands alone accounted for 12 per cent of ordinary revenue in the Napoleonic period.[9]

For a time, the English crown was somewhat better-off than the French. In the 1470s Sir John Fortescue estimated that Edward IV received a fifth of the total yield of temporal property in his kingdom, though by the end of his reign this no longer sufficed to cover royal expenditure.[10] Henry VII was so successful in raising domain revenue that he had to turn to parliament for taxation only once, in 1504; while his son gave a brief boost to the royal balance sheet by seizing the lands of the monasteries. However, most of these were quickly sold off to finance wars against France and Scotland: by the last years of Edward VI, seven-eighths had gone.[11] His sister, Elizabeth I, could not hope to live of her own. Indeed, the crown's lack of independent means was the main reason for the growth in the power of parliaments in the late sixteenth and seventeenth centuries. Although the restored monarchy recovered extensive lands after the Civil War, it was henceforth dependent on parliament for additional funding. In 1760 George III made over the revenues of the royal estates to parliament; since then the monarchy has largely been financed out of taxation through the Civil List and other subsidies.[12]

Further east, the "domain state" persisted for longer. In 1630 the Swedish royal domain, which included silver, iron and copper mines, accounted for 45 per cent of royal revenues and the Danish for 37 per cent; though by 1662 the Danish proportion was down to just 10 per cent, and by the end of the eighteenth century the Swedish royal domain had all but disappeared.[13] Prussia was perhaps the longest-lived domain state, and among the most entrepreneurial. In 1740 revenue from the royal estates accounted for around 46 per cent of total revenue, and this fell only slightly in the subsequent fifty years. Even in 1806 its share was still as high as 30 per cent, and the development of a state railway network and other industrial concerns in the nineteenth century led to a slight increase.[14] In 1847 more than a third of revenues came from state enterprises; ten years later 45 per cent; and in 1867 slightly more than half.[15] This upward trend continued after German unification. Total entrepreneurial revenues rose as a proportion of total (ordinary and extraordinary) income from 48 per cent in 1875 to 77 per cent in 1913. Of course, these gross figures exaggerate how much disposable revenue the enterprises generated. But even when the costs of running the state enterprises are deducted, their importance was considerable: they covered 16 per cent of total ordinary and extraordinary expenditure in 1847 and 1857, 25 per cent in 1867. However, the net revenue declined steadily in importance after unification, from 6 per cent in 1875 to less than 2 per cent on the eve of the First World War.[16] In Britain, by contrast, the railway system had been built almost entirely with private finance.

Prussia was not unique, however. Other German states in the eighteenth and nineteenth century were also entrepreneurial: Württemberg, for example, or Hesse-Cassel—though the principal source of the latter's entrepreneurial income was the state's mercenaries, which paid for roughly half of all government spending between 1702 and 1763. As Landgrave William VIII put it: "These troops are our Peru."[17] By the turn of the century, his son was one of the richest men in the world: managing just a part of his huge investment portfolio started the Rothschilds on the road to banking greatness.[18] Russia too had a substantial royal domain, to which was added a large railway network and heavy industrial sector in the later nineteenth century. By 1913 net receipts of the railway network accounted for around 8 per cent of total public revenue.[19] Even nineteenth-century Britain, for all its reputation as a "night-watchman state," derived an average of 20 per cent of its gross revenues from the postal, telephone and telegraph services which the state monopolized.[20] This was much more than in France, where state properties declined as a proportion of total revenue from more than 10 per cent in 1801–14 to just over 3 per cent under the Bourbon and Orléanist regimes, and less than 2 per cent from 1848 until 1914.[21]

State monopolies have also been established on the production and sale of commodities. The T'ang dynasty in China introduced a salt monopoly in 758; by 780 it accounted for half of all central government revenue. Salt monopolies were also introduced in Venice, Genoa, Siena, Florence, France and Austria, and were often linked to a tax (usually called the *gabelle*). Russia too introduced a salt monopoly, though its monopoly on vodka after 1895 was more lucrative: by the eve of the First World War the latter was providing just under a fifth of total revenue—an astonishing figure.[22] The French monopoly on tobacco accounted for over 7 per cent of revenue at its peak in the eighteenth century.[23] One of Bismarck's abortive schemes to free himself from partial dependence on the democratic German parliament he had called into being was to create a similar tobacco monopoly. State monopolies on alcohol sales are still to be found in many countries. Around 5 per cent of American state and local government revenue comes from state utilities and liquor stores.[24] State lotteries play a similar role: in each case the state monopolizes the gratification of a particular vice. The profits such monopolies make are essentially taxes on drinkers or gamblers. And like the vices themselves, the revenues they generate can be hard to give up. One of the greatest blunders of Mikhail Gorbachev was his campaign against alcohol abuse in the Soviet Union: the reduction of vodka consumption led to a drastic drop in revenue from this source.[25]

Spending on infrastructure by states is sometimes portrayed as developmental: the state substitutes for insufficient private sector investment in strategically important sectors. In fact, most state enterprises have generally had a narrower, revenue-raising purpose. In undemocratic regimes, such public enterprises were indeed capable of making money, or at least of breaking even. But in many democratic states and in the planned economies of the twentieth century the public sector soon turned into a channel for covert subsidies to the poor and, at the same time, a sponge for soaking up surplus labor. Concealed unemployment, and the attendant stagnation or outright decline of productivity, meant that state enterprises after 1914 were more often net recipients of state funds than revenue generators. A good illustration of this point is the way the German railways went from being a substantial source of revenue before the First World War to being a vast job-creation scheme in the Weimar Republic and the Third Reich.[26] On average, 30 per cent of the Reich deficit between January 1921 and November 1923 was accounted for by net expenditures on the Reichsbahn. A substantial part of the railway deficit was due to over-manning, as well as to the government's failure to index passenger fares.[27] This policy was continued by the Nazis, who increased the number of railway employees by nearly a million. The contrast with the pre-war position in Prussia could hardly be more stark.

The British nationalized industries provide another melancholy example. Nationalization in fact predated 1945: Churchill had brought the Thames dockyards into public ownership in 1908, while the Forestry Commission, the Central Electricity Generating Board, the British Broadcasting Corporation, the London Passenger Transport Board and British Overseas Airways were all inter-war creations. Between 1945 and 1951, however, state ownership was extended to coal, aviation, roads, railways, gas, electricity and steel. Whatever the motives behind these decisions—and the desire to avoid job-losses or wage cuts undoubtedly took precedence over boosting productivity or net revenue—the losses subsequently incurred were colossal. In 1982 the total cost in capital write-offs and grants was estimated at around £40 billion. The £94 billion of public money invested in the nationalized industries was "yielding an average return to the Exchequer of minus 1 per cent." The car manufacturer British Leyland alone cost the taxpayer close to £3 billion in the space of a decade.[28] It is not surprising, in the light of these figures, that the Thatcher government was attracted to the possibility of "privatization": sale of these and other state-owned assets raised around £100 billion. This income should not have been, but generally was, counted as current revenue, allowing the government to paint a rosier picture of its finances than was justified. On the other hand, there was little substance to the former premier Harold Macmillan's complaint that the "family silver" was being sold off cheap.[29] The shares in the privatized utilities were not systematically undervalued by the Treasury; and the productivity improvements subsequently achieved in most of the privatized industries have amply justified the policy, since widely imitated.[30]

"TAXES ON EVERY ARTICLE"

The simplest taxes to levy are those on easily monitored transactions: partly for that reason, customs duties on imports have been a source of revenue since ancient times. Ancient Athens imposed an average duty of 1 per cent on all imports.[31] Rome too had its *portoria*, which accounted for around a quarter of revenues in the reign of Augustus.[32] In medieval England, King John set a precedent by collecting a general *ad valorem* duty of 16 pence in the pound on a wide range of imports and exports. Although this was initially imposed with the consent of merchant assemblies, the duty gradually came to be regarded as part of the ordinary revenue of the crown (hence "customs"). After 1294 the crown also imposed extraordinary taxes on wool exports; and these too became customary: from 1398 life grants of the wool tax were made to the monarch along with the subsidy on wine and other merchandise (tunnage and poundage).[33]

Yet the taxation of trade has its disadvantages. If taxes on commerce are set too high, they may have the effect of reducing the volume of trade and hence the amount of revenue. The high duty on English wool exports in the fourteenth century may well have been a factor in the sector's slow decline.[34] High import duties, on the other hand, encourage smuggling. Even an island state like Britain found it impossible to prevent large-scale evasion of duties in the eighteenth century, when the figure of "Smuggler Bill" attained heroic status and as many as 20,000 people were involved in illegal trade. More importantly, import duties discriminate against foreign goods which might otherwise be cheaper than those which are domestically produced. From a liberal perspective, tariffs are not only a burden on consumers (here was the electoral appeal of "Free Trade"); they also diminish the efficiency of the international economy as a whole by sheltering from competition mediocre firms that happen to be on the right side of a national border. It was the practical argument that lower tariffs would increase trade volumes, allied to a distinctly Protestant view of the economy as a divinely ordained and self-regulating mechanism, which converted the majority of the British political elite to free trade, beginning with the Liberal Tories in the 1820s.[35] In the event, duties were reduced so much that when trade dipped and military expenditure rose Sir Robert Peel had to accept (in 1842) the necessity of a peacetime income tax to balance the budget.

Continental states followed the British example of free trade to varying degrees, a process of trade liberalization that culminated in the early 1870s. However, the decline of agricultural and industrial prices in course of the 1870s (due in large part to steep reductions in rail and sea freight rates) soon precipitated a revival of protectionism. "Manchesterism" had been criticized since the 1840s by economists such as Friedrich List, who realized that infant German textile firms stood little chance of competing with superior British mills in the absence of protective tariffs. But the protectionist revival owed more to the fundamental political utility of tariffs as a way of buying support from biddable interest groups such as farmers.[36] Protective tariffs on agricultural and industrial imports were restored by Bismarck in Germany in 1878 and reached a pre-war peak in 1902: not only did they benefit his own social class, the landowning *Junker*, they also had the merit of dividing his liberal opponents. On the eve of the First World War, according to League of Nations figures, average German tariff rates had risen to 12 per cent, compared with 18 per cent in France (the figure for Britain was still zero). Continental tariffs on wheat had risen to 36 per cent in Germany and 38 per cent in France; in Italy, Spain and Portugal the rates were higher still. In Russia and the United States, by contrast, it was imported manufactures that were heavily taxed; the same was true in Latin America.[37] Between 1861 and 1871 the ratio of American duties to imports rose from 14 per cent to as much as 46 per cent, before levelling off at around 30 per cent.[38] The 1902 Fordney–McCumber Act empowered a new Tariff Commission to impose duties on a case-by-case basis; of course, once a tariff had been introduced, it tended to remain in place regardless of changes in relative prices.[39]

In the aftermath of the First World War, protectionism continued its upward drift. In the major industrial economies, the value of customs collected as a proportion of total imports rose from 11 per cent (1923–6) to 18 per cent (1932–9).[40] A crucial factor in the Great Depression was the plodding passage between October 1929 and June 1930 of the American Smoot–Hawley tariff bill, which specified duties on no fewer than 21,000 items.[41] Even Britain, the erstwhile champion of free trade, opted for protection, imposing a 10 per cent *ad valorem* duty in March 1932 and finally adopting Empire-wide protection ("Imperial Preference") in July 1932.[42] As in the nineteenth century, protectionism had articulate defenders. In a lecture he gave in Dublin in April 1933, Keynes declared that he "sympathise[d] . . . with those who would minimise rather than with those who would maximise economic entanglement between nations."[43] Only gradually did economists and politicians come to see that this was a destructive game of "beggar-my-neighbour." While it undoubtedly made more sense to impose tariffs than uni-laterally to pursue a free trade policy in a protectionist world, it made even more sense to reduce trade barriers collectively, first by bilateral agreements, then, after the Second World War, through the multilateral General Agreement on Tariffs and Trade. The lesson first taught by Adam Smith in the eighteenth century—that lower import duties would lead to higher revenues by boosting trade—had to be painfully re-learned.[44]

There is, of course, no reason in logic why a transaction that involves moving goods across a border should be treated differently from a transaction within a border. Throughout history, states have also had recourse to taxes on domestic transactions. Ancient Athens had an excise on sales of slaves.[45] Rome had a similar 4 per cent sales tax, as well as a tax on the manumission of slaves and a 1 per cent sales tax on other goods.[46] In medieval France the Ordnance of December 1360 "revolutionized" royal finance by imposing a duty (the *gabelle*) on salt and *aides* of 5 per cent on the sale of most commodities apart from wine, which was taxed at a higher rate (at first 8, later 25 per cent).[47] Renaissance Florence depended for a fifth of its revenue on a similar salt duty, levied at the city's gates.[48] Habsburg Castile had the *alcabala*, a 10 per cent sales tax.[49] Even before the introduction of the vodka monopoly, the excise on spirits was one of the Russian state's principal sources of revenue, accounting for as much as a third of the total in 1815.[50]

Few states in history have relied as heavily on the taxation of domestic consumption as Hanoverian Britain; and this is of particular interest as it was the regime which presided over the first industrial revolution.[51] In fact, the excise—defined succinctly in Dr Johnson's dictionary as "a hateful tax levied upon commodities"—had its origins in the Stuart period: Charles I had levied duties on cloth, starch, soap, spectacles, gold and silver wire and playing cards; and in 1643 Parliament had introduced excises on tobacco, wine, cider, beer, furs, hats, leather, lace, linen and imported silks.[52] By 1660 excises were also being levied on beer, salt, saffron, hops, lead tin, iron and glass. In the course of the next hundred years, these taxes became the British state's principal source of revenue.[53] To help finance the war with revolutionary France, the Younger Pitt added hats, gloves, mittens, perfumery, shops and female servants to the list of dutiable goods, to say nothing of bricks, horses and hunting.[54] By the end of the Napoleonic Wars, it seemed that scarcely anything in Britain was not taxed. Writing in the *Edinburgh Review* in 1820, Sidney Smith bemoaned:

[T]he inevitable consequences of being too fond of glory;— TAXES upon every article which enters into the mouth, or covers the back, or is placed under the foot; taxes upon everything which is pleasant to see. hear, feel, smell, or taste; taxes upon warmth, light and locomotion; taxes on everything on the earth, and the waters under the earth, on everything that comes from abroad or is grown at home; taxes on the raw material; taxes on every fresh value that is added to it by the industry of man; taxes on the sauce which pampers man's appetite, and the drug which restores him to health; on the ermine which decorates the judge, and the rope which hangs the criminal; on the poor man's salt, and the rich man's spice; on the brass nails of the coffin, and the ribands of the bride; at bed or board; couchant or levant, we must pay. The schoolboy whips his taxed top; the beardless youth manages his taxed horse, with a taxed bridle, on a taxed road;—and the dying Englishman, pouring his medicine, which has paid 7 per cent, into a spoon which has paid 15 per cent, flings himself back upon his chintz bed, which has paid 22 per cent, and expires in the arms of an apothecary who has paid a license of a hundred pounds for the privilege of putting him to death. His whole property is then immediately taxed from 2 to 10 per cent. Besides the probate, large fees are demanded for burying him in the chancel; his virtues are handed down to posterity on taxed marble; and he is then gathered to his fathers to be taxed no more.[55]

How far this reliance on taxing consumption helped or hindered British economic growth remains a matter for debate. The Hanoverian tax system certainly encouraged exports (which were not only duty free, but in some cases subsidized by bounties); but it is doubtful that the large transfers from consumers to untaxed rentiers had beneficial macroeconomic effects.[56] It is striking that contemporary critics of Spanish and Dutch finance—among them Adam Smith—believed that excessive reliance on taxes on consumption tended to push up labor costs and inhibit internal trade.[57]

The seventeenth-century Swedish Chancellor Axel Oxenstierna called indirect taxes "pleasing to God, hurtful to no man, and not provocative of rebellion." Some modern political scientists agree, arguing that consumption taxes are less "visible" and hence less politically sensitive than direct taxes.[58]

Yet no state can subsist for long on indirect taxes alone: in a tax system which is too regressive, the conflict of interest between a powerful, propertied patriciate and a poor, powerless populace will sooner or later lead to unrest—a point apparent to Machiavelli in the light of Florentine experience.[59] Protests against indirect tax were a recurrent feature of life in early modern Europe. Tax figured among the grievances that sparked off the revolt of the Netherlands against Spain, the German Peasants' War, the *Comuneros* uprising in Hungary and a variety of disturbances in Ottoman lands between 1590 and 1607.[60] In 1630 a new salt tax had to be withdrawn after protests in the Basque country. In 1647 there were riots in Palermo and Naples against new excise taxes.[61]

Nowhere were such protests more frequent than in *ancien régime* France. The combined squeeze on peasant incomes of rising taxes and rising rents triggered the uprising of the Pitauds against the *gabelle* in Guyenne in 1548; while collection of the 5 per cent sales tax known variously as the *sol pour livre*, the *pancarte* or the *subvention générale* had to be abandoned twice—in 1602 and 1643—because of popular resistance, and as late as the 1660s was still only collectable by force in the provinces of Dauphiné and Guyenne.[62] In 1648 a major rebellion in France began with a tax strike against Cardinal Mazarin's new fiscal measures.[63] Among the other revolts against taxation in early modern France were the revolt of the *Croquants* in Quercy in 1624; the revolt of the Guyenne towns against the wine sales tax in 1635; the revolt of the *Nu-pieds* in Normandy against the abolition of their exemption from the *gabelle* in 1639; and the Breton revolt against the *papier timbré* in 1675.[64] Historians since Tocqueville have, of course, seen taxation as one of the key factors in the origins of the French Revolution, though the regressiveness of the tax system before 1789 owed more to the many exemptions and anomalies in the system of direct tax (see below) than to the overall level of the tax burden.

As Edmund Burke observed, "To tax and to please, no more than to love and to be wise, is not given to men." Not surprisingly, the proliferation of the excise in Hanoverian Britain was also the cue for popular protests. In 1733 a mob besieged parliament chanting "No slavery — no excise — no wooden shoes!" in a temporarily successful protest against Sir Robert Walpole's Excise Bill.[65] Yet Hanoverian Britain is interesting partly because such protests never escalated, as they did elsewhere, into large-scale revolt. This partly reflected the fact that "necessities of the poor" were taxed relatively lightly: duties were higher on spirits, wines and tobacco than on beer, candles, soap, starch and leather, while the only agricultural products taxed were hides, malt, horses and tallow.[66] When eighteenth-century rural crowds imposed "popular taxation" (i.e. "just" prices) on wheat, flour and bread, it was the free market, not fiscal policy, they were reacting against.[67]

The difference between the British and French experience in the eighteenth century suggests that it is not the level of indirect taxation which matters but the range of commodities that are liable to taxation. In the nineteenth century, taxes on bread continued to be a key cause of unrest among the urban poor. Nothing better illustrates the enduring political importance of the bread tax than its role in generating support for the German Social Democratic Party in Wilhelmine Germany. In fact, the regressive impact of the tariff on imported grain was much less than the socialist press claimed. Tariffs accounted for only 10 per cent of total public sector revenue in 1913; and according to modern calculations the effect of protection was to raise the price of bread by no more than 8 per cent, equivalent to around 1.5 per cent of the average working class family's income.[68] But the claim that "dear bread" was paying for "militarism"—that the revenue from grain tariffs was financing the construction of the Kaiser's navy—proved to be a potent vote-winner, and was a major contributory factor in the SPD's election triumph in 1912. In a similar way, what scuppered Joseph Chamberlain's campaign for Tariff Reform after 1900 was the association of tariffs with high bread prices before the repeal of the Corn Laws. At Liberal meetings in 1905, old women whose memories stretched back to the 1840s were hauled onto the platform to remind voters of the bad old days before Free Trade.

By contrast, taxes on legal and other transactions—often called "stamp taxes"—have seldom been controversial, because by their nature they tend to fall on the better-off. The French state in particular came to rely heavily on these: by 1913 stamp and registration taxes accounted for more than a fifth of total revenue.[69] The exceptions that prove the rule were, of course, the duties on legal documents, newspapers, cards and dice imposed on the American colonies by the Stamp Act of 1765, which provoked so violent a reaction that they were hastily repealed. As we shall see, however, it was the constitutional propriety of the taxation more than the financial burden that caused the trouble.[70]

Modern governments have learned something from the past. In late-twentieth-century Western Europe, the development of the Value Added Tax has given the state a lucrative new form of indirect tax which consumers have been remarkably ready to pay and businesses have been remarkably ready to administer. Between 1979 and 1999 the share of total British revenue from VAT has doubled and now stands at nearly 16 per cent.[71] At the time of writing (2000), 55 per cent of consumers' expenditure is liable for VAT at a rate of 17.5 per cent. In France VAT is even more important, bringing in some 45 per cent of total revenue.[72] The relative lack of resistance to VAT can be explained in several ways. First, governments have been careful to reduce or forgo the tax on politically sensitive goods. In Britain, for example, food and water are zero-rated, as are medicines on prescription, books and newspapers. Rents, school fees, bets and funerals (among other things) are all exempt; while domestic fuel is taxed at a lower rate. Second, the rate has been increased in careful stages. Third, it has been linked to reductions in other taxes. When it was introduced in Britain in 1972 the rate was just 8 per cent. In 1979 it was raised by the new Thatcher government to 15 per cent, but with the ostensible aim of financing a popular reduction in the basic rate and higher rates of income tax. In 1991 the increase to the present level was "sold" as part of a package to replace the unpopular Community Charge.[73] When the government sought to levy VAT on domestic fuel, it attempted to phase it in, beginning at a lower rate of 8 per cent. As the Major government's majority in the House of Commons was whittled away, it proved impossible to raise this rate any further.

As a result of such finesse, VAT is not (as is sometimes assumed) a regressive tax.[74] However, the old and distinctly regressive excise lingers on in Britain in the form of the immensely high duties on tobacco, alcohol and fuel. Together, excise duties and VAT account for 88 per cent of the price of a gallon of diesel, 82 per cent of the price of a packet of cigarettes and 64 per cent of the price of a bottle of spirits.[75] As a result, the overall burden of indirect taxation is in fact slightly regressive in Britain: in 1995 a father of two on less than average earnings paid 13.5 per cent in VAT and other indirect taxes; whereas a father of two on more than average earnings paid 12.8 per cent.[76] Put differently, in 1993 households in the bottom fifth of the population paid around 30 per cent of their disposable income in indirect taxes; for those in the top fifth, the figure was closer to 15 per cent.[77] In particular, the tax on tobacco is regressive, as lower income groups not only spend a bigger proportion of their income on cigarettes, but also smoke more.[78] Other countries tax smoking, drinking and driving, of course; but few tax them so punitively. In the United States, taxes on these simple pleasures amount to a mere 2.6 per cent of total government revenue. The equivalent figure for Britain is 12.2 per cent.[79]

The high British excises on tobacco, alcohol and fuel are no longer intended solely to raise revenue: they are also intended to deter people from consuming the commodities in question for medical and environmental reasons.

Unfortunately, as could easily have been predicted, the high rates of duty have tended to encourage smuggling as much as to discourage consumption; while revenue has fallen in relative terms (in the case of tobacco, from 15 per cent of total taxation in 1947 to less than 3 per cent by 1990).[80] Nor should the efficacy of VAT be exaggerated. A substantial part of the so-called "black economy" exists because small businessmen wish to avoid becoming liable for VAT and other taxes which fall on enterprise. According to European Union estimates in 1998, the "shadow" labor market in Britain is equivalent to around 12 per cent of GDP. Detailed research on the Austrian economy suggests that the avoidance of indirect tax has been an increasingly important motive for the growth of the black economy.[81] As in the case of import duties, there are limits to how much money can be raised from taxes on consumption and value added, particularly in a world of highly mobile people and goods—witness the European fuel protests of 2000.

"PICKING OVER THE FRUITS": DIRECT TAX

The simplest form of direct tax is the poll tax, which requires a payment from everyone. Poll taxes were a feature of English finance in the fourteenth century and again in the mid-seventeenth; the French *ancien régime* also had its *capitation* (first introduced in 1695) from 1701 until 1789.[82] The "soul tax" was the basis of Russian taxation from the time of Peter the Great until the Revolution.[83]

The difficulty with poll taxes is that they are regressive, requiring the poor to give up a much larger proportion of their income than the rich. For this reason they too have sometimes provoked tax revolts. These occupy a special place in English history because it was a poll tax—a shilling per head on all adults over 15 except beggars—that triggered the 1381 Peasants' Revolt; and because it was the introduction of the Community Charge to England that struck the fatal blow to Margaret Thatcher's position as prime minister in 1990.

For this reason, poll taxes have more often been imposed on minorities than whole populations. The Athenians imposed a poll tax on foreign-born residents only.[84] The early Abbasid caliphate collected a poll tax from all non-Muslims; though this had to be abandoned as more and more infidels responded to the obvious incentive by converting to Islam.[85] The Holy Roman Empire demanded a poll tax from Jewish communities.

One direct tax that very clearly exempts the poor is a land or property tax, which is imposed in proportion to an individual or community's holding of real estate. This was the basis of the Anglo-Saxon *geld* levied to finance the defence of the kingdom against the Danes.[86] It was also the basis of the "subsidies" that developed in both England and France to help finance their crusades and wars in the twelfth and thirteenth centuries, with payment of tax by landowners substituting for their notional obligation to perform military service for the crown.[87] The French *taille* was a geographically apportioned tax assessed on landed incomes; augmented by various surtaxes, it was still the biggest direct tax in France as late as 1780. More than 60 per cent of the revenues collected by Suleiman the Magnificent from Ottoman-controlled Egypt in the sixteenth century came from the land tax.[88] Likewise, the land tax in Tokugawa Japan amounted to 40 per cent of rice product and may have yielded as much as a quarter of national product.[89] In Mughal India at the end of the reign of Akbar the land tax amounted to around a sixth of national product.[90]

In many ways, the land tax is the natural tax for a mainly agrarian society. Indeed, to the French Physiocrats, a tax on the net income from land was the sole necessary tax.[91] Joseph II of Austria also dreamt of reforming Habsburg finances on this basis. However, more commercial societies have also taxed land, though differentially: the Dutch United Provinces taxed agricultural land at 20 per cent of rental values, but built-on land at just 12.5 per cent. Business profits were tax-free.[92] Before the First World War, Lloyd George too advocated a levy on land values and a capital gains tax on land; though his aim was redistribution of land once the national land valuation had been completed.

The disadvantages of a land tax are twofold: first, it discriminates against landowners as compared with holders of financial and other moveable assets; secondly, it requires accurate knowledge on the part of the tax assessors of the structure of land ownership and the productivity of individual holdings. The latter is the greater defect: for in the time that it takes to carry out an accurate survey of landownership, who knows how many acres will have changed hands? Even in the Italian city-states this proved problematic. Fifteenth-century Florence based its property tax on a survey of property ownership, the *catasto*, which was regularly updated (eight times between 1427 and 1495) before finally being abandoned in favour of a simple 10 per cent tithe.[93] Cardinal Wolsey's attempt to arrive at an accurate survey of English wealth—"the Great Proscription" of 1522—had to be abandoned in the face of aristocratic opposition.[94] The assessment that formed the basis of the 1692 English land tax (approximately a fifth of total rents) rapidly became out of date because of the eighteenth-century agricultural revolution, though the "quotas" derived from it continued to be used until the 1790s. In the words of Adam Smith, a land tax necessitated "the continual and painful attention of government to all the variations of the state and produce of every different farm in the country."[95] French fiscal reformers of the *ancien régime* dreamt of a new cadastral survey, but were put off by the thought that it would take more than three thousand surveyors to do the job.[96] A survey was finally initiated by Napoleon in 1808; it was already out of date by the time it was completed forty-two years, eleven million proprietors and 126 million plots of land later.[97] Thereafter, the tax on which it was based was not only whittled away by rising productivity but also became less fair because no account could be taken of differential improvements. By 1914 the land tax on brought in a mere 2.3 per cent of total revenue.[98]

One way around this problem is to levy taxes on property at the time it is inherited. As Lloyd George wryly remarked: "Death is the most convenient time to tax rich people." Ancient Rome had such an inheritance tax (the British slang "death duty" is more vivid), which was levied at a rate of 5 per cent and accounted for a little more than the same proportion of total revenues.[99] Although commonly seen as a twentieth-century innovation in Britain, it was in fact as early as 1853 that so-called "succession duties" were extended to real estate. And although the Liberal Chancellor Sir William Harcourt usually gets the credit (or blame) for introducing modern "death duties" in 1894, his Conservative predecessor George Goschen had anticipated him in 1889 with his one per cent duty on all estates above £10,000 in value. As critics predicted, this was the thin end of the wedge. By the time of Lloyd George's "People's Budget," raising "death duties" had become almost routine for left-of-center Chancellors. Even conservatives on the continent turned to the inheritance tax. When the German government sought to increase the Reich's share of direct taxation (which was largely in the hands of the federal states), the first major proposal was for an inheritance tax. In both cases, there was fierce but ultimately vain opposition from aristocratic interests.

Though inheritance tax rates rose to punitively high levels for the rich in the course of the twentieth century, there have never been enough rich people—to be precise, enough rich people without accountants—to raise significant sums. Today inheritance tax brings in less than 1 per cent of total public revenue in both Britain and America, and conservative politicians in both countries have begun to argue for its extinction.

The main alternative to inheritance tax has been some kind of general tax on income which, in its simplest form, requires the same proportional sacrifice from everyone, regardless of the source of their income. The first of Adam Smith's four "canons" of taxation was that "the subjects of every state ought to contribute towards the support of the government, as nearly as possible, in proportion to their respective abilities; that is, in proportion to the revenue which they respectively enjoy under the protection of the state."[100] A similar formulation formed part of the French revolutionaries' "Declaration of the Rights of Man and the Citizen." Taxes must be "apportioned equally among all citizens according to their capacity to pay."[101] This was hardly a new concept. In ancient times, tax was often set at a tenth of annual income. Such was the form of the eighth-century Abbasid *ushr*;[102] the fourteenth-century English tithe on the clergy as well as the parliamentary "tenth" (supplemented later by a fifteenth);[103] the Venetian *decima*;[104] the short-lived eighteenth-century French *dixiéme*, later the *vingtiéme*.[105] The first English attempt at an income tax was a 20 per cent levy on all incomes introduced in 1692.[106] But it is Pitt's income tax of 1798—again a 10 per cent levy—which is usually seen as the real milestone in the history of taxation, ultimately providing nearly a third of the additional revenue needed to win the wars with France.[107]

In fact, Pitt's tax was repealed in 1802; and the modified version introduced by his successor Addington when war resumed the following year was voted out of existence as soon as the war ended in 1815. That naval officer spoke for many who declared in 1799: "It is a vile, Jacobin, jumped up Jack-in-Office piece of impertinence—is a true Briton to have no privacy? Are the fruits of his labor and toil to be picked over, farthing by farthing, by the pimply minions of bureaucracy?"[108] It was not until 1842, as we have seen, that a peacetime income tax was introduced by Peel, and it was (and, in a spirit of defiant parliamentary hope, remains to this day) formally a temporary measure.[109] Despite repeated pledges by both Gladstone and Disraeli to do away with this "unjust, unequal and inquisitorial" measure, it has proved indestructible. Moreover, the years since 1876 have everywhere seen a sustained rise in the rate at which the tax is levied. At its lowest level after 1842 (the mid-1870s), the standard rate of British income tax was less than 1 per cent. By the eve of the First World War, however, it had risen to just under 6 per cent. By the end of the war, the figure was 30 per cent. It was only 1 per cent lower on the eve of the next war. By 1945 the figure was 50 per cent. The standard rate fell only slowly in the post-war years: in 1972 it was still just under 39 per cent, and reductions of what became known as the basic rate in the 1970s were compensated for by higher rates for higher incomes (see below). Only with the election of Margaret Thatcher in 1979 was there a real effort to reduce income tax, though the basic rate at the time of writing (23 per cent) is still higher than the average for the First World War years.

There are a number of ways to refine the income tax. It is possible to exempt poorer taxpayers by setting a threshold below which no tax is payable. In thirteenth-century England, householders with movable property valued below 10 shillings enjoyed such an exemption; after 1334 the proportion of the population which was below the direct tax threshold fluctuated between a tenth and a half.[110] Pitt's tax exempted incomes below £60 a year; while Peel's income tax, introduced at a rate of 7 pence in the pound (3 per cent), exempted all those whose incomes were below £150 per annum.[111] Thereafter, tinkering with the threshold became a favourite occupation of Victorian Chancellors of the Exchequer. In 1853 Gladstone lowered it to £100, which he called "the equatorial line of British incomes." In 1874 Disraeli put it back up to £150.[112] Another form of partial exemption is the allowance, which effectively raises the threshold for specific groups by making an additional tranche of their income tax-free. In 1909, for example, Lloyd George introduced an allowance of £10 per child for parents.

Aristocratic polities, of course, were just as likely to grant exemption from tax to the rich: indeed, for most of the early modern period exemption from tax was as much a privilege of high rank as of low income. This was the principal defect of the French *taille*, which was unpopular mainly because the large number of exemptions drove up the burden on those who did pay.[113] Nor was it easy to get rid of such privileges once they were established. Attempts in Catholic states to increase clerical taxation at the time of the Reformation led to a strike by the clergy of Castile in 1532.[114] Between 1561 and 1788 the proportion of total French expenditure paid for by clerical taxation fell from 15 per cent to just 1 per cent.[115] Attempts to increase the taxation of the French nobility after 1749 generated loud complaints; and even Calonne assumed in his plans for fiscal reform that the nobility would not have to pay the *taille*, or indeed the *capitation*.[116] Nor was it only the nobles and clergy who avoided paying the taille: magistrates, royal officials and some urban elites were also exempt. Prussian landowners regarded exemption from taxation as a privilege of their rank, and persisted in evading tax even once it had legally been imposed upon them; something they could easily do in their capacity as local tax-collectors.

The converse has proved less true: left-wing governments, whatever else they may have achieved, have failed to preserve the Victorian exemption of the working class from income tax. The main reasons for this have been the huge costs of the world wars, which necessitated a widening of the tax net; the rise of working-class income far above subsistence level; and the effect of inflation, which has lowered the real value of thresholds (the phenomenon of "bracket-creep"). In Britain the number of income tax payers more than trebled from 1,130,000 in 1913 to 3,547,000 in 1918, while the proportion of wage-earners paying tax rose from zero to 58 per cent.[117] In Germany after 1918 tax deducted from wages at source accounted for a steadily rising share of total direct tax revenue as middle-class taxpayers delayed payment of their tax bills, leaving inflation to reduce them in real terms.[118] Lowering allowances, or allowing inflation to lower them, remains the simplest means of increasing income tax. It was one of the ways Britain financed the Second World War, though in this case the additional tax paid as a result of the reduced personal allowances was subsequently repaid (albeit in depreciated pounds). Since the war, the tax threshold has crept relentlessly downward. In 1949 a father of two on average manual earnings paid no income tax; but twenty years later he began paying tax as soon as his earnings exceeded 53 per cent of the average. Conservative rule in the 1980s and 1990s did nothing to halt this trend. In 1979 a father of two had to earn just 35 per cent of average manual income to become liable for income tax. By 1995 the figure had fallen to 30.7 per cent.[119]

It is also possible to differentiate between different sources of revenue, so that (for example) income from investments is taxed at a higher rate than income from wages. An early example of differentiation was the subsidy introduced in the reign of Mary I, which was set at 4 shillings in the pound for landed incomes, but just 2 shillings and 8 pence for income from other forms of property.[120] When Addington reformed the income tax in 1803, he introduced the five "Schedules" still used by the Inland Revenue today which distinguished the different sources of an individual taxpayer's income: A (income from land and buildings), B (farming profits), C (public annuities), D (self-employment and other items) and E (salaries, annuities and pensions). Although he made no attempt to tax the schedules differently, a mechanism to do so had been put in place. The introduction of tax deductions for business expenses already implied a discrimination between earned and "unearned" (i.e. investment) income as early as 1853. However, it was not until 1907 that differential rates were introduced by Asquith, who raised the rate on earned income to 9 pence in the pound, but the rate on unearned income to a shilling. Lloyd George proposed a further 2 pence on the unearned rate two years later. Penalizing investment income remained the norm in twentieth-century British budgets until the 1980s.

An income tax can also be *graduated* so that the tax rate rises in some kind of (seldom exact) proportion to the size of one's income. An early example of a progressive income tax was the short-lived French *fouage*, which was intended to produce an average of 3 francs per hearth, but rose from 1 to 9 francs depending on the wealth of the household.[121] The idea was formalized in the eighteenth century by (among others) Jean-Louis Graslin, who argued for a direct tax scale rising from zero to 20 per cent on the highest incomes.[122] During the Revolution Robespierre took up the idea: "Those citizens whose incomes do not exceed what is necessary to their subsistence shall be exempted from contributing to public expenditure; the others shall support it progressively, according to their fortune."[123] The association of graduation with Jacobinism took a long time to fade, and not only in France: Gladstone detected in graduation "a distinct tendency towards communism."[124] It might, he warned, "amount to confiscation."

Yet Gladstone himself admitted that "the principle of graduated taxation had already been recognized by the income tax exemptions"; and he himself introduced an element of graduation to the income tax in 1853, when a lower rate was introduced for income between £100 and £150; and in 1863, when he introduced a £60 allowance for tax-payers earning less than £200, a device developed further by Disraeli in 1874. The real departure, however, was the introduction of higher rates of tax for higher income groups: this came in 1909 with Lloyd George's "People's Budget," which introduced three different rates: 3.75 per cent on incomes up to £2,000 a year, 5 per cent on incomes up to £3,000 and 5.83 per cent on incomes above £3,000. In addition a new "super-tax" ("surtax" for short) of 2.5 per cent was levied on income above £5,000. Lloyd George's (defeated) Finance Bill of 1914 envisaged a lower threshold for this higher band and a steeper "gradient," as well as proposing graduation for death duties.[125] By 1939 the "surtax" rate was 41 per cent; by 1945 it was 48 per cent (for incomes over £20,000). Again, it was not until the 1980s that these rates were lowered—to 40 per cent in the case of the higher rate.

Finally, the twentieth-century has seen the advent of tax on the incomes of companies as well as individuals. In Britain, the First World War once again was the watershed, with the introduction of the Excess Profits Duty, which taxed the difference between pre-war and war-time profits. The same measure was adopted in the Second World War, when the rate rose to 100 per cent; though there was a 20 per cent rebate after the war. In 1965 the Labor government introduced Corporation Tax on company profits and a Capital Gains Tax on the appreciation of assets.

The crucial difficulty of income tax remains the method of assessment. Should income be assessed by the state according to "objective" indicators, as was the case in the France until 1914? Or can the state trust citizens to declare their annual income, assuming that the majority will not understate their earnings by too much? If not, how much power of inquisition can the state be allowed? The French preference for assessed taxation—not only of land, but also of businesses, individuals, movable property, doors and windows—proved costly, as the "objective" values in each case tended to lag behind economic growth. The collection of the *vingtiéme*, for example, depended heavily on local verification of assessments; but only a fifth of parishes in the *pays d'élections* co-operated with this in the 1770s.[126]

In the United States and in Britain, by contrast, a system of individual declaration evolved. It remains intact in the United States today, where the number of individual tax returns each year now exceeds 120 million. But the enormous financial costs of the Second World War, combined with the rising money incomes of manual workers, brought to an end the purely declaratory system in Britain. Ever since the introduction of Pay As You Earn—PAYE—in 1944, British employers have been required to deduct tax "at source" from the wages and salaries they pay. Even so, income tax is still considerably more expensive to collect than customs and excises. In 1992–3 Customs and Excise collected only 16 per cent less tax than the Inland Revenue, but at roughly half the cost: just over 1 per cent of the total tax collected, compared with a figure of 2 per cent for the Inland Revenue, which employs more than double the number of staff.[127] At least part of the explanation for this discrepancy lies in the complexity of the system that has developed as one Chancellor after another has tinkered with tax reliefs in the hope of pleasing selected interest groups. In 1989 the Labor MP Frank Field estimated that if all tax allowances and reliefs were abolished, a standard rate of 12–15 pence in the pound would be possible.[128]

There is no question that income tax has been the crucial lever of modern fiscal policy. In most states it rose steadily from the 1890s until the 1970s (see Figure 5). However, its importance has varied from place to place. The individual German states followed the British example in the second half of the nineteenth century, but the Reich itself did not secure control of income tax until after the First World War. ("How jubilant the German people would be," observed the economist Gustav Schmoller in all seriousness in 1909,

Figure 5. Income tax as a percentage of taxation, 1866–1999

Sources: Flora et al., *State, Economy and Society,* vol. i, pp. 299, 305, 339; Butler and Butler, *British Political Facts,* pp. 391 f.

"had it so adaptable a factor of revenue . . .")[129] During the Civil War, the United States introduced a federal income tax, but it was abolished after the war, and declared unconstitutional by the Supreme Court in 1893.[130] The radical principle that the state should not be allowed to probe the individual's private affairs meant that France did not introduce an income tax until as late as 1914. This difference persists. In Britain and America today income tax accounts for a quarter of total public revenue; in Germany for as much as 36 per cent; in France for a mere 17 per cent.

Only belatedly (and at much higher rates than Victorian opponents of "confiscation" had expected) did diminishing returns set in. By 1947 the standard rate of income tax in Britain was 45 per cent; that of surtax was 52 per cent. Taking into account the special contribution payable when a person's total income exceeded £2,000 (50 per cent for investment income over £5,000), the effective rate of tax on investment income above that threshold for a higher-rate taxpayer was 147.5 per cent.[131] Twenty years later the situation was little different: by then the effective rate on such income was 136 per cent. Under James Callaghan in the mid-1970s the top rate of tax was raised to 83 per cent, producing a top marginal tax rate of 98 per cent on investment income.[132] It is hard to imagine much stronger economic disincentives than these; though as with indirect taxation, punitively high rates on income are more likely to encourage evasion than abstinence, to say nothing of promoting the art of avoidance. Ultimately, the excessive income tax rates of the post-war period affected enough people directly or indirectly (through their undoubted dampening effect on aggregate growth)[133] to generate a political reaction, strongest in Britain and the United States, in the 1980s.

Yet the extent to which the Thatcher and Reagan governments were able to alter their respective fiscal systems should not be exaggerated. The high costs of taming inflation made it difficult to cut taxes across the board; and the net effect of reductions in tax rates was much less than might be expected. True, the marginal rate of taxation in Britain fell between 1978 and 1995 from 53 per cent to 44 per cent. But whereas a married father of two on average earnings paid 20.9 per cent of his gross income in income tax and national insurance contributions in 1978, twelve years later the figure was 20.8—hardly a huge tax cut. Moreover, the figure rose under the Major government to 22.5 per cent in 1995. On average, those on lower incomes (say three-quarters of average earnings) did slightly worse under the Conservatives than those on higher incomes (50 per cent higher than average). But more striking than this is the general consistency of direct tax rates and indeed the tax burden as a whole.[134] It should also be remembered that the proportion of total income tax paid by the top 1 per cent of taxpayers went up from 11 to 15 per cent under Margaret Thatcher: a good example of lower tax rates bringing in higher revenues.[135]

THE TWO SISTERS

The balance between direct and indirect taxation has thus varied a great deal over time and between different states. Indirect taxes accounted for nearly all of the tax revenues of the English crown in the fourteenth and fifteenth centuries, but by the 1550s for little more than a tenth. Throughout the sixteenth century they only exceeded 50 per cent five times; and during the Commonwealth they averaged just 20 per cent. It was not until the 1750s that the share of indirect taxes rose back to between 70 and 80 per cent.[136] In the first half of the nineteenth century, despite the sustained reduction of import duties, this did not change much, since the liberal theory that cutting duties would increase revenue proved to be broadly true. However, the intro-duction of the peacetime income tax confirmed that a liberal trade policy could not be reconciled with continued imperialism without direct tax.[137]

In Gladstone's rather labored metaphor, direct and indirect tax were like "two attractive sisters, who have been introduced into the gay world of Lon-don; each with an ample fortune." Throughout his career, he continued to dream of abolishing income tax, but had to admit that, "whether it be due to a lax sense of moral obligation or not . . . as Chancellor of the Exchequer . . . I have always thought it not only allowable, but even an act of duty, to pay my addresses to them both."[138] Yet the proportion of total gross rev-enue coming from direct tax remained remarkably low for much of his career. When he entered parliament in 1832 customs and excise alone accounted for over 70 per cent of gross revenue; in 1875 it was still 64 per cent. Only gradually did the share of direct tax in total taxation rise, from a third in 1868 to 57 per cent in 1910.[139] The First World War and its subse-quent costs drove the figure up to just under 70 per cent in 1920, a peak not exceeded until 1975, after which the direct tax burden has tended to dimin-ish. At the time of writing, direct taxes account for around half of total UK government revenue.

France had relatively high direct taxation under the *ancien régime*—it accounted for some 41 per cent of total revenue—and this remained the case at the end of the First Empire, by which time the figure was 43 per cent.[140] But subsequently the balance shifted in the other direction, not least because the various assessed taxes proved to be very inelastic sources of revenue.[141] Between 1815 and 1913 direct tax fell steadily as a proportion of total rev-enue from 34 per cent during the Bourbon Restoration, to 24 per cent under the Second Empire, to just 13 per cent on the eve of the First World War. The proportion coming from indirect tax rose from 22 to 55 per cent.[142] Thus, as has rightly been remarked, "the principle of justice in the sense of equal-ity of incidence was increasingly infringed *de facto* though ever more strongly entrenched *de jure*."[143] The pendulum swung back the other way under the influence of the world wars: between 1920 and 1945 the share of total revenue coming from direct tax rose from 26 per cent to 52 per cent. However, between 1950 and 1975 the proportion averaged just 37 per cent. That was also the figure in 1997.

It therefore appears that the high tide of direct taxation has passed, though it is not clear whether a new equilibrium has been reached. It is often said that the appetite of the British and American electorates for cuts in direct taxation has waned since the 1980s; and there are those who maintain that

British voters would pay more income tax if they believed it would lead to an improvement in public services. The reality is that, as international barriers to the migration of skilled labor have fallen, so the degree of tax competition between nation states has tended to rise. We are therefore unlikely to see a return to the punitively high marginal rates of taxation seen in the 1970s, though that is not to say that the aggregate revenue from direct taxation might not increase even as rates are further reduced. The fact remains that indirect taxation, whether on consumption or on turnover, is cheaper to levy and on balance less objectionable to those who pay it. People are much less likely to emigrate to escape 70 per cent cigarette duties than to escape a 70 per cent income tax bracket. On the other hand, excessive indirect taxation will tend to encourage smuggling and the black economy. Like Gladstone, modern finance ministers must therefore continue to pay their addresses to both the sisters—unattractive though they appear to the taxpayer.

THE POET AS TAXMAN

This chapter began with a famous exchange about the inevitability of taxation between Benjamin Franklin and Jean-Baptiste Le Roy in November 1789. Without unpopular taxes, it might be said, Franklin would not have found himself the plenipotentiary of a new republic. And without political problems not unrelated to taxation—about which more in the next chapter—Le Roy might have lived the rest of his life under an absolute monarchy. Another man who, by temperament and conviction, would have made a fine revolutionary in the same era was the Scottish poet Robert Burns. Lowborn, a Freemason, a religious sceptic, a nationalist, a drinker and a womanizer, Burns might, with a little less levity, have been Scotland's Danton. As early as 1785 he was penning risqué verses in celebration of "LIBERTY'S . . . glorious feast"; events in France after 1789 served to politicize him further. By the mid-1790s he counted among his "most intimate" friends Dr William Maxwell, who had been among the guards in attendance at Louis XVI's execution—an event Burns dismissed scornfully as "the delivering over [of] a perjured Blockhead . . . into the hands of the hangman."[144] Filled with egalitarian zeal, it was Burns who gave the revolutionary era one of its most enduring anthems in "A Man's a Man for a' that":

> For a' that, and a' that,
>   It's comin yet for a' that,

That Man to Man the warld o'er,
Shall brothers be for a' that.[145]

A less well-known example of Burns's radicalism is his populist attack on the excise tax, "The De'il's awa wi' th' Exciseman," composed in 1792, which nicely captures popular attitudes towards the British state's ubiquitous revenue-gathering agency:

We'll mak our maut and we'll brew our drink,
    We'll laugh, sing and rejoice, man;
And mony braw thanks to the meikle black deil,
    That danc'd awa wi' th' Exciseman.[146]

Yet Burns's revolutionary potential never came to fruition, as it might have done had he been born in France or emigrated—which he briefly contemplated—to the colonies. And one reason for this lies in the simple fact that, from 1788, he himself was in the employ of the Excise, on a starting salary of £50 per annum, plus commissions on goods seized.[147] This was no post for a would-be Jacobin. In December 1792, when Burns was accused of "disaffected . . . political conduct" during a revolutionary commotion at the Dumfries playhouse, he had to write a grovelling letter of denial to his patron, Robert Graham of Fintry, the Commissioner of the Scottish Board of Excise. Admitting to having been France's "enthusiastic votary in the beginning of the business" (meaning the Revolution), Burns now solemnly pledged to "seal up [his] lips."[148] He would sing the revolutionary Ça ira no more.

As we shall see, the strength of the Hanoverian British tax system lay precisely in the way it combined élite sanction through parliament with public compliance—and complicity—through bureaucracy. Even in his letter of exculpation, Burns still ventured to assert that "an alarming System of Corruption has pervaded the connection between the Executive Power and the House of Commons." But the point was that, for the sake of his job with the Excise, he would cease to voice such beliefs. The "System of Corruption" had him firmly in its grip.

It is to the relationships epitomized by Burns's predicament—between taxation, representation (or lack of it) and administration—that we now turn.

3

The Commons and the Castle:
Representation and Administration

In moderate states, there is a compensation for heavy taxes; it is liberty.
In despotic states, there is an equivalent for liberty; it is the modest taxes.

Montesquieu[1]

For most of history, direct taxes could be collected only with the co-operation of the richer groups in society. For that reason, the widening of the direct tax "base" has very often been associated with extension of political representation, as taxpayers have traded shares of their income for participation in the political process, a fundamental part of which is the enactment of tax legislation. In this model, the process of democratization is inseparable from the growth of the band of income and property tax payers. The slogan "no taxation without representation" neatly encapsulates the trade-off.

However, an alternative—or, more often, additional—direct tax-raising strategy has been to create a competent civil service paid by the state to collect tax. In this model, there is representation of a sort; but participation in administration clearly differs from participation in legislation. If liberty is well served by the representation of taxpayers in legislatures, it is generally diminished by the growth of a tax-collecting bureaucracy.

This chapter is about the interaction of these related processes: tax raising; the growth of political representation; and the growth of civil services. Though its starting-point will be familiar to any political theorist, its development is novel. The key point is that far from leading to a gradual parliamentarization (the "Whig" paradigm caricatured by Herbert Butterfield[2])—or, for that matter, to a happy "post-historical" equilibrium—the interaction of taxation, representation and administration can produce a variety of different outcomes, not all of them benign.

An important measure introduced here is the ratio of voters to taxpayers, and particularly income tax payers. If that ratio is significantly above unity—if there is representation without taxation, in other words—then the executive

can be susceptible to political pressures for increased non-military expenditure from the untaxed or less taxed voters. Also potentially important is the ratio of public employees to taxpayers. It is not coincidental that democratization often coincides with a growth in public employment, transforming the relatively exclusive system of patronage of the *ancien régime*—lampooned as "old corruption" by nineteenth-century reformers—into a new form of corruption in which the voter-clients of democratic political machines are rewarded with "jobs for the boys." The bureaucracy, which to begin with optimized the state's revenue raising power, becomes itself an expense.

Both the expansion of the franchise and the expansion of public sector employment tend to push up non-military expenditure. This was the "law of the growing activity of the state" discerned by the German economist Adolph Wagner as early as 1863.[3] At the same time, the importance of transfers from one social group to another tends to increase, as the budget is increasingly used as a device for the redistribution of income. In addition to public employment, the cost of publicly funded *un*employment tends to rise as the proliferation of doles distorts the labor market. The gap between revenue—what the electorate is prepared to pay—and expenditure—what they expect the welfare state to provide—becomes institutionalized. It was these processes that prompted the great Austrian sociologist Joseph Schumpeter to diagnose the "fiscal crisis of the tax state" more than eighty years ago.[4]

TAXATION AND REPRESENTATION

Ever since the time of ancient Athens, the link between taxation and political representation has been the crux of democracy, though the *demos* itself has been (and continues to be) variously defined. The Athens of Pericles expected the propertied class to pay for public festivals and warships; and in 428 B.C. introduced a property tax to help pay for the Peloponnesian War. The corollary of this was the advent of democracy (though of course only the propertied élite were represented): decisions on taxation were made by mass meetings of adult male citizens and administered by a council of five hundred.[5]

Conversely, undemocratic regimes prefer sources of revenue independent of popular consent. The maintenance of the royal domain as a source of Prussian revenue into the nineteenth century, for example, was part of a political strategy to preserve monarchical power. As Baron vom Stein put it:

The income from the domains is the economic foundation of the sovereign kingdom and therefore of independent internal and external state building, because the crown's domain is the foundation of the material independence of the king against the . . . corporations of the estates [i.e. representative assemblies]. Hence, domains exist and will continue to exist as long as there are kingdoms.[6]

The difficulty, as we have seen, is that such non-consensual sources of revenue have generally proved less elastic than taxation based on consent. For that reason, it is tempting to rephrase Montesquieu: it is precisely liberty—in the sense of representative government—that permits high taxation. Or does it?

The country with the longest unbroken history of consensual taxation is England. It was during the Hundred Years War that the convention took root that the extraordinary taxation necessary to finance the conflict with France required parliamentary approval.[7] Edward I may be said to have begun the practice of summoning parliaments of the crown's lay and ecclesiastical tenants-in-chief, as well as representatives of the shires and towns. From the fourteenth century onwards the lords and later the commons begin to present "lists of grievances which they linked implicitly (and occasionally more explicitly) to the grants of supply," expecting remedial legislation in return for "supply." A key moment came in 1306 when the crown commuted a "gracious aid and tallage" in return for a general subsidy authorized by parliament. By the middle of that century it was widely accepted that most formal legislative acts could only be made in Parliament.[8]

The key to English constitutional development in the sixteenth and seventeenth centuries was the structural dependence of the monarch on sources of revenue controlled by parliaments: the tenth and fifteenth and the subsidy. The relative decline during the reign of Elizabeth I of the other sources of revenue which the crown controlled directly—domain income and customs—placed her Stuart successors in a position of serious weakness.[9] As James VI and I put it: "The only disease and consumption which I can ever apprehend as likeliest to endanger me, is this eating canker of want, which being removed, I could think myself as happy in all other respects as any other King or Monarch that ever was since the birth of Christ."[10] Innovations such as "impositions" on trade, forced loans, sales of monopolies or titles and purveyance tended to arouse parliamentary and judicial opposition.[11] Yet there was nothing predestined about the triumph of parliament in the 1640s: Charles I's attempt to expand extra-parliamentary sources of finance (particularly the extension of the coastal defence levy known as "Ship

Money" to inland counties) might well have succeeded had it not been for his expensive and unsuccessful war against the Scots. By the later 1630s Ship Money was already bringing in three times as much as parliamentary subsidies and threatened (as one parliamentarian anxiously put it) to become "an everlasting supply of all occasions."[12] It was Charles's failure to keep order in his multiple kingdoms that allowed the parliamentary principle to triumph. This had been enunciated clearly enough as early as 1628 in the Petition of Right's "prayer" that "no man hereafter be compelled to make or yield any gift, loan, benevolence, tax or such like charge without common consent by act of parliament." It was constitutionally secured by the "Glorious Revolution" of 1688 which gave parliament the exclusive authority to raise new taxes and the right to audit government spending.[13]

The pattern in France was quite different, not least because the French nobility had no desire to offer the king their money as well as their counsel. As early as the late fifteenth century Sir John Fortescue was contrasting France's *dominium regale*, where the sovereign could tax at will, with England's *dominium politicum et regale*, where the monarch required consent to tax.[14] Although Philip V (1316–22) used representative assemblies to raise tax, his inability to secure a subsidy in peacetime meant that the practice did not take root. The French Estates met again in 1355 and 1356 but, even with King John II a prisoner and a ransom demand before them, they failed to produce adequate money.[15] Prior to 1789 they only met four times (in 1484, 1560–1561, 1588 and 1614–15); an Assembly of Notables was summoned twice.[16] Only the *parlements* continued to claim and exercise a right of remonstrance and were able to exert some influence over fiscal policy by refusing to register new royal loans (as in 1784 and 1785).[17]

When, in 1786, Calonne advised Louis XVI to convoke an "Assembly of Notables" to sanction his planned reform of royal finances—principally a new land tax—he was therefore reviving a long-dormant representative principle. Although the Assembly was supposed to be a rubber-stamp, Calonne's decision to pack it with representatives of the clergy and nobility proved to be a miscalculation, since they at once objected to any diminution of their tax exemptions, and demanded a permanent commission of auditors to supervise royal finances as well as, crucially, the summoning of the Estates General. When Louis appointed Brienne with a brief to press ahead with the reforms regardless, he found that the *parlements* would not register the new taxes. Louis exiled the *parlement* of Paris to Troyes, but Brienne was nevertheless obliged to drop the land tax. When the King sought to force registration of new loans at a "Royal Session" of the reconvened *parlement* on

19 November 1787—with the hubristic and by now anachronistic words "it is legal because I wish it"—the die was cast. In May 1788 the *parlement* asserted that taxation must have the consent of the Estates General and that they must meet regularly. On 8 August Brienne was forced to announce that the Estates General would meet the following May.[18]

The revolutionary import of the tax–representation nexus had also manifested itself twelve years before in Britain's American colonies.[19] The Americans were not, of course, the first people to seek independence from distant rulers in the face of taxes imposed on them without their consent; nor the last. (It was the introduction by Spain of a new property levy which prompted the Portuguese bid for independence in 1640, for example.) But the American case is the best known, not least because the causal link between the British decision to impose import duties on the thirteen American colonies and the Declaration of Independence nine years later is drummed into every American schoolchild.

It was not the amount of taxation that rankled. Indeed, in many ways it was really a tax *cut* elsewhere in the Empire that provoked the Boston Tea Party: the reduction of the duty on East India Company tea imported to Britain for re-export to America.[20] What was at stake was a constitutional question, namely that the colonies had no say in such matters. The principle was phrased eloquently by the Whig Lord Camden in February 1766: "Taxation and representation are inseparable . . . whatever is a man's own, is absolutely his own; no man hath a right to take it from him without his consent either expressed by himself or [his] representative; whoever attempts to do it, attempts an injury; whoever does it, commits a robbery; he throws down and destroys the distinction between liberty and slavery." The colonists put it more pithily: "Taxation without representation is tyranny." Yet for the colonists to raise the issue of representation in connection with a duty on their external trade was from the outset revolutionary. Adam Smith's counterfactual of giving the Americans representation in a kind of "states-general of the British Empire" in return for extending the full range of British taxes to the colonies may have been logical, but that was not what the colonists were after.[21] Their aim was to enhance the power of their local assemblies and ultimately—as became clear at the first Continental Congress—to give their institutions legislative parity with the Westminster parliament. But that ran counter to the doctrine of the sovereignty of parliament made sacrosanct by Sir William Blackstone's *Commentaries* and affirmed by the majority of British MPs.[22] The whole point of Townshend's 1767 tea duty was that it was intended to raise revenue to pay "independent Salaries for the civil officers in North America"—in other words, to make royal governors *more* independent of the colonists' assemblies.[23]

REPRESENTATION WITHOUT TAXATION

Representation is of course a matter of degree: there was a world of difference between the democratic republic envisaged by Tom Paine and the "virtual representation" supposedly enjoyed by voteless British subjects at Westminster. Yet virtual representation in a parliament of the propertied was better than no representation in an absolute monarchy. Was it also better in a practical sense?

It is sometimes assumed by political theorists that "representative institutions, not absolute monarchy, [are] superior in revenue extraction."[24] This, as we have seen, was Montesquieu's view. But, true as this was of Britain and France in the eighteenth century,[25] the correlation between representation and taxation has not been universal. A representative assembly can easily act as a serious check on the state's tax-raising capacity if the assembly does not approve of the government's spending priorities. When Sir Francis Bacon declared that the Englishman was "most master of his own valuation of any nation in Europe" in the seventeenth century, he might have added: "and therefore the least heavily taxed."[26] Eighteenth-century Poland was the *reductio ad absurdum*: almost no taxation *because* of representation. The nobility represented in the *Sejm* interpreted liberty as liberty from taxation, with the result that the country's revenues—and consequently the size of its army—stagnated, with fatal consequences.[27]

Paradoxically, the overthrow of the absolute monarchy in France and the triumph of the principle that taxes must have the consent of a bicameral legislature did not increase the willingness of the populace to pay tax: the new taxes introduced by the National Assembly (the *contribution foncière*, the *contribution mobilière et personnelle* and the *patente*) were failures in large part because of high levels of non-payment.[28] Even the British parliament sometimes succumbed to fiscal irresponsibility. The income tax was abolished with indecent haste almost as soon as the Napoleonic Wars ended— "amidst the greatest cheering and the loudest exultation ever witnessed within the walls of the English Senate"—despite the fact that expenditures exceeded revenue even with the income tax.[29] It is a good measure of the reckless mood of the Commons that a motion was passed that all books and records relating to it be destroyed was passed; fortunately, or unfortunately, copies had already been sent to the King's Remembrancer.[30]

Nevertheless, the course of British history between 1832 and 1918 can be understood as a parallel and in some measure complementary extension of both the franchise and the direct tax "net." Until 1884 the British franchise was in fact based on rental values (essentially, freeholders, leaseholders and householders whose properties exceeded a certain rental value were entitled to vote); but liability to local taxation was also a requirement in both county and borough constituencies. Proposals for electoral reform were also frequently related, both by opponents and proponents of reform, to fiscal criteria. "There ought," reasoned Gladstone, "to be an affinity between electoral privileges and contributions to taxes." If the former were to be limited so as to exclude the poor, then so must the latter be. "Financial feebleness and extravagance," in short, were "the sure means of generating excessive demands for reform."[31] His arch-rival Disraeli went so far as to propose as one of his "fancy franchises" in 1867 that all 20-shilling income tax payers be given the vote. Nor was this some subtle political arithmetic obscure to electors. A placard of the early 1860s, supporting Gladstone in his criticism of Palmerston's costly foreign adventures, makes this clear:

TAXPAYERS! . . . How long will you suffer yourself to be Humbugged by PALMER-STONIANISM and Robbed by the "Services," and others interested in a War Expenditure, even in times of Peace? . . . THE CHANCELLOR OF THE EXCHEQUER APPEALS TO YOU TO HELP HIM. . . . Reform the House of Commons, AND DO IT THOROUGHLY THIS TIME.[32]

Franchise reform, in other words, was a way of increasing the representation and power of taxpayers.

However, the expansion of the electorate tended to occur at a far faster rate than the expansion of the income tax bracket. Between 1832 and 1914 the proportion of adult males enfranchised rose from 18 per cent to 88 per cent (though around a third of these were still informally excluded because of the registration system, which depended on a prolonged period of residence in a constituency). But the number of income tax payers remained remarkably static—and low—in relation to the population. In short, while there was no taxation without representation, there was a great deal of representation without direct taxation. Under these circumstances, it is hardly surprising that there was growing pressure to increase direct taxation in the wake of the 1884 Reform Act: between 1867 and 1913 it more than quadrupled as a proportion of total revenue from 8 to 36 per cent. The standard rate of income tax rose from just 2 pence in the pound in 1876 to 14 pence in 1913.[33]

The significance of this link from democratization to rising direct taxation was not lost on contemporaries. Lord George Hamilton noted the way the 1884 Reform Act led to an increase in public pressure for higher naval spending: "The great addition to the electorate . . . had, to a large extent, swamped the old niggardly and skinflint policy of the Manchester School. . . . [T]he mass of the recently enfranchised escape direct taxation out of which new burdens of expenditure were mainly defrayed; but independently of this personal consideration, the wage earning classes are very proud of the Navy."[34] As Prime Minister, Salisbury took a similar view. The 1884 Act, he argued, had substantially diluted the representation of income tax payers in the Commons. Consequently, there was bound to be pressure for increased expenditure from those MPs representing tax-exempt sections of the electorate. Warning his Chancellor against financing new naval spending exclusively from income tax, Salisbury observed astutely: "It is dangerous to recur to realized property alone in difficulties because the holders of it are politically so weak that the pernicious financial habit is sure to grow."[35] It was not only Conservatives who thought this way: the Liberal Robert Lowe foresaw a conflict of interest between an enlarged electorate and the taxpaying élite during the debates on the 1867 Reform Bill. Such fears had respectable intellectual progenitors in Bentham, Tocqueville and John Stuart Mill.[36] By 1913 it was almost the conventional wisdom that (in the words of Sir Bernard Mallett): "[In] the modern democracy . . . policy may ultimately [be] controlled by, and in the interests of, the majority of an electorate consisting mainly of the poorer classes, while revenue is obtained mainly from a minority of wealthier persons."[37]

Because the First World War increased the number of income taxpayers by more than the number of voters, its effect was to lower the ratio of voters to taxpayers slightly, from 7 : 1 to 6 : 1. However, subsequent electoral reform between the wars—principally the lowering of the female voting age—pushed the ratio up even higher than its pre-war level: by 1935 it was more than 8 : 1. In the words of the authors of the definitive history of modern British public spending, "The widening of the franchise increased the political importance of the group most likely to believe that public expenditure should be increased for their benefit, but that the necessary revenues should be raised from others (the richer) by such means as a progressive taxation."[38] Perhaps the surprising thing in the light of this figure is that there was not more pres-sure to increase public spending in response to the Depression; we shall return to this conundrum later. The tendency since the Second World War has been for the ratio of voters to income tax payers to fall from more than 2 : 1 after the war to an equilibrium level of around 1.7 : 1—in other words, a situation in which there are roughly 70 per cent more voters than income tax payers. That ratio has varied only slightly since the mid-1960s.[39] What it means is that—contrary to the claim that in the welfare state "universal suffrage is combined with almost universal income taxpayer status"[40]—British democ-racy enfranchises more than eighteen million people who do not pay income tax (though needless to say they nearly all pay at least some indirect tax). In addition to those workers whose earnings fall below the income tax thresh-old, that figure includes the unemployed, other welfare recipients, poor pen-sioners, the medically incapacitated and students. Given the size of this group, it is perhaps surprising that Conservative efforts to reduce the overall burden of direct taxation achieved anything in the 1980s.[41]

The shift from taxation without representation to representation without direct taxation was by no means peculiar to Britain. Many nineteenth-cen-tury states defined eligibility to vote on the basis of direct taxation. In France between 1824 and 1830 suffrage was restricted by high direct tax minima and the highest taxpayers also elected 40 per cent of deputies. Just half of 1 per cent of men over 19 had the vote.[42] The 1830 Revolution scarcely changed this. Under Louis Philippe's "bourgeois monarchy," there contin-ued to be a direct tax minimum which was only slightly lower (now some-thing like 1 per cent of men over 19 could vote). When Guizot was chal-lenged about the high level of the threshold for qualification, his response was simple: "Enrichissez-vous!"—"So get rich!" In Italy too the suffrage included a minimum tax requirement until 1913, though the threshold was lowered in 1882 and continued to apply to voters between the ages of 21 and 29 until 1919.[43] In Prussia until as late as 1918 the ingenious three-class franchise for the lower house was based on direct tax payment: taxpayers were ranked according to the amount of tax they paid and divided into three groups each of which paid the same total *amount* of tax, the top third nat-urally having far fewer individuals than the others, but all three groups being given the same representation in the *Landtag*. Most of the member-states of the Reich restricted the vote in some such way; it was only at the federal level that there was universal adult male suffrage. Figure 6 shows how the exclu-siveness of European franchises diminished from the mid-nineteenth century onwards. It is worth noting that Britain lagged behind both France and Ger-

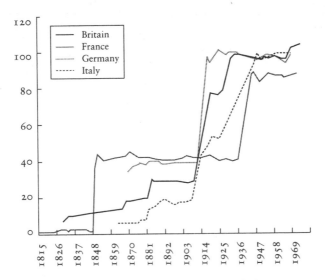

Figure 6. Electorate as a proportion of population aged above 20, 1815–1974

Sources: Flora et al., *State, Economy, and Society,* vol. i, pp. 113, 117 127,149.

many in the race to democratize before 1914, while Italy lagged behind Britain. After the First World War, however, the link between taxation and representation was broken.

In most modern democracies, there is now a considerable discrepancy between the number of people entitled to vote and the number who pay income tax. The British case is not so unusual. In the United States, the equivalent ratio since the war has been between 1.6 : 1 and 1.8 : 1. However, many voters (a high proportion of them non-taxpayers) do not exercise their right to determine who represents them. Only in the early 1960s did the number of active voters in elections to Congress exceed the number of income taxpayers. In 1990 just over 61 million Americans voted; nearly 114 million (almost twice as many) paid income tax. Millions of Americans today are liable to taxation without representation; unlike their colonial forebears, however, their disenfranchisement is largely voluntary.

KAFKA'S CASTLE

Yet it would be a mistake to regard the relationship between taxation and representation as implying some kind of paradigm of fiscal democratization:

the Whig theory of history translated into the realm of finance. Many modern authoritarian states have been able to extract high tax revenues without granting any representation to the populace. Tax can be collected without parliamentary consent, as it was (to name the obvious examples) in both fascist and Communist regimes after the First World War. But to do so effectively an army of tax collectors is needed: in short, a bureaucracy.

The origins of public employment lie in courts: institutions for dispensing justice and other forms of royal influence. The expenses of courts were in fact remarkably high in the early modern period, and not only in Europe. In the sixteenth century most of the expenditure of the Japanese shogunate went on the court.[44] The costs of his court, harem and stables seem to have accounted for nearly all the Mughal Emperor Akbar's expenditure.[45] But these institutions were seldom concerned with such humdrum matters as tax collection.

The emergence of bureaucracy in the modern sense—an organization of salaried officials charged with executing the executive's commands—was no more a linear development than the emergence of representative assemblies. In the medieval and early modern period, the temporal power was hampered by the fact that the Church all but monopolized the training of clerks capable of drafting and executing written instructions. The partial secularization of education created a supply of laymen willing to hold offices; but this should not deceive us into antedating the emergence of the modern bureaucracy.[46] The motivation of the "new men" often lauded by historians was more often to secure a stream of income for themselves (whether in the form of a salary or the 'perquisites' of office) than to rationalize administration in the Weberian sense. Indeed, many monarchs were tempted to treat offices as state assets—which they were, in the sense that they generated revenue—and simply sell them to the highest bidder.

This could take one of two forms: the sale of specific taxes to so-called "tax farmers" or the sale of specific offices to individuals. Tax farming was not unknown in England. From the reign of Elizabeth I until the Long Parliament, certain customs duties were farmed out.[47] However, it was far more important in France. In the first half of the seventeenth century, the three main farms (of the *gabelle*, the *aides* and the so-called *cinq grosses fermes* which controlled customs duties after 1584) accounted for 80 per cent of the income from all indirect taxation. In 1681 Colbert merged all the various excises and customs with the new tobacco monopoly, leasing them in their entirety to a syndicate of forty tax farmers known as the Farmers-General.[48] These leases were renegotiated every six years. The main disadvantage of tax farming is obvious: left to their own devices, the tax farmers creamed off a far larger share of the revenue passing through their hands than was in the interests of the executive. Half of total revenues simply never reached the French government.[49] Although there were attempts during the eighteenth century to move to a system of *régies* (whereby the government paid the tax farmers salaries and bonuses), the resistance of vested interests to thorough-going reform proved insuperable.[50] The Hôtel des Fermes came to be reviled as "an immense and infernal machine which seizes each citizen by the throat and pumps out his blood."[51]

The other fiscal device on which the French *ancien régime* came to depend was the sale of offices. This has been called "a second system of public debt," in the sense that office-holders invested some capital in an office, the income from which was equivalent to the interest on a government bond.[52] By 1660 there were around 46,000 office holders, whose offices had an approximate capital value of around 419 million livres. There may well have been politi-cal advantages to this system from the point of view of the French monar-chy. Contemplating the overthrow of James II in 1688, Louis XIV's advisers concluded that:

if England had as many officials supported by the king as France does, the revolution would never have occurred. For it is certain that so many officials means so many committed people attached to the maintenance of royal authority. Without that authority they would be naught. If it were destroyed they would instantly lose the large sums of money with which they bought their positions.[53]

The difficulty was that the fiscal costs of the system outweighed this apparent benefit. Although only a minority of offices were paid a salary, they represented a large liability for the crown, which could only partly be offset by taxes on office-holders such as the *paulette*. As early as 1639 annual payments to office-holders exceeded new income from sales of offices. By Colbert's time the crown was receiving 2 million livres in taxes from office-holders, but paying out 8.3 million livres in salaries. Though Colbert was successful in abolishing around 20,000 offices, his work was partly undone by the high costs of the Dutch War of the 1670s.[54] The attempt by Maupeou to reduce the number of offices in 1770 cut the total number by only 5 per cent.[55]

In place of tax farming and a venal officialdom, Britain developed, in the Department of Excise, the prototype of a modern bureaucracy, based on "recruitment by examination, training, promotion on merit, regular salaries and pensions, and standardized procedures."[56] The Excise still attracted rent-seekers like the poet Robert Burns; but he soon found he had to work for his salary. At the same time, there was a shift towards centralization of other revenue collection. By the end of the reign of Charles II, tax farming had been done away with and the Exchequer was in sole charge of accounting for the income and expenditure of all central government departments, a role ultimately taken over by the Treasury.[57] These reforms were little short of "an administrative revolution" with dramatic results:

In the 1670s, Charles II disposed of 2.7 times as much revenue as his benighted father had managed with such difficulty to collect just half a century earlier. Fifty years later, the revenues of the newly established Hanoverian regime were eight times, and in the 1770s eleven times, greater than those spent by Charles I. After the wars with Napoleon, the British state commanded thirty-six times as much revenue as that fiscally embarrassed and unfortunate Stuart monarch had garnered two centuries earlier.[58]

It was in this institutional regard, more than in their absolute economic resources, that the continental great powers lagged behind Britain. According to one rough calculation, there was one "fiscal bureaucrat" for every 1,300 people in Britain. The comparable figure for France was one per 4,100, for the Netherlands one per 6,200 and for Prussia—often wrongly portrayed as a more bureaucratic state than Britain—one per 38,000.[59] The fiscal bureaucracy more than trebled between 1690 and 1782: revealingly, the Excise became known as "the monster with 10,000 eyes."[60] The French Revolution—so Bosher has argued—was partly about achieving a similar transition to bureaucratic rather than "corrupt" (or rather, entrepreneurial) finance—a transition which had in fact been set in motion by Necker and Brienne before 1789.[61] Symbolically, 36 tax farmers were arrested during the Revolution, of whom 28 were guillotined on 8 May 1794.[62] Among them was the great chemist Antoine Lavoisier, who had financed his researches out of his income as a tax farmer.[63]

In the wake of the Napoleonic Wars, there was a sustained drive in most states to reduce the number of public employees. Reductions in indirect taxation were not only justified on the basis of *laissez faire, laissez passer*, but also as a means of shrinking the tax-gathering bureaucracy. Although much has been written about the modernization of government in the mid-nineteenth century, the statistics make it clear that for most of the century the "night-watchman state" was a reality. In 1891 total government personnel amounted to less than 2 per cent of the total labor force in Britain. The figures on the continent were higher, but not by much. For Italy in 1871 the equivalent figure was just 2.6 per cent; for Germany in 1881 3.7 per cent. Even the famously elaborate Habsburg bureaucracy was small in relation to the swelling population of the Empire. But from the turn of the century onwards there was a sustained growth in the public sector almost everywhere. By the 1920s public employment exceeded 5 per cent of the workforce in Italy, 6 per cent in Britain and 8 per cent in Germany.

In his monumental *Economy and Society* Max Weber portrayed the modern bureaucracy as admirably rational: "rules, means, ends, and matter-of-factness dominate its bearing."[64] Yet even as he wrote, disillusionment with bureaucracy was growing, not least in the wake of the enormous expansion of the public sector during the years of war and inflation, a phenomenon more closely associated with proliferating red-tape and corruption than with rationality. The reality of modern bureaucracy turned out to be closer to Kafka's *Castle*, in which enigmatic files are trundled up and down grey corridors, being allocated apparently at random to faceless pen-pushers behind identical office doors.[65] The *Beamte*—once admired as the epitome of Prussian virtue—became the personification of sloth and self-interest. During a violent political riot in Vienna in 1927, Elias Canetti vividly recollected seeing a distraught official outside the burning Palace of Justice, "flailing his arms and moaning over and over again":

"The files are burning ! All the files!"

"Better files than people!" I told him, but that did not interest him; all he could think of was the files. . . . He was inconsolable. I found him comical, even in this situation. But I was also annoyed. "They've been shooting down people!" I said angrily, "and you're carrying on about the files!" He looked at me as if I weren't there and wailed repeatedly: "The files are burning! All the files!"[66]

The files—*die Akten*—had become an end in themselves.

Significantly, bureaucracy was one of Hitler's bugbears.[67] Dining with Himmler in January 1942, he outlined a characteristically infantile scheme to "reduce the bureaucracy to a third of its importance" by simplifying the German tax system:

As regards direct taxes, the simplest is to take as a basis the amount paid the previous year. The tax-payer is told: "You'll pay the same sum as last year. If this year your earnings are lower, you'll report the fact. If they're higher you'll immediately pay a proportionate supplement. If you forget to announce the increase in your income, you'll be severely punished." . . . Everything could be done by means of an extremely simple piece of apparatus, and the Chinese puzzle of declaring one's taxes would be done away with. . . .

If I explain this system to the Ministry of Finance . . . the reply will be, after an instant's reflection, "My Führer, you're right." But within six months they'll certainly have forgotten everything.

Hitler subscribed to the conventional view that bureaucracy is self-perpetuating. "The snag is that a tax which is easy to collect doesn't suit these gentlemen of the administration. What would be the use of having been to a University? Where would one find jobs for the jurists? There's be no more work for them." Yet the way Hitler himself fomented competition between overlapping state and party institutions tended to encourage bureaucratization, as he himself all but admitted:

One decides to create a group of the Hitler Youth at Salzburg. Suddenly they need a building of five hundred rooms. . . . I created the Ministry of Propaganda with the idea that it would be at everybody's service. . . . Yet there practically doesn't exist a Ministry today that hasn't its own press-service. . . . Göring wanted to get from me a decree conferring powers on Stuckart and Reinhardt [the Ministers of Finance and the Interior] so that they could undertake the reorganization of our administrative services with a view to simplifying them. I refused. Why entrust these men with such a mission when it's precisely the Ministr[ies] of Finance and Interior . . . whose adminitrations are plethorically swollen?[68]

In the Soviet Union, of course, there was no other employer than state and party; and that remained true until the 1980s. Yet it was not only in totalitarian regimes that the public sector tended to expand. By 1950, thanks mainly to nationalization, the proportion of public employees in Britain had risen above 10 per cent of the workforce.[69] Figure 7 shows that this growth has since continued in more or less every developed country and has been substantially reversed in only one. In twelve out of seventeen OECD countries, government employment has scarcely declined at all since reaching a peak in the mid-1990s. In Sweden, Norway and Denmark the proportion of total employment which is in the public sector is in excess of 30 per cent. In France, Finland and Austria the figure is above 20 per cent. Portugal, Spain, Italy and Germany all saw public sector employment exceed 15 per cent of the workforce in the 1990s; Switzerland and Greece are not far behind them. The exceptions to this pattern are the United States, where government employment peaked in the mid-1970s, and Britain, Ireland, Belgium

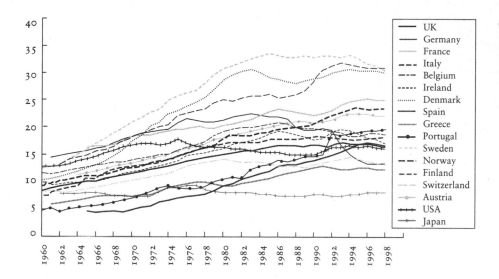

Figure 7. Government employment as a percentage of total employment,
1960–1999
Source: OECD.

and Japan, where the peak occurred in the 1980s. But only in Britain has
there been a significant decline since that peak. In 1983 government employment reached a post-war high of 22 per cent of total employment; in 1999
the figure had fallen to 13.6 per cent, lower even than the figure for the
United States. Among developed economies, only Japan and Greece have
smaller public payrolls.

Whatever the macroeconomic costs of high levels of public employment,
the immediate fiscal problem lies in determining the pay of public employees in the absence of the kind of information that allows productivity to be
measured in the private sector; and (usually) in the presence of public sector
unions and other pressure groups agitating for pay rises ahead of inflation.
The sheer size of the wage-bill is staggering. In 1992 total public sector pay
accounted for fully a third of general government expenditure in Britain.[70]
In the United States the figure is a fifth.[71] Small pay rises can therefore have
very large fiscal implications. Indeed, one of the paradoxes of modern
democracy is the tendency of governments to respond to criticisms of public services by increasing public pay. In fact, to give a British example, pay
rises for nurses in the National Health Service may imply real reductions in
the amounts of money spent on hospitals, beds, equipment and medicines,

and therefore a further deterioration in patient-care—though an improvement, no doubt, in nurses' living standards.[72]

SERVILE STATES

States have long been able to secure substantial portions of national income by taxation: it is quite wrong to think that high tax burdens are a phenomenon of the twentieth century. The total revenues of the Abbasid caliphate in the late eighth century amounted to between a sixth and a quarter of national product.[73] Venetian tax revenues at the end of the sixteenth century amounted to between 14 and 16 per cent of GNP;[74] while the total revenues of the United Provinces around 1688 were equivalent to around a quarter of national income.[75] According to one calculation, the tax burden in France as a percentage of national income declined from 18 per cent in 1450 to just 10 per cent in 1525; but then rose rapidly in the seventeenth century to 31 per cent in 1683 and reached as much as 38–40 per cent in 1789.[76] The great economic historian Alexander Gerschenkron estimated the Russian tax burden at roughly two-thirds of the entire grain harvest in 1710, a level of fiscal extraction not seen again until Stalin's time.[77]

The history of Britain's rise to great power status is also, and not coincidentally, the history of a rising tax burden. Royal revenue in the reign of Elizabeth I 'never exceeded 2 per cent of national product,' or at most 5 per cent if one includes occasional forced loans, charges by officials and local levies.[78] Even as late as 1698, according to estimates by the early political economist Charles Davenant, Britons were paying a smaller proportion of their national income in tax than their continental neighbours: whereas the Dutch paid up to a third of national income in tax and the French a fifth, the British proportion was just an eighth.[79] However, in the course of the eighteenth century the British tax burden rose rapidly. Total expenditure as a percentage of national income went up from under 4 per cent in the mid-1680s to peaks of between 17 and 20 per cent in the war years of the eighteenth century.[80] Even then, the absolute amount of tax revenue raised in Britain was less than in under-taxed France: it is easily forgotten that as late as the 1780s French GNP was more than twice that of Britain. One reason Britain was able to mount such an effective military challenge to her larger neighbour was her higher rate of taxation.[81] As a percentage of GNP, total taxes were nearly double what they were in France in 1788 (12.4 per cent compared with 6.8 per cent). If France had only been able to raise more tax her fiscal crisis might have been averted.[82]

As Chapter 1 demonstrated, the principal cause of increases in the level of state expenditure and hence of taxation has, for most of history, been war. In peacetime, expenditure and taxation tended to fall substantially. This was one reason why the nineteenth century was also a time when tax burdens fell to historic lows in most countries. In the twentieth century, by contrast, there was a ratchet effect. In the aftermath of both the world wars, public spending failed to revert to its pre-war level, whether in absolute terms, in inflation-adjusted terms, in per capita terms or in relation to GDP. In 1990 prices, total public expenditure in Britain was £15.3 billion in 1913; £27.5 billion ten years later; and it never fell below £60 billion after the Second World War.[83] Moreover, in both real and per capita terms, public spending since 1945 has continued to rise decade by decade, despite the absence of a major war. Even as a proportion of GDP, the trend was upwards until the 1980s and 1990s, when a plateau was reached. In the same way, federal government outlays as a percentage of US GDP were just 16 per cent in 1950, 18 per cent in 1960, 19 per cent in 1970 and 22 per cent in 1980 and 1990.[84] The peak for total US public sector outlays came in 1992 (36.6 per cent); they were projected to fall to 32 per cent in 2000. Spending ratios rose even higher in Europe: to peaks of 45 per cent in Britain (1993), 50 per cent in Germany (1995), 55 per cent in France (1996) and 57 per cent in Italy (1993). The highest spending ratios in the developed world were in Scandinavia: the Swedish figure peaked at 71 per cent in 1993, while in Denmark the figure was 60 per cent.[85] This was quite different from the experience of previous centuries, when such levels of public expenditure were seen only in time of war.

The familiar explanation for this almost universal phenomenon is the rise of the "welfare state." But what exactly is the meaning of this well-worn phrase, first used in English by the Anglican bishop of Manchester, William Temple, in 1928? If by the welfare state we mean public spending designed to reduce income inequalities—whether by direct supplements to those on low pay or the provision of services to the poor at below market prices— then that too is not a wholly modern invention. Nearly half the adult male population of fifth-century BC Athens received some form of payment from the state. Around 10 per cent of state spending in Augustan Rome went on 'doles' to the Roman plebs. However, most transfers in the medieval and early modern period were from taxpayers to relatively well-off groups: lawyers, soldiers, arms suppliers and financiers.[86] In Mughal India, the emperor and 122 nobles—a tiny fraction of a total population of 110 million—received roughly an eighth of the total national product.[87] However, attitudes to poverty in Western societies oscillated, with public relief sometimes being made available in a crisis, but more often the responsibility for care of the needy being left to charity and self-help, leaving the state to perform a more disciplinary role towards marginal groups.

The extent of what could be done to relieve poverty and sickness without the state's intervention is often forgotten. In Victorian Britain, "Friendly Societies" were responsible for an astonishing volume of prudential saving. Until just before 1914, spending by registered and unregistered charities, friendly societies, trade unions and other benevolent and self-help institutions was more than the annual budget of the poor law and dwarfed the central government's expenditure on social welfare.[88] As early as 1803 there had been over nine thousand mutual or 'friendly' societies, with more than 700,000 members. By 1877 total membership of registered friendly societies had risen to 2.75 million, and less than forty years later it stood at 6.6 million. In addition, more than two million people were members of unregistered societies.[89] When national insurance was introduced in Britain in 1911, over three-quarters of those covered by the new scheme were already members of friendly societies. Even thereafter, private insurance grew even more rapidly than national insurance: by the eve of the Second World War, premiums on private insurance policies exceeded the total contributions to the state schemes for health, unemployment and pensions.[90] Self-help, in short, was more than a pious Victorian aspiration; for a substantial proportion of the working population it was a reality. And its corollary was often a deep suspicion of the interference of the state: in particular (to quote a Longton miner interviewed by the Fabian R. H. Tawney in 1912), irritation at outsiders "mak[ing] us ignorant people live in the way they think we ought."[91] It was not only libertarians like Hilaire Belloc who were hostile to "the servile state."[92]

Moreover, help for those who could not help themselves was also forthcoming, unprompted by the state. Donations to charities amounted to a substantial "voluntary tax" funding a myriad of good causes, principally in education and health-care. In Britain the total income of the registered charities was £13 million in 1910, more than total local authority expenditure on poor relief (£12.3 million); and this figure excludes smaller charities and sums raised informally and distributed by parish churches and Nonconformist chapels. Samples of wills suggest that an average of 13 per cent of wealth was being bequeathed to charities in the years before 1899.[93]

Nevertheless, the political arguments for more state activity became irresistible around the turn of the century, thanks to a combination of socialist theory, "New" Liberal repudiation of *laissez faire* doctrine and conservative fears of the declining "national efficiency" exposed by the Boer War. The Right was as responsible as the Left for the rise in public spending before 1914. In Britain free elementary education and subsidies to Irish peasants— "the price we have to pay for the Union"—were both introduced by Salisbury's Conservative government. But the real watershed was the Liberal government of 1905–15. The Liberals introduced school meals and compulsory school medical inspections. Adapting a system that had originated in Bismarckian Germany, they conferred a non-contributory old-age pension as an entitlement from the age of 70.[94] And for those on lower incomes, they brought in a system of compulsory national insurance against both ill health and unemployment, with the state supplementing employers' contributions.

Like many continental systems, national insurance built on existing networks of friendly societies and insurance companies. Nor can it be regarded as a failure. True, dependants were excluded from the scheme, and the Treasury maintained a tight control on payments made and benefits available.[95] On the other hand, between 1912 and 1938 the number of people covered by the scheme rose by a factor of more than four. Henceforth, transfers to the old, the sick and the poor were an integral and growing part of total public expenditure.

The increase in spending was also marked at the local level. In Britain local government expenditure had been held in check for much of the nineteenth century by the New Poor Law of 1834, which effectively deterred all but the desperately poor from claiming the austere relief of the workhouse. That began to change in the 1880s. In 1885 a Royal Commission recommended that the London county council be empowered to improve housing in the capital. In 1902 the county councils also acquired responsibility for education. Between 1870 and 1913 local spending increased by a factor of five.[96] In Germany the federal system gave even more latitude to state and local governments: their expenditure on education, welfare, health and housing rose steadily, so that in all these items accounted for nearly half all public sector spending in 1913.[97]

As is well known, the First World War not only increased expenditure on defence, but also expanded significantly the range of non-military governmental activities. In Britain, there were new ministries not only for Munitions and Air, but also for Food (1916) Labor (1916) and Health (1919), not to mention the short-lived departments for National Service and Reconstruction. Although the ambitious schemes for post-war expenditures on "homes fit for heroes" foundered on the rocks of retrenchment, it proved impossible to roll back the state to its pre-war position. In terms of new dwellings completed, the public sector outbuilt the private sector in 1921 and 1922, fell back thereafter but then forged ahead in every year from 1941 until 1959.[98] Indeed, the unprecedented unemployment of the inter-war years forced governments everywhere to spend more money, no matter how they strove to avoid it. The pre-war schemes for compulsory insurance could not cope with such high and sustained unemployment (and in countries that had experienced hyperinflation, their funds were largely wiped out). Governments found themselves having to pay doles to the unemployed or using public money to give them work, which seemed the more expensive option. Much used to be made of the power of Treasury orthodoxy in resisting pressure for higher public spending during the Slump. But in terms of public expenditure on transfers and public works of various sorts, the Treasury yielded much ground before 1939.

Still, it is probably true that authoritarian regimes between the wars were more ambitious in this area, not least because they were less respectful of the traditional fiscal orthodoxy that had helped kill off prototype welfare states like the Weimar Republic.[99] Though rearmament had come to dominate the German economy by 1938, the Nazis initially pursued policies which were not mere spin-offs of military expenditure, spending up to 5 billion reichsmarks on job creation to the end of 1934 and devoting still more to the construction of 4,000 kilometres of *Autobahn*, a program which employed 120,000 workers at its peak. "Each measure," declared Hitler in July 1933 "is to be judged [according to the criteria]: what are its consequences? Does it create more employment or does it create more unemployment?"[100] As is well known, the regime's policy of state investment in infrastructure and armaments had achieved full employment by the mid-1930s, though historians continue to argue about the relative importance of civilian schemes and rearmament.

Welfare too had been a Nazi preoccupation even before Hitler came to power. In 1931 Goebbels took the Berlin-based Nazi People's Welfare Association under his wing; after May 1933 it spread to cover the whole Reich, swallowing up private charitable institutions in the process. By 1939 it covered over half of all households and was second in its membership only to the German Labor Front. Of course, National Socialist conceptions of welfare were distinctive, not least because "ethnic aliens" were systematically excluded and an ethos of public activism was encouraged to promote the sense of "ethnic community" Hitler craved. But in other respects there were disquietingly "modern" aspects to the Nazi welfare state: the compulsory deductions of Winter Aid from pay slips, the procreation-friendly child allowances, the subsidized "Strength through Joy" pleasure cruises and holiday camps.[101]

The welfare state was thus no invention of William Beveridge, nor of the 1945 Labor government which implemented the recommendations of his famous report. Most of the key elements of that government's economic policy—progressive taxation, national insurance, publicly funded education and state ownership of key industries—predated the 1940s. Even the notion that fiscal policy could be geared to maintain full employment had occasionally been put into practice before Keynes gave it intellectual respectability in his *General Theory*. What was new in Britain after 1945 was the aim of universal coverage, to allow the abandonment of means-testing. The implication of this was that, unless national insurance contributions were regularly adjusted to take account not only of inflation but also of the demand for health care or unemployment benefits, entitlements would almost inevitably outstrip what claimants could expect to receive under a real system of insurance. The breaking of the link between contributions made and entitlements received was to prove the crucial flaw of the British welfare system.

The original effect of national insurance was in fact regressive so long as contributions (and benefits) were flat-rate.[102] The first deviation came in 1959 when earnings-related supplements were introduced for both pensions and contributions, significantly increasing the progressivity of the tax system. The second came in the 1980s, when the Conservatives did away with the link between earnings and state pensions. This has significantly reduced the British government's liabilities for state pensions compared with many other European countries: by the mid-1990s, the effective cut in pensions implied a saving of over 3 per cent of GDP.[103] But the fact that the link between earnings and national insurance contributions was *not* broken amounted to a further step towards treating national insurance contributions as a shadow income tax.[104] It is too seldom pointed out that, although she cut income tax rates, Mrs Thatcher raised the standard rate of employees' national insurance contributions from 6.5 per cent to 9 per cent. For those on half average earnings, national insurance contributions became almost as burdensome as income tax.[105] In 1949 income tax accounted for a third of all taxes, national insurance contributions for less than a tenth. By 1990 the proportions were, respectively, 28 per cent and 18 per cent. Even then, the rule whereby the fund should not fall below one-sixth of total national insurance expenditures would have been broken in the 1990s without "top-up" payments from the Treasury.

In the same way, the creation of a National Health Service funded out of taxation but supposedly "free at the point of use" has imposed all the rising costs of an ageing population (to say nothing of increasingly sophisticated medical treatments) directly on central government finances. According to government estimates in the 1980s, an extra 1 per cent expenditure per year in real terms was necessary to maintain real spending per head at a constant level; the figure for the 1990s was closer to 2 per cent.[106] But the pressure on governments of both parties to restrain total public spending means that from time to time such a real increase is not achieved. In effect, the NHS is a system of central rationing—to call it planning would be to flatter successive ministers—the effect of which is to hold total expenditure on health as a proportion of GDP substantially below the European and North American averages.[107]

FROM WARFARE TO WELFARE

Taken together, the processes described in Chapters 1 to 3 help to explain the transformation of the warfare state into the welfare state. The processes of parliamentarization and bureaucratization were first made necessary by the cost of war. But in the twentieth century they developed a momentum of their own, increasingly diverting resources away from military towards civilian employment and redistributive transfers.

Perhaps the simplest way to illustrate the extent of the transformation is to compare government finance in Britain in 1898 and 1998. In 1898 gross public expenditure was equivalent to just 6.5 per cent of GDP. In 1998 the comparable figure (total managed expenditure as a percentage of GDP) was 39 per cent. In 1898 the biggest item of the budget was defence (36 per cent), followed by debt service (21 per cent) and civil government (20 per cent). Just over 10 per cent was spent on "Education, Art and Science." In 1998 the biggest outlays went on social security (30 per cent), health (17 per cent) and education (12 per cent). The two biggest items of a century before, defence and debt service, now account for just 7 per cent and 9 per cent of spending. No less striking are the changes on the revenue side. The biggest sources of gross public revenue in 1898 were the excise (29 per cent), followed by customs (19 per cent), income tax (15 per cent) and death duties

(13 per cent). In 1998 the main sources of government revenue were income tax (26 per cent), national insurance contributions (16 per cent) and VAT (also 16 per cent). Inheritance tax now brings in less than 1 per cent of total revenue; customs duties a mere half of 1 per cent.[108]

As these figures show, there is nothing novel in the idea of the budget as an instrument of redistribution: the high proportion of debt service in 1898 represented a transfer not much smaller in relative terms than the social security system in 1998. It is the nature of the transfer that has changed, as we shall see: from a system that was socially regressive, as a consequence of the way it financed its wars, to one that regards the reduction of material inequality as its primary function.

In the light of the seemingly inexorable growth of welfare spending, we may well ask: is there "a limit to taxable capacity"?[109] As Calvin Coolidge is said to have remarked, "Nothing is easier than spending the public money. It does not appear to belong to anybody. The temptation is overwhelming to bestow it on somebody." Yet even the most *dirigiste* social democrats had to draw the line somewhere if there was to be a meaningful distinction between their creed and outright socialism. Thus the Labor Home Secretary Roy Jenkins declared in 1976: "I do not think you can push public expenditure significantly above 60 per cent and maintain the values of a plural society with adequate freedom of choice. We are here close to one of the frontiers of social democracy."[110]

In fact, there is no need for politicians to devise such "lines in the sand" for themselves. For there are real economic constraints that explain why the state's expenditures and employment tend not to rise far above, respectively, a half of output and a third of employment. One of these we have already seen: the limit on how much can be raised in taxation to finance expenditure before diminishing returns set in, not only in terms of revenue, but in terms of aggregate economic growth.[111] We now turn to the other variable in what economists call the "inter-temporal budget constraint": the limit on how much a state can *borrow*.

SECTION TWO
PROMISES TO PAY

4

Mountains of the Moon: Public Debts

Great is Bankruptcy.
Carlyle

If you walk up 6th Avenue to 43rd Street in Manhattan, you used to see a thirteen-digit number on a billboard above you. The last time I saw it (on 17 October 1999), the number was:

5,601,723,423,979

Above it were three words: "Our National Debt." Before it was the dollar sign. And below it there were two small calculations: "Your Family Share: $73,192" and "Increase per second: $10,000."

It is a little piece of history, that sign: a relic of the once acrimonious debate about American public finance which played such an important role in the politics of the late 1980s and early 1990s. In 1986 critics of Ronald Reagan's fiscal policy took out an advertisement to warn readers of the *New York Times* that the burgeoning debt would lead to "the death of [the] Republic." Paul Kennedy cited the total debt for 1985 (then a mere $1.8 trillion) as one indicator of impending American overstretch, adding darkly: "Historically, the only other example which comes to mind of a Great Power so increasing its indebtedness in *peacetime* is France in the 1780s, where the fiscal crisis contributed to the domestic political crisis."[1]

If that $10,000-per-second figure was to be believed, the national debt would have become a fourteen-digit number by the beginning of the year 2001: ten trillion dollars. Yet President Clinton was able to claim in February 2000 that, under his last budget plan, all US public debt would be repaid by 2013,[2] which might seem to imply an "increase per second" of the order of *minus* $1,000. Whatever happened to the American debt crisis? To answer this question it is necessary to set those thirteen digits above 6th Avenue in a rather broader historical and economic perspective. A long-run view of public debt reveals that an apparently large "mountain" of debt may be far from disadvantageous, provided the institutions of a country's financial system are

equal to the task of its management. In the uneven geographical development of these institutions—above all, the institution of a funded national debt—lies one of the keys to modern history.

THE ORIGINS OF PUBLIC DEBTS

Though the history of private debt may be traced back as far as the second millennium BC, the history of public debt is much shorter.[3] Neither ancient Greece nor ancient Rome had formalized public debts. Nor did the early Abbasid caliphate, though the central treasury in Baghdad still had to borrow for short periods in anticipation of tax receipts, illegally paying interest or rewarding lenders with non-cash privileges.[4] The late development of public debts is somewhat surprising, since in the modern world states are generally (though not always correctly) seen by investors as less likely than private debtors to default on loans. Many of the essential institutions of credit predated large-scale public borrowing. Ways had been found to circumvent the laws against usury—condemned alike by Catholicism, Protestantism and Islam—by the early Middle Ages; bills of exchange were in use in Genoa from the twelfth century, and the first negotiable bills, which could be transferred to a third party through endorsement, date from the fourteenth century.[5] As we shall see, however, the early modern risk premium was more often paid by rulers than by merchants.

It was the simple fact of taxation—of more or less predictable revenue streams—that provided the basis for the earliest systems of public debt in medieval Italy. The Venetian public debt, which originated in the twelfth century, was secured on the state salt monopoly, the revenues of which were earmarked for debt service and redemption. In the thirteenth century the increasing use of forced loans (*prestiti*) as a form of taxation further increased the importance of the debt. Something similar happened in the sixteenth century, when the Monte Nuovo[6] was established to administer the repayable tax known as the *decima*. In Genoa the salt tax revenues themselves were sold at auction to *comperisti*, a system which, in the fifteenth century, was put under the control of a quasi-public bank, the Casa di San Giorgio.[7] A similar system evolved in Florence, where the communal debt, administered by the Monte Comune, was systematically increased by the fisc's heavy reliance on forced loans (*prestanze*). An important development here was the transferability of claims on the Monte, which could be sold to other citizens freely or, with authorization, to outsiders.[8] In 1526 a Monte della Fede was established to manage the papal debt.[9]

North European city-states evolved somewhat different arrangements based on the sale of perpetual, terminable or life annuities. In each case, an investor lent his capital to the state in return for a stream of income. In the case of a perpetual bond, that income stream was notionally infinite: the state would go on paying a percentage of the face value of the bond for ever, but of course the investor never got his capital back. A redeemable bond, by contrast, paid interest for a fixed period, after which the bond "matured," meaning that original capital was repaid. Life annuities, then as now, paid interest only for the duration of the investor's or another specified life. From the late fourteenth century, Cologne offered perpetual but redeemable annuities paying from 5 to 5 and a half per cent.[10] Such redeemable bonds were usually called "purchases of money" or "sales of dues," and tended to be secured on a piece of immovable property like a town; interest was called a "gift" to circumvent the usury laws. Dutch cities, on the other hand, issued *liffrenten* (lifetime annuities) and *losrenten* (perpetual loans). In 1586 the Receiver General of the Union between the Dutch states began issuing *obligaties*, which were more easily transferable than urban bonds—and hence more attractive to investors, who might wish to liquidate their investment before a bond matured. However, the greater part of Dutch borrowing in the subsequent centuries was done at the regional level, mainly by the province of Holland, since it was the provinces that controlled the bulk of tax revenues.

Medieval monarchs, by contrast, tended to rely on loans from wealthy banking families to finance their deficits. Siennese and Florentine bankers lent to the kings of England; Tuscan bankers to the Roman curia; South German bankers to the Habsburgs; Swiss and Italian bankers to the French.[11] The Spanish crown turned first to Genoese merchant bankers (*hombres de negocios*), then Portuguese *marranos*.[12] It made sense to rely on international financiers when, very often, the money was needed to pay for armies fighting abroad.[13] But it is important to remember that these were often little more than personal loans to individual rulers, like the £300,000 borrowed by Edward III.[14] Only in Catalonia in the late fifteenth century was there anything like the system that had evolved in the Italian and German city states. The Catalan system guaranteed investors regular interest out of revenues that were earmarked for the purpose (hypothecated) and managed by a special commission.[15]

Haltingly, in the course of the sixteenth century, the other European monarchies learned to mimic the techniques of urban public debt. In France, for example, the Paris Hôtel de Ville issued perpetual 8 per cent annuities known as *rentes*. The money was handed to the crown in return for certain royal revenues" being assigned to the Paris Receiver General; the advantage to investors was that the General Farm paid the interest payments directly from its coffers, rather than via the less than reliable royal fiscal administration.[16] The volume of rentes grew substantially in the course of the seventeenth and eighteenth centuries: by the 1780s Necker put the capital sum at around 3.4 billion livres, and this may well have been an underestimate.[17] The Spanish crown developed a two-tier system of short-term, high-interest loan contracts (asientos) and long-term, lower-interest bonds assigned on ordinary revenues (juros), which by the 1560s had become transferable, and which could be purchased in perpetual, lifetime or redeemable forms.[18] Likewise, life and perpetual annuities in the Habsburg Netherlands in the 1540s were serviced by the revenues from excise and property taxes.[19]

An important innovation which spread from Italy throughout Europe in the course of the seventeenth century was the public bank. Here it is important to distinguish between two functions that were originally performed by distinct institutions: the management of the state's debt and the management of forms of money other than coinage (which tended to be entrusted to a separate mint), in particular the system of clearing that was so vital to the development of large-scale commerce. Although there were forerunners of these public banks in Genoa and the Florence of the Medicis, the first true public banks were the Banco della Piazza di Rialto (founded in 1587), which reformed the Venetian currency and payments system by accepting deposits, effecting transfers between accounts and accepting bills of exchange payable to its clients; and the Banco del Giro (1619), which converted a part of the Venetian state's short-term debt into interest-bearing and transferable bonds (*partite*).[20] The Amsterdamse Wisselbank (1609) performed similar functions to the Rialto Bank, but also dealt in bullion and minted coins. It was soon imitated in Middleburg (1616), Hamburg (1619), Delft (1621) and Rotterdam (1635); and later in Austria (Wiener Stadtbank, 1703), Denmark (Kurantbanken, 1736), Sweden (Riksen Ständers, 1762), Prussia (Königliche Giro- und Lehnbank, 1765) and Russia (Assignationsbank, 1768). The Sverige Riksbank in Sweden (1668), on the other hand, was more like the Venetian Giro Bank, as was the Bank of England (1694). Unlike the Amsterdamse Wisselbank, the Bank of England's primary function was to manage the government's debt. However, its regional monopoly on note issue and its extensive commercial business gave it a natural interest in (and hence, over time, responsibility for) currency stability, which meant maintaining the convertibility of paper notes into specie.[21]

In France, by contrast, public banking was discredited for two generations by the disastrous bubble generated by John Law's Banque Royale (see below). The Caisse d'Escompte established in 1776 was designed to discount commercial bills and did not begin lending to the government—at first covertly, then openly—until 1787.[22] It too was short-lived: Necker's efforts to convert it into a national bank were thwarted by opponents of a new "plutocracy" (notably Mirabeau and the comte de Custine), and in 1793 it was suppressed along with all joint-stock companies. "We have nothing to gain from making ourselves English, bankers and financiers," declared the baron de Batz; a very erroneous judgement.[23] It was not until 1800, after a brief period of "free banking," that the Banque de France was founded by supporters of Napoleon Bonaparte's coup of 18 Brumaire. Unlike the Banque of England, the Banque de France was partly owned by the government, which acquired shares in it in return for depositing its new Sinking Fund.[24] As Napoleon himself declared in 1806, three years after the Banque had been granted its monopoly on Parisian banknote issue: "The Banque does not solely belong to its shareholders; it also belongs to the state which granted it the privilege of creating money."[25]

The evolution of public banks was only part of a Dutch financial revolution in the seventeenth century. It was not only that the debt of Holland, the wealthiest of the United Provinces, grew rapidly. It was also the fact that it took the form of life and redeemable annuities, providing the merchant élite of the United Provinces with an investment that was secure, yet easily marketable. At the same time, a new kind of security developed in the form of shares in the chartered trading monopoly known as the Dutch East India Company (Vereenigte Oost-Indische Compagnie), a semi-private vehicle for Dutch commercial and colonial expansion.[26] These innovations crossed the Channel when William III, Stadholder of the Netherlands, became king of England and Wales after the Glorious Revolution. [27]

The cost of the ensuing War of the League of Augsburg soon required the application of Dutch financial techniques in England; but with important modifications. While sales of life annuities and lottery tickets proved disappointing in 1693, the issue of £1.2 million of special bonds paying a guaranteed 8 per cent was fully subscribed the following year. The subscribers were attracted by the fact that specific taxes had been earmarked to pay the interest on the bonds, and by the right the subscribers acquired to incorporate themselves as a new "Bank of England" with an effective monopoly on government borrowing. The new institution redeemed Exchequer "tallies" and allowed the Treasury to issue Bank "sealed bills" instead, as well as accepting government credit notes as deposits or as subscriptions to new public loans, of which there was a steady, war-induced stream from 1702 until 1713. The Bank in turn issued shares of its own. This was only the first of a series of flotations by monopoly companies: the New East India Company (1698), the United East India Company (1708) and the South Sea Company (1710) soon followed. As a result of these issues, London was soon outstripping Amsterdam in terms of the range of tradable assets available to investors. But it is important to bear in mind how much of the business of this nascent stock market was still the government's. The South Sea Company was set up primarily in response to the strain of war finance, with the aim of funding some £9 million of short-term government obligations. The company accepted these at face value in exchange for its shares, and then swapped the short-term debts for new 6 per cent government annuities. By the time of the Peace of Utrecht (1713), the total government debt was divided in approximately equal shares between annuities, lottery stake money and loans funded by the Bank and the South Sea Company. Four years later, much of the lottery money was "consolidated" into—in other words, exchanged for—a new 5 per cent stock managed by the Bank.[28]

It was the experiments with these companies—including the traumatic experience of the South Sea Bubble which ultimately produced an asset ideally suited to the needs of government. In the short run, the capital gains of shares in the South Sea and other trading companies made them far more attractive than government-issued annuities, and investors rushed to exchange them for company stock when this was offered by the South Sea Act of March 1720. However, the collapse of the Bubble revealed to investors the sad fact that share prices can go down as far as they can go up: much further in either direction than is likely with a fixed-interest bearing bond. To bail out the many investors who had exchanged annuities for South Sea shares, the company converted the shares into annuities; initially paying 5 per cent (later falling by stages to 3 per cent). The South Sea annuity was followed by the first Three Per Cent Bank Annuity in 1726, a redeemable bond secured on economies in the Civil List. After the Consolidating Act of 1751 the government itself could issue what became known as the "consol," the forerunner of the modern "gilt."[29]

BONDS, BANKS AND BUBBLES

The birth of the consol marks the beginning of the history of modern public debt.[30] Whereas the annuities of the pre-1720 period had been relatively illiquid, consols were liquid, redeemable at par but otherwise perpetual. In other words, an investor who bought consols could be confident of receiving the specified percentage of his nominal capital, paid twice yearly, for ever, or until he wished to sell. The risk that the selling price would be far below what he had initially invested certainly existed, but it soon became apparent that it was a significantly smaller risk than for any similar asset. Consols became a byword for financial security, the benchmark against which all other investments' riskiness came to be measured. And from the government's point of view, the credibility of consols meant that, in a crisis, much larger sums could be raised by selling them than by raising taxation, without incurring a crippling interest burden in the future. Though there were later innovations—such as the introduction by the Younger Pitt of a sinking fund, which required annual payments for amortization of the debt—consols reigned supreme as the key component of the national debt until the time of the First World War. True, consols were never the sole debt instrument the government could issue. Particularly in times of crisis, short-term Exchequer bills—loosely modelled on the commercial bills which financed an increasing amount of British trade—could also be sold to the public or to institutions. But the mass of new debt issued henceforth took the form of consols. On average, less than 4 per cent of the total debt between 1801 and 1914 was "unfunded," that is, short-term.[31]

The British system differed from the two principal continental alternatives—the Dutch and the French—because the institutions of debt management co-existed with a centralized, bureaucratic system of tax collection, a transparent process of parliamentary budget-making and a nascent central bank—though it should be noted that the maintenance of the convertibility of paper banknotes into gold was an important but *not* an indispensable part of the system. When the Bank of England was forced to suspend "cash payments" between February 1797 and May 1821, the effect was not fatal to the system.[32] In addition, the system benefited from the development of a large and liberally regulated financial market capable of trading not only government bonds but also a range of private sector financial assets.[33] Alongside the market for consols, there flourished markets for private sector bonds and early equities, as well as (at the nearby Royal Exchange) the discount market for commercial bills, to say nothing of the various commodity and insurance markets. Peacetime expansion of private sector asset markets deepened and widened the capital market, increasing its capacity to absorb government debt in the event of war.

Of all the great powers, France had the greatest difficulty in evolving a stable system of public debt management: a distinct disadvantage for a power which ran a deficit in every year between 1610 and 1800 apart from the nine years between 1662 and 1671.[34] This was not for want of trying. Under Louis XIV, Jean-Baptiste Colbert had laboured mightily to raise tax revenues and to establish in the form of the *caisse des emprunts* an institution of modern debt management. It was abolished after his death.[35] In 1718 the Scotsman John Law set out to modernize French borrowing—which under Louis XIV had relied increasingly on innumerable short-term loans (often little more than paper "IOUs") from tax farmers, accountants and contractors[36]—by combining the best of the Dutch and British systems. Boldly, Law sought to unite the functions which had been carried out separately in Britain by the Bank of England and the South Sea Company. His Banque Générale was rechartered as the Banque Royale and, in return for exchanging its own stock for the existing government debt, gained the right to issue banknotes. However, from the outset the Banque Royale's fortunes were inseparable from those of the Compagnie d'Occident, which had been granted monopolies on French trade with the Caribbean and the exploitation of the drainage of the Mississippi river basin. A quarter of the Banque Royale's capital was held as shares in the Compagnie d'Occident; the boards of the two entities also overlapped; and Law himself was a director of the Compagnie. There was a confusion of priorities, in which the stability of the currency came at best third.

In May 1719 Law merged the Compagnie d'Occident with two other trading companies to form the Compagnie des Indes, then used issues of new Banque Royale banknotes to chase up the prices of the new company's shares. He then proceeded to take over the royal tobacco monopoly and the United General Farms, the corporation of the principal tax farmers. Between August and December 1719, shares in the Compagnie des Indes soared from around 3,000 livres each to over 10,000 livres. At the zenith of his "system," Law accepted the office of Comptroller General and merged the Banque Royale and the Compagnie des Indes. It was too much. The combination of monetary inflation and the interest-rate cap on new loans which Law himself imposed burst the bubble, and in June the Compagnie des Indes shareprice plummeted back below 6,000 livres. By September the shares were "almost worthless"; in October the notes of the Banque Royale ceased to be legal tender; and in December Law fled France.

The collapse of Law's schemes, it is generally agreed, more or less "demolished the existing credit structure in France."[37] It is worth pausing to ask why the same thing did not happen in England, which also had its South Sea Bubble. The price of South Sea shares had in fact experienced a not dissimilar rise and fall: from 128 on 1 January 1720 to 950 on 1 July, slumping to 775 two months later and touching just 170 on 14 October.[38] The average price in 1722 was just 92.[39] Yet the institutional damage was much less in England. In France both the Compagnie des Indes and the Banque Royale were dissolved. Moreover, a very large part of the assets and cash Law had created—which had an estimated face value of some 4 billion livres—was simply repudiated: only 1.6 billion were recognized by the liquidating commission know as the *Visa*, and these were converted into government bonds paying just 2 or 2.5 per cent interest.[40] In England, by contrast, the Bank of England and the pound—the value of which had been fixed in gold only three years before—remained intact, while holders of South Sea stock came off with tolerable losses.[41] The authorities recognized that the Company was too big to fail: its debts were partly taken over by Parliament, while £4.2 million of its nominal capital (which totalled over £38 million) was bought for cash by the Bank of England and converted into bonds paying 5 per cent. In 1723—by which time the Company's shares were back above par—half of its capital was converted into bonds. Those who had exchanged life annuities (which often yielded as much as 14 per cent) for South Sea shares were undoubtedly worse off; as were those who had speculatively bought shares during the Bubble. But the scale of losses was far smaller than in France, where many investors and creditors lost everything.

Because of Law's failure and the drastic way it was dealt with, France remained locked in a system in which private credit was restricted to the "information network" provided by an élite of public notaries;[42] while public credit increasingly depended on the old forms of short-term loan ("assignations," "anticipations" and "rescriptions")[43] and the sale of offices. For, as we have already seen, the money invested in offices was not so different from the money invested in the British national debt, except that the interest was paid in the form of salaries. In 1660 Colbert estimated the value of the capital invested in offices by some 46,000 office-holders at 419 million livres; when the Revolution finally liquidated the system, the compensation paid to officeholders was almost twice that sum.[44] By the middle of the eighteenth century it was clear that the sale of offices was no longer the solution to the *ancien régime*'s fiscal problems, but a fundamental part of them, since officeholders were one of the most powerful interest groups opposed to root and branch fiscal reform. In their search for new sources of revenue after 1750, ministers turned to life annuities (*rentes viagéres*), which increasingly took the place of sales of office as the crown's readiest source of funds. However, a rising proportion of these were sold at a flat rate without regard to the ages of the purchasers.[45] Between 1777 and 1781 Necker borrowed some 520 million livres by this and other means, but for terms seldom exceeding twenty years.[46] His successors Calonne and Brienne could not equal this and, despite the forcible registration of new loans in the *parlement* of Paris in November 1787, royal finances became increasingly dependent on renewing the short-term *anticipations* of future tax revenue, which now amounted to some 240 million livres. When the government attempted to override the *parlement*'s demand that the Estates General be convened, "the government's usual creditors refused to lend." In August 1788 Brienne was forced to suspend payments, even on long-term rentes. It was this debt crisis which obliged the government to summon the Estates General.[47]

Only after another great financial collapse—that caused by the Revolution—were steps taken to remodel French finance in something like the British image. Henceforth government borrowing took the form of issues of *rentes perpetuelles* bearing interest of 5 or 3 per cent. The rente now became a standardized, liquid security like the consol. They were not bearer bonds (i.e. freely transferable between buyers and sellers): the names of rentiers were inscribed in the *Grand Livre de la Dette Publique*.[48] By contrast, the coupons of a bearer bond could be clipped off and exchanged for cash when interest was due by whoever possessed them.

The contrast with the financial system which developed in the other great revolutionary regime of the age is striking. Under the influence of Alexander Hamilton, the United States acquired a system of public debt that resembled in essentials that of Britain—though its federal fiscal system was much more like the Dutch. As early as 1779–80 Hamilton outlined a plan to "accomplish the restoration of paper credit, and establish a permanent fund for the future exigencies of government . . . select[ing] what is good in [Law's] plan and any others that have gone before us, avoiding their defects and excesses."[49] In 1789 he successfully funded the old debt of the bankrupt Confederation, converting them into new 6 per cent federal bonds ("Hamilton 6s"), redeemable at par like consols. And two years later he overcame the opposition of Thomas Jefferson and others to establish the Bank of the United States, modelling its charter on that of the Bank of England and issuing Bank shares ("the hot . . . initial public offering of mid-1791"), just as had been done in England a hundred years before. As is well known, Hamilton's central bank subsequently fell victim to political opposition, which culminated in President Andrew Jackson's 1832 veto of the bill to recharter the Second Bank of the United States. And Hamilton's intention to give the dollar a metallic basis was undermined by the tendency of silver to drain away to Latin America. For most of the nineteenth century America had "free banking" and paper money, with up to 1,600 banks issuing as many as 10,000 different kinds of banknote (though until the Civil War the link to silver was maintained, at least in theory). Only in 1863 were steps taken to reduce the number of note-issuing banks and to create a standardized national bank-note; only in 1879 was the dollar restored to a metallic exchange rate, though *which* metal remained controversial; and only in 1913 was a central bank finally created in the form of the Federal Reserve. Nevertheless, the British-style national debt Hamilton had created did survive. Indeed, in many ways the American financial system went further than the British in encouraging private sector issues of securities to deepen and widen the capital market.[50]

For reasons to be discussed in Chapter 10, the nineteenth century saw the global spread of the British system of public debt, just as the institutions of parliamentary budget-making, bureaucratic tax collection and metallic (increasingly gold) currency were also widely copied. The consol became the model for long-term bonds, and indeed the benchmark against which their performance was conventionally measured (though some countries preferred to issue bonds with specified if remote maturities). The Bank of England was imitated, though with significant national variations, in Finland (1811), Holland (1814), Norway and Austria (1816), Denmark (1818), Portugal (1846), Belgium (1850), Spain, Germany and Bulgaria in the 1870s, Japan, Romania and Serbia in the 1880s, and Italy in 1893.[51] Where there continued to be diversity was in the structures of commercial banking systems. For example, the American National Banking Act of 1864 restricted branching by national banks and currency could only issued if government bonds were held by the issuing bank.[52] The German banking system, with its industry-financing "universal" banks was different again.[53]

Despite the breadth and depth of the London stock market, the British government came to rely on an élite of bankers to manage its borrowing through the mechanism of competitive auctions by the Bank of England. Until at least the time of the Crimea, the Rothschilds played a leading role, though competition subsequently drove down the profits to be made from underwriting issues of consols—the practice whereby banks guaranteed the government a certain price for a new issue and then sold them on to the public. The continuity from the early modern period is striking: Nathan Rothschild had made his reputation in London conducting, albeit on an unprecedented scale, precisely the kind of wartime transfers of money across the Channel which had been carried out by men like Horatio Pallavicino in the 1570s and Edward Backwell in the 1650s.[54] Where banking was less developed, the Rothschilds' multinational partnership came closer to monopolizing new bond issues. This was true to varying degrees in France, Belgium, Austria and Italy, while the Barings came to dominate Russian public borrowing and the Morgan group that of the United States. Rulers who chafed at the power of the haute banque sought to encourage rivals like the Crédit Mobilier in France and its many imitators throughout Europe. But it was only gradually that the new joint-stock banks really took over from the private partnerships like Rothschilds.[55]

The alternative to reliance on banking intermediaries was direct sale via subscription to the public. Such an operation was tried as early as 1506 in Basle, but its success depended on the existence of a relatively developed and broad capital market. For bigger political entities, the risks of public subscription for a long time seemed too high, and it was not until the later nineteenth century that states like Italy sought to liberate themselves from the dominance of the Rothschilds by selling bonds this way.

In practice, however, all debt-issuing agencies tended to deal more with financial intermediaries than with individual private investors.[56] There was considerable variation in the precise channels through which government bonds were sold. In London a dedicated profession of "jobbers" evolved whose sole function was the purchase of new securities (while stockbrokers sold them on to investors). The system in the United States, by contrast, remained closer to the nineteenth-century model of competitive auctions between big institutions. In France there was something more like a cartel of big banks. Nevertheless, the crucial relationship everywhere was between debt management departments and the major financial institutions like pension and insurance funds which were now holding a growing proportion of bonds in their portfolios.

WAR DEBTS AND THEIR LEGACY

In Ford Madox Ford's First World War tetralogy *Parade's End*, the hero Christopher Tietjens is introduced in the "perfectly appointed railway carriage" of a train which "ran as smoothly . . . as gilt-edged securities."[57] This, however, was on the eve of a conflict that would pose a formidable challenge to the smooth running of government debts.

The immense expenditures occasioned by the war, which not even the most pessimistic pre-war commentators had forecast accurately, required a transformation in the techniques of government borrowing. It was not long before the language of mobilization which had been adopted to justify the creation of mass armies was applied to war finance too. The system of selling bonds directly to the public by subscription was widely adopted during the First World War, when buying war bonds was portrayed in official propaganda as a matter of patriotic duty. The British films *You!* and *For the Empire* (commissioned by the Committee on War Loans for the Small Investor) exhorted audiences to invest in war bonds; the latter went into great detail to show "the quantity of munitions" an investment of 15s. 6d. would provide.[58] A German poster of 1917 depicted a naval officer explaining to a soldier as they watch an enemy ship sinking: "That's how your money helps you to fight. Turned into a U-boat, it keeps enemy shells from you. So subscribe to war loans!"[59] "A man who can't lend his government $1.25 at the rate of 4 per cent interest," declared the American Treasury Secretary William Gibbs McAdoo in 1917, "is not entitled to be an American citizen."[60]

However, as the war wore on it became steadily harder (especially for the Central Powers) to persuade their subjects to put their cash into war bonds.[61] For that reason, the First World War also saw a revival and development of short-term debt instruments, principally Treasury-bills. By the end of the war, 32 per cent of the German national debt was in this form—of which more than two-fifths were held by the Reichsbank—and 37 per cent of the French. The continental states at first relied on sales of long-term bonds to the public; when demand for bonds waned, sold short-term Treasury bills to fill the gap; and when the public declined to buy these, sold them to the central bank (with consequences for monetary policy to be discussed in the next chapter). The British also reduced their long-term debt. The funded national debt (mainly consols) had accounted for 90 per cent of the total debt in March 1914; five years later consols accounted for less than 5 per cent of the total debt.[62] However, the Treasury sought to mop up the excess liquidity generated by its own short-term borrowing by issuing a variety of medium-term instruments with maturities longer than Treasury Bills. Around 31 per cent of the British national debt in December 1919 was therefore made up of bonds due for redemption after periods of between one and nine years.[63] "Gilts" (short for gilt-edged government securities) were now available with a range of maturities. This was the real difference between British and continental war finance. On average, only 18 per cent of the British wartime debt was short-term. The United States, which spent in relative terms less on the war, was unique in being able to rely almost entirely on long-term bonds.[64]

The significance of the more complicated "term structure" of national debts in after 1914 was twofold. First, the diversification of bond maturities added to the flexibility of the system by giving investors wider choice. Secondly, and less positively, the growth of short-term debt created complex and not always well-understood links between fiscal and monetary policy. In particular, central banks which were statutorily obliged to discount short-term treasury bills simply monetized short-term debt, leading to considerable inflationary pressure during and after the First World War (see Chapter 5). Moreover, the need regularly to renew or "roll over" short-term debts could expose modern states to funding crises not dissimilar from the one that had undermined the French *ancien régime*. Few countries after 1919 shared the British readiness to run budget surpluses in order to repay short-term debt or to "fund" it by converting it into long-term debt.[65] Indeed, in France, Belgium and Italy, "funding crises"—a refusal by lenders to roll over short term debts—led to serious monetary instability in the mid-1920s. In 1925 long-term bonds accounted for just over half of the total French debt; the same was true in Belgium. In Italy the proportion was roughly two-thirds, but here too a funding crisis struck.[66] One of the keys to the stabilization of war debts in the 1920s was a reduction of the proportion of short-term debt.[67]

In the Second World War British policy aimed at maximizing sales of medium- and long-term debt instruments by restricting other investment opportunities through the Capital Issues Committee. A wide range of bonds and bills was used to soak up liquidity: Defence Bonds, National Savings Certificates, War Bonds and Exchequer Bonds for institutions.[68] The maturity structure by the end of the war was rather shorter than it had been in 1918/19, but the difference was small.[69] The balance was similar in the United States, where borrowing from the public and money creation financed roughly equal proportions (a quarter apiece) of total wartime spending.[70] But the Axis powers relied heavily on short-term borrowing which in effect meant printing money. In Germany and Japan wartime monetary growth was roughly sevenfold; in Italy eighteenfold.[71] As in the First World War, the lion's share of the expansion was due to the monetizing of short-term government debt by the central bank.

The real difference between 1918 and 1945 in Britain was that after the Second World War there was much less of a drive to fund the short-term debt run up during the war. As a result, it was Britain which now experienced the problems associated with substantial levels of short-term debt and artificially low short-term interest rates. For most of the post-war period, it was assumed that there was a relationship between the structure of public debt and the supply and demand for money. The authorities therefore strove to limit the stock of liquid assets available to the banking system, at the same time relying on direct controls to limit bank lending. Instead of trying to convert short-term gilts into long-term gilts, the Bank of England adopted a passive "tap" system of funding, whereby the quantity of long-term securities sold was determined by the jobbers in the market.

This somewhat unsatisfactory (and theoretically flawed) system was swept away in the 1980s as a result of the abandonment of the credit "Corset," the revival of the Bank of England's base rate as the primary tool of monetary policy and the institutional "Big Bang" which did away with the jobbers as intermediaries between government and investors. Henceforth, new gilts were sold directly to the big institutions in auctions, much as had been done in the 1850s and early 1900s. However, the shifting attitudes of Conservative Chancellors towards government borrowing as an influence on the money supply led to inconsistencies in debt management. In the early 1980s the authorities actually sold more gilts than the deficit required ("over-funding"), hoping to increase the proportion held by private investors other than banks, which it was assumed would merely use additional gilts as the basis for new lending. This practice was abandoned when monetary targets were dropped by the Treasury. Instead, a "full funding" rule was adopted, whereby all public sector borrowing was absorbed outside the banking system. But in the recession of the early 1990s the government once again allowed itself to count sales of gilts to banks as funding. Finally, the Debt Management Review of July 1995 declared the complete separation of debt management and monetary policy, a theoretical break institutionalized by the decision to entrust monetary policy to the "operationally independent" Bank of England (1997) and debt management to the new Debt Management Office of the Treasury (1998).[72] This separation of public debt management from central bank control of monetary policy is in some ways historically novel, given the origins of most central banks as managers of public debt. Perhaps significantly, it coincided with a rapid fall in the government's borrowing requirement.

SCALING THE MOUNTAINS

So much for the techniques of government borrowing. Now let us turn to the question of scale. How big were past deficits and debts?

In the century after the Glorious Revolution all the great powers tended to spend more than they raised in taxation. Between 1692 and 1815, for example, the average British budget deficit amounted to approximately 3.3 per cent of national income.[73] A strikingly high proportion of Britain's expenditure during the wars of the eighteenth century was financed by loans: nearly 40 per cent between 1776 and 1783 and as much as 27 per cent between 1793 and 1815.[74] Russia's deficit was around 18 per cent of expenditure in 1764 and 29 per cent in 1796.[75] When Louis XVI's comptroller-general Calonne laboriously calculated the extent of royal insolvency in 1786, he estimated the deficit at 19 per cent of expenditure.[76] However, revolutionary France ran far larger deficits: 70 per cent of total expenditure in 1791, 40 per cent in "the Year III" (1794–5) and nearly 50 per cent in the Year V (1796–7).[77] The wars against France of the eighteenth and early nineteenth centuries were indeed, as George III said, in some measure "wars of credit."[78] So obvious did it seem to Kant that public debts had become the basis for war finance that Article 4 of his *Thoughts on Perpetual Peace* (1795) envisaged a ban on "debts . . . contracted in connection with the foreign affairs of the state . . . either from without or from within the state."[79]

Calculated as percentages of total expenditure, total deficits in the nineteenth century—commonly thought of as an era of "sound finance"—were also far from negligible. Only in Britain, and only after the Napoleonic Wars, was the balanced central government budget the norm. Between 1816 and 1899 the UK government ran a deficit in excess of 1 per cent of GNP in only four years. Indeed, if payments for debt service are excluded, the British primary budget surpluses of the nineteenth century were remarkably large: averaging 4.6 per cent of GDP every year between 1816 and 1899, and reaching a peak of 11.1 per cent in 1822. The figures would be even larger if payments to the new sinking fund after 1875—counted as current expenditure under the Treasury's idiosyncratic conventions—were also omitted.[80] When not at war the American federal government also tended to run surpluses.[81] But most continental countries ran budget deficits most years. France had a budget surplus in only seven years between 1816 and 1899. Italy ran a deficit every year of its existence from 1862 until 1899; the same was true of the German Reich until 1924. Between 1870 and 1913 the Austrian budget was only balanced in two years, 1892 and 1893; Russia had only three surplus years between 1890 and 1913.[82] To be sure, deficits tended to be quite small in relation to national income before 1914 (see Table 2). Only the German Reich's averaged more than 3 per cent of net national product between 1890 and 1913, and most of the federal government's

Table 2. Average annual central government budget deficits as a percentage of national product, selected periods

	UK	France	Italy	Germany	Austria	Russia	US	Japan
1830–59	−0.1	−1.5						
1860–89	0.0	−1.6	−2.4	−1.0	0.4			
1890–13	0.1	0.0	−0.9	−3.2	−1.1	−1.9	0.0	1.9
1914–18	−35.9	n/a	−23.5	−38.3	−2.7	3.2		
1919–38	1.2	−4.3	−9.9	−5.4	−1.8	1.9		
1939–45	−30.9	n/a	−23.9	−21.2	−22.2	−12.4	1.6	
1946–69	2.9	−1.1	−5.7		−0.3	1.4		
1970–89	−1.0	−2.1	−10.4			−2.7	−3.1	
1990–99	−3.8	−3.6	−7.2	−2.7	−3.1	−7.8	−1.5	−2.2

Sources: US, France and Italy: Masson and Mussa, "Long-term Tendencies" (original data kindly provided by Professon Masson). UK: Goodhart, "Monetary Policy." Germany: 1890–1913: Mitchell, *European Historical Statistics*; Hofmann, Grumbach and Hesse, *Wachstum*; 1914–18; Roesler, *Finanzpolitik*, pp. 197 ff.; Witt, "Finanzpolitik," p. 425; 1919–38; Balderston, *German Economic Crisis*, p. 226; Bresciani-Turroni, *Economics of Inflation*, pp. 437 f.; James, *German Slump*, p. 375; 1939–43: Hansemeyer, "Kriegswirtschaft," p. 400. Austria: 1890–1913; Mitchell, *European Historical Statistics*; Hobson, "Military-extraction Gap and the Wary Titan." Russia: 1890–1913; Mitchell, *European Historical Statistics*, and Gregory, *Russian Natoinal Income*, pp. 58 f.; 1939–45 (in fact only available for 1942–5): Harrison, "Soviet Union", p. 275. All figures for 1990–1999 from OECD, except for Russia which are from the IMF and cover the period 1993–9.

deficit was financed by "matricular contributions" from the member states, rather than by borrowing.[83] However, when we take into account the relatively small size of pre-1914 government budgets the deficits look more significant.

By any measure, the world wars resulted in vastly larger deficits in all combatant countries. In Britain the deficit exceeded 30 per cent of GNP between 1915 and 1918; in Germany it rose above 40 per cent, and may even have exceeded 60 per cent in 1917; in Italy it averaged 22 per cent. In the Second World War, the orders of magnitude were similar: deficits in 1943 ranged from between 19 per cent of net material product in the Soviet Union to 36 per cent of GNP in Germany.[84] Between the wars most states sought to return to balanced budgets. Of the former combatants, few apart from Britain succeeded (though the United States did in the 1920s); and even Britain slipped briefly into the red in 1933.[85] This was also the pattern after the Second World War, though in the period to 1969 not only Britain but also the defeated powers Germany and Japan were able to run surpluses.

The absence of deficits in Britain in every year between 1948 and 1972 (with the partial exception of 1965, when expenditure was recategorized) gives the lie to the idea that there was a "Keynesian revolution" in public finance prior to the 1970s, in the sense of deliberate strategy of using public borrowing to raise the level of domestic demand. To be sure, Keynes began arguing for "loan expenditure" as a way of increasing effective demand as early as 1933. But he always saw deficit finance as "a desperate expedient." Keynes's argument against Treasury proponents of the perennial balanced budget was that "there is no possibility of balancing the budget except by increasing national income, which is the same thing as increasing employment." During a depression, in other words, deficits in the short term would yield balanced budgets in the medium term. Moreover, Keynes wished the deficit to be seen in the context of a "capital budget," in other words to finance public investment, not current government spending.[86] In practice, even those politicians who thought of themselves as Keynesian found themselves unable to pursue a counter-cyclical policy, not least because of the recurrent conflicts between the pursuit of full employment and the maintenance of a stable exchange rate. Possibly the only authentic attempt at a Keynesian fiscal expansion was Anthony Barber's 1972 budget, which ushered in sixteen years of deficits. After a febrile boom in 1973, when GDP rose by 7 per cent, the economy collapsed as the balance of payments deficit ballooned, sterling slumped and inflation soared.[87]

The lack of deficits before 1973 also casts doubt on the theory of the inherent "democratic deficit," which predicts that democratic governments will tend to run deficits because the electorate favours public spending but is averse to taxation.[88] The preponderance of voters over direct taxpayers in the twentieth century described in the previous chapter might have been expected to give rise to such a politically induced deficit. But in the British case, deficit finance only became a feature of policy after the oil shock of the early 1970s. The same has been true of Japan.

Nevertheless, it is possible that Britain and Japan are merely the exceptions that prove the rule. Table 2 shows that central government deficits were the norm in both France and the United States in every period except 1890–1913. The Italian state has always run a deficit (even in the period when the franchise was based on a narrow tax qualification). Moreover, the period between 1970 and 1999 was marked almost everywhere by deficits higher than any previously recorded in peacetime. Especially noteworthy was the way Japan, having traditionally run budget surpluses (even in war periods), plunged into deficit. Britain too continued to run deficits—with the exception of the years 1988–90—despite the efforts of a consciously anti-Keynesian government to bring fiscal policy under control. Reductions in the redefined "Public Sector Borrowing Requirement" were a key objective of successive budgets under Margaret Thatcher, culminating in Nigel Lawson's hubristic declaration in 1988 that "henceforth a zero PSBR will be the norm." By 1994 it had risen to 8.3 per cent of GDP. Indeed, by the old measure the deficit was even wider. The bottom line was in many ways disguised in the Thatcher years by a combination of reduced capital expenditure and counting receipts from sales of public assets (privatization) as current revenue.[89]

What of past debts? In 1427 the Florentine public debt amounted to some 5 million florins, roughly ten times what it had been a century before. This was probably rather more than total national product.[90] The combined public debt of the Dutch United Provinces was still bigger: it was around 100 per cent of national product by the 1690s, and rose still higher in the years of French rule between 1795 and 1806.[91] By contrast, early modern monarchies were less indebted. The French debt in 1561, for example, was around 20 per cent of GNP.[92] The debts of the English crown remained tiny in relation to national income until the late seventeenth century. In the course of her reign, Elizabeth I's debt fell from £227,000 to zero and then rose again to £350,000: this last figure amounted to no more than 1 per cent of national product. Even at the time of the Glorious Revolution, the royal debt of £3 million represented little more than 5 per cent of national product.[93] In the seventeenth century the Swiss Confederation had no debts whatever; indeed, some of its constituent republics had considerable assets. In 1600 around a third of the total expenditure of Lucerne, for example, was invested in loans to other states and individuals.[94]

In the century after the Glorious Revolution, however, Britain's debt rose with only a few peacetime pauses to 215 per cent of national income in 1784. After a brief peacetime decline in the following decade, it rose again to 222 per cent of national income in 1815 and reached a peak of 268 per cent in 1821.[95] Small wonder the national debt became a byword for immensity. "My master is the best of all husbands in all the five quarters of the globe," wrote Leopold of Saxe-Coburg's secretary Baron Stockmar in 1816, shortly after his master's marriage to Princess Charlotte, daughter of the Prince Regent, "and his wife bears him an amount of love, the greatness of which can only be compared with the English national debt."[96] The British debt burden was indeed exceptionally high. Not only was the French debt lower in absolute terms; French national income was higher. According to one estimate, the total French debt in the late 1770s was equivalent to just 56 per cent of GNP;[97] though another source implies a figure of over 80 per cent in 1787, and a third estimate for 1789 puts it at 150 per cent.[98] Even the highest estimate is considerably below the equivalent British figure.

Figure 8 attempts to present the longest possible view of public debt in Britain, France, Germany and the United States. As is immediately obvious, the British experience has been of two great mountains of debt, due to the eighteenth century wars against France between 1688 and 1815 and the wars against Germany between 1914 and 1945. Though of equal height—in 1946 the debt/income ratio only just exceeded the post-Napoleonic peak—the two peaks are distinguished by their gradients, the slopes of the later debt mountain being much steeper on both the ascent and the descent. The "south face" of the earlier mountain is in fact a series of lesser summits (in 1698, 1721, 1750, 1764 and 1784); while the later mountain has a jagged triple summit (1923, 1933 and 1946).

By comparison, both France and Prussia emerged from the Napoleonic period with debt/national product ratios below 50 per cent. Indeed, the French debt burden remained below 50 per cent until the war of 1870, but thereafter rose sharply to reach a peak of 117 per cent in 1887, then declining gradually to just 66 per cent on the eve of the Great War. The Prussian debt burden fell sharply from 42 per cent in 1815 to 11 per cent in 1848 and was still only 14 per cent in 1872. Its subsequent rise should be seen alongside the rise of the federal debt of the German Reich. While the Prussian debt burden came close to 50 per cent in 1892, the Reich debt grew rapidly to a peak of 47 per cent of net national product in 1894. In other words, the major continental powers had rising debt/GNP ratios at a time when Britain's was being reduced.

All three European powers experienced dramatic and comparable increases in the ratio of debt to GNP during the First World War. After 1919, however, their paths sharply diverged. While the British and French debt burdens rose in the immediate post-war years, the German declined precipitously to zero in 1923, for reasons to be discussed in the next chapter. After peaking at 185 per cent of GNP in 1922, the French burden also fell sharply in the years to 1930, though it remained in excess of 100 per cent of GNP. The British debt burden by contrast hardly fell at all in the 1920s and actually rose between 1930 and 1933. The German debt burden remained relatively lower than the

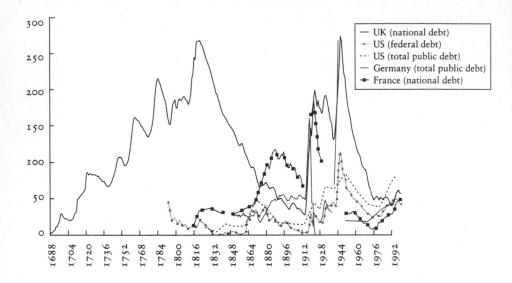

Figure 8: Debt/GNP Ratios since the Late Seventeenth Century

Sources: Goodhart, "Debt Management", statistical appendix. I am grateful to Ryland Thomas for supplying the complete database used by professor Goodhart. US: Brown, "Episodes", pp. 245–51; from 1980: Statistical Abstract 1999, table 542; Federal Reserve Bank of St. Louis, website. Germany: (1850–1914) Hoffman et al., *Wachstum*, pp. 789 f.; (1914–23) Balderston, "War Finance"; Webb, *Hyperinflation*, p. 49; Witt, "Finanzpolitik und sozialer Wandel", p. 424; Mitchell, *European Historical Statistics*, p. 390; Holtfrerich, *Inflation*, pp. 67 f.; (1925–38) Hoffman, Grumbach and Hesse, *Wachstum*, pp. 789 f.; James, *German Slump*, pp. 52, 375; (1939–45) Braun, *German Economy*, pp. 112, 115; 1950–1998: Statisches Bundesamt, *Statistisches Jahrbuch* 1997, tables 24.3, 20.5; Deutsche Bundesbank, *Monatsbericht* (August 1998), p. 56. France: Schremmer, 'Public Finance'; Flandreau, 'Public Debts'; 1920–9; Alesina, "End of Large Public Debts"; 1960–99: OECD (gross debt as a percentage of gross national income).

Note: These series are not perfectly comparable. British and American figures are expressed as a percentage of GNP; German figures as a percentage of NNP. The debt figures are not exactly comparable either, as the British and French figures exclude local government debt, the American figures exclude state and local debts, as well as federal debt held by the government or Federal Reserve system; while the German figures are for total public debt, including all levels of government.

British and French during the Great Depression; but after 1933 it soared with astonishing speed, overtaking that of Britain in 1943. Yet after the Second World War it fell once again to less than 20 per cent of GNP in 1950. The French debt burden was also much reduced after 1945, and indeed continued to decline in the 1950s and 1960s: from above 30 per cent in 1958 to less than 8 per cent in 1974.

The American federal debt burden has followed a lower and somewhat moother path, declining from above 60 per cent after the War of Independence to zero in the 1830s, then rising sharply from 2 per cent in 1860 to 41 per cent in 1878. Even when state and local debts are included, total American public debt was low in the nineteenth century: around 10 per cent of GNP in 1825, rising to 15 per cent in 1843, then declining slightly to 12 per cent in 1860. Its highest level was in 1870, after the Civil War, when it reached 49 per cent of GNP; but thereafter the ratio fell back to just 14 per cent in 1913.[99] Even the First World War caused a far smaller increase than the European states experienced: in 1919 the federal figure was a mere 30 per cent, compared with European figures of around 150 per cent. The debt burden rose during the Great Depression, from a low of just 16 per cent in 1929 to 45 per cent in 1939 (the total public sector debt was by now around 100 per cent of GNP); and went even higher as a result of the Second World War, at the end of which the federal debt alone amounted to 114 per cent of GNP. Like Britain, however, the US saw a sharp fall in its debt burden in the post-war years, in the American case to just 23 per cent of GNP in 1974. In 1980 the total public debt of all three tiers of American government was just 38 per cent of GNP. Set in this comparative perspective, the subsequent increase of the debt under Ronald Reagan—which at the time caused commentators so much *Angst*—was modest, as the figure makes clear.

Using the OECD definition of total gross government debt, the post-Reagan US figure peaked at just over 63 per cent of GDP, a lower figure than for at least nine other OECD members. Moreover, the debt burden had risen more steeply during the same period in seven other OECD economies.[100] Even on the broader definition used in the *Statistical Abstract of the United States*, total public sector debt was no more than 82 per cent of GDP in the mid-1990s. If one thinks of this debt as at least in part a consequence of winning the Cold War, the figure is strikingly close to the equivalent figure in 1946, immediately after the Second World War had been won. And as we have already seen, the budget surpluses of the late 1990s have raised the prospect of substantial if not total repayment of the federal debt. In Britain too buoyant government revenues in 2000 prompted the Chancellor of the Exchequer to talk—perhaps hubristically—of debt redemption.

By comparison, four OECD member states in 1999 had debt/GDP ratios in excess of 100 per cent (Italy, Belgium, Japan and Greece). And even these figures pale into insignificance alongside the external debt burdens of many less developed and post-Communist economies. In Guinea-Bissau total debt exceeds 500 per cent of GNP; in both Nicaragua and the Republic of Congo the figure is above 300 per cent. Five other countries—all in sub-Saharan Africa—have total debts in excess of two years' GDP.[101]

DO PUBLIC DEBTS MATTER?

How high is too high? According to Mr Micawber, any deficit at all was excessive: "Annual income twenty pounds, annual expenditure nineteen nineteen six, result happiness. Annual income twenty pounds, annual expenditure twenty pounds ought and six, result misery."[102] This is the view some American politicians take of public finance: they would like to see a balanced budget amendment to the federal constitution similar to those already in force in some states. Europeans are less Micawberish. The Maastricht Treaty specified that countries wishing to qualify for single currency membership should not have deficits in excess of 3 per cent of GDP, nor debts in excess of 60 per cent; though neither criterion was rigidly enforced. The British Chancellor of the Exchequer, Gordon Brown, has recently suggested that the British debt should be stabilized "over the economic cycle" at around 40 per cent of GDP.

Yet the long-run experience—and especially that of Britain—would seem to fly in the face of all such rules. Any theory of the economic significance of public debt must explain why Britain was not only able to overcome economically and demographically superior antagonists in both the eighteenth and the twentieth centuries; but also why she managed to avoid the internal political crises associated with high debt burdens in both France and Germany; and, above all, why she emerged as the "first industrial nation" despite carrying a public debt burden of unparalleled size and duration.

Anxiety about the macroeconomic impact of large public debts is not new. When David Hume contemplated Britain's growing national debt in 1752 he saw "the seeds of ruin . . . here scattered with such profusion as not to escape the eye of the most careless observer."[103] Sir James Steuart, writing fifteen years later, agreed: "If no check be put to the augmentation of public debts, if they be allowed constantly to accumulate, and if the spirit of the nation can patiently submit to the natural consequences of such a plan, it must end in this, that all property, that is income, will be swallowed up by taxes."[104] Adam Smith argued in *The Wealth of Nations* that loan finance tended to crowd out private investment and hence to depress private capital formation.[105] Ricardo called the national debt "one of the most terrible scourges . . . ever invented to afflict a nation . . . the overwhelming incumbrance which palsies all effort."[106] The moralistic nature of this critique exerted a powerful influence on Victorian politicians. In March 1854, arguing vainly that the Crimean War could be paid for out of current taxation, Gladstone described "the expenses of war" as "a moral check which it is pleased the Almighty to impose upon the ambition and lust of conquest which are inherent in so many nations."[107] "To resort to the money market for a loan," he declared, "would be a course not required by our necessities and therefore unworthy of our character." Citing (selectively) John Stuart Mill and McCulloch, he argued that "capital taken in loans" might be "abstracted from funds either engaged in production or destined to be employed in it" so that "their diversion from that purpose [would be] equivalent to taking the amount from the wages of the working classes." Raising taxes, on the other hand, would encourage "the community" to take "the first and earliest prospects of concluding an honourable peace."[108] It was the mid-Victorian conventional wisdom that "taxes are taken from income, and loans from capital."[109] On this basis, Stanley Jevons argued (in his *Coal Question* of 1865) that the national debt should be paid off entirely because Britain's coal reserves—a key component of the national wealth—would be exhausted after a century. This so alarmed Gladstone that he sketched plans to eliminate the debt over the next two hundred and fifty years by a combination of budget surpluses and a pacific foreign policy.[110]

Yet there has long been a counter-argument that public borrowing can have beneficial effects. The eighteenth-century writer Isaac de Pinto claimed that national debts might be a positive stimulus to growth, since "the debts, never becoming due, and having no critical period to dread, are as if they did not exist." Each new loan, he argued, "create[s] a new artificial capital which did not exist before, which becomes permanent, fixed and solid, as if it were so much real treasure." "When once a fund is created, the numerary remains, and the contributive faculty increases as well as circulation, and without too great an increase of specie . . . A light tax is drawn from the nation, into whose hands it returns again, with a general benefit to the whole."[111] Thomas Malthus opposed repayment of the national debt on the ground that, by dint of what would now be called a "wealth effect," bondholders' consumption boosted aggregate demand.[112] At a rather less sophisticated level, a national debt could be seen as enhancing a state's power—even its prestige. In 1781 Alexander Hamilton, the genius of early American public finance, declared: "A national debt, if it is not excessive, will be to us a national blessing. It will be a powerful cement to our nation."[113] Some eighty years later, in his "Biglow Papers," James Russell Lowell satirized the Confederate leader Jefferson Davis's claim to independence on this basis: "We've a war, an' a debt, an' a flag; an' ef this ain't to be independent, why, wut on airth is?"

More sophisticated defences of public debt have been advanced in the twentieth century. The early Keynesians argued that "functional" deficit finance could be used to stimulate an economy operating below full employment: public sector deficits and therefore debts would be a good thing in a crisis.[114] More recently it has been argued that the growth of public debts can, if markets are incomplete, assist capital formation and economic growth by encouraging the development of financial institutions (to be precise, "by introducing new securities that expand risk-sharing opportunities").[115] Historians have suggested that this helps explain Britain's economic success in the eighteenth century, despite a high burden of debt. The positive relationship between debt and capital formation was especially strong, it is claimed, in the later phase of the Napoleonic Wars, when loans were used to pay for British ships and armaments.[116] It is certainly true that government borrowing effectively created the market for private sector bonds and shares, as Table 3 shows. In 1853 British government bonds accounted for 70 per cent of the securities quoted on the London Stock Exchange. By 1913 the figure had fallen below 10 per cent, but the effect of the world wars in increasing the government debt and stifling private sector issuance drove the proportion back up to 55 per cent in 1950. Even as late as 1980, gilts accounted for more than a fifth of the market value of all securities on the London Stock Exchange and 60 per cent of the nominal value.

Another justification for public debts is that the transfers they effect simply do not matter that much. In his *Essai politique sur le commerce* (1736), the French theorist Jean-François Melon argued that a national debt was made up of "debts from the right hand to the left, by which the body is not weakened if it has the necessary nourishment and knows how to distribute it."[117] This anticipated the idea that debt is not necessarily worse in macroeconomic terms than tax because (in the economist Robert Barro's words) "households view as equivalent a current aggregate tax of $1 and a current

Table 3. *The growth and structure of the London Stock Exchange, 1853–1990*

	Total value (£ millions)	UK government share (per cent)
1853	1,215	70.2
1863	1,683	53.6
1873	2,270	37.6
1883	5,677	24.0
1893	6,561	16.5
1903	8,834	13.4
1913	11,263	9.0
1920	16,626	32.6
1933	18,476	35.3
1939	18,507	35.7
1945	24,701	49.3
1950	25,063	54.9
1960	45,060	31.9
1970	107,414	15.0
1980	280,328	21.7
1990	2,098,492	5.9

Source: Michie, *London Stock Exchange*, pp. 88 f., 175, 184, 320, 322, 360 ff., 419, 421, 440, 473, 521 f., 589 f.
Note: To 1933: Nominal values; from 1939 market values.

budget deficit of $1."[118] The key assumption here is that, to any household with a sense of obligation to the next generation, a tax tomorrow (to pay for current borrowing) amounts to the same as a tax today.[119] Government deficits, in this view, merely influence "the timing of real economic activity" in that they influence the timing of taxation. Indeed, when taxes are distortionary—in other words, when they impose distortions on the economy that will tend to reduce growth below its optimal level—deficits can play a beneficial tax-smoothing role, allowing the payments for exceptional events like wars or recessions to be deferred until more prosperous periods.[120] Since taxes usually are distortionary, this is an important argument for public borrowing in a crisis. The point was anticipated nearly a century and a half ago by Sir George Cornewall Lewis, the British Chancellor of the Exchequer who replaced Gladstone during the Crimean War. "Taxes which

cripple enterprise and derange industry or interfere with the ordinary distribution of capital," he argued in April 1855, "are more detrimental to the
community than loans effected by the Government." Or, as the Oxford economist G. K. Rickards put it in a lecture that same year: "Better to succeed to
a mortgaged patrimony than to an exhausted estate."[121]

Yet all this may be a debate about a flawed concept. It is widely acknowledged already that the term "deficit" is an ill-defined one. To take the British
case, what contemporaries regarded as the bottom line of the central government's budget (the balance of the "consolidated fund") from the 1870s
until the 1930s tended to understate the size of current surpluses by counting payments to the sinking fund as expenditure.[122] The Treasury also made
a somewhat arbitrary distinction between expenditure "above the line" and
"below the line," which notionally but not exactly distinguished between
current and capital expenditure. Moreover, the consolidated fund does not
include the national insurance fund, nor does it include the borrowings of
local authorities and public corporations (which *were* included in the Public
Sector Borrowing Requirement, the measure of the deficit introduced in
1976).[123] And this too is considered by some economists a measure inferior
to the cyclically adjusted Public Sector Fiscal Deficit, which seeks to exclude
the influence of public sector financial transactions (such as privatization)
and the cyclical fluctuations of economic growth.[124]

There are even more profound definitional problems.[125] In the modern
dynamic theory of fiscal policy, the key concept is the government's inter-
temporal budget constraint. This means that the sum of the "generational
accounts" of those now alive plus those of future generations has to be equal
to the sum of future government purchases plus the government's net debt.
Generational accounts represent the sum of the present values of the future
net taxes (taxes paid minus transfer payments received) that members of a
birth cohort can be expected to pay over their remaining lifetimes, assuming
current policy is continued. The sum of the generational accounts of all members of all living generations is how much those now alive will pay towards
the government's bills. The government's bills, on the other hand, are the present value sum of all of the government's future purchases of goods and services plus its official net debt (its official financial liabilities minus its official
financial assets, including the value of its public-sector enterprises). Bills not
paid by current generations *must* be paid by future generations. This is the
zero-sum nature of the government's inter-temporal budget constraint.
Essentially, existing debt must be fully funded in the long run by cumulative
budget surpluses.

However, different choices of fiscal labels can alter the present generation's accounts and the government debt by equal absolute amounts, leaving the next generation's accounts and the government's future purchases unchanged. Suppose, for example, that the British government had chosen in 1998–9 to label workers" national insurance contributions a "loan" and the additional Basic and State Earnings Related Pension benefits paid to workers in old age in recognition of those contributions "payment of interest and principal" on those "loans," less an "old age tax" (levied at the time contributors receive their benefits). This alternative set of words would have increased the government deficit by roughly £45 billion, instead of the surplus officially claimed. The government's debt would also have risen. However, so would the generational accounts of currently living generations, since their future "old age tax" would now be included in their accounts. The burden on future generations would therefore remain the same. And the economic position of the present generation would also be unaffected by the change of labels. Each worker would have handed the government the same amount of money in 1998 and would receive the same amount of money from the government in the future.[126]

The fact that the government uses one set of words rather than another is therefore a matter of semantics not economics. Each set of words results in a different measure of the deficit. But there is nothing in economic theory to lead one to prefer one measure to another. This approach to public finance—known as generational accounting—is little more than a decade old, but it has already been adopted in more than twenty countries.[127] We shall return to its distributional and political implications in chapter 7.

DEBT SERVICE

The most economically important measure of public debt may therefore not be the current outstanding nominal amount of debt, but the relationship between present and future tax burdens. On the other hand, the most *politically* important measure of public debt is more likely to be the current cost of debt service as a proportion of government expenditure. This is certainly the most visible measure to a government struggling to make ends meet, for the simple reason that every penny spent on debt service—in effect, the ongoing cost of past policies—is a penny that cannot be spent on present policies.

When state budgets were relatively modest, debt charges could be immense. In fifteenth- and sixteenth-century German towns, debt service averaged around a third of total budgets. In princely states and kingdoms, there was wider variation. In the first half of the sixteenth century the state of Hesse paid between 2 and 9 per cent of total spending on debt service. The figure for Württemberg in the same period was 80 per cent. Somewhere in the middle was Spain, where by 1543 nearly two-thirds of ordinary revenue was going on interest on the *juros*.[128] France too ended the sixteenth century with burdensome debts—four-fifths of annual revenue was already assigned at the start of Henry IV's reign[129]—but thanks to the reforms of Sully, her debt burden declined in the course of the seventeenth century to around a fifth of total spending between 1663 and 1689. Naples, by contrast, paid as much as 56 per cent of the budget on debt charges in 1627.[130] Papal debt service was also high, rising from 36 per cent in 1526 to a peak of 59 per cent in 1654.[131] By comparison, eighteenth-century Austrian debt service was low, at between a quarter and a third of total spending.[132]

History provides plentiful examples of political crises due to the rising burden of debt service. The ability of German city-states to preserve their independence often hinged on this: thus Mainz, which by 1411 was paying almost half its total revenue to the holders of annuities, lost its independence in the fifteenth century; while Lübeck and Hamburg, where debt service was lower, did not.[133] The Spanish monarchy's difficulties in the late sixteenth and seventeenth century were closely related to recurrent debt crises. As early as 1559 total interest payments on the *juros* exceeded ordinary revenue; and the situation was not better in 1584 when 84 per cent of ordinary revenue went to bondholders. By 1598 the proportion was back to 100 per cent.[134] The Dutch Republic was able to sustain much higher absolute levels of debt than its continental rivals, yet paid relatively small amounts to service the debt. In the 1640s, for example, debt service accounted for just 4 per cent of the total budget. But even here a limit was finally reached. By 1801, six years after the provincial and union debts had been consolidated into one, debt service amounted to 41 per cent of the budget. The French Republic which had overrun Holland in 1795 was, by contrast, unburdened by debt, for reasons to be discussed below.[135]

Pre-revolutionary France is perhaps the most notorious case of a state brought low by the costs of debt service. Between 1751 and 1788 interest and amortization payments rose from 28 to 49 per cent of total expenditure, or from just over a quarter of tax revenue to 62 per cent.[136] In fact, the cost of debt service to France's main military rival was not much less. Between 1740 and 1788 British debt charges rose as a proportion of tax revenues

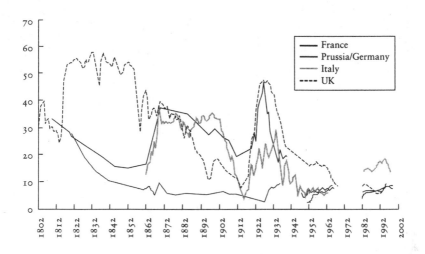

Figure 9. Debt service as a percentage of government expenditure, 1802–1999

Sources: Flora et al., *State, Economy and Society,* vol. i, pp. 381 ff., except: France 1802–22: Mann, *Sources of Social Power,* vol, ii, p. 373; UK 1802–1914: Mitchell and Deane, *Abstract of British Historical Statistics,* pp. 396–9; Prussia: Gerloff, "Der Staatshaushalt," p. 5; *Jahrbuch für die Statistik des Preussischen Staats* (1869), pp. 372–443, 466–545. All figures from 1982 to 1999 are from OECD.

Note: German figures for 1870 to 1914 are for general government; as are all figures from OECD. Other figures are for central government.

from 37 per cent to 56 per cent.[137] But the key point is that France had a substantially lower debt than Britain both in absolute terms and as a proportion of national income. Between 1776 and 1782 French debt charges amounted to around 7.5 per cent of the total debt, compared with a figure of 3.8 per cent for Britain. In other words, the cost of servicing the same amount of debt was roughly *twice* as high for France. This crucial disadvantage was only partly due to higher payments for amortization; the main reason will be explored in the next chapter.

Figure 9 presents figures for debt service in relation to budgets since the early nineteenth century, showing that it was not until the 1870s that other major states approached Britain in this respect. The British data show that for almost the entire period between 1818 and 1854 more than half of gross central government expenditure was going on debt service, close to the debt burden carried by the French *ancien régime* on the eve of the Revolution. But Britain was able to reduce the burden of debt gradually from the late 1830s, as the figure shows, while French (and Italian) debt charges caught up as a result of the wars fought from Sebastopol to Sedan. From the end of the 1860s until the mid-1880s, Britain, France and Italy were all spending around a third of their budgets on debt charges. Rising expenditure on other civil and military functions caused the proportions to fall towards the Prussian level (below 10 per cent) in 1913, except in France where the figure remained just above 20 per cent.

The figure also makes clear how different were the burdens the four states carried after the First World War. Whereas in Britain and France debt service peaked at around 44 per cent of total government spending, in Italy the average figure for the 1920s was just under 18 per cent. In Germany—for reasons we shall soon see—debt service was just 2 per cent of total spending in 1925. Interest and debt repayments have mattered far less in Germany and France since 1945, though in both cases the share of total spending has been going up since the early 1980s. In Britain debt service tended to fall from the 1950s to the 1990s, whereas in Italy the trend was in the opposite direction, culminating in the mid-1990s, when more than a fifth of total government expenditure was going on the national debt.

The obvious explanation for the declining importance of debt service as a proportion of government spending might simply be that government budgets in the nineteenth century were so small. As we have seen, the growth of the welfare state had barely begun in this period, so that payments to bondholders were the principal transfers made through national treasuries. This is certainly a part of the story, to which we shall return in Chapter 7. There are, however, other reasons why debt was so much less expensive for Britain than for her eighteenth- and nineteenth-century rivals; and why, at least for the developed economies of the West, debt today is relatively less expensive than in the past. These are the subject of the next chapter.

5

The Money Printers:
Default and Debasement

"To whom it may concern, this note of hand
Is worth a thousand ducats on demand . . ."

. . .

You signed: as if by sleight of hand, behold,
That night provided copies thousandfold,
And, so that all might have the boon to share,
We stamped the total series then and there.
Tens, Thirties, Fifties, Hundreds, all to date,
You cannot think how people jubilate.

. . .

None now has power to stay the flying chits,
They ran as quick as lightning on their way,
And money-booths kept open night and day,
Where every single note is honoured duly
With gold and silver—though with discount, truly.

Goethe, Faust[1]

In 1912 the German Union of Women's Suffrage held a well-attended meeting on the subject of "Inflation." At that time, consumer price inflation in Germany—as measured in the price of food—was just under 5.3 per cent per annum. This was its highest level since 1880: the average annual inflation rate since the foundation of the German Reich in 1871 had been little more than 1 per cent. The Suffragists' meeting was one of many expressions of public anxiety about high prices: as one newspaper commentator had remarked the year before, "Everyone talks about the rise in the cost of living."[2] But talking about inflation is not the same as understanding it.

In 1924 the UWS met again to consider not inflation but stabilization. As a result of the previous year's disastrous hyperinflation—which had seen the annual rate of inflation peak at 182 billion per cent—the society's assets were

now worth precisely five marks and fourteen pfennigs. Though they had been denied the vote before and during the First World War, they had patriotically invested their funds in German government bonds.[3] Those purchased during the war were now worth precisely nothing.

Twice in the space of twenty-five years, the German government debt all but vanished as a result of the total collapse in value of the currency. Twice those who put their faith in the credit of the German Reich were left with worthless paper. It was as if there had been a collective failure to read to the end of Goethe's masterwork (though, as it happens, the Vice-President of the Reichsbank during the first hyperinflation was a distinguished Goethe scholar).[4] In the scene in Part Two, Act I, from which the epigraph above is taken, the printing of money at first seems to bring prosperity. The paper money flows "to wine-shops, butchers, bakers, / With half the world as glutton merry-makers." Clothiers, tailors and restaurateurs do a roaring trade. "Such paper-wealth," declares Mephistopheles, "is practical."[5] But in Act IV Mephistopheles reveals that these were "bogus riches"; and the country on which he bestowed them has "collapsed in anarchy":

> With men both high and low emmeshed in feud,
> Brother by brother murderously pursued.
> Castle fought castle, town invaded town,
> And guilds had plots to pull the nobles down,
> Chapter and flock against the bishop rose,
> And nowhere could men meet, except as foes,
> In church they stabbed to kill, before the gate
> The travelling merchant met a bloody fate . . .
> So they . . . limped on, fell, rose again perhaps,
> Then, losing balance, lurched to a collapse.[6]

Writing shortly before his death in 1832, Goethe probably had the French experience during the 1790s in mind. But this passage also foretells uncannily the early history of the Weimar Republic.

The German experience of inflation has been by any standards extreme. The memory of hyperinflation was still being cited as a factor in German politics in the late 1980s, as politicians sought to persuade voters that a new European currency would be as sound a currency as the deutschmark (which in fact depreciated by 75 per cent in the fifty years of its existence). Yet the experience of default through inflation is in many ways universal—as universal as the story of Faust. Since 1899 the price of a packet of cigarettes in

Britain has risen by a factor of 15; the price of a loaf by a factor of 32; and the price of a pint of beer by a factor of 456. The average weekly wage has risen by a factor of 89.[7] By contrast, a British government consol with a face value of £1,000 has actually fallen in price.

HOW NOT TO PAY

There are five ways to reduce transfer payments in the form of debt interest and repayment when they reach what is judged (politically) to be excessive. First, part or all of the debt can simply be paid off. One obvious way of doing this is by levying a one-off capital levy on the bondholders or, for that matter, all wealthy groups. Secondly, the interest paid on the debt can be reduced by legislative act, an operation known as a "conversion." Thirdly, payments to bondholders can be suspended by fiat. Fourthly, an unanticipated rise in inflation can reduce the real value of both debt and interest payments, provided the debt is not index-linked or denominated in foreign currency (or gold). This has often been seen as the easier political option; and, as we shall see, twentieth-century governments found it hard to resist. The final option—the hardest but best way to reduce a debt burden—is to achieve an increase in the real rate of growth; though under certain circumstances the very existence of a large public debt may make this difficult.

The most politically "respectable" way to reduce the real debt burden is by repayment, that is by running recurrent primary budget surpluses (meaning surpluses greater than current debt interest). Occasions when a debt has been wholly repaid are in fact relatively few. Between 1816 and 1834, to give one of the rare examples, the total US federal debt was paid back.[8] However, both the United States and Britain regularly managed to *reduce* their total debts by running primary surpluses. Between 1822 and 1914 the British national debt was reduced by about a quarter in nominal terms as a result of a sustained program of debt repayment. In the United States there were also debt reductions between 1805 and 1811, 1871 and 1893, 1920 and 1930, and again (though on a much smaller scale) between 1947 and 1953.[9]

For reasons to be analysed in Chapter 7, raising taxation across the board to pay off bondholders is seldom politically popular. It is also economically problematic, since the income and consumption taxes conventionally used to finance such repayments are, as economists say, distortionary.[10] An alternative policy which is not distortionary is to levy a one-off capital levy on the bondholders themselves: in effect to pay them off with their own money.

However, the occasions when this has been politically possible have been relatively few; and the occasions when it has been successful even fewer.[11] The attempt of the German Finance Minister Matthias Erzberger in 1919 to reduce the Weimar Republic's deficit with a one-off, steeply progressive "Reich Emergency Sacrifice" (*Reichsnotopfer*) on all property-owners failed miserably, for the simple reason that the tax could be paid in instalments over periods ranging from 25 to 47 years, with interest charged at only 5 per cent after December 1920. So long as inflation remained above 5 cent, delayed payment could be relied upon to erode the real value of the liability.[12]

The simplest solution to a problem of excessive debt is, of course, not to pay at all. Outright default was the habitual response of medieval and early modern monarchs when the costs of debt service were consuming too much of their income. Edward III ruined the Bardi and Peruzzi families this way in the 1340s.[13] Jacques Cœur, the fifteenth-century French financier fell victim to a similar default by Charles VII.[14] In the early modern period defaults by the great powers became so frequent that they were more or less institutionalized; it may indeed be more accurate to think of them as moratoria, reschedulings or forced conversions of debt, rather than state bankruptcies.[15] Thus Spain defaulted on all or part of her debt fourteen times between 1557 and 1696.[16] What happened was that existing debts were effectively rescheduled—usually by converting short-term *asientos* into long-term *juros*—and new borrowing resumed shortly afterwards. However, even habitual defaulting had a cost. After 1627 Genoese financiers limited their exposure to *asientos*, foreseeing yet another bankruptcy which would leave them holding lower-yielding *juros*. The decline in the outstanding amount of *asientos* from its peak in 1625 (12.4 million ducats) to little more than 1 million in 1654 reflected Spain's narrowing fiscal room for maneuver. This had direct political implications at a time when France and the United Provinces were able to borrow more at home and abroad.[17] Moreover, Spanish finances remained prone to episode throughout the nineteenth century: there was another major episode in the mid-1870s.

France too was a regular defaulter in the early modern period. Sir George Carew had said of Henry IV that he "wringeth them [financiers] like sponges and ransometh every three or four years."[18] It was a practice his successors were obliged to imitate. The royal government defaulted wholly or partially in 1559, 1598, 1634, 1661, 1648 and 1698, and again in 1714, 1721, 1759, 1770 and 1788. As in the Spanish case, default became part of a more or less predictable pattern: "Borrow to fight the war, struggle in vain to raise taxes sufficiently to pay the debt, borrow even more to service the debt and . . .

ultimately default on part of the debt to restore balance."[19] It is possible to distinguish between three kinds of default: temporary suspension of reimbursement payments; "reform," which meant restoring the interest on debts to 5 per cent; and outright repudiation, when the interest rate was reduced below 5 per cent.[20] Since the reign of Francis I, the government had used periodic *chambres de justices*—special commissions to inquire into financial fraud—not only to purge the fiscal system, but to default on various obligations. There were eleven such episodes between 1597 and 1665.[21] It was Louis XVI's refusal to default in the usual manner, it has been suggested, that forced him to summon the Estates General, and thereby unleash the revolutionary crisis. Yet this merely postponed—and at the same time worsened—the fiscal crisis. The default of 1797 affected fully two-thirds of the entire national debt, overshadowing even the *Visa* that followed the collapse of Law's schemes.

David Hume cynically observed that if Britain had defaulted as France had in the eighteenth century, the effects would have been minimal: "So great dupes are the generality of mankind, that, notwithstanding such a violent shock to public credit, as a voluntary bankruptcy in ENGLAND would occasion, it would probably not be long ere credit would again revive in as flourishing a condition as before."[22] Hume was right in one respect: defaults may raise the price of borrowing for a country, but they seldom scare lenders away for long. England had indeed experienced a kind of default in 1672, when Charles II decreed a moratorium on all "orders of payment" not repayable from an earmarked source of future revenue. This "Stop of the Exchequer" had disastrous consequences for the London goldsmiths who had been giving the government short-term credits in this form since 1665. In the 1680s interest payments on the Exchequer debts were suspended, and were not resumed again until 1705.[23] Nevertheless, the costs of default are usually quantifiable in terms of the higher interest rates (and therefore higher debt charges) paid by defaulting governments on new post-default borrowing. As we shall see, the best explanation of the differential between British and French financial strength in the eighteenth century lies here.

Although the American federal government never defaulted on its debt, the same cannot be said of the American states themselves. In the recession of 1837–43, there were defaults on around half of the outstanding state debts; 10 per cent of the total amount owed by the states was repudiated altogether. There were further rashes of default in 1857 and again in the 1870s.[24] Latin American states were the perennial defaulters of the nineteenth and twentieth centuries. There were waves of default in the 1820s, the late 1880s (Argentina and Colombia), the pre-1914 period (Brazil and Mexico), the 1930s and again in the 1980s. The Middle Eastern states were not much better. There was a calamitous Turkish default after 1875, which also hit holders of Egyptian bonds. The collapse of the Ottoman Empire after the First World War led to another major default; though not on the scale of the Russian default of 1917, perhaps the biggest in financial history. However, these cases were all complicated by the fact that a substantial proportion of bondholders were foreigners, raising quite different economic and political questions from a purely domestic default. We will return to this point in Chapter 9.

Conversion—the exchange of one kind of bond for another paying a lower coupon—is distinct from default, provided investors consent to the exchange. In 1672, as we have seen, the English Crown susupended payments on its "orders of payment," but ultimately converted the debt into perpetual annuities;[25] and in 1715 the Dutch Generality suspended and then reduced interest payments, an operation repeated in 1753.[26] There were more or less successful conversions of parts of the British national debt in 1707–8, 1716–17, 1727, 1749–50, 1756, 1822, 1824, 1830, 1834 and 1844; but in 1853 Gladstone's bid to convert 490,000 of "consolidated" and "reduced" annuities into a new $2^1/_2$ per cent stock foundered; and it was thirty-five years before another such operation was attempted by Goschen, who succeeded in reducing the interest on a substantial portion of the debt to $2^3/_4$ per cent.[27] A crucial conversion was that of 1932, which belatedly cut the coupon on £2.1 billion of the First World War debt still outstanding from the by then excessive level of 5 per cent to $3^1/_2$ per cent. The success of this immense operation—involving a quarter of the entire national debt, equivalent to around half a year's national income—brought the government an annual saving of £30 million.[28]

Unlike defaults, such operations were managed in a transparent and predictable way, in response to perceptible declines in market interest rates. More importantly, conversions are based—or should be—on consent. A conversion like that of 1932 effectively invited investors to switch to a longer and lower-yielding asset: when the Midland Bank refused to accept the Bank of England's terms, it was not forced to. On the other hand, smaller investors were cajoled into accepting the conversion not only by patriotic propaganda, but also by carrots and sticks. Bonds that were not converted ceased to be eligible for rediscount at the Bank, for example.[29]

The British tradition of negotiated conversions has in many ways been exceptional, however. When the French premier Villèle tried a British-style conversion in 1824 he encountered stiff opposition in the aristocratic Upper Chamber, and the scheme ultimately foundered. The vicomte de Chateaubriand claimed it was an Anglo-Austrian ruse to defraud the French *rentier*, while the fact that some of the proceeds would have financed compensation to aristocratic victims of the Revolution added to the political difficulty.[30] When negotiated conversions have proved impossible, authoritarian governments have sometimes used compulsion. This was the key to Mussolini's stabilization of the Italian debt in the 1920s. There were two man-datory conversions (*conversione forzosa*) in 1926, when short-term bonds were converted into 5 per cent long-term bonds (*titoli del Littorio*), and again in 1934, when these new bonds were converted into 25-year $3^1/_2$ per cents.[31]

As these examples make clear, there is in truth no clear-cut distinction between default and conversion; what matters is the way creditors are induced to reduce their claims on the state, and the extent to which those claims are reduced.

THE INFLATION TAX

Capital levies, defaults and conversions are all overt ways of reducing a debt burden. However, there has long been recognized that there is a covert way too; namely, to debase the unit of account in which a debt is denominated. The issuing of money to cause an unanticipated rise in the price level operates as a fiscal tool in a number of ways. First, it permits a government to swap intrinsically worthless pieces of paper (or their electronic equivalents) for actual goods and services. This real transfer to governments, or "seigniorage," is paid for by the private sector through a decline in the real value of their money balances generated by the policy's attendant inflation. Secondly, raising prices by "printing" money reduces the real value of non-price-indexed government wage payments, transfer payments, and official debt repayment. Inflation simple reduces the real value of the government's debt, provided it is denominated in local currency. Thirdly, inflation permits the government to push the public into higher tax brackets.

Historically, this is how most states have coped with severe fiscal imbalances. The "inflation tax" on holders of money and financial assets was no invention of the twentieth century, though that century saw its most extensive and ruthless use.

Though precious metals have been the foundation of the monetary system since the third millennium BC, coinage did not come into existence until around the seventh century BC.[32] From Roman times at the latest it appears to have been understood that reducing the gold and silver content of coins was a source of revenue. There was sustained debasement of the Roman denarius after the reign of Marcus Aurelius, reducing its silver content by nearly 99 per cent by the time of Diocletian.[33] In medieval and early modern France revenue from seigniorage was high—as much as eleven times more than other sources of royal income in 1421. Between 1318 and 1429 the French coinage was debased four times.[34] There were debasements in Florence in the fourteenth century, Castile and Burgundy in the fifteenth, England in the sixteenth and much of Germany in the early seventeenth century. In the 1540s Henry VIII issued debased coins with a face value of £4.4 million, twice the price of the metal they contained. He made a profit of 46 per cent on every coin, or some £2 million.[35] The metallic content of gold coins was reduced by around 25 per cent and of silver coins by 80 per cent.[36] In the same way, the silver content of the French *livre tournois* fell by around half between 1513 and 1636.[37] The legitimacy of such operations had been asserted in the fourteenth century by the writer Nicolas Oresme, whose *De moneta* argued that, in a just cause, debasement was a legitimate form of tax.[38] But this was not a popular view, and the practice was supposed to be secret. Henry VIII's Secretary Thomas Wriothesley called the Mint "our holy anchor," but urged that its operations be kept secret, "for if it should come out that men's things coming thither be thus employed, it would make them withdraw and so bring a lack."[39] Germans remembered the time of the Thirty Years War as the *Kipper- und Wipperzeit*: the age of the coin-clippers.

The correlation between debasement and price inflation was seldom exact: early modern prices were influenced as much by international specie flows, to say nothing of agricultural and demographic fluctuations, and there were in any case physical limits on how much the money supply could be expanded by debasement. Nevertheless, the apparent link between debasements and sixteenth-century price rises provoked a theoretical and practical reaction. To Jean Bodin, writing in 1568, it was "a fraud and a pure trumpery of courtesans to claim that the king and the people gain [from debasement]"; the king might well, but the people patently did not.[40] By the seventeenth century successive debasements had led to something verging on monetary chaos in Europe. In 1610 there were around a thousand different gold and silver coins in circulation in Amsterdam, pushing up the transaction costs of commerce.[41] At the same time, the returns of seigniorage tended to diminish with each successive debasement.

In response, two countries endeavoured to adopt systems of fixed exchange rates. In 1638 the Dutch guilder was set at slightly less than 10 grams of silver, though the unit of account at the Amsterdamse Wisselbank remained the 1544 guilder. This facilitated the creation of a unified system of payments, but with flexibility in the exchange rate between the coinage in circulation, mainly used for domestic transactions, and the bank guilder, reserved for foreign trade. In England the practice of clipping silver coins was halted after a burst of wartime depreciation with the great recoinage of 1696.[42] Since the aim was to establish a bimetallic system, the price of the gold guinea was fixed in terms of silver; however, the rate chosen undervalued silver relative to France and Holland, causing silver coins to be removed from circulation. The drift to gold continued in 1717 when the Master of the Mint, the great physicist and mage Sir Isaac Newton, set the mint price of gold at £3 17s. 10$^{1}/_{2}$ d. per ounce; once again gold was overvalued relative to silver, and silver coins effectively vanished from circulation. For larger transactions the place of silver was gradually taken by paper money backed by gold. In 1774 silver ceased to be legal tender for sums in excess of £25.[43] For similar reasons, the coinage of the United States, formally bimetallic under the 1792 Coinage Act, was first predominantly silver (because of undervaluation of gold at the mint), then after 1834 predominantly gold (because of undervaluation of silver).[44]

However, the development of paper money—which can be traced as far back as eleventh-century China, but did not begin in the West until 1690—created new opportunities for levying the inflation tax.[45] Between 1704 and 1707 the French *caisse d'emprunts* issued up to 180 million livres in interest-bearing notes, though the market soon knocked these down to around two-thirds of their face value.[46] As we have seen, one of the key elements of John Law's disastrous experiment with French finances was a massive expansion of the supply of paper money to some 2,235 million livres in 1720, compared with 344 million livres in 1708.[47] There was another, less blatant, expansion of the paper money circulation in the second half of 1789 as a result of government borrowing from the Caisse d'Escompte.[48] After 1768 Russia too relied heavily on printing paper money (as well as debasing the coinage) to finance her deficits.[49] So did Spain, though the *vales reales* issued by Charles III from 1780 were interest-bearing.[50] In the same way, a substantial part of the Austrian debt between 1790 and 1820 was financed by issuing paper *Zettel*.[51] Often the paper notes in question were technically short-term debt instruments rather than cash proper; but the inflationary effect was much the same.

The most spectacular of all eighteenth-century inflations was that of the *assignats* issued by the French National Assembly in anticipation of sales of confiscated royal and church property. Although originally intended to reimburse and indeed replace the so-called *dette exigible*[52] of the old regime, the assignats swiftly became a device to finance the revolutionary regime's large wartime deficits. The original 400 million livres issued in December 1789 were interest-bearing, but from October 1790 the assignats ceased to pay interest and the volume in circulation rose swiftly from 1.2 billion that September to 2.4 billion in October 1792. By February 1796, when the printing machines were publicly smashed, 40 billion had been issued—about eight times the nominal amount of the *ancien régime*'s debt.[53] The assignats' purchasing power in terms of gold fell from 91 per cent in January 1791 to 0.5 per cent in 1796.[54] This wiping out of the debts of the eighteenth century meant that, by 1818, the per capita burden of debt was fifteen times higher in Britain than in France.[55] On the other hand, the experience of the assignats left a lasting scar on the French psyche, in the form of a reluctance to rely on paper money which persisted for the better part of a century. In 1850 more than 90 per cent of all transactions in France were settled in specie, compared with just over a third in England and only a tenth in Scotland.[56]

The French experience was not unique. Between 1786 and 1815 the circulation of paper roubles increased by a factor of 18. The equivalent figure for Austria between 1790 and 1811 was 37.[57] Napoleon was right that paper money was one of the foundations of Austrian war finance: in September 1809 he even ordered the printing of 100 million gulden of fake Austrian banknotes in order "to depreciate this paper issue, and to force Austria back onto a metal currency," which would "compel her to reduce her army."[58] Moreover, while France achieved a successful and enduring currency stabilization under Napoleon with the creation of the franc germinal in 1803, the East European states were much slower to wean themselves off paper money.

Even in Britain war and the suspension of gold convertibility in 1797 led to inflation, though the scale was much less than on the continent—prices rose by around 80 per cent between 1797 and 1818, and by 1822 had more or less returned to their pre-war level as a result of the return to gold. Unlike on the continent, there was confidence throughout the war that the authorities had the intention and the means to return to gold convertibility after the fighting was over.[59]

The nineteenth century is usually seen as a time when the spread of the gold standard more or less eliminated the possibility of debt-reduction via currency depreciation. This is not quite true. The American Civil War saw an assignat-style inflation in the states of the Confederacy, and a depreciation of the paper "greenback" in the Union too, with corresponding reductions in the real value of public debts.[60] The convertibility of the dollar was suspended from 1862 until 1879, and even after that doubts about the American commitment to gold persisted into the 1890s. War and internal crisis also tended to undermine the attempts to peg the Russian and the Austrian currencies to silver, forcing governments to monetize deficits. Between 1847 and 1853, for example, short-term debt rose from 8 per cent to over 25 per cent of total Austrian debt.[61] In the three years 1849–51 high powered money also rose by 25 per cent; while the cost of living peaked in 1854 at 29 per cent above its level seven years before. There were similar problems as a result of the three wars Austria fought between 1859 and 1866.[62] Italy too was off gold from 1866 until 1883, and again after February 1894; in 1883 Spain also suspended convertibility. Between 1880 and 1914 Chile, Argentina and Brazil all suffered currency depreciation of between 50 and 80 per cent.[63] Even within the gold system, a measure of inflationary debt "relief" was possible. The fact that a large number of European countries saw their debt burdens fall from the 1890s until 1914 has been attributed not only to higher growth rates but also to the global expansion in the gold supply and hence higher inflation (compared with negative rates in the 1870s and 1880s).[64]

Nevertheless, the significance of this mild inflation was minimal compared with what happened after 1914, when specie payments were suspended by nearly all the First World War combatants (Japan and South Africa excepted) and deficits were financed to varying degrees by resort to the printing press. The extreme case was that of Germany, where wholesale prices rose between 1914 and 1923 by a factor of around 1.3 trillion. Something of the shock this inflicted on ordinary people used to the stability of gold-backed marks can be gauged from Elias Canetti's memoir of life in Frankfurt in 1923:

It was more than disorder that smashed over people, it was something like daily explosions. . . . The smallest, the most private, the most personal events always had one and the same cause: the raging plunge of money. . . . I [had] regarded money as something boring, monotonous . . . But now I suddenly saw it from a different, an eerie side—a demon with a gigantic whip, lashing at everything and reaching people down to their most private nooks and crannies.[65]

For some it was too much: the great art historian Aby Warburg suffered a nervous breakdown and was haunted thereafter by visions of cultural devaluation, with art reproductions being churned out like banknotes from the printing press.[66] Others, however, remembered their Goethe. The *Nordwestdeutsche Zeitung* even published a topical parody of Mignon's Song from *Wilhelm Meisters Lehrjahre*:

> Do you know the land where the currencies bloom,
> [Where] in dark night the clip joints shine?
> An icy wind blows from the nearby chasm—
> Where the Mark stands low and the dollar high.[67]

Yet, as Table 4 shows, inflation was an almost universal phenomenon after 1914, affecting even neutral states. In addition to Germany, four countries—Austria, Hungary, Poland and Russia—all suffered something that can be

Table 4. European price inflation during and after the First World War

	Peak of wholesale prices in terms of paper currency (1914 = 1)	Date
Switzerland	2	1921
Spain	2	1920
Netherlands	3	1919
Denmark	3	1920
UK	3	1920
Sweden	4	1920
Norway	4	1920
Italy	6	1926
France	7	1926
Belgium	7	1927
Finland	12	1921
Czechoslovakia	14	1921
Austria	14,300	1922
Hungary	23,466	1922
Poland	2,484,296	1924
Russia	4,146,849	1923
Germany	1,261,600,000,000	1923

Sources: Mitchell, *European Historical Statistics*; Bresciani-Turroni, *Economics of Inflation*, pp. 23 f., 161–5; Capie, "Conditions in which Very Rapid Inflation has Occurred"], table 6; Sargent, "Ends of Four Big Inflations", tables.

described as hyperinflation.[68] The timing of stabilization also varied: in most countries, prices had stopped rising by 1921; but in the more extreme cases, inflation continued into 1922 and 1923. Italy, France and Belgium were unusual in that inflation continued until around 1926, but never boiled over into hyperinflation. The French experience was something of a helter-skelter, with annual inflation peaking at over 50 per cent in 1920, then turning negative in 1921, peaking again at over 40 per cent in 1926, then turning negative again in 1927. France experienced deflation for most of the period between 1930 and 1936; but inflation soared back above 30 per cent in mid-1937.[69]

The causes of post-war inflations, though complex, were undeniably rooted in the short-term borrowings of governments and their monetary financing by central banks. Inflation only stopped when it was clear that these practices would cease—which (especially in the countries that suffered hyperinflation) necessitated a substantial "regime change," meaning a change of the monetary and fiscal policy regime. In the Italian case there was a change of political regime as well.[70] The consequences of high inflation were also in large part fiscal. Above all, the divergent paths of inflation had radically different effects on the real debt burdens of the countries concerned. In Britain and the United States the decision to return to the gold standard at the pre-war exchange rate required deflation. Despite some debt repayment, the combined effect of falling prices and reduced growth caused substantial increases in the real debt burden. Between 1920 and 1931 the nominal value of the British national debt was reduced by around 5 per cent; but the real debt burden, allowing for deflation, rose by a staggering 60 per cent. In the United States in the same period, debt repayments and deflation simply cancelled one another out, leaving the real debt burden unchanged. Yet countries which went down the inflationary road emerged with much, if not all, of their internal war debt gone. In the extreme case, German public debt was reduced to virtually zero in 1923. Although subsequent "revaluation" legislation did something to compensate the holders of pre-war bonds—like the hapless women suffragist—the same treatment was not accorded to war bonds.[71] In a parody of the motto on the soldier's Iron Cross, the German public gave their gold in return for worthless paper.[72] Somewhere in between lay countries like France and Belgium. In France the total internal debt rose in nominal terms between 1920 and 1929 by about 37 per cent. But in relation to net national product it fell by almost exactly the same amount.[73]

In many ways, this story repeated itself during and after the Second World War. In Germany there was an even steeper increase in both public debt and paper currency, and only strict price controls prevented an inflationary explosion during the last two years of the war. When the regime collapsed in 1945, the reichsmark went with it almost immediately, and was followed with astonishing rapidity by the occupation currency printed by the Americans and (in excessive quantities) the Soviets, forcing victors and vanquished alike to improvise with cigarette money and other substitutes until the currency reform of June 1948. Other countries which experienced very high post-war inflation were Greece, China and Hungary; in two of these cases civil war was a primary cause of the problem.[74] By contrast, Britain succeeded in keeping monetary expansion and inflation below the First World War levels: prices rose by just over 50 per cent relative to 1938.[75]

Between 1914 and 1945 the world veered between inflation and deflation. With only a few exceptions—American consumer prices fell by small amounts in 1949 and 1955, for example, and Japan experienced slight deflation of less than half of one per cent in 1980, 1995 and 1999—the world since 1945 has been inflationary, though with distinct phases of low and high inflation. In the 1950s and 1960s most economies experienced mild inflation under the gentle strictures of the Bretton Woods system (see Chapter 11). In the 1970s and 1980s, however, the breakdown of that system led to a more or less global adoption of paper money. The consequence was a general increase in inflation, though there was considerable variation between countries, depending on the way fiscal and monetary authorities reacted to the higher oil prices imposed by the OPEC cartel in 1973 and 1979. (To give an impression of this variation, compare the average inflation rates for Germany, the United States, Britain and Portugal between 1961 and 1999, which were respectively 3.3, 4.6, 7.1 and 12.0 per cent.) Since the late 1980s, however, there has been a marked decline in inflation rates in most countries. Portuguese inflation, which exceeded 50 per cent in May 1977, fell below 3 per cent in 1999. French inflation, which reached 14 per cent in November 1981, fell to just 0.2 per cent. A few bold commentators have even ventured to speak of the "death of inflation."

RULES AND DISCRETION

The great variations in inflation over time and between countries are perhaps as well explained by institutional changes as by universal economic laws like the quantity theory of money or its derivatives.[76] Figure 10 presents long-run evidence on British consumer price inflation since 1871, showing that there are indeed rough correlations between the inflation rate and monetary

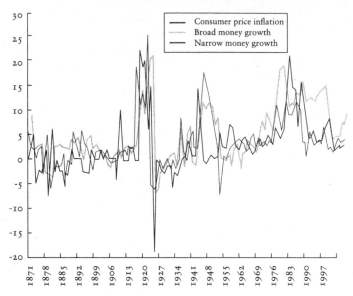

Figure 10. British money supply and inflation (annual growth rates), 1871–1997

Source: Goodhart, "Monetary Policy;" Capie and Webber, *Monetary History.*

growth rates (that is, the rate of growth of the money supply, whether defined narrowly to include just notes and coins in circulation, or broadly to include bank deposits).[77] But the relationships have clearly changed as the nature of money and the institutions that generate it have evolved. A good example of the difficulties that confront a narrowly monetarist interpretation of inflation is the divergence between broad money and inflation in the mid-1980s, a period when, ironically, government policy was avowedly monetarist.

An institutional approach emphasizes the changing role played by central banks, in particular the fundamental difference between "rules" and "discretion." In the first instance, as we have seen, most note-issuing public banks existed to help governments finance their mainly war-induced deficits. However, the gold standard evolved as a system designed to limit the discretion of central banks to lend too freely in peacetime. Only gradually did the idea evolve that the central bank should be responsible for the management of the currency and the stability of the banking system as a whole.[78]

In the theory developed by classical economists, price stability was *not* the main goal of the gold standard. Rather, the appeal of maintaining a fixed rate between gold and the currency was that it automatically kept the international and domestic economy in equilibrium by relating the domestic money supply to the external balance of payments. According to the "price-specie-flow" theory first propounded by David Hume, an outflow of gold would act on the domestic price level, causing it to fall, while at the same time raising the external price level, leading to an increase in exports, a reduction in imports and a reflux of gold.[79] Under the nascent "rules of the game" (the phrase was not in fact coined until 1930), the Bank of England was supposed to respond to such an outflow of gold by raising its discount rate,[80] thereby restricting credit, so as to maintain the ratio between notes and gold. The resulting monetary tightening would, in theory, reduce prices in Britain relative to the rest of the world and therefore increase the competitiveness of British exports, while at the same time depressing domestic demand for imports. This was the underlying rationale behind Sir Robert Peel's Bank Charter Act of 1844, which separated the Bank's note-issue department from its commercial banking operations and imposed a fixed one-to-one ratio between gold and the note issue beyond a fixed quota (initially £14 million).[81]

It is important to distinguish between the formal statutory rules governing the gold reserve and note issue and the unwritten "rules of the game." It is often assumed that the rules were simply that the bank should raise its discount rate when the gold reserve diminished and lower it when it increased. This was not always the case. As far as the Bank was concerned, "the rate of discount charged . . . [was] regulated more by the proportion of the reserve[82] to liabilities than by any other consideration."[83] Changes in this proportion were monitored on a daily basis, though Bank rate was announced weekly when the Court of Directors met. In addition the Governor could order an increase (or decrease) in the rate at any time on his own authority, as happened in the 1907 crisis. Modern research has confirmed that changes in the gold reserve were indeed the principal determinant of changes in Bank rate.[84] However, the Bank's reaction to changes in its reserve was not perfectly symmetrical. As a spokesman put it in a statement to the American National Monetary Commission in 1909: "The Bank rate is raised with the object either of preventing gold from leaving the country, or of attracting gold to the country, and lowered when it is completely out of touch with the market rates and circumstances do not render it necessary to induce the import of gold."[85] The Bank Directors also took into account the movements of foreign (mainly European) exchange rates, on the ground that these acted as an indicator of impending reserve changes.[86]

Nor should it be assumed that the Bank was "setting" short-term interest rates for the money market as a whole. In his classic account, *Lombard Street* (1873), Walter Bagehot questioned the extent of the Bank's influence over the market:

The value of money is settled, like that of other commodities, by supply and demand . . . A very considerable holder of an article may, for a time, vitally affect its value if he lay down the minimum price which he will take, and obstinately adhere to it. This is the way in which the value of money in Lombard Street is settled. The Bank of England . . . lays down the least price at which it will dispose of its stock, and this, for the most part, enables other dealers to obtain that price, or something near it. . . . The notion that the Bank of England has control over the Money Market, and can fix the rate of discount as it likes, has survived from the old days before [the Bank Charter Act of] 1844 . . . But even then the notion was a mistake.[87]

Bagehot thought it desirable that the Bank should increase its control over the money market. But for much of the period before 1914 it clearly struggled to make its rate "effective."[88]

The most common contemporary explanation for this was the decline in the Bank's size relative to the rest of the financial sector, particularly joint stock banks. Between 1826 and 1858 the Bank's original monopoly as the country's only joint-stock bank was whittled away, allowing the growth of large commercial banks (which together developed the clearing system) and discount houses (which worked in the market for commercial bills).[89] In theory the Bank of England still had "the largest paid-up capital of any bank in the world" even after the turn of the century (£14.5 million, plus a further £3 million of "accumulated and undivided profit"). But this was not vastly greater than the biggest of the City's merchant banks, N. M. Rothschild & Sons, which had total capital of £8.4 million in 1905. Indeed, the Bank of England was smaller than the Rothschild bank if one adds together the Rothschilds" London, Paris and Vienna houses, which formed a united partnership with around £37 million capital until that date.[90] Moreover, the growth of joint-stock commercial banks, which seldom borrowed from the Bank, further reduced its leverage.[91] For the years 1894 to 1901 the Bank's reserve averaged just over 3 per cent of the deposits, current accounts and note circulation of all UK banks.[92] This alarmed contemporaries. Palgrave was only one of many critics who urged "the attainment of really sufficient reserve." In vain: it remained a "thin film of gold."[93] In addition to Bank rate changes, the Bank therefore had to evolve a variety of supplementary devices designed to make its rate "effective": prototype open market operations (mopping up excess cash in the money market by selling consols "spot" and repurchasing them forward); borrowing from major customers like the India Office, the Bank of Japan, or even (as in 1905–6) from the clearing banks; curtailing its loan and rediscount facilities to the market; and manipulating its buying and selling prices for foreign gold (bar and coin).[94] There is even some evidence that the Bank occasionally reacted counter-cyclically, cutting rates to mitigate commercial downturns.[95] Indeed, it sometimes reduced its reserve as interest rates went up, the very opposite of the sequence required by the rules of the game.[96] In all this, long-run price stability was a mere by-product of monetary policy. Indeed, short-run *instability* was a corollary of pre-1914 monetary policy (a point we shall return to in Chapter 11).

The key point is that the Bank continued to have multiple roles: a political duty to attend to the government's financial needs, largely in abeyance in the Victorian era; a statutory duty to maintain the convertibility of banknotes into gold; and a commercial duty to pay dividends to its shareholders. With the 1870s came the recognition of a fourth role: as "lender-of-last resort" to the banking system as a whole. That it should perform such a function was the conclusion Bagehot drew from its actions during the financial crises of 1825, 1839, 1847, 1857 and 1866, when the huge discount house of Overend Gurney had failed.[97] The Bank had occasionally bailed out ailing banks in the past;[98] but in "lifeboat operations" such as that which rescued Barings in 1890, the Bank was able to use its special relationship with government to underwrite a salvaging operation by the principal merchant banks.[99] The crisis of July–August 1914 extended the role of lender of last resort further: after the traditional emergency measures had been adopted (suspension of the 1844 Act, suspension of gold convertibility), a moratorium on bills of exchange led to the Bank's taking over an unknown (but large) quantity of bad debts; this bailed out the bill-brokers whose foreign remittances had dried up as a result of the diplomatic crisis. The issue of new £1 and £10 Treasury notes also acted as an injection of base money.[100] Though the circumstances of 1914 were certainly exceptional, this represented a significant extension of the Bank's public role: having once been able to focus its gaze on "the proportion," it now had to be concerned about general financial, and by extension even macroeconomic, stability.[101] It was only gradually in the course of the twentieth century that economists became conscious of the problem of "moral hazard" that followed from the central bank's new role as lender of last resort. If banks could more or less rely on being bailed out by the authorities if they were "too big to fail," then they were likely to be even less risk averse in their business. (The same problem arose with the system of deposit insurance introduced in the United States in the 1930s.)

This was the British model, then: a synthesis of Peelite principle and Bagehotian pragmatism. But it should be stressed that the evolution of central bank functions varied considerably from country to country. Rules governing gold reserves were not all the same, and not all countries redeemed in coin and bullion.[102] Moreover, other countries broadened the remit of their central banks beyond specie convertibility from the very outset. According to its 1875 statute, the German Reichsbank was supposed "to regulate the money supply in the entire Reich area, to facilitate the balancing of payments and to ensure the utilization of the available capital."[103] The American Federal Reserve system as it was established by the Act of December 1913 was supposed to relate its monetary policy to the volume of "notes, drafts and bills of exchange arising out of actual commercial transactions"—an echo of the "real bills" doctrine advanced by the British opponents of "bullionism" in the 1810s.[104]

In some respects, the First World War and its aftermath tended to diminish these differences, on paper at least. For all the combatants, the war took central bank–state relations back to the eighteenth century: the government deficit came first, while the suspension of gold convertibility was a means not only of avoiding a general liquidity crisis but also of centralizing the gold needed to finance ballooning trade deficits. More novel was the way central banks everywhere in Europe sought to manage their exchange rates in the absence of the gold peg. Exchange controls and requisitions of overseas assets in private portfolios were designed to limit depreciation against the dollar. After the war, on the other hand, the banks sought to reassert themselves by regaining or increasing their independence from government—in the words of the 1921 Brussels Conference, all "banks of issue should be freed from political pressure"[105]—and proclaiming their faith in the "rules" of the restored gold standard. The Genoa Conference held in 1922 issued a clarion call for central bank independence and gold convertibility—a model adopted in the wake of currency reforms in Austria (1922), Hungary (1923) and Germany (1924), as well as in Chile (1926), Canada (1935) and Argentina (1936).[106]

Why then was there such a divergence in monetary experience after 1918, with some countries inflating and others deflating? The answer is that behind their outward similarities the bankers' priorities were quite different. Rudolf Havenstein, President of the Reichsbank throughout the inflation years, regarded the maintenance of German industrial production and employment as his principal objectives; currency stability he disregarded, possibly because he subscribed to the view that the depreciation of the mark would persuade Britain and the United States to reduce the reparations burden imposed on Germany, perhaps because he sincerely believed Knapp's legalistic "state theory of money" (which, in true Prussian fashion, maintained that paper money would retain its value if the state said it did).[107] His successor, Hjalmar Schacht, though outwardly a devotee of gold and central bank independence, also saw monetary policy as a potential instrument of revisionist diplomacy, ultimately aligning himself with Hitler.[108] In Britain, by contrast, the restoration and defence of the pre-war exchange rate was seen as indispensable if confidence in London as a financial center was to be restored; and this became Montagu Norman's mission as Governor of the Bank of England. Meanwhile, France and the United States attached more importance to domestic conditions than the rules of the game: both countries systematically sterilized gold inflows to prevent their large balance of payments surpluses translating into higher domestic inflation.[109] Partly because of this—but also because sterling was overvalued after the return to gold—the British attempt to turn back the clock of monetary history ended with the great international financial crisis of 1931, after which one country after another abandoned gold.

The Federal Reserve Bank of New York developed an especially aberrant monetary theory after the death in 1928 of its President, Benjamin Strong. Focusing on nominal rates of interest and bank borrowing, convinced that there had been excessive monetary expansion in the 1920s, the Fed repeatedly did the wrong thing: failing to halt contraction after the Wall Street crash (October 1929); sterilizing gold inflows and even inducing a perverse monetary contraction; raising interest rates to stem gold outflows (September 1931 and again in February 1933) and discontinuing open market purchases of government securities in 1932 even when its reserve ratio was double the required minimum.[110] If a single human agency can be blamed for the severity of the Great Depression, it was to be found here.

FROM INDISCRETION TO INDEPENDENCE

Revolution, depression and another world war between them led to the subordination of central banks almost everywhere to governments. Given the mess they had made of the 1920s and 1930s, it was a fate most of them deserved. The extreme case was in the Soviet Union, where credit was entirely centralized within the framework of the Five Year Plans. In Germany the Reichsbank under Schacht imposed an array of controls on the financial system, only to find itself in turn subjugated by Hitler, who responded to Schacht's warnings about the inflationary effects of rearmament by sacking him. But the erosion of central bank power happened in democracies too:

even before the Second World War the Danish, New Zealand and Canadian central banks had all been nationalized. The Federal Reserve system was effectively subordinated to the Treasury under the New Deal (though this did not prevent another avoidable recession in 1936–7, when the Fed needlessly raised reserve requirements).[111] By the end of the Second World War even the Bank of England was so manifestly the money-printing wing of the Treasury that nationalization was barely resisted.[112] Today it is still the case that most central banks are state-owned.[113]

The logic of nationalization was that the private ownership of central banks was incompatible with their macroeconomic responsibility, which in practice meant maintaining low interest rates, while fiscal policy did the serious Keynesian work of achieving the ideal level of demand. In the words of the Radcliffe Committee report (1959), "Monetary policy . . . cannot be envisaged as a form of economic strategy that pursues its own objectives. It is a part of a country's economic policy as a whole and must be planned as such."[114] In practice—and this was especially true in Britain—it was the struggle to maintain successive dollar pegs under the Bretton Woods system that really dominated monetary policy. The Bank of England no longer relied on changing the discount rate; it now had a wide range of credit controls at its disposal. Successive Chancellors tinkered with these in an almost impossible struggle to maintain full employment without weakening sterling.[115] In the United States, by contrast, the Federal Reserve retained considerable freedom to engineer economic contractions to reduce inflation (or "lean against the wind"): it did so on six occasions between 1947 and 1979, with substantial and enduring real effects. On average, a shift to anti-inflationary policy led to a reduction of industrial production of 12 per cent and a two-percentage-point increase in unemployment.[116] This was what William McChesney Martin—Governor of the Federal Reserve from 1951 until 1970—meant by "tak[ing] away the punch bowl just when the party is getting going."

Two events exposed the inflationary dangers of central bank impotence: the Vietnam War which, along with the "Great Society" welfare program, pushed American deficits up (though not by as much as is often asserted);[117] and the oil crises triggered by the Yom Kippur War of 1973 and the Iranian Revolution of 1979. The collapse of the Bretton Woods system—because of European refusals to revalue against the dollar—removed the external check on monetary expansion. To proponents of the "political business cycle" theory, there was nothing now to prevent politicians manipulating monetary policy so as to secure re-election—except the rapidly worsening trade-off between inflation and employment as popular expectations adjusted and the "non-accelerating inflation rate of unemployment" ("nairu") rose (see Chapter 8).

How far the high inflation of the 1970s was directly responsible for low growth remains a matter for debate. Some economists maintain that reducing inflation to zero would promote growth, since inflation creates a bias in favour of consumption over saving;[118] others that pushing the unemployment rate below the "nairu" has only mild inflationary effects.[119] But even if it is true that inflation is only detrimental to growth at rates of more than 40 per cent—and may even be helpful at around 8 per cent[120]—there were other obvious reasons for checking the acceleration in inflation, not least the questionable legitimacy of income and wealth redistribution by this means.[121]

There were three intellectual responses to the "stagflationary" crisis. The first was that central banks should now make price stability their paramount, if not sole, objective. The second was that they should do this by targeting the growth of the money supply. The third was that they should be made more independent from governmental pressure.

Never have the rules of the game changed as rapidly as they did in the 1970s, as various central banks experimented with a plethora of monetary targets (such as M0 and M3 in Britain and non-borrowed reserves in the United States).[122] In itself "monetarism" was a compromised revolution almost from the outset, as the economic theorists disapproved of the bankers" reliance on the old interest-rate tool (they wanted the monetary base to be directly controlled to achieve the target for the monetary aggregate). In any case, the deregulation of the financial system which accompanied the new policy (especially in Britain) had the perverse effect of changing the very monetary aggregates that were being targeted. Almost as soon as they had abandoned one system of fixed exchange rates, European politicians began to devise a new system for themselves; even the British and Americans acknowledged by the mid-1980s that exchange rates could not simply be left to their own very volatile devices. The real significance of monetarism was as part of the broader regime change symbolized politically by the elections of Margaret Thatcher and Ronald Reagan and the accession to power of Helmut Kohl in Germany. The monetary shocks inflicted in 1979–82 as nominal interest rates rose sharply broke the upward spiral of inflationary expectations.

This success compensated for the theoretical failure, however: behind the scenes "rules" were quietly dropped in favour of "discretion"—by which was meant a reliance on a multiplicity of rules, not all of them explicit or consistent with one another. The nemesis of this incoherence was most painful in Britain, where monetary targeting was abandoned by Nigel Lawson in favour of "shadowing" the deutschmark, and ultimately joining the Exchange Rate Mechanism at the very moment when German reunification was driving German interest rates upwards.[123] In the aftermath of sterling's ignominious exit from the ERM, the Bank followed the example of the Bank of New Zealand in targeting neither money nor the exchange rate but inflation itself. In the course of the 1990s this approach was adopted by more than fifty other central banks—though not the Federal Reserve, which still chooses to pursue its dual statutory goals of "maximum employment" and "stable prices" using open market operations and with reference to an eclectic mixture of variables.[124]

The 1990s are sometimes seen as "the age of the central bankers."[125] Thanks to the proliferation of new nations, there were more central banks than ever: from just 18 in 1900 and 59 in 1950, their number had risen to 161 by 1990 and 172 by 1999. Over 90 per cent of all members of the United Nations now have their own central banks.[126] Great power is frequently attributed to the élite handful of these institutions. Before Economic and Monetary Union, the Bundesbank was portrayed as "the Bank that rules Europe."[127] In the United States first Paul Volcker and then Alan Greenspan were so successful in enhancing the power and prestige of the chairmanship of the Federal Reserve Board that the latter came to be seen as more economically powerful than the President. The fact that inflation had been discernibly lower in countries with independent central banks[128] persuaded many theorists, bankers and politicians that a separation of economic powers was the key to price stability (if not to higher growth).[129] This was, as so often in the history of economic policy, an old idea in a new guise. In the 1930s the Bank of England's roving monetary expert Otto Niemeyer (Keynes's arch-rival since their Cambridge days) had spelt out the principle in a report presented to the New Zealand House of Representatives in 1931:

The bank must be entirely free from both the actual fact and the fear of political interference. If that cannot be secured, its existence will do more harm than good, for, while a Central Bank must serve the Community, it cannot carry out its difficult technical functions and hope to form a connecting-link with other Central Banks of the world if it is subject to political pressures or influences other than economic.[130]

The rediscovery of this argument has led to greater autonomy for a rising proportion of the world's central banks. Within less than a week of coming to power in 1997, the new Labour government unexpectedly granted the Bank of England "operational independence," meaning freedom to set interest rates so as to achieve a publicly announced inflation target.[131] So high is the esteem in which the Chairman of the Federal Reserve is held at the time of writing that he is absolved from explicit targets, instead dispensing occasional Delphic utterances.

FROM INDEPENDENCE TO IRRELEVANCE?

Nevertheless, the ultimate power of the executive and legislature over the central bank should never be lost sight of: even the most independent central bank in the world will ultimately have to yield to the wishes of the government in a national emergency. This does not necessarily have to be a war, as the Bundesbank discovered to its discomfort in 1990, when Chancellor Kohl overruled President Karl-Otto Pöhl on the terms of German monetary reunification. Arguably, central banks have only gained more independence because the political will to achieve lower inflation has grown; there is no evidence that they achieve lower inflation at a lower cost in terms of growth and employment than banks that are not independent.[132]

More importantly, the dramatic expansion and evolution of financial markets since the 1980s have significantly reduced the leverage central banks can exert over private sector credit. As Benjamin Friedman has pointed out, the total volume of reserves that banks and other financial institutions maintain with the Federal Reserve System is less than $50 billion, a tiny fraction of total US GDP (0.5 per cent). By comparison, the outstanding volume of securities issued by the US Treasury is $3.7 trillion; add the issues of government sponsored or guaranteed institutions, and the total comes to $7.1 trillion; and if private-sector bonds are included the total US bond market amounts to $13.6 trillion. The equity market is even larger. True, the central bank is still the monopoly supplier (or withdrawer) of bank reserves; so relatively small changes in its policy may in theory influence the financial system as a whole. But innovations in the payments system—electronic money and "smart cards"—may begin to reduce the need for traditional bank reserves and centralized national clearing systems.[133]

Already the growth of non-bank credit—loans by institutions which are not banks on the basis of liabilities other than bank reserves—is tending to limit the importance of bank reserves. Pension funds, insurance companies and mutual funds do not hold reserves; yet their share of the US credit market has been increasing steadily. In 1950 the commercial banks accounted for more than half the total US credit market; by 1998 their share was down to less than a quarter. This reflects the improvements in data processing and information technology, which have significantly reduced informational "asymmetries"—the very *raison d'être* of traditional commercial banks. At the same time, the growth of "securitization," whereby traditional forms of bank loan are sold on to non-bank investors and packaged into aggregated portfolios, has further weakened the link between the central bank's reserve system and the credit system as a whole. For all these reasons, Friedman has characterized the modern central bank of the (near) future as "an army with only a signal corps."[134] In any case, central banks that rely on changes in short-term interest rates to maintain price stability are reliant on forecasts of price inflation at least two years into the future.[135] So the signals they send may turn out to be the wrong ones if the forecasts are wrong.

There are those who maintain that central banks will survive so long as people prefer the anonymity of cash to traceable e-money; so long as they need banks to help them distinguish between good and bad credit risks when disposing of their assets; and so long as governments wish to risk taxpayers' money in trying to control short-term interest rates.[136] On the other hand, it has long been recognized that central banks could be dispensed with.[137] Indeed, there have been past experiments with "free banking": the United States in the nineteenth century, for example. It is far from self-evident that this did not work. True, the Federal Reserve System was set up after the 1907 financial crisis in the belief that having a lender of last resort would increase the stability of the American financial system. Yet it is worth remembering that, as we have seen, the far worse financial crisis which devastated the American economy in the years after 1929 had a great deal to do with the way the Fed misused its powers. It is at least arguable that if American monetary policy had not been under the Fed's control, the Great Depression would not have been so severe—and not only in the United States.

To pursue such arguments further, however, it is necessary to turn our attention to a concept that has so far been deliberately left out of account: the rate of interest. The curtain accordingly falls on Goethe's *Faust*; and rises on Shakespeare's Shylock.

6

Of Interest

I *don't* believe in princerple
But oh, I *du* in interest.
James Russell Lowell

In *The Merchant of Venice*, we never learn at what rate Shylock might have been willing to lend Bassanio three thousand ducats for three months, before the malicious thought occurs to him to lend the money on the security of a pound of Antonio's flesh. An educated guess would be around 10 per cent.

In the sixteenth century interest rates in Italian commercial centers fell substantially. In the first quarter of the century the interest paid on the forced loans of the city-state of Venice ranged between 6.75 and 9.62 per cent. By the end of the century, when Shakespeare was writing, rates in Genoa (for which we have better records) were as low as 1.88–4.38.[1] On the other hand, that was the rate of discount on the declared dividends of the Bank of St George, a semi-public institution with an impeccable reputation; whereas Bassanio wanted to borrow from Shylock on the strength of his merchant friend Antonio's business. Antonio himself may have been confident that "within two months, that's a month before / This bond expires, I do expect return / Of thrice three times the value of this bond." But Shylock had every reason to be skeptical:

Yet his means are in supposition: he hath an argosy bound to Tripolis, another to the Indies; I understand, moreover, upon the Rialto, he hath a third at Mexico, a fourth for England, and other ventures he hath, squandered abroad. But ships are but boards, sailors but men: there be land-rats and water-rats, water-thieves and land-thieves, I mean pirates, and then there is the peril of waters, winds and rocks.[2]

To ask that Antonio pledge a pound of his own flesh—in effect, his life—to guarantee the debt was perhaps to demand an excessive risk premium.

Shylock was nevertheless right to recognize that lending on the security of Antonio's ships was a very different proposition from lending to the Venetian state or the Genoese bank.

YIELDS

This chapter is concerned with rates of interest, and particularly the rates paid by states when they borrow, in the first instance from their own citizens. Largely omitted from the discussion are the rates merchants like Antonio have had to pay for credit through the ages, though it is important to be aware that as early as the sixteenth century a differential had begun to emerge between the rate that a financially well-established state could expect to pay and the rate on commercial bills or bonds. Here the interest rate—usually the yield on a government's bonds—is of interest because it is the crucial determinant of the cost of government borrowing.

For the sake of uninitiated readers, a few words of explanation may be in order. The "yield" an investor receives from a government bond he has purchased—in effect, the long-term interest rate—is seldom identical with the nominal coupon the bond pays, because bonds generally sell at a price below their face value ("par"). Thus the 3 per cent coupon on a typical nineteenth century perpetual bond like a rente in fact represented a yield of $3^3/_4$ per cent when the price paid for the bond in question was 80 per cent of par.

But what was it that determined yields? One possibility that has long intrigued economists is that there might be some kind of positive relationship between nominal interest rates and inflation (the "Gibson paradox" or "Fisher effect"). The long-run British experience suggest that it was the peculiar fiscal effects of war which produced such an effect.[3] As might be expected, there are also statistically significant relationships between the yield on consols (the principal British long-term bond) and measures of monetary growth. One possibility which can apparently be discounted, however, is that of a clear-cut relationship between debt/GDP ratios and yields. Statistical analysis of long-run British data from 1727 until 1997 reveals only negative or very weak relationships between the consol yield and the main indicators of fiscal policy (both the debt/GNP ratio and the deficit/GNP ratio). The only fiscal indicator that comes close to having a statistically significant relationship with consols is the burden of debt service.[4] Even when the period is broken up into sub-periods, the results are not much better. One possibility is that it was the increased *spending* associated with wars, not the increased borrowing, which periodically pushed up interest rates in eighteenth- and nineteenth-century Britain. But it is impossible to separate the effects of increased spending and increased debt as the two moved closely together; and higher yields may partly have reflected changes in the default premium on British bonds and expectations about the future convertibility of the currency into gold.[5]

One possible explanation for this is that contemporaries simply did not know about debt/GDP ratios. Though the concept of national income or wealth was not unknown,[6] estimates were too imprecise and too infrequent for such figures to be calculated on a regular basis. However, even when similar calculations are done for a similar sample of countries over the period 1960–99, the correlation between the debt/GDP ratio and the long-bond yield is negative instead of positive in five out of seven cases.[7] The extreme case is that of Japan, where rapid growth in debt has been accompanied by an almost equally rapid decline in yields. Between 1990 and 1999 Japanese gross government debt rose from 61 per cent of GDP to 108 per cent, and was forecast to reach 130 per cent in 2000. Yet long-term Japanese bond yields fell from above 8 per cent in September 1990 to a nadir of less than 1 per cent in November 1998.[8] The reason for this lack of close correspondence between debt burdens and yields is that the current amount of debt outstanding in relation to output is only one of many measures which influence investors' perceptions; in some cases it may not influence them at all. In the industrialized countries during the 1990s, investors' expectations of falling inflation—and in the Japanese case of outright deflation—counted for much more than rising debt/GDP ratios.

In economic theory, the yield on a bond is the "pure" or real rate of interest (which is equivalent to the marginal efficiency of capital in the economy) plus a premium for uncertainty which takes into account first the risk of default by the borrower and, secondly, the lender's expectations of inflation and/or depreciation, with the size of the premium generally being larger the more remote the redemption date. In the simplest possible model, "bond rates . . . reflect the sum of real growth expectations and inflation expectations."[9] In reality yields are also influenced by the liquidity of markets and particularly the availability and relative attractiveness of alternative assets; as well as by legal rules and restrictions (such as those obliging pension funds and life assurance companies to hold government bonds); and by taxation of "unearned" income. But at root yields ought mainly to reflect expected growth and inflation. This is how Keynes put it:

The rate of interest . . . is a measure of the unwillingness of those who possess money to part with their liquid control over it. . . . It is the "price" which equilibrates the desire to hold wealth in the form of cash with the available quantity of cash . . . A necessary condition failing which the existence of a liquidity-preference for money as a means of holding wealth could not exist . . . is the existence of *uncertainty* as to the future of the rate of interest.[10]

Expectations about the future course of inflation and the chances of future default are reflected in the "yield curve," which plots the yields of bonds according to their maturity. When (to give the obvious example) inflation is anticipated, the yield curve slopes upwards, meaning that short-term interest rates are lower than longer-term rates.[11] Major distributional changes will tend to occur when expectations are badly wrong: to be precise, when there are unanticipated defaults or unforeseen changes in the price level. Problems will also arise when (as happened in the 1980s) expectations of inflation raise the anticipated inflation rate above the actual realized rate.[12]

The key relationship in debt management is therefore between interest rates, inflation and growth. In particular, when the real interest rate (meaning long-term bond yields less expected inflation) is greater than the real growth rate of the economy, then the debt/GDP ratio is "intrinsically explosive."[13] Taking the example of Britain since 1831, Figure 11 shows the difference between real growth and real interest rates (calculated as the difference between the yield on consols in a given year and the average inflation rate for the preceding five years).[14] As is clear, there have been relatively few periods when real interest rates have consistently exceeded growth. The worst period in this regard was 1920–1932, and the result was indeed a very rapid increase in the debt burden. (Contrast the French experience between 1921 and 1929, when the real interest rate averaged –2.8 per cent and real growth averaged 6.25 per cent per annum.)[15] Periods when growth has exceeded the real interest rate—such as the early 1950s and the late 1970s—have of course had the opposite effect.

A complicating factor—which could make debt potentially explosive—is the possibility that high debts may actually drive up real interest rates. For the period 1970–1987, for example, there were significant positive correlations between rising debt/GDP ratios in the world's main industrial economies and rising real interest rates. Rising debt service burdens have also coincided with falling public sector investment.[16] Some recent work suggests a global link between public debts and real interest rates,[17] though this is not universally accepted.[18]

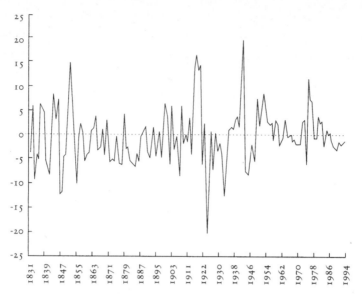

Figure 11. The real growth rate minus the real interest rate in Britain, 1831–1997

Source: Goodhart, "Monetary Policy."

In order to illustrate the interaction of debt, inflation and growth, Table 5 attempts to distinguish the impact on the British national debt of the three key influences: new bond issuance (or amortization); inflation (or deflation); and growth (or recession). The striking point is the distinct periodization which emerges. In the period 1822–1914 there was almost no debt reduction through inflation, but rather a reliance on nominal debt repayments, which reduced the debt by about a quarter in absolute terms, and growth, which reduced it by 90 per cent in real terms over as many years. Between 1915 and 1923 there was an immense sevenfold increase in the nominal debt, which was only offset slightly by inflation, and hardly at all by growth. Between 1924 and 1941, however, the debt was more or less static in both nominal and real terms, but fell by 31 per cent in relative terms thanks to higher growth. Between 1941 and 1946 the debt rose again by a factor of 2.4, an increase which was only slightly mitigated by growth and scarcely at all by inflation. But between 1947 and 1975 inflation and, to a lesser extent growth, wholly negated the effects of a 79 per cent increase in the nominal amount of debt. In real terms, the debt fell by 61 per cent, and relative to GNP by 82 per cent. Between 1976 and 1997 there was a more muted interplay between the three factors. Nominal debt increased by a factor of over 7, but inflation reduced this to a factor of just under 2, and

Table 5. Increase or decrease in the British national debt by sub-periods, 1822–1997

	Multiple			Percentage change		
	Nominal	Real	As a percentage of GNP	Nominal	Real	As a percentage of GNP
1822–14	0.7	0.8	0.1	−26	−24	−90
1915–23	7.0	5.0	4.9	598	396	388
1924–40	1.0	1.0	0.7	3	−1	−31
1941–46	2.4	2.3	1.9	138	133	94
1947–75	1.8	0.4	0.2	79	−61	−82
1976–97	7.4	1.9	1.2	642	88	23

Source: Calculated from figures in Goodhart, "Monetary Policy."

growth cut the increase to just over 20 per cent. Similar calculations are possible for the United States, and show a broadly similar trend, though with different peaks and troughs. Between 1969 and 1997, for example, the US federal debt rose in nominal terms by a factor of 13; in real terms by a factor of 3.5; but relative to GNP by a factor of just 1.6.[19] These figures reveal the importance of price movements and growth in determining how far large nominal debt burdens persist in real terms.

The ease with which real debt burdens have been reduced by inflation in the twentieth century makes it tempting to conclude that such periodic "jubilees" are a recurrent feature of modern political economy. Yet the inflation tax is an effective means of reducing debt burdens only under certain circumstances. When the structure of the debt is tilted towards short-term instruments, lenders may anticipate or swiftly react to inflation by raising the interest rates they demand.[20] Even when a government relies mainly on long-term bonds, a rise in inflation will lead to a rise in yields, increasing the cost of any new borrowing. Moreover, inflation is easier to start than to stop under conditions of high public indebtedness. A central bank aiming to halt inflation by raising the short-term interest rate would be likely to fail if the government continued to run high deficits.[21] The problem is that the central bank's rate increase, and expectations of lower inflation, would also tend to raise the real interest rate on government debt, increasing the cost of debt service, widening the budget deficit and thereby undermining the credibility of the bank's policy. Higher interest rates also tend to reduce seigniorage, as well as reducing revenues and increasing expenditures because of their negative effects on growth.[22]

Clearly, much depends on the nature of expectations. If these are "adaptive"—if there is only a gradual response to a change in monetary policy because workers and firms base their expectations on an average of current and past inflation—an anti-inflationary policy will inevitably have negative effects on output and employment. If expectations are rational, on the other hand—meaning that economic agents immediately infer lower future inflation from a policy change—then inflation could be brought under control at a lower cost, provided the policy change was "once-and-for-all, widely understood and widely agreed upon . . . and therefore unlikely to be reversed."[23]

In the light of the "unnecessary randomness" of "partial default *via* inflation," some economists have concluded that "overall, nominal debt seems to be a bad idea" and that index-linked (i.e. inflation-proof) bonds are to be preferred.[24] However, this course was followed only to a limited extent as inflation fears abated during the 1990s. Instead, many governments have effectively ruled out the possibility of an inflationary default by issuing a high proportion of short-term debt. Table 6 shows that short-term debt counts for relatively little in the total debts of Austria, Germany and the Netherlands, but constitutes more than a third of Italian, French and Spanish debts. In Britain something like a quarter of the total national debt in 1997 had a maturity of five years; more than a fifth has a maturity greater than fifteen years.[25] But in the United States around a third of the privately held federal debt has a maturity of less than a year; and 72 per cent—nearly three-quarters—has a maturity of less than five years.[26]

Such a reliance on short-term bonds stands in marked contrast to the nineteenth century. Quite apart from deterring governments from trying to inflate away their debts, it makes government debt charges a great deal more sensitive to fluctuations in interest rates. This can be advantageous when rates fall, as happened in the 1990s: according to one estimate, the long maturities of British government bonds cost taxpayers in 1999 £3 billion more in debt charges than they would have had to pay on short-term equivalents.[27] But short-term debt can quickly lead to trouble when the direction is the other way.

EXPECTATIONS: THE PAST AND THE PRESENT

Whether adaptive or rational, expectations are in large measure historically based. To be sure, most financial markets are "weak-form-efficient" in the

Table 6. The structure of European national debts, circa *1993*

Country	Short-term debt as percent of domestic debt
Austria	0.4
Belgium	21.1
Finland	27.9
France	42.4
Germany	3.9
Italy	39.4
Netherlands	4.9
Spain	52.7
Norway	35.4
Sweden	15.3
UK	29.6

Source: Eichengreen and Wyplosz, "Stability Pact," p. 103.

sense that "the sequence of past prices provides no exploitable information as to the sequence of future price movements": they follow what economists like to call a "random walk."[28] But even the most sophisticated econometric models—as well as the more or less informal models on which small investors make their decisions—need some past data to chew on. The significance of defaults and inflations such as those described above and in the preceding two chapters lies here.

From the investors' point of view, a major reason for fearing that a country might default or depreciate its currency is the simple fact that it has done so in the past. This explains why the short-term benefits of default or depreciation in reducing a government's debt burden must be set against the longer-term costs of loss of reputation, which usually raises the cost of future borrowing. This is a crucial point if we are to understand why some countries have been able to sustain much higher absolute levels of debt than others.

Early modern evidence confirms the link between past misdeeds and present interest rates. Most obviously, creditworthy city-states could borrow at lower interest rates than default-prone monarchs. Yields on the consolidated debt of Genoa in the second half of the fourteenth century fluctuated between 5 and 12 per cent.[29] This was not unusual: in fifteenth-century Florence yields ranged between 5 and 15 per cent.[30] By contrast, Habsburg *aides* in Antwerp yielded as much as 20 per cent in the 1520s and 1530s (though they fell to 10 per cent in 1550). The yields on short-term *asientos* rose steadily during the sixteenth century as the Habsburg regime's credit-rating declined due to successive defaults: from 18 per cent in the 1820s to 49 per cent by the 1550s.[31]

It was the Dutch system of public finance that proved most successful in lowering interest rates. Dutch yields fell steadily from above 8 per cent in the 1580s to 5 per cent in the 1630s, 3 per cent in the 1670s and just 2.5 per cent by the 1740s.[32] Yet this was at a time when the United Provinces were steadily increasing their debt, confirming that there is no automatic correlation between the absolute size of a debt and the yield on the bonds that constitute it. The same was true of the Swiss cantonal debts and the yields on them for most of the sixteenth century.[33]

By contrast, French yields in the eighteenth and nineteenth centuries reveal starkly the impact of fiscal unreliability on investor confidence. The effect of France's institutional difficulties—above all, the *ancien régime*'s bad habit of defaulting every few decades—was not only to limit the absolute amount France could borrow, but to push up the *cost* of borrowing far above the equivalent Dutch or British figures. Because of the complex structure of the French debt, it is possible to calculate a variety of different yields. Rentes were considered *biens immeubles*, like land, and were not easily traded. Life annuities—the largest part of the debt by 1789—were not bought and sold after the lives had been specified. The best available rate which can be compared with that for Britain is therefore probably that for the *emprunt d'octobre* (October Loan) created by the new Compagnie des Indes in 1745, though it should be remembered that this represented only a small fraction of the total French debt. Nevertheless, the figures clearly indicate the extent of the fiscal difference between France and Britain. Between 1745 and 1780 there was a significant differential between the yields on French and British government bonds of the order of between 100 and 200 basis points (one or two percentage points). As Figure 12 shows, the spread was at its widest in the early 1770s, when the yield on the French October Loan rose above 10 per cent at a time when consol yields were steady at around the 3.5 per cent mark. Other French bonds carried even higher yields.[34] True, between 1780 and 1785 the spread fell below 100 basis points, and indeed all but disappeared in March 1785. But averaging out the figures for 1754 to 1789, it is clear that the cost of borrowing was significantly higher for France than for her rival across the Channel: of the order of 244 basis points, or nearly $2^1/_2$ per cent.

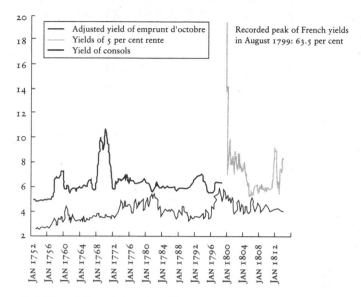

Figure 12. British and French bond yields, 1752–1815

Sources: Neal, *Rise of Financial Capitalism,* pp. 241–57, for consol prices; French data kindly supplied by François Velde.

These differentials were based on past experience of which bonds were most likely to be defaulted upon: there was an element of "prepaid repudiation."[35] But there was also clearly a jump in yields in the aftermath of defaults in 1759 and 1770, suggesting that the market was not wholly clairvoyant.[36] Moreover, the amount the French government had to pay on new loans issued in the period was almost always significantly higher than the yield on the October Loan. The ten-year loan issued in May 1760 yielded 9.66 per cent to investors, at a time when the October Loan yield was 6.87 per cent. The life annuities which were the most common form of new loan yielded as much as 11 per cent in 1771.[37] These were far higher rates than the British government had to pay for old or new loans. Because both countries were on a fixed specie standard from 1726 until the 1790s—gold in the British case, bimetallic in the French—the differential mainly reflected the greater French default risk (though the greater liquidity of the British market doubtless played a part).[38] This was what Bishop Berkeley meant when he said that credit was "the principal advantage which England hath over France."[39] As Isaac de Pinto put it in 1771, when French yields were soaring: "It is not credit that has ruined the finances of France . . . On the contrary, it was the failure of credit in time of need that did the mischief."[40]

The key difference between France and Britain in the eighteenth century, then, was not a matter of economic resources. France had more. Rather, it was a matter of institutions. Britain had the superior revenue collecting system, the Excise. After the Glorious Revolution, Britain also had representative government, which not only tended to make budgets transparent, but also—more importantly—reduced the likelihood of default, since the bondholders who had invested in the National Debt were among the interests best represented in Parliament.[41] The National Debt itself was largely funded (long-term) and transparently managed (especially after the advent of the consol). And the Bank of England—which again had no French analogue—also guaranteed the convertibility of the currency into gold (save in an extreme emergency), reducing if not eliminating the risk of default through inflation. It was these institutions which enabled Britain to sustain a much larger debt/GDP ratio than France because they ensured that the interest Britain paid on her debt was substantially less than France paid on hers. If one seeks a fiscal explanation for Britain's ultimate triumph over France in their global contest, it lies here.

But the crucial point is that financial institutions depend for their effectiveness on credibility. It is highly significant, in this context, that each time the chances of a Stuart Restoration rose—for example during the 1745 Jacobite Rising—so too did the yield on government bonds.[42] To contemporaries, there was no guarantee that the regime change brought about by the Glorious Revolution would endure, and that the lineal descendants of the Hanoverians would still reign in Britain more than three hundred years after the deposition of James II. The possibility could not wholly be dismissed—even after the crushing of the '45 at Culloden—that a combination of the French abroad and the Highland Scots at home might restore the Stuarts. But by comparison with the risks of default facing investors in French bonds, the danger was remote.

It is at first sight surprising, in this light, that the political crisis of 1789 did not have a bigger impact on French yields. Though the yields on the new loans issued in 1782 and 1784 rose above 11 per cent, this happened a year earlier, in 1788. They oscillated around the 9 per cent mark in 1789 and 1790, but then fell to between 5 and 6 per cent in the first half of 1791. The October Loan was even less affected by the first phase of the Revolution, as Figure 12 shows, never rising above 8 per cent, far less than the yield peak in 1771.[43] What this suggests is that the market initially welcomed the advent of constitutional government, not least because the alternative was clearly another major default.[44] As the 1790s went on, however, the trauma of war, the Terror and default sent French yields soaring from around 6 per cent to above 60 per cent.[45] The French Revolutionary Wars could be financed only by printing money: for most of the 1790s substantial long-term government borrowing was simply out of the question.

It was only slowly that French credit recovered from these shocks. Under Napoleon, yields declined from a peak of around 12.5 per cent in 1802 to below 6 per cent in late 1807, and held more or less steady at around 6 per cent until the winter of 1812, when defeat in Russia dealt a fatal blow to Napoleon's ambitions. The decisive reverse at Leipzig in October 1813 saw French yields leap up to 10 per cent; and their subsequent recovery was cut short in March 1815 by the news of Napoleon's return from Elba and the Hundred Days that culminated at Waterloo. Napoleon's defeat and the substantial reparations imposed on France kept yields high thereafter: in 1816–17 they averaged between 8 and 9 per cent. But with the withdrawal of Allied troops and the normalization of the restored Bourbon regime's relations with the victors of Waterloo, yields declined steadily, falling below 5 per cent in 1825 for the first time since 1753.[46] French institutions gradually became more like British ones: the tax system was reformed by the Revolution and Empire; the Chamber of Deputies became more representative after 1830; the issuance of 5 and 3 per cent *rentes perpetuelles* became the basis of public borrowing; and the Banque de France, another legacy of Bonaparte, managed the specie currency. Nevertheless, recurrent revolutionary episodes—in 1830, 1848 and 1870–1871—periodically revived in investors' minds the memory of the 1790s. Not until 1901 did French yields for the first time fall before British.

The French experience of past default and depreciation as a cause of higher bond yields is far from unique. To provide a long-term perspective, Figure 13 shows yields since 1700. Another obvious case when a major default led to a sustained risk-premium on a country's bonds can be seen from the 1920s until the 1950s. Like the French experience of the 1790s, the German hyper-inflation of 1919–23 left scars on investors' memories that were legible in bond yields for years afterwards. And the high yields on post-1923 German bonds had profound effects. For example, it was the tightness of the bond market in the later 1920s that choked off local government investment in housing, a key habringer of the approaching Slump.[47] Moreover, a "Keynesian" response to the Slump at the Reich level was more or less ruled out by the fear that deficit finance would reignite persistent public fears of a second great inflation.[48] Only by covertly issuing the so-called "Mefo-bills"—in reality, short-term government bills—through the bogus "Metallurgical

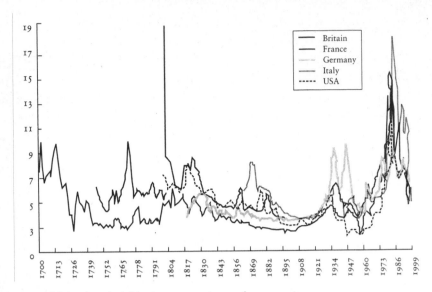

Figure 13. Major bond yields since 1700 (annual averages)

Sources: France 1746–1793: Velde and Weir, 'Financial Market'; France, Germany, Italy to 1959: Homer, *History of Interest Rates*; from 1960: OECD; Britain 1700–1800: Global Financial Data; 1800–50, 1914–59: Mitchell and Deane. *British Historical Statistics*; 1850–1914: Klovland, 'Pitfalls', p. 185; from 1960: ONS; US: Global Financial Data. Notes: UK: Consols (corrected yield); France: 1797–1824: 5 per cent rentes; 1825–1949: 3 per cent rentes; 1950–59: 5 per cent rentes; Germany: To 1869: Prussian 4 per cents, 3.5 per cents; 1870–1908: Reich 3 per cents; 1909–26: High grade corporate bonds; 1927–44: government loans; 1948–53: High grade bonds; 1956–59: government loans; Italy: 1924–49: 3.5 per cents; 1950–69: 5 per cents. All countries except Britain 1960–99: long-term bonds (OECD standardized measure).

Research Office" was Schacht able to finance the first phase of Nazi rearmament.[49] Yet it was not only hyperinflation that traumatized bondholders and thereby circumscribed future fiscal policy. As a *de facto* default, the Italian "forced conversions" of 1926 and 1934 had a comparable effect, pushing up the cost of any subsequent borrowing by the fascist regime and necessitating illegal devices such as secret loans from the cities of Milan and Rome.[50] The French experience of high but not hyper-inflation in the 1920s might seem like the optimal post-war policy, but the experience was one reason the French government adhered grimly to the gold standard in the 1930s, while Britain was able to reap the benefits of devaluation.[51] We shall revert to this point in Chapter 11.

"EVENTS, DEAR BOY"

Yet it would be misleading to suggest that past behaviour is the sole determinant of yield differentials. For investors in bonds are as much interested in any current indications of a government's future fiscal and monetary policy as they are interested in the policies of the past. This presents an awkward problem for economic theory, in that investors do not rely purely on economic data when forming their expectations of future policy. They are as much interested in political events.

To illustrate this point in the context of a large and liquid domestic debt market, I have calculated the annual percentage increase in the yield on consols since 1754.[54] Such a measure differs from the more usual measure of absolute increases or decreases in yields expressed in terms of basis points. The reason for using the percentage change is simply that an increase of 100 basis points pushes up the cost of borrowing by more in relative terms when yields rise from 2 to 3 than when they rise from 7 to 8. By this measure the twentieth century has been only slightly more volatile than the eighteenth, with the nineteenth an interlude of comparative stability. The troubled year 1974 occupies a special place at the top of the league table of rises in British bond yields, with the average annual long-bond yield going up by some 38 per cent. Second only to 1974 in the list of yield hikes was 1797, the year of the suspension of gold payments by the Bank of England: Pitt's "Political Ravishment" of "The Old Lady of Threadneedle-Street."[53] 1998, however, witnessed the biggest ever annual *decline* in yields, one of that year's least commented-upon historic firsts and in large part a response to the successful transition to Bank of England operational independence.[54]

Inferences about political causation can be made with slightly more confidence when the same calculation is made using monthly figures (see Figure 14).[55] Here the months that stand out are November 1792, March 1778 and March 1803, in each of which the yield on consols rose by more than 14 per cent. In fourth place comes June 1974 (an increase of just under 13 per cent), followed by March 1814 (12 per cent). It is possible that all these dramatic fluctuations were due to monetary factors: in all but one case Britain was off gold. On the other hand, it is at least suggestive that each jump in yields coincided with a major international or domestic political crisis. On 6 November 1792 French forces defeated the Austrian army at Jemappes and overran the Austrian Netherlands (modern Belgium); on the 19th, the French National Convention offered its support to all peoples wishing to overthrow their governments. Similarly, the collapse in bond prices in March 1778 came

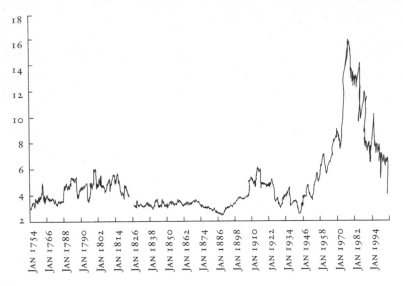

Figure 14. The yield on consols (end-of-month figures), 1754–1998
Sources: 1753–1823: Neal, *Financial Capitalism*, pp. 241–57; 1824–42: *Spectator*
(closing prices on last Saturday of each month); 1843–1849: *The Economist*;
1850–1914: Klovland, 'Pitfalls', pp. 184 f.; 1914–62: Capie and Webber, *Monetary
History*, pp. 514–527: 1963–98: ONS, Financial Statistics.

NOTE: The possibility existed that is consols reached 100 they could be redeemed.
This creates difficulties for the calculation of correct yield figures in the late nineteenth century, which have been addressed by Klovland.

shortly after the United States had signed two treaties with France, leading
Britain to declare war on France. In March 1803 Napoleon's annexations of
Italian territory and interference in the affairs of Switzerland were causing
grave concern in London: war broke out again with France in May. The rise
in yields that occurred in March 1814 is the exception, since it coincided with
Napoleon's defeats at Laon and Arcis-sur-Aube, and the fall of Boulogne (12
March) and Paris (31 March). However, the 13 per cent rise in June 1974
came after a catalogue of political reverses for the newly installed Labour government: the collapse of the Sunningdale agreement in Northern Ireland (28
May) and the explosion of a bomb outside Westminster Hall (17 June) sig-
nalled a serious deterioration in the Ulster crisis; while the government suffered a succession of parliamentary defeats, leading ultimately to a second dissolution on 20 September, a mere seven months since the previous election.

The apparent link between political events and the bond market is even closer if one considers the experience of inter-war France (see Figure 15). The biggest increase in the yield on rentes at any time in the history of the Third Republic came in August 1925, when the rate rose by more than 10 per cent.[56] This might seem surprising. In June a preliminary agreement had been signed with Germany confirming the existing West European borders, a deal finalized that October at Locarno. On 13 July French troops had evacuated the Rhineland. However, events elsewhere were less peaceful. A revolt in Morocco against Spanish and French rule had broken out in May 1925; the government resolved to crush it, sending General Pétain to lead a substantial force against the rebels. The war went on until May 1926.[57] The other major crises on the French bond market are easier to fathom. On four occasions between 1933 and 1939, yields rose by between 8.5 and 10 per cent: March 1933, March 1935, April 1937 and January 1939. It seems at least plausible that the deterioration of Franco-German relations and the possibility of another great war were behind these rises. On 5 March 1933 the Nazis consolidated their power in Germany with a sweeping election victory; eleven days later the new government sank the latest British disarmament plan at Geneva by insisting that the brown-shirted Nazi stormtroops (the SA) should not be counted as part of Germany's armed forces. And the Enabling Law of 23 March gave Hitler dictatorial powers. On 1 March 1935 the Saarland was restored to Germany; two weeks later Hitler repudiated the disarmament clauses of the Versailles Treaty and reintroduced conscription. April 1937 saw Belgium released from her obligations under the Locarno Treaty and Guernica bombed flat by German aircraft. The crisis of January 1939 differed only because it related to Italy rather than Germany (indeed, on 6 December 1938 France and Germany had signed a pact confirming the inviolability of their existing frontiers). But on 17 December Italy had denounced its 1935 agreement with France regarding Corsica and Tunisia, prompting the French prime minister Édouard Daladier to make a defiant visit to both places. The ground was cut from under Daladier on 10 January when Chamberlain and Halifax visited Rome for talks with Mussolini.

It is illuminating to compare the fluctuations in the German bond market over the same period, though the data are not complete because of the disruptions caused by the 1923 hyperinflation, the 1931 banking crisis and the 1935 law imposing maximum interest rates. When the market was able to function more or less normally, however, the role of political events is once again apparent—in this case, mainly domestic political events. The two biggest jumps in yields occurred in June 1932 (8 per cent) and July 1934 (9

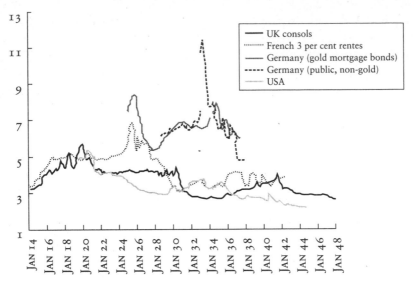

Figure 15. Monthly bond yields, 1914–48

Source: NBER, except German data kindly supplied by Joachim Voth.

per cent). The first coincides with the political instability following Papen's decision to dissolve the Reichstag and hold new elections, a decision that played into the hands of the Nazis and triggered unprecedented political violence in German cities. In 1934 the main political upheaval was the "Night of the Long Knives" on 30 June, when over 170 radical Nazis and other politically "suspect" individuals were murdered, including the leader of the SA, Ernst Röhm, and the former Chancellor General Schleicher.[58] The reaction of the bond market to Hitler's appointment as Chancellor was ambivalent: yields fell 6 per cent in January 1933 but rose the following month; fell again in March and April, but rose 4 per cent in May, the month of the anti-Jewish boycott.

For the rest of the Nazi period it is necessary to look outside Germany's controlled economy for evidence of investor expectations. One illuminating study has looked at the fluctuations of prices of German bonds traded in Switzerland, which suggest a high level of investor pessimism about the Third Reich's chances of victory in the Second World War. The Swiss market for German bonds fell by some 39 per cent in September 1939; it had already fallen 17 per cent in the wake of the invasion of Czechoslovakia the previous March. There were further drops as a result of reverses during the war—notably the entry of the United States into the war after Pearl Harbor (minus 5 per cent) and the Russian counter-offensive at Stalingrad in November 1942 (minus 7 per cent). And prices finally collapsed (by 34 per cent) after the Allied powers resolved to demand unconditional surrender at the Yalta Conference.[59]

A similar exercise can be carried out for American yields since 1919. Remarkably, the five biggest percentage rises in the yield on US long-term bonds all occurred between 1979 and 1984 (see Figure 16). It is at least arguable that the bond market was simply following the Federal Reserve's increases in short-term interest rates. That was certainly the case in October 1979, when Paul Volcker introduced his new policy of controlling non-borrowed reserves and raised interest rates to 12 per cent.[60] In the same month the long-bond yield rose 9 per cent or 76 basis points. However, yields rose twice as much (18 per cent or 152 basis points) in February 1980. Was this another response to monetary tightening? Or was it a reaction to the superpower tension sparked by the Soviet invasion of Afghanistan? This had begun on Christmas Day the previous year and had been denounced by President Carter on 8 January as the biggest threat to world peace since the Second World War. On 23 January, a day after martial law had been proclaimed in Kabul, Carter had gone further, warning the Russians against any interference in the Persian Gulf. A similar coincidence between politics and the bond market occurred in January 1982. On 29 December 1981 President Reagan had imposed economic sanctions on the Soviet Union in retaliation for the introduction of martial law in Poland. Bond yields rose by 10 per cent (85 basis points). There were somewhat smaller though still substantial rises in yields—both of the order of 8.7 per cent—in August 1981 and May 1984. On 9 August 1981 Reagan announced his decision to proceed with the manufacture of the neutron bomb; ten days later US planes shot down two Libyan fighters. On 24 May 1984 Iranian planes attacked oil tankers off the coast of Saudi Arabia, prompting the US to send Stinger anti-aircraft missiles to the Saudis.

At this stage, it would be unwarranted to regard these as any more than coincidences: a formal demonstration that there is a causal relationship between political events and bond market crises comes later. However, it is possible to strengthen the presumption of a causal link by making use of weekly data and comparing these with contemporary financial commentary. To this end, I have calculated weekly fluctuations in consol yields for the period 1845–1910 and analysed the editorial analysis of the London market in *The Economist*. As this was the period when yields were at their most stable—the market was liquid, Britain was on gold and, with the budget usu-

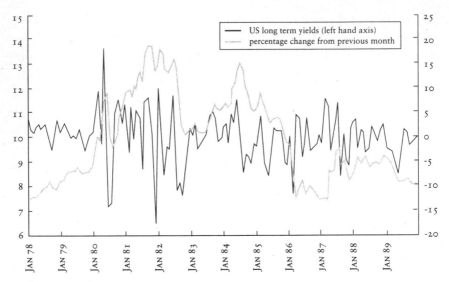

Figure 16. U.S. long-term bond yields, 1979–1989

Source: Federal Reserve Bank of St. Louis.

ally in surplus, there was no question of default risk—weekly fluctuations were relatively low. However, there were significant movements and, because of the importance of the consol market to its readers, *The Economist* followed these closely.

Once again it is remarkable that the biggest short-run jumps in yields occurred on dates that mean more to the political than the economic historian. Thus the biggest shock to the bond market in the period happened immediately after the outbreak of the 1848 revolution in Paris (which began on 22 February, too late to affect British markets in the week ending 24 February). Between that date and 3 March, the yield on consols rose by 7.6 per cent.[61] As in 1830, a French revolution was worrying to British investors mainly because memories of the 1790s led them to expect war with a revolutionary France. On 31 March *The Economist* described a further 2.4 per cent rise in yields as a "consequence of the increased likeliness of war breaking out."[62] Wars also seem to account for the second and third biggest jumps in yield, in the weeks ending 31 March 1854 (4.2 per cent) and 29 April 1859 (6 per cent). On 28 March 1854 Britain had declared war on Russia. On 17 November the magazine noted another steep fall in consol prices, attributing the decline to "the impression that there was a great deal more work for the English troops to do in Crimea than had previously been expected."[63]

Austrian forces crossed the Sardinian frontier on 29 April 1859, ten days after their ultimatum to Count Cavour's government to disarm: as *The Economist* remarked, "hopes of peace had clearly been cherished up to the latest moments."[64]

If the analysis had been extended seven years further, second place would have been taken by the week ending 31 July 1914, when consol yields rose 6.6 per cent. Had the stock market remained open after 1 August 1914, the following week would have seen an even bigger rise in yields than in 1848. The 5 per cent drop in bond prices on the day Germany declared war on Russia (1 August) was, according to *The Economist*, unprecedented, as was the widening of the bid-ask spread to a full percentage point, compared with a historic average of one-eighth.[65]

But how can we be sure that these were not exceptional coincidences between political and economic crises? Table 7 presents an analysis of *Economist* editorial comments on significant movements in the consol market. For the sake of clarity, I have distinguished between 22 different explanations offered by the magazine for increases in UK yields, adopting the distinctions made at the time even when these seem by modern standards to overlap.

Such statistics should, needless to say, be used with caution. However, they do offer some insight into the way contemporaries thought, and hence into the way that expectations were formed. A striking result is the very high proportion of movements in the consol market attributed by *The Economist* to exogenous political events: primarily the possibility of war, or some other international development. Together these account for more than a quarter of the explanations the magazine offered for significant market movements. The proportion of references to changes of fiscal and monetary policy was only fractionally higher, with action by the Bank of England the single most frequent explanation for movements in yields. (Interestingly, *The Economist* usually distinguished between changes to short-interest rates that it saw as arising spontaneously in the money market, and those that were due to specific action by the Bank of England.) Certainly, the table serves to illustrate the wide range of influences that acted on the bond market, including even the weather (primarily because of its impact on agriculture). Yet there is no question that political events loomed large.

To the economic determinist, it is economic change that shapes political events. But in the financial markets political events have economic consequences too. In fact, the direction of causation runs both ways. When a political crisis causes a rise in yields of as much as 178 basis points (as happened

Table 7. Determinants of fluctuations in the price of consols, 1845–1900, as cited in The Economist

Event	Number	Percent of total
War	237	15.7
Domestic politics	32	2.1
Foreign politics	134	8.9
POLITICAL	403	26.6
Fiscal policy	43	2.8
Debt conversion	12	0.8
Commissioners of National Debt	34	2.2
Bank of England	318	21.0
POLICY	407	26.9
Money market	192	12.7
Settlement day	76	5.0
Railways	28	1.8
Stock market	5	0.3
Industry	6	0.4
Speculation	51	3.4
Investment	64	4.2
Hedging	9	0.6
Failures	19	1.3
DOMESTIC MARKETS	450	29.7
Balance of payments	1	0.1
Gold	90	5.9
Foreign bonds	65	4.3
Bills market	3	0.2
Foreign market	45	3.0
FOREIGN MARKETS	204	13.5
Weather	48	3.2
Agriculture	2	0.1
TOTAL	1514	100.0

Note: The system employed here was to take notes from each issue of *The Economist* in which explicit explanations for changes (or lack of changes) in the price of consols were published and to divide explanations into categories. The above total refers to the number of references to particular factors. The total number of editorials from which notes were taken was 889. Often, a single editorial offered more than one explanation. Percentages may not sum exactly due to rounding.

in Britain in June 1974), its economic consequences extend far beyond the bond market as the whole structure of interest rates in the economy changes. Above all, the government faces a rising cost of borrowing in nominal if not in real terms—a matter of some importance when, as was the case then, both the deficit and debt interest amounted to more than 4 per cent of GDP.

Asked to name the principal danger that any government faced, Harold Macmillan famously replied: "Events, dear boy, events." The dictum applies to all who borrow money—as Antonio found out when events sank his ships. But it applies with especial force to a government with a large amount of short-term debt.

SECTION THREE
ECONOMIC POLITICS

7

Dead Weights and Tax-eaters:
The Social History of Finance

This is the way that our crew *beat* the people of France. They laid out,
in the first place, *six hundred millions* which they borrowed, and for
which they *mortgaged* the revenues of the nation. Then they contracted
for a *dead weight* to the amount of *one hundred and fifty millions*. Then
they stripped the *labouring classes* of the commons, of their kettles, their
bedding, their beer-barrels; and, in short, made them all paupers, and
thus fixed on the nation a permanent annual charge of about 8 or 9 *millions*, or a gross debt of £200,000,000. By these means, by these anticipations, our crew did what they thought would keep down the French
nation for ages; and what they were sure would, for the present, enable
them to keep up the *tithes* and other things of the same sort in England.
But the crew did not reflect on the *consequences of the anticipations!* . . .
These consequences . . . are coming . . .

Cobbett, Rural Rides[1]

There is no need to subscribe to Marxism to believe that class division was
the most important social consequence of capitalism. Émile Zola memorably
described in *L'Assommoir* (1877) how the workers led the social cavalcade
that began every day at 6 a.m. in the Boulevard de la Chapelle, near the Gare
du Nord:

You could tell the locksmiths by their blue overalls, masons by their white jackets,
painters by their coats with long smocks showing underneath. From a distance this
crowd looked a uniformly nondescript plaster colour, a neutral tone made up chiefly
of faded blue and dirty grey. Now and again some workman would stop to light his
pipe, but the others tramped on round him with never a smile, never a word to a
mate, pasty faces all turned towards Paris, which swallowed them one by one . . .

By 8 o'clock, however, the scene had changed:

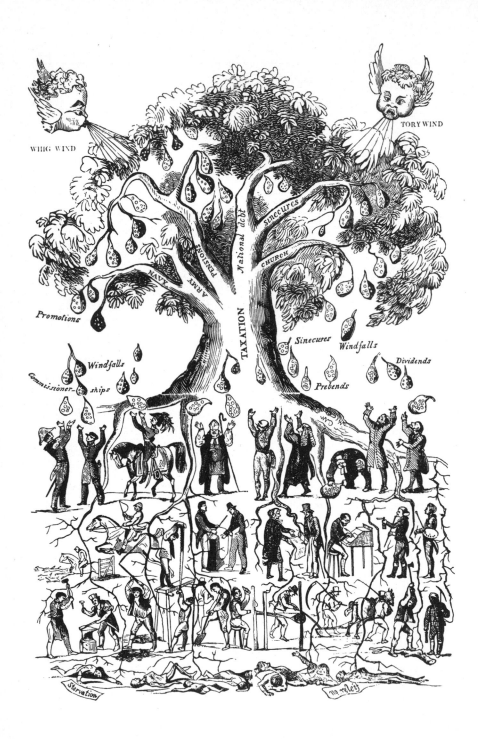

After the workmen came the workgirls—polishers, dressmakers, florists, huddled up in their thin dresses, tap-tapping along the outer boulevards in threes and fours, chattering away and giggling, darting keen glances about them . . . Next the office workers passed along, blowing on their fingers and munching their penny rolls as they walked; lean young men in suits a size too small . . . or little old men with toddling gait and faces tired and pale from long hours at the desk, looking at their watches to regulate their speed within a second or two. And finally . . . the local well-to-do . . . taking their stroll in the sun.[2]

The seriously rich—like the family which had financed the construction of the magnificent Gare du Nord itself, the Rothschilds—would rarely have been seen in such a quarter.

As Zola's description makes clear, there were numerous gradations within the working class, according to occupation, sex and age: these different strata were even distinguishable by the time they got out of bed. Yet—and this was Marx's point—these were manifestly less important than the fundamental division between the property-less mass and a propertied élite. Nor is there any doubt that the processes of industrialization and urbanization made that division wider. Merchants, industrialists, proprietors and rentiers held 53 per cent of all wealth in Paris in 1820. By 1911 the figure was 81 per cent.[3] The same was true elsewhere. Between 1850 and 1880 the British economy grew in real terms by around 130 per cent. According to the most recent research, however, average real earnings rose by just 25 per cent.[4] During the same period, thirty-nine individuals died leaving estates worth more than a million pounds: eighteen industrialists, twelve bankers, four landowners, two merchants, two shipowners and a builder. The combined value of their estates—£57 million—was equivalent to around two-fifths of gross national product.[5]

Yet for all their obvious utility and subjective resonance,[6] the categories of class have their limitations. In particular, the role of the state as an instrument of redistribution is not easily explained in terms of class, unless the state is simplistically regarded (as Heinrich Heine once jokingly suggested) as the "supervisory board of . . . bourgeois society."[7] For large public debts have, since their origin on the eve of the industrial revolution, generated conflicts of interest between bondholders and taxpayers: groups that have seldom been as entirely distinct as the propertied and the property-less.

It is, of course, possible to translate fiscal conflicts into the language of class using the tripartite model favoured by economists since Ricardo, and adopted by Marx, which divides society into rentiers, entrepreneurs and workers. But such an approach, however theoretically convenient, presupposes a somewhat unrealistic separation between social groups and indeed between different fiscal policies. For the growth in the number of state creditors—including not only bondholders but pensioners—creates complex overlaps which cannot be overlooked. Moreover, public debts also transfer resources between generations because, as we saw in Chapter 4, government borrowing today implies cuts in spending or increases in taxation at some future date. Given the fact that future generations do not vote and therefore have only indirect political representation (in the form of one or two legislators with abnormal foresight), the former relationships—between current taxpayers and recipients of benefits—tended for most of the twentieth century to be uppermost in the minds of policy-makers. But there is now a growing awareness that generational conflicts are no less important; and may indeed hold the key to the future of public finance.

THE BIRTH OF THE RENTIER

When monarchs relied on individual bankers for loans—and they continued to do so in many German states until the end of the eighteenth century—the bankers were, as we have seen, always vulnerable to default, often in the guise of prosecution for alleged fraud. In 1451, for example, the financier Jacques Cœur was forced to flee France after being accused of embezzlement.[8] Periodic "purges" of royal creditors soon became institutionalized in the form of *chambres de justice*. Even into the eighteenth century financiers remained vulnerable to such treatment, especially if they were Jews, as the case of Josef Süss Oppenheimer illustrates. Oppenheimer rose from being the Duke of Württemberg's *Hoffaktor* (court agent) to become his privy councillor and, in 1733, his envoy in Frankfurt. Four years later, however, he was executed, having been found guilty of wielding excessive political power and undermining the position of the Württemberg estates (*Stände*). Contemplating the much greater power of the Rothschilds in his own day, Thomas Carlyle looked back with malign nostalgia on King John's use of the "pincer": 'Now Sir, the State requires some of these millions you have heaped together with your financing work. You wont? Very well'—and the speaker gave a twist with his wrist—'Now will you[?]'—and another twist, till the millions were yielded."[9]

When public creditors formed a more numerous class, by contrast, they could become politically formidable. As early as the Renaissance, the sophisticated public debt systems of the Italian city-states brought into being rentier-like groups. In Genoa the *comperisti* were able to secure permanent political representation in 1323 in the form of elected *protectores comperarum*.[10] In Florence there were about 5,000 creditors of the Monte in 1380, heavily concentrated in the top decile of wealth holders.[11] The nearest equivalent in medieval England was the power of the merchants of London. Indeed, it has been suggested that Henry VI's fall from power was related to the decision by the London merchants to end their financial support of the Lancastrian regime.[12] Charles I too owed his downfall in part to lack of credit. Though historians once tried to explain the English Civil War in terms of class—and memories of the "storm over the gentry" have not altogether faded—the Stuarts' failure to win the confidence of a relatively small group of actual and potential creditors mattered more. The Glorious Revolution saw the transformation of the sovereign debtor from the Crown into "the King-in-Parliament." The emergence of the bondholders as an influential lobby within parliament reduced the risk of default by the British state and thereby increased the state's capacity to borrow cheaply.[13]

In *ancien régime* France, the range of people who invested in the debt of the crown was probably wider: the class of rentier was said to include "nobles and bourgeois, bishops and ecclesiastics, office holders and state servants, merchants and artisans, male and female servants."[14] However, most of these had no institutional form of political "voice"—which helps to explain the frequency of default in eighteenth-century France. At the same time, it may also explain the reluctance of the revolutionary National Assembly—where they were represented—to default overtly on the long-term debt of the crown; instead attention focused on other liabilities, such as venal offices and short-term advances from tax farmers. Yet attempts by Necker to convert the short-term debt into something like a modern long-term debt by turning the Caisse d'Escompte into a proper public bank foundered in the face of venomous attacks on "plutocracy" (*plutonarchie*) by mainly aristocratic deputies. "I have never been able to understand," declared the comte de Custine, "the necessity . . . of having a court banker and several fiscal agents to make payments . . . and to provide funds." They were "bloodsuckers on the body politic . . . with fortunes made by the sweat and blood of the people." "Let us fear capital," urged Mirabeau, "which has long had a habit of seeking opportunities for fortune in the needs of the State."[15] This revolutionary critique of "parasitical" finance had its roots in the work of the *philosophes*. Both Montesquieu and Hume had disapproved of public debts because they increased the size of an idle rentier class.[16] By the eve of the Revolution "Anti-Finance" had become a slogan of the Parisian pamphleteers.

Although the British system of public debt after 1688 is generally considered an institutional triumph compared with what happened in France,[17] it provoked a very similar anti-financial critique of its distributional consequences after the Napoleonic Wars. In his *Rural Rides*, which he began in 1822 and published in 1830, William Cobbett portrayed English agriculture groaning under the burden of the debt incurred during the Napoleonic Wars. Dismissive of contemporary economists like Ricardo (himself a retired stockbroker) who defended the government's wartime reliance on loans, Cobbett directed his fire at the social and political consequences of the debt. Its political purpose, he argued, had been "to crush liberty in France and to keep down the reformers in England";[18] but its principal effect after the war was redistributive. "A national debt, and all the taxation and gambling belonging to it, have a natural tendency to *draw wealth into great masses . . . for the gain of a few*." "The Debt, the blessed Debt" was "hanging round the neck of this nation like a millstone." The funds were a "vortex," sucking money from the poor to new plutocracy. And the government's decision to return to the gold standard could only make matters worse by increasing the burden in real terms. Astutely, Cobbett saw the proliferation of government pensions during and after the war as the link between the old élite and the new. It was these pensions—the "*Dead Weight*" on the budget—that reconciled the aristocracy to the growing power of the bondholders. Only too late were the landowning "jolterheads" coming to appreciate that they too would lose out as their rents declined. There must, declared Cobbett, be "a struggle between the *land* and the *funds*." Otherwise, estate by estate, the country would fall into the hands of "those who have had borrowed from them the money to uphold this monster of a system . . . the loan-jobbers, stock-jobbers . . . Jews and the whole tribe of tax-eaters."[19]

Like most Radicals, Cobbett saw electoral reform rather than revolution as the necessary remedy. After all, "the *House* [of Commons] made all the loans which constitute the debt: *the House* contracted for the Dead Weight: *the House* put a stop to gold-payments in 1797: *the House* unanimously passed Peel's Bill [to return to gold]."[20] Reform of the Commons would dilute the power of both the "Old Corruption" of royal patronage and the new corruption of the fundholders and pensioners. Cobbett was also (like Carlyle) a romantic conservative at heart, regretting the decline of rural life in the South East as the "Great Wen" of London sprawled inexorably outwards. Yet there are still detectable traces of his analysis in much early socialism. Cobbett himself had identified a causal link between the national debt, the concentration of wealth and the development of manufacturing industry.[21] In *Capital*, Marx echoed *Rural Rides* when he associated the growth of the British national debt with the "sudden emergence of [the] brood of bankocrats, financiers, *rentiers*, brokers, stock-jobbers, etc.:" this, he agreed with Cobbett, had been the prelude to the emergence of industrial capitalism proper.[22] A less dedicated German revolutionary than Marx, Heine, also shared Cobbett's view that the bondholders would oust the traditional aristocracy of landed wealth. "The system of state bonds," he argued, had "destroyed the predominance of land, by . . . mobilizing property and income and at the same time endowing money with the previous privileges of the land."[23]

The anti-Semitic note in Cobbett's work also found an echo on the racialist Right, however, after this separated itself from the socialist Left in the wake of 1848. Nearly all the early leaders of the German anti-Semitic movement denounced the "rapacious capital" of the stock exchange and called on the German *Volk* to free itself from the "interest slavery" of the Jewish financiers.[24] The same theme could still be heard in early Nazi propaganda. Dietrich Eckart's address "To All Working People" (1919) was a denunciation of the Rothschilds and their ilk which could equally well have come from the anti-Semites of the 1880s:

[They] only need to administer their wealth, to see that it is nicely placed, they do not need to work, at least not what we understand by work. But who provides them and their like with such an enormous amount of money? . . . Who does this? You do it, nobody but you! That's right, it is your money, hard-earned through care and sorrow, which is drawn as if magnetically into the coffers of these insatiable people.[25]

Yet Cobbett's invective against Jews—so offensive to the modern reader who knows where such talk ultimately led—should not distract us from the underlying validity of his argument about the socially redistributive effects of the national debt.[26] In the Britain of the 1820s, debt service was financed largely out of regressive taxation on consumption, so the transfer was indeed from the property-less majority to a tiny, very wealthy élite.

THE TAX-EATERS

It is not easy to be sure just how many people were in fact bondholders. We know how many *accounts* there were for the various different stocks issued by the government. According to the latest estimates, there were around 300,000 in 1804, 340,000 in 1815 and 300,000 in 1822; excluding life annuities payable at the Exchequer the figures come to 296,500, 334,500 and 290,000. By 1850 the number had fallen to 274,000; and by 1870 it stood at 225,500. But it was possible for one individual to hold more than one account; to arrive at figures for bondholders we therefore need to reduce these totals by around 20 per cent. That suggests that there were around 300,000 bondholders in 1815; and just 200,000 fifty-five years later. As a percentage of the population of England and Wales, bondholders were therefore a tiny and dwindling élite: from 2.7 per cent of the population when Napoleon I was defeated to just 0.9 per cent when the same fate befell Napoleon III.[27]

Cobbett was also right about the rewards this tiny elite enjoyed. Figure 17 shows how high the real returns were on British bonds at the time of his *Rural Rides*: more than 9.6 per cent between 1820 and 1829. The same phenomenon arose again in the 1870s, the time of the so-called "Great Depression"—"great deflation" would have been more accurate—when falling prices drove up the real returns on bonds as high as 12 per cent in the United States.

And the fiscal transfers involved were indeed profoundly regressive. As Table 8 shows, the nominal value of the wealth held in the form of bonds was equivalent to more than 200 per cent of British national income in 1804. The total annual interest payments the bondholders received on their investments were equivalent to more than 7 per cent of national income; and as a proportion of total government expenditure, interest payments rose from just under a quarter in 1815 to very nearly a half in 1822, and were still around two-fifths in 1850 and a third in 1870. As we have already seen, the lion's share of government revenue in Britain in the 1820s came from indirect taxation: as much as 69 per cent in 1822, falling only slightly over the next fifty years. American taxation was also regressive in the 1870s, when the real returns on bonds were at their height.[28] These figures do indeed represent an astonishingly inequitable system of transfers from the poor majority to the bondholding minority.

Moreover, the nineteenth century saw not the demise of "moneyocracy" yearned for by Cobbett and other Radicals, but a marked increase in the bondholders' security against default and other forms of expropriation. The spread of the gold standard, it has been argued, reflected the bondholding bourgeoisie's preference for stable prices and exchange rates to protect their investments.[29] In the same way, the stability of the international monetary

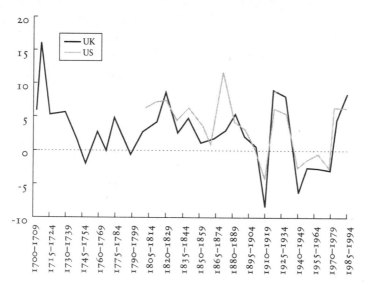

Figure 17. *Real returns on British and American bonds since 1700 (decennial averages)*

Source: Global Financial Data.

system before 1914 can be linked to the persistence of non-democratic, non-proportional systems of parliamentary representation, which ensured that the rentier class remained over-represented.[30]

The power of the bondholders lay not only in their over-representation within parliaments and political élites. Their ownership of the national debt gave them real economic leverage over governments. For the movements of prices of existing government bonds—the products of past fiscal policy—have, as we have seen, an important bearing on present and future fiscal policy. To put it simply, if a government wishes to borrow more by issuing more bonds, a fall in the price of its existing bonds is a serious discouragement, as it means that the yields on any new issues will have to rise, meaning that the government will get less for every nominal £100 of debt it sells to the public. Indeed, a fall in the price of a government's bonds can be interpreted as a "vote" by the market against its fiscal policy, or against any policy which the market sees as increasing the likelihood of default, inflation or depreciation.

Bond prices and yields thus have a political significance that historians have too rarely appreciated. They are, of course, the product of multiple assessments by individual and institutional investors of the economic situa-

Table 8. *The bondholders and the British national debt, 1804–1870*

	Approximate number of bondholders	Bondholders as percentage of population	Total funded national debt (£ millions)	Total interest payments (£millions)	Total funded national debt as percentage of National Income	Total interest payments on the funded national debt as a percentage of National Income	Total interest payments on the funded national debt as a percentage of total government expenditure	Customs and excise as a percentage of total government revenue
1804	237,200	2.5	504.3	17.9	204	7.2	33.8	63.7
1815	267,600	2.4	684.6	25.6	191	7.1	22.7	56.9
1822	232,000	1.9	798.5	28.4	n/a	n/a	48.6	69.2
1850	219,200	1.2	775.7	24.2	145	4.5	43.6	65.3
1870	180,400	0.8	741.5	22.4	64	1.9	33.4	58.8

Sources: J. F. Wright, private communication; Mitchell and Deane, *Abstract of British Historical Statistics*, pp. 8 f., 392–9, 402–3; O'Brien, *Power with Profit*, pp. 34 f.; Mitchell, *European Historical Statistics*, p. 408.

tion as a whole. But they are also, in some respects, a kind of daily opinion poll, an expression of confidence in the bond-issuing regimes. Of course, they are an opinion poll based on a highly unrepresentative sample by democratic standards. Only bondholders (or, nowadays, fund managers) get to "vote" and they can express an opinion about any country whose bonds they chose to buy or sell. On the other hand, this was not such an unrepresentative kind of poll in the nineteenth-century context; for the kind of people who bought and sold government bonds were, in most countries for much of the period, the kind of people who were represented politically—not to mention the politicians themselves.[31] To put it simply—but in terms any contemporary would have understood—if they bid up the price of a government's bonds, that government could feel secure; if they did the reverse, that government was quite possibly living on borrowed time as well as money.

The irony is—to give a specific example—that one of the decisive blows struck for the cause of electoral reform was the slide in bond prices following the Duke of Wellington's defiant claim in 1830 that the electoral system was "as perfect as the wit of man could devise." At this, consol prices fell from 84 to $77^{1}/_{2}$ (an increase in the yield of some 30 basis points), suggesting that even if they did not favour Reform, the bondholders understood the perils of resisting it.[32] Conversely, when Lloyd George confronted the grandees of the City of London in 1909–10 over his "People's Budget," it was the fact that yields held steady that helped ensure his victory. Whatever the self-appointed spokesmen of the City might say against his increases in income tax and death duties, the bond market as a whole favoured them as a step towards balancing the budget.[33]

Still, the power of the nineteenth-century bondholder should not be exaggerated. With the exception of the investor in consols (or any bonds underwritten by the British government), the bondholder's position was not a great deal more secure in the less democratic half-century before 1880 than it was in the more democratic half-century after 1914. On either side of this brief "golden age," wars, defaults and devaluations periodically disturbed the calm of the coupon-clippers—and to describe such events as "well-understood emergencies" is to understate their unpredictability.[34]

Moreover, although Cobbett's hopes for some kind of legally imposed reduction of the national debt were disappointed, relief from the "blessed Debt" did come, in the form of debt redemption, reduced real interest rates and higher economic growth. Between 1850 and 1870, as Table 8 makes clear, there were substantial falls in both the size of the debt burden and the cost of servicing it relative to national income. The interest on the funded national debt amounted to less than 2 per cent of GDP by 1870. Elsewhere, the spread of the gold standard not only reduced the risk of investing in the bonds of countries with records of default or depreciation; for precisely this reason it also caused bond yields to decline. When this decline continued even after growth and inflation picked up in the mid-1890s,[35] the effect was significantly to reduce the real returns on bonds, as Figure 17 shows. In both Britain and the United States, real returns on bonds fell close to 3 per cent in the 1890s and were close to zero in the decade beginning in 1900. The golden age of the bondholder was over at least ten years before the gold standard itself was plunged into crisis.

THE EUTHANASIA OF THE RENTIER?

This process whereby the bondholders' due was painlessly reduced by growth, gentle inflation and low yields came to an abrupt end in 1914. The First World War returned Europe as a whole to the position Britain had been in a hundred years before. By 1918 all had incurred immense debts—the British and American debts rose ninefold, the German sixfold, the Italian fourfold and the French threefold—and all had seen prices at least double or treble following the suspension of the gold standard and the wartime expansion of the circulation of banknotes. Few, however, opted to favour the minority of bondholders with a policy of deflation, as Britain had after 1815—few, that is, apart from Britain once again. Why was this?

In an analysis that owes much to the pioneering work of Charles Maier on the experience of France, Italy and Germany after the First World War,[36] Alberto Alesina has set out a simple schema for understanding such redistributive conflicts. In this model, as in the familiar class system, there are three groups, each with a different view of the national debt. The rentiers naturally oppose default or high inflation, and are in favour of tax increases, provided these fall predominantly on consumption rather than high incomes (for they also tend to be in higher tax brackets). Businessmen, however, prefer inflation and even debt default, though they agree with the rentiers that taxation should be regressive rather than progressive. The advantage of inflation to them is that it reduces the real value not only of the government debt but also the debts of their own enterprises; it may also reduced real wages and, if associated with a weakening exchange rate, boost their sales abroad. Naturally businessmen are averse to taxes on wealth if they extend to physical capital. Finally, the workers favour debt default, since they are not bondholders; but they also favour progressive income tax and taxes on all forms of wealth. They are ambivalent about inflation: it may reduce real wages if they are unable to bargain effectively; on the other hand, it may be associated with expansionary fiscal and monetary policies which boost employment.[37] Thus the reason for high inflation in Italy, France and Germany after the First World War was that "socialist 'workers' were strong enough to represent a credible threat . . . [so] the 'rentiers' and the 'businessmen' could not impose overly harsh measures on the working class for fear of communist insurrections."[38] Germany in particular saw a state-sponsored "inflationary consensus" between big business and organized labour: the classic combination characterized by some later writers as "corporatism."[39] In Britain this was not the case. Rentiers and businessmen, united by a "conventional wisdom" in favour of fiscal orthodoxy, succeeded in imposing the costs of deflation on the workers in the form of high unemployment.[40]

In much of the modern literature on the German hyperinflation, there has been a readiness to view what Keynes called the "euthanasia of the rentier" in a positive light. In his *Tract on Monetary Reform* (1923), Keynes argued that, though inflation was "worse" than deflation "in altering the *distribution* of wealth," deflation was "more injurious" in "retarding the *production* of wealth"; he therefore favoured the former, "because it is worse in an impoverished world to provoke unemployment than to disappoint the rentier."[41] This analysis has encouraged many historians to conclude that "the balance of material gains and losses" of the German hyperinflation was "on the side of gains."[42] Perhaps the most economically sophisticated history of the inflation echoes this conclusion, showing that the inflation resulted in a more equal distribution of the income, if not of wealth.[43] The inflation was thus a modern-day version of Solon's *seisachtheia*: a jubilee in which all debts were simply wiped out, including those of the state, to the benefit of the indebted majority.[44]

British policy-makers were well aware that a policy of deflation would, by contrast, have regressive social consequences. As early as January 1918 the Treasury produced a paper on "The Conscription of Wealth" which anxiously foresaw the post-war conflict of interest:

So long as we have a national debt of £6,000,000,000 to £8,000,000,000 with an annual debt charge of £300,000,000 to £400,000,000 the rentier will be the subject of perpetual jealousy and perpetual attack: the owners of other forms of capital wealth whose property would, at any rate in the opinion of a large section of the public, be appropriated to meet the rentier's claims will be in a position scarcely less vulnerable. The slower the restoration of general prosperity, the heavier will become the pressure of taxation and the greater the popular discontent.[45]

As in the 1820s, deflation meant a rapid increase in the real value of the debt burden and the cost of servicing it. As in the 1820s, the bondholders were a wealthy Élite: in 1924 nearly three quarters of all British government securities issued after 1914 and held in private hands were owned by individuals whose estates were valued at more than £10,000.[46] And, as in the 1820s, the real returns they enjoyed on their investments were exceptional high, as Figure 17 shows: 9.5 per cent in the 1920s and only 1 per cent less in the 1930s.

On the other hand, the number of bondholders was certainly a much higher proportion of the population than in 1815, thanks to the success of wartime efforts to sell bonds to small investors and the growth in importance of savings institutions. Around 12 per cent of the internal British national debt was held by small savers by 1924. Moreover, many of the biggest holders of war bonds were institutional rather than individual investors—insurance companies, savings banks and so on—whose large wartime purchases were effectively made on behalf of small savers. For example, 5.5 per cent of the British debt in 1924 was held by insurance companies.[47] The tax system after 1918 was also significantly more progressive than it had been after 1815.[48] Finally, it is important to remember the benefits of lower interest rates enjoyed by all countries that returned to gold.[49]

Nor should we understate the risks of the inflationary course. In view of his later (caricatured) reputation as an inflation "dove," it is worth remembering that few contemporaries described the perils of this policy more vividly than John Maynard Keynes. In his *Economic Consequences of the Peace* (1919), he was harshly critical of the effects of high inflation on the distribution of wealth:

By a continuing process of inflation, governments can confiscate, secretly and unobserved, an important part of the wealth of their citizens. By this method, they not only confiscate, but they confiscate *arbitrarily*; and, while the process impoverishes many, it actually enriches some. The sight of this arbitrary rearrangement of riches strikes not only at security, but at confidence in the equity of the existing distribution of wealth. Those to whom the system brings windfalls . . . become "profiteers," who are the object of the hatred of the bourgeoisie, whom the inflationism has impoverished not less than of the proletariat. As the inflation proceeds . . . all permanent relations between debtors and creditors, which form the ultimate foundation of capitalism, become so utterly disordered as to be almost meaningless. . . . There is no subtler, no surer means of overturning the existing basis of society.[50]

Or, as he put it in the *Tract*: "Inflation . . . impoverish[es] . . . the middle class, out of which most good things have sprung . . . [and] destroys the psychological equilibrium which permits the perpetuance of unequal rewards."[51] There is certainly much to be said for the view that, regardless of the macroeconomic costs and benefits, the damage to the German bourgeoisie's trust in liberal institutions was fatal to the Weimar system.[52] It is significant that Keynes did not relax his hostility to inflationary finance during the Second World War, when he recommended "deferred pay" in preference to "voluntary saving." Reliance on the traditional system of government borrowing, he argued, would simply lead, as in the First World War, to a "vicious" and "ridiculous" wartime inflationary spiral.[53]

It is an irony then that the policies which produced the inflations of the 1970s were so often stigmatized as "Keynesian." For if the euthanasia of the British rentier had been decisively rejected between the wars, after 1945 a policy of slow starvation was adopted. In every decade between 1940 and 1979 the real return on British government bonds was negative: on average, minus 4 per cent.[54] American bondholders fared only slightly better. This was the period when the real value of the debts incurred during the world wars was dramatically reduced not only by growth but by inflation. In effect, to adopt a modern political phrase, bondholders paid the greatest "stealth tax" in history. Perhaps the most surprising thing is how slowly they responded to these low returns. Bondholders in Weimar Germany—like the members of the Women's Suffrage Union whose plight we encountered in Chapter 5—could claim, not wholly implausibly, to have been the victims of a swift and unforeseeable hyperinflation. But even the nominal returns on bonds in the 1950s and 1960s were meagre; a powerful "money illusion" (or institutional inertia) must have been at work to persuade investors to stick with gilts and treasuries into the inflationary 1970s.

THE NEW TAX-EATERS

The euthanasia of the rentier was not the only way in which fiscal policy in the mid-twentieth century became more egalitarian in its distributional effects. As we have seen, taxation in most industrial countries was already becoming more progressive by 1900, while public expenditure was rising on "social" policies which directly or indirectly redistributed income from the rich to the poor. In the aftermath of the First World War these tendencies were accelerated. In the inter-war period welfare essentially represented a transfer from the rich (a minority of direct tax payers) to the poor (the unemployed and impoverished elderly, again a minority). However, the universalist welfare systems that emerged in Western Europe after the Second World War had the potential to adjust the incomes of nearly everyone.

In 1948 there were a million Britons on national assistance (2 per cent of the population); by the mid-1990s over five million people were on its equivalent, Income Support (close to 9 per cent). Roughly half the income of all pensioners now comes from social security.[55] Of the final household income of households in the bottom quintile of the British population, a staggering 74 per cent consists of benefits in cash and kind (net of tax).[56] In other words, a *fifth* of all households rely on the state to provide *three-quarters* of their income (see Table 9). Yet these are just the dependent minority. For the welfare state's goal of universal provision means that nearly everyone is a recipient of some form of transfer payment. In 1993 the Department of Social Security estimated that the number of people receiving at least one social security benefit totalled 46 million: nearly 80 per cent of the population, or four out of every five Britons.

It was the nineteenth-century French liberal Frédéric Bastiat who called the state "the great fictitious entity by which everyone seeks to live at the expense of everyone else."[57] Hyperbole in Bastiat's own day, this nicely describes the welfare state of the late twentieth century. For at the same time, of course, nearly everyone is a taxpayer, even if they pay only indirect taxation.

"Who whom?" was Lenin's famous question. In the welfare state the ques-

Table 9. Redistribution of income through taxes and benefits, United Kingdom 1992, by quintile groups of households (£ per year)

	Bottom	Next	Middle	Next	Top	All
Total original income	1,920	5,020	12,860	20,850	39,370	16,000
Gross benefits	8,060	7,350	6,110	4,410	3,140	5,810
Gross taxes	2,500	3,150	5,800	8,320	14,220	6,790
Net contribution from state	5,560	4,200	310	-3,910	-11,080	-980
Final income	7,480	9,220	13,190	16,940	28,270	15,020
Percentage of final income from (to) state	74	46	2	(23)	(39)	(7)

Source: *Social Trends 1995*, table 5.17. The figures are for 1993.

tion is who pays for whom? In the absence of an integrated system of taxation and social security, it is in fact far from easy for some individuals to be sure if they are net winners or losers. One estimate suggests that 46 per cent of households are net gainers, while 54 per cent are net losers; but it is doubtful that most households know into which group they themselves fall. Consider the middle fifth of households in terms of disposable income. Table 9 shows that they receive almost exactly as much in the form of benefits in cash and in kind as they pay in the form of taxes. To quote two critics of the British welfare system: "In its modern, climactic absurdity, taxation has at last fused the shearers and the shorn into one."[58] This policy of taxing the right pocket to fill the left is not merely pointless, but also costly. As the last column shows, the expense of the entire redistributive exercise leaves the average household worse off in net terms, to the tune of just under a thousand pounds a year. Even more perversely, the bulk of benefits under the universal welfare system—including all public subsidies to health, education and transport—flow not to the poor but to the rich. According to one estimate, the wealthiest fifth of the UK population receive 40 per cent more public spending on health than the poorest fifth; with respect to secondary education the figure is 80 per cent, to university education 500 per cent and to railway subsidies a staggering 1,000 per cent.[59]

Nevertheless, mainly because of the effects of progressive taxation, the European welfare state does substantially reduce inequality. As Figure 18 shows, in the absence of taxes and transfers nearly all major industrial economies would generate a considerable amount of what has been called "deep [relative] poverty." In eleven out of fifteen countries covered by the chart, more than a fifth of all families would be on incomes below 40 per cent of the median family income were it not for the welfare system. The chart shows that in all the continental European countries, taxes and transfers reduce the proportion of families in "deep poverty" to 5 per cent or less. Britain and her former colonies Canada and Australia have slightly more poverty after fiscal redistribution. But the United States stands out because, even after taxes and transfers, nearly 12 per cent of families are still in deep poverty. Put another way, all but one of the fiscal systems covered in the chart reduce deep poverty by more than two-thirds; the Belgian reduces it by more than 90 per cent. The American system reduces it by just 44 per cent.

But is there a downside to equality? Do Europe's more egalitarian welfare systems explain its relatively slower economic growth in recent years? The empirical evidence is ambiguous on this point.[60] Despite the widening gap between the United States and Europe in terms of productivity growth since 1994, there is still no compelling proof that the more egalitarian system is

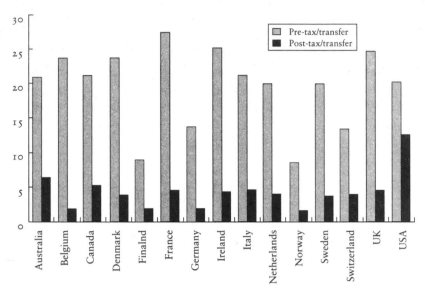

Figure 18. Relative poverty rates before and after taxation and transfers, 1991

Source: Solow, "Welfare," p. 21.

Note: Poverty rates are defined as percentage of families with an income less than 40 percent of the median.

ultimately the more sluggish.[61] What is undeniable is that universal welfare systems are more likely to create perverse incentives, encouraging patterns of behavior which in turn necessitate higher government spending. The failure of the British Conservatives to limit the duration of unemployment benefit was a costly mistake, given the empirical evidence that unlimited entitlement discourages job-seeking. Another glaring instance is the way fiscal policy in the past few decades has penalized married couples with children relative to single parents and childless couples. Taking into account all taxes and benefits, the real weekly earnings of a single mother of two in the lowest income "decile" rose by 145 per cent between 1971 and 1993. The equivalent figure for a married man with a non-working wife and two children was 38 per cent.[62] The strains on the housing stock and social security budget have been increased by what amount to incentives to remain single or to divorce. Between 1981 and 1995 spending on lone parents rose four and a half times.[63]

In a sense, then, it does not matter whether these and other skewed incentives directly retard growth. The real question is how far such systems can be sustained in fiscal terms. Given their burgeoning costs and the ways in which they are being financed (or not), there are reasons for doubt.

Between 1960 and 1992 transfers and subsidies rose from 8 per cent of the GDP of industrial countries to 21 per cent in 1992. As we have seen, a high proportion of this rising cost was financed by borrowing. But the rise of public debt reintroduces an old variable into the redistributive equation (omitted from Table 9): the traditional transfer from taxpayers to bond-holders in the form of debt interest. One unforeseen consequence of the welfare state has in fact been a revival of the rentier, rumours of whose demise turn out to have been exaggerated.

The bondholder of the early twenty-first century has learnt from the past, however. Far more than in the nineteenth century, he now enjoys safety in numbers, since a very large proportion of modern national debts are held on his behalf by institutions such as pension funds. Insurance companies, pension funds and investment trusts accounted for just 29.5 per cent of total holdings of gilts in 1975. By 1999 the proportion had risen to 62.3 per cent. Individual holdings had meanwhile fallen from 18 per cent to less than 9 per cent.[64] True, investments in government bonds represent a declining fraction of total private sector wealth, thanks to the spread of home-ownership and equity ownership. In Britain the value of gilts amounted to 40 per cent of wealth in 1970; twenty-five years later the proportion was just a quarter.[65] Nevertheless, the growing proportion of the population that held bonds indirectly through institutions by the late 1970s may help explain, in terms of political economy, why there was a return to positive real rates of interest in the 1980s and 1990s. Real rates of return on British bonds rose above 9 per cent in the first half of the 1990s: more or less what they were in the 1820s and 1920s (Figure 17 again). A British investor who invested in gilts at the beginning of 1997 enjoyed a total return of 14.85 per cent over the year.[66]

Still, even today's institutionally organized bondholders should feel a certain unease. For the expansion of public debts may yet prove to be an unsustainable process in some developed countries. The threat to the modern rentier is not posed by a politically powerful inflationary coalition of workers and entrepreneurs, however. Rather it is posed by the largest of all the disenfranchised groups left in today's democracies: the young and unborn.

GENERATION GAMES

The "Ricardian" theory of public debt is, as we have seen, that an increase in government borrowing today will be offset by an increase in private saving, because the present generation knows that, without such saving, the next generation will have to repay the government's debt out of its own income. Even when individuals do not have an infinite planning horizon, the fact that generations are linked by bequests to heirs should suffice. Experience suggests that this is not the way the world really works.[67] Whether because of "fiscal illusion" or indifference to the next generation's financial fate, present generations do not seem to behave with perfect altruism with regard to their heirs. Rather, they tend to "overlook future liabilities and to assume that debt-financed public services come for free."[68] In doing so, they leave unpaid bills to the next generation over and above what could be justified by "tax smoothing." To put it differently, "the stock of debt is the cumulative amount of transfers that past taxpayers have received from future ones."[69] The extent of this phenomenon is best captured using the new technique, introduced in Chapter 4, known as generational accounting.[70]

Generational accounts are simply total net taxes over entire lifetimes—to be precise, the sum of all future taxes citizens born in any given year will pay over their lifetimes, given current policy, minus transfer payments they will receive. Comparing the generational accounts of current newborns with the accounts of future newborns, with due adjustments for population and economic growth, therefore provides a precise measure of generational balance or imbalance.[71] If future generations face higher generational accounts than current newborns, today's policy is generationally unbalanced and therefore unsustainable. Because of the unbreakable inter-temporal budget constraint, the government simply cannot collect the same net taxes from future generations as it would collect, under current policy, from today's newborns.

The calculation of generational imbalance is an informative counterfactual, not a likely policy scenario, because it imposes the entire fiscal adjustment needed to satisfy the government's inter-temporal budget constraint on those born in the future. Nevertheless, such a calculation delivers a clear message about the need for policy adjustments. The question then becomes how to achieve generational balance without foisting all the adjustment on future generations. As an example, we can calculate the reduction in total future government purchases that would be necessary to lower the size of the generational accounts of future generations by enough to achieve generational balance. Whatever the size of that reduction in percentage terms, the policy could be implemented by an immediate and permanent cut in the annual flow of those purchases by the same percentage. Alternatively, there could be an immediate and permanent increase in annual tax revenues. This would raise the collective generational accounts of those now alive, and therefore reduce those of future generations.

When "generational accounts" are constructed they clearly show that in most developed countries today fiscal policy is indeed "enabl[ing] members of current generations to die in a state of insolvency by leaving debts to their descendants."[72] Figure 19 is based on generational accounting results for nineteen countries. It shows two mutually exclusive ways these countries could achieve generational balance: either by increasing all taxes or by cutting all transfer payments. Each of these policies is described in terms of the immediate and permanent percentage adjustment required. The magnitudes of these alternative adjustments provide an indirect measure of countries' generational imbalances.

The figure shows that seven countries would need to increase all taxes by more than 10 per cent to achieve generational balance. In the case of Austria and Finland the necessary increase is not far short of 20 per cent. If Germany were to rely exclusively on across-the-board tax hikes, then tax rates at all levels of government (federal, regional and local) and of all types (value added, payroll, corporate income, personal income, excise, sales, property, estate, and gift) would have to rise overnight by over 9 percent. The equivalent figure for the United States is nearly 11 per cent; for Japan it is 16 per cent. If countries relied solely on income tax increases, then Austria, Finland and France would each have to raise their income tax rates by over 50 per cent.[73] A number of countries could achieve generational balance with relatively modest tax increases of under 5 per cent: Australia, Belgium, Canada, Denmark, Portugal and Britain. Only Ireland and New Zealand would not have to raise taxes to achieve generational balance. Indeed, Ireland could cut its income tax rates by about 5 percent before needing to worry about burdening future generations.

It goes without saying that tax increases are seldom politically popular. What about the alternative, namely a reduction in government transfers (the source, after all, of much of the recent growth in spending and borrowing)? Figure 19 shows that five of the nineteen countries would need to cut all government transfers by more than a fifth to achieve generational balance: Austria, Finland, Japan, the Netherlands and the United States. Worst off is Japan, which would have to cut transfers by over 25 per cent. Best off once again is Ireland, which could legitimately increase transfers by 4 per cent. New Zealand too could afford a slight increase.

These figures are sobering. They show that only two or three of the world's developed economies have generationally balanced fiscal policies. The two biggest economies in the world—the United States and Japan—are among the countries furthest from equilibrium. Among other things, this exposes as illu-

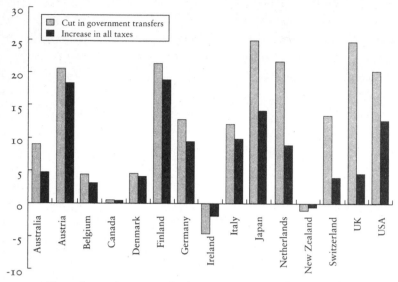

Figure 19. Two alternative ways of achieving generation balance (percentage increases required)

Source: Kotlikoff and Raffelheuschen, "Generational Accounting." The two different policies are considered under a definition of government expenditure that treats education as a transfer payment rather than a government purchase. It should also be noted that the figures are for all levels of government. For an earlier version which provides more methodological detail see Kotlikoff and Leibfritz, "International Comparison of Generational Accounts."

sory the budget surpluses realized and blithely projected in the United States since 1998. While presidential candidates debated how to spend these supposed surpluses, the generational accounts of the United States were among the worst in the world: worse, according to the measures used here, than those of Italy.[72] Only if official projections of growth prove to be too pessimistic will the American position improve. Otherwise there will almost certainly have to be reform of the state pension system—revealingly described by Vice-President Gore as "a solemn compact between the generations."

It is also striking that generational accounting produces a very different ranking of European fiscal weakness from the conventional measures of debts and deficits as ratios of GDP specified in both the Maastricht Treaty and the 1997 Stability and Growth Pact. On the basis of the debt/GDP ratio (which the Maastricht Treaty vainly stipulated should not exceed 60 per cent in any country wishing to participate in Economic and Monetary Union),

Belgium, Italy and the Netherlands have the most serious fiscal problems.[75] But in terms of generational balance, it is Austria, Finland, Spain and Sweden which are in trouble. Among developed economies, Britain and her former colonies—Australia, Canada, Ireland and New Zealand—are the countries with least to worry about. Indeed, Britain's generational imbalance would entirely disappear if labour productivity were to be 0.25 per cent higher than projected, and if government expenditures were not raised in line with the increase in the tax base. On the other hand, if there is no such improvement in productivity and no fiscal tightening, the British position is likely to deteriorate. If the government wished to achieve generational balance solely by increasing income tax—an unlikely scenario, admittedly—then there should have been an immediate and permanent 9.5 per cent income tax hike in 1999. But by 2004 the increase would need to be 11 per cent and 15 per cent ten years after that.[76]

What explains these differences between countries? The answer is partly differences in fiscal policy, but mainly differences in actual and future demographic structure. Table 10 gives figures for dependency ratios, meaning the ratio of the population over and above working age (under 15 or over 64) to the population aged from 15 to 65, or (in the last two columns) to the active employed population. These figures show that, contrary to some more alarmist predictions, dependency ratios today are lower in most major economies (except France) than they were a hundred years before. The difference is that

Table 10. Dependency ratios, actual and projected, 1900–2050

	Dependency ratios*					Effective economic dependency ratios**	
	1900	1938	1950	2000	2050	2000	2050
US	0.62	0.47	0.51	0.52	0.66	0.72	0.93
Japan	0.63	0.71	0.48	0.47	0.86	0.63	1.16
Germany	0.61	0.42	0.52	0.47	0.69	0.75	1.11
France	0.52	0.52	0.57	0.53	0.73	0.91	1.26
UK	0.59	0.44	0.56	0.53	0.69	0.77	0.99
Italy	0.68	0.62	0.55	0.48	0.78	0.91	1.47

Source: Economist, *World in Figures*, p. 17; McMorrow and Roeger, "Economic Consequences of Ageing Populations."

*0–14s + 65s and over/15s–64s

**0–15s + 65s and over/active employment

in 1900 most dependants were children: on average a third of the population of these countries was under 15. Today that figure is just 17 per cent,
while the proportion of the population aged 65 or over has risen from an
average of 5.6 per cent to 16 per cent. What makes the biggest difference to
the various generational accounts is the extent to which this ageing of the
population is projected to increase in the next fifty years. In all six cases in
Table 10, the expected "greying" of the population will increase the dependency ratios to unprecedented heights by the year 2050. If the "effective economic dependency" ratio is used, the dependent population will actually out-
number the working population in Japan, Germany, France and Italy.[77] In
those countries, more than a fifth of the population will be aged 65 or over
in just ten years" time. The German position is worsened by the extent of
early retirement, which in the 1970s and 1980s was naïvely believed to be a
way of increasing job opportunities for the young. Only 39 per cent of Germans aged between 55 and 64 now work.[78] By comparison, a country like
Thailand is blissfully young: the proportion of the population aged over 64
will be just 10 per cent by 2010.[79] This, along with distinctive features of the
tax system, explains why the generational imbalance in Thailand is positive—in other words, to the advantage of future generations.[80]

What these figures tell us is that a new kind of distributional conflict is
taking the place of the traditional class-based model that dominated the
twentieth century. In a sense, the welfare state was designed to end the old
struggles between rentiers, entrepreneurs and workers, and largely succeeded
in doing so. But the price of success was the creation of a system of universal entitlements that has become unaffordable. If the generational accounts
are out of kilter—as they are in most of Europe, Japan and the United
States—substantial future cuts in expenditure or increases in taxation are
inevitable. In one scenario, the next generation ends up paying in higher
taxes for the present generation's pensions and other transfers, including
interest on bonds (a large part of their private pensions). Alternatively, entitlements to the elderly end up being reduced—for example by a cut in state
pensions, a default on government bonds, or a big and unanticipated increase
in inflation—and the bill is handed back to the generation which incurred it
years before.

Redistribution between generations is not new, of course. Large public
debts and unfunded public pensions have always meant a transfer from the
young and unborn to the old, just as public spending on education transfers
resources from the old to the young.[81] However, the current scale of generational imbalances is probably unprecedented. The old are substantial net

beneficiaries of most "first world" fiscal systems, not only because of pensions but because they are the biggest consumers of subsidized health care; they are therefore the obvious targets for policies aimed at reducing spending. But, unlike the young and unborn, they also have votes. The question this raises is how far objective conflicts of interest between generations could become subjective political conflicts.

In the past, generations tended to quarrel more about politics, art and hair-length than about the redistributive effects of fiscal policy. Bazarov has many grievances in Turgenev's *Father and Sons*, but the cost of supporting the older generation is not among them. Even today, generational conflict over finance is limited by the fact that those who may be most disadvantaged by current policy are not enfranchised: in the words of the Italian economist Guido Tabellini, "If the young could vote on the decision to issue debt, they would all oppose it."[82] Nevertheless, it seems plausible that debates over pension reform could make generational conflicts more financially explicit in the future.

A good illustration of the changing importance of age in politics is provided by the case of Britain since 1979. The Thatcher government inherited a dual system of state pensions: the long-established basic pension, which was increased each year in line with the higher of two indices: the retail price index and the average earnings index. In addition, there was a new State Earnings Related Pension introduced in 1978.[83] In its first budget, the new government amended the rule for increasing the basic pension so that it would rise in line with the retail price index only, breaking the link with average earnings. Six years later the additional pension was also made less generous. The short-run fiscal saving involved was substantial, since the growth of earnings was substantially higher than inflation after 1980 (around 180 per cent to 1995, compared with 120 per cent). The long-run saving was greater still (the UK's unfunded public pension liability is a great deal smaller than those of most continental governments: as little as 5 per cent for the period to 2050, compared with 70 per cent for Italy, 105 per cent for France and 110 per cent for Germany).[84] In the words of Nigel Lawson, Chancellor between 1983 and 1989, "this politically brave decision . . . was a critical part of regaining control of public expenditure."[85] No doubt; but it also represented a substantial inter-generational transfer, to the detriment of those in or approaching retirement. The surprising thing is the slowness and mildness with which the losers reacted.

Age has not been seen as a decisive political cleavage in British politics. It is, however, striking that the young tend disproportionately to vote Labor, and the old to vote Conservative. The reduction of the minimum voting age from 21 to 18, according to Britain's leading psephologist, "probably cut [the Conservative] majority from 60 to 30 in 1970 and made the decisive difference in the two 1974 elections" won by Labour.[86] And it was those aged under 30 who defected from the Conservatives to Labour in the greatest numbers in 1997.[87] The old, by comparison, have remained remarkably loyal to the Conservatives despite the Thatcherite cuts in state pensions. In 1992 nearly half of voters over 64 voted Tory, 4 per cent more than the figure for the electorate as a whole. The percentage fell by just 3 per cent in 1997, compared with a national decline in the Conservative vote from 43 per cent to 31 per cent. Pensioners were in fact the only age group that gave the Tories more support than Labour.[88] It is nevertheless significant that one of the principal campaign issues of the 1997 election was the Labour claim that Social Security Secretary Peter Lilley was contemplating the complete abolition of the state pension. According to the Conservatives' own polls and "focus groups," the Labour attack on Lilley's reform proposals was followed by a sharp dip in Tory support among the over-65s, though aggressive rebuttals may have reversed this effect before polling day.[89] Al Gore tried the same tactic in 2000. It would be very remarkable if such "playing on the fears of the elderly" did not become an increasingly important theme of elections in other countries in the coming decades. In the words of a European Commission paper published in November 1999:

With an increasing proportion of national resources being transferred to the retired population, it is difficult . . . to speculate as to the extent which these changes in the distribution of societies [sic] resources, between the employed and dependent populations, will be capable of being resolved without major crises and inter-generational conflicts. . . . The economic impact of the "greying" of the population over the next 50 years will . . . become unbearable for the Community in the event that its labour markets, and by implication its tax and social security systems, remain in their present state . . .[90]

AN UNWELCOME ANSWER

An obvious solution to the problem of "greying" populations—though one not mentioned in the EC report cited above—is, of course, increased immigration, since immigrants are generally of working age, with above-average economic motivation. This is happening. In the early 1990s around 80 million people were estimated to be living outside the country of their birth; by the year 2000 that figure had risen to 120 million, around 2 per cent of the world's total population.[91] The huge influx of new migrants to the United States since the 1980s—around 850,000 a year on average—may well represent the best hope for the American social security system, provided the newcomers are quickly integrated into the tax system.[92] Germany too is likely to benefit (as it did in the 1950s) from large-scale immigration: there are now 7.3 million foreigners resident in the country, around 9 per cent of the population.[93]

Unfortunately, a number of those countries most in need of immigrants are among those least inclined to admit them. The Austrian fiscal system suffers from one of the most serious generational imbalances in Europe. Yet nowhere have anti-immigration policies attracted more popular support, to the extent that the openly xenophobic Freedom Party entered government in 2000. Moreover, anti-immigration laws have a perverse effect: because most borders are in practice impossible to seal, they create a large category of illegal immigrants who are outside the tax system, and therefore make no direct contribution to the fiscal system. In the European Union, for example, there are an estimated 3 million illegal immigrants; in the United States roughly 2 million out of 7 million Mexican-born residents are there illegally. The total number of illegal immigrants in the US is estimated to be around 6 million.[94] If the past is any guide, however, there is little reason to expect these semi-enforceable laws to be relaxed in the near future. It was precisely at the zenith of the last age of globalization that the United States and other labour-importing states began to restrict immigration, beginning with the exclusion of migrants from China and Japan before the First World War.[95]

The enactment of anti-immigration legislation is a good example of the way a democratic preference can run counter to a society's long-run economic interests. (As a rule, immigration tends to erode the real wages of unskilled workers, but it benefits the host economy as a whole.) In the same way, most proponents of generational accounting are pessimistic about the chances that their recommendations—whether for tax increases or spending cuts—will be heeded. Politicians, it tends to be assumed, are incapable of looking further than the next election. They are certainly not likely to favour policies that are in the interests of voters as yet unborn if they involve sacrifices by voters today.

To pursue this issue further, the next chapter moves from the realm of distributional conflicts into the arena of politics. Cobbett's belief was, as we have seen, that democratization would lead to an improvement in fiscal policy: the widening of the franchise would put a stop to the reign of the "tax eaters" by forcing politicians to reduce (by some unspecified means) the "blessed Debt." In practice, however, new debts have piled up—and the ranks of the tax eaters have swollen not shrunk. Why?

8

The Silverbridge Syndrome:
Electoral Economics*

"... It's the game I looks to. If the game dies away, it'll never be got up
again;—never. Who'll care about elections then?"

Trollope, Can You Forgive Her[1]

When Anthony Trollope's dashing young hero Phineas Finn stood for Parliament as a Liberal, the election was a foregone conclusion. There were only 307 registered electors and "the inhabitants were so far removed from the world, and were so ignorant of the world's good things, that they knew nothing about bribery." In any case, the local grandee, the Earl of Tula, withdrew his support from the Conservative incumbent, his brother, with whom he had quarreled.[2] However, when Trollope himself became a parliamentary candidate—the year after he had completed Phineas Finn—he was less fortunate. The constituency he contested was Beverley, in the East Riding of Yorkshire, one of the most notoriously corrupt in England. Since arriving on the scene in 1857 the Conservative member, Sir Henry Edwards, had systematically "bought" the electors, to the extent that "the Working Classes [newly enfranchised in 1867] look[ed] upon the privilege of the vote only as a means to obtain money."[3] The publicans too were paid by Edwards to dispense free beer. Even in municipal elections, the Conservative agents would sit in the aptly named Golden Ball tavern, dispensing coins and carefully noting the names of the recipients in a book. Trollope spent £400 on his campaign, but came bottom of the poll with 740 votes, compared with Edwards's 1,132. So brazen was the bribery that a Royal Commission was set up to investigate the Beverley election. It found that more than 800 voters had been bribed, and duly abolished the constituency.[4]

To read Trollope's fictionalized versions of this experience in *The Prime Minister* and *The Duke's Children* is to realize how little English political life

---

*This chapter was co-authored with Glen O'Hara

had changed between the 1750s and the 1860s. In the imaginary constituency of "Silverbridge," candidates are forced to hand over checks for £500 to local attorneys, "honest citizens" brazenly ask for "the smallest pecuniary help" in return for their votes, the local brewer is defeated by the protégé of the local aristocrat and a defeated candidate threatens to horsewhip one of his rivals.[5] Two major Reform Acts had been passed in 1832 and 1867; yet Trollope's Silverbridge seems only marginally less disreputable than the Hanoverian election so vividly depicted by William Hogarth in 1753.

Nothing of the sort would happen in a modern-day Silverbridge, it might be thought. These days, an MP can be turned out of the House of Commons if he is found to have exceeded the legally fixed minimum for campaign expenditures even by a few pounds. And of course, none of the money spent by today's candidates goes directly into the pockets of voters. Yet there are other respects in which the politics of the early twenty-first century do recall the age of Trollope. Votes in modern democracies are not bought directly; but money still has to be spent in order to secure them.

ARE YOU BETTER OFF NOW?

It has become an axiom of modern politics that there is a causal relationship between economics and government popularity: to be precise, that the performance of the economy has a direct bearing on the electoral success of an incumbent government. A good illustration of this new economic determinism was the widespread explanation of the failure to impeach President Clinton for perjury and the obstruction of justice in connection with his numerous sexual misdemeanors. By February 1999 a majority of Americans believed Clinton was guilty of the charges against him, but only a small minority wanted him to resign as president. According to Senator Robert Byrd—and many other commentators—the explanation was simple: "No president will ever be removed . . . when the economy is at record highs. People are voting with their wallets in answering the polls."[6]

This, the *Financial Times*'s correspondent suggested, was the difference between Clinton and Richard Nixon, who was forced out of the White House in August 1974. In the year and a half leading up to Nixon's fall, his "approval rating fell from about 60 per cent . . . to less than 30 per cent. . . . Over that period, output suffered its most severe slowdown since the Second World War, unemployment rose by almost 1 million and the inflation rate doubled

. . . On Wall Street the stock market fell by a third." But Clinton's approval rating rose from a low of 40 per cent (when Kenneth Starr was appointed Special Prosecutor in 1994) to above 70 per cent at the end of 1999, a year dominated by the Monica Lewinsky scandal. This was because, the *FT*'s man suggested, "since the Lewinsky affair broke . . . the US has created more than 3 million jobs, the unemployment rate has dropped to a 40-year low and growth has been at its strongest sustained level in more than a decade. On Wall Street, the Dow Jones Industrial Average has risen more than 15 per cent." At first sight, Figure 20 seems to bear out this analysis. In other words, Clinton's own campaign watchword during the presidential race of 1992—"It's the economy, stupid"—appears to have been vindicated by his experience in office.

The idea of the primacy of economics in American politics antedates the Clinton era, however. In 1980, during a televised debate with Jimmy Carter, Ronald Reagan declared: "When you make that decision [at the polls], you might ask yourself, 'Are you better off now than you were four years ago?' . . . Is there more or less unemployment in the country than there was four years ago?"[7] British politicians too have long been economic determinists; indeed, the idea that the state of the economy could decide a government's electoral success can be traced as far back as the mid-Victorian period. A Liberal leaflet published in Manchester in 1880 compared the numbers of inmates and recipients of out-door relief at the Salford Workhouse "When Gladstone took office" and "When he retired," compared with "When Lord Beaconsfield took office" and·"on 1st January, 1880." The figures had fallen under the Liberals and risen sharply under the Tories. The leaflet's conclusion was ironical: "So much for TORY RULE with its Bad Trade, Heavy Rates & Taxes. IF YOU HAVE NOT HAD ENOUGH OF THESE, VOTE FOR THE TORIES."[8] Disraeli himself was sufficiently impressed by such arguments that he told Salisbury: "'Hard Times,' as far as I can collect, has been our foe and certainly the alleged cause of our fall."[9]

In 1930, as the international depression deepened, Winston Churchill declared: "It is no longer a case of one party fighting another, nor of one set of politicians scoring off another. It is the case of successive governments facing economic problems and being judged by their success or failure in the duel."[10] Harold Macmillan, the most successful Conservative politician of the 1950s, was quite explicit in regarding gentle inflation and low unemployment as the bases of Conservative political success. "Let us be frank about it," he famously told Bedford Conservatives in July 1957, "most of our people have never had it so good."[11] Two years later the party's election slogan was "Life's Better With the Conservatives: Don't Let Labour Ruin It."

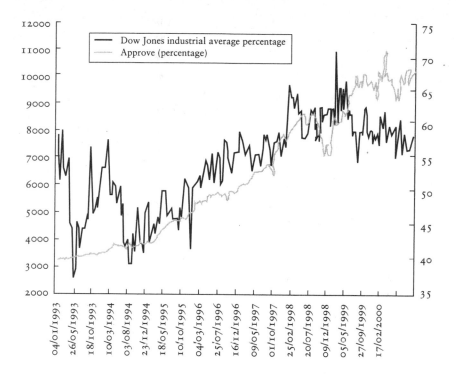

Figure 20. President Clinton's approval rating and the Dow Jones index, 1993–2000

Sources: Gallup Organization; Economagic.

Notes: Dow Jones Industrial Average index, daily closing, "Approve": percentage of those surveyed who answered "Approve" to the question: "Do you approve or disapprove of the way Bill Clinton is handling his job as president?"

When the Liberals won the Orpington by-election in March 1962 Macmillan blamed his own Chancellor's economic policies.[12] It did not take long for the Labour Party to adopt the same mode of operation. In 1968 Harold Wilson he told the *Financial Times*: "All political history shows that the standing of a Government and its ability to hold the confidence of the electorate at a General Election depend on the success of its economic policy."[13]

By the 1970s the idea that government popularity depended on economic performance—and that economic policy could and should be manipulated to maintain popular support—had become almost axiomatic. In July 1975 Barbara Castle gloomily concluded that "unemployment levels continuing at 3 per cent right up to 1978–79" would be "a scenario for another Tory victory just in time for them to reap the harvest of our bitter self-sacrifice."[14]

In September 1978 Wilson's successor Jim Callaghan wound up a Cabinet meeting by saying: "Don't forget, Governments do well when people have money in their pockets. How do we do it?"[15]

Though they had little else in common with their predecessors in office, the Conservatives of the Thatcher era were equally firm believers in the view that the economy was the key to political success. From "Labour isn't Working" in 1979 to "Labour's Tax Bombshell" in 1992, economic issues were central to the election campaigns run for the Tories by the Saatchi brothers. Of course, the 1979 campaign's emphasis on the dole queue soon proved to be a double-edged sword, as unemployment soared in the wake of Geoffrey Howe's deflationary budgets to a peak of 3.2 million, two and a half times the level the Tories had inherited. In her memoirs, Margaret Thatcher herself explained her own early unpopularity in strictly economic terms.[16] She had "no doubt" that the result of the 1983 election "would ultimately depend on the economy." In the same way, as the 1987 election approached, she saw "economic recovery" as providing "an effective salve" for political "wounds" such as the Westland Affair: "Our policies were delivering growth with low inflation, higher living standards and . . . steadily falling unemployment." When the 1986 Conservative Party Conference coincided with "increasing evidence of prosperity, not least the fall in unemployment," it "gave us a lift of morale and in the polls which . . . set us on course for winning the next election."[17] Nearly all Thatcher's Cabinet colleagues echoed this analysis. Her Chancellor of the Exchequer Nigel Lawson's chapter on the 1987 election was entitled simply: "An Election Won on the Economy."[18] Indeed, according to Nicholas Ridley, Margaret Thatcher not only lived but died by the economic sword too:

Her personal popularity ratings in the polls was [sic] at a very low point in the autumn [of 1989]. . . . The single most vital electoral attribute of the Tories—that they were seen as much the best party at managing the economy—suddenly became questionable. Historically, there seems to be an almost direct relationship between the interest rate and the popularity of a government. Over a long period, the higher the interest rate the less popular has a government been in the opinion polls, and vice versa.[19]

A PROBLEM FOR THE THEORY

Yet for the politicians quoted above who were around to witness the general election of May 1997, the result was not so easy to explain. Labour's landslide victory signified a complete breakdown of the supposedly traditional relationship between the economy and government popularity.[20] The Conservative manifesto's opening chapter was entitled "Doubling Living Standards."[21] The party's key campaign slogan, "Britain is Booming," was based on the assumption that economic prosperity would once again lead voters to re-elect them.[22] And Britain *was* booming. Since April 1992, the date of the previous election, Bank base rates had fallen from 10.5 to 6 per cent; inflation had fallen from 4.3 per cent to 2.6 per cent; unemployment had fallen from 9.5 per cent to 7.2 per cent; real GDP had risen by 15.8 per cent; and average annual growth was a healthy 2.4 per cent. What is more, voters in 1997 *knew* that the economy was doing well. An opinion poll published on 24 April, a week before the election, showed that nearly half of the electorate agreed that "the Government has built strong foundations for Britain's recovery." Unfortunately for the Tories, however, only a fifth of those polled believed that they deserved to win.[23] Although they managed to reduce considerably the Labour lead between December 1994 and the election, the Conservatives' share of the vote still fell by nearly 11 per cent, and the number of seats they held in the Commons fell by 170. "Recessions . . . destroy governments," the former Deputy Prime Minister Michael Heseltine was heard to declare in February 1999.[24] But it was anything but a recession that destroyed the Major government.

Predictably, economic commentators struggled to make their models fit the facts. According to the Institute for Fiscal Studies, although it was true that incomes had risen since 1992, they had not risen by as much as in previous electoral periods. After tax, the real income of an average family with two children had risen by £765 a year between 1991 and 1996. But the figure for the period 1983–7 had been twice as high and that for the period 1987–92 three times as high. There was, in short, not enough "fuel for the feelgood factor" in 1997.[25] The journalist Will Hutton argued that the "success" of the economy since 1992 was superficial: nothing had changed in the "underlying performance of the economy," and voters recognized this.[26] A third theory advanced was that the Conservatives had simply not been forgiven for the economic mismanagement which had resulted in the 1990 recession and the 1992 departure of sterling from the Exchange Rate Mechanism.[27] This indeed was the explanation offered by the principal architect of the Conservative campaign:

Only one thing changed between the 1997 election defeat and the four election victories that preceded it. There was a 40 point turnaround against us, from +20 to

– 20, in answer to the standard . . . question: "With Britain in economic difficulties, which Party has the best policies for managing the economy?" *The only thing that changed* between victory and defeat was the perception of the parties' relative economic competence.[28]

This distinction between economic reality and perception is crucial, as we shall see.

To set the election of 1997 in perspective, figure 21 compares the government's lead in the opinion polls with a "misery index," which simply adds together the unemployment and inflation rates. Superficially, there are traces of the inverse relationship predicted by the feelgood model, namely that rises in unemployment and inflation would make governments less popular. When the misery index rose sharply in 1951, the popularity of the Attlee government fell, leading to its defeat in the election that October. The subsequent troughs of the misery index seem to coincide closely with the peaks of Conservative popularity in the summer of 1955 and the autumn of 1960; while the rise of the misery index above 7 in May 1962 saw a slump in the Tory lead. But from the mid-1960s onwards the relationship is less distinct. At a Cabinet meeting on 14 July 1966 Wilson commented revealingly on a poll that showed Labour 16 points ahead of the Conservatives: "He couldn't understand how or why! It appeared the more unpopular the measures we took, the more popular we became."[29] Yet when the government's lead collapsed almost immediately thereafter, its loss of popularity was out of all proportion to the rise in misery captured by the index. The comparable collapse between 1974 and 1977 seems more readily explicable in economic terms; but comparably high misery had much less of an effect on the Thatcher government's popularity in 1980 and 1981. Thereafter, the government lead appears to move more or less independently of the misery index.

Using more sophisticated statistical methods to distinguish the effects of unemployment, inflation and interest rates,[30] we can be quite precise about the decline of the feelgood factor (see Appendix B). It was certainly present at the beginning of the period, as Figure 21 suggests. Under the Conservative governments of the 1950s, a 1 per cent rise in unemployment was associated with a fall in the government lead of nearly 5 per cent; the effect of rising inflation and interest rates was also negative, though less damaging. For the first Wilson government, the effect of rising unemployment was even more serious: a rise in unemployment of just 1 per cent could reduce government popularity by nearly 10 per cent. Rising interest rates were also

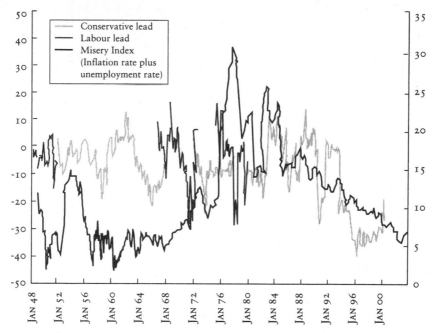

Figure 21. Government lead (left-hand axis) and the "misery index" (right-hand axis), 1948–2000

Sources: Butler and Butler, *British Political Facts*; Central Statistics Office, *Monthly Digest of Statistics*; id., *Retail Prices* 1914–1990; HMSO, *Ministry of Labour Gazette*; Recent data are from the following websites: Bank of England, HM Treasury, www.statistics.gov.uk, except for the opinion poll data, which are from the Gallup Organization (as published in the *Daily Telegraph*).

Note: The indicators used in the analysis are as follows: Government lead: Percentage of respondents who would vote for governing party if an election were held tomorrow less percentage who would vote for principal Opposition party. RPI: retail price index, percentage change over the previous year. Unemployment figures (defined from January 1971 as the claimant count) are given without seasonal adjustment.

associated with falls in government popularity, though higher inflation seems to have had no significant effect. Interestingly, the figures under Heath were extremely close to those under his Conservative predecessors. And unemployment was associated with bigger falls in support under Wilson and Callaghan between 1974 and 1979.

However, only unemployment had a statistically significant relationship with the popularity of the Wilson-Callaghan governments. Indeed, for all subsequent governments only one of the three indicators is significant: interest rates in the case of the Conservatives, unemployment in the case of Labour. This suggests that Mrs Thatcher may have been successful in shifting the attention of voters away from unemployment, which had a slightly positive but insignificant relationship with government popularity between 1979 and 1992. It is perhaps more surprising, given Thatcher's anti-inflation rhetoric, that the correlation between inflation and government unpopularity was not stronger. But Ridley's "law"—"the higher the interest rate, the less popular has a government been in the opinion polls"—does appear to have held: every 1 per cent increase in base rates correlated with a 3 per cent drop in government popularity.

What of the period leading up to the 1997 election? Given John Major's public commitment to price stability as a "gain" worth substantial "pain," it is not surprising that the correlation between inflation and government popularity was strongly negative between 1992 and 1997. The most striking feature of the years 1992–7, however, was the perversity of the correlation between interest rates and the government's position in the polls. Bizarrely, a one per cent rise in the Bank of England base rate was associated with an increase in government popularity of around 8 per cent; or, to be exact, falling interest rates after September 1992 coincided with a collapse in government support. It was this inversion of the feelgood model—on which they had faithfully based their campaign—that condemned the Conservatives to defeat. Even more perplexing is the positive relationship between unemployment and government popularity since 1997, which shows that public support for the Blair government has actually declined as unemployment has continued to fall—an unprecedented phenomenon in the history of the modern Labour party.

In other words, there was only a relatively short period—the heyday of "Keynesian" demand management in the 1960s—when the relationship was even close to the linear one implied by the feelgood theory. Otherwise, there has seldom been a stable causal link from economic to political success. There seem to have been two reasons for this. First, political attempts to manipulate the economic cycle have generally had unanticipated negative consequences: this was painfully obvious in the 1970s, when (as we saw in chapter 5) fiscal and monetary policies aimed at boosting unemployment were blamed for accelerating inflation. Secondly, voters do not simply reward incumbents when the economy has grown and punish them when it has not: their responses to economic change are far more complex.

THE POLITICAL BUSINESS CYCLE

There are two ways of explaining why electoral outcomes might not—or at least not always—be determined by economics. One is that politicians simply lack the skill to manipulate the economy successfully.

In his *Economic Theory of Democracy* published in 1957, Anthony Downs proposed that "parties formulate policies in order to win elections, rather than win elections in order to formulate policies" and that, once elected, "democratic governments act rationally to maximize political support."[31] This formed the basis of William Nordhaus's theory of the "political business cycle," which suggested that governments would tend to manipulate the economy so that the economic cycle would peak shortly before they came up for re-election. Quite apart from politicians' own admissions, there is some empirical evidence to back this up. In some countries at least—the United States, Germany and New Zealand, for example—unemployment has appeared to follow a political cycle, rising in the first two years of government and falling in the last two years.[32] As we have seen, the British data do not show the same pattern. However, it has been demonstrated, using slightly different methods, that in two-thirds of election years up until the 1970s, the increase in disposable income rose above the mean in the pre-election year.[33]

The trouble with the expansionary policies used to get unemployment down was, of course, that they generated higher than anticipated inflation. As politicians primed the pump with increasing frequency, the Phillips curve—the apparently close relationship between employment and inflation—began to steepen. The conclusion many commentators drew was that the political business cycle might after all be unsustainable because, in the words of Samuel Brittan, it gave rise to "the politics of excessive expectations."[34] To Peter Jay, writing in the mid-1970s, "a crisis of political economy" seemed imminent.[35] In Britain and America that crisis took the form of a counter-inflationary backlash under Thatcher and Reagan.

The polarization of politics that occurred in the late 1970s prompted a "partisan" modification to the political business cycle theory. Perhaps different parties had different policy preferences: left-wing politicians worrying more about unemployment because of their working-class constituents, while conservatives worried more about inflation because of their rentier supporters. One influential study done in 1977 calculated that, on average, post-war unemployment had been higher in Britain under the Conservatives than under Labour.[36] Democrats too were likely to aim for lower unemployment and higher inflation than Republicans.[37] The election of conservative governments in many countries therefore did not represent the end of political manipulation of the economy, so much as a realization that the benefits of inflation had been overtaken by the costs. As Brittan constantly lamented during the 1980s, and as the politicians' memoirs confirm, the political business cycle lived on under the Conservatives, with interest rate changes carefully timed with one eye (or both) on their political impact. There seems little doubt that in the period 1983–7 the Tories did "manipulate the money supply . . . in order to influence public opinion," responding to evidence of their own unpopularity by relaxing monetary policy.[38] A further theoretical explanation for the well-timed profligacy of some conservative administrations is that conservatives may raise fiscal deficits (through tax cuts) precisely in order to constrain left-wing rivals if the latter are likely to come to power, by forcing them to limit or even cut public spending.[39]

However, such political tinkering with nominal indicators might have less visible real effects if voters could see through the politicians' intentions. In that case, the political business cycle would be more likely to show up in the budget or monetary policy than in growth, employment or inflation data. Studies comparing all the OECD countries appear to bear this out.[40] One possible explanation of the decline of the feelgood factor after the 1970s might therefore simply be public disillusionment as the policies of one government after another generated new economic grievances. To put it another way, the more a government targeted one particular variable, the more likely it was to cease to correlate closely with its popularity, as other problems developed elsewhere in the economy—a variation on Goodhart's famous law that the very act of basing policy on one indicator may undermine its predictive power.

There is, however, a second explanation for the non-existence or decline of the political business cycle. This relates to the other—and much more complex—human variable in the electoral equation, namely the voters.

THE VOTE FUNCTION

The political scientist Helmut Norpoth has written: "The economy is a concern that almost everywhere bonds electorates and governments as tightly as Siamese twins joined at the hip. . . . Economic voting . . . is hard-wired into the brain of citizens in democracies."[41] Yet the evidence suggests that the circuitry is highly complex and may occasionally blow a fuse. Indeed, any idea of a simple causal link from prosperity to popularity must be abandoned in the face of a mass of empirical research from around the democratic world.[42]

Using data from thirty-eight countries, but comparing only the vote for the major party in office in the most recent elections and the poll and pre-poll figures for real GDP growth, Norpoth has found (using a simple regression) that "for every percentage point that real GDP grows in the election year, the major incumbent party stands to gain roughly $1^{1}/_{2}$ per cent of the vote above its normal share."[43] Another study found similar evidence of "economic voting" in Europe and the US in the early 1980s.[44] However, Paldam's 1991 survey of the "vote function" in seventeen OECD countries over four decades found only superficial relationships between votes for parties in power and a variety of economic indicators (the change in unemployment, price rises and GDP growth). When subjected to more rigorous statistical tests, these relationships turned out to be weak, even when allowance was made for such variables as the political complexion of the government, the number of parties, and the size of the country.[45] Only by making adjustments to take account of differences in the degree of the responsibility of government parties for economic performance (given differing political systems), and by considering inflation and unemployment in comparative rather than absolute terms, can significant links from the economy to elections be found.[46]

More detailed work on specific countries (a great deal of which, it should be stressed, focuses on the United States) has raised eight questions about the way the economy and voting behavior are related:

1. Do voters care about inflation, unemployment or some other measure of economic well-being?
2. Are voters motivated by individual self-interest or do they have regard for the common good?
3. Do voters view the economy differently according to which party they identify with?
4. Do voters view the economy differently according to which class they belong to?
5. Do voters act asymmetrically, punishing failure more than they reward success?
6. Are voters backward-looking or forward-looking?
7. Are voters myopic or rational?
8. Is "feeling good"—meaning the perception of prosperity—more important to voters than actually being better off?

The following paragraphs summarize the main answers political scientists have come up with.

1. *Economic Indicators.* It is clear from numerous individual country studies that there is considerable variety in the economic indicators that matter to voters. For instance, one study of US congressional elections between 1896 and 1964 found a significant correlation between changes in real income and election results, a slightly weaker negative correlation between prices and voting, but no real relationship with unemployment.[47] Looking at twentieth-century presidential elections, Ray Fair found changes in both real GNP and the rate of unemployment in the pre-election year to have been significant: specifically, a 1 per cent rise in real GNP gave the incumbent an additional 1.2 per cent of the vote, while an equivalent rise in the rate of unemployment cost as much as 2.3 per cent of the vote.[48] An updated version of this model, based exclusively on pre-election growth data, was a source of solace to Al Gore's supporters in the early stages of the 2000 campaign, when their candidate was lagging behind in the polls.[49]

In Britain more attention has been paid to the trade-off between inflation and unemployment. A pioneering study of British elections published in 1970 found that both indicators had influenced government popularity in the post-war period (after allowing for a six-month lag in the effect of unemployment changes, "euphoria" after the election of a new government, and "backswing" to a government just before an election).[50] Comparable results have since been produced for the UK under the Thatcher government.[51] However, other analysts have argued that inflation was the more important indicator for Britain in this period.[52]

Growing public concern about inflation may help explain why Britain produced a more radical conservative reaction in the 1980s than other European countries. For West Germany, by contrast, there is evidence that unemployment mattered more than inflation between 1971 and 1986 in persuading voters to change parties.[53] In France between 1978 and 1987 both indicators correlated closely with public approval for the party in power.[54] But then inflation in those countries never reached British levels in the 1970s. The maximum inflation rate in Britain was 27 per cent in August 1975, at a time when French inflation was just 11 per cent and German less than 6 per cent. On the other hand, the British Conservatives had to work hard to defend an anti-inflationary policy that had as its principal side-effect a doubling of unemployment.

Although most studies of the "vote function" focus on real incomes, inflation and unemployment, there are of course other possibilities. Tax policy probably deserves more investigation, given the importance in recent years of promises like George Bush's infamous "Read my lips: no new taxes" pledge in August 1988.[55] Trade policy too can play an important part in elections (as it did in the nineteenth century): witness the extraordinary swings in party allegiance on the eve of the 1988 Canadian general election as a result of the Liberals' decision to stall the passage of the North American Free Trade Agreement.[56] There is also some evidence that privatization did attract new voters to the British Conservatives in the 1980s.[57] One strong possibility is that the importance of specific indicators changes over time (and indeed from place to place).[58] In the United States, for example, the relationship between family income and government popularity was strong in the 1950s, weak in the 1960s and then strong again in the early 1970s.[59] This is precisely the volatility that made the feelgood model so unreliable in Britain after the 1960s.

2. *Self-interest or the Common Good?* Some research on the United States has suggested that voters are more likely to be influenced by general economic conditions than by their own individual economic circumstances in their voting decisions, implying that voters are "sociotropic" or altruistic in their behavior; or, alternatively, that "self-reliant" Americans tend not to attribute their own individual fortunes to the government.[60] In 1984, for example, only around 5 per cent of American voters attributed changes in their own personal economic circumstances to government tax policy.[61] However, it is not at all easy to distinguish personal and general economic influences on voting decisions.[62] And a number of forecasters still regard the question "Are you better off or worse off than you were a year ago?" as a good indicator to voting intentions.[63]

3. *Partisan Asymmetry.* A further complication is that voters may have different economic expectations of different parties: they may *expect* lower inflation but higher unemployment from right-wing governments, and the converse from left-wing governments.[64] If nothing else, this seemed a helpful way to rationalize the failure of voters to turn away from the Thatcher and Reagan governments when unemployment rose during the early 1980s.[65] However, closer inspection has required some substantial qualifications to this story: for example, it emerges that in 1979 British voters regarded Labour as better than the Conservatives at dealing with inflation, which polls still showed to be the most important economic issue of that election. Yet Labour lost. Moreover, when unemployment rose in the subsequent three years, voters turned not to Labour but to the new Social Democratic Party.[66]

4. *Class Voting.* Thus far we have tended to imagine voters as a homoge-

neous group. However, political scientists have long sought to demonstrate that voters' economic preferences are in some measure a function of their social class. It is often claimed that the link between social class and party allegiance has weakened since its zenith in the 1950s.[67] Early proponents of "feelgood" politics such as Anthony Crosland were deeply influenced by this, arguing that as voters abandoned old class allegiances they would simply follow whichever party delivered the lowest prices and the highest employment. More recently, it has been argued that class has been superseded by other social attributes: now it is ethnicity or church attendance that matter more (though some of the "new" determinants of voting behavior such as trade union membership and home ownership can hardly be distinguished from class).[68] This raises the possibility that the stronger correlations between economics and politics in the 1950s and 1960s were in fact related to the persistence of class allegiance, whereas after around 1970 the dissolution of class identities reduced the significance of macroeconomic indicators. Nevertheless, there are those who maintain that class still matters. True, it appears to have declined if one uses a simple measure like the "Alford index" which measures the difference between the percentage of manual workers and non-manual workers who vote for Labour. But more sophisticated methods—for instance, controlling for the decline of manual workers as a percentage of the population—seem to show the persistence of class-political affinities. Studies are legion showing that, even in more recent times, a rise in unemployment tends to increase support for the Left among the working class more than among other social groups.[69]

5. *There's No Gratitude . . .* Some political scientists argue that voters act "asymmetrically," punishing politicians for bad economic developments more than they reward them when things go well.[70] Among British voters polled in 1963 and 1964, for example, those who believed their economic situation had worsened over the previous year were twice as likely to "swing" against the government than those who believed their situation had improved.[71] Yet the rapid growth of the economy since the Tories had come to power in 1951 should have ensured that the losers were in a clear minority. Contemplating the government's plummeting popularity since 1960, Harold Macmillan mused that perhaps "after ten years of unparalleled prosperity, the people are bored."[72] In other words, the majority of winners who had never had it so good were less ready to reward the government than the minority of losers were to punish it.

6. *Peasants or Bankers?* However, this assumes that voters judge politicians retrospectively on their past performance, as opposed to prospectively

on their expected future performance. To pose the question in academic jargon: are voters backward-looking "peasants" or a forward-looking "bankers"? There is some evidence of retrospective voting in the United States,[73] though the effect appears to be stronger in presidential than congressional elections, while retrospective judgments are clearly mingled with other factors, such as long-term political allegiance ("We've always voted Republican in this family/street/town").[74] It would, of course, be wiser for voters to act on the basis of what they think a future government will do rather than what a past government has done. And some Americans research does indeed suggest that forecasts rather than memories are what motivate voters.[75] In Britain too the 1992 election can be seen as an example of prospective voting: rather than punishing them for the past recession, voters re-elected the Conservatives on a wave of rising financial expectations.[76] According to one argument, Tory voters had indeed voted prospectively throughout the 1980s—though their judgment of Labour remained firmly retrospective.[77] For this reason, answers to the question "Who *would* make the best prime minister?" may provide a more reliable guide to voting intentions than approval ratings, supposedly based on past performance.[78]

Of course, this is almost certainly a false dichotomy, since expectations must in some measure be based on past experience.[79] Yet even a model based on both the past *and* the future can be wrong. The Conservatives' "great hope" before the 1997 election was that "rises in real personal disposable income in the previous twelve months would be followed by rises in householders' net expectations about their financial position in the next twelve months, which would be followed by rises in voting intention for the Conservative Party."[80] It did not happen.

7. *Fooling the People.* The peasants-or-bankers question raises a more fundamental theoretical division between those who assume—with the original proponents of the political business cycle theory—that voters are "myopic," and do not foresee the inflationary costs of pre-election "bribes";[81] and those who prefer to assume that voters act rationally and with foresight, and therefore "cannot be routinely fooled by the government." This, the argument runs, is why American voters tend to switch allegiance in the middle of a presidential term.[82]

8. *Feeling versus Being.* A final and related possibility it that "feeling good" may be something different from actually *being* better off: in the words of Maurice Saatchi, it is "economic perceptions" not "economic facts" that count.[83] If that is so, fooling people may be more important than filling their pockets.

When voting behavior is open to so many different interpretations—nearly all of which rest on some empirical evidence—it is perhaps no wonder that the history of economics and politics has an apparently "chaotic" character, in the sense that electoral behavior appears stochastic and is unpredictable. Political equations are in fact non-linear.[84] Another way of putting this is to say that economic relationships, even if they do have some element of linearity, are frequently "drowned out" by political events. Three notable examples in recent British history are the Falklands War, victory in which undoubtedly helped to avert a Conservative election defeat in 1983;[85] the entirely avoidable crisis precipitated by the introduction of the poll tax in 1990, a measure which defied political as well as economic rationality; and the departure of sterling from the Exchange Rate Mechanism in 1992, which was at root a consequence of the rise in European interest rates caused by German reunification. To devise an equation that relates economic performance to electoral success in the British case, it is necessary to incorporate political dummy variables designed to quantify the impact of precisely these events.[86]

Does such an exercise salvage the theory of the feelgood factor? It seems doubtful. Of the eight components of David Sanders's equation designed to explain the Conservative vote between 1979 and 1997, only two are economic variables—the change in the tax index and the balance of positive over negative household financial expectations—compared with four political dummy variables (in addition to the three listed above, the advent of Tony Blair as a credible Labour leader has been included).[87] There is of course no reason why more such dummies should not be added at the author's discretion whenever the need arises to realign the model's predictions with an inconveniently diverging reality.

POLITIKVERDROSSENHEIT

If the advertising agents and "spin doctors" who have come to dominate British and American politics are right, however, then the breakdown of the relationship between *real* economic indicators and government popularity may not matter. If it is only perceptions that count, then politicians need only concentrate on buying the most effective possible election campaign, the theme of which should ideally be: "You have felt good under our party for the past few years; you will feel even better if you re-elect us for another few."

There are three reasons why this strategy is unlikely to be effective for long. The first is simply that marginal increases in human satisfaction from economic growth appear to be subject to diminishing returns. Richer people may be happier than poorer people, according to some surveys; but if all the people surveyed are asked again after five years of rapid economic growth, their reported happiness will not have increased as much as their incomes. In Japan, to give an example, real incomes have risen by a factor of five since the 1950s, but according to the surveys there has been no change in happiness.[88] Nor are the richest countries in the world home to the happiest people: according to one attempt to gauge global happiness, the United States is only the thirteenth-happiest country in the world. Iceland is the happiest. Yet in terms of GDP per capita, the United States is ranked seventh to Iceland's sixteenth.

One interpretation is that an increase in economic growth may provide a boost to the credibility of the government order, but then the effect fades as prosperity becomes the norm, or levels off. In other words, it may have been the novelty of growth that caused its electoral impact in the 1950s and 1960s: the essence of the experience of the 1950s and 1960s was not so much feeling good as feeling *better*-off.[89] A more radical possibility is that beyond a certain point rising incomes do not necessarily increase "well-being": in the psychologist Donald Campbell's striking phrase, the rich find themselves trapped on a "hedonic treadmill" of unfulfilling consumption.[90] The more frenetic pace of life in conditions of rapid growth may also heighten feelings of insecurity.[91] Alternatively, it may simply be that the conventional indicators we use to measure prosperity do not capture "disamenities"—negative side-effects—of growth, such as pollution and traffic congestion.[92]

The second reason why voters may be less and less inclined to believe political pledges to make them feel better is the phenomenon of disillusionment with politics in general. The Germans call it *Politikverdrossenheit*, which is perhaps best translated as "politics fatigue." One obvious symptom of this is the phenomenon of falling turnout at elections. There are those who maintain that turnout is mainly governed by the perceived "salience" of elections, and that provided an election appears to be important and that voting in it seems likely to have some bearing on the result, voters will not stay at home. But this overlooks the point that elections *in general* may seem less "salient" than they did thirty years ago.[93] Turnout in British general elections has fallen from 85 per cent in 1959 to 70 per cent in 1997.[94] It has declined even more markedly in local and European elections: in the latter, from 57 per cent in 1994 to just 49 per cent in 1999.[95]

At the same time, there has been a marked increase in electoral volatility:

the fickleness of voters. The proportion of British voters with a "very strong" party affinity was 47 per cent in 1964; in 1987 it was just 16 per cent.[96] In Ireland in 1981, 24 per cent of voters said they did not feel "close" to any party; eight years later, the proportion had more than doubled to 58 per cent.[97] On the continent too volatility has risen in the 1990s. The Pederson index of volatility for thirteen European systems (which adds together the change in each party's share of the vote between elections and divides by two) shows an increase from around 8 per cent for the period 1948–89 to 14 per cent for 1990–4.[98] Using an alternative measure of volatility based on the net aggregate shift in votes from one election to the next (equivalent to the total gains of all winning parties), the Italian elections of 1994 saw volatility of 37 per cent, one of highest figures for any European election between 1885 and 1989.[99] (For Germany in the post-revolutionary year 1919 the figure was 48 per cent, for France after the end of the Nazi Occupation, 36.)

The phenomenon of political fatigue is of particular concern in Germany, for obvious historical reasons; it is therefore worth pausing to consider the evidence in the German case more closely. It would certainly be misleading to lay too much stress on the fall in the percentage of Germans declaring themselves "interested in politics" from 57 per cent in 1990 to just 40 per cent in 1997. German reunification was responsible for boosting public interest in politics after 1989, an effect that wore off in 1992 but was still making itself felt in 1994 and 1995. In any case, positive interest in politics had been significantly below 40 per cent in the 1950s and 1960s (in June 1952 only 27 per cent of the population declared themselves interested in politics).[100] Nevertheless, there has undoubtedly been a marked change in attitudes towards politicians as a group in the past twenty years. In 1972 some 63 per cent of West Germans answered "Yes" to the question "Do you believe that one needs considerable abilities to become a Bundestag deputy in Bonn?" Just 23 per cent said no. In 1996, by contrast, 25 per cent of those asked said yes while 59 per cent said no. The process of disillusionment has been even more rapid in the former East German states since their accession to the Federal Republic. In 1991 some 44 per cent of former East Germans answered "Yes" to the question about Bundestag deputies' abilities; by 1996 the figure was down to 22 per cent.[101] More than two-thirds of Germans surveyed in 1995 thought that a Bundestag deputy's most important role was to represent citizens' wishes and interests, but only a third believed that their elected representatives actually gave this function priority. Almost as many thought that deputies cared as much about "the realization of their own personal ideas and goals." And more than half of those questioned in the same survey regarded their elected representatives as overpaid, while 78 per cent were opposed to a decision to increase parliamentary salaries—a point we shall return to below.[102]

The periodic surges of disillusionment with all four major political parties are also striking. In 1983 just 29 per cent of West German voters expressed themselves "disillusioned" with all the big parties; ten years later that figure reached a peak of 57 per cent. Although disillusionment declined sharply in 1993 and 1994, it rose back above 50 per cent in April 1997. East German attitudes have moved in an almost identical way since 1990.[103] Perhaps even more perplexing is the decline in public understanding of the German system of proportional representation, which gives each voter two votes, one for a constituency candidate and one for a party list; the latter vote determines the actual balance of the parties in the Bundestag. This basic fact was understood by 54 per cent of voters in 1980. In recent surveys, however, only around a quarter of voters are aware that the second vote is the decisive one.[104]

It would be quite overblown to describe these as "Weimar symptoms." The majority of today's Germans have been taught and have learned from the past to reject anti-democratic political options, especially those dressed up in nationalist or racialist garb. In any case, the phenomenon of *Politikverdrossenheit* is not peculiarly German. When French voters were asked in November 1999 how they reacted when they thought of politics, 57 per cent replied "with suspicion," 27 per cent "with boredom" and 20 per cent "with disgust." Only 25 per cent thought they were well represented by a political party or leader.[105] Nevertheless, it is always worth recalling that the most spectacular collapse of any democracy was preceded by at least some of these signs of malaise: electoral volatility, splintering of parties and public perceptions of political corruption.

There is, however, a third reason why governments may find it increasingly difficult to persuade voters that they "feel good." That is the simple fact that to do so—especially in the face of diminishing returns from materialism and mounting politics fatigue—may call for advertising campaigns more expensive than modern political parties can actually afford.

In 1956 the Democrat Presidential candidate Adlai Stevenson told his party's convention: "The idea that you can merchandize candidates for high office like breakfast cereal—that you can gather votes like box tops—is . . . the ultimate indignity to the democratic process."[106] He retained his dignity, but lost two successive elections to Dwight Eisenhower. Perhaps, as the feelgood theory suggests, Ike owed his victory to the rapid growth of the American economy in the 1950s. But the possibility that he owed it to superior campaigning cannot be ruled out. It is to that cash nexus—the link between party finance and electoral success—we now turn.

POLITICS AS BUSINESS

On the morning after the Labour Party's May 1997 election victory the *International Herald Tribune* hailed the election of "Blair & Co." Three months later the new prime minister gave an insight into his own thinking when justifying the use of "citizens' juries" to sample public opinion on specific policies: "If you're running a business like Sainsbury's or Marks and Spencer, you keep having to test what you're doing." As the *Guardian* commented: "CEO Tony Blair wants to keep his job, so he gives the customers what they really want."[107] The *Observer*, meanwhile, urged Blair to manage his party "like a modern company," giving everyone "a stake in the new governing enterprise." Such rhetoric was rapidly matched by action. There have never been so many Labour ministers drawn from the world of business as there were in Tony Blair's government in 1997. The Conservatives, the undisputed party of business in Britain since the days of Stanley Baldwin, hurried to imitate this new model of the party *as* business. In the wake of their crushing defeat, they turned for leadership to a former McKinsey's management consultant and the chairman of the Asda supermarket chain. William Hague and Archie Norman hurried to give the party a new managerial structure that vested supreme decision-making power in a "Board."[108]

This is not a peculiarly British phenomenon. All over the world, the language of management and the language of politics are tending to converge. Ross Perot's bids for the presidency in 1992 and 1996 were based on the idea that only a businessman could "turn the US round," as if it were some enormous but unprofitable company. In July 1999 the chief executive of Siemens urged the German Chancellor Gerhard Schröder to base his fiscal policy on the idea of "benchmarking . . . a familiar concept in companies, but . . . less usual in the political world."[109] In the same month the head of the Russian security council, Boris Berezovsky, explained why he believed more businessmen should seek election to the parliament: "Crudely put, capital hires the authorities for work. The form of hiring is called elections. And so far as elections take place in a competitive way, then this choice is rational."[110] Berezovsky himself made millions in car dealing and advertising before entering politics. The *Wall Street Journal* was saying much the same when it described ideas as "the only commodity in the political marketplace . . . The best ideas are what sell, the consumers are the voters, and they make their selections in the voting booth."[111] A widespread assumption is that businessmen can bring to politics distinctive skills, acquired in the corporate sphere but applicable in government: this is the essence of the media mogul Silvio Berlusconi's political appeal in Italy. In its extreme form, however, this is reduced to the notion that politics itself is simply a business.

But how far has the winning of votes become a business like any other? Perhaps the best way to pursue this analogy is to think of elections as takeover battles for the control of a major utility, which in view of its core business we might call "Welfare Inc." Welfare Inc. is a troubled behemoth, despite having a near monopoly in a number of mass markets, a vast client base of consumers (taxpayers and their dependants), most of whom are also shareholders (voters), a large number of whom receive dividends known as benefits. The company provides consumers with a wide range of services. It runs hospitals, schools and an immense road network. It is also a security company operating the police, prison and armed services. And it has controlling stakes in a range of other businesses, ranging from universities to a broadcasting company. The problem with Welfare Inc. is that—to take the British case—in nearly every year since 1973 it has made a loss. In order to carry on paying dividends it has been forced (a) to slash capital investment (b) to put up the prices of its services across the board (c) to impose periodic pay freezes on its huge workforce (d) to reduce the real value of dividends and to cease paying them altogether to certain classes of shareholder and (e) to increase central control of its regional and local branches. Small wonder that consumers (around 58 million), shareholders (43 million) and employees (3.6 million) are all dissatisfied.

Now turn to the political parties. These are much smaller entities, whose prime objective is to win and retain control of Welfare Inc. To do this, the main opposition party has to wage a protracted takeover campaign, pointing out the shortcomings of the current management. The aim of these campaigns is to persuade the shareholders (voters) to vote in favor of their bid at the next quinquennial general meeting (general election). If the opposition party succeeds in this, there follows a merger between it and Welfare Inc., as a result of which the board of Welfare Inc. is replaced by the board of the opposition. It is also possible for the opposition to assist its takeover campaign by gaining control of Welfare Inc. subsidiaries (such as local government) and infiltrating its workforce, though in recent years the centralization of public finance and the decline of the public sector unions have made these tactics less effective.

One of the most obvious differences between the business of politics and real business is the inherent implausibility of nearly all take-over bids. In opposition, a political party is little more than a cross between a think tank, an advertising agency and a leisure club (though the last of these functions has all but withered away). Unless it has substantial local or regional power, the opposition party is not in fact engaged in the business of governing that it claims to be good at. In power, however, a party is charged with managing the vast corporation that is the modern state. As in the nineteenth century, voters must be persuaded to change their allegiances, but this can no longer be achieved simply by providing free beer at the hustings. Instead they must be wooed by promises of future improvements in the management of Welfare Inc., whether in the form of higher investment, lower prices (taxes), better conditions for employees, higher dividends (benefits) or some kind of restructuring to enhance efficiency. The governing party, however, can offer all of these immediately; moreover, it has far greater resources to carry out research and to propagate policy.

It is here—in the realm of finance—that the crucial difference between politics and business is to be found. Perhaps the most striking feature of modern democracy is the wide discrepancy between the budgets of parties and that of the state they seek to manage. While the latter has, as we have seen, tended to rise in relation to gross domestic product over the past century, the former have declined dramatically. Total expenditure by candidates on the 1880 election exceeded £1.7 million.[112] In 1997 prices this amounts to over £20 per vote, compared with a figure in 1997 of 42 pence. In relation to GDP expenditure by candidates on general elections has fallen by an astonishing 98 per cent since 1880 (Figure 22).

Nevertheless, there has been an undeniable rise in the operating costs of parties in the past two decades. They now rely less on volunteers working for nothing and more on professional administrators and consultants. This was the main reason why the 1997 election was significantly more expensive than that of 1992. The Conservatives spent £24 million, Labour spent £17 million and the Liberal Democrats just under £3 million—in all £44 million, compared with total expenditures by the three major parties of £32 million five years before.[113] Figure 23 adjusts for inflation to show the marked *real* increase in election expenditure by the major parties since the 1970s. In 1997 the Conservatives spent nearly three times what they had spent in February 1974, as did Labour. Even as a proportion of GDP, total party expenditures have risen by almost 55 per cent since 1979. Moreover, these figures do not take account of the rising costs of day-to-day party management. When fig-

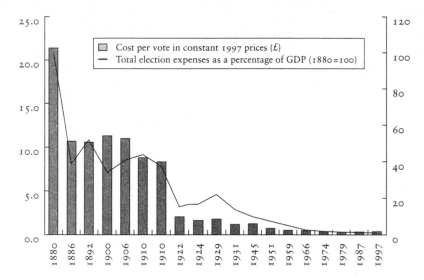

*Figure 22. The real cost of elections: candidates, declared general election
expenses, 1880–1997*

Sources: Pinto-Duschinsky, *British Political Finance,* p. 27; Butler and Butler,
British Political Facts, p. 241; Butler and Kavanagh, *General Election of 1997,*
p. 223.

ures for central party expenditure, including routine, non-election payments,
are analyzed (Figure 24), the upward trajectory of party expenditures is confirmed, most obviously for the Labour Party. The Conservatives too experienced a clear upward shift in their routine expenditures from the mid-1980s.

This problem is far from unique to Britain. In Europe the pattern has been
the same. Austrian campaign expenses doubled between 1975 and 1990; so
did those in Sweden between 1982 and 1988. Irish parties have also been
spending more and more on electioneering: Fine Gael's budget for this
quadrupled in real terms between 1969 and 1989.[114] (The Netherlands is the
exception that proves the rule: campaigns there seem to have got slightly
cheaper.)[115]

The American case is especially notorious. According to estimates in mid-
1999, the campaign to elect President Clinton's successor could cost as much
as 50 per cent more than the 1995–6 campaign.[116] Candidates for the United
States House and Senate spent $459 million in the 1987–8 two-year election
cycle, more than double the figure of ten years before. Candidates in presidential primaries spent a further $250 million, while the presidential candidates

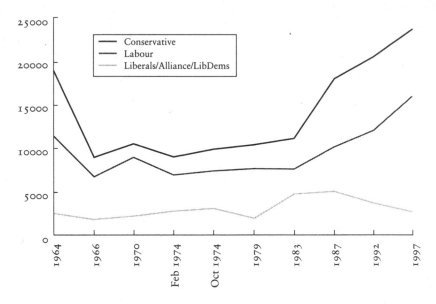

Figure 23. Total general election expenditure of the three main British parties, 1964–1997 (thousands of 1997 pounds)

Sources: Paul D. Webb, "Party Organizational Change in Britain: The Iron Law of Centralization?" in Katz and Mair, *How Parties Organize*, p. 112; Butler and Kavanagh, *General Election of 1997*, pp. 223, 242. Figures deflated using cost-of-living index.

themselves spent $90 million.[117] The equivalent figures for 1995–6 were $765 million, around $244 million and at least $153 million.[118] The round numbers are daunting by European standards. The British general election cost the three major parties little more than $66 million; yet the total cost of the federal electoral process in 1995–6 (including primaries, presidential race and elections to Congress and the Senate) exceeded $2 billion.

As in the British case, it is true, there is a need for a long-term perspective. In nominal terms, the total cost of a presidential electoral cycle may have risen by more than a quarter between 1987–8 and 1995–6. But in real terms, adjusting for inflation, the cost was more or less unchanged. And in relation to GNP, the cost of a presidential election cycle has actually *fallen* from 0.016 per cent to 0.014 per cent. As those tiny numbers suggest, the cost of American democracy is not as burdensome as is commonly supposed. It is worth remembering that the entire amount spent on elections in 1996 was slightly

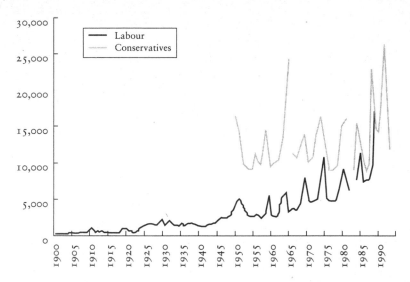

Figure 24. Conservative and Labour parties, central expenditure (routine and election), 1900–1992 (thousands of 1997 pounds)

Sources: Pinto-Duschinsky, *British Political Finance,* tables 11, 15, 21, 23, 25, 28, 31, 38; *idem,* "Trends in British Party Funding," tables 1 and 2; Butler and Butler, *British Political Facts,* pp. 133, 151.

less than the advertising budget of the Philip Morris tobacco company the year before.[119]

Nevertheless, there are a number of crucial ways in which the cost of American politics has tended to rise. Adjusted for inflation, total spending by the two major parties on federal elections rose by more than a fifth between 1983–4 and 1995–6. The increase was almost entirely registered by the Democrats, whose inflation-adjusted expenditures rose by 86 per cent. Also in real terms, the amount of federal funds contributed to presidential candidates rose by 28 per cent between 1980 and 1996. Although total expenditures on Congressional Senate elections remained more or less constant in real terms during the 1990s, the decline in the number of contested elections concealed rapidly rising spending in contested seats. Spending by Political Action Committees has also risen in real terms: by 54 per cent in the case of contributions to candidates for the House, 64 per cent in the case of the Senate.[120] And there has been a surge in the amount of "soft money," raised by National Party Committees for so-called "party-building activities," from $86 million in 1992 to $262 million in 1996.[121]

The difficulty is that parties are seeking to win votes, not to sell a product that generates revenues. They are therefore reliant on sources of finance that are, from a business viewpoint, abnormal. Membership dues can, of course, be likened to subscriptions to newspapers, but neither parties nor newspapers can rely on these alone (and parties cannot sell advertising). In any case, party political membership is nearly everywhere in decline.

In Britain in 1953, as Table 11 shows, the Conservatives could claim to have nearly three million members. By the late 1990s the figure had fallen by 86 per cent to just 400,000. The number of individual members of the Labour Party peaked in 1952 at 1,015,000; there were more than five million corporate (mainly trade union) members.[122] Despite the success of the New Labour recruitment drive, individual membership at the time of writing remains around two-fifths of its 1953 peak.[123]

The full extent of the crisis is best gauged by calculating individual party membership as a percentage of the UK population. Figure 25 shows that in relative terms Labour Party membership in the 1980s had sunk to a level not seen since the 1920s.

A similar process is now discernible on the continent. In Austria, for example, membership of the main parties peaked in around 1980 and has since fallen. Despite the success of the Freedom Party (FPÖ) in attracting new members, total party membership as a percentage of the electorate fell from 29 per cent in 1962 to 23 per cent in 1990.[124] In Denmark membership of

Table 11. Individual membership of the three major British political parties, 1953–1997

	Labour*	Conservative	Liberals/Alliance
1953	1,005,000	2,805,832	n/a
1960	790,192	2,800,000	243,600
1969	681,000	1,750,000	n/a
1974	691,889	1,500,000	190,000
1983	295,344	1,200,000	n/a
1987	288,829	1,000,000	137,500
1992	279,530	500,000	100,000
1997	420,000	400,000	103,000

*Excluding corporate members.
Sources: Webb, "Party Organizational Change," p. 113; Butler and Butler, British Political Facts.

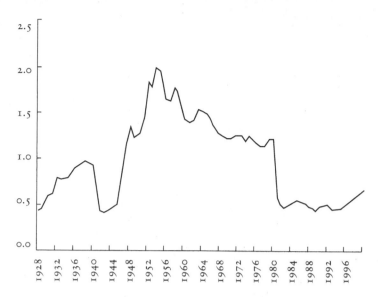

Figure 25. Individual Labour party membership as a percentage of the UK population, 1928–1997

Source: Butler and Butler, *British Political Facts*, pp. 146f., 323.

the four main parties fell from 600,000 in 1960 to 220,000 by end of 1990; the four new parties which emerged in that period managed to recruit a mere 28,000 members, just 0.7 per cent of electorate.[125] Holland too has seen party membership fall from 745,000 in 1960 to 320,000 at beginning of the 1990s: from 15 per cent of the electorate in 1946 to less than 4 per cent.[126] In Italy there has been a collapse of membership of the three main parties since 1993, which new organizations like the Northern League have not been able to compensate for. Labour and Conservative party membership is also down in Norway; and a large proportion of those who choose to remain party members do not pay their dues.[127] As the distractions of modern life have multiplied, it seems, political activity has lost its social and economic appeal. Members are no longer content to turn up at party gatherings just to lick stamps and be addressed by some minor party figure; nor are many willing to spend their leisure time pounding the pavements to canvas local voters.[128]

The only exceptions to this flight from the parties are Sweden and Belgium. In the former, total membership has remained constant at around 1.5 million, so that its share of the population has only declined slightly (from 21 per cent in 1960 to 18 per cent in 1989).[129] Remarkably, the Swedish Social Democrats can still claim membership equal to 46 per cent of their total vote.[130] In Belgium too, party membership as a percentage of the total electorate has held steady, albeit at the much lower level of 8–10 per cent.[131]

The effect on party finances of declining party membership everywhere else can readily be imagined. In the case of the British Conservative Party, constituency income (that is, from party members) declined from 14 per cent of total party income in 1988–9 to below 6 per cent in 1994–5.[132] In Austria membership dues have fallen as a percentage of the Socialists' total income from 43 per cent (1975–8) to 36 per cent (1986–9).[133] In Germany, it is true, membership dues still account for around half the Social Democrats' total income, 40 per cent of Christian Democrats' and 25 per cent of Bavarian CSU's—rather more than in the 1960s.[134] But no European party can expect to rely on membership dues as a source of income on this scale for much longer.

The decline of party membership, coinciding as it has with the rising cost of elections, has plunged many parties into an acute financial crisis. The Conservatives' accumulated deficit rose from just £500,000 in 1975 to £19 million in 1992, though this has since been reduced to around £10 million. In 1999 Labour's debts were estimated at £3.5 million plus an overdraft of £4.75 million—and this despite the fact that a substantial number of the marketing experts working for the Shadow Communications Agency gave their services for free. In 1992–3 the Irish political parties were estimated to have debts of around £I 5.5 million, an immense sum for such comparatively small organizations.[135]

All this explains the increasing reliance of so many political parties on private donations. In recent years the veils that have traditionally concealed Conservative Party finance have been drawn back. In 1987, for example, the party raised nearly £15 million, of which £4 million came from public companies, another £4 million from private companies and around £6 million from individuals.[136] As a proportion of Tory party income, it has been estimated, company and individual donations rose from just under 78 per cent in 1988–9 to 83 per cent in 1994–5.[137] For the following year, a detailed breakdown is available of donations by public companies, which reveals that the Conservatives received 120 donations totalling £2.88 million, including seven of over £100,000.[138] Between 1979 and 1993 United Biscuits led the field, donating more than a million pounds to the party.[139] A more complete disclosure by the party itself in November 1998 revealed a list of thirty-three donors who had given £5,000 or more, though the total sums were not specified. The party was to all intents and purposes bailed out after its 1997 defeat by its party treasurer, the Belize tycoon Michael (now Lord)

Ashcroft.[140] This reliance on foreign money was not new: the party had received around £7 million from foreign backers before the 1992 elections. Among the foreign donors were the Greek shipping tycoon John Latsis and the suspected fraudster Asil Nadir.[141]

A more novel feature of the past decade has been the increasing importance of business donations to the Labour Party, which had, as we have seen, traditionally relied on the trade unions for the bulk of its funding (92 per cent in 1974).[142] Business fund-raising accounted for hardly any Labor revenue in 1986, while nine years later *Labour Research* was able to identify only 12 business donations totaling £1.25 million. By 1996 the figure was over £6 million, compared with trade union contributions of £8 million.[143] Altogether between June 1996 and March 1997 the party raised no less than £15 million from business.[144] Despite talk of increasing trade union contributions in 2000, it seems unlikely that the party will ever be able to return to its previous reliance on organized labor.

In many ways, the dependence of British parties on big individual donors represents organizational *regression*: a return to the political institutions of the age of Trollope.[145] But British political donations are small change by American standards. According to the Washington-based Center for Responsive Politics, federal parties and candidates were able to raise around $1.5 billion in the form of individual contributions, donations to Political Action Committees and "soft money" in the 1997-8 election cycle—a period in which there was no presidential election. Contributions from the Finance, Insurance and Real Estate Sector alone amounted to more than $154 million.[146] Though most of this money comes from a relatively small number of rich institutions, there are some signs of an increase in "small political investors." By July 1999 around 160,000 individuals had made donations to the campaigns of George W. Bush and Al Gore.[147]

The question is: why not?

THE POLITICAL ECONOMY OF SLEAZE

Gibbon ironically called corruption "the most infallible symptom of constitutional liberty."[148] Certainly, the 1990s saw a rash of corruption scandals in nearly all the major democracies. By the end of 1996 two-thirds of the British electorate regarded the Conservative Party as "sleazy and disreputable."[149] Where power has changed hands more regularly than in Britain, such sentiments are felt towards politicians in general. For example, a survey in Austria in 1989 found that 69 per cent of people agreed that "politicians were corrupt or bribable," nearly twice the figure a decade before.[150] In November 1999 some 61 per cent of French voters agreed with the statement that "elected politicians and political leaders in France are generally corrupt." The statement was endorsed by 75 per cent of voters between the ages of 18 and 25.[151]

But is modern politics especially venal? Suppose it was revealed that the British prime minister had taken a decision which had caused shares of a particular company to rise by 25 per cent. Such things are far from unknown. But then suppose it turned out that the prime minister personally owned shares in that firm with a market value before the decision of £17 million. As a direct result of his action, his shares had increased in value by £7.5 million. It is hard to believe that even the popular Mr Blair would survive such a scandal.

It was in fact William Ewart Gladstone who in late 1875 acquired £45,000 (nominal) of the Ottoman Egyptian Tribute loan of 1871 at a price of just 38 per cent of par (£17,100). As the editor of his diaries revealed, he had added a further £5,000 (nominal) by 1878 (the year of the Congress of Berlin); and in 1879 bought a further £15,000 of the 1854 Ottoman loan, which was also secured on the Egyptian Tribute. By 1882, these bonds accounted for no less than 37 per cent of his entire portfolio (£51,500 nominal). Even before the British military occupation of Egypt in 1882—which he himself ordered—these proved a good investment: the price of the 1871 bonds rose from 38 to 57 in the summer of that year. The British takeover brought the prime minister still greater profits, however: by December, the price of 1871 bonds had risen to 82—a total overall capital gain of nearly £20,000 on his initial investment in 1875.[152] Assuming a 25 per cent rise in the value of his total holdings of Egyptian-Ottoman bonds in the second half of 1882, Gladstone personally made £12,785 from the decision to occupy Egypt. In today's prices, that amounts to at least half a million pounds. Allowing for growth as well as inflation, the present-day equivalent of Gladstone's gain from the invasion would indeed be £7.5 million.

The belief that modern-day politicians are more corrupt than in the past is almost universal. The 1997 British election campaign was dominated, and in some respects won, by allegations of "sleaze" directed against the Conservatives by all the opposition parties. By Victorian standards, however, British politicians are remarkably scrupulous in separating their public role and their private interests.

It is important when speaking of "sleaze" to distinguish between sexual transgressions, a part of the human condition; inconsequential venality, another such; and authentic corruption, when government policy is constrained or determined by private interests, whether of donors or ministers themselves. Although there was no shortage of the first two kinds of scandal in the government of John Major, the third was largely conspicuous by its absence.

Leaving aside the comical but essentially trivial first category, the majority of Conservative financial scandals in fact related to the efforts of MPs to bolster their own salaries by, for example, asking parliamentary questions in return for money, or otherwise acting in support of a private interest.[153] Venality of this sort is tempting to professional politicians, not least because their salaries are pegged below those of their peers in other professions. In real terms British MPs' salaries doubled between 1911 and 1964; but for the next thirty years they stagnated, averaging less than £30,000 a year (in 1997 prices). Although the allowance for office expenses was increased in real terms after its introduction in 1969 (and actually exceeded the basic salary in 1986), this cannot really be regarded as equivalent to pay.[154] Even the 26 per cent increase to £43,000, agreed in 1996, can hardly be said to make the job a financially attractive one—though it may be asked what kind of private sector job is equivalent to that of a legislator. Moreover, the tightening of the rules requiring the declaration of MPs' interests has made it hard for politicians to accept paid directorships or consultancies to supplement their income. Trollope would have been mystified by the notion of a Member of Parliament with no outside interests and income.

Even harder to justify is the discrepancy between ministerial salaries and those of senior executives managing comparably large budgets. When the Senior Salaries Review Body looked into this it explicitly compared the prime minister's job with that of "a huge multinational company in a sector (such as oil) requiring massive capital investment and exerting a clear influence on the world economy." But on this basis, the prime minister ought to be paid at least £450,000; and his Cabinet colleagues, as executive directors of the same company, at least £375,000. Instead, it was recommended that Cabinet ministers' pay should rise from £69,651 to £103,000, and the prime minister's from £84,217 to £143,000. In his capacity as chairman of Unilever, the head of the self-same Review Body, Sir Michael Perry, had received a total annual package the previous year amounting to £2.94 million.[155] It is hardly surprising that politicians seek to supplement their salaries as directors and consultants.

But to repeat: to be meaningful, the term "corruption" must signify that private interests influence government policy, presumably—though this is assumed more often than it is proven—to the detriment of the public interest. For this reason, payments to ministers give more cause for concern than payments to MPs, whose job it is to represent interests. The only serious complaint that can be made against an MP who accepts money for posing a question on behalf of a company is that he is neglecting to represent the rest of his constituents, who as taxpayers pay his salary, when he does so. But then every question an MP asks on behalf of a constituent implies a neglect of the interests of the rest. The idea that all interests can be represented equally is (as eighteenth-century parliamentarians understood) a fiction. When ministers accept cash or gratuities it is another matter. Jonathan Aitken's gratis stay in the Paris Ritz in 1993 differed from Neil Hamilton's a few years later mainly because Aitken was a junior defence minister at the time, and his bill was picked up by the Saudi government, which was bidding to lease some British submarines.[156] Similarly, when it was revealed in 1998 that Peter Mandelson's London home had been purchased with an undeclared loan of £373,000 from his fellow-minister Geoffrey Robinson, the real scandal lay in the fact that Mandelson's own department was conducting an investigation into Robinson's business affairs at the time he owed the money.[157] In neither case, however, does it seem very likely that policy was influenced one way or the other: it was the denial or concealment of the transactions that constituted the mischief.

One reason why overt purchases of policy have been relatively rare in recent British history is the role of the honors system. The sale of honors was supposedly made illegal by the Honours (Prevention of Abuse) Act of 1925, after Lloyd George flagrantly auctioned off peerages for £50,000 apiece. However, the persistence of the practice can hardly be denied. No more than 6 per cent of companies make donations to the Conservative Party, but half of all knighthoods and peerages have gone to directors of those companies.[158] On the other hand, it is far from self-evident that this is an unacceptable trade-off, particularly in the case of purely honorific knighthoods. As a form of recompense for political donations, decorations and titles—though not seats in the Upper House—are fairly unobjectionable, a point usually overlooked by critics of the honors system. In the United States no such system exists, though the offer of a night in the White House's Lincoln bedroom for $250,000 might be considered roughly analogous.

Somewhat less innocent is the practice of selling access to members of the executive. Here too Bill Clinton has been a pioneer, as videotapes of White House coffee mornings for donors revealed. In 1998 it emerged that advisers to Labour Ministers were also selling access to their superiors for cash donations to the party.[159] Yet coffee with the head of the executive is just coffee: ground beans, hot water—but no binding policy pledge. The crucial question is how far donations are tied to specific political commitments. It seems clear, for example, that President Clinton gave licenses to Democrat-funding companies to export high-technology equipment to China, with potentially deleterious consequences for American national security. This kind of transaction is particularly overt with respect to certain agricultural interests: some protective American tariffs and subsidies (notably those for peanut- and sugar-producers) undoubtedly owe their continued existence to conditional donations. The practice is less overt in Britain, though business-men (and trade union leaders) have certainly attempted—who knows how often?—to secure policy pledges in return for money. Before the 1997 election, for example, Bernie Eccleston tried to secure, by means of £1 million donation to the Labour Party, an exemption for Formula One from the party's proposed ban on tobacco advertising in sport.[160]

It is here that the analogy between business and politics breaks down. For there is a fundamental incompatibility between the ethos of modern democracy and that of modern business with respect to the returns on investment. In theory, a donor to a political party is making a gift, no different in purpose from a donation to a charity distributing medicines to the poor of Africa. The "return" on a gift is the intangible fulfillment of an ethical imperative. In practice, most large political donors do expect a return; and in that sense they regard payments to politicians as investments, or at least insurance premiums, rather than pure gifts. But precisely this idea of a policy return on a political investment is regarded as illicit by most liberal political theorists—a view shared by the electorate. It is primarily for this reason that most democracies have introduced legislation to regulate political finance. The effect of this legislation, however, is to distort the political market so much that parties are simply unable to behave in the way that firms in other sectors do.

FROM PRIVATE TO PUBLIC CORRUPTION

Politicians have an interest in trying to limit the costs of electioneering. The public has an interest in limiting the influence of rich donors over policy.[161] These may seem straightforward rationales for regulating political finance. But both statements need qualification. For politicians, the costs of election campaigns pose a classic game-theoretical problem akin to the famous prisoners' dilemma. If two rival parties co-operate to limit campaign expenditure, the total cost of an election is held down to the benefit of both winner and loser. But the temptation not to co-operate is very great, since the benefit of winning—power—exceeds the cost of even an expensive election. Whatever the rules say, both "prisoners" are likely to renege on any deal in the belief that doing so may secure victory. At the same time, the public also has an interest in leaving the cost of running political parties to someone else. The reluctance of individuals to join political parties suggests a fundamental lack of interest in this form of representation. If rich individuals and corporations are willing to pick up the bill for election campaigns, the majority of voters may not object, even if the result is that elected representatives are "in hock" to investor-donors. It is these dilemmas that make the regulation of political finance so difficult.

A clear majority of democracies now have some kind of statutory control of campaign finances: only the Netherlands, Sweden and Thailand do not. Most democracies have sought to regulate party finance in three ways: by trying to cap political expenditures; by trying to cap private donations; and by offering public funding to political parties as an alternative to private money. In Britain limits on local expenditures date back to the Corrupt Practices Act of 1882, which imposed a ceiling on candidates' individual election expenses (excluding Returning Officers' charges) according to the number of electors in a constituency. This had the effect of halving the average amounts spent by those contesting seats. The expenditure limit in the late 1980s, following successive revaluations in every General Election since the 1960s, was £3,240, with an additional 3.7p for each voter in the counties and 2.8p in the boroughs.[162] Certain types of expenditure by candidates have also been outlawed, such as radio transmissions, posters, transport to and from the poll, and bribery in cash or kind.[163] Only recently has the idea of a cap on central spending been raised. In October 1998 the Committee on Standards in Public Life chaired by Lord Neill recommended that national general election spending be limited to £20 million per party; and that campaigns by pressure groups on behalf of parties should not exceed £1 million in cost. To adopt this would be to follow the example of Canada, where the Election Expenses Act of 1974 placed strict limits on party spending both at the center and in the constituencies.[164] The Canadian experience, however, shows that spending caps do not necessarily narrow gaps between different parties' financial strength. Campaign expenditure limits have simply caused parties to focus their attention on their regular operating costs.[165] Most countries now also impose at least indirect caps on expenditure by banning paid-for political advertisements on television (only 12 out of 45 countries in a recent survey allow these, while France also bans press advertising, posters and even free phone lines). Here too the effect is more to divert than to dam the flow of cash.

Attempts to limit expenditure in the United States have been more limited. Amendments to the Federal Election Campaign Act of 1974 aimed to impose mandatory spending caps, but these were struck down two years later by the Supreme Court (Buckley *v.* Valeo), on the ground that they limited free speech and therefore violated the First Amendment. As a result, the main check on political finance is the $25,000-a-year ceiling on an individual's political donations which was the 1974 Act's main provision; and the more recent ban on foreign donations.[166] In theory, companies and trade unions were also banned from contributing under the Act, though "voluntary contributions" by shareholders or employees were declared legal in 1975.[167] More importantly, the two main parties' National Committees have been able to raise hundreds of millions of dollars in "soft money" for "party building," "getting out the vote" and other purposes supposedly not specific to particular candidates' campaigns. In practice, the "issue ads" funded by soft money are indistinguishable from other campaigning propaganda.

The only real check on American political finance, then, is the fact that information on the sources of campaign funds is relatively easy to obtain: all donations over $250 have to be declared. Other countries (including Britain and Canada) rely mainly on disclosure rather than ceilings to regulate private donations. Thus Lord Neill recommended that only foreign donations to British political parties be banned, but that all national donations in excess of £5,000 should be declared. In Germany any gift of more than DM20,000 ($10,300) must be published; in France anything above a mere 1,000 francs ($150). The French also limit donations to Assembly candidates to 50,000 francs.

The regulation or limitation of private political donations forms part of a wider transformation of party finance, however. Nearly all democracies have gone a step further by offering substantial public funding directly to parties. Only around seven democracies today give parties no direct subsidies, though systems vary (the most common gives money to parties on a per vote or per seat basis). Today—startlingly—private sources of funding count for more than public sources in only three major democracies: the Netherlands, Britain and the United States.[168] Moreover, thirteen systems give additional indirect subsidies (such as tax breaks for contributions to parties, as in the

US, Canada and Germany); while at least twenty-three democracies give parties free television airtime.

Even in Britain public funding of parties is growing. Between 1979 and 1992, the principal Opposition parties received more than £9 million in so-called "Short money" to assist their parliamentary work: Labour alone received £7.2 million.[170] This is intended to counter the advantage enjoyed by the party in power in the form of civil service resources. In addition, meeting-halls, postal services and television airtime are provided free at election time; while gifts to political parties are exempt from some taxes.[170] In the United States too, state funding is more extensive than is generally recognized. The Presidential Election Campaign Fund matches the first $250 of each individual contribution made to primary candidates in return for a promise that they will remain within an inflation-adjusted fund-raising limit; and then gives presidential candidates a lump sum in return for not accepting any further private donations. In 1996 the two main candidates received about $13.5 million apiece in Federal Matching Funds. Each major party is also entitled to a public subsidy ($11 million in 1992) to cover the costs of the presidential nominating convention.[171]

The role of the state is proportionately greater in Europe. Already in 1989 state payments to Irish parties amounted to I£ 4 million, compared with total party income from other sources of just I£ 2.7 million.[172] In Holland state funding as a share of party income ranges from 14 per cent to 31 per cent.[173] German parties that gain more than 2 per cent of the vote have their election expenses automatically reimbursed, while the state pays increasing amounts to the "party-near" foundations like the Social Democrats' Friedrich Ebert Foundation. The number of party *Fraktion* employees paid for by the state has also risen from 115 in the 1960s to 619 in the late 1980s, and Bundestag deputies contribute a share of their salaries to their parties, which could be regarded as a form of state funding.[174] After a series of arms sales scandals, the French introduced state reimbursement of presidential candidates, amounting to 6 million francs if they attracted less than 5 per cent of the vote on the first round of the contest, and 30 million if they were able to get more than 5 per cent. Central parties were granted their own subsidies, which amounted to 262 million francs by 1991.[175] Almost everywhere in Europe the story is the same:

- In Denmark the total direct public subsidy to the main parties increased from 57,262 krone in 1965 to 72.4 million in 1990.[176]

- In Austria national and regional subsidies for parties have risen in the past twenty years from less than 400 million schilling to around 1.75 billion.[177]
- In Italy state funding to parliamentary groups and election campaign funds rose from 60 billion lire to 183 billion between 1974 and 1985.[178]
- In Norway the total state subsidy to the parties has risen from 8 million krone in 1970 to 58.7 million in 1991.[179]
- In Spain parties' private fund-raising is limited to just 5 per cent of their state subsidy.[180]

Indeed, it is not too much to say that the political parties of the West are slowly being nationalized. They run the risk of becoming mere appendages of the state.

But is state funding a genuine remedy for the problem of corruption (to be precise, of conditional private donation)? Or might it be (as Karl Kraus once said of psychoanalysis) "the disease of which it pretends to be the cure"? In the first place, it is far from clear that public funding displaces private funding. It may just as easily supplement it, even when caps are imposed on private funding. Despite public subsidies, it has been estimated that Italian parties received a total of 60 billion lire a year (in 1986 prices) in illegal funding between 1979 and 1987. Another estimate of these *tangenti* in 1993 put them at a staggering 3.4 trillion lire a year, ten times the parties' official income.[181] State funding does not seem to have sufficed for the German Christian Democrats either: witness the sums raised illegally by the party under Helmut Kohl.[182]

Even if such malpractice can be prevented, it must seriously be doubted whether the increasing identity between political parties and the state is desirable. If one views the modern state as the impartial arbiter of Weberian theory, this may indeed be a step towards the nirvana of "unpolitical politics." But if one regards the state as possessing a "grabbing hand"—as being the custodian of its own self-interest, rather than the public interest—then it is disquieting to see the political parties losing their traditional autonomy. In the old German Democratic Republic there was a variety of political parties when people went to the polls: but they were all integral parts of the state and therefore constituted no real alternative to the Socialist Unity Party. Western Europe will end up recreating a rather different but almost as artificial democracy if once independent parties become beholden to Finance

Ministries. What is the electorate to make of politicians who seek election in order to pay themselves money . . . to seek re-election?

TOWARDS THE POLITICAL MARKET

Clearly, no amount of regulation is likely to reverse the organizational evolution of established parties from mass-membership voluntary associations into quasi-firms bidding with ever more sophisticated and expensive campaigns to manage Welfare Inc. Increasing regulation of party finance may serve merely to increase the level of hypocrisy and mendacity in democratic life.

One possible development is that, partly because of the regulations imposed on them, the established parties may find themselves challenged, if not actually replaced, by single-issue pressure groups or (as they prefer to be called) non-governmental organizations (NGOs). In Britain today, around twenty times more people belong to voluntary or self-help groups than are members of political parties.[183] The Royal Society for the Protection of Birds alone has more members (a million in total) than the three principal political parties put together.[184] The protracted debate about whether or not to ban fox-hunting in Britain nicely illustrates the different forms such new "grassroots" organizations can take: on the one hand, a number of comparatively small but aggressive and active animal rights groups; on the other, a loose "alliance" of hunters, farmers, rural dwellers and suburban sympathizers. What is more, electronic communication clearly makes it easier than in the past to mobilize large numbers of people rapidly in support of a particular cause.

Yet it is striking that, to date, the opponents of hunting have come closest to achieving their aim—a nationwide ban on hunting with hounds—by donating £1 million to the Labour Party. This kind of interaction between extra-parliamentary organizations and parties is not new: similar roles were played by the Anti-Corn Law League in the mid-nineteenth century, the Temperance movements in both Britain and the United States until the 1920s, or the Campaign for Nuclear Disarmament and its continental equivalents in the 1950s and 1980s. To say that single-issue groups will play an important role in the democracy of the future is to say, once again, that the future will be like the past. The difference is that today's pressure groups, like today's parties, must organize themselves in a far more business-like way than those of the past. And although they can currently count more on voluntary support than established political parties, sooner or later the NGOs are likely discover that the costs of effective lobbying in an increasingly expensive political market are outstripping their revenues from membership dues and one-off appeals. In strictly economic terms it is not efficient to create a new political organization, with all the attendant overheads, each time one wishes to achieve a policy objective. One reason the Liberal Party came into existence in the nineteenth century was precisely because a host of Victorian single-issue groups saw the wisdom of pooling their resources for the purpose of securing power in the legislature.[185]

The real question is whether or not the established parties should be freed from the present, largely perverse, constraints on their activities. What would be the effect of ending not only the restrictions on private funding of political activity but also the anomalies in the system of public funding? Suppose that instead of disbursing taxpayers' money to all candidates for election to parliament, there was a redistribution of resources to make ministerial salaries comparable with equivalent private sector employment. It is at least possible that high ministerial salaries would attract more talented people into politics as a career, while reducing the pressure on ministers to act on behalf of rich backers when in office. Suppose too that the only regulation imposed on party finance was the requirement to disclose the source of donations and to publish accounts to the standard expected of public companies.

The conventional argument is that such a "free market" in politics would benefit the rich and exclude the poor from political influence. Perhaps it would—though it would not change the fact that in a democracy all "shareholders" in the state have equal voting rights, regardless of their contributions to party finances. A party whose platform consisted of tax cuts for the top 0.5 per cent of taxpayers might raise a fortune in donations from the rich, but would almost certainly lose to a party that campaigned to deliver improved public services without altering the tax burden—provided the second party could secure a donation of at least a pound from every beneficiary of such a policy. On balance the risks of a political free market may be less than the risks of excessive regulation.

The essential point is that political parties—those essential institutions of a functioning democracy—are being denied the funding they need by rules aimed to curb private influence, and at the same time forced into an unhealthy dependence on the state. Yet the stigmatizing of private donations to parties is in many ways irrational; it is a little like saying that the rich should not be allowed to buy more shares in a company than small investors, or to donate more money to charity than average earners. Worse, the nationalization of the parties threatens to replace genuine competition between free political associations with the machinations of a homogeneous state *apparat*.

A political market in which there were no restrictions on overt private donations and minimal public subsidies would not necessarily breed corruption: it might well reduce it by removing the need for subterfuge. This is not to recommend a return to Trollope's Silverbridge; but rather to suggest that Western politics is already uncomfortably close to a new kind of corruption every bit as bad for democracy as that which thwarted Trollope's political ambitions.

SECTION FOUR
GLOBAL POWER

9

Masters and Plankton:
Financial Globalization

The Masters of the Universe were a set of lurid, rapacious plastic dolls
that his otherwise perfect daughter liked to play with. . . . They were
unusually vulgar, even for plastic toys. Yet one fine day, in a fit of euphoria, after he had picked up the telephone and taken an order for zero-
coupon bonds that had brought him a $50,000 commission, *just like
that*, this very phrase had bubbled up into his brain. On Wall Street he
and a few others—how many?—three hundred, four hundred, five hundred?—had become precisely that . . . Masters of the Universe.

Tom Wolfe, Bonfire of the Vanities[1]

TERRIFYING EVERYBODY

Early in Bill Clinton's first, unsteady hundred days as President, his campaign
manager James Carville remarked that, if there was such a thing as reincar-
nation, he wanted to come back, not as the President or the Pope, but as the
bond market—because that was what really ruled the world. "That way,"
as he put it, "you can terrify everybody."[2] He was alluding to the market's
(mildly) nervous reaction to the arrival at the White House of the first Democrat president since Jimmy Carter. In the two months before Clinton's election, as his chances of success grew, the markets had pushed up US long-term
bond yields by 35 basis points[3] at a time when yields in most other major
economies were declining. Early Clinton initiatives on health care and homo-
sexual soldiers were not reassuring to the masters of the universe.

The global bond market is certainly terrifyingly big. Between 1982 and
1997 it increased in size by a factor of six, to around $25 trillion.[4] By mid-
1999 the total value of bonds outstanding had reached $34 trillion. That
exceeds not only the total capitalization of all the world's stock markets
($27.5 trillion in 1999) but also the total GDP of all the world's countries
($30.1 trillion in 1997). More than half of all bonds in 1999 were issued by

governments or other public sector agencies. And just under half of all bonds were of American origin.

The rise—or rather, renaissance—of the bond market in the 1980s is often associated with the mercurial career of Salomon Brothers.[5] Salomon's star has since waned; but American institutions remained the principal market makers in the 1990s. In 1997 around 90 per cent of total bond issuance was issued by just twenty firms (of which Merrill Lynch, Morgan Stanley and J.P. Morgan accounted for around a fifth).[6] The point of Carville's remark was, however, that despite its dominance by American banks, the bond market is not the president's to command—even a president who has just won a decisive election victory. There are too many individual and institutional investors with too much money—and too many of them are not American. At the time of Clinton's inauguration, more than 13 per cent of US federal government bonds were in foreign hands.

The extraordinary growth of the bond market has to be seen in the context of a broader process of financial "globalization." Flows of capital have increased dramatically in the past twenty years. In 1980 cross-border transactions in bonds and equities (shares issued by companies) were equivalent to just 8 per cent of Japanese GDP; in 1998 the figure was 91 per cent. For the United States, the increase has been even greater: from 9 per cent to 230 per cent. German cross-border transactions have risen from 7 per cent to 334 per cent of GDP.[7] International bank lending too has expanded exponentially. Between 1993 and 1997 gross international bank claims rose from $315 billion to $1.2 trillion. Though the growth of lending was lower in 1998, the total outstanding stock of international bank claims still reached a record high of $11 trillion at the end of that year.[8] The daily turnover on the world's foreign exchange markets rose from $1.6 trillion in 1995 to $2.0 trillion in 1998, implying annual flows of more than $400 trillion.[9] And the growth of international derivatives markets has been even more rapid. The total amount of futures and options instruments traded on exchanges rose from $7.8 trillion at the end of 1993 to $13.5 trillion at the end of 1998. The amount of so-called "over-the-counter" (OTC) instruments traded outside established exchanges rose from $8.5 trillion to an astonishing $51 trillion.[10] The OTC derivatives market is now by any measure the biggest financial market in the world—more "terrifying" even than the $34 trillion bond market.

Strictly speaking, only around 14 per cent of bonds are international; around $29 trillion were classified as domestic in 1999, meaning they were issued within the borrowing country (see Appendix C). Moreover, the public sector accounts for less than a third of international bonds. But the proportion of government bonds that are held by foreign investors is still remarkably high. Even in the early 1990s, as Table 12 shows, external debts amounted to between a sixth and a half of the national debts of most major economies. In Britain and the United States the trend has been clearly upwards since the end of the 1970s. Non-residents hold 19 per cent of UK long-term bonds ("gilts" for short) in 1999, compared with less than 6 per cent in 1979. Foreigners held 23 per cent of the gross US federal debt in 1998, nearly double the proportion fifteen years before. That represents more than 14 per cent of American GNP. For most of the 1990s, foreign purchases of US long-term bonds (usually known as "Treasuries") played a crucial part in financing the American balance of payments deficit, which in 1999 reached its highest level since 1960 (3.9 per cent of GNP). Net foreign investment in the United States also reached a record level in 1999 at 14.6 per cent of GNP.[11]

Is this financial globalization unprecedented, as cheerleaders of the "new economy" would have us believe?[12] Does the bond "mountain" pose "a latent threat to the global financial system," as some have warned?[13] And does it matter that the world's only superpower is so heavily indebted to foreigners—in stark contrast to the net creditor position of Great Britain in her

Table 12. Foreign holdings of developed countries' national debts, circa 1993

Country	Foreign debt as percent of total debt
Austria	19.1
Belgium	15.8
Finland	65.1
Germany	48.7
Italy	14.5
Netherlands	21.3
Spain	17.0
Norway	29.9
Sweden	50.5
US	14.2
UK	16.6

Source: Eichengreen and Wyplosz, "Stability Pact," p. 103, except US (Federal Reserve Bank of St Louis) and UK (Bank of England).

heyday? This chapter shows how the institutions of public debt management described in Section Two were internationalized in the course of the nineteenth century; and draws some historical lessons from the way the international bond market functioned—and then malfunctioned—in the first age of globalization.

CAPITAL FLOWS: BETWEEN POLITICS AND THE MARKET

International capital flows are not a new phenomenon. They have always occurred when there have been large-scale international movements of goods and people.

For most of modern history, capital export has been motivated by a mixture of economics and politics. The economic rationale of capital export is to secure higher returns than would be possible from a domestic investment. Even short-term credits would not have been granted to foreign merchants in medieval times if there had not been the prospect of better profits than from internal trade. Yet from the time of the Hundred Years War, if not before, cross-border capital flows also tended to be necessitated by overseas military campaigns. The English kings who laid claim to all or part of France sent armies across the Channel to enforce their claim. Only a fraction of their supplies could be shipped over from England; it was always easier to transport money and buy provisions where the action was. It was better still, as later governments realized, to pay another state already on the right side of the Channel to do the fighting for you. Both operations necessitated the transfer of funds from London to an overseas theatre of war. A very large part of the history of international capital markets is bound up with this basic military exigency.

In theory, it ought to be possible to distinguish between private, profit-motivated capital export and public, strategically motivated capital export. In practice, however, the categories tend to overlap. Often, private overseas investment has been officially sanctioned and has sometimes therefore come with political strings attached. There are numerous cases of loans intended to help foreign governments reform themselves—if only to turn them into more dependable allies. The most obvious examples in the late nineteenth century were the immense French loans to Russia, which were designed not only to finance the Russian railway network but also to secure Russia's allegiance in the event of a war with Germany.[14] For investors, on the other hand, their own government's backing has the attraction of reducing the risk of default by the foreign borrower. Sir Ernest Cassel said of the Rothschilds—who accounted for roughly a quarter of all foreign government bond issues in London between 1865 and 1914—that they "would hardly take up anything that did not have the British government guarantee about it."[15] This was an exaggeration, but a pardonable one. When the German banker Max Warburg was approached by the Japanese government to float a loan in 1904, during the Russo-Japanese War, he "did what any sound banker has to do in such a case: I went to the Foreign Office in Berlin."[16]

There are three fundamental problems with foreign (as opposed to domestic) investment as a purely economic proposition—though they are also part of its allure. It is harder to ensure that a foreign borrower honours his obligations than to ensure payment of interest and capital from a borrower living under the same national jurisdiction as the lender. Defaults present more serious problems for foreign than for domestic bondholders, because the former have no voice in representative institutions and may be less able to use the legal system to press their claims against the government.[17] It is also harder to be sure that a foreign borrower will put overseas funds to good use: what economists call "informational asymmetries" are generally greater the further the lender is from the borrower. Finally—though this has not always been the case—lending across borders can involve an additional risk quite distinct from default risk; namely the risk that the exchange rate of the currencies of lender and borrower may unexpectedly change, to the disadvantage of one of the parties depending on the terms of the loan contract.

At the same time, there are three fundamental problems with the idea of conditional foreign lending as a political lever. The first is that, as with the basic problem of lending, it is far from easy to oblige a foreign borrower to carry out any promised reforms or international obligations. Indeed, once money has been handed over, it may allow a bad government to resume or even worsen its wicked ways. (This was the perennial problem of lending to the Ottoman Sultan.) The second problem is that the costs of debt service may, particularly when a tax system is regressive, generate revolutionary political developments within the borrower country which are the very opposite of those desired by the lender. Thirdly, there is the possibility that, for purely economic reasons of the sort described above, capital may be withdrawn at short notice despite the political arguments for continued lending. The deleterious effects of sudden capital outflows may undo the benefits of previous inflows. Only if a loan is effectively nationalized—as happened when the United States government took over Britain's war debts from J. P. Morgan in 1917—can the political rationale prevail over the economic.

Underlying this analysis, of course, is the assumption that there will be one or more capital-exporting powers with a political or strategic agenda. As we shall see, this has usually been the case. What makes the late twentieth century unusual is the absence of such a financially hegemonic power.

ORIGINS OF THE BOND MARKET

Though medieval monarchs often turned to foreign bankers for loans,[18] and some Italian cities allowed obligations to be sold to non-citizens,[19] an international bond market in the modern sense did not begin to emerge until the sixteenth century.[20] Philip II and Philip III did not finance their wars simply by moving bullion from the Americas via Spain to the Netherlands; they also relied on the development of an international market in *asientos* and *juros* to fill the perennial gap between tax revenue and military expenditure.[21] As early as the reign of Elizabeth I, a substantial proportion of the English crown's debt was also financed in Antwerp;[22] though London began to develop as an international financial centre in its own right during the seventeenth century.

By the middle of the eighteenth century there was a high degree of integration between the London and Amsterdam markets. Shares in the Dutch and British East India companies, the Bank of England, the South Sea Company and later British consols were traded with minimal price differentials or time-lags in both centres. The bubbles of the 1720s inflated and burst in all the major financial centres with remarkable synchronization.[23] Evidence of market integration can also be found in the registers of shareholders' names. By 1750 total foreign holdings in the big three British companies stood at over 19 per cent. A significant proportion of the total national debt—in the region of 14 per cent—was also held by foreigners, mainly Dutch investors, a figure which rose above 16 per cent by 1776.[24] Frankfurt meanwhile played a comparable role in financing the debt of the Habsburg Empire and channelling the capital of the wealthy Elector of Hesse-Kassel into a variety of European bonds.[25] Austrian bonds were also sold and traded in Antwerp, Amsterdam, London, Geneva and Genoa.[26]

Hanoverian Britain had long made war indirectly by subsidizing continental allies. Between 1757 and 1760, for example, Frederick the Great had received British subsidies worth £670,000 a year.[27] But the scale, duration and cost of the wars of the period between the Declaration of American Independence and the Battle of Waterloo meant that such transfers spiralled upwards. Between 1793 and 1815 Britain paid £65.8 million in the form of subsidies to her allies, half of it in the last five years of the war.[28] That represented between a fifth and a quarter of a year's national income. By 1823 the total advances to Austria alone amounted to £23.5 million, of which the government ultimately had to write off all but £2.5 million.[29] The combined cost of such payments and the need to put ever larger British armies in the field necessitated enormous cross-border transactions. These could not have been achieved without the existence of two complementary markets: the market for government bonds and the market for commercial bills.[30]

Bonds might raise funds internally in advance of taxation; but they could not be sold to foreigners in sufficient quantities to facilitate transfers to the actual theatres of war. In the Seven Years War the Exchequer purchased bills of exchange from London merchants which were drawn on their correspondents abroad; these were then sent to the quartermasters in the field who could use them to pay troops and purchase supplies. Foreigners were happy to accept bills drawn on London, because they could be exchanged for sought-after British manufactures and colonial goods. Napoleon's continental system was an attempt to thwart this by choking off British exports to the continent. But continental merchants were generally happy to hold on to their bills on London, or to invest their balances in consols, in the expectation of an ultimate British victory.[31] When bills could no longer be used in payment other than at ruinous discounts, Nathan Rothschild stepped in, using his own extensive credit network to buy up bullion wherever he could and then advancing it to the British government. In 1815 alone Rothschild and his four brothers lent the government a total of £9.8 million which they paid directly to Britain's armies and allies.[32] As soon as this operation ceased to be profitable, they invested the proceeds in consols, in the correct expectation that prices would appreciate as the pound was restored to convertibility and the budget restored to balance.

Britain's foes were capable of similar transactions, though they could not match the scale of Rothschild operations. Of the $77 million of 6 per cent bonds issued by Alexander Hamilton to fund the deficit of the new-born United States, $12 million were purchased by foreigners; nearly half the US debt was in foreign hands by 1803. Indeed, the Louisiana purchase would have been impossible if Napoleon had not been willing to accept such bonds in payment.[33] The Emperor also invested a million francs of his own in a Prussian state loan; in 1811 he put over three millions in Saxon bonds.[34] But

Napoleon preferred to conquer and tax rather than to borrow money from abroad; and this limited his resources just as it ultimately limited Hitler's after him. There was a certain complementary quality to the British and French systems: the British lent the Austrians money, the Austrians lost in battle and Napoleon then seized some of the originally British funds by imposing an indemnity.[35] Yet Napoleon might have got more out of his victories—for example, if he had tapped rather than choked the Amsterdam capital market. By 1803 per capita taxation in the "Batavian" Republic—as the conquered Netherlands were renamed—was more than four times higher than in France; but the bourse which had once been the world's largest was prostrate.[36]

"THE TRUE LORDS OF EUROPE"

After 1815 there was a gradual spread of what contemporaries came to think of as the British financial system. As we have seen, the defining characteristics of this system were: a professional tax-collecting bureaucracy, parliamentary and public scrutiny of budgets, a funded national debt guaranteed by parliament and a central bank with a partial monopoly over note issue. The gold standard and free trade were later and optional adjuncts to this system. But free capital movement was from the outset an integral part of it, for it was only through the London bond market that the continental European fiscal systems—to say nothing of the North and South American republics that had secured their independence in the war years—could be stabilized in the post-war period.

Between 1818 and 1832 twenty-six loans were floated in London on behalf of foreign governments with a nominal value of £55.8 million.[37] One of the first of these, the Prussian loan of 1818, illustrates the way attempts were made to export the British institutional model along with British capital.[38] From the outset of the negotiations, Nathan Rothschild argued that any loan would have to be secured by a mortgage on Prussian royal domains guaranteed by the representative estates of the domains concerned. When the Prussians demurred, Rothschild spelt out his reasons for wanting such a guarantee:

[T]o induce British Capitalists to invest their money in a loan to a foreign government upon reasonable terms, it will be of the first importance that the plan of such a loan should as much as possible be assimilated to the established system of borrowing for the public service in England, and above all things that some security, beyond the mere good faith of the government . . . should be held out to the lenders . . . Without some security of this description any attempt to raise a considerable sum in England for a foreign Power would be hopeless[;] the late investments by British subjects in the French Funds have proceeded upon the general belief that in consequence of the representative system now established in that Country, the sanction of the Chamber to the national debt incurred by the Government affords a guarantee to the Public Creditor which could not be found in a Contract with any Sovereign uncontrolled in the exercise of the executive powers.[39]

In short, a constitutional monarchy was seen in London as a better credit risk than a neo-absolutist regime.[40]

Admittedly, Rothschild was prepared to settle for much less than parliamentary control in the Prussian case: the final contract merely stated that "for the security of the creditors" there would be a special mortgage on the royal domains, which were "wholly disposable according to the House[hold] Law of November 6, 1809, passed by H.M. the King of Prussia and the princes of the royal house with the assent of the provincial estates."[41] This was a long way from British-style parliamentary control. On the other hand, there is an obvious link from Rothschild's negotiations to the subsequent Clause 2 of the "Decree for the Future Management of the State Debt" of January 1819, which imposed a ceiling on the state debt, earmarked revenues from the royal domains for debt service, and declared: "If the state should in future for its maintenance or for the advancement of the common good require to issue a new loan, this can only be done in consultation with and with the guarantee of the future imperial estates assembly."[42] This meant that any future loan by the Prussian state would automatically lead to the summoning of the estates; in other words, it conceded the link between public borrowing and constitutional reform. The 1819 decree explains why of all the German states Prussia borrowed the least in the 1820s and 1830s and why, when the policy of retrenchment broke down in the 1840s, the consequences were revolutionary.

As the key player in the world's biggest market, Rothschild was the prototype financial master of the universe. In May 1818 he fired off a letter to the Director of the Prussian Treasury which perfectly captures his sense of his own power—the power of money: "The cabal there [opponents of the Rothschild loan at the Prussian court] can do nothing against N. M. Rothschild, he has the money, the strength and the power, the cabal has only impotence and the King of Prussia . . . should be well pleased and thank Rothschild, who is sending you so much money [and] raising Prussia's credit."[43] Small wonder, then, that Carville-esque remarks about the power of the Rothschilds and their rivals turn up time and again in the correspondence of nineteenth-century politicians, as well as in the writings of journalists, novelists and poets. "Who hold the balance of the world?" asked Byron in Canto XII of *Don Juan* (1823):

> Who reign
>   O'er Congress, whether royalist or liberal?
> Who rouse the shirtless patriots of Spain?
>   (That make old Europe's journals squeak and gibber all.)
> Who keep the world, both old and new, in pain
>   Or pleasure? Who make politics run glibber all?
> The shade of Bonaparte's noble daring?—
> Jew Rothschild, and his fellow Christian Baring.
>
> Those, and the truly liberal Laffitte,
>   Are the true lords of Europe. Every loan
> Is not a merely speculative hit,
>   But seats a nation or upsets a throne.

In Disraeli's *Coningsby* the elder Sidonia is described as having foreseen in 1815 that "after the exhaustion of a war of twenty-five years, Europe must require capital to carry on peace. He reaped the due reward of his sagacity. Europe did require money, and Sidonia was ready to lend it to Europe. France wanted some; Austria more; Prussia a little; Russia a few millions. Sidonia could furnish them all." As a result he became "lord and master of the money-market of the world and of course virtually lord and master of everything else. He literally held the revenues of Southern Italy in pawn; and monarchs and ministers of all countries courted his advice and were guided by his suggestions."[44]

The key to the power of the Rothschilds is that they were a truly multinational partnership, with "houses" in London, their birthplace Frankfurt, Vienna, Naples and Paris. It was not only Nathan who inspired contemporary fascination; it was the fact that he was the *primus inter pares* of five "Finance Bonapartes" (the phrase was coined by Metternich's Secretary Friedrich von Gentz). Balzac's Nucingen, for example, is very obviously modelled on Nathan's brother James: a "Louis XIV of the counting house," an "elephant of finance," who "sells deputies to the ministers and the Greeks to the Turks"—in short, the personification of "the age of gold in which we live."[45] To the young Heine, writing in the 1820s, James and his elder brothers appeared to be a bulwark of the reactionary post-Vienna order:

Without the Rothschilds' help, the financial embarrassment of most states would have been exploited by subversives wanting to mislead the populace into upsetting whatever order or disorder constituted the status quo. Revolutions are generally triggered off by deficiency of money; by preventing such deficiencies the Rothschild system may have served to preserve peace in Europe.[46]

MEASURING POLITICAL RISK, CIRCA 1830–1870

Yet despite such contemporary assessments of the Rothschilds' power, the bond market was prone to violent and unpredictable crises which were beyond the control of even the biggest player.

In the early 1820s the London market was inundated with bond issues by South American states (including a number that did not actually exist); but the tightening of fiscal and monetary policy in Britain, combined with political instability in the debtor states, led to a disastrous crash in 1825. Brazilian bonds which the Rothschilds had issued at a price of 85 fell to 56; Mexican, Colombian and Peruvian bonds all fell below 20.[47] Latin monarchies proved no more reliable than Latin republics. Portugal and Spain attracted investors in the 1830s, but they proved almost as unreliable as the Latin American states in the 1820s. By the late 1830s the Rothschild brothers privately referred to Iberian bonds in their correspondence as "shit." Nor was it only Hispanic states that defaulted. Between 1837 and 1843 eight North American states did so too.[48] The years 1847–9 witnessed the worst European financial crisis of the century, the effects of bad harvests and revolution. Recovery in the 1850s was also precarious. A succession of wars beginning with the Crimean War and continuing with the wars over Italian and German unification generated new bond issues in Europe, but at the same time increased the risks to investors. Because few countries joined Britain on the gold standard before the 1870s, these risks included not only default but depreciation.

In making their assessments about sovereign bonds, modern investors tend to look first at the most recent indicators of fiscal and monetary policy, for example budget deficits as a percentage of GDP or monthly monetary growth rates; their assessment will be in some measure informed by knowledge of the figures of preceding years. In the words of one celebrated bond salesman: "The American bond market . . . lurches whenever important economic data is [sic] released by the US Department of Commerce. . . . The markets decide what is important data and what is not. One month it is the US trade deficit, the next month the consumer price index."[49] In the past, however, there were fewer economic data on which to base judgements about default-risk or future inflation and depreciation. Early nineteenth-century investors had fairly good and regular information about certain commodity prices, gold reserves, interest rates and exchange rates, but fiscal information apart from annual budgets was few and far between, and there were no regular or reliable estimates of national income. In non-parliamentary monarchies, even annual budgets were not always available or, if they were published, could not be relied upon. There was no headline cost-of-living index before the First World War.

Instead, evidence from contemporary sources strongly suggests that mid-nineteenth century investors were more likely to infer changes in fiscal and monetary policy from political events. Among the most influential bases for such inferences were four assumptions:

1. that a political move to the left, ranging from outright revolution to a change of ministry due to elections, would tend to loosen fiscal and monetary policy;

2. that a new and radical government would be more likely to pursue an aggressive foreign policy which might, in turn, lead to war;

3. that any war would disrupt trade and hence lower tax revenues for all governments (in the words of the French premier Villèle in the mid-1820s, "Cannon fire is bad for money");[50] and

4. that direct involvement in war would increase a state's expenditure as well as reducing its tax revenues, leading to substantial new borrowings.

Though to some extent truisms, it is clear that all these assumptions owed much to the experience of the period between 1793 and 1815: war involving a revolutionary France was the markets' biggest nightmare. Indeed, the experience of the 1790s—when revolution, war, default and inflation had sent the yields on French securities soaring from 6 to 60 per cent[51]—reverberated, like the Marseillaise, for nearly a century: in 1830, in 1848 and in 1871. Each time Paris sneezed, to paraphrase Metternich, the European markets caught cold (though London tended to rally as capital left Paris for the safer market across the Channel). Nevertheless, it was only with the end of the Boulanger crisis (1887–8) that the fear finally disappeared of a French domestic political upheaval leading to a European war.

Figure 26 allows us to trace quite precisely—on a weekly basis—the fluctuations of the bond yields for four of the five great powers in the London market between 1843 and 1871 (prices of Prussian bonds were not quoted in the source for the data).[52] The stories are markedly different. British yields were lower than other yields throughout. Austrian yields tended to rise, while French and Russian yields followed markedly different paths in between. Part of the explanation for these differences was obviously the divergence of exchange rates, since only Britain was on gold, while France was bimetallic and both Russia and Austria were on (and sometimes off) silver. However, exchange rate regimes can only explain a part of the volatility of yields in this formative period. Of equal, though not entirely separable, importance were political events, particularly wars and revolutions. Indeed, anyone with an elementary knowledge of European history will be able to formulate a persuasive *prima facie* explanation for nearly all the major yield increases in the figure.

Table 13 summarizes the magnitude of bond market crises precipitated by the principal wars and revolutions of the period. A number of striking points emerge. For example, the biggest crisis on the European bond market in the nineteenth century occurred during the two months after the outbreak of the 1848 revolution in Paris. In London, Austrian and French bonds were both severely hit, with yields rising by as much as 662 basis points in the former case and 505 in the latter. But even Russian bonds were affected, though there was no revolution there. Only British bond yields fell in this period, reflecting as much the recovery of the British money market from the financial crisis of 1847 as the switching of investors from continental bonds into safer consols. Clearly, the market as a whole had no expectation of a revolution in London, which was used as a safe haven by many continental investors.[53] The outbreak of the Crimean War had an effect on all major bonds, including even consols, for obvious reasons: but it is interesting that Austrian yields rose even faster than Russian (by 243 basis points as against 175). This differential between a manifestly over-stretched Habsburg regime and its rivals widened disastrously in the wars of 1859 and 1866: Austria's defeat by France and Italy pushed yields up by more than 400 basis points, and her defeat at the hands of Prussia by just under 300. (Consol yields also rose in 1866 but, since this was due to the financial crisis caused by the collapse of the Overend Gurney discount house, I have omitted the figures.)

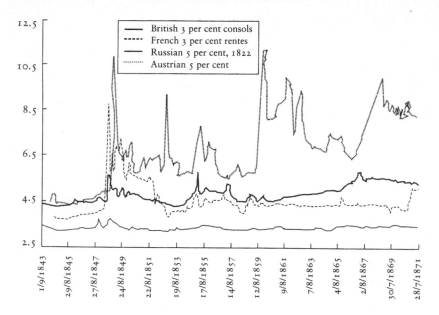

Figure 26. Unadjusted yields on European bonds, London prices, end of week, 1843–71

Source: The Economist.

Note: Breaks are due to markets being closed (in 1847–8) or prices not being quoted in London (especially true in the case of Austria before 1870).

Austrian yields remained high because after May 1870 they were formally excluded from the London stock exchange following the 1868 conversion operation, which had been combined with a tax on foreign as well as domestic bondholders.[54]

That nineteenth-century investors priced bonds in response as much to political news as to less accessible fiscal or monetary indicators is not difficult to demonstrate. Thus we find James de Rothschild assessing the implications of the revolution in France in October 1830: "You can't begin to imagine what might happen should we get war, God forbid, for if that were the case, then all the securities would suffer such a fall that it would be impossible to sell anything."[55] A month later he sought to quantify the risk: "We have a holding of 900,000 rentes; if peace is preserved they will be worth 75 per cent, while in case of war they will drop to 45 per cent . . . I am convinced that if peace is maintained rentes will improve on three months by at least 10 per cent . . ."[56] From an early stage it was the possibility of

Table 13. Wars, revolutions and the bond market, 1830–1914

	Event	Britain		France		Russia		Austria	
	Starting date	Peak date	Increase	Peak date	Increase	Peak date	Increase	Peak date	Increase
1	27/7/1830	8/2/1831	67	2/4/1831	273				
2	22/2/1848			7/04/1848	505	7/4/1848	172	28/4/1848	662
3	2/6/1853	31/3/1854	52	7/4/1854	106	24/3/1854	175	31/3/1854	243
4	19/4/1859	29/4/1859	18	20/5/1859	50	27/5/1859	46	24/6/1859	426
5	7/6/1866			8/6/1866	9	8/6/1866	29	26/4/1867	298
6	2/7/1870			31/3/1871	181				
7	24/4/1877	4/5/1877	5	27/4/1877	12	27/4/1877	60	27/4/1877	59
8	4/2/1904					10/5/1906	129		
9	28/6/1914	31/7/1914	22	31/7/1914	5	31/7/1914	52	31/7/1914	42

Key:

1 1830 Revolution: revolt against Charles X's 5 ordinances
2 1848 Revolution: revolt in Paris after ban on banquets
3 Crimean War: British fleet ordered to Dardanelles
4 Austro-Italian War: Austrian ultimatum to Sardinia to disarm
5 Austro-Prussian War: Prussian troops occupy Holstein
6 Franco-German War: Leopold of Hohenzollern's acceptance of Spanish throne
7 Russo-Turkish War: Russia declares war on Turkey
8 Russo-Japanese War and 1905 Revolution: outbreak of war
9 Approach of First World War: assassination at Sarajevo

Source: *The Economist* (except for the figures for 1830, which are based on data from Rothschild Archive and the *Spectator*).
Note: All increases in basis points (one per cent = 100 basis points). Figures for 1914 not strictly comparable because of market closure after 31 July.

war that concerned him far more than the change of dynasty. After all, as the poet and journalist Ludwig Börne remarked wryly, the new king's relations with the *haute banque* were so close that he had "taken the title Emperor of the five per cents, King of the three per cents, Protector of bankers and exchange agents." James's brother Salomon was relieved to watch Louis Philippe take the coronation oath to uphold a slightly revised constitution: "Thank God that we have come so far that the matter has ended so well, for otherwise the rentes would not have stood at 79 but would have fallen to

39, God forbid."[57] But there was always the danger that Louis Philippe would not be able to restrain his ministers, some of whom found memories of the 1790s distinctly intoxicating. As James's nephew Nat put it, during a later French crisis, "In general when troops begin to move bondholders are frightened . . ."[58]

Towards the end of his career, James de Rothschild's tendency to assess political events in these terms had become the stuff of bourse legend. "So, M. le baron," the Piedmontese premier Cavour was heard to ask James de Rothschild a month before his country's French-backed war against Austria in 1859, "is it true that the bourse would rise by two francs the day I resign as Prime Minister?" "Oh, monsieur le comte," replied Rothschild, "you underestimate yourself!"[59] Rothschild responded similarly to Napoleon III's inflammatory speech at Auxerre on 6 May 1866, in which the Emperor denounced the treaties of 1815. Once Napoleon had assured France's neighbours, "L'Empire, c'est la paix" ("The Empire means peace"). But now, declared Rothschild, "L'Empire, c'est la baisse": literally, "the Empire means a falling market."[60]

It was not only bankers who thought this way. In 1840, as Palmerston intransigently rejected the French premier Thiers's bids for a face-saving compromise over the Eastern Question, King Leopold of the Belgians told his niece Queen Victoria:

Politics are uppermost in people's minds, and everybody has been more or less loosing [sic] by the funds and other securities tumbling head over heels I see with some satisfaction that the English funds that were before the [abortive Anglo-French] Convention at 91 are now at 87 and were even less, I hope this will rouse our friend Melbourne [the British Prime Minister].[61]

Disraeli was another eminent Victorian who grasped the interrelatedness of war crises and financial crises. In January 1859, on the eve of the Franco-Italian challenge to Austria, he wrote to the Earl of Derby: "The alarm in the City is very great: 'the whole of the Mediterranean trade is stopped.' The reduced value of securities is not less than 60 millions sterling, the greater part in France. Another such week will break the Paris bourse. 'And all because one man [meaning Napoleon III] chooses to disturb everything.'"[62] Even the Marquess of Salisbury occasionally lapsed into the idiom of the Stock Exchange, observing drily (with respect to the lack of outside investment in Ireland): "Capitalists prefer peace and 3 per cent to 10 per cent with the drawback of bullets in the breakfast room."[63]

Nor was this a peculiarity of British "gentlemanly capitalism." When reflecting in January 1865 on the likely outcome of the struggle for mastery in Germany, one French diplomat commented shrewdly, if not quite accurately, that "Prussia stood above par in politics as on the bourse."[64] Bismarck too appreciated the significance of the bond market. Indeed, he relished putting one over on Amschel von Rothschild in February 1854, when he heard the news of the Russian ambassador's recall from Paris: "I considered whom I could best frighten thereby. My eye fell on [Amschel] Rothschild. He turned as white as chalk when I gave him the news to read. His first remark was, 'If only I had known it this morning'; his second, 'Will you do a little business with me tomorrow?' I declined the offer in a friendly way, thanking him and left him to his agitated reflections."[65] Bismarck himself later became the object of speculation. When the British ambassador Lord Ampthill called on Gerson Bleichröder in 1882, he reported seeing a telegram (from the Paris Rothschilds) asking for immediate news of the Kaiser's health. "I asked Bleichröder what effect French financiers expected from the Emperor's death upon the Paris Bourse. 'A general *baisse* of from 10–15 per cent,' he replied, 'because of the uncertainty of Bismarck's tenure of office under a new reign.'[66]

EMPIRE

It is often forgotten that, until the end of the 1860s, France and Britain were more or less neck and neck as foreign lenders. Between 1861 and 1865 the value of government loans floated in Paris was almost exactly the same as the value of loans issued in London.[67] It was only after the German defeat of France in the war of 1870–1 that Britain forged decisively ahead. If Europe was, in Herbert Feis's famous phrase, "the world's banker," then from 1870 until 1914 Britain was the bank's head office.[68]

There were two great waves of British capital export between 1870s and the First World War. Between 1861 and 1872 net British foreign investment rose from just 1.4 per cent of GNP to 7.7 per cent, falling back to 0.8 per cent in 1877. It then climbed back to 7.3 per cent in 1890, before once again dipping below 1 per cent in 1901. In the second upswing, foreign investment reached an all-time peak of 9.1 per cent in 1913—a level not subsequently surpassed until the 1990s.[69] In absolute terms, this led to a huge accumulation of foreign assets, rising more than tenfold from £370 million in 1860 to £3.9 billion in 1913—equivalent to more than 140 per cent of GNP.[70] Put differently, the share of British wealth invested abroad rose from 17 per cent in 1870 to 33 per cent in 1913.[71] No other country came close to this level of foreign investment: the closest, France, had foreign assets worth less than half the British total, Germany just over a quarter. Britain accounted for something like 44 per cent of all foreign investment on the eve of the First World War.[72] Far from "starving" British industry of investment, as has sometimes been alleged, this capital outflow effectively paid for itself. In the 1890s net foreign investment amounted to 3.3 per cent of gross national product, compared with net property income from abroad of 5.6 per cent. For the next decade, the figures were 5.1 and 5.9 respectively.[73]

The reasons for the outflow have been endlessly debated ever since J. A. Hobson's *Imperialism* (1902), which argued that Britain's unequal society was generating more savings than could be invested at home. This does not appear to have been the case.[74] Lenin's argument during the war was that overseas investment had been a response to declining domestic returns; and subsequent research has found some evidence for this. Returns on domestic investments were markedly lower between 1897 and 1909 than they had been in the 1870s. Moreover, even allowing for the higher degree of risk involved, the returns on foreign securities were rather better (by between 1 and 2 per cent) than those on domestic securities when averaged out over the period 1870–1913.[75] This averaging conceals substantial fluctuations, however. Domestic securities were sometimes a better investment than comparable overseas securities—for example, in the decade 1887–96 and in the last three pre-war years.[76] A more recent interpretation relates capital flows to the high dependency ratios in the New World, where couples married young and had more and healthier children than their counterparts in the old country; savings rates were correspondingly low.[77]

As Hobson's title suggests, writers have long tended to assume that there was a link between British capital export and British imperialism. There is certainly no question that the boom in overseas lending from London coincided with a dramatic expansion of British colonial rule. In 1909 the territorial extent of the British Empire was 12.7 million square miles, compared with 9.5 million square miles in 1860: an increase of exactly a third. Some 444 million people lived under some form of British rule on the eve of the First World War, a quarter of the world's population. Only one in ten British subjects lived in the British Isles themselves.

It is true that between 1865 and 1914 only around a quarter of total British investment went to the Empire, whereas 45 per cent went to other foreign economies. Moreover, the overall rates of return on investments in the

Empire seem to have declined in relative terms: they were around two-thirds higher than returns on domestic investments in the period before 1884, but two-fifths lower thereafter.[78] By the late nineteenth century strategic considerations increasingly outweighed economic ones in extending the imperial frontier.

Yet this is not to say that overseas investment outside the Empire had no political significance. Between 1865 and 1914 around 35 per cent of all British overseas investments in quoted securities was in public sector bonds; while most of the rest was concentrated in sectors general characterized by a high level of government interest, if not intervention, such as railways, mines and public utilities. Only 4 per cent was in manufacturing.[79] In 1862 it was calculated that the aggregate capital of national debts in the world was £2.6 billion, of which more than a quarter was quoted on the London Stock Exchange. Ten years later the total had risen to £4.6 billion and the proportion quoted in London to 53 per cent.[80] Foreign or colonial government issues rose from around 6 per cent of the total value of securities quoted on the London Stock Exchange in 1853 to 26 per cent in 1883 (see Figure 27). There were many countries which Britain could not govern directly, but whose governments were nevertheless dependent on British investors.

The relationship between capital export and British imperialism—both formal and informal—is well illustrated by the contrasting cases of Egypt and Turkey. In the aftermath of the Crimean War, both the Sultan in Constantinople and his vassal the Viceroy (or "Khedive") in Cairo had begun to accumulate huge and ultimately unsustainable domestic and foreign debts. Between 1855 and 1875 the Ottoman debt increased from around 9 million Turkish lire to around 251 million. In relation to the financial resources of the Ottoman government this was a colossal sum: as a percentage of current revenue the burden rose from 130 per cent to around 1,500 per cent; as a percentage of expenditure, interest payments and amortization rose from 15 per cent in 1860 to a peak of 50 per cent in 1875.[81] By 1877 the Turkish debt had reached 251 million lire, of which, after commissions and discounts, the Treasury in Constantinople had received just 135 million. Nor was the money put to good use. Millions were squandered by the Sultan Abdul Mejid on the new Dolmabahçe palace, a seraglio with the proportions of the Gare du Nord.

The Egyptian case was similar: between 1862, the date of the first Egyptian foreign loan, and 1876, the total public debt rose from 3.3 million Egyptian pounds to 76 million, roughly ten times total tax revenue; in addition, the Khedive Ismail owed around 11 million pounds on his own private

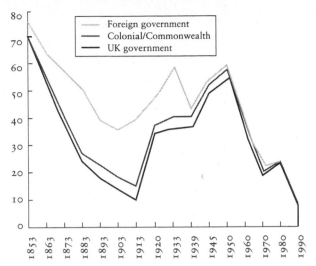

Figure 27. Government bonds as a percentage of all securities quoted on the London Stock Exchange, 1853–1990

Source: Michie, *London Stock Exchange*, pp. 88 f., 175, 184, 320, 322, 360 f., 419, 421, 440, 473, 521 F., 589 f.

Notes: From 1883, figures include foreign government bonds payable abroad but quoted on the London Stock Exchange. To 1933 nominal values; from 1939 market values.

account. In the 1876 budget, debt charges amounted to more than half (55.5 per cent) of all expenditure.[82] Compared with other major borrowers on the international market (such as Brazil or Russia), Turkey and Egypt were out of control. Brazilian and Russian debts were never much more than three times greater than total tax revenue, while debt service typically accounted for less than 15 per cent of total spending. In fact, the closest parallel to the Middle Eastern experience was in Spain, which also defaulted in the 1870s.

The gradual transformation of Egypt from an Ottoman fiefdom into a British dependency began with the declaration of Turkey's bankruptcy in October 1874. It was this that forced the Khedive to offer his shares in the Suez Canal to the British government for £4 million—an enormous sum, equivalent to more than 8 per cent of the entire British budget net of debt charges, but one the Rothschilds were able to advance Disraeli in a matter of days, if not hours.[83] In the wake of this coup, a new Caisse de la Dette Publique was established to place Egyptian finances under the supervision of representatives of Britain, France, Italy and Austria—the main creditor countries. It fixed the consolidated debt at £76 million (a figure which did not include £15 million of private debts secured on the Khedive's lands and a substantial floating debt which may have been as much as £6 million).[84] In 1878 the Caisse recommended that an "international" government be appointed with an Englishman as Finance Minister and a Frenchman as Minister of Public Works.[85] In April 1879, however, the Khedive dismissed the international government, which had predictably made itself unpopular with Egyptian taxpayers. The powers duly re-imposed their authority by replacing the Khedive with his son Tewfiq; but a nationalist military revolt led by Arabi Pasha finally drove the British government to direct military intervention. In July 1882 Alexandria was shelled, and by September Arabi had been overthrown. It was the beginning of a prolonged, though never unabashed, occupation. Between 1882 and 1922 Britain felt obliged to promise the other powers no fewer than sixty-six times that she would end her occupation of Egypt. British troops did not leave until June 1956, returning briefly and ignominiously the following November in a vain attempt to prevent the nationalization of the Canal.

Though the occupation of Egypt was partly a strategic riposte to French activities in Tunisia, the financial rationale of the British action was thinly veiled. In 1884 the First Lord at the Admiralty, Lord Northbrook—a member of the Baring banking family—was despatched to Egypt to enquire into the country's finances; his cousin Evelyn Baring (later Lord Cromer) was already in Cairo as consul-general. It was the latter Baring who did much of the work of stabilizing Egyptian finances.[86] The absolute debt burden was reduced from a peak of £106 million in 1891 to just £94 million in 1913; simultaneous increases in taxation meant that the debt/revenue ratio halved. Yet Cromer was also able to raise enough new foreign money to carry out substantial infrastructural investments.[87] This can hardly have been bad for Egyptians. It was certainly good for foreign bondholders. The British occupation of Egypt in 1882 pre-empted complete default and ensured an exceptionally high real rate of return on Egyptian bonds.[88] The Canal shares also proved to be an extraordinarily good investment for the British Treasury. By January 1876 they had risen from around £22 to more than £34, an increase of more than 50 per cent. The market value of the government's stake was £24 million in 1898, £40 million on the eve of the First World War and £93 million by 1935 (around £528 a share).[89] Between 1875 and 1895 the government received its £200,000 a year from Cairo; thereafter it was paid proper dividends, which rose from £690,000 in 1895 to £880,000 in 1901.[90]

By contrast, Russian and later German interest in Constantinople made it impossible to go beyond great power supervision of Ottoman finances (the pagoda-like offices of the international Administration de la Dette Publique can still be seen in Istanbul today). As a result, Turkish government and finances carried on much as before. In 1889, after the major debt rescheduling of 1881, the debt/tax revenue ratio was 8.7 : 1; by 1909 it was back above 10, as it had been in 1879. As a percentage of expenditure, debt service rose from 12 per cent in 1890 to 33 per cent in 1910, the year of the Young Turks' revolt.[91] The real returns on Ottoman debt were correspondingly low (1.6 per cent, compared with an anticipated return of 7.4 per cent).

The problem with "informal imperialism"—investment in the absence of direct political control—was that financial control was harder to impose, so that the risk of default remained high. Between 1880 and 1914 nearly all the biggest defaults, apart from that of Turkey, were in Latin America (Argentina in 1890, Brazil in 1898 and 1914 and Mexico in 1910). As Table 14 makes clear, countries under British control—Australia, Canada and Egypt— offered overseas investors markedly higher real returns than independent states like Japan, Russia and Turkey. On average, Latin American states lay somewhere in between, though Mexico stands out because of its repeated defaults.

THE PARADOX OF CONVERGENCE, 1870–1914

From the 1870s until 1914 there was a marked convergence in the long-term interest rates of most major economies. Yield spreads between British consols and more or less equivalent French, German, Russian, Italian and American long-bonds all tended to fall. For example, Italian yields, which were close to double British yields in 1894, had fallen to just 54 basis points above them by 1907.[92] Figure 28 presents monthly data for yield spreads relative to consols for a sample of seven countries for which monthly data are available. Although part of this convergence was due to the rise of consol yields from their all-time nadir of 2.25 in July 1896 to 3.6 per cent in July 1914, the main reason for convergence was the decline in yields on the bonds of the other great powers.

Economic historians have offered three distinct, though not mutually exclusive, explanations for this phenomenon. One is simply the high level of integration of global capital markets. A number of studies have shown that there was an extraordinary—and as yet unmatched—disconnection between saving and investment in the period 1880–1914 because of international

Table 14. Anticipated and real premiums on selected international bonds, 1850–1983

	1850–1914		1915–1945		1945–1983		Total amount lent for whole period
	ex ante	*ex post*	*ex ante*	*ex post*	*ex ante*	*ex post*	*in m. 1913 US$*
Argentina	2.15	1.71	2.05	1.95	4.93	4.70	1,943
Brazil	1.91	0.88	3.34	1.48			1,278
Chile	2.42	1.48	3.30	−1.90			501
Mexico	2.87	−2.72			2.39	2.31	565
Australia	1.34	1.01	1.16	1.21	0.95	0.72	4,874
Canada	1.30	1.27	0.64	0.65	2.23	2.25	969
Egypt	4.07	2.92	−0.65	−0.73			409
Japan	1.47	1.25	3.24	2.26	2.91	2.25	1,346
Russia	2.01	−1.63					3,341
Turkey	4.23	−1.56	1.00	−0.88	0.11	−0.34	919
TOTAL	2.36	−0.13	1.75	1.21	1.38	1.3	16,146

Definitions: premium—difference between rate of return on foreign bond and rate of return on UK or US (according to country where foreign bond was issued) long bond for equivalent holding period; ex ante—internal rate of return implied by the bond issue price and repayment terms; ex post—real realized rate of return deflated by consumer price index of lending country.

Source: Lindert and Morton, "How Sovereign Debt Has Worked," tables II and III. Lindert and Morton's sample consisted of 1,557 external bonds issued by the public sectors of ten major countries. They include bonds outstanding in 1850 and all those issued between 1850 and 1970.

financial flows, falling transaction costs and unrestricted arbitrage.[93] In fact, a comparison of prices for identical securities in different markets during seven financial crises between 1745 and 1907 suggests that financial integration may have been somewhat less in the early twentieth century than it had been in the mid-eighteenth century.[94] However, these snapshots may be distorted by problems of market liquidity associated with crisis periods. Given the growth in volume of asset arbitrage after 1870[95] and the increased

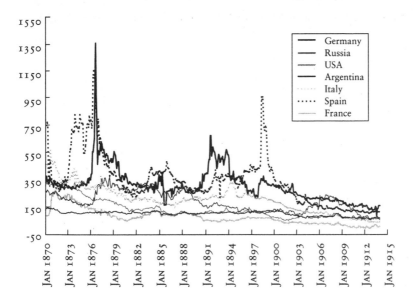

Figure 28. Yield spreads over consols, 1870–1915

Source: Batley and Ferguson, "Event Risk."

ease of communications following the introduction and proliferation of the telegraph,[96] a gradual process of international financial integration seems undeniable, albeit one that was punctuated by occasional and severe crises.

A second possible explanation for the convergence seen in Figure 28 lies in the realm of fiscal policy. According to one line of argument, interest rate differentials were related to debt/gross domestic product ratios: they can therefore be seen as "a broad measure of default risk," though "countries had to plunge quite deep into debt before they started feeling the pain" in the form of higher yields.[97] Yet debt/GDP ratios tell us relatively little. Some of these countries had very high proportions of long-term debt, others had substantial short-term liabilities.[98] Some countries (notably Russia) had substantial external debts; others (Britain and France in particular) held nearly all their debt domestically. Some denominated much of their debt in gold; others did not. In any case, debt/GDP ratios were unknown to contemporary investors since—as we saw in Chapter 4—gross domestic product is a twentieth-century concept, and only a few attempts to estimate national wealth and income had been made in the period before the First World War.

Appendix D gives some of the measures with which late nineteenth-century investors would have been more familiar. Here debt is related to government revenue and exports (the latter ratio being especially important to countries like those of Latin America or the Middle East with large proportions of debt in foreign hands and currency). In addition, debts have been adjusted to take account of the higher interest coupons on peripheral countries' bonds, as well as state assets on the other side of the balance sheet (important in the case of countries that had financed their railway networks through government bond issues). In order to give an impression of the extent of nineteenth-century globalization, the table includes all the countries surveyed in *Fenn's Compendium* of 1889, one of the most comprehensive manuals for investors in the later part of the century. The approach taken in the *Compendium* seems to have been typical of the period. There are methodological similarities between Fenn's calculations and the debt/national wealth ratings devised by Michael Mulhall in the 1890s; while Crédit Lyonnais based its credit ratings on net debt service as a proportion of tax revenue, allowing for past episodes of default.[99]

Do figures such as these provide a better explanation of yield spreads and fluctuations than anachronistic debt/GDP ratios? One way of answering this question is to test statistically the relationship between bond yields and contemporary fiscal measures. The results, however, are disappointingly ambiguous: only one out of six countries for which data are available for the period 1880–1913 evinced a strong positive relationship between the deficit/revenue ratio and the bond yield (France); in two cases (Britain and Germany) the relationship was actually negative.[100] This is perhaps not altogether surprising. Measures of the sort described above exaggerated the debt burdens of industrialized countries like Britain and France, which had big debts but also big economies. On the basis of the debt/revenue ratio, only two countries in the 1880s (or four if only central government is counted for Germany and Switzerland) were as "creditworthy" as Britain in the 1980s; and in the case of the other two—China and Bulgaria—their low debt burden primarily reflected their lack of access to domestic or international bond finance.[101] In the same way, the Crédit Lyonnais ratings placed Russia—the biggest debtor in the world[102]—in the "first division" along with the United States but would, if rigorously applied, have put Britain in the second division along with Romania, Egypt, Austria, Hungary and Spain.[103]

The third explanation for yield convergence is that the rise in the number of states on the gold standard reduced currency risk as a factor in investors' calculations.[104] According this view, adherence to gold standard was a signal of fiscal rectitude which "facilitated access by peripheral countries to capital from the core countries of western Europe." Gold standard membership

indicated that a country followed "prudent fiscal and monetary policies."
The exception that proved the rule was "a well-understood emergency such
as a major war"; but if a country went off gold in such an emergency, the
public understood that the suspension was temporary. The gold standard
was thus a "contingent rule or a rule with escape clauses"; it delivered the
benefit of lower interest rates at the affordable cost of balanced budgets in
peacetime. To be precise, a commitment to gold reduced the yield on government gold-denominated bonds by around 40 basis points.[105]

There is, however, a difficulty with this analysis too: namely, the assumption that wars were "well understood emergencies." The historical reality is
that the period 1890–1914 was characterized by a growing danger of a war
of unprecedented magnitude and unforeseeable duration between all the
great powers. This was hardly unknown to investors. The Polish financier
Ivan Bloch predicted as early as 1899 that "the immediate consequence of
[a great] war would be to send securities all round down from 25 to 50 per
cent, and in such a tumbling market it would be difficult to float loans."[106]

How are we to explain the paradox of yield convergence at a level significantly below the average of the 1870s at a time of rising international tension? One possibility is that investors simply forgot what a full-blown political crisis could do to the international financial markets.[107] In the 1980s,
after all, "the guiding principle of Salomon Brothers in the department of
customer relations" was said to be that "customers have very short memories."[108] Table 15 above gives some indication of how that forgetfulness
might have been encouraged in the four and a half decades between 1870
and 1914. Compared with the preceding forty years, the biggest political
crises of that period had a markedly less dramatic impact on international
bond yields. The French debacle of 1870–1871, for example, hardly influenced other countries' bonds. The Eastern Crisis of 1876–8 also had a relatively muted impact on yields (though of course Turkish bonds were hit hard
by default). Even the power of a revolution to alarm investors seems to have
diminished over time; witness the 129 basis point rise in Russian yields in
the crisis of 1904–6.

In the light of this tendency for political crises to have diminishing financial repercussions, a plausible hypothesis may be that investors grew over-
confident. Like the liberal journalist Norman Angell, they came to believe
that nothing—neither war nor revolution—could long disrupt the business
of the world's stock exchanges. "The delicate interdependence of international finance"—according to Angell's best-selling book *The Great Illusion*—meant that a war between the great powers had become more or

less impossible.[109] The illusion was all Angell's of course. The historical significance of his book is that it shows how *ill* understood the First World War was on the eve of its outbreak.

On 23 July 1914 the British Foreign Secretary, Sir Edward Grey warned the Austrian ambassador that a major war "must involve the expenditure of so vast a sum of money and such an interference with trade, that [it] would be accompanied or followed by a complete collapse of European credit and industry."[110] A continental war, he told the German ambassador the next day, would mean "total exhaustion and impoverishment; industry and trade would be ruined, and the power of capital destroyed. Revolutionary movements like those of the year 1848 due to the collapse of industrial activities would be the result."[111] The prediction of a commercial collapse proved accurate in the very short term; and Grey was also prescient about what would ultimately happen in East and Central European countries. What he and many others failed to foresee was that the suspension of gold convertibility and the expansion of domestic and international bond markets would suffice to finance a global conflict for more than four years.[112]

THE CRISIS OF THE INTERNATIONAL BOND MARKET: LESSONS FOR TODAY?

The convulsion that seized nearly all financial markets in 1914 forced stock exchanges all over the world to close. Even the London Stock Exchange did not reopen after the Bank holiday of 3 August 1914 until the end of the year. Yet this did not spell the death of the international bond market. On the contrary, the First World War was decided as much by flows of capital as by spilling of blood. By 1917 Russia owed foreign creditors around £824 million.[113] Italy and France too were substantial net foreign debtors.[114] By 1919 Britain had lent her Dominions and wartime allies £1.8 billion, equivalent to 32 per cent of GNP, and had borrowed £1.3 billion (22 per cent of GNP) from the United States and other foreign countries.[115] The US was a net creditor to the tune of more than $7 billion, around 9 per cent of GNP. The years 1914–18 were by some measures the historic peak of international lending.

Moreover, these immense wartime transactions were followed in the 1920s by a new wave of international lending. The mean value of net foreign investment as a percentage of national income for ten major economies fell only slightly from its peak of 5.5 per cent in 1915–19 to 4 per cent in

1920–4, a higher figure than in 1910–1914.[116] All told, international capital flows totalled around $9 billion between 1924 and 1930. Now, however, America was the world's banker. Total long-term foreign lending from the United States between 1919 and 1928 amounted to $6.4 billion, of which more than half went to national and provincial governments.[117] Just as the Rothschilds had lectured nineteenth-century foreign borrowers on the need to Anglicize their institutions, "money doctors" like Edwin Kemmerer toured the world preaching Americanization in return for dollar loans.[118]

Yet signs of impending crisis were already manifesting themselves. The Bolshevik regime in Russia had enacted perhaps the biggest default in history after the October 1917 revolution, affecting bonds worth around £800 million. As in the Turkish and Mexican revolutions of seven years before, foreign creditors were soft targets for a radical new regime, particularly one avowedly at war with the bourgeoisie. Investors could hardly be oblivious to the pledges of Trotsky to export the Russian revolution to the rest of the world. Secondly, the new German Republic defrauded foreign and domestic investors alike by allowing its currency, and hence all government bonds denominated in marks, to depreciate to the point of worthlessness. The net capital flow into Germany between 1919 and 1923 may have been as much as 6 or 7 per cent of net national product; but much of the money foreigners put into German securities and currency was wiped out by the inflation: a form of "American Reparations to Germany."[119] Thirdly, many of the major international loans of the 1920s were, on closer inspection, designed to refinance pre-war sterling loans in post-war dollars.[120] Fourthly, the flows from the principal lenders (US, UK and France) were significantly lower in real terms: in 1913 prices, the average annual outflow was just $550 million from 1924 until 1928, compared with $1,400 million between 1911 and 1913. Finally, short-term lending—"hot money"—was significantly more important than it had been before 1914; and among the biggest short-term debtors were the principal net long-term creditors.[121] The most striking thing about capital flows in the inter-war period is how quickly they were reversed—and with what devastating consequences.[122] In the short run, capital withdrawals intensified recessions that had begun in most primary producing countries in the mid-1920s. But after 1931 defaults and devaluations led to major redistributions of resources from creditor to debtor countries.[123] There were defaults by Turkey, China, most of Eastern Europe and all of Latin America.[124] Bolivia defaulted in January 1931, followed by Peru, Chile, Cuba, Brazil and Columbia. Hungary, Yugoslavia and Greece defaulted in the following year, Austria and Germany in 1933.[125] By 1934 all debtor countries except Argentina, Haiti and the Dominican Republic had suspended debt service.[126]

The purpose of this chapter is not to offer an explanation of why this collapse of the global financial system happened; the answer to that question is so bound up with the workings of the international monetary system that it properly belongs in the next chapter. The point here is simply that financial globalization *did* collapse. This raises two questions. The first is: Could it happen again? The second is: Was there a connection between the collapse of global finance between the war and the decline of Britain's capacity to act as a hegemonic power, politically underwriting international financial stability through formal and informal imperialism?

GLOBALIZATION PAST AND PRESENT

Economic historians disagree about whether or not globalization today is greater than it was in the decade or so before the First World War. The answer to the question depends on which indicators they choose to look at—as well, perhaps, as which country they come from. A glance at the external debt/GNP ratios of big international debtors like India and Russia would suggest that the present and the past are uncannily alike: the ratios before 1913 were between 25 and 30 per cent, as they were again in 1997.[127] However, few large economies today are as heavily reliant on foreign capital as Argentina was before 1914, when around half the capital stock was foreign-owned and current account deficits ran as high as 10 per cent of GDP. Between 1870 and 1890 Argentinian capital imports amounted to nearly 20 per cent of GDP, compared with a figure of just 2 per cent in the 1990s.[128] As we have seen, the zenith of capital export was in fact the First World War, when the average current account reached around 5 per cent of GDP, compared with a nadir of 1.2 per cent in the years 1932–39. The figure for the period 1989–96 was still only 2.3 per cent.[129]

Table 15 gives some more comprehensive indicators of globalization, however. By these measures, it is clear that the global markets for goods and for capital are more open today than ever before. Merchandise exports amounted to at most 9 per cent of world GDP in 1913; the figure in 1990 was 13 and is almost certainly higher now.[130] This reflects the fact that international tariff barriers are currently lower than they were in the early 1900s: it was the fall of freight costs more than liberal economics that boosted trade

Table 15. Indicators of commercial and financial globalization

	Merchandise exports as percentage of world GDP	Foreign assets as a percentage of world GDP
1870		6.9
1890	6.0	
1900		18.6
1913	9.0	17.5
1930		8.4
1945		4.9
1950	7.0	
1960	8.0	6.4
1970	10.0	
1980		17.7
1990	13.0	
1995		56.8

Source: Crafts, "Globalization and Growth," pp. 26, 27.

before 1914.[131] Foreign assets were equivalent to around 18 per cent of world GDP in 1913; in 1995 the figure was an astonishing 57 per cent. The table also shows that capital exports declined far more drastically than merchandise exports from the 1930s until the 1960s. At their lowest recorded point, in 1945, foreign assets amounted to less than 5 per cent of world GDP. In other respects too, globalization today exceeds that of a century ago. Direct investment (as opposed to portfolio investment mediated through stock exchanges) is much greater now because of the growth of multinational corporations.[132] Information flows are both faster and greater in volume, greatly facilitating cross-border investment decisions. What is more, this process could go further. According to the IMF, 144 countries still had capital controls on foreign direct investment in 1997, while 128 still regulated all international financial transactions.[133] If such controls were to be dismantled, cross-border capital movements would get even bigger.

On the other hand, the global labour market is almost certainly less open than it was a century ago. The first age of globalization witnessed two massive waves of migration, the first enforced, the second voluntary. By 1820 around 8 million Africans had been shipped as slaves to the Americas and the Caribbean. In the century that followed no fewer than 60 million Europeans emigrated, three-fifths to the United States.[134] Total net emigration from the United Kingdom alone between 1881 and 1890 was more than 3.2 million, around 7 per cent of the mean population.[135] German emigration—1.3 million in the same period—reached annual peaks in 1854 and 1881 of 7 and 5 per thousand of the population, or nearly 3 per cent for the 1880s as a whole.[136] Ireland was, of course, the great exporter of people: total emigration in the 1880s was equivalent to 14 per cent of the population. Despite the relaxation of US restrictions in the 1980s and 1990s, immigration has still not reached the heights attained in the decade after 1900, when total immigration was equivalent to around 10 per cent of the population. (For Argentina in the same period the figure was a staggering 29 per cent.[137]) The US immigration rate in 1990 was less than a third of what it was a century before.

This is a profoundly important difference between the past and the present, since it was migration that did most to reduce inequalities in incomes between countries in the first age of globalization. When flows of capital predominate the gap between rich and poor countries tends to widen. This is because when humans move, the poor go to richer countries where labour is relatively scarce. But when capital moves, it tends to avoid really poor countries, not least because of the low productivity of their workers.[138]

For many commentators, globalization is a force for good, promising nothing less than "A Future Perfect."[139] The sociologist Anthony Giddens approves of the way economic globalization subverts not only the nation state, but also "traditional" cultures and even the family.[140] Yet there can be little doubt that free trade and capital movement without a proportionate volume of international migration are leading to unprecedented levels of inequality around the world. In 1999 the United Nations estimated that the assets of the world's three leading billionaires were greater than the combined GNPs of the world's poorest countries, the inhabitants of which number 600 million people. In the 1960s the richest fifth of the world's population had a total income thirty times greater than the poorest fifth's; in 1998 the ratio was 74 : 1.[141] According to the World Bank, some 1.3 billion people now live in abject poverty, meaning on an income of less than $1 a day. And the way the world is going, the gap between rich and poor nations may widen further.[142] If the first age of globalization saw a substantial measure of convergence of incomes, this age is seeing a pronounced divergence. Recent academic writing about the "first era" of globalization before 1914 has been haunted by the question: Could there be "another backlash" in the early twenty-first century, whether in the form of protectionism, xenophobia or even international conflict?[143] But that is to presuppose that the "backlash" will come from the developed economies.

Another qualification relates to the very different roles played by the hegemonic powers in the two eras of globalization. Significantly, those who believe the present is more global than the past tend to be Americans relying on mainly American data.[144] But as Table 16 shows, British data tell a quite different story; and since Britain was the "hegemonic" power of early twentieth century globalization, these figures may be a more appropriate benchmark. British merchandise exports were equivalent to nearly 30 per cent of GDP in 1913 or 76 per cent of merchandise value added, compared with figures for the United States in 1990 of, respectively, 8 and 36 per cent. American economists argue that exports of services are more important now than they were then, but while this is true of the United States, it is not true of the UK.[145] American trade policy is certainly more liberal than ever, but it is still not as liberal as British trade policy before 1914. And Britain was a net exporter of people before 1914, whereas America today is once again a significant importer, if not on the scale witnessed in the first decades of the century.

Perhaps the crucial difference between then and now, however, is that Britain was a net exporter of capital while the United States today is the opposite. For the United States has used its dominance of the international bond market not to *export* capital—which in net terms it did until around 1972—but to import it. This greatly reduces the financial leverage of its foreign policy: for you cannot have "dollar diplomacy" without dollars. In short, the global hegemon of the present age of globalization has much less financial leverage than that of the first age. And this is one of the reasons why, although the United States has a few quasi-colonial dependencies, it cannot exercise the kind of formal and informal control over the world economy wielded by Britain in her imperial heyday.

PLANKTON

Does that matter? Some would say not. In 1999 the American journalist Thomas Friedman imagined a conversation between the former US Treasury Secretary Robert Rubin and the Malaysian prime minister, Mahathir bin Mohamad, inspired by the latter's denunciation of globalization at the 1997 World Bank meeting in Hong Kong:

Table 16. A tale of two hegemons, 1870–1995

	United Kingdom					United States				
	Merchandise exports as percentage of GDP	Merchandise exports as percentage of merchandise value added	Average tariffs on manufactures	Net foreign investment as a percentage of GDP	Emigration rate per 1,000 population	Merchandise exports as percentage of GDP	Merchandise exports as a percentage of merchandise value added	Average tariffs on manufactures	Net foreign investment as a percentage of GDP	Immigration rate per 1,000 population
1870				5.0	5.0					6.4
1875	27.3		0.0	4.3	5.3			45.0		
1890		61.5		7.3	8.6	5.6	14.3			9.2
1910	29.8			7.7	7.0					10.4
1913		76.3	0.0	9.1		6.1	13.2	44.0		
1930					4.7					3.5
1935			17.0					48.0		
1950			23.0		3.0			14.0		0.7
1960	15.3	33.8				3.4	9.6		2.4	
1970	16.5	40.7				4.1	13.7		1.5	1.7
1990	20.6	62.8	5.7		0.5	8.0	35.8	4.6	-4.7	2.6
1995			4.6					3.0	-5.3	

Source: Crafts, "Globalization and Growth," pp. 26, 27, 30, except for British emigration figures from Mitchell, *European Historical Statistics*, pp. 5, 8, 47; *Social Trends*, 1995, p. 23, table 1.14.

Ah, excuse me, Mahathir, but what planet are you living on? You talk about participating in globalization as if it were a choice you had. Globalization isn't a choice. It's a reality. There is just one global market today and the only way you can grow at the speed your people want to grow is by tapping into the global stock and bond markets, by seeking out multinationals to invest in your country and by selling into the global trading system what your factories produce. And the most basic truth about globalization is this: *No one is in charge*, not George Soros, not "Great Powers" and not I. I didn't start globalization. I can't stop it and neither can you . . .[146]

Here, as at the beginning of this chapter, we encounter the idea of the international financial markets as a power beyond human agency—certainly beyond the control of the United States government. To Friedman, this is a good thing: a check on politicians, and a marked improvement on the first age of imperialist globalization. (In this same book, Friedman gloats to the prime minister of Thailand that he helped bring him to power by selling shares in East Asian emerging markets, hence contributing to the depreciation of the Thai currency, and hence undermining the prime minister's predecessor.)[147]

Yet can the huge and volatile markets of the present really be thought of as powerful in their own right? A shoal of plankton may occupy more water than a sperm whale. But to say that the financial markets rule the world is to say the plankton rule the sea. The movement of plankton is not predictable; nor is it the product of a single conscious will. Friedman uses a similar metaphor: he describes international investors and the supposed "masters of the universe" who act on their behalf as an "electronic herd." The trouble is that a herd—especially one without a herdsman—is prone to stampede.

The next two chapters consider, first, the impact of capital mobility on the history of stock markets and, secondly, the various attempts that have been made to reduce the risk of stampedes—sudden capital withdrawals and currency crises—by erecting monetary "fences."

10

Bubbles and Busts:
Stock Markets in the Long Run[1]

As is well known to the wise in their generation, traffic in Shares is the one thing to have to with in this world. Have no antecedents, no established character, no cultivation, no ideas, no manners; have Shares. Have Shares enough to be on Boards of Direction in capital letters, oscillate on mysterious business between London and Paris, and be great. Where does he come from? Shares. Where is he going to? Shares. What are his tastes? Shares. Has he any principles? Shares. What squeezes him into Parliament? Shares. Perhaps he never of himself achieved success in anything, never originated anything, never produced anything? Sufficient answer to all; Shares. O mighty Shares! To set those blaring images so high, and to cause us smaller vermin, as under the influence of henbane or opium, to cry out, night and day, "Relieve us of our money, scatter it for us, buy and sell us, ruin us, only we beseech ye take rank among the powers of the earth and fatten on us!"

Dickens, Our Mutual Friend

HOW HIGH THE DOW?

On 29 March 1999 the Dow Jones Industrials index for the first time closed ahead of the totemic 10,000 mark (figure 29). The Dow, of course, has had its share of downs, most notably between 1929 and 1932, when it fell by some 89 per cent from peak to trough. But the long-run tendency of the US stock market since the index began in 1897 has been ebulliently upwards.[3] Any thirty-year old who had the nerve to begin tracking the index in the very depths of the Great Depression would have increased his investment roughly tenfold by the time he retired in 1957. If his thirty-year old son had held on to his inheritance and continued tracking the index, he would have celebrated his 72nd birthday in 1999 having notched up a further twenty-fold

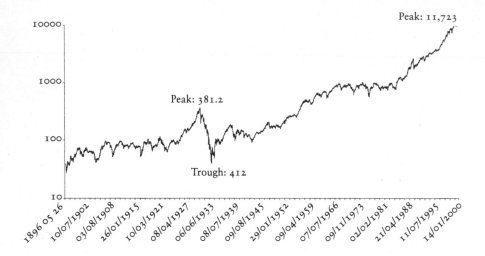

Figure 29: The Dow Jones industrial average daily closing price, 1896–2000 (log. scale)

Source: www.economagic.com

gain. In the long run we may all be dead, as Keynes famously said; but if we track the Dow, it seems, we at least die rich.

The 1995–99 bull market in the US has done much to undermine the credibility of an historical approach of to financial analysis and to vindicate the famous judgment of Henry Ford that "history is bunk." Commentators were warning as long ago as April 1997 that the US market was over-valued by any historical measure.[4] For a moment in August 1998 it appeared that the bears were to be vindicated, but an easing of monetary policy allayed the fears aroused by the crises in Asia and Russia.[5] The market reached a record high on 14 January 2000 of 11,723. At the time of writing (September 2000) many analysts continue to maintain that it will rise further. In April 2000 Abby Joseph Cohen of Goldman Sachs forecast that the Dow would end the year at 12,600.[6] The American Enterprise Institute predicted that the Dow Jones could hit 36,000 in the foreseeable future.[7]

There are numerous justifications offered for these rosy forecasts. One is simply that—as figure 29 suggests—the long-run ascent of the American stock market has been seriously interrupted only once, by the 1929–32 crash. Compared with the history of other stock markets, it is an exceptional story. William Goetzman and Philippe Jorion's study of 39 stock markets in the twentieth century found that the 4.73 per cent annual compound real return enjoyed by investors in the US stock market between 1921 and 1995 was unmatched any-where else. The mean figure for all the 39 markets they surveyed was in fact negative: –0.28 per cent. Sixteen out of the 39 (including Belgium, Italy, Spain and New Zealand) returned below zero over the long run.[8] The slogan "Stocks for the Long Run," coined by Jeremy Siegel, therefore needs to be seen for what it is: advice to investors in Wall Street, not investors with a global portfolio—and, it is tempting to add, advice to investors in Wall Street between twenty and a hundred years ago, not necessarily investors today.[9] In many other countries, a strategy of "buy and hold" over the twentieth century would have been dis-appointing, if not disastrous. Americans who invested in Germany or Japan before the Great Depression would have had to start all over again, having lost every cent by the end of the Second World War. As figure 30 shows, the long-run trajectory of the US stock market has been more smoothly upward than the British, French, German or Japanese. Stock markets in these and many other countries experienced a collapse during the Second World War far more severe than anything ever witnessed on Wall Street. Nothing disagrees with a stock market quite like being overrun by a foreign invader.

This historical point, however, is heard less often than self-consciously unhistorical explanations, which lay stress on the novelty of the present. The economist Robert Shiller lists the following "conventional" explanations for the high valuations of the current market:

1. "The Arrival of the Internet"—in other words, technological change with implicit productivity and profitability gains;
2. "Triumphalism and the Decline of Foreign Economic Rivals"—not only the end of the Cold War but the travails of Japan or, put more gener-ally, international peace and security;
3. "A Republican Congress and Capital Gains Tax Cuts" and "The Expansion of Defined Contribution Pension Plans"—that is, changes in fiscal policy favorable to investment in shares;
4. "The Baby Boom"—meaning demographic trends favorable to invest-ment in shares, in this case the impact of large numbers of people cur-rently in their thirties, forties and fifties making provision for a pro-tracted retirement;
5. "The Growth of Mutual Funds" and "The Expansion of the Volume of Trade"—in other words, innovations in financial services;
6. "Cultural Changes Favoring Business"—which might be summed up as a new mood of materialism;
7. "An Expansion in Media Reporting of Business News" and "Analysts'

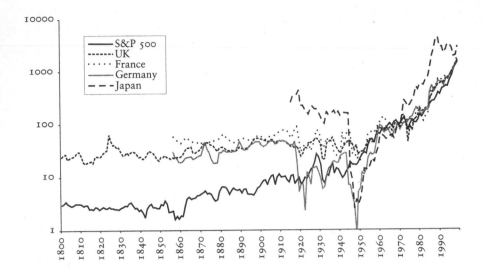

Figure 30: Stock market indices since 1800 (log. scale in dollars, 1969=100)

Source: Global Financial Data.

Increasingly Optimistic Forecasts"—a growth in the volume of financial information and advertising;

8. Decline of Inflation and the Effects of Money Illusion"—encouraging greater confidence in financial assets generally; and

9. "The Rise of Gambling Opportunities"—since these encourage speculative behavior in other spheres.[10]

It should be said at once that these explanations are not all wholly fanciful. There is now little doubt that there was some improvement in labor productivity in the US economy in the course of the 1990s, though by some calculations the annual growth rate of total factor productivity is still below that achieved in the 1950s and 1960s.[11] The end of the Cold War has undoubtedly reduced the risk to financial markets of a superpower confrontation.[12] Fiscal and demographic factors have also tended to encourage investment by middle-aged Americans anticipating a protracted retirement. Just as happened in Japan in the 1980s, there has been a correlation in 1990s America between the proportion of the population aged between 35 and 64 and share prices.[13] Financial markets have become more liquid, transactions costs have fallen and investors can reduce risk by diversifying and hedging much more easily than in the past.

However, Shiller does not regard any of this as sufficient to explain the steep rise in American stock markets since 1995. This he attributes to a combination of investor ignorance and media hype, resulting in "feedback loops" or an "amplification process," whereby short-run capital gains encouraged investors to expect future capital gains—a prophecy which could be self-fulfilling, but not forever. Indeed, Shiller goes so far as to compare the rise of the US stock markets to a "naturally occurring" Ponzi scheme. (In a Ponzi scheme, naïve investors are persuaded to part with their money by the promise of alluringly high returns, which are in reality financed by the next cohort of even more naïve investors. Obviously, such schemes can only be sustained as long as the number of investors continues to grow at a rate greater than the returns investors have been promised.[14])

Even if it is not quite a Ponzi scheme, the US stock market was still at the time of writing substantially over-valued according to nearly all historical yardsticks. Consider the following:

1. The price/earnings ratio on the Standard & Poor's composite index (meaning the price of shares divided by their dividends) reached a record high of 33.4 in 1999, its highest level since the Great Depression, and more than double its post-1945 average.[15] And even this calculation understates the extent of overvaluation because it takes no account of inflation. According to Shiller, the ratio of the real price to a ten-year average of real earnings reached an unprecedented 45 in 2000, compared with a previous peak of 33 in 1929. In the technology sector of the S&P 500 index, the price/earnings ratio stood at nearly 64 in February 2000.[16]

2. To put the same point another way, the dividend yield (dividends as a percentage of share prices) fell to its lowest level since 1871, 1.14 per cent.[17] The equivalent figure for Britain in 1999 was around 2.1 per cent. This is exceptionally low. Over the long run, returns on shares have tended to be markedly higher than returns on bonds in both America and Britain, giving rise to the notion of the "equity risk premium": the extra return companies have to offer investors in equities to compensate them for the greater risk associated with investment in equities as compared with government bonds. According to one study, the American equity risk premium averaged 5.8 per cent for the years 1925 to 1999; the British figure was slightly lower (5.0 per cent).[18] Yet current dividend yields can only be regarded as sustainable if one believes the equity risk premium—or the dividend yield/bond yield ratio, a measure some analysts prefer—has shifted markedly downwards.[19] It has sometimes been suggested that the equity risk premium may be about to disappear, as investors come to see equities, with their historically higher

returns, as being at least as safe an investment as government bonds. But this is not a plausible argument. States generally last longer than companies, because the core functions they perform are perennial and their revenue sources (taxes) are relatively stable. Companies, by comparison, are vulnerable to the obsolescence of their technology and to competition from other companies. Nothing has changed in the past ten years to make states significantly less likely to default on their bonds than companies to disappoint their shareholders. This is why the *ex ante* equity risk premium is unlikely to disappear. It should not be confused with the *ex post* differential between returns on shares and returns on bonds, which—as figure 31 shows—has varied considerably over time, and has not invariably been positive. Returns on UK bonds were higher than returns on gilts not only in the 1990s, but also from 1710 to 1729, from 1810 to 1839, from 1890 to 1909 and in the 1930s. On Wall Street, returns on bonds were higher throughout the first half of the nineteenth century and again in the 1870s and 1930s.

3. The ratio known as "Tobin's Q," after the economist James Tobin—that is, the ratio of the stock market valuation of companies to their net worth or replacement cost, which appears historically to revert to a mean of around 1—was higher in 2000 than it was even in 1929.[20] At the time of writing, Q was approximately 2, implying that it in mid-2000 it was twice as expensive to buy a company on the stock market than to create a replica of it from scratch. Not even the growth of unmeasured intangible assets can justify such valuations.

4. The future earnings implied by recent valuations imply improbably high future profits. According to surveys in 1999, many equity analysts were anticipating rises in corporate earnings of the order of 13 per cent a year, twice the overall nominal return forecast by the IMF and the expected growth in nominal GDP.[21] In the technology, media and telecommunications sector, current valuations imply expected returns of 21 per cent a year for the next ten years.[22] According to one survey of 133 Internet companies that have gone public since 1995, they would need to expand their revenues by more than 80 per cent every year for the next five years to justify their valuations at the end of 1999.[23] Yet in 1999 the Internet sector—priced on Wall Street at over $1 trillion—*lost* $3.4 billion.[24]

5. If demography has played a part in driving the market up, it can only have the reverse effect as the "Baby boomers" retire and begin to live off their accumulated assets.[25]

These are only some of the reasons for skepticism about the durability of the 11,000 Dow, much less the attainability of even higher stock market val-

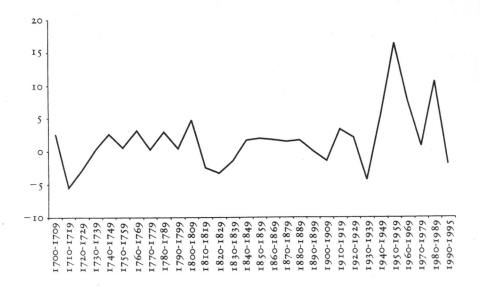

Figure 31: The UK 'Equity Risk Premium' (ex post returns on stocks less returns on bonds), 1700–1995

Source: Global Financial Data.

uations. Another striking piece of evidence is that the rise of indices like the S&P 500 or the Dow Jones Industrial Average has come to depend on the exceptional performance of a minority of companies, nearly all of them in the technology sector. Nearly two-thirds of the total return on the S&P 500 in 1999 was accounted for by just ten companies. Between them, Microsoft and Cisco Systems accounted for a fifth of the total return, while more than half the stocks in the index actually declined over the year.[26] Since 1998 the difference between the number of shares rising and the number of shares falling each day has been going down. Much of the bull market of 1999 was accounted for by the performance of a few computer, internet and telecommunications giants.

At the same time that the advance of the stock market has been narrowing, so the investing public has been widening. More than half of American households now own shares; in 1987 the proportion was around a quarter. Many Americans have treated a proportion of their $10 trillion in capital gains since 1994 as money they can spend: the so-called "wealth effect" may have added as much as one percentage point to the annual growth rate since 1996.[27] Such a process has the potential to work in reverse, with falling share prices leading to cuts in private consumption and recession. The increased volatility of prices, linked to the marked increase in the number of times the average share changes hands in a year, makes the possibility of a sudden downturn in the market seem even greater than it was in 1987.[28]

For all these reasons, investors with long memories or historical knowledge are haunted by the fear that, far from soaring onwards and upwards to 36,000, the Dow could one day plummet as far as it did between 1929 and 1932. This has been a recurrent fear: witness the headlines when the Dow Jones experienced its biggest one-day collapse in 19 October 1987.[29] The experience of Japan in the early 1990s—when the Nikkei index collapsed from above 38,000 to 14,000, ushering in a decade of economic stagnation—had already prompted some pessimists to forecast a second Great Depression as early as 1992.[30]

THE SHADOW OF 1929

A second Great Depression would, if financial history were to repeat itself exactly, take the Dow down from over 10,631 (where it stood on 26 September 2000) to around 1,275 by July 2003. Is this a realistic possibility? Superficially, of course, there are resemblances between the 1920s and the 1990s. Then, as now, indicators like the price/earnings ratio and the dividend yield were out of alignment with their long-run averages. There was also a good deal of rose-tinted talk about a "new economy" based on new technologies (electrical power, the internal combustion engine and chemicals)—talk which many historians regard as more justified than recent claims about the economic impact of the computer and the internet. The number of investors grew rapidly as first-time buyers of shares were drawn into the market by the promise of easy capital gains. The press fuelled speculation, just as it has in the recent past. Cross-border flows of "hot" money (short-term lending and investment) magnified both boom and bust. A general backlash against economic globalization led to higher tariffs and other measures that made matters worse rather than better.[31]

Yet for all these resemblances, it is important not to lose sight of the differences between the 1920s and the 1990s. Two are worth emphasizing. First, recent Federal Reserve policy has been self-consciously based on learning lessons from the Great Depression. It is almost inconceivable that Alan Greenspan could make mistakes comparable with those made by the Federal Reserve Bank of New York between the wars.

This is not to suggest that (as dealers at one London bank were heard to chant in 1999) "the Fed is God," however. There can be little doubt that a part of the explanation for the dramatic rise in the American stock market since the mid-1990s has been the relatively loose monetary policy of the Federal Reserve. The American money supply (M3) grew at an accelerating rate between 1995 and 1999, peaking at more than 10 per cent per annum. US private sector debt rose from below 80 per cent of GDP to 130 per cent by the end of 1999. There were close links between this expansion of credit—in part due to the effects of banking deregulation—and the rise of the stock market. In 1998 alone non-financial businesses increased their debt by more than $400 million; significantly, over half the money was used to finance share buy-backs, with obvious implications for share prices as the supply of tradable shares was reduced. Margin loans (credit provided to investors against the collateral of the shares they buy), also rose from $100 billion in 1997 to $173 billion in 1999. The private sector financial deficit (firms' and households' savings minus investment) rose to an unprecedented 5 per cent of GDP in 1999, having rarely been above zero at all since 1960; private sector debt now stands at 165 per cent of private disposable income.[32]

At the same time, Fed policy has encouraged many investors to believe that, in the event of a crash, they would be bailed out by the monetary authorities. An important precedent was set by the way the Fed injected liquidity to bolster the market in October 1987. The belief that this action had averted a second 1929 undoubtedly informed the way the Fed managed the two international financial crises of 1997 and 1998.[33] In September 1998, when the partial default of the Russian government blew apart the arbitrage operations of the Long Term Capital Management hedge fund, the Fed organized a successful rescue operation by a consortium of American and European banks, then cut interest rates three times. Critics of the Fed would argue that Greenspan has used monetary policy to prop up the stock market, giving the investors the impression of an asymmetrical policy which cuts rates promptly when the market falls, but is slower to raise them when the market rises. The apparent reluctance of the monetary authorities to countenance a major bank failure has clear connotations of "moral hazard."

The best argument on the other side is that it is not part of the central bank's job to prick asset bubbles. "How do we know," Alan Greenspan asked on 5 December 1996, "when irrational exuberance has unduly escalated asset values . . . And how do we factor that assessment into monetary policy?"[34] Since he asked that—apparently rhetorical—question, the Dow Jones index has risen by two-thirds. The question has not got any easier to answer. According to a few economists, central banks should include asset price inflation in the inflation rate they monitor.[35] But this is easier said than done, given the technical difficulty of integrating commodity and asset prices. (Apart from anything else, asset prices are themselves based on assumptions about future interest rates, so there is a certain circularity about using them as a guide to what interest rates ought to be.) It is far from clear that the Fed would have made a better job of monetary policy in the 1920s if it had targeted asset prices.[36] When the German Reichsbank sought to counter asset price inflation in the mid-1920s, it did no great good. And there is strong evidence that the policy of the Fed was a prime cause of post-war recessions.[37] The question implied by Greenspan's policy is whether the Fed does any good in "taking away the punch bowl" when there is no sign of rising inflation as conventionally measured.

Above all, it is the role of international capital that makes the job of domestic monetary authorities so awkward in such situations. Foreign investors have played a major part in the bubble of the 1990s: witness the growth of America's net foreign liabilities to $1.5 trillion (20 per cent of GDP), and the steep decline of the euro since its launch at the beginning of 1999, which has been largely a consequence of substantial flows of European capital into the US stock market. The problem is that any attempt by domestic monetary authorities to prick asset bubbles by raising interest rates can have the perverse effect of attracting foreign investors. This brings us to a second important difference between 1999 and 1929. A crucial transmission mechanism of the Great Depression was the gold standard; today, by contrast, foreign investors operate in a world of floating exchange rates, and have to rely on hedging rather than pegged rates to guard against currency risk.

OTHER BOOMS AND BUSTS

If 1929 is not necessarily the ideal point of comparison for today's stock market, what other analogies can be drawn? There is certainly no shortage of past booms and busts with which comparisons can be drawn. Charles Kindleberger lists the following twenty financial crises in which Britain was involved between 1700 and 1990: 1720, 1763, 1772, 1793, 1797, 1810, 1815–16, 1819, 1836, 1847, 1857, 1866, 1890, 1920–1, 1931–3, the 1950s, the 1960s (*sic*), 1974–5, 1979–82 and 1982–7.[38] The monetarist view is that by themselves stock market crashes are not financial crises: only contractions in the money supply really qualify, especially when associated with banking failures. Thus Schwartz argues that after 1866 there was no true financial crisis in Britain, in that potential crises were averted by appropriate monetary policy in 1873, 1890, 1907, 1914 and 1931.[39] Bordo nevertheless identifies severe monetary contractions in the UK in 1872–8, 1890–3, 1900–1, 1902–3, 1907–8, and 1928–31.[40] Mishkin has suggested rather similar years for American financial crises: 1857, 1873, 1884, 1890, 1893, 1896, 1907 and 1929–31.[41] In their analysis of international financial crises before 1914, Goodhart and Delargy single out 1873, 1890–91, 1893 and 1907.[42] Other such lists could easily be cited. Without exception, these monetary contractions were accompanied by downward "corrections" of asset prices.

Leaving aside for a moment the monetary dimension, let us focus on the prices of equities—to be precise, the price of the selected groups of equities that go to make up indices. Figure 32 shows a composite annual UK stock market index since 1700, adjusted for inflation. Three points are worth noting. First a caveat: in splicing together these very different indices we are ignoring the profound changes in the composition of the stock market that occurred in this extended period. Secondly, it is striking that, when allowance is made for inflation, the increase in asset values in the 1990s was much less in the UK than in the US. According to one estimate, the real rise in the American stock market index between 1994 and 1999 was of the order of 165 per cent. The equivalent British figure was roughly half that: 86 per cent.[43] Thirdly, even as late as 1999 the Financial Times ordinary share index had still not managed to regain its 1968 level in real terms.

If it serves no other purpose, such a long-run index enables as to compare bubbles and busts over the long run. According to these figures, the biggest real (inflation-adjusted) annual rise on the British stock market was in 1720 (93 per cent); and the biggest real fall came the following year (–57 per cent). Even the disastrous years 1974 and 1826 saw smaller real declines in asset prices than when the South Sea bubble burst.

Figure 33 carries out the same exercise using the available monthly indices, adjusting for inflation in the period after 1885 (a) because monthly inflation data are not available for the earlier period and (b) because long-run inflation was effectively zero in this period.

The biggest monthly rises in the stock market since 1811 (omitting the period 1935 to 1962, for which figures were unavailable) came in January 1825 (71 per cent) and February 1975 (41 per cent); in third and fourth places came November and December 1824, showing the remarkable magnitude of the asset price increases in the 1824–5 bubble. The biggest falls came in November 1987 (–22 per cent) and December 1973 (–18 per cent),

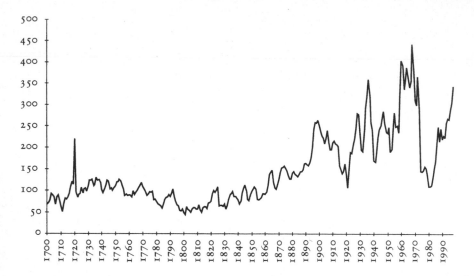

Figure 32: Inflation-adjusted UK stock market index, 1700–1998

Source: Mitchell, *British Historical Statistics*, pp. 687–9; ONS, *Financial Statistics*.

with April 1825 in third place. By rights the date August 1914 should figure near the top of this list, but the Stock Exchange was closed on 31 July, for the first time since its foundation, preventing the full force of the collapse of commercial credit from making itself felt on asset prices.[44]

Is there any obvious explanation for these "extreme observations"? Michael Bordo's ten-part definition of a financial crisis begins with "a widespread change in expectations associated with a fear of a change in the economic environment." As he observes, "such a change in expectations was often triggered in the past by some real event such as a war or a harvest failure, but also by monetary events," such as a currency devaluation.[45] And of course many so-called "monetary events" have their origins in real—meaning political rather than climactic—events. We have already seen that political events, and especially wars, have frequently acted as triggers for bond market instability. However, the connections are less evident in the case of equity markets. Although it is often assumed that major movements in share price indices are caused by news, empirical studies have failed to find a significant correlation between political or economic news and big movements in the market. Sometimes a big story has no impact; sometimes there are big shifts without big stories.[46] This is not surprising. A stock market index is composed of the shares of a sample of companies, not all of which

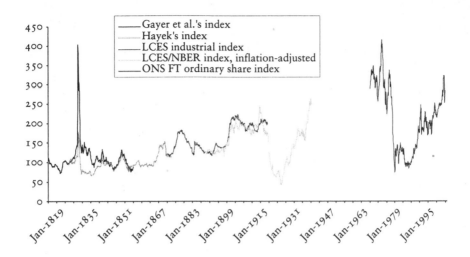

Figure 33: British share indices since 1811 (inflation-adjusted for the 20th century)

Sources: 1820–1868: Gayer, Rostow and Schwartz, *Growth and Fluctuation*, vol. I, p. 456; 1868–1914: London and Cambridge Economic Services, *Special Memorandum*, No. 37, pp. 8–19; 1914–1918: *Bankers' Magazine* (computed by NBER); 1919–1935: London and Cambridge Economic Service, *Special Memorandum*, No. 33, p. 14; 1930–1935: NBER; 1963–1998: ONS, *Financial Statistics*.

Notes: No monthly index available from 1935 to 1962.

will be equally affected by specific items of international or national news, and some of which may be very significantly affected by company-specific or sector-specific information. By contrast, the price of a government bond will tend to be quite closely correlated to news that has implications for that government's future fiscal and monetary policy. Technically, both share prices and bond prices follow a "random walk"—a kind of financial Brownian motion in which prices, like particles in physics, are moved by innumerable minute and random collisions. The difference is that it is easier to discern big collisions in the bond market.

Nevertheless, it would be wrong to think of stock markets as being uninfluenced by politics. One important reason not to understate the relationship between politics and asset prices is the simple fact that stock markets owe their origins to public finance. Because the market for equities has benefited from the expansion of the institutions necessary to fund state borrowing, while at the same time competing with the bond market for investors' funds, the two cannot really be viewed separately. Given the way in which, as we have seen, political events have often determined movements in nominal interest rates, and given the vital importance of interest rates for assessing the present value of public companies' future revenue streams, it would be odd if politics had no impact on the stock market.

THE FIRST BUBBLE

At first, it is true, there were only limited connections between corporate finance and public finance. The first partnerships with transferable shares can be traced back to fifteenth-century Italy, where the distinction was already recognized between share capital (*corpo*), which received shares in the company's overall profits (or losses), and *sopracorpo*, in effect corporate bonds, which received only a guaranteed interest.[47] By 1600 there were about a dozen joint-stock companies in England, though they remained small and primitive organizations. The real take-off came in the seventeenth century, with the advent of the Dutch East India Company, the first of a succession of European trading companies established to exploit monopolies of overseas markets.[48] As a growing number of trading companies issued more and more shares in smaller and more affordable denominations, something like a regular stock market became possible.

The bourse at sixteenth-century Antwerp was originally a center for cash settlements and commodities contracts, including options; later a secondary market developed there for trading government bonds like rentes and annuities.[49] But it was in the rival Amsterdam bourse that a market for company shares first developed. Amsterdam was the center of what is sometimes considered the first true "bubble," the "tulip mania" of 1636–37, though this involved speculation in commodity futures rather than shares.[50] The seventeenth-century Amsterdam market's sophistication—it was already possible to trade options and futures there—can be gleaned from Joseph Penso de la Vega's engagingly titled *Confusion de Confusiones* (1688).[51] The emergence in the 1690s of regular financial journals, notably John Castaing's *Course of the Exchange*, widened the circle of market participants and improved the flow of information. By the early eighteenth century there was already a remarkable degree of international financial integration. On the Paris Bourse (opened in 1724) shares could be traded on margin or with the use of put (sell) and call (buy) options, increasing market liquidity and reducing transaction costs.[52] It was also possible to hedge in forward markets to reduce risk.[53] In London and New York there were already informal stock markets long before such institutions were formally constituted in respectively 1801 and 1817.[54]

Yet despite appearances it was principally the market for government debt that stimulated the growth of European stock markets. The companies whose shares became the objects of speculation in 1719–20 were nominally monopolistic trading companies; but their real function was to convert (or "engraft") government annuities into shares, in order to reduce the cost of public debt service. This was true of both the Mississippi Company in France and the South Sea Company in England. The ultimate failure of this experiment—so catastrophic for the development of the French financial system—led in Britain to the emergence of the modern bond market, in which governments fund their deficits by sales of fixed interest bearing long-term or perpetual bonds. Until the late nineteenth century, because of the immense debt incurred by Britain in fighting the Napoleonic Wars, this market remained far larger in volume than the market for shares in joint-stock companies. Indeed, that market was in a stagnant state for much of the second half of the eighteenth century.[55] As late as 1853 British government bonds accounted for 70 per cent of the securities quoted on the London Stock Exchange. By 1913 the figure had fallen below 10 per cent, but the effect of the world wars in increasing the government debt and stifling private sector issuance drove the proportion back up to 64 per cent in 1950. Even as late as 1980, more than a fifth of the market value of all securities on the London Stock Exchange—and 60 per cent of the nominal value—was in the form of gilts.[56] The failure of the infant equity markets successfully to absorb the public liabilities of Britain and France had profound and enduring consequences for financial history.

Instead of brooding about the possibility of another 1929, equity market analysts would do better to study what happened 210 years before. As figure 34 shows, what happened in 1719–20 was not only the first true stock market bubble; it also has a good claim to have been the biggest bubble in history—bigger even than the bubble of the 1920s in the United States. Although the European capital markets were still in their infancy at this time, in a number of respects the circumstances bear comparison with those of the late twentieth century:

1. The economic setting was one of rapid commercial expansion, facilitated by improvements in ship-building technology and the colonization of overseas markets.

2. There was a government-sponsored attempt to shift out of bonds and into equities.
3. A small number of very big firms dominated the stock market.
4. The future earnings of those firms were exaggerated on the assumption that they would be able to maintain monopolistic positions in their markets.
5. The managements of the bubble companies had a vested interest in pushing up their share prices.
6. First-time investors provided the "cannon-fodder" for the bubble.
7. Monetary expansion played a crucial role in inflating the speculative bubble.
8. "Hot" foreign money helped both to inflate and deflate the Paris and London share markets.

Indeed, nearly all of Robert Shiller's preconditions for the bubble of the 1990s had their counterparts in Western Europe in 1719: the improvement in communications technology; international peace following the end of the War of the Spanish Succession in 1713; a discernible shift (in Britain at least) towards a more capitalist culture; the dominance of fiscal policy (again in Britain) by the wealthy elite; the beginnings of a demographic revolution; the growth of a financial press; the development of new financial institutions, namely the bond and stock markets; the stabilization of the (British) currency on the gold standard and the spread of a gambling culture.

The man who exemplified the fusion of gambling and finance was John Law.[57] The son of a successful Edinburgh goldsmith (and therefore money-lender), Law spent a dissolute youth in London, fleeing to the continent in 1694 to escape hanging for murder. After circumnavigating the gaming tables of the continent, Law returned to Scotland in 1704 and began drafting schemes of economic reform revolving around the advantages of paper money. When his hopes of a royal pardon were dashed, he returned to the Continent (along with his French mistress and two illegitimate children), attempting to sell his monetary schemes to various governments. Law's chance came in September 1714, when the susceptible duc d'Orleans became Regent of France following the death of Louis XIV.

In May 1716 Law secured a charter for a new Banque Generale which, in addition to issuing banknotes, offered basic financial services such as transfers. To boost confidence in Law, the Regent deposited a million livres with the new bank; and in October ordered French tax collectors to remit payments to the Treasury in Law's banknotes; soon after, the public were also

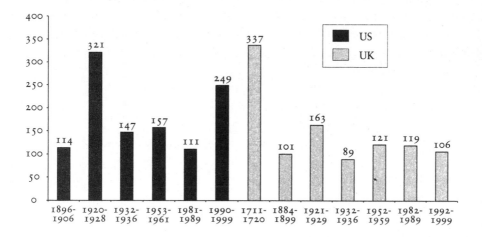

Figure 34: American and British stock market bubbles (percentage increases in inflation-adjusted annual indices)

Source: Global Financial Data.

allowed to pay taxes in notes. In December 1718, by which time the bank's assets exceeded 10 million livres, it was transformed into the Banque Royale and branches were opened in Lyon, La Rochelle, Tours, Orleans and Amiens. In effect, Law had gained control of the French money supply.

Law's next move was to bid for the Compagnie d'Occident (Mississippi Company) trading concession when it was relinquished by its previous owner in lieu of tax arrears. Law offered to turn it into a joint-stock company, exchanging shares with a face value of 500 livres for short-term government *billets* and reducing the interest on the debt. In effect, Law was converting a part of the French national debt into shares in his company. Not content with the Compagnie d'Occident, he then bid for the Compagnie d'Orient, issuing 50,000 new shares (these were known as the *filles*, to distinguish them from the first shares issued, the *mères*). Payment was in ten monthly installments (later increased to twenty). Law himself offered to buy 90 per cent of the new shares for 25 million livres, effectively underwriting the offering. The new merged company was named the Compagnie des Indes and the price of its shares soon rose rapidly, fuelled by the money being printed by the Banque Royale, also controlled by Law. As new shares were issued, existing shareholders were given preferential treatment: to buy a new share, one had already to own four old ones, for example. To maintain public enthusiasm, Law also announced a 12 per cent dividend for the following year. Between May and August, as figure 35 shows, the price of the shares rose from 490 livres (slightly below par) to 3,500 livres.

In July 1719 Law continued his extraordinary sequence of mergers by buying the rights to the Royal Mint for 50 million livres, issuing a further 50,000 shares (known as *petites filles*). His next and boldest stroke was to offer to convert the entire national debt (1.2 billion livres) from annuities into company shares or 3 per cent annuities. At the same time, he offered 52 million livres for the right to take over royal tax collection from the Receivers General.[58] Again this was financed by new issues of shares: 100,000 were issued on 13 September priced at 5,000 livres, once again with a nominal price of 500. Two more issues of 100,000 followed, then a final one of 24,000. By this point, mobs of would-be investors were besieging Law's offices in the rue Quincampoix, turning the street outside into a *de facto* stock market. By October the price of Mississippi shares had reached 6,500 livres, and by the end of November the price was up to 10,000. The price dipped in the middle of December to 7,500, but rallied to 9,400 by the end of the year. At the peak of the bubble, Law began to sell call options (known as *primes*), allowing investors to pay a deposit of 1,000 livres for the right to buy a share priced at 10,000 livres for delivery within the next six months.

Law's company was only notionally concerned with trade. The economic prospects of Louisiana were much too bleak to justify such valuations: indeed, Law was reduced to conscripting orphans, criminals and prostitutes to populate his God-forsaken Mississippi *entrepôt*. The business he was really doing was financial reform. Yet no matter how far he was able to reduce the national debt, and how far he was able to increase net tax revenues, he could never hope to generate profits large enough to justify a twenty-fold rise in the company's share price. The Mississippi bubble depended on three things: rampant money creation, the attraction of foreign capital and in the last resort state power. Share issues and banknote issues moved closely together, as figure 36 shows. Law allowed investors to buy shares in instalments, paying 10 per cent of the purchase price each month, with the option to defer the first two months to the third. At the same time, he provided loans from Banque Royale on the security of shares.[59] As he controlled both the central bank and the stock market, he was in a position to engineer a spectacular

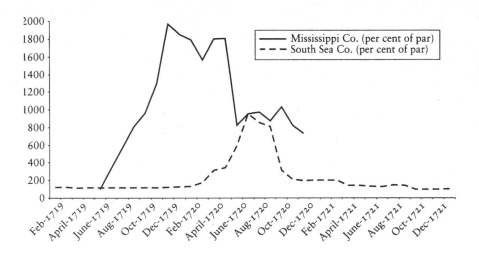

Figure 35: The Mississippi and South Sea bubbles, 1719–1720

Source: Murphy, *John Law*, p. 208, table 14.1; Neal, *Financial Capitalism*, pp. 234f.

asset price inflation. Between 25 December 1718 and 20 April 1720, issues of notes by Banque Royale rose from 18 million livres to 2,557 million livres.[60] By May 1720 the public held more than 2.4 billion livres in bank-notes. Exchange rate movements show the distinct role of foreign capital in fuelling the bubble, as Larry Neal has demonstrated. However, when foreign investors began to realize their gains in early 1720, Law was forced to rely on his new powers as controller general to try to stem the outflow of capital. On 28 January 1720 he banned the export of coins and bullion. On 4 February he banned the purchase and wearing of diamonds and other gems. On 18 February he banned the production and sale of gold ornaments. On 27 February he banned the possession of more than 500 livres of silver or gold and required that all payments of more than 100 livres be made in banknotes. In the end he was reduced to trying to demonetize silver and gold altogether in a vain attempt to halt a simultaneous depreciation of both his banknotes and the company's shares. Amid riots and an outbreak of plague, Law was

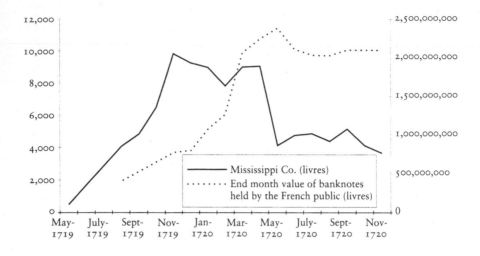

Figure 36: The Mississippi bubble: money and share prices

Source: Murphy, *John Law*, table 19.2, p. 306.

forced to abolish the paper currency, close the Banque and impose a levy on shareholders. In December 1720 he fled the country under a false passport.

The story of the South Sea Company differs from that of the Mississippi Company in three ways. First, because of the parliamentary political system in Britain, there was never a serious possibility that the company would succeed in gaining control of all the key financial institutions as Law had. Corrupt it may have been, but at least the British system had rival parties. The Whig-controlled Bank of England, created in 1694, remained outside the control of the Tory-backed South Sea Company, founded in 1711, so that the latter never wielded the control over the monetary system enjoyed by Law. Secondly, and for the same reason, the Company could not rely on the arbitrary devices adopted by Law when its share price began to fall: the Bubble Act of June 1720, designed to limit the formation of rival companies, required parliamentary sanction, unlike Law's exchange control regulations. But in other respects, the story repeated itself in London. As in the French case, the principal objective was to transform the national debt into the share capital of a company, in other words to convert annuities into equities and thus, it was hoped, reduce the cost of the debt.[61] In the initial conversion operation with which the Company began, debt-holders were essentially exchanging yields of 9 per cent for yields of 4.5 per cent; the incentive was simply that the South Sea stock was more liquid.[62] This was a process in which everyone gained, according to Neal.[63]

On 21 January 1720 it was announced in parliament that the South Sea Company would take over the entire British national debt, absorbing annuities with a capital value of around £30 million. The company would issue shares with a nominal value of £31.5 million (315,000 new shares at £100 each); it was entitled to issue new stock up to the nominal par value of the government debt it was able to convert. For this privilege, the Company would pay the government £7.5 million. Even before the measure was enacted on 7 April, the share price rose rapidly from 128 in January to 187 in mid-February.[64] Between 13 and 27 April it rose from 288 to 335. By 1 July it had reached 950.

Apart from the bribes paid to ministers and MPs, four things tended to propel the price upwards. First, the company never committed itself to a fixed conversion price for the old debts it was acquiring.[65] Secondly, stock was not made available for transfer until December, eight months after the first issue. Thirdly, as in France, shares could be paid for in installments over prolonged periods, but could instantly be used by purchasers as collateral for loans from the Company. Finally, as in Paris, exchange rate and the other interest rate data point to large-scale foreign speculation, first from France, then from Holland. And as in Paris, the smart foreign money got out at the top of the market.[66]

Until mid-June, according to Neal, the bubble was "rational." This seems implausible since Law's bubble had burst in May, offering investors in South Sea stock an alarming vision of their own future. Regardless of events in Paris, the Company's future prospects could hardly justify its share price. The announcement in 21 June of a 30 per cent dividend and a guaranteed 50 per cent dividend for the next twelve years was sheer fantasy. Moreover, there was always the danger that, because the South Sea Company could not print its own money—it relied on the promissory notes of the Sword Blade Company, which were not legally banknotes at all—and because it was slow to prevent other companies competing with it for funds, share prices might outrun the resources of the money market.[67] This was what happened in June, when the Company opened its third subscription to new investors (as opposed to holders of old government annuities). When stock worth £50 million was subscribed, the drain on the money market was too much.[68] By August there was "a desperate credit crunch in the London money market" and the price slipped to 810.[69] On 24 September the Sword

Blade Company suspended payments and the price collapsed to 310. Unlike Law, those responsible did not escape unpunished. The Chancellor of the Exchequer and several directors of the Company were consigned to the Tower of London.

What lessons, if any, can be learned from the experience of the Mississippi and South Sea Bubbles? Now, as then, a relatively small number of companies have attracted investors with implicit or explicit promises of high and prolonged monopoly profits. Now, as then, a fundamental shift is occurring—or being attempted—from public sector bonds to private sector equities. In the modern case, it is not a direct conversion that is being attempted, but rather an indirect and piecemeal transition. First, there are countries like Britain and the United States, which are actively reducing their outstanding national debts. One consequence of this policy is to reduce the availability of long-term government bonds. Secondly, there are countries such as Germany, while seeking to reduce their unfunded public pension liabilities, which have the potential greatly to increase their funded debt in the foreseeable future. Thirdly, all these countries are actively encouraging their citizens, by a variety of incentives, to provide for ill health or retirement by investing directly or through mutual and pension funds in the stock market. In combination, these forces are causing an unprecedented shift in the balance of financial forces, so that (for example) the market capitalization of the New York Stock Exchange is now four times greater than the stock of US Treasuries.[70] In theory, it is without doubt preferable to pay pensions through investment earnings from private pension funds rather than through taxation and social security ("Pay As You Go"). But in practice, as the British experience shows, simultaneously increasing private investment in pension funds while reducing the national debt and hence the availability of gilts can have the perverse effect of driving down yields and hence rates of return below the real growth rate.[71] Under an unfunded state pension system, the old can be defrauded by political fiat if taxpayers insist on a reduction in the real value of entitlements. But in a funded scheme pensioners can lose out too if the weight of their own savings drives down the real returns they can hope to enjoy.

Finally, international capital flows are exerting an exceptionally large influence on stock markets, just as they did in 1719–20. The economic journalist Anatole Kaletsky put his finger on this when he wrote in August 1999: "The entire US economy has in effect become a sort of gigantic investment fund, borrowing money cheaply from financially unsophisticated foreigners (especially the Japanese) and then reaping the profits for investing it more imaginatively in riskier ventures at home and abroad."[72] The experience of the eighteenth century suggests that a shift in the sentiment of foreign investors could have dire consequences.

CALCULATING "THE MADNESS OF PEOPLE"

It is always hard to argue against a bull market. Sir Isaac Newton, the genius of his age, lost heavily on South Sea stock by buying, selling, and then re-entering the market on the eve of its collapse. "I can calculate the motions of the heavenly bodies," he commented ruefully, "but not the madness of the people."[73]

Unlike Newton, Karl Marx believed that the motions of human history could be calculated on the basis of the economic laws he discerned. Yet the author of *Capital* was unable to succeed where Newton had failed. On 4 June 1864 Marx wrote to his long-time collaborator Friedrich Engels that he had "made a killing on the Stock Exchange here. The time has come again when, with wit and a very little money, it's possible to make money in London."[74] According to his most recent biographer, Marx may have been tempted to become a day-trader by the German socialist Ferdinand Lassalle, who had boasted of his stock market speculations when the two met in 1862.[75] Three weeks later Marx enlarged on his activities to another correspondent:

I have, which will surprise you not a little, been speculating—partly in American funds, but more especially in English stocks, which are springing up like mushrooms this year (in furtherance of every imaginable and unimaginable joint stock enterprise), are forced up to quite an unreasonable level and then, for the most part, collapse. In this way, I have made over £400 and, now that the complexity of the political situation affords greater scope, I shall begin all over again. It's a type of operation that makes small demands on one's time, and it's worth while running some risk in order to relieve the enemy of his money.[76]

If the mid-Victorian stock market could lure even the most influential of all critics of capitalism, its charms were potent indeed.

Will the bubble of the late 1990s continue to inflate, stabilize or burst? Who can predict a random walk? The elusiveness of a relible predictive model of stock market behavior is not however, an argument for "the end of economic history."[77] Rather it demonstrates that predictive models are not what historical study can hope to construct. In studying financial history, we are studying systems more complex and chaotic than the weather: systems in which the particles—human beings—are subject to unpredictable mood swings ranging from the "irrational exuberance" of the late 1990s to the equally irrational "fear itself" of the 1930s. The task of the financial historian is not to find the economic equivalent of Mr Casaubon's "Key to all Mythologies," but to reveal the wide range of possible outcomes, even within quite similar institutional frameworks. One possible outcome at the time of writing is that the market has already entered a phase of consolidation, and will bump along at the 10,000 mark for some time to come. As figure 29 above shows, there have been such plateaus before, notably from 1906 to 1924, and again from 1966 to 1982. Still, it is worth remembering that it was Irving Fisher, professor of economics at Yale, who declared on the eve of the 1929 crash: "Stock prices have reached a permanent and high plateau." If nothing else, that should illustrate the difficulty of making any prediction about the future path of asset prices. Fisher knew a lot about economics. So did some of those who predicted a stock market crash back in 1997.

I I

Golden Fetters, Paper Chains:
International Monetary Regimes

Ex uno plures.
Converse of the motto printed on every US dollar bill (E pluribus unum).

In Ian Fleming's *Goldfinger* (1959), the implausibly titled Colonel Smithers of the Bank of England gives James Bond a brief explanation of the gold standard in the era of Bretton Woods: "Gold and currencies backed by gold are the foundation of our international credit," he explains to the great secret agent, whose ignorance of monetary matters outside the casino seems more or less complete. "We can only tell what the true strength of the pound is, and other countries can only tell it, by knowing the amount of valuta we have behind our currency." But gold is being stolen from the Bank by the sinister bullion-dealer Auric Goldfinger, who has already accumulated £20 million of the stuff. And while demand for gold continues to grow inexorably—for hoarding, for dental fillings and for jewelry, as well as for central bank reserves—the supply is nearing exhaustion:

"Just to show you, from 1500 to 1900 . . . the whole world produced about 18,000 tons of gold. From 1900 to today we have dug up 41,000 tons. At this rate, Mr Bond," Colonel Smithers leaned forward earnestly, "— and please don't quote me— but I wouldn't be surprised if in fifty years' time we have not totally exhausted the gold content of the earth!"

Finally, Smithers comes to the point. "The Bank can do nothing about [Goldfinger's smuggling], so we are asking you to bring Mr Goldfinger to book, Mr Bond, and get that gold back. You know about the currency crisis and the high bank rate? Of course. Well, England needs that gold, badly— and the quicker the better."[1]

In fact, it turns out that Goldfinger has bigger fish to fry than the Bank of England. As Bond aficionados will recall, he plans, with the aid of the Mafia

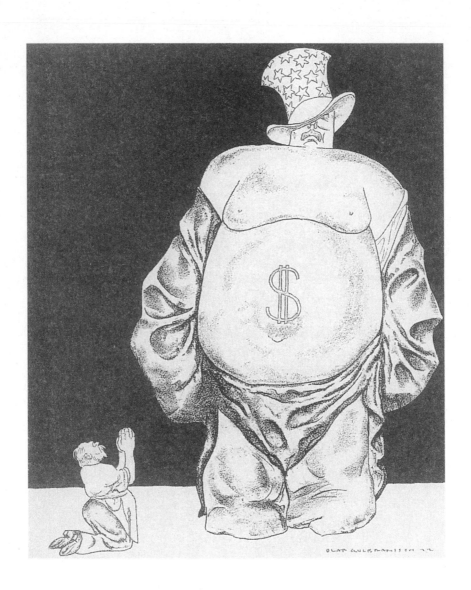

and a lethal nerve gas, to rob the US gold reserve at Fort Knox, which at that time contained $15 billion of gold bullion ("approximately half the supply of mined gold in the world"). Moreover, Goldfinger himself is a mere operative of the Soviet counter-espionage organization SMERSH. Their ultimate objective is nothing less than "to take the golden heart of America" to Russia.

In 1959 Goldfinger would have been stealing precious metal worth $35 dollars an ounce. It seems reasonable to assume that the disappearance of such a large quantity of gold from the US reserves would have driven the dollar price of gold up sharply, thereby destabilizing if not demolishing the Bretton Woods system of fixed exchange rates. In the event, however, there was no need for a Goldfinger to bring this about. Bretton Woods disintegrated just over a decade after Fleming's book was published, the victim not of a Soviet-backed heist, but of the rising costs of the war in Vietnam and the "Great Society" welfare program. On 15 August 1971, after prolonged pressure on the dollar–gold exchange rate, President Nixon suspended convertibility of the dollar by "closing the gold window." Henceforth it would no longer be possible for anyone in the United States to exchange dollar bills for the precious metal. The dollar price of gold immediately took off; which is to say that the gold price of the dollar collapsed. By January 1980 the price of gold had reached an historic peak of $850 per ounce.

More than forty years on, it is tempting to wonder if it would now be worth Goldfinger's while to rob Fort Knox, with the price of gold down to around $260 per ounce. Such a robbery would certainly come too late to save the Soviet system, SMERSH and all. But there is an organization which might derive benefit from such a robbery: that of the world's gold producers. If they still yearn to see the price of the yellow metal return to its 1980 peak, then the only man capable of doing it is Goldfinger.

Since the late 1990s it has been the gold producers who have felt themselves the victims of robbery. In May 1999 the British Treasury announced the government's decision to sell 415 tonnes[2]—more than half—of its gold reserve held in the vaults of the Bank of England. What would Colonel Smithers have made of this? Almost immediately the price of gold fell by more than 10 per cent. For most of January and February 1999 it had hovered around $290 an ounce. By the second week of June the price was just over $258, the lowest price in twenty years. Shares in gold mines fell by around a quarter. And of course the value of the Bank of England's gold fell too, at a notional cost to the British taxpayer of some $660 million.

It was not just the British decision to start selling off gold that alarmed the bullion market in 1999. Potentially of equal importance were the implications for gold of European Economic and Monetary Union (EMU). The European Central Bank did not—as it might have done—exclude gold completely from its balance sheet. But its decision to hold 15 per cent of its reserves in gold (860 tonnes) was more than counterbalanced by the diminished needs of the eleven national central banks which, in January 1999, became to all intents and purposes subsidiaries of the ECB. In all, the National Central Banks held some 12,447 tonnes of gold on the eve of EMU, around 17 per cent of their total pre-EMU reserves. But under the single currency they could no longer count other EMU currencies as foreign currency reserves, and they were also obliged to value gold at its market price (something a number of them, including the German Bundesbank, had not been doing). This meant that on 1 January 1999 the proportion of gold in their reserves rose overnight to almost a third of the total.[3] It therefore seemed likely that other European countries would at some point join Britain in selling gold. The Swiss central bank was also poised to start reducing its gold holding from 1,300 tonnes, around half its total reserves.[4] As the year 2000 approached, the International Monetary Fund came under political pressure—not least from the British Chancellor of the Exchequer Gordon Brown—to fund developing country debt "forgiveness" by selling off part of its large reserves, the second largest in the world.[5] The twilight of gold appeared to have arrived.

True, total blackout is still some way off. There were bouts of gold-selling by some Western central banks in the 1970s and 1980s, but these did not escalate into demonetization.[6] Moreover, the bullion market was granted a stay of execution in September 1999, when the European central banks announced a five-year ceiling on gold sales of 400 tonnes per year.[7] It is nevertheless worth pondering what would happen if, like the Bank of England, all major central banks decided or were told to reduce their gold holdings by around 50 per cent. If Germany, France, Italy, the Netherlands, Portugal, Spain and Austria were to do so, 5,753 tonnes would be released onto the market. If (and this seems much less likely) the United States and Japan were to reduce their gold reserves by half, then a further 4,446 tonnes would be for sale. If these figures are added together with anticipated British, Swiss and IMF sales, the total amount of disposable gold could be as much as 12,224 tonnes: about four to five years of total world mining production.[8] And of course it is a great deal easier to get gold from a central bank vault than from under the ground, provided one knows the combination.

THE TWILIGHT OF GOLD

In long-term perspective, of course, the fall in the price of gold was to be expected. On the basis of the average purchasing power parity of gold over two hundred years, the price of gold should have been just $234 per ounce in 1997.[9] The surge in gold prices that occurred during the 1970s was historically anomalous, reflecting a sudden increase in demand for gold following the American suspension of convertibility and the rapid depreciation of most Western currencies relative to oil and other commodities.

Gold has a future, of course—but mainly as jewelry, the demand for which accounted for more than three-quarters of all the gold sold in 1992. The average Saudi bride wears five kilograms of 24-carat gold jewelry. India alone consumes around 700 tonnes of gold per annum, compared with less than 300 tonnes in 1993; all told, the Indian public holds approximately 10,000 tonnes. To set this figure in perspective, the world stock of gold above ground at the end of 1997 amounted to 134,800 tonnes, of which central banks held less than a quarter (31,900 tonnes). The annual production of all the world's gold mines in 1998 was 2,500 tonnes—less than four times the annual consumption of India alone. Luckily for gold producers, the cultures most addicted to gold as a decoration are currently enjoying rapid growth of both population and income.[10]

Gold also has a future as a store of value in parts of the world with primitive or unstable monetary and financial systems. This is because of its long-run "tendency . . . to return to an historic rate of exchange with other commodities."[11] Since 1899 the price of a loaf of bread in Britain has risen by a factor of 32; the price of an ounce of gold by a factor of 38.[12] Indeed, an ounce of gold buys approximately the same amount of bread today as it bought in the time of Nebuchadnezzar, king of Babylon, more than 2,500 years ago.[13]

It should be emphasized that, contrary to popular belief, gold has been a poor hedge against inflation in Britain and the United States.[14] The purchasing power of gold has actually increased more in periods of deflation like the 1880s and 1930s; whereas during war-induced inflations it has lost ground relative to industrial commodities needed for military purposes.[15] The real attraction of gold is that it is accessible and exchangeable even when established monetary institutions fail. In the American banking crises of the pre-1914 period, in the extreme hyperinflations of the early 1920s and in the banking collapses of the early 1930s—these were the times when a hoard of gold was worth its proverbial weight. In the Second World War, as national financial systems buckled in the face of invasion and aerial bombardment, gold was the one asset that proved indestructible. It was Britain's ability to ship it in large quantities to the United States in 1938–40 that kept the flow of imports coming across the Atlantic. Even when ships carrying gold were sunk—as happened to the SS *Fort Sitikine* in Bombay Harbour in April 1944—the gold could still be recovered, albeit in a somewhat battered condition.[16] Much of the gold that the Nazis managed to steal from the countries they plundered has since been found: it survived, though its rightful owners perished. In any country that has experienced hyperinflation in the past century, gold has also been a better investment over the hundred years than both bonds and equities. Even in the recent Asian crisis, it was remarkable how many financially stricken individuals were saved from complete insolvency by their nest-eggs of gold. Gold will continue to have an appeal as a store of value anywhere where currencies or banking systems are fragile, the countries of the former Soviet Union being obvious examples.

Nevertheless, as part of the first tier of central bank reserves in developed economies, gold appears to have had its day. Inexorably, we are moving towards a demonetization of gold comparable with the demonetization of silver that began in the 1870s.

From the point of view of the private investor in the West, where the possibility (or at least the memory) of political or financial catastrophe has receded, the twilight of gold makes some sense. As an investment, gold has signally under-performed stocks and government bonds in the United States and Britain in the past century: if your great-grandfather had bought and bequeathed to his heirs an ounce of gold in the 1890s, you would still have an ounce of gold; but if he had bought shares in a UK tracker fund—had such a thing existed—you would now be able to buy around 88 ounces with your inheritance.[17] On the other hand, the real returns from holding gold from 1968 to 1996 varied inversely with the real returns from holding stocks and bonds, so that a portfolio which included some gold in that period offered on average a higher return and lower risk than a portfolio composed exclusively of shares.[18] But that begs the question: should central banks make decisions about their reserves in the same way that investors structure their portfolios?

In historical perspective, the creeping demonetization of gold is another difference between the globalization of the period 1870–1914 and the globalization of our own time. The process of financial globalization described in the previous chapter went hand in hand with the extension of a system of fixed exchange rates based on gold. In the eyes of many contemporaries, the gold standard was the *sine qua non* of large scale international investment. Yet today's financial globalization is taking place at a time of considerable exchange rate volatility, and apparently with little need for gold reserves.

There have been four periods of global exchange rate stability since the period of monetary chaos caused by the Revolutionary and Napoleonic Wars (see Figure 37). Between 1819[19] and *c.*1859 an informal bimetallic system function relatively smoothly. Between 1859 and 1871 a succession of wars in Europe and North America disrupted this system. After 1871 the world entered a second phase of currency stability which lasted until 1914: gradually more and more countries abandoned silver in favour of the monometallic gold standard. The nine years of war and revolution from 1914 to 1923 saw renewed exchange rate volatility; but from 1924 until 1931 a restored gold exchange standard operated, only to disintegrate in the face of the Great Depression. The fourth era of international currency stability—under the Bretton Woods dollar standard—ran from 1947[20] until 1971, when the decision to end the convertibility of the dollar ushered in the current era of more or less freely floating rates.

Although there have been myriad efforts to limit exchange rate volatility in the form of more or less ephemeral international agreements (from the Smithsonian in 1971 to the Louvre in 1987), national currency pegs and boards, regional exchange rate systems and monetary unions, the most important rates are primarily determined by the foreign exchange markets. This may well be the best available arrangement. As Milton Friedman long ago argued, movements in exchange rates offset inflation and productivity differentials with much less friction than adjustments of nominal wages and prices under fixed rates. This is certainly true over the long run. In the short run, however, the rates set by the foreign exchange markets tend to overshoot and undershoot relative to purchasing price parities—that is, the rates implied by differentials in national inflation rates.[21] Whatever the reason for this—and economists are divided, if not downright baffled—it is plainly a source of periodic and severe regional instability. Currency crises in Mexico and Asia in the 1990s led to severe recessions as exchange rates nose-dived, busting banks with large foreign currency liabilities, crunching domestic credit and driving the incomes of millions of people sharply downwards.[22]

Two alternatives suggest themselves, both of which merit historical assessment. Should the world attempt to return—with or without gold—to a

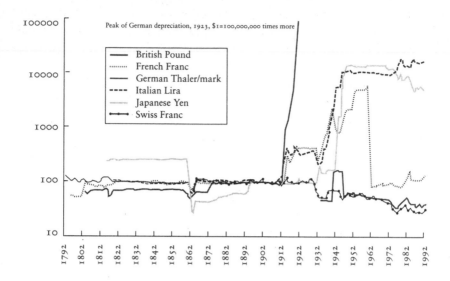

Figure 37: Exchange rates of major currencies per US dollar, 1792–1992 (1913=100)
Source: Global Financial Data.

system of fixed exchange rates? Or does the future lie not with fixed exchange rates but with outright monetary unions like the one established by eleven European countries in 1999?

THE YELLOW BRICK ROAD

In *The Wizard of Oz*, Dorothy, the Scarecrow, the Tin Man and the Lion have to follow a winding and hazardous "yellow brick road" in order to reach their destination. Few devotees of the classic Judy Garland movie are aware that the original 1900 book by Frank Baum was in part a satire on America's entry into the gold standard.[23]

The road to an international gold standard was indeed more tortuous than is often acknowledged. For most of the nineteenth century two of the five great powers—Austria and Russia—had widely fluctuating exchange rates.[24] The United States suspended convertibility as a result of the Civil War in 1862 and remained on a paper standard until 1879. Although the redemption of US bonds was restored to a gold basis in 1869 and the silver dollar was dropped from the coinage in the so-called "crime of 1873," there was a sustained political campaign against gold lasting into the 1890s.[25] (In the eyes of the Populists, the gold standard was a British and/or Jewish racket to depress mid-western farm prices and enrich the financiers of Wall Street.) In 1868 only Britain and a number of its economic dependencies—Portugal, Egypt, Canada, Chile and Australia—were on the gold standard. France and the other members of the Latin Monetary Union, as well as Russia, Persia and some Latin American states were on the bimetallic system; while most of the rest of the world was on the silver standard. Not until 1900 was the transition to gold more or less complete. By 1908 only China, Persia and a handful of Central American countries were still on silver. The gold standard had become, in effect, the global monetary system, though in practice a number of Asian economies had a gold exchange standard (with local currencies convertible into sterling rather than actual gold) and a number of "Latin" economies in Europe and America did not technically maintain convertibility of notes into gold.[26]

How exactly the gold standard worked has been debated *ad nauseam* by economists. As an international system, its primary function was obviously to fix exchange rates: or to be precise, to narrow the band of fluctuation down to the so-called "gold points," the rates at which it became profitable to import or export gold.[27] As we saw in Chapter 5, the classical model of the system derived from the "price-specie-flow" mechanism, which was supposed to adjust trade imbalances through the effects on relative prices of gold flows. Later theorists discerned a more swiftly adjusting mechanism at work, whereby short-term capital flows responded more or less instantaneously to increases or decreases in discount rates. Keynesians concentrated on the effects of the gold standard on incomes and demand in peripheral countries such as Argentina.[28] Monetarists, meanwhile, have sought to show that the gold standard did not operate through changes in the terms of trade because arbitrage kept the prices of all internationally traded goods the same around the world.[29]

According to the "rules of the game," central banks were supposed to mediate between the international and domestic economy by varying interest rates in response to gold flows. However, there is considerable evidence of outright breaches of these rules, for example by the French and Belgian central banks.[30] Some central banks were more likely to increase rates in response to an outflow than to decrease them in response to an inflow; some manipulated the price of gold to change the gold points.[31]

What were the benefits of the gold standard? Clearly, fixed exchange rates remove an element of uncertainty from international trade. But there is little reason to think that this was the reason for the increased volume of trade between 1870 and 1914, which might just as easily have occurred without fixed exchange rates. What the gold standard is usually said to have delivered is long-run price stability. The average annual change in wholesale prices between 1870 and 1913 was –0.7 per cent in Britain and 0.1 per cent in the United States. Table 19 shows average inflation rates for twenty-one countries since 1881, subdivided according to regions and exchange regimes. Though it would not be true to say that the pre-1914 gold standard delivered the lowest inflation for all twenty-one countries in the sample—that accolade belongs to the deflationary inter-war period—it is clear that prices were most stable in the industrialized economies when they were on gold.

True, such figures conceal considerable short-run fluctuations and significant movements over shorter periods. Between 1849 and 1873 British prices rose by 51 per cent; then fell by 45 per cent between 1873 and 1896, only to rise by 39 per cent between 1896 and 1913. American prices followed a

Table 17. Exchange rate regimes and inflation

	Gold Standard	Gold Exchange	Bretton Woods	Floating
	1881–1913	1919–1938	1946–1970	1974–1990
US	0.3	–1.8	2.4	5.6
UK	0.3	–1.5	3.7	9.4
Germany	0.6	–2.1	2.7	3.3
France	0.0	2.2	5.6	8.8
Other Western Europe (1)*	0.6	–0.5	3.1	4.0
Scandinavia (2)	0.4	–0.6	5.0	8.1
Dominions (3)	0.5	–0.8	3.6	6.8
Southern Europe (4)	0.3	2.0	5.6	14.7
Latin America (5)	4.0	2.3	25.0	82.8
Japan	4.6	–1.7	4.5	2.6
All	1.2	0.2	7.3	19.0

* 1 Belgium, Netherlands, Switzerland; 2 Denmark, Finland, Norway, Sweden; 3 Australia, Canada; 4 Greece, Italy, Portugal, Spain; 5 Argentina, Brazil, Chile. Source: Bordo, "Gold as a Commitment Mechanism," pp. 32 f. Inflation defined as the annual mean of the GDP deflator.

similar path.[32] Nevertheless, statistical analysis reveals these movements to have been a "random walk" or "white noise" process, meaning that they showed no tendency to persist.[33] No matter what the short- or medium-term movements of the price level, people could be confident that prices would ultimately revert to their historic mean.[34]

Was this economically beneficial? In theory (or at least in some theories) price stability always is. And there is some empirical evidence to suggest that the gold standard was. In Britain and the United States, real per capita income was less variable between 1870 and 1913 than it was thereafter. Unemployment was lower than between the wars.[35] So too were long-term interest rates, though not necessarily real rates.[36] However, it is not certain that these differences can be attributed solely or even partly to the presence or absence of gold. It has been argued persuasively that bimetallism would have been preferable to monometallism: the real "crime of 1873" was the French decision to abandon silver, and hence to give up Paris's role as the key center of international monetary arbitrage.[37] Moreover, the greater short-run variation of inflation and output under gold may have been more distressing to contemporaries than the lower long-run inflation emphasized by gold standard enthusiasts.[38] Keynes's famous remark—"In the long run we are all dead"— bears repeating: people are generally far more conscious of short-run ups and downs of the economy than of secular movements of prices and output. From the point of view of achieving low and stable inflation and high and stable growth, the Bretton Woods system of which Keynes was a principal architect was superior—though other factors almost certainly contributed more to post-war success than the exchange rate regime.[39]

The fluctuations in prices mentioned above were partly a result of changes in the global stock of gold. The worldwide shift to gold might have had disastrously deflationary consequences had the supply of gold not proved relatively elastic. In the 1840s world gold production averaged 42 tonnes a year, of which more than half came from Russia. By the 1850s total production had risen to 965 tonnes, with around half the increase from California and half from Australia.[40] Thanks to the development of the Rand goldfields in South Africa and the Kalgoorlie field in Western Australia in the 1890s, as well as discoveries in Colorado, the Klondike and Siberia, world gold stocks more than trebled between the 1850s and 1900s.[41] As Figure 38 shows, the additions to the world gold stock were far from gradual, ranging from 88 per cent in the 1850s to just 11 per cent in the 1880s.[42] Changes in the technology of gold processing such as the discovery of the cyanide process also had an influence.

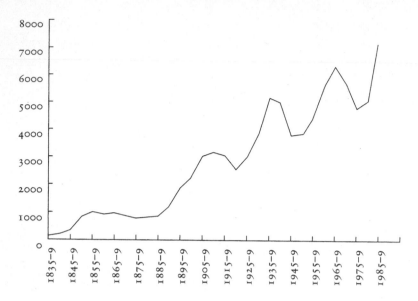

Figure 38. World gold production, five yearly totals, 1835–1989 (metric tonnes)
Source: Green, World of Gold, pp. 364f.; id., "Central Bank Gold Reserves."

At the same time, it is important to recognize that the gold standard was not rigidly bound to the gold supply. Financial innovation, as the use of paper money and cheques became more widespread, loosened the golden fetters. The greater part of the monetary expansion that occurred between 1885 and 1913 was due to the fivefold growth of demand deposits; by comparison gold reserves grew only three and a half times.[43] Remarkably, given its much-vaunted "hegemonic" position, the UK accounted for just 3.6 per cent of all gold held by central banks and Treasuries in 1913.[44] The Bank of England was like a "man with little flesh on his bones . . . [with] only a slim gold reserve surrounding a vulnerable gold standard frame."[45] The disadvantage was that there was a clear trade-off between the size of the gold reserve and the volatility of short-term rates: countries with bigger reserves (such as France) needed to change the discount rate less frequently.[46]

A rather different justification of the gold standard is that, by removing exchange rate risk and affirming a country's commitment to "sound" fiscal and monetary policies, it reduced the cost of international borrowing for countries that joined. It was a "commitment mechanism": going onto gold was a way of forswearing "time-inconsistent" fiscal and monetary policies such as printing money to collect seigniorage or defaulting on debt.[47] However, so the argument runs, gold convertibility was "a contingent rule, or a rule with escape clauses": it could be suspended "in the event of a well understood, exogenously produced emergency, such as a war, on the understanding that after the emergency had safely passed convertibility would be restored at the original parity."[48] In some cases there was a second legitimate exception to the rule: in banking crises (such as 1847, 1857 and 1866 in Britain) the authorities could temporarily suspend the golden rule to act as lender of last resort.[49]

As has already been suggested, the idea of wars or financial crises as "well understood emergencies" is the weak link in this argument. Its proponents merely infer from statistical data that such exceptions to the gold convertibility rule were "well understood"; they provide almost no historical evidence that contemporaries regarded them as such. Nor is it entirely clear why some emergencies were regarded as legitimate reasons for departing from the rule, while some were not.[50] It is certainly true that countries bearing the "Good Housekeeping seal of approval" conferred by gold standard membership could borrow money on better terms than those which did not. However, the premiums involved were surprisingly low in view of the very substantial depreciations experienced by Argentina, Brazil and Chile between 1880 and 1914. Already by 1895 the currencies of all three had depreciated by around 60 per cent against sterling. Yet the premiums they had to pay on gold-denominated bonds amounted to no more than two percentage points relative to gold-adhering borrowers like Canada and Australia. The average yield on Chilean paper-denominated bonds over the period as a whole was just 7 per cent, compared with a figure for the United States of just over 4 per cent. But by 1914 the Chilean currency was down to 20 per cent of its 1870 exchange rate; whereas the dollar was at par.[51] The limits of this approach may well be revealed by the fact that the same calculations for the inter-war period produce similar results.[52] Being on gold was worth between 100 and 200 basis points on a country's yields. But what were the costs in terms of output of being on gold?

It is also worth noting that a commitment mechanism might be possible without fixed exchange rates. For example, the current fashion for inflation targeting or the adoption of some other form of explicit rule by independent national central banks could amount to a form of credible commitment. However, it remains to be seen how far heterogeneous national targets could ever constitute an international commitment mechanism comparable with the gold standard.[53] Given the well-established tendency for monetary targets to drift in the 1970s and 1980s, it seems doubtful that inflation targets will ever attain the credibility associated with a gold convertibility rate.[54]

Still, with all these qualifications, the combination of long-run price stability, a commitment to time-consistent fiscal and monetary policies and lower interest payments on foreign debt makes the gold standard sound quite attractive. Indeed, there was a period (in the aftermath of the collapse of the Bretton Woods system) when many American economists—including the young Alan Greenspan—argued seriously for a return to gold for precisely these reasons. This view is by no means defunct. Pointing to the high costs of the enormous number of foreign exchange transactions carried out every year in the absence of fixed rates, the economist Robert Mundell has argued for "the introduction of [an] international composite currency" with, at least to begin with, some kind of "confidence-building identification with gold."[55] In May 1999 Greenspan himself reassured the House Banking Committee that gold still represented "the ultimate form of payment in the world;" indeed, he had told a Bank of England symposium five years before that "the pressure towards . . . focusing central bank activity to the equivalent of the gold standard [would] become increasingly evident."[56]

The reason most economists are skeptical of such arguments is perhaps best summed up by the idea of a policy "trilemma." In essence, the trilemma is that a country can have at most two out of three economic policy objectives: a fixed exchange rate; free capital movements; and an independent monetary policy.[57] Members of the gold standard or any successor system generally had the first two, but could not have the third. The possibility therefore existed that the monetary policy required to maintain exchange rate stability in the context of free capital movements might be inappropriate from the viewpoint of the domestic economy. This had been Keynes's point in the *Tract on Monetary Reform*:

In truth, the gold standard is already a barbarous relic. All of us, from the Governor of the Bank of England downwards, are now primarily interested in preserving the stability of business, prices, and employment, and are not likely, when the choice is forced on us, deliberately to sacrifice these to outworn dogma, which had its value once, of £3 17s 1 $^1/_2$ per ounce. Advocates of the ancient standard do not observe how remote it now is from the spirit and the requirements of the age.[58]

For this reason, the price of gold standard membership was not necessarily as low as some calculations might seem to imply. A government that committed itself to a fixed exchange rate might find the domestic costs outweighing the benefits. The credibility of the exchange rate would weaken as the domestic costs rose but, in a vicious circle, attempts to reaffirm credibility by raising interest rates would merely increase the pain for domestic borrowers. Beyond a certain critical point, the speculators would begin to circle overhead and, in the absence of effective external assistance, the central bank's ability to intervene (to buy the currency as fast as others were dumping it) could quite quickly be exhausted.

Currency crises like these have been fairly regular events because, even in the absence of an international system of fixed rates, many developing countries with external debts denominated in foreign currency will tend to peg their exchange rates rather than risk a market-led depreciation. One way of assessing the costs of fixed exchange rates is to compare financial crises[59] before 1914 with financial crises since the collapse of Bretton Woods. There is in fact some evidence that crises in the gold standard era were, if not less severe—the crisis in Argentina in 1890 was worse even than Thailand's in 1997—then at least shorter in duration than equivalent crises in the modern world of more or less freely floating rates. This has been cited as evidence in favour of the "commitment mechanism" view of the gold standard: because countries were seen to be committed to convertibility, their breach of the rules in a crisis was seen as only temporary, encouraging investors to return.[60] Yet the differences are fairly marginal, and firm conclusions are hazardous given the difficulty of finding data from a strictly comparable sample groups of countries.[61] Moreover, if there was greater rapidity of adjustment in the pre-1914, it may have been a function of quite different factors:[62] greater flexibility of prices and wages, greater mobility of labour in the absence of restrictions on cross-border migration, limited political representation of the social groups hardest hit by such crises and perhaps also the widespread adoption in colonial economies of British legal and accounting standards.[63] On the other hand, emerging markets before 1914 tended to lack effective lenders of last resort, so that recovery from banking crises ought to have been slower than in the 1990s.[64]

The experience of the inter-war period also suggests that fixed exchange rates run the risk of exporting financial crises: the phenomenon known as "contagion." Few historians would now dispute that disastrous errors were made by the American monetary authorities in the 1930s.[65] But the sterilization of gold inflows in the 1920s,[66] the over-reaction to gold outflows in September 1931 and the failure to continue open market operations in 1932 had catastrophic effects not only on the United States but on all economies with currencies pegged to the dollar. That meant most of the world since, at the system's high noon in 1929, no fewer than forty-six nations were on the gold exchange standard.[67] It was only when countries abandoned the gold standard in the 1930s that they began to experience recovery.[68]

By the same token, the system of "fixed but adjustable" exchange rates established at Bretton Woods ultimately subordinated the rest of the world to American monetary policy.[69] Although it coincided with a period of rapid economic growth, it is important to remember how unstable the Bretton Woods system was as a system of fixed exchange rates. Almost from the out-set, there was doubt about the sustainability of the dollar–sterling rate, in view of British balance of payments problems. After a failed attempt to restore convertibility in 1947, sterling was devalued in September 1949 and again in November 1967. The franc was also devalued three times. Mean-while, the deutschmark was revalued twice. Until 1959 only the dollar was fully convertible; capital and exchange controls were retained elsewhere because of the shortage of international reserves outside the United States. Thereafter, pressure on the dollar increasingly required international inter-vention (the "gold pool") and other devices to limit conversion of dollars into gold. From March 1968, when the pool was suspended, the system was in terminal decline, as dollar reserves accumulated in Germany and Japan, both of which were running large current account surpluses with the United States.[70] The fundamental reason for the breakdown of the system was the reluctance of the other members—France in particular—to import rising American inflation.[71]

The crisis of the European Exchange Rate Mechanism in the 1990s was analogous to the demise of Bretton Woods, in that the members of the ERM were essentially hostages to German monetary policy. Established in 1979, by the end of the 1980s the ERM appeared to confer on its members the ben-efits of German monetary policy, namely a credible commitment to low infla-tion, and therefore relatively low interest rates. This was the main reason for the British decision to join, six weeks before Margaret Thatcher's deposition in 1990. However, this coincided fatefully with the collapse of the Soviet empire in Eastern Europe and the reunification of Germany, leading to a dra-matic increase in the German federal deficit. The resulting surge of new Ger-man bond issues to finance unification with the former German Democratic Republic pushed up not only the German debt/GDP ratio but also German interest rates. (To be precise, German public debt rose from 42 per cent of GDP in 1991 to just over 60 per cent in 1996, almost twice the figure for 1980; the average public sector deficit for the years 1991–6 was 5.5 per cent of GDP.) In the absence of the ERM, the deutschmark would certainly have appreciated against other European currencies. The rules of the system, however, required interest rates to rise throughout the system. By 1992 it was apparent that the domestic political costs of higher interest rates—not least those on Conservative voters' mortgages—were proving intolerable in Britain and in Italy and in September of that year both currencies were forced out of the system by a speculative onslaught which the various central banks were unable (or perhaps, in the case of the Bundesbank, unwilling) to resist. Spain, Portugal and Ireland were also forced to devalue; and in the summer of 1993 pressure on the French franc led to a widening of the bands within which the remaining currencies were allowed to fluctuate against one another.[72]

Finally, it is possible to have contagion on the periphery even in the absence of a major policy shock emanating from the core. Once the credibility of one currency peg was lost in Asia—when the Thai *baht* was allowed to float, or rather sink, on 2 July 1997—the credibility of neighbouring currencies soon followed.[73] This was partly because foreign investors did not make distinctions between Asian emerging markets, but also because the related problems of unhedged foreign exchange borrowing, short-term loans to finance long-term investments and moral hazard (the presumption that the government or IMF would bail the private sector out in a crisis) were present in most of the affected economies.[74]

Like clouds, currency crises have silver linings. The main beneficiaries of the Asian crisis were Americans, all of whom benefited from sharply reduced import prices—and particularly American economists, who were supplied with a fresh subject for study just as interest was fading in the problems of post-Soviet "transition." Some analysts blamed the Asian economies for practicing "crony capitalism," a shorthand for myriad problems of inadequate financial regulation. Others blamed the IMF for failing to act as an international lender of last resort.[75] Policy prescriptions of every hue abounded. It was claimed that the Asian crisis illustrated the need for controls or at least brakes on short-term international capital flows of the sort introduced in Chile in the 1980s. Another school of thought recommended the development of deeper domestic capital markets to allow more long-term borrowing in domestic currencies. One argument was simply for (a return to) a "dollar standard" for Asia, including Japan as well as the emerging markets.[76] But perhaps the most surprising argument to resurface in the wake of the crisis was the need for "dollarization," meaning the complete substitution of the US currency for the *baht et al.*, a policy long ago adopted by Panama.[77]

This argument for currency union with the United States had its parallel in the argument in 1992 (advanced by *The Economist* among others) that the breakdown of the Exchange Rate Mechanism demonstrated the need for European monetary union. It is to this alternative solution to the exchange rate problem that we now turn.

CURRENCY UNIONS

From conception, through gestation, birth and into its early infancy, the euro has consistently proved the sceptics wrong. Some thought that chauvinistic voters would reject the single currency in referenda. Others doubted that all the applicants would fulfil the Maastricht deficit criterion. Still others predicted that disputes over the European Central Bank's presidency might abort the entire enterprise. Yet Economic and Monetary Union has thus far proceeded according to plan. The electorate's "petit oui" in the French referendum may have required a little gentle massaging, and the Maastricht Treaty's convergence criteria may have been honoured partly in the breach. But the important point is that the fixed exchange rates within the "Eurozone" have held firm, despite divergences in economic fundamentals, and prophecies of speculative attacks on individual members during the transitional phase have yet to be fulfilled.[78]

It is true that the new currency has been subject to 20 per cent depreciation against the dollar between its launch and the time of writing (May 2000). But nobody ever claimed that the euro would have a fixed rate against the dollar, or any other currency for that matter. Nor can anyone be certain whether it will go up or down in the next twelve months. On the one hand, as Figure 39 shows, compared with the performance of its predecessor, the unit-of-account ecu, the euro is still some way above its historic nadir. On the other, there is some reason to expect the euro sooner or later to recover against the dollar when the latter weakens, a likely consequence of the widening US balance of payments deficit and accumulating external debt described in the previous chapter.[79] If that happens, the prophets and architects of the single currency will no doubt relish their moment of—apparent—vindication, just as their opponents have savoured the "progress" of the euro in the foreign exchange markets since its launch. The pro-euro triumph is likely, however, to prove a fleeting one. For no monetary union can long endure when the mobility of labour is so hampered by cultural barriers and regulation; and, perhaps more importantly, when the fiscal policies of its member states are so out of kilter.[80]

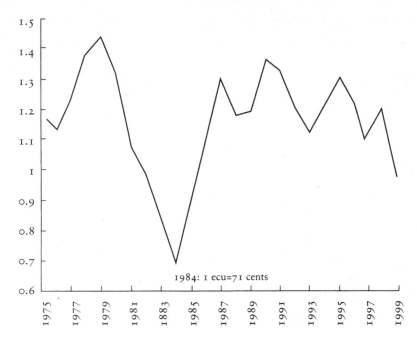

Figure 39: 'Progress' of the Ecu/Euro
Source: Global Financial Data.

The proposition that monetary unions can be undone by fiscal imbalances rests in part on comparative history. The difficulty is in deciding which previous monetary unions most closely resemble EMU; none does exactly. Indeed, given the fact that all EMU members are democracies and that monetary policy is today regarded as "the primary macroeconomic stabilization instrument," it is arguable that there are no real historical parallels.[81] True, a number of authors have sought to draw comparisons with the pre-1914 gold standard. However, others maintain that EMU is more like a national monetary union, because there is a common central bank (or, at least, a system of central banks) and no prescribed right to exit EMU; we should therefore compare it with the experience of Italy and Germany in the nineteenth century, when monetary unification was an integral part of national unification, or possibly with the more protracted process in the United States.[82]

None of these parallels is in fact very illuminating. As we have seen, the gold standard was an informal system without a single central bank from which states always had the option to exit in an emergency: it was much more like a large-scale version of the pre-1999 Exchange Rate Mechanism.[83] On the other hand, comparing EMU with the monetary unions achieved in the United States, Italy or Germany is unconvincing. Even the success of the Dutch United Provinces as a monetary union was inseparable from their political unification. In each case, political (and hence fiscal) union came before monetary union. Nor is it helpful to compare currency unions between giants and dwarves (such as that between France, Andorra and Monaco). The best analogies are with monetary unions between multiple states with only loose (if any) confederal ties and negligible fiscal centralization. Two such systems exist in francophone Africa: the West African Economic and Monetary Union and the zone of operation of the Central Bank of Equitorial Africa.[84] But these are essentially satellites of the French monetary system (and therefore now of EMU itself), since their currencies are pegged to the franc.

In fact, there is no need to look so far afield for antecedents of EMU. A monetary union of this sort has precedents in European history. One possible analogy is with the Austro-Hungarian monetary union after 1867, since the Habsburg Dual Monarchy was "an economic entity providing for the free circulation of goods and capital, with a unique central bank, and with *complete* fiscal autonomy for each part of its constituences" as well as multiple nationalities.[85] (Unlike the EU, however, there was a common army.) Both Austria and Hungary regularly ran quite sizeable deficits in the period up until 1914, but these were absorbed by the domestic and international bond markets with little difficulty. However, the dramatic but asymmetric increase in expenditure and borrowing occasioned by the First World War caused inflation to accelerate. The political disintegration of the Dual Monarchy at the end of the war led almost immediately to the disintegration of the monetary union, beginning with the Yugoslavian decision to secede by literally stamping all currency in its territory in January 1919. Its example was quickly followed in March by the new Czech and Austrian governments. When the Austro-Hungarian Bank protested, the Czech Minister of Finance replied that the action was a necessary response to the Bank's "systematic destruction [through inflation] of the Austro-Hungarian krone." Once the process had begun, it was hazardous for other former Habsburg states not to follow suit, since the Austro-Hungarian Bank continued to print unstamped notes until it was liquidated in September 1919. These unstamped notes quickly went to a premium since they could be used wherever the policy of stamping had not been adopted (Poland and Hungary until the spring of 1920).[86]

An even more illuminating precedent is the Latin Monetary Union (1865–1927), which made the coinages of France, Belgium, Switzerland,

Italy, the Papal States and (later) Greece freely exchangeable and legal tender within a single currency area. True, there was no Latin Central Bank. But one obvious parallel with EMU is that the LMU had a consciously political motivation. A driving force behind the LMU Convention of 23 December 1865 was the Frenchman Félix Parieu, who dreamt that the LMU would ultimately lead to a "European Union" with a "European Commission" and "European Parliament."[87] However, the costs to the other members of Italian (and especially Papal) fiscal laxity were high. The Papal government financed its deficits by issuing silver subsidiary coinage with high seigniorage profits—in short, debasing the coinage and allowing private agents to export it to the rest of the Union. This was a flagrant breach of the rules of the Convention. At the same time, to finance its deficits (11 per cent of GDP in 1866, on top of an existing debt of 70 per cent of GDP), the Italian government issued largely inconvertible paper currency, which broke the spirit if not the letter of the Convention. This helps explain why, despite initial efforts to attract new members, none was admitted after Greece, despite applications from Spain, Austria-Hungary, Romania, San Marino, Colombia, Serbia, Venezuela, Bulgaria and Finland.[88] The war of 1870 removed the political rationale of a French continental hegemony; and the only reason the LMU survived after 1878 was "to avoid the cost of dissolution."[89] Like the more modest Scandinavian Monetary Union founded in 1873 by Sweden and Denmark, the LMU was belatedly pronounced dead in the 1920s.

More recently there have been three monetary unions which have scarcely survived more than a few years after the break-up of earlier political unions: that between the eleven members of the Confederation of Independent States of the former Soviet Union; that between the former members of the Federal Republic of Yugoslavia; and that between the Czech Republic and Slovakia after they separated. In two cases, the break-up was associated with hyperinflation as internally weak member states raised revenue the easy way by printing money.

Past experience therefore tends to suggest that asymmetric fiscal problems—often, but not necessarily generated by war—quickly cause monetary unions between politically independent states to dissolve. In the case of present-day Europe, it seems quite possible that the strains caused by unaffordable social security and pension systems could have a similar centrifugal effect: the Habsburg scenario, with welfare substituting for war as the fatal solvent.

As Chapter 7 showed, the majority of EMU member states have severe generational imbalances, though they vary considerably in scale. Yet it is extremely hard to imagine any of the policy options necessary to eliminate these imbalances being adopted by any of the nine EMU members which need to act, much less all of them. To recap: in order to achieve generational balance, Finland needs to increase all taxation across the board by 17 per cent; Austria by 18 per cent; Spain by 14 per cent and Italy by 10 per cent. Even Germany needs to increase taxes by 9.5 per cent, or cut all government transfers by 14 per cent.[90] The main reason such increases will not happen is obvious: there would be insuperable political opposition, whether fiscal reform took the form of cuts in government consumption, cuts in government transfers, increases in all taxes or just increases in income tax. The political conflicts over tax increases and/or welfare cuts are easy enough to imagine: indeed, in Germany and Italy they have already begun. One reason for the fall of government of Massimo D'Alema in April 2000 was its inability to achieve reform of the Italian state pension system—the most expensive in the EU, with an annual cost of nearly 14 per cent of GDP—in the face of trade union opposition. It is especially unfortunate that so many continental Social Democrats persuaded themselves in the 1980s that early retirement schemes would boost employment opportunities for the young, a theory with disastrous fiscal implications wherever it was put into practice. Nor does it help that short-run macroeconomic arguments against fiscal tightening can so easily be devised: plainly, the problem of high unemployment in Germany and other EMU member states would hardly be improved by tax increases— and indeed the Schröder government has opted for tax cuts. The worsening fiscal situations of many European states could, of course, be eased by a permanent increase in the average rate of growth. However, there are good reasons to be doubtful about the likelihood of this happening in the core European countries. In particular, the rigidity of the European labour market has suggested to many economists that monetary union is premature.[91] (One reason the pre-1914 gold standard could function as it did was the high level of international labour mobility that went with it.[92])

The stark choice facing nearly every country in the Eurozone (leaving aside an end to immigration restrictions) is therefore between increases in taxation unprecedented in peacetime or reductions in public expenditure greater than anything achieved in the 1980s. Neither option is likely to be popular. Indeed, it seems more likely that most governments will allow generational imbalances to worsen in the short term.

What then are the monetary implications of this impending fiscal gridlock? One assumption often made is that various countries will find it progressively harder to keep within the specified budgetary limits set out in the Maastricht

Treaty and the Growth and Stability Pact. However, the possibilities for creative accounting with traditional measures of debts and deficits have not yet fully been exhausted. As the Maastricht criteria are based on measures of debt which are economically arbitrary, there is every reason to expect them to be laxly enforced: indeed, this has already happened. No fewer than eight of the EMU members had debts above the Maastricht 60 per cent threshold in 1997.[93]

In any case, rising borrowing by the EMU member states is not really the issue. Past experience (for example, the German monetary union after 1871) suggests that monetary unions can co-exist with federal fiscal systems in which some member states issue substantial volumes of bonds. Different levels of issuance may also result in a divergence of bond yields after the convergence of the pre-EMU period. But the existence of yield spreads are not incompatible with monetary union: markets cannot be forbidden from attaching different default risks to different member states. This can already be seen in the case of Austrian yields, which rose by around 20 basis points above German yields as it became clearly that the xenophobic Freedom Party was likely to enter the Austrian government. There is no more reason for European bond yields to be uniform than there is for companies issuing euro-denominated bonds to offer investors the same returns. Nor is the point that high levels of state borrowing necessarily lead to inflation, as is sometimes assumed.[94] Much depends on the international bond market's demand for grade AAA or AAB sovereign debt, and with more and more people living for two decades after retirement that demand should, if anything, strengthen.

The implications of generational imbalance are not simply that European states will have to run deficits. Because generational accounts are based on the idea of the inter-temporal budget constraint, it is already assumed within the calculations that they will. The figures imply not an increase in future borrowing, but an inevitable need to raise taxes, reduce expenditure or issue money. The real question is what happens when Austria, Finland or Spain—or all three—reach a political impasse on taxation and public spending.

At this point it seems plausible to expect that the countries with the most severe generational imbalances will attempt to exert pressure on the European Central Bank to relieve the pressure on them by loosening monetary policy.[95] Time and again in history, as we saw in Chapter 5, a leap in inflation has been the line of least resistance for governments in fiscal difficulties: the defeated powers after the First World War, for example, or Russia and the Ukraine since the collapse of the Soviet economy. This, of course, would be the moment of truth for the single currency. One possibility—which cannot be ruled out—is that the ECB will cave in, allowing the euro to depreciate and inflation in the Eurozone to rise. It seems unlikely, however, since the Bank is explicitly prohibited from acceding to a request for monetary financing under the institutional framework established by the Maastricht Treaty. To be precise, there is a strict "no bail-out rule" enshrined in Article 104 of the Maastricht Treaty (now Article 101 of the Treaty establishing the European Community) and in Article 21 of the Statute of the European System of Central Banks. This is the crux of what has been called the "unprecedented divorce between the main monetary and fiscal authorities" brought about by EMU.[96]

It is therefore not difficult to foresee a series of collisions between national governments, struggling to bring their finances under control, and the European Central Bank, which is bound to maintain price stability[97] as its primary objective (under Article 2 of the Statute of the European System of Central Banks). The ECB is likely to ignore the "unpleasant monetary arithmetic" implied by the budgetary imbalances of the member states, and to retort with some "unpleasant fiscal arithmetic" of its own by raising interest rates.[98]

If all countries were in approximately the same predicament, a political resolution of this conflict might be conceivable. But because there is such variation in the scale of the generational imbalances within the Eurozone, and indeed in their rates of growth and inflation, some countries will get into difficulties sooner than others. It is not hard to foresee the kind of inter-country conflicts this could lead to.[99] Most attempts to assess the likely durability of EMU have sought to estimate the effects of an "asymmetric" shock to the system.[100] Generational accounting suggests that the system already has the asymmetry and may not need a very large shock.

Then what? Legally, withdrawal from EMU is impossible: unlike the gold standard, there is no escape clause. But historically there is always an exit. If a country's only politically viable policy option is to print money and inflate away some of its liabilities (in other words, to levy the inflation tax), and if the EU institutions abide by the "no bail-out rule," then secession will need to be considered. The only remaining question is what the costs of secession from EMU would be.

First, there would be higher interest rates in the short term, and much would depend on the speed with which this impacted upon the government's debt service bill. In this context, the different term structures of the various national debts are important: a country with a lot of short-term debt will stand to gain much less from a rise in inflation. More than half of Spain's domestic debt is short-term, for example, compared with 0.4 per cent of Austria's: so Spain would find it much harder to inflate away its obligations.[101] Secondly, the exchange rate of the new (or restored pre-EMU) currency of the seceding state would weaken relative to the euro and other major currencies. This might provide a stimulus to exports, though whether this would compensate for the higher interest rates that would almost certainly be needed is impossible to predict. Moreover, there would also be all kinds of legal tangles as creditors and debtors (foreign and domestic) fought over whether the pre-secession debts should be treated as euro- or national-currency denominated. This could severely destabilize the seceding country's financial system, as well as those of other countries. Again, the implications would be graver the more of a country's debt was held externally. In short, secession from EMU would be far more difficult than secession from the ERM, a point to be borne in mind by countries like the UK which are still considering whether or not to join.

It is possible that the political will to implement spending cuts and tax increases may be strengthened by these obvious disincentives. Less likely, but also conceivable, there could be a weakening of the ECB's anti-inflation resolve; or, alternatively, a shift towards greater fiscal centralization to allow the continent's generational imbalances to be dealt with collectively.

Still, the fact remains that history offers few examples of democratically agreed budgetary adjustments on the scale necessary in certain European countries today. What it does offer are several examples of monetary unions between sovereign states disintegrating when the exigencies of national fiscal policy became incompatible with the constraint imposed by a single international currency.

I 2

The American Wave:
Democracy's Flow and Ebb

It is evident to all alike that a great democratic revolution is going on among us, but all do not look at it in the same light. . . . A kind of religious awe [is] produced in the author's mind by the view of that irresistible revolution which has advanced for centuries in spite of every obstacle and which is still advancing in the midst of the ruins it has caused.

Tocqueville[1]

When the American sociologist Francis Fukuyama proclaimed "The End of History" in 1989, his role model was the philosopher of history and master of the dialectical method Georg Wilhelm Friedrich Hegel.[2] For Hegel, world history was "governed by an ultimate design . . . a divine and absolute reason." "The spirit [of reason] and the course of its development" were "the true substance of history," Hegel argued; and this spirit he equated with "the idea of human freedom." Thus the historical process could be understood as the attainment of self-knowledge by this idea of freedom through a succession of "world spirits." In Hegel's tortuous prose, "the concrete manifestation" of "the unity of the subjective will and the universal"—"the totality of ethical life and the realisation of freedom"—was the state.[3] As a young man, Hegel had been inspired by the French Revolution ("a glorious sunrise . . . a sublime emotion"); but his model state turned out to be the Prussian.[4] Fukuyama's inspiration was the East European revolutions of 1989; yet his model remains the liberal capitalist democracy of the United States.

Like Hegel, Fukuyama is anything but an economic reductionist. The progressive, dialectical relationship he discerns between democracy and growth is mediated by culture.[5] And he has acknowledged that (particularly in Asia) "political development could turn away from democracy" because of cultural resistance to the individualism associated with democracy. Nevertheless, ten years after "The End of History," he remains confident of "a long-term

progressive evolution of human political institutions in the direction of liberal democracy." Indeed, Fukuyama concluded his most recent book, *The Great Disruption*, with an unabashedly Hegelian claim: "In the political and economic sphere, history appears to be progressive and directional, and at the end of the twentieth century has culminated in liberal democracy as the only viable alternative for technologically advanced societies."[6]

The view that democracy and economic progress are mutually reinforcing is close to becoming a new orthodoxy. The political economist Mancur Olson's posthumously published *Power and Prosperity* advanced the argument that democratic systems are more conducive to wealth creation than their undemocratic predecessors for the same fundamental reason that in the Middle Ages a tyranny was preferable to anarchy. A monarch—or "stationary bandit" in Olson's striking phrase—has an "encompassing interest" in the long-term prosperity of his subjects, which is not true of a wandering band of brigands. The brigands "tax" at a rate of 100 per cent and then move on, indifferent to the fact that by preventing present investment and discouraging future investment, they are reducing the future output of those they plunder. The stationary bandit, by contrast, will tend to "reduce his rate of tax theft down to the point where what he gains (from tax theft on a larger output) is just offset by what he loses (from taking a smaller share of output)." He also has an incentive to provide public goods out of his own resources if they will increase the output of his subjects.[7] But democracy is even better, because the governing majority gains not only from redistributing tax revenues towards itself, but also from maximizing its income from market transactions: hence "the optimal tax rate for the majority is bound to be lower than the autocrat's."[8] In the same way, the greater encompassing interest of a democratic majority will incline it to spend more of its resources on public goods which benefit everyone. There can even be "super-encompassing interests" (i.e. majorities which do not include all of society) which are so broad that they tax and spend out of self-interest exactly as much as if their motives were entirely altruistic. Olson had argued in earlier works that the protection of property rights and the security of contracts were crucial in stimulating economic activity; now he asserted that these were more likely under democratic governments.[9] This argument echoes earlier work by Douglass North, who argued that democratic government offers "greater political efficiency" because it "gives a greater and greater percentage of the populace access to the political decision process, eliminates the capricious capacity of a ruler to confiscate wealth, and develops third-party enforcement of contracts with an independent judiciary."[10]

The Nobel laureate Amartya Sen too has lent his support to the idea that democracy is economically beneficial. Sen argues that freedom, desirable in its own right, also has an economically instrumental justification. True, he concedes, China, Singapore and (until recently) South Korea have enjoyed rapid economic growth in the past two decades despite the absence of democracy. But these examples of authoritarian "tiger" economies do not suffice to rebut the economic case for democracy. There are counterexamples like Botswana, a rapidly growing oasis of democracy in Africa. More tellingly, democracies are better at avoiding economic disasters than autocracies. "No substantial famine," Sen argues in *Development as Freedom*, "has ever occurred in a democratic country—no matter how poor . . . because a government in a multiparty democracy with elections and free media has strong political incentives to undertake famine prevention."[11] Here the contrast between India's experience since independence and China's is in the former's favour.

Such arguments find echoes in the work of less-well-known scholars too. One recent study compared the "quality of citizen's lives" in over a hundred mainly developing countries and concluded that democratic states meet the basic needs of their citizens "as much as 70 per cent more" than non-democratic states."[12] A similar comparison has been made for the pre-industrial period between self-governing European towns and those under absolutist rulers, showing that growth was faster when towns were governed by their local merchant élites.[13] A partly political explanation has also been suggested for the superior economic performance of post-Communist Poland, with its comparatively vibrant democratic institutions, as compared with Russia where democratization has been impeded by "kleptocratic" élites.[14] The general refrain has been taken up by policy-makers too. The Bonn Conference on Economic Cooperation in Europe summed up the new conventional wisdom: "Democratic institutions and economic freedom foster economic progress."[15]

It is certainly a plausible historical hypothesis that economic growth encourages the evolution of democratic institutions. But is it so certain that the causation runs in the opposite direction too? Can democratization be relied upon to boost growth? If so, then history may well have ended—and like a fairy-story: They all lived happily (or at least, democratically and prosperously) ever after. This is the "double helix" theory in its essence: democracy and economic progress spiralling upwards together, each dependent on the other.

There are, however, reasons for caution. One of Olson's bolder sallies is that "the Whig interpretation of history was right" in discerning an upward trajectory in British constitutional history. No historian can feel entirely comfortable with such an ingenuous conclusion, based as it is on an admixture of mathematics and a barely recognizable caricature of historical events.[16] Fukuyama's dialectical optimism should also make us pause. We seem to confront here an improbable alliance of Hegel and Lord Macaulay.[17]

A PARISIAN IN AMERICA

Of Macaulay's generation, perhaps the shrewdest analyst of democracy was the French aristocrat, historian, sociologist and politician Alexis de Tocqueville. In *Democracy in America* (1835), based on a nine-month journey to the United States in 1831–2, Tocqueville gave a qualified welcome to the "institutions and mores" he had encountered there. Among the strengths of American democracy he identified the decentralization of government; the power of the law courts; the strength of associational life; the role of lawyers as a surrogate aristocracy and the vigour of religion ("if [man] is free, he must believe"). Strongly influenced by the Federalists, Tocqueville was not blind to the defects and potential hazards of American democracy. Political parties were "an inherent evil of free governments;" the press was excessively violent and prone to muck-raking; the people tended to vote mediocrities into high office (he badly underestimated Andrew Jackson); above all there was the danger of the "tyranny of the majority." Tocqueville was also alive to the intolerance of minorities—and particularly of blacks, whether enslaved or free. But his conclusion was optimistic: the strengths of American society would be enough to compensate for these deficiencies. Democracy was the future, he argued in his introduction, and—in America at least—it worked.

Whether it could work as well elsewhere was another question, however. In France, "the democratic revolution [had] taken place in the body of society without that concomitant change in the laws, ideas, customs, and morals which was necessary to render such a revolution beneficial." Democracy had been "abandoned to its wild instincts" and its "lawless passions."[18] In England (which Tocqueville visited in 1833 and 1835), a new "manufacturing aristocracy" had arisen which, he warned, might succeed in restoring the "permanent inequality of conditions" of the pre-democratic social order. Above all, Tocqueville noted that in Europe, unlike in the United States, public administration was becoming "more centralized . . . more inquisitive and minute. . . . It gains a firmer footing every day about, above and around all private persons, to assist, to advise, and to coerce them."[19] In a startlingly prescient passage towards the end of the second volume he identified

the novel features under which despotism may appear in the world. The first thing that strikes the observation is an innumerable multitude of men, all equal and alike, incessantly endeavouring to procure the petty and paltry pleasures with which they glut their lives. Each of them, living apart, is a stranger to the fate of all the rest; his children and private friends constitute to him the whole of mankind. . . . Above this race of men stands an immense and tutelary power, which takes upon itself to secure their gratification and to watch over their fate. That power is absolute, minute, regular, provident and mild. . . . It provides for their security, foresees and supplies their necessities, facilitates their pleasures, manages their principal concerns, directs their industry, regulates the descent of property, and subdivides their inheritances; what remains, but to spare them all the care of thinking and all the trouble of living? . . . Every day it renders the exercise of the free agency of man less useful and less frequent . . . The principal of equality has prepared men for these things. . . . I have always thought that servitude of the regular, quiet and gentle kind which I have just described . . . might . . . establish itself under the wing of the sovereignty of the people.[20]

In the 1830s and 1840s Tocqueville remained hopeful that France could achieve the transition to a form of democracy similar (though not identical) to the American; above all, one which preserved individual liberty and limited the power of the central state. But by the time *L'Ancien Régime et la Révolution* appeared in 1856—the first and only volume of his projected history of the French Revolution—he had become less optimistic. It had proved impossible to introduce democracy in France without an intolerable sacrifice of liberty. The aristocracy and the Church against which the Revolution had directed its energies had in fact been bastions of liberty under the old regime. Once they had been destroyed, the process of centralization—which long antedated the revolution—could accelerate unchecked. Equality trumped liberty, and the result was despotism:

For while the urge to freedom is forever assuming new forms, losing or gaining strength according to the march of events, our love of equality is constant and pursues the object of its desire with a zeal that is obstinate and often blind . . . Hence the fact that the French nation is prepared to tolerate, in a government that favours and flatters its desire for equality, practices and principles that are, in fact, the tools of despotism. . . . Every time that an attempt is made to do away with absolutism the most that [can] be done has been to graft the head of Liberty onto a servile body.[21]

Admittedly, Tocqueville's bleaker view of French democracy owed much to the frustration of his own political career following the revolution of 1848. Appointed Foreign Minister in September 1849, he had been dismissed after less than two months by the President, Louis Napoleon; even more bruisingly, his thirteen-year parliamentary career had been cut off when Napoleon staged his coup d'état and restored the Empire in December 1851.[22] Mindful of these events, modern historians have been at pains to point out the many anachronisms in Tocqueville's account of eighteenth-century France: his portrayal of the intendants as prototypes of Bonapartist prefects, for example. Yet as a work of political theory Tocqueville's *Old Regime* deserves to be reread, along with the concluding book of the *Democracy in America*, and not least as a corrective to the neo-Hegelian effusions of Fukuyama and Olson's updated Whiggery. Democracy may indeed be destined to triumph over autocracy around the world. But we cannot take it for granted that liberty—including economic liberty—will always share in that victory.

Tocqueville had little interest in the economic implications of his presentiment that in democracies egalitarianism and centralization would pose a threat to liberty. But twentieth-century political theorists—Adam Przeworski, for example—have drawn the obvious inference. According to Przeworski, there is a fundamental conflict between the market, in which individuals cast "votes" using the resources that they own—which are distributed unequally— and the state, "a system that allocates resources which it does not own, with rights distributed differently from the market." In the case of a democracy, the rule of "one citizen, one vote" gives everyone the same right to influence the allocation of resources through the state:

It is hardly surprising that distributions of consumption produced by the market differ from those collectively preferred by the electorate, since democracy offers those who are poor . . . or otherwise dissatisfied with the initial distribution of endowments an opportunity to seek redress *via* the state. Endowed with political power in the form of universal suffrage, those who suffer as a consequence of private property will attempt to use this power to redistribute wealth. . . . Democracy inevitably threatens "property rights."[23]

Might there after all be a conflict between an economic progress which depends primarily on liberty and a democracy which, as Tocqueville warned, tends to give preference to equality?

THE ASCENT OF DEMOCRACY

For the past twenty-five years democracy has been spreading across the globe just as Tocqueville predicted. It began in the Iberian peninsula in the mid-1970s, spread to Latin America and parts of Asia in the 1980s, and between 1989 and 1991 swept across Central and Eastern Europe, as well as parts of sub-Saharan Africa. "For the first time in history," according to the Institute for Democracy and Electoral Assistance, "more people are living in democracies than under dictatorships. . . . And the trend . . . is towards enlargement of the democratic mandate."[24] Democracy has become "a global phenomenon."[25] Its spread has been a benign version of the "domino effect" Americans used to fear during the Cold War.[26] It has even been predicted that "the democratic community might reach the 90 per cent level toward 2100."[27]

Though it may seem, with the benefit of hindsight, to have been predictable, the success of democracy is one of history's bigger surprises. When the central question of Western political theory—monarchy, aristocracy or democracy?—was first debated, the proponent of democracy lost. In Book III of his *Histories*, Herodotus imagines how the Persian conspirators who slew the Magi decided on the future form of their country's government. Otanes argued for democracy: "First, [the rule of the people] has the finest of all names to describe it—equality under the law; and secondly . . . under a government of the people a magistrate is . . . held responsible for his conduct in office, and all questions are put up for open debate." But Megabyzus argued for oligarachy, on the ground that

The masses are a feckless lot—nowhere will you find more ignorance or irresponsibility of violence. . . . A king does at least act consciously and deliberately; but the mob does not. Indeed, how should it, when it has never been taught what is right and proper . . . ? The masses have not a thought in their heads; all they can do is to rush blindly into a politics like a river in flood.

Finally, Darius made the case for monarchy, and he too had words to say against democracy:

In a democracy, malpractices are bound to occur . . . corrupt dealings in government services lead . . . to close personal associations, the men responsible for them putting their heads together and mutually supporting one another. And so it goes on, until somebody or other comes forward as the people's champion and breaks up the cliques which are out for their own interests. This wins him the admiration of the mob, and as a result he soon finds himself entrusted with absolute power—all of which is another proof that the best form of government is monarchy.

Darius won. Significantly, Otanes's last democratic act was to secede from the new monarchical order.[28]

For centuries Western political thought was against Otanes. Only belatedly, in the seventeenth and eighteenth centuries, did the case for a democratic polity begin to find proponents; and even in the nineteenth century relatively few of these were willing to contemplate universal suffrage. Moreover, the first half of the twentieth century seemed to herald not the triumph of democracy but of socialism. In 1942 Joseph Schumpeter argued that democracy was inexorably undermining capitalism, and that socialism was the shape of things to come. But how would democracy fare under socialism? "Socialist democracy," he concluded grimly, "may eventually turn out to be more of a sham than capitalist democracy ever was."[29] Another Austrian exile, Friedrich von Hayek, warned that utopian socialism would lead post-war Britain down "the road to serfdom," just as National Socialism had led Germany to totalitarianism.[30]

Schumpeter and Hayek can be forgiven their pessimism, writing as they were in the wake of the worst depression of modern economic history and in the depths of the Second World War—a war which was waged not only against an array of dictatorships but also in alliance with one of the most repressive and murderous of them all. Yet the events of the past twenty-five years have belied their forebodings.

Though there is academic disagreement as to how exactly democracy should be measured,[31] the extent of the democratic triumph is unmistakable. Among the most systematic attempts to quantify the advance of democracy is the Freedom House Survey, which has been published annually since 1973 and which awards marks for "political rights" and "civil liberties"[32] on a scale from 1 (the highest degree of freedom) to 7 (the lowest). Countries whose combined averages for political rights and for civil liberties fall between 1.0 and 2.5 are designated "free;" those who score between 3.0 and 5.5 are classified as "partly free;" while a mark of between 5.5 and 7.0 signifies "not free." Summarizing the 1998 Survey, the Freedom House president Adrian Karatnycky calculated that

88 of the world's 191 countries (46 per cent) [are now] rated as Free, meaning that they maintain a high degree of political and economic freedom and respect basic civil liberties. . . . Another 53 countries (28 per cent of the world total) were rated as Partly Free, enjoying more limited political rights and civil liberties, often in a context of corruption, weak rule of law, ethnic strife, or civil war. . . . Finally, 50 countries (26 per cent of the world total) that deny their citizens basic rights and civil liberties were rated as Not Free.[33]

Whatever reservations one may have about its methodology, the Freedom House Survey indicates that freedom (by its own definition, at least) has been making a sustained advance. In 1998 India, the Dominican Republic, Ecuador, Nicaragua, Papua New Guinea, Slovakia and Thailand were all promoted from "partly free" to "free;" while a further three countries formerly ranked as "not free" were now rated as partly free.[34] Altogether twenty-two countries saw their freedom score improve (i.e. go down), compared with just twelve which were judged to have become less free. Only thirteen states qualified for the worst possible score of 7: Afghanistan, Burma, Cuba, Equatorial Guinea, Iraq, Libya, North Korea, Saudi Arabia, Somalia, Sudan, Syria, Turkmenistan and Vietnam. The Survey implies that nearly 2.4 billion people (or 40 per cent of the world's population) now live in free societies, compared with 1.6 billion (26 per cent) who are partly free and just under 2 billion (34 per cent) who are not free. That is liberty's best showing since the Survey began twenty-six years ago. Then just 30 per cent of countries were free; 24 per cent were partly free; and 46 per cent were not free (see Table 18).

Table 18. Free, partly free and not free countries: the freedom house surveys for 1972–3 and 1998–9

	1972–3		1998–9	
	No. of countries	*Percentage*	*No. of countries*	*Percentage*
Free	43	30	88	46
Partly free	34	24	53	28
Not free	67	46	50	26
TOTAL	144	100	191	100

Source: Freedom House, *Annual Survey of Freedom*.

Admittedly, the Freedom House definition of freedom is not the same as democracy. As Fareed Zakaria has pointed out, there are a number of democracies that are not especially liberal when one considers closely their respect for civil rights.[35] The Survey counted (at the end of 1998) a total of 117 "electoral democracies,"[36] representing over 61 per cent of the world's countries and 55 per cent of its population. Yet only 40 per cent of people live in countries Freedom House regards as free, implying that 15 per cent of human beings now live in democracies that are not wholly free. (This would not have surprised Tocqueville.) Nevertheless, the trend would now appear to be in the direction of liberalism as well as democracy. In 1995 the Survey rated 76 of the 117 electoral democracies free (just under 65 per cent), 40 partly free (over 34 per cent), and one—Bosnia-Herzegovina—not free. Today, out of the same number of electoral democracies, 88 (over 75 per cent) are free, while all the others are partly free.[37] The illiberal democracies may therefore prove to be a transient phenomenon. Still, the point is well taken that the introduction of free elections based on universal suffrage does not automatically guarantee the rule of law and respect for civil rights.

It is worth pausing at this point to ask what precisely we mean by "democracy," given the significant differences that exist within this broad and antique category. Take the most basic democratic mechanism, the franchise itself. While most parliamentary systems have, in the course of the last century, ceased to discriminate against women and the poor, the age of entitlement to vote still ranges from 15 (the Philippines) to 21 (India). The number of years between general elections also varies from two to five. Diversity is especially marked with respect to electoral systems. Among fifty-three countries in a survey conducted in 1996, nearly half (twenty-five) had a version of proportional representation (though with different formulas for Lower House composition and different kinds of list); twelve used the British "first past the post" system; eleven had a mixed system, combining elements of PR and FPTP; and two had a majority or "run-off" system (leaving two which defied categorization).[38]

Another area of divergence is the number of parties represented in democratic legislatures around the world. According to one estimate (which weights parties by the number of seats they win), the number of "effective" parties in legislatures in the early 1990s ranged from two to twenty-three (Ukraine). This is not just a matter of custom or culture. There does seem to be a link between the electoral system used and the number of parties represented, though the difference is less than might be expected. A recent analy-sis of 509 elections in twenty countries found that, on average, majority sys-tems had seven parties and PR systems had eight.[39] The referendum also plays a role of varying importance: at one extreme, the Swiss have had no fewer than 275 since 1945. At least thirteen democracies make voting com-pulsory; partly for this reason, turnout in recent general elections has ranged from 21 per cent (Mali) to 96 per cent (Australia). Most but not all systems are bicameral. In 1997 there were 58 two-chamber parliaments in the world, but in China, Denmark, New Zealand, Portugal and Sweden—not to men-tion Nebraska and Queensland—there is only a single chamber. Some are directly elected; some indirectly; a few (like the "reformed" House of Lords in Britain) are entirely appointed by the executive.[40] Only twenty-eight out of fifty-three democratic states in the sample mentioned above have popu-larly elected heads of state, and not all of these are truly presidential. It has long perplexed American political scientists that so many West European democracies stubbornly choose to retain hereditary heads of state.[41]

Such institutional differences can have major implications for the success of democracy. The evidence suggests strongly that parliamentary democra-cies are more stable than presidential systems: of thirty-one democracies that have lasted for at least twenty-five years, twenty-four are parliamentary and only four presidential.[42] There are also reasons to think that proportional representation can "exacerbate divisions and conflicts within societies by re-creating them and relocating them in its legislature with a multitude of polit-ical parties."[43] Certainly, there is little doubt that it tends to produce shorter-lived governments: in eighteen OECD countries between 1950 and 1990, the average government lasted just 1.9 years under PR, compared with 3 years in majority systems.[44]

And there are other important differences. Some democracies (such as Britain and France) are very centralized, while others (Switzerland, the United States, Germany, Canada and Australia) have federal systems. Fed-eral systems naturally strike Americans as preferable; yet it remains very hard to conceive of a federal Britain, even after the creation of national assemblies in Scotland, Wales and Northern Ireland, unless England were to be in some way subdivided. Some states concede more power than others to unelected bodies, such as the judiciary and the central bank. As we have seen, the trans-fer of control over monetary policy back to more-or-less independent banks run by unelected experts was a widespread response to the problems of infla-tion in the 1970s and 1980s. Yet there are those who would see this as a diminution of democracy. In Britain considerable power has also been vested in so-called "quangos" (quasi-non-governmental organizations), which are appointed by the incumbent executive and are barely accountable to parliament. Finally, some democracies are more ready than others to delegate powers to supra-national organizations. The European Union illustrates well that the whole of such an organization can sometimes be less democratic than the sum of its parts.

In short, even if the world is "on a roll" towards democracy, it is not clear which form of democracy is likely to predominate in the future. Democracy is even understood by some to extend beyond the sphere of politics. In his Reith lectures, Anthony Giddens spoke with evident enthusiasm of the democratisation of family life, eagerly looking forward to a "democracy of the emotions in everyday life"[45]—whatever that may mean.

THE THREE WAVES

But can we be sure that the trend towards democracy will continue? It is at least arguable that the quarter century covered by the Freedom House Survey is too short a period on which to base projections, much less confident predictions. Moreover, it is important to remember that much of the dramatic change summarized in Table 18 above occurred in a very short period between 1989 and 1991, when the Communist bloc in Eastern Europe and the Soviet Union itself collapsed.

If there had been a Freedom House Survey for the past century, what would it have shown? Looking back in the summer of 1900 on the three previous decades, an earlier author might also have concluded that liberty and democracy were making inexorable progress in the world. True, much of the world was under imperial rule by the European great powers; while Latin American countries were prone to coups and civil wars. But there were unmistakable moves towards greater liberty and democracy elsewhere. In Russia, Turkey, Portugal and China, absolutist monarchies were driven to liberalize by revolutions or overthrown altogether. Admittedly, there were drastic declines in freedom, if not in democracy, between 1914 and 1916, as the combatant powers in the First World War curtailed political and civil liberties in the name of national emergency. But from 1917 until around 1921 democracy won major victories, with as many new states being constituted as democracies as there have been since 1989.

Yet this advance was not sustained. The imposition of Bolshevik rule in Russia and most of the old Tsarist empire represented a profound setback for Eastern Europe, the Caucasus and Central Asia, as the new regime was in many ways even less liberal than its Tsarist predecessor. Moreover, there was a collapse of nearly all the new democracies in the years from 1922 to 1938. By that date, democracy survived only in Britain and its white Dominions, the United States, Czechoslovakia, France, Belgium, Holland, Switzerland and Scandinavia. In the following five years Nazi Germany and her allies overran all but two of the remaining continental democracies. And although the defeat of Germany restored democracy in north-western Europe, it did not do so in Eastern Europe or Iberia. Nor did decolonization in Asia and Africa advance the cause of democracy, for in few cases did the new rulers long tolerate political opposition. (As the white Rhodesian leader Ian Smith sardonically observed, African democracy meant "One man, one vote—once.") Moreover, both sides in the Cold War installed or propped up undemocratic regimes in Latin America, Asia and Africa. For these and other reasons, fully a third of the democracies that existed world-wide in 1958 had been snuffed out by the mid-1970s.[46] The failure of parliamentary regimes in sub-Saharan Africa after decolonization was as big a setback for democracy as events in Eastern Europe since 1989 have been an advance.[47]

These points can be presented more formally using the Polity III database, which applies a rather more complex 11-point scale for a much longer period than the Freedom House Survey. Here the score for democracy is based on four criteria: "competitiveness of political participation" (maximum score 3 points), "competitiveness of executive recruitment" (maximum score 2), "openness of executive recruitment" (maximum score 1) and "constraints on the chief executive" (maximum score 4): the maximum score is therefore 10, the minimum—for a wholly undemocratic state—zero. Over 160 states are covered and there are data for many countries from as long ago as 1800.[48]

The most striking point is that, though it is undoubtedly true that the world has never been more democratic than it was in 1998, the trajectory of democratization has not been smoothly upwards (see Figure 40). There have in fact been three peaks of global democratization: in 1922, 1946 and 1994—hence Samuel Huntington's idea of the current "third wave" of democratization. The crucial point, of course, is that both the two previous waves receded.[49]

Nor has the progress of democracy between uniform around the world. Table 19 presents a simplified overview of the Polity figures, taking twenty-

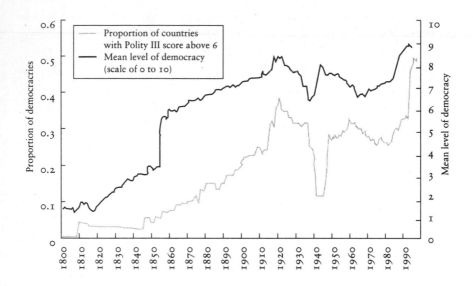

Figure 40: The rise of democracy, 1800–1996
Source: Polity III database.

Table 19. Average democracy score per country, by regions, 1800–1998

	Americas	West Europe	East Europe	Africa	Middle East	Asia	World
1800	7.0	0.4	0.0	1.0	0.0	1.4	0.9
1825	2.4	0.6	0.0	1.0	0.0	1.4	1.0
1850	1.8	1.6	1.5	4.0	0.0	1.4	1.6
1875	2.5	3.1	2.0	4.6	0.0	3.7	2.7
1900	3.6	5.5	1.9	3.4	0.0	3.3	3.6
1925	3.1	8.7	4.1	4.8	1.3	4.0	4.6
1950	3.0	8.1	1.7	3.5	3.9	3.3	4.1
1975	3.2	9.2	2.5	1.0	1.4	3.0	2.8
1998	7.7	9.9	6.8	2.8	1.5	4.4	5.2

Source: Polity III database.

five-year samples of regional averages. The Middle East emerges as consistently the least democratic region, Western Europe the most democratic. There has been no clear trend in Africa, Asia or the Americas. The erratic and uneven character of democratization is borne out by other attempts to quantify the progress of democracy or freedom in the long run.[50]

To illustrate the point in more detail, it is worth considering the experience of Europe in the first half of the twentieth century. In 1918 the American president Woodrow Wilson declared: "Democracy seems about universally to prevail. . . . The spread of democratic institutions . . . promise[s] to reduce politics to a single form . . . by reducing all forms of government to Democracy."[51] As Figure 41 shows, Wilson's optimism seemed well-founded between 1916 and 1922, during which time the average democracy score in Europe more than doubled. But thereafter it began to slide downwards, touching 5.7 out of 10 in 1931, 4.6 in 1938, and a nadir of 1.9 during the Second World War. Of the 29 countries covered, nearly all had acquired some form of representative government before during or after the First World War. Yet six had become dictatorships by 1925; a further four by 1930; six by 1935 and eight by 1940. Russia, of course, was first to go when the Bolsheviks shut up the National Assembly in 1918. In Hungary the franchise was restricted as early as 1920 and Gömbös's presidency (1932–6) was to all intents and purposes a dictatorship. Mussolini seized power in Italy with the approval of the king and the army in 1922. In Turkey Kemal established what was effectively a one-party state in 1923. A coup in Lithuania imposed authoritarian rule under Smetona and Voldemaras in 1926; while Pilsudski set up a military dictatorship in Poland. Zogu installed himself as king of Albania in 1928; Salazar came to power in Portugal in 1932; and Dollfuss took control of Austria in 1933—the same year that another Austrian became Chancellor of Germany. In Latvia an authoritarian regime was established under Kviesis in 1932–4; much the same happened in Estonia under Päts. In Bulgaria an army coup in 1934 was followed a year later by a royal dictatorship under Boris III; meanwhile in Greece a republican coup attempt in 1934 was the prelude to the royal-sponsored dictatorship established by Metaxas two years later. Romania too slid into royal dictatorship under Carol II in 1938. In Yugoslavia King Alexander staged a coup in 1929, restored parliamentarism in 1931 and was assassinated in 1934. In Spain there was a constitutional monarchy from 1917 until 1923, then a military dictatorship under Primo de Rivera until 1930, then a highly unstable republic, civil war and finally Franco's dictatorship. In those few countries where democracy survived, invasion by Germany,

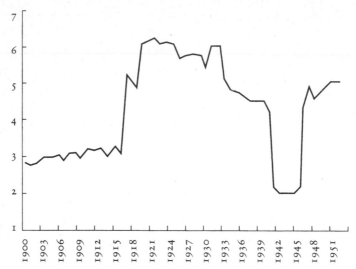

Figure 41: *The average democracy 'score' for 29 European countries, 1900–1950*
Source: Polity III database.

Russia or Italy had snuffed it out by 1940. The exceptions were Britain and the neutrals Eire, Sweden and Switzerland.

Viewed in a longer-term perspective, then, there has been no rule of natural progression from autocracy to democracy. It is only legitimate to speak of "a long-term progressive evolution of human political institutions in the direction of liberal democracy" if by "long-term" we mean the last twenty-six years. To some, of course, that seems a long time. By a strange irony, it was the Portuguese premier Antonio Gutteres who orchestrated, as chair of the European Union, the diplomatic sanctions against Austria following the formation of a coalition government including the Freedom Party in January 2000. Portugal was, of course, the last West European state to embrace democracy—in 1974, exactly twenty-six years before.[52]

An optimist might retort that the long run really means the last two and a quarter centuries since the American Revolution. But that period has been characterized by too many extreme dips to justify confidence in an unstoppable progressive trend. Indeed, given the vastly enhanced capabilities of the modern state to interfere in the lives of individual citizens, it might even be argued that there is somewhat less liberty in the Anglo-American world than there was at the turn of the last century. That, of course, had been Tocqueville's fear. Only by redefining liberty to encompass such notions as "freedom from unemployment" or "freedom from relative poverty" can justifications be devised for the diminution of liberty in its classical sense.

DEMOCRACY AND PROSPERITY

At first sight, Francis Fukuyama's claim that democracy and economic growth are positively correlated might seem self-evident. In economic terms, the triumph of democracy is even more impressive than any measure previously considered. Democracies today account for a huge proportion of the world's wealth. The world's fifty biggest economies have an average democracy score (using the Polity III measure) of 8.8. Of these, the democracies scoring ten account for almost exactly three-quarters of world GNP; and that proportion would rise above 80 per cent if all countries scoring ten were included.[53] The Freedom House statistics also seem to bear out the idea that that democracy and economic prosperity go hand in hand. Interestingly, Karatnycky echoes Fukuyama's emphasis on "the links between economic freedom and political freedom:"

Not only does economic freedom help establish the conditions for political freedom by promoting the growth of prosperous middle and working classes, but successful market economies appear to require political freedom as a barrier against economic cronyism, rent seeking, and other anticompetitive and inefficient practices. Open and democratically accountable societies and economies have also shown themselves capable of weathering economic setbacks . . .[54]

There are, in fact, two distinct propositions here: the first, that economic growth leads to democratization; the second, reversing the direction of causation, that democratization promotes economic growth.

The first proposition is much the less controversial. Numerous studies based on different samples and periods have identified strong statistical links between economic development—to be precise, per capita income—and democracy. A certain level of prosperity, it is generally argued, is one of the "social requisites" of democracy. In 1959 the American political scientist Seymour Martin Lipset pointed out the correlation between democracy and wealth, industrialization, urbanization and education.[55] Lipset was careful to avoid a crude determinism: his findings, he insisted, did "not justify the optimistic liberal's hope that an increase in wealth, in the size of the middle class [and] in education . . . will necessarily mean the spread . . . or the stabilizing of democracy."[56] In his view, the legitimacy of democratic institutions depended as much on the cultural setting, the development of civil society and a country's past (especially colonial) experience, as on economic performance.[57] However, subsequent research has tended to play down these other factors.[58] A characteristic determinist conclusion is that "a democracy can be expected to last an average of about 8.5 years in a country with per-capita income under $1,000 per annum, 16 years in one with income between $1,000 and $2,000, 33 years between $2,000 and $4,000, and 100 years between $4,000 and $6,000. . . . Above $6,000, democracies are impregnable . . . [they are] certain to survive, come hell or high water."[59]

The most sophisticated analysis to date of the relationship between democracy and living standards concludes that there is indeed "a strong positive linkage from prosperity to the propensity to experience democracy." The economist Robert Barro's analysis of data from around a hundred countries between 1960 and 1990 suggests that various measures of living standards (real per capita GDP, life expectancy, and the size of the gap between male and female educational attainment) do indeed stimulate the development of democratic institutions.[60] In an ambitious study which focuses on the *rate* rather than the level of growth, Benjamin Friedman too argues that "the link . . . between rising living standards and an open democratic society" holds good. According to his version of the rule, "a society is more likely to become more open and tolerant and democratic when its citizens" standard of living is rising, and to move in the opposite direction when living standards stagnate."[61]

Yet there are many exceptions to challenge this apparent historical law. The events of the 1990s provided a salutary reminder that quite economically advanced societies can turn away from liberal democracy. Fifteen years ago Yugoslavia appeared economically better placed than most East European countries; yet democracy has fared worse there than in almost any other post-Communist country. Moreover, it was chronic economic stagnation, not growth, that led to the democratization in most of the Soviet bloc after 1989. Conversely, China has experienced extremely rapid economic growth in the past decade and a half; yet there is little sign so far that its gerontocracy will relax its grip on political power. The same goes for Singapore. Conversely, the success of democracy in poor countries like Papua New Guinea and Sri Lanka seems to defy the determinist model.[62] Nor is it easy to explain the crisis of democracy in relatively prosperous Latin American countries like Argentina, Chile and Uruguay in the 1960s and 1970s.

One possible explanation for some of these anomalies is that "the strain flowing from economic growth may undermine democratic stability."[63] Though the data are problematic, it may also be that the increased inequality initially caused by rapid development tends to undermine democratic institutions.[64] This point can be reinforced by comparing the Freedom House

Survey with some other cross-country data. An analysis of a sample of fifty-nine countries reveals a striking absence of the alleged positive correlation between liberal democracy and growth. On the contrary, for the period 1990–1997 there was a positive relationship between *lack* of political freedom and growth.[65] Or consider the long-run development of total factor productivity in the British, American and German economies. Both Germany and the United States outstripped the United Kingdom in the twentieth century; but it would be less than easy to tell from the available data that one of the two had spent only the period 1919–33 and 1947 to the present under democratic forms of government.[66]

Perhaps the most that can be said is that major economic crises such as high inflation and depression can undermine representative institutions, especially when these are of comparatively recent origin.[67] The tendency for economic losers to blame liberal policies for their troubles and to vote for equality and even dictatorship in preference to democracy is well documented. Indeed, it is typically argued that "the immediate effect of the economic crisis in Europe was to increase domestic political and social tensions, to bring Hitler to power in Germany and to encourage the development of fascist movements elsewhere."[68] Yet there are problems even here. Figures 42 and 43 present the available figures for real growth of national product for two groups of European countries: those that successfully sustained democratic institutions throughout the inter-war period; and those that failed to do so ("dictatorships" for short). It will be immediately apparent that there is no significant difference in economic performance between the two groups. To take two specific examples, the Depression was only slightly worse in Germany, where democracy failed, than in the Netherlands, where it did not. Moreover, as the figures in Appendix E show, there is simply no correlation between the severity of the Great Depression (measured in terms of the decline in real GNP from peak to trough) and the ease with which dictatorships were established in the 1930s; if there had been, then Czechoslovakia and France would also have turned fascist in, respectively, 1935 and 1936.[69] In any case, in eight of the fourteen dictatorships democracy failed before 1928. Nor, indeed, is it possible to identify any straightforward correlation between an economic or socio-economic indicator and the durability of democracy in the period. Neither the proportion of the population in education nor the relative size of the armed forces—to take two examples—bear any relationship to the political stability of the countries in the sample. The only faint statistical correlation is that the more urban a society was, the more likely democracy was to endure. The problem with this statistical finding is that two of the "outliers"

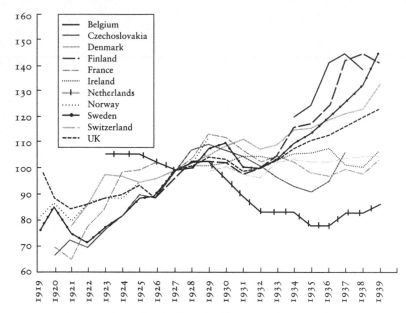

Figure 42: Real national product indices for European democracies, 1919–1939 (1927=100)

Sources: Lethbridge, 'National Income,' pp. 542, 555, 571, 575, 582, 592; Flora *et al.*, *State, Economy and Society*, vol. ii, pp. 370–400; Mitchell, *European Historical Statistics*, pp. 409–16.

were none other than Germany and Austria, which were second only to Britain in the relative size of their urban populations.

Similar anomalies arise when one considers the relationship between economic crisis and democracy in other periods and settings. Economic crises may have been responsible for the failures of Latin-American democracy in the mid-1960s; but democracy in the region survived the debt crisis of the 1980s and the financial crises of 1990s. High inflation appears to have increased the likelihood of democratic breakdown from 1950 until the mid-1970s, but not in the 1980s.[70]

What of the converse proposition that democracy is good for economic growth? It ought by now to be uncontroversial that the undemocratic socialist regimes of the post-1917 period failed in the long run to generate sustainable growth compared with their declared democratic capitalist foes. Even the long-cherished belief of Marxists like Eric Hobsbawm that Stalin's policies of forced collectivization and industrial planning were necessary to modernize the Russian economy can hardly be sustained when the human

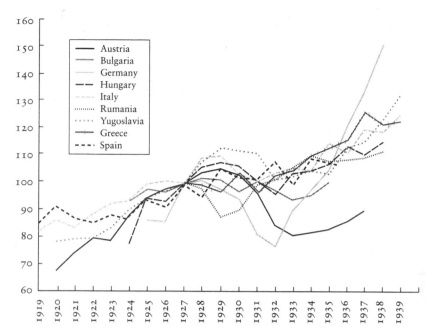

*Figure 43: Real national product indices for European 'dictatorships,' 1919–1939
(1927=100)*
Source: As for figure 42.

cost is set alongside the contemporaneous increases in physical output. To
put it brutally, for every nineteen tons of steel produced under Stalin, *at least*
one Soviet citizen died as a result of man-made famine, deportation, incar-
ceration in the gulag or execution.[71] The evidence is compelling that the communist system was so wasteful of resources and so perverse in its incentive
structure as ultimately to be self-destructive. According to one recent estimate, allowing for new investment and human capital, Soviet growth was
"the worst in the world" between 1960 and 1989.[72]

However, when the comparison is extended to include non-socialist autocracies, the evidence from a multitude of empirical studies is ambiguous to
say the least.[73] It was not only the democratic states of Western Europe that
grew faster than those of Communist Eastern Europe between 1950 and
1989; it was also countries like Greece, Portugal and Spain, which were
undemocratic for much of the period.

One possibility is that democracy is *not* in fact a crucial determinant of
economic success. According to Barro, the key contributions a government
can make towards growth are:

1. providing or encouraging the provision of secondary and higher education;
2. providing or encouraging the provision of effective health care, since there is a correlation between growth and life expectancy;
3. promoting birth control;
4. avoiding "non-productive government expenditures, since "big government is bad for growth;"
5. enforcing the rule of law;
6. keeping inflation below around 10 per cent per annum.

This conclusion is echoed in *The Wealth and Poverty of Nations* by David Landes, who suggests that "the ideal growth-and-development" government would:

1. secure rights of private property, the better to encourage saving and investment;
2. secure rights of personal liberty . . . against both the abuses of tyranny and . . . crime and corruption;
3. enforce rights of contract . . .
4. provide stable government . . . governed by publicly known rules . . .
5. provide responsive government . . .
6. provide honest government . . . [with] no rents to favour and position;
7. provide moderate, efficient, ungreedy government . . . to hold taxes down [and] reduce the government's claim on the social surplus . . .[74]

(Suprisingly, Landes omits the provision of good education.) But both he and Barro agree that such an ideal government need "not necessarily [be] democratic." The latter's figures show that the fact of a government's being democratically elected is statistically insignificant as a determinant of growth. In other words, both sets of growth-promoting policies could be delivered as readily by a non-democratic as by a democratic government. Barro himself cites a number of examples of growth-promoting dictatorships: the Pinochet government in Chile, the Fujimori administration in Peru, the Shah's regime in Iran, as well as the now familiar Asian examples.[75] It is also worth recalling that most developed economies experienced their industrial revolution some time before they enacted universal suffrage.[76]

On closer inspection, there are no hard and fast rules linking democracy and growth. Clearly some dictatorships ("right wing" or "technocratic" ones) do deliver high growth, while others ("populist" or "kleptocratic" ones) do not.[77] The relationship between democracy and growth, on the other hand, appears to be non-linear: graphically represented, it is shaped like an inverted U. Democratization is initially beneficial to growth—up to a point roughly halfway along Barro's scale—but thereafter the relationship appears to turn negative.[78] In short, democracy is not "a critical determinant of growth:"

At low levels of political rights, an expansion of these rights stimulates economic growth. However, once a moderate amount of democracy has been attained, a further expansion reduces growth. A possible interpretation is that, in extreme dictatorships, an increase in political rights tends to raise growth because the limitation on governmental authority is critical. However, in places that have already achieved some political rights, *further democratization may retard growth because of the heightened concern with social programs and income redistribution.*[79]

This is a crucial caveat.

To the historian, Barro's finding is not surprising. The inter-war period furnishes a number of striking examples of new democracies pursuing disastrous economic policies. Indeed, the real significance of the inter-war failure of democracy in Europe may lie here. It has been argued that it was the combination of proportional representation and deep economic divisions which produced the most severe policy failures (such as hyperinflation) after the First World War.[80] In fact, the evidence suggests that more or less any form of democracy failed to deliver sustained growth in the 1920s because of conflicts between fiscal and monetary policy, the former in the hands of universal suffrage parliaments, the latter still largely controlled by financial élites. And the point is not simply that "democracies that arise without prior economic development . . . tend not to last."[81] Germany, Austria and Italy were economically far advanced by 1919, with relatively high levels of per capita income.

Another line of argument stresses not the character of a regime (democratic or autocratic) but its *stability*. A recent survey analyzed the experience of over a hundred countries from the 1950s or 1960s until 1982 and concluded that political instability is more harmful to growth than the absence of democracy.[82] This too accords with historical evidence of the interwar period, when many new democracies suffered from myriad forms of instability (large-scale strikes, street violence, assassinations and attempted coups).

None of this, of course, should be construed as in any sense an argument against democracy. As Churchill said, "democracy is the worst form of Government—except all those other forms that have been tried from time to time."[83] This is true. It is simply that democracy is not guaranteed to be economically superior to those alternative forms of government.

THE SPIRIT OF DEMOCRACY

In his famous essay on "The Protestant Ethic and the Spirit of Capitalism," Max Weber suggested that the rise of modern capitalism had its roots in the cultural changes wrought in north-western Europe and exported to America by the Reformation. In particular, Calvinism encouraged a pattern of behaviour which had—as a benign side-effect—a qualitative and quantitative improvement in wealth-creating activity. The key was its ethos of asceticism, which exalted hard work and deferred consumption as outward proofs of godliness. The capitalist "calling" was, in other words, religious in origin: "To attain . . . self-confidence [in one's membership of the Elect] intense worldly activity was recommended . . . Christian asceticism . . . strode into the market-place of life."[84] This link from theology to behaviour, Weber suggested, [was] the best explanation for the fact that "sober, bourgeois capitalism with its rational organization of free labor" had been much slower to take hold in Catholic, Orthodox or, for that matter, non-Christian parts of the world.[85]

Though frequently criticized since its first publication in 1904—and certainly ambiguous in tracing the origins of a rational process of accumulation back to a fundamentally irrational ethos of self-denial[86]—Weber's cultural model has never been wholly discredited. What has tended to happen is that the distinction he made between Protestantism and other forms of Christianity has been blurred, in order to emphasize the difference between European and non-European cultures. Thus the divergence of European patterns of family formation from those of Asia—the "origins of individualism"—has been sought as far back as the seventh century, when the Church sought to undermine the extended kinship group by prohibiting marriage between close relatives.[87] Stretching the thesis even further, Judaism has been identified as having a related pro-capitalist ethos. Landes retains a strongly Weberian element in his account of world economic history, seeking explanations for Europe's economic "triumph" over China, Turkey and India in the realm of religion and culture; but his "spirit of capitalism" is rooted in a Judaeo-Christian ethic.[88]

There is a link between the Weberian thesis about the rise of capitalism and Tocqueville's interpretation of the rise of democracy. For Tocqueville, it was the strength of the Protestant religious sects that made the United States an ideal environment for a democratic system which was also friendly to liberty. By contrast, the disrepute of the Church in eighteenth-century France, and the consequent hostility of the Revolution towards religion, helped to explain the illiberal turn French democracy had taken. (Writing nearly a century before,

Gibbon had advanced the complementary argument that it had been the rise of Christianity which had fatally undermined the Roman Empire.)

The idea persists that Christian culture is at once more friendly to capitalism and more hostile to despotism than the religious cultures of Asia. According to the Freedom House Survey, for example, Christian societies are more likely to be democratic and free. Of the 88 countries that qualify as "free" in the 1998 edition, no fewer than 79 are "majority Christian (by tradition or belief);" whereas only 11 of the 67 most illiberal countries are. By contrast, only one country with a Muslim majority—Mali—is free; 14 are partly free and 28 are not free. Evidence of this sort has encouraged Samuel Huntington to posit an impending "clash of civilizations" by way of a substitute for the late and in some quarters lamented clash of ideologies between the United States and the Soviet Union.[89]

This simple correlation between Christianity and liberty hardly stands up to close scrutiny, any more than the assumption (central to Huntington's thesis) that there is a correlation between Islam and violence, or between Islam and weak nation-states. After all, many Catholic countries were illiberal and undemocratic when the Freedom House Survey began. Moreover, two of the three most murderous regimes of the twentieth century arose in originally Christian societies, even if the ideologies of all three were anticlerical: Hitler's National Socialism evinced pagan leanings, while "Socialism in One Country" was as aggressively atheistic in Stalin's Soviet Union as in Mao's China. However, a more sophisticated approach, which groups countries according to which of nine major religious groups predominates and relates this to their level of democratisation, produces a different picture. Table 20 gives the average of the democracy score (in this case, the maximum is 1.00) for the period 1975 to 1994. This kind of evidence persuades some political scientist (notably Lipset) that the chances of democratization are enhanced if a country is Protestant rather than Catholic, and Christian rather than Islamic.[90]

Yet there is a danger here that correlation may be mistaken for causation. A more careful statistical analysis casts doubt on the explanatory significance of religion: in the case of Protestant countries, the higher standard of living appears to have been the key to the relative success of democracy, rather than their Protestantism *per se*. This merely brings us back to the Weber thesis: was it Protestantism that lay behind the higher standard of living? The difficulty is to decide what the dependent variable is. To take another example: former British colonies have had more success with democracy than the erstwhile possessions of France, Portugal, Holland or Belgium.[91] But is this a legacy of settlement by Protestant emigrants and the work of British

Table 20. Average democracy score (maximum 1.00, minimum 0.00) for 136 countries, 1975–1994

Dominant religion	No. of countries	Average of democracy indicator
Jewish	1	0.85
Protestant	24	0.78
Hindu	5	0.66
Catholic	49	0.60
Buddhist	4	0.56
Shinto etc.	3	0.45
Other	17	0.28
Muslim	32	0.26
Atheist	1	0.10

Source: Barro, "Determinants of Economic Growth," p. 48.

missionaries? Or was it the secular aspects of British rule that laid the foundations for later developments?

One strong possibility raised by the example of former British colonies is that both growth and democracy benefit, independently of one other, from the development of the rule of law—to be precise, the kind of law which attaches paramount importance to individual property rights. This is certainly the argument advanced by the Peruvian development economist Hernando de Soto, who sees defective legal institutions rather than poverty *per se* as the principal cause of under-development.[92] It is a line of argument with obvious appeal to economists like Douglass North, who have long argued that the English (and even more so the American) legal systems provided the best available setting for capitalism in the eighteenth and nineteenth centuries.[93]

There is, however, a paradox about this gratifying Anglo-American success story. In both cases, the institutions that proved so favourable to the growth of both capitalism and democracy emerged out of civil wars fought within religiously mixed and multi-ethnic societies.[94] It is to the vexed question of ethnicity that we must now turn.

13

Fractured Unities

> After the collapse of the Austro-Hungarian monarchy, the Bukovina became part of Romania. While in Austrian times its linguistically and sartorially kaleidoscopic mixture of people had given an attractive touch of colour to the placid and mannered everyday life of a flourishing crown land, the opposite now occurred: a thin foil of civilization appeared to have been superimposed on an untidily assorted ethnic conglomerate from which it could be peeled off all too readily. . . . Those who remained in Romania split into groups determined by nationality. The Romanians holding important government posts established themselves as the new masters . . . The so-called Bukovina Swabians . . . segregated themselves in a flag-waving Great Germany clannishness . . . The Ruthenians refused to have anything to do with the former Austrians, who they felt had always treated them as second-degree citizens, or the Romanians, who cold-shouldered them in return. Poles, Russians and Armenians . . . now more than ever kept to themselves. All of these despised the Jews, notwithstanding that the Jews . . . played an economically decisive role . . .
>
> Gregor von Rezzori, *The Snows of Yesteryear*[1]

When the news of the outbreak of the First World War reached Gregor von Rezzori's mother in the Bukovina, her immediate reaction was to flee the advancing Russians to Trieste. On their way there—through a pass in the Carpathian mountains and on via Bistrice, Budapest and Vienna—they were entirely dependent on the linguistic skills of the boy's wetnurse Cassandra, who spoke "snatches of Romanian, Ruthenian, Polish and Hungarian, as well as Turkish and Yiddish, assisted by a grotesque, grimacing mimicry and a primitive, graphic body language." It was the beginning of an era of ethnic chaos that would shatter the Habsburg unity she personified.

By the time they family returned to Tschernowitz at the end of the war, the town was on the verge of being handed over to Romania under the Treaty

of Trianon: as Rezzori recalled, "sinister species in rags had begun to fill the streets." For twenty years thereafter, the different nationalities co-existed fractiously in what was now Cernati: youths from the Romanian Youth Movement crossing swords with ethnic German student fraternities, both despising the Hasidic Jews with their clothes stalls and synagogues.[2] Then in 1940, under the terms of the Nazi-Soviet Pact, the Red Army occupied the town and the German population was unceremoniously expelled. A year later, in the wake of Operation Barbarossa, the Germans returned—in the form of Sonderkommando 10b, part of Einsatzgruppe D, one of the mobile task forces entrusted with the task of massacring the Jews of Eastern Europe. They found that the Romanians had already begun their work for them. Between them, the Germans and Romanians killed two thousand Jews and set about deporting the others to the killing fields of Transnistria.[3] In the summer of 1944 the Soviets returned. Today the town is called Chernovsty, a backwater of Ukraine, only slowly emerging from the monotonous uniformity imposed by the Communists—who, like the Nazis before them, claimed they had found the "solution" to the nationalities question.

The history of Tschernowitz–Cernati–Chernovtsy is a microcosm of the mayhem unleashed by ethnic politics in the twentieth century. But as more recent events in places as far afield as Kosovo, Rwanda and Indonesia remind us, ethnic politics—and ethnic conflict—show no sign of abating. Indeed, the politics of ethnicity may have fewer ideological rivals at the dawn of the twenty-first century than a hundred years ago.

A BALKAN WORLD?

The previous chapter considered the relationship between democracy and economics, and concluded that they were both dependent variables of other institutional factors such as religion and the law. Another and more controversial characteristic of states which is sometimes said to influence both their economic and their political development is ethnic composition. Ninety years ago, when Werner Sombart wrote his distasteful rejoinder to Weber, *The Jews and Economic Life* (1911), the question was whether some races were more adept at capitalism than others, for better or for worse.[4] Nowadays, a more commonly asked question is how far ethnic homogeneity is a prerequisite for democratization. The two questions are not unrelated.

The Freedom House Survey, to take a recent example, suggests that countries without a predominant ethnic majority are less successful in establishing open and democratic societies than ethnically homogeneous countries (defined as countries in which over two-thirds of the population belong to a single ethnic group). Of the 114 countries in the world which possess a dominant ethnic group, 66—more than half—are free. By contrast, among multi-ethnic countries only 22 of 77 are free—less than a third.

This need not be read simply as an argument for the creation of homogeneous states, however. Rather, what it may imply is that most multi-ethnic states can be held together only by illiberal regimes. One theory is that there is a trade-off between the economies of scale which favour the creation of large nation-states (public goods can be provided more cheaply per capita for big political units), and the alienation experienced by geographically peripheral groups when the center of government is very remote. As democracy spreads, this alienation tends to find expression in the demands of peripheral groups for compensation for their political exclusion, and the complaints of core groups about "parasites" on the fringe. Democratization may therefore to lead to secessions by groups on the periphery.

That was arguably the inter-war experience, when there was a relatively close (though not exact) correlation between the presence of large ethnic minorities in countries like Poland, Romania and Yugoslavia and the failure of democracy. Nearly 30 per cent of the population of Poland were not considered Poles: the rest were Belorussians (5 per cent), Ukrainians (14 per cent), Jews (8 per cent) and Germans (2 per cent). Nearly a fifth of the people of Romania, as the case of Tschernowitz illustrates, were not Romanians: 8 per cent were Hungarian, 4 per cent Germans, 4 per cent Jews and 3 per cent Ukrainians.[5] Minorities also accounted for roughly 20 per cent of the populations of Spain and Albania. In Turkey around two-fifths of the population belonged to minorities.[6] Without the grip of authoritarianism, the argument runs, the forces of self-determination will always cause such multi-ethnic states to break up into homogeneous "statelets." Events in Yugoslavia and, on a much larger scale, the Soviet Union in the decade after 1989 would seem to bear this out. To date Yugoslavia has fragmented into nine separate entities; and the process may not yet be complete. As a consequence of the collapse of the Soviet Union in 1991, the world has been blessed with fourteen new independent states—fifteen, if the Russians should ever tire of retaining Chechnya by force. This fissiparity of post-Communist Europe has prompted the "historian of the present" Timothy Garton Ash to suggest that "a contemporary European state with a less than 80 per cent ethnic majority is inherently unstable."[7]

There are reasons to be skeptical of such ethnic determinism, it is true. In the inter-war period there were obvious exceptions to the supposed rule that ethnic heterogeneity means either authoritarianism or fragmentation. In fascist Italy ethnic minorities accounted for around 2 per cent of the population, while in Nazi Germany the figure was just 1.6 per cent. Yet democracy survived until the Third Reich snuffed it out in heterogeneous Czechoslovakia, where minorities were a third of the population, as well as in multi-ethnic Belgium and Switzerland. And it should not be forgotten that the two most successful capitalist democracies—Britain and the United States—are themselves multi-ethnic states, the former with its Celtic and more recently ex-colonial minorities, the latter largely populated by immigrants from Europe, Africa, Asia and Latin America and their often proudly "hyphenated" descendants.

None the less, it is impossible to ignore what appears to be a long-run historical trend towards ever more ethnically homogeneous states; and it may well be that at least some of the above counter-examples will one day also fragment: Czechoslovakia already has, while in Belgium and the British Isles the centrifugal forces of ethnic politics have seldom been stronger, as the "invented traditions" of the eighteenth and nineteenth centuries slowly fade.[8]

MEN AND MAPS

This was not at all what the early nationalists anticipated. When trying to imagine an ideal map of Europe in 1857, the Italian nationalist Giuseppe Mazzini imagined eleven nation states.[9] At that time the map of Europe was dominated by four multinational empires—the British, Russian, Habsburg and Ottoman—seven medium-sized monarchies—France, Prussia, Spain, Portugal, Holland, Belgium, Denmark and Sweden—a republican confederation—Switzerland—and a plethora of smaller states in Germany, Italy and the Balkans. Nationalism looked like the great simplifier, rationalizing the borders of Europe. William Penn's *Essay towards the Present and Future Peace of Europe* (1693) had envisaged a European "league," but this would have included, in addition to the major powers, "Venice, the Seven [Dutch] Provinces, the Thirteen [Swiss] Cantons, the dukedoms of Holstein and Courland." Likewise, in his tract *Perpetual Peace* (1712) Charles de Saint-Pierre's ideal "European Union" consisted of twenty-four states, including Savoy, Venice, Genoa, Florence and the Papacy; as well as Bavaria, Lorraine, Courland, Saxony, Hanover, the Palatinate and the ecclesiastical electorates of the Holy Roman Empire.[10] When Rousseau sought to refine de Saint-Pierre's scheme he still had to reserve places for the Elector of Bavaria, the Elector

Palatine, the ecclesiastical electors, the Republic of Venice, the King of Naples and the King of Sardinia.[11] How much simpler, in Mazzini's view, to have less than a dozen big nation-states, united on the basis of language and ethnicity.

Yet the history of modern Europe has exposed Mazzini's vision as a chimera. For one thing, the process of state-building in the nineteenth century owed little, if anything, to nationalism: new states like Greece, Bulgaria or Romania were more the products of great power rivalry than of indigenous aspirations; while the most famous of the unifiers—Cavour and Bismarck—were in many ways playing the old game of extending their royal masters' domains. The entities that emerged were as much Greater Piedmont and Greater Prussia as Italy and Germany. Moreover, there were few parts of Eastern Europe where the ideal of a homogeneous nation-state was easily applicable. It was no coincidence that the First World War had its roots in the Balkans, where the notion of a Serb-led South Slav state not only clashed with the patchwork ethnography of Bosnia-Hercegovina but struck at the very heart of the Austro-Hungarian system of dual power. There is a telling scene at the end of Joseph Roth's *Radetsky March* when the news of the Archduke Franz Ferdinand's assassination by a Serb terrorist is broken at a riotous ball in provincial Hungary. The first response of the local Magyar nobility is delight—particularly in the case of the former Jew among them, who is especially eager to affirm his Hungarian chauvinism. Meanwhile in far-off Bohemia, Jaroslav Hašek's Good Soldier Švejk is incensed, but erroneously holds the Turks responsible for "our Ferdinand's" death.

It was Woodrow Wilson who unwittingly exposed the impracticality of the Mazzinian model. As early as December 1914 Wilson had argued that any peace settlement "should be for the advantage of the European nations regarded as Peoples and not for any nation imposing its governmental will upon alien people."[12] In May 1915 he went further in a speech to the League to Enforce Peace, stating unequivocally that "every people has a right to choose the sovereignty under which they shall live."[13] He repeated the point in January 1917: "Every people should be left free to determine its own polity;"[14] and elaborated on its implications in points five to thirteen of his Fourteen Points.[15] The League of Nations was not simply to guarantee territorial integrity of its member states but was empowered to accommodate future territorial adjustments "pursuant to the principle of self-determination."[16] This was not novel, of course. British Liberals since John Stuart Mill had been arguing that the homogeneous nation-state was the only proper setting for a liberal polity, and British politicians had spasmodically stuck up for the right to independence of their pet minorities (notably the Greeks and the Italians, whom they tended to romanticize). But never before had the principle been accorded such international recognition as it was at the Paris peace conference in 1919.

Applying self-determination to the map of Europe proved far from easy, however, especially in view of the ethnic heterogeneity of Central and Eastern Europe. For one thing, there were at least nine and a half million Germans outside the borders of the post-1919 Reich — around 13 per cent of the total German-speaking population of Europe. The adoption of "self-determination" as a guiding principle of the peace was perilous because it could not be applied to Germany without aggrandizing her far beyond the territory of the pre-1919 Reich. From the outset there had to be inconsistency, if not hypocrisy: no *Anschluss* of the rump Austria to the Reich; but plebiscites to determine the fate of North Schleswig, eastern Upper Silesia, Eupen-Malmedy and later the Saarland. In addition to Istria, part of Dalmatia and the Dodecanese islands (added in 1923), Italy acquired South Tyrol, which included numerous Germans. France reclaimed Alsace and Lorraine, lost in 1871, despite the fact that the map of Alsace-Lorraine used by the American expert Charles Homer Haskins showed the "vast majority of districts with at least 75 percent German speakers."[17]

There were other exceptions too. Several million Hungarians found themselves outside the rump Hungary. The creation of what became Yugoslavia was a negation of self-determination, as it lumped together Serbs, Croats, Slovenes, Bosnian Muslims, Kosovar Albanians and Vojvodina Hungarians. And no serious objections were raised when Turkey (in breach of the Treaty of Sèvres) partitioned briefly independent Armenia with Russia.[18] This was "self-determination" in the British sense: a Victorian veneer for whatever borders suited the great powers. As James Headlam-Morley, the assistant director of the Political Intelligence Department of the Foreign Office, sardonically noted: "Self determination is quite demodé." He and his clever colleagues "determine[d] for them [the nationalities] what they ought to wish . . ."[19] There were, it is true, serious attempts to write "minority rights" into the various peace treaties, beginning with Poland. But here again British cynicism and self-interest played an unconstructive role. Revealingly, Headlam Morley was as skeptical of minority rights as he was of self-determination. As he noted in his *Memoir of the Paris Peace Conference*:

Some general clause giving the League of Nations the right to protect minorities in all countries which were members . . . would give [it] the right to protect the Chinese in Liverpool, the Roman Catholics in France, the French in Canada, quite apart from more serious problems, such as the Irish . . . Even if the denial of such a right else-where might lead to injustice and oppression, that was better than to allow every-thing which means the negation of the sovereignty of every state in the world.[20]

If the League was not going to act to protect minority rights, then who would? The Greek premier Venizelos pointed the way ahead when he sought, with Italian connivance, to grab additional Greek-inhabited territory from the Turks. The ensuing war ended in victory for the Turks under the leadership of Kemal in August 1922; its most tangible consequence was the "repatria-tion" of 1.2 million Greeks and half a million Turks.[21] Similar transfers of population happened with varying degrees of compulsion all over Central and Eastern Europe. Three-quarters of a million German-speakers had quit the "lost territories" for the Reich by 1925.[22] Between 1919 and 1924, 200,000 Hungarians left the enlarged Romania; 80,000 left Yugoslavia. Some 270,000 Bulgarians left their homes in Greece, Yugoslavia, Turkey and Romania.[23]

This was only the beginning of the bloody process of ethnic conflict and forced population transfers that would culminate in the horrors of the 1940s. The Germans were without question the worst offenders. In addition to mur-dering between five and six million Jews, their racial policies were responsi-ble for the deaths of around three million Ukrainians, 2.4 million Poles, 1.6 million Russians, 1.4 million Belorussians and a quarter of a million gyp-sies.[24] All this was done in a fulfilment of a vast plan to transform the eth-nic map of Europe, extending the "living space" of the Aryan "master race" thousands of miles eastwards, expelling, starving or ultimately murdering the Jewish and Slav "sub-humans" who lived there. The scale and sophisti-cation of Nazi policy sets it apart; that and the fact that it emanated from a highly developed and apparently civilized society. Nevertheless, "ethnic cleansing" was not a Nazi invention. The Turkish genocide against the Arme-nians during the First World War was an influence Hitler acknowledged. Nor should we overlook the fact that over one and a half million members of eth-nic minorities—Poles, Germans, Chechens, Tatars, Meskhetians, Koreans, Kalmyks, Ingushi, Karachai and Greeks—perished as a result of Stalin's ver-sion of ethnic cleansing. Formally, they were sentenced to deportation, but under such harsh conditions and to such inhospitable terrain that between 10 and 30 per cent of the peoples affected did not survive.[25]

The motivations for these murderous policies were myriad; but economics played a part. For example, the new states established after the First World War were more likely to harass minorities when they were wealthy. "Land reform" became a device for expropriation in the interests of the less well-off members of the majority people. There is no question that a significant part of the appeal of anti-Jewish policy to those without strong racialist prejudices was quite simply that it was an opportunity to plunder the richest of all Europe's minorities. From the first boycott of Jewish stores through the "Aryanization" of Jewish firms and the "taxation" of emigrants to the final pitiless extraction of gold rings and tooth-fillings at the death camps, the Nazis wasted no opportunity to mulct their victims. The art collections of the Rothschilds were only the crowning glory of a vast heap of stolen goods. According to one recent estimate, the total value of the property stolen by the Nazis from the Jews of Europe amounted to between $8 and $12.6 billion.[26] Table 21 offers some intriguing evidence of the extent of Jewish "over-representation" within the economic élites of various countries for which statistics are available on wealth ownership by ethnic group. The ratio in the last column is no more than a very rough indication, since the definition of the economic élites varies significantly from country to country. Nevertheless, the statistics have their uses. The German and American ends of the spectrum make it tempting to argue that anti-Semitism was more severe where the Jews were over-represented within the economic élites. But the British and Polish figures seem to be the wrong way round if such a theory is to be sustained.

Table 21. *The Jews in economic élites: selected statistics*

Country	Jews as a percentage of population	Jews in the economic élite	Ratio of "over-representation"*
Germany	0.95 (1910)	31 per cent of richest families (1908–11)	33
Britain	0.56 (1915)	8.5 per cent of estates of £500,000 or more (1809–1939)	15
Hungary	5.1 (1910)	62.3 per cent of top business taxpapers (1887)	12
Russia	4.1 (1913)	35 per cent of merchant class (1914)	9
Poland	10.5 (1929)	45 per cent of highest income-earners outside agriculture (1929)	4
Australia	0.4 (1911)	3.45 per cent of largest estates left in New South Wales, (1817–1939)	9
US	3.2 (1911)	6.5 per cent of "super-rich" ($20–$30 million plus, 1865–1970)	2

*Percentage of economic élites divided by percentage of population.
Source: Rubinstein, "Jewish Participation," tables 1 and 6.

The crucial point about ethnic or religious minorities is that they have often been associated with entrepreneurial aptitude. It was not just the Jews who out-performed majority groups in the countries where they settled; it was also island Greeks, overseas Chinese, Armenians, Parsees and, for that matter, Germans in Eastern Europe and Scots in the British Empire.[27] For majority populations, the difficulty is to choose between the long-run indirect benefits that flow from accommodating such over-achieving minorities; and the short-run temptation to give in to feelings of envy and pillage them. In Britain the minorities were tolerated and the economy as a whole reaped the benefit. In Central and Eastern Europe armed robbery prevailed, with the predictable consequence of long-term impoverishment.

UNTYING THE NATIONS

The upshot of the Paris peace treaties of 1919–20 was that Europe consisted of twenty-six sovereign states. Looking at the map more than eighty years after the Treaty of Versailles, it is tempting to conclude that the continent has come full circle. The new states created in the ruins of the Romanov and Ottoman empires remain much as they were after 1919. In north-eastern Europe Poland has shifted westwards, but Lithuania, Latvia, Estonia and Finland are much as they were in 1919, namely independent of Russia. In the Middle East the map reads Israel where once it read Palestine, and Jordan has lost its prefix "Trans-," but otherwise not much has changed, save for the fact that the British and French "mandates" are no more, just as they have disappeared in the former German colonies in Africa. Even more striking, the republics of Armenia, Georgia, Azerbaijan, Ukraine and Belorus, which by 1921 had been restored to Russian rule by the Bolsheviks, have regained their independence. Only the post-Habsburg order in central and south-eastern Europe looks significantly different. Gone are those multi-ethnic compounds, Czechoslovakia and the "Kingdom of Serbs, Croats and Slovenes" (as Yugoslavia was originally and cumbersomely known). Gone too are the large ethnic minorities of the main Central European states: from 30 per cent of the population of Poland in the 1930s to just 2.7 per cent today; from 33 per cent of the population of Czechoslovakia to just 4.5 per cent.[28] By mainly foul means, the nationalist utopia of ethnically homogeneous states has been brought closer.

And, like some unstoppable process of fission, "self-determination" continues to generate yet more sovereign states. In all, there are as many as forty-eight separate entities in Europe today on the broadest definition of geography and autonomy (including Russia and Turkey): more than four times the number Mazzini had in mind.[29] And it is perfectly possible that the process of fragmentation is not over yet. From Scotland to Montenegro, would-be nation-states are waiting in the wings.

This fissiparous tendency is not confined to Europe. Excluding sub-Saharan Africa, there were 64 independent countries in the world in 1871. Forty-three years later, on the eve of the First World War, imperialism had reduced the number to 59. The aftermath of the war was not as dramatic globally as it was for Europe. In all, including Africa, there were 69 countries in 1920. But since the Second World War there have been sustained increases. In 1946 there were 74 independent countries; in 1950, 89. By 1995, as Table 22 shows, the number was 192, with the two biggest increases coming in the 1960s (mainly Africa, where 25 new states were formed between 1960 and 1964) and the 1990s (mainly Eastern Europe).

To be sure, the degree of fragmentation should not be exaggerated, given the acceleration of population growth in the period since 1871. The "average country" has not in fact shrunk at all since Bismarck's day: it has grown from 22 to 28 million inhabitants. However, there does appear to have been an increase in the number of very small states. Of the 192 independent states in existence in 1995, 87 had less than 5 million inhabitants, 58 less than 2.5 million and 35 less than 500,000. More than half of the world's countries have fewer inhabitants than the state of Massachusetts.[30] Iceland (the population

Table 22. World population and the number of independent states since 1871

	World population (millions)	Number of countries	Average country population (millions)
1871	1,416	64	22.1
1914	1,854	59	31.4
1920	1,946	69	28.2
1946	2,400	74	32.4
1950	2,478	89	27.8
1995	5,457	192	28.4

Source: www.census.gov/ipc/www/worldhis.html; Alesina, Spolaore and Wacziarg, "Economic Integration," pp. 1, 23.

of which is around 270,000) has about as large a population as Leicester; yet it is a fully-fledged member of the OECD, with its own language, currency and airline.[31]

Between the wars, political fragmentation came with a high price-tag in terms of economic growth and political stability. Could world "Balkanization" have the same negative consequences? Eric Hobsbawm likens the new map of the world to that of the Middle Ages when interstitial economic centers flourished as territorial enclaves: in this view, city-states, extraterritorial "industrial zones" and "tax-havens [on] otherwise valueless islands" signify a regression to the days the Hanseatic League.[32] Alberto Alesina and his collaborators make the point that from a purely economic point of view, the process of political disintegration leads to "an inefficiently large number of countries."[33] To be sure, small can be beautiful, in the sense that the richest country in the world (in terms of per capita GDP) is among the smallest: Luxembourg. On the other hand, the public sector of small states tends to be larger, since the per capita cost of providing public goods will be higher than in big countries.[34]

Moreover, the number of regional conflicts may be higher as large countries fragment, and this may mean an increase in the per capita cost of defence.[35] This is because fission in the world of politics, as in the world of particles, is explosive: for many of the new states, the transition to independence has involved at least some measure of conflict with neighbours or former colonial powers. It has been argued persuasively that "the formation of many new countries may actually increase the mass of observed conflicts" because an increase in the number of countries "increases the mass of international interactions that can, potentially, lead to conflict."[36] The case of the Balkans is only the best-known example in our own time. In Rwanda the massacre of around 800,000 Tutsis by Hutu interahamwe in April–July 1994 took place *after* international efforts to democratize the regime.[37] In Indonesia the most bitter fighting in East Timor came *after* the collapse of President Suharto's dictatorship in May 1998 and the island's democratic vote for independence in August the following year.

Figure 44 gives annual figures for the number of wars covered by the Singer and Small "Correlates of War" database between 1816 and 1992. It will be seen at once that the late 1980s and early 1990s saw more wars in progress than at any time since the defeat of Napoleon. To be sure, this increase may be partly due to bias in the data: minor wars outside Europe were no doubt rather better reported in the late twentieth century than in the nineteenth. And of course the number of wars tells us nothing about the scale of global conflict since many of the most recent wars have been little more

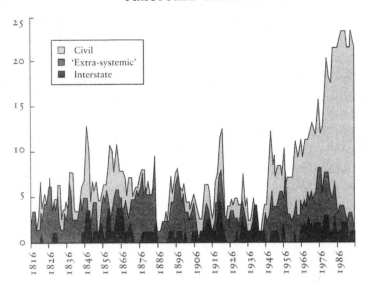

Figure 44: Number of wars in progress per year, 1816–1992
Source: Correlates of war database.

than border skirmishes, barely passing the Singer–Small threshold of a thousand casualties a year.

On the other hand, it is incontestable that nearly all of the increase in the number of wars in the world since 1945 is due to the spread of civil war. Throughout the period covered by the figure, civil wars account for just under half of all wars. For the period since 1945, however, the proportion is closer to two-thirds. It may be that civil war is more closely associated with undemocratic than with democratic regimes; it is certainly more closely associated with poor states than with rich ones, and the latter, as we have seen, are more inclined to be democratic. Nevertheless, there is some evidence to suggest that steps in the direction of democratization—especially in ethnically polarized societies—increase the likelihood of civil war as the minority takes up arms against a feared tyranny of the majority.[38] Civil wars are in fact often the preludes to those secessions which produce new countries; and may well be followed by further conflict between the now separate states.

UNITING THE NATIONS?

In many ways, the metaphor of "Balkanization" does not do justice to the phenomenon of global fragmentation. Perhaps we need to think of the world's political geography in the terms astronomers have used to describe the cosmos. Usually historians confine themselves to the metaphor of the satellite to describe a client state, but there are wider parallels to be drawn. The bigger nation states, like stars, are formed by powerful centripetal forces. During their lives, the give off heat and light in varying degrees. To push the analogy a little further, some radiate goods, some radiate people and some radiate money. Around them, while they are strong, mini-states orbit like planets. But after a time their lustre begins to fade. As their lustre dims, they become "red dwarves." Ultimately they explode into supernovae. Some may even become black holes.

Yet the break-up of a few big stars may not matter if the galaxy as a whole is thriving. According to one argument, the process of political fragmentation has as its corollary the growth of supra-national organizations. Economic globalization, so the theory runs, is being accompanied by political globalization.

Certainly, the growth of supra-national trading blocs like the European Union and the North American Free Trade Area, and the increasing influence of the World Trade Organisation (formerly the General Agreement on Tariffs and Trade) mean that more small countries are economically viable than was the case in the era of protectionist national trade policies. There is, in other words, an inverse relationship between global trade liberalization and the size of countries.[39] At the same time, the International Monetary Fund and the International Bank for Reconstruction and Development (or World Bank) have acted as sources of capital for new states; for all their defects,[40] they have been far more successful than their predecessor, the Bank of International Settlements.[41] And these are only the best-known organizations: between 1952 and 1984 the number of intergovernmental organizations in the world rose from 123 to 365.[42] Nor should we overlook the growing importance of international non-governmental organizations. According to the *Yearbook of International Organizations*, there were 6,000 of these in 1990; now there are around 26,000. Membership of the Worldwide Fund for Nature has increased tenfold since the mid-1980s to 5 million; while Greenpeace has 2.5 million members and Amnesty International 1 million members. If critics see these as the missionary societies of a new Western imperialism, others hail them as the foundations of an international civil society.[43]

In addition to delegating aspects of economic and social policy to such organizations, small states can also seek to enhance their own security by adhering to existing military alliances: the rush by East European states to join NATO in the 1990s provides an obvious illustration. Indeed, it could be argued that the more power accrues to international organizations, the more illusory the sovereignty of the small states becomes. The more utopian internationalists—and the more paranoid of conspiracy-theorists—look forward, with respectively eagerness and dread, to an era of world government under the auspices of the United Nations, which will extend its original remit to include the defence of human rights, regardless of national sovereignty. In this vision, the remaining multi-ethnic states will eventually dissolve into autonomous regions, until every ethnic group, from the East Timorese to the English themselves, is left in possession of its own more or less impotent statelet.

There is, however, a difficulty with this scenario; and that is the fundamental weakness of most supra-national organizations. In financial terms, these behemoths—including the biggest of all, the United Nations—are midgets. The total operating expenses of the UN, the World Bank, the IMF and all UN programs and agencies amounted to $18.2 billion a year in 1999.[44] The US federal budget was approximately a hundred times larger. The same kind of calculation should be borne in mind when the idea is floated that the European Union could become a federal "super-state." The EU's total expenditure in 1999 was little more than one per cent of EU GDP; expenditure by national governments accounted for around 48 per cent.[45] Global purchasing power remains concentrated in the rich nation-states, a fact symbolized by the $1.7 billion owed by the United States to the United Nations. Even the international NGOs are more powerful than their governmental counterparts. The World Trade Organisation's annual budget is £43 million, less than a quarter of the Worldwide Fund for Nature's and half that of Oxfam.

This helps to explain the very patchy record of the United Nations as a global policeman. The UN is usually compared favourably with its predecessor, the League of Nations. But the League also had some successes, and faced bigger problems. Of sixty-six international disputes it had to deal with (four of which had led to open hostilities), it successfully resolved thirty-five and quite reasonably passed twenty to the channels of traditional diplomacy. It failed to resolve just eleven conflicts—unfortunately, the most serious ones.[46] The UN's record is not much better; it only looks better because it has never faced threats to compare with 1930s Germany, Italy and Japan. For most of the Cold War, the UN Security Council was deadlocked, and achieved little more than a series of truce-maintaining interventions in minor civil wars and border disputes. Only in the exceptional circumstances of

1991, with the Soviet Union in its death throes, was it possible to overturn Saddam Hussein's annexation of Kuwait on the basis of an unequivocal UN mandate. Since then its record has been dismal. Between 1992 and 1999 the Security Council authorized a series of humanitarian interventions in Somalia, Bosnia, Rwanda, Haiti, Cambodia, Albania and East Timor. The last of these operations was successful; but the majority of these operations were at best ineffective, and at worst disastrous. The fiasco of the US Rangers' mission to Mogadishu in 1993; the abject failure of the Security Council to reinforce the French contingent in Rwanda in 1994; the Dutch impotence and possible complicity in the massacre at Srebrenica in 1995—these episodes cast grave doubt on the ability of the UN to react rapidly and effectively enough to crises.[47]

Nothing illustrates more clearly the limits of the power of supra-national institutions than the events of 1999, when ethnic cleansing was once again unleashed by a government—that of the rump Yugoslavia—against a minority, the Albanians of Kosovo. Because Kosovo was and remains an integral province of Serbia, the Yugoslav government was legally protected from external intervention by Article 2(4) of the UN Charter, which states that "all Members shall refrain . . . from the threat or use of force against the territorial integrity or political independence of any State;" and Article 2(7) which prohibits intervention "in matters which are essentially within the domestic jurisdiction of any state." It was also covered by the General Assembly's 1970 Declaration on Principles of International Law, which denies members "the right to intervene, directly or indirectly, for any reason whatever, in the internal affairs of any other state." Under the UN Charter, force may be used only in self-defence or with the explicit authorization of the Security Council in response to an act of aggression (Article 51 and Chapter III).[48] No such authorization could be obtained because of Russian opposition on the Security Council—the old story.

Only by ignoring the UN Charter (or, in the words of Tony Blair, "qualifying . . . the principle of non-interference . . . in important respects") could the military intervention by NATO on behalf of the Albanians of Kosovo be justified. In this respect, Kosovo forms part of a pattern. Massive human rights violations were stopped when India intervened in Pakistan in 1971, when Vietnam invaded Cambodia in 1978 and when Tanzania invaded Uganda in 1979. Not one of these operations was authorized by the UN. The intervention of the Economic Community of West African States in Liberia in 1990 was only retrospectively authorized by the UN. The decision by the

United States, Britain and France to establish a "safe haven" for the Kurds of Northern Iraq was not authorized at all.[49]

The prevention of mass expulsions and massacres of minority populations is without doubt a good thing. Unfortunately, as long as there is cross-border migration, and as long as there are ethnic differentials in economic performance, it is a phenomenon likely to go on repeating itself, no matter how often the map of the world is redrawn; no matter how many times the story of Tschernowitz is re-enacted. But history suggests that there is little point expecting the United Nations to prevent ethnic cleansing. Not only does it lack the right to do so; it lacks the means. The question is whether the United States and her allies are willing to devote sufficient resources to defend minority rights effectively. As we shall see in the final chapter, there is reason to doubt it.

14

Understretch:
The Limits of Economic Power

> Go, bind your sons to exile
>   To serve your capitives' need;
> To wait in heavy harness
>   On fluttered folk and wild . . .
>   *Kipling*[1]

Why is the United States so powerful? Why is the United States not more powerful?

Many commentators would answer the first question with a single word: economics. There is, Paul Kennedy argued in his influential *Rise and Fall of the Great Powers*, "a very significant correlation *over the longer term* between productive and revenue-raising capacities on the one hand and military strength on the other." To be sure, Kennedy warned against "the trap of crude economic determinism," and acknowledged "geography, military organisation, national morale, the alliance system . . . individual folly . . . and extremely high battlefield competence" as factors that can influence military outcomes too. But he nevertheless insisted on "a very strong correlation between the eventual outcome of the *major coalition wars* for European or global mastery, and the amount of productive resources mobilized by each side. . . . victory has repeatedly gone to the side with the more flourishing productive base:"[2]

The fact remains that all of the major shifts in the world's *military-power* balance have followed alterations in the *productive* balances; and further, that the rising and falling of the various empires and states in the international system has [*sic*] been confirmed by the outcomes of the major Great Power wars, where victory has always gone to the side with the greatest material resources.[3]

Thus the rise of Habsburg Spain, the Dutch Republic, the British Empire, Russia and, finally, the United States had their roots in the realm of economic

history; as did the failure of Germany and Japan to achieve the global power to which they aspired in the 1930s and 1940s.

However, Kennedy argued, the decline of great powers can also be understood in economic terms:

Wealth is usually needed to underpin military power, and military power is usually needed to acquire and protect wealth. If, however, too large a proportion of the state's resources is diverted from wealth creation and allocated instead to military purposes, then that is likely to lead to a weakening of national power over the longer term. In the same way, if a state overextends itself strategically . . . it runs the risk that the potential benefits from external expansion may be outweighed by the great expense of it all. Great powers in relative decline instinctively respond by spending more on "security," and thereby divert potential resources from "investment" and compound their long-term dilemma.[4]

The point was that if a power became strategically overextended, the costs of defending its empire would "leave less room for 'productive investment,'" leading to a "slowing down" of economic output which could only have "dire implications for [its] long-term capacity to maintain both its citizens' consumption demands and its international position."[5] It was "increasingly difficult," according to Kennedy, "to argue against the proposition that *excessive* arms spending will hurt economic growth:"

There looms today a tension between a nation's . . . search for strategic security . . . and . . . its search for economic security, which depends upon growth (which in turn flows from new methods of production and wealth creation), upon increased output, and upon flourishing internal and external demand—all of which may be damaged by excessive spending upon armaments. . . . A top-heavy military establishment may slow down the rate of economic growth and lead to a decline in the nation's share of world manufacturing output, and therefore wealth, and therefore *power*.[6]

Kennedy left his readers in no doubt that this general proposition had specific relevance to the United States, which he claimed already ran "the risk . . . of what might roughly be called "imperial overstretch." The US, he noted, spent too much on military research and development compared with Germany and Japan, which were able to concentrate on more productive civilian R&D.[7] The implication was clear: that Germany and Japan, relatively unburdened by military commitments, would sooner or later outstrip America economically; after which a shift in the balance of economic power would be more or less inevitable. "In the largest sense of all," he concluded, "the only answer to the question increasingly debated by the public of whether the United States can preserve its existing position is "no."[8]

This argument owed a substantial debt to the British experience of imperial "overstretch" and economic decline from the late nineteenth century onwards. Kennedy himself pointedly remarked that maps of "Major US Military Deployment Around the World" [in the 1980s] . . . look[ed] extraordinarily similar to the chain of fleet bases and garrisons possessed by that former world power, Great Britain, at the height of its strategic overstretch."[9] His words of warning to the United States were therefore a conscious echo of those Victorian and Edwardian critics of British imperialism, who insisted that the cost of maintaining naval bases, colonial armies and subsidized governments across a vast proportion of the globe was higher than any economic benefits could justify. The same point has been made with the benefit of hindsight by a number of economic historians, who argue that Britain could have enjoyed the advantages of free trade without the expense of formal empire; and, more importantly, that the money that taxpayers would have saved as a result of an Edwardian decolonization could have been spent on electricity, cars and consumer durables, thus encouraging industrial modernization at home.[10]

Kennedy's is only one of a number of economic theories of power. In his *Rise and Decline of Nations* (1982), Mancur Olson suggested that strength or weakness might have more to do with the internal structure of a country's political economy than its external commitments. It was the growth of "parochial" cartels and special-interest lobbies that tended to undermine the vitality of an economy: hence the relative success of post-war Germany and Japan, whose various vested interests had been smashed by the experience of dictatorship, total war and defeat, compared with the Britain's decline into the stagflation of the 1970s.[11] One somewhat counter-intuitive inference from this is that occasional military defeat may be economically preferable to consistent victory. Certainly, Olson's policy prescriptions—the "repeal [of] all special-interest legislation or regulation and . . . [the application] of rigorous anti-trust laws to every type of cartel or collusion that uses its power to obtain prices or wages above competitive levels"—are more likely to be achieved by an army of occupation than the normal democratic process.[12]

What is not clear from such economic theories of power is how far the rise and fall of states are due to a self-equilibriating or cyclical mechanism, with prosperity leading to power, and then overstretch or internal sclerosis leading inexorably to decline. In the ambitious models of Modelski and Wallerstein, the cycles of global hegemony have a strongly deterministic character. According to the former, there have been five cycles of "relative naval power" since 1500—the Portuguese, the Dutch, two British and the American—and in each there have been four phases: "global war," "world power," "delegitimation" and "deconcentration." In Wallerstein's model, which takes a Marxist view of capitalist development, there have been four cycles since 1450—the Habsburg, the Dutch, the British and the American—and again, within each of these, four phases: "ascending hegemony," "hegemonic victory," "hegemonic maturity" and "declining hegemony."[13] However, Kennedy's argument (like Olson's) seems to have a policy implication: namely, that governments should try to restrain defence spending to avoid economic, and ultimately military, decline.

Kennedy has been much criticized for exaggerating the danger of decline facing the United States in the 1980s. Yet such criticisms overlook the fact that politicians in the US, and indeed throughout the NATO alliance, have apparently heeded this advice. As we saw in Chapter 1, defence spending among the Western powers has sunk to historically low levels in the years since Kennedy published *The Great Powers*. The 1997 defence expenditure to GDP ratios for the major Western powers—3.4 per cent for the US, 3 per cent for France, 2.7 per cent for the UK, 2 per cent for Italy and just 1.6 per cent for Germany—were the lowest since the 1920s, and in the French and Italian case since the 1870s. At the same time, the growth rate of the American economy has risen significantly, suggesting that hopes of a post-Cold War "peace dividend" have been fulfilled. But does that mean that the United States has solved the problem of incipient decline?

The answer to that question depends on three things: the scope of American foreign policy; the scale of the foreign opposition to it; and the use America is able to make of her unmatched economic resources. The follow-up question posed here is how far the United States and her allies now run the risk of *under*stretching themselves: spending too little on their military establishments to achieve their foreign policy goals in the face of what are best described as multiple nuisances.

Under President Clinton, the aims of American foreign policy were extended beyond the defence of allied states—the number of which has increased as a result of NATO enlargement—to include the termination of civil wars in a number of politically sensitive regions, and the occasional use of military force to protect the rights of persecuted minorities in certain countries. Whatever one may think of these objectives, it is worth asking how far recent cuts in Western defence establishments are compatible with their effective realization. The United States, it is suggested here, has no shortage of economic power. But economic power is mere *potential* if it is not harnessed. That requires not only a readiness to divert resources from civilian consumption to military use—to turn butter into guns, in the old image, or taxes into divisions. It also requires the moral resolve to make the optimal use of military resources to deter or defeat the opponents of US policy. Without legitimacy— in the case of a democracy, public support—the foreign policy of a Goliath can be thwarted by a David, particularly if there is more than one David.

THE ILLUSION OF PEACE

The disarmament of the Western powers would not matter if the chances of war were diminishing proportionately. According to one strand of liberal theory, this ought to be the case, since war is economically irrational and becomes more so as the world becomes more economically integrated.

The idea that war is obsolescent in an economically liberal world dates back to the eighteenth century. "If war enriched some of the peoples of antiquity," wrote the Physiocrat François Quesnay, "it impoverishes and makes miserable the peoples of modern times."[14] In his *Perpetual Peace*, Kant agreed that the "spirit of commerce" was "incompatible with war."[15] "The civil wars of Flanders," noted Adam Smith towards the end of *The Wealth of Nations*, "and the Spanish government which succeeded them, chased away the great commerce of Antwerp, Ghent, and Bruges. . . . The ordinary revolutions of war and government easily dry up the sources of that wealth which arises from commerce . . ."[16] It was on this basis that Smith was critical of mercantilist policies that subordinated market forces to grand strategy. This view attracted many adherents in the nineteenth century. Though Comte conceded that in previous centuries "efforts . . . to discover and improve military apparatus . . . were not entirely without value for the progress of industry," he saw the subordination of war to industrial development as a distinctive feature of his own times.[17] For Richard Cobden, peace and prosperity were mutually reinforcing: hence the title of his 1842 pamphlet, *Free Trade as the Best Human Means for Securing Universal and Permanent Peace*. Norman Angell's *The Great Illusion* (1910–1911) is a monument to the persistence of this belief. According to Angell, war was economically irrational: the fiscal burdens of armaments were excessive, indemnities difficult to collect from defeated powers, and colonies not a source of profit. "What is the real guarantee of the good behaviour of one state to another?" asked Angell. "It is the elaborate interdependence which, not only in the economic sense, but in every sense, makes an unwarrantable aggression of one state upon another react upon the interests of the aggressor."[18]

Such beliefs have proved remarkably resilient in the face of repeated and bitter disappointment. On the very eve of the war over Kosovo in 1999, the cover of the British magazine *Prospect* bore the legend "The End of War?," recalling Ivan Bloch's *Is War Now Impossible?* a hundred years before. Perhaps the most hubristic passage in Thomas Friedman's *The Lexus and the Olive Tree* is his assertion that globalization "increases the incentives for not making war and increases the costs of going to war in more ways than in any previous era in modern history." To reinforce his point, Friedman propounds "The Golden Arches Theory of Conflict Prevention," according to which no two countries, both of which have at least one McDonald's franchise, have gone to war.[19] Friedman's book was published on 17 May 1999, less than two months after the United States had gone to war with the Republic of Yugoslavia—apparently oblivious to the well-advertised presence of McDonald's in Belgrade. This does not make Friedman as wrong as Norman Angell, of course; not yet, at least. But he manifestly shares with him the belief that economic rationality should discourage war—a belief Angell lived to see exposed as the authentically great illusion it was.

Time and again in the twentieth century, states ignored the liberal appeal to economic rationalism by going to war. They did so even when the potential costs of defeat were huge; indeed, they did so when even the potential costs of victory were high. One possible explanation for this is simply myopia—a kind of "bounded rationality" which habitually understates the costs of war and overstates its benefits. However, a better explanation may be that in a non-democratic regime the aggregate and long-run costs of war may be irrelevant. Provided the immediate benefits of war flow to the ruling élites and the costs are borne by the unenfranchised masses, war can be a perfectly rational policy option.

GIVING WAR A CHANCE

From the point of view of an autocratic state, expenditure on war can generate a visible return in the form of booty, indemnities from vanquished states or territory (which can widen a state's tax base or natural resource endowment)—not forgetting glory.[20] In some cases, such returns may even exceed the costs of achieving victory; but if the costs of war are largely borne by an unenfranchised peasantry, this may be a minor consideration.

The Ottoman Sultan Suleiman the Magnificent is said to have run a surplus of around a third of annual revenue, largely consisting of tributes from conquered territory.[21] The French Revolution brought into being another regime that came to rely on the exploitation of conquered territory as a major source of income. By its last years, the Directory could count on the levies imposed in the occupied Netherlands for around a quarter of total revenue; altogether between 1795 and 1804 the Dutch paid some 229 million guilders to the French, more than a year's Dutch national income.[22] Napoleon's campaigns of 1806–7 were not only self-financing, but covered at least a third of ordinary French government expenditure. In Italy between 1805 and 1812 fully half of all the taxes raised went to the French treasury.[23] Britain too knew how to make war pay in the nineteenth century: something in the region of 40 per cent of the total defence budget for 1842 was covered by the £5.8 million indemnity exacted from China under the Treaty of Nanking; Palmerston even boasted to the House of Commons that the war had shown a profit.[24] Russia was able to squeeze increasing sums of money out of Turkey in the successive peace settlements of 1829, 1878 and 1882. As proportions of Russian defence spending those sums represented, respectively, 9 per cent, 42 per cent and 115 per cent. Even the last figure was dwarfed by the indemnity wrested from China by Japan in 1895, which amounted to more than three times total Japanese military spending in that year and around double the cost of the war.[25]

But it was Prussia which perfected the art of profitable war—made war, as Mirabeau said, its "national industry." Frederick the Great had pointed the way ahead with the seizure from Austria of mineral-rich Silesia between 1740 and 1745. Though the costs of retaining the province in the subsequent Seven Years War proved heavy, Silesia was an asset which yielded a healthy industrial return for two centuries. Bismarck's victory over the German Confederation in 1866 was also close to self-financing: while total Prussian military spending in that year was at most 111 million thaler, the fruits of victory—in addition to the annexed territory of Holstein, Hanover, Hesse-Cassel, Nassau and Frankfurt—included indemnities worth 40 million thaler from Austria, a further ten from Saxony, six from Frankfurt, to say nothing of the seized treasure of the deposed king of Hanover, worth 16 million thaler, and a smaller sum from Württemberg.[26] Probably the most profitable war of the entire nineteenth century was that waged by the Prussian-led

North German Confederation against France in 1870. The immense sum of 5 billion francs imposed as part of the 1871 peace agreement—equivalent to around a quarter of French GDP—amounted to four times the previous year's Prussian defence budget. In addition the French had to pay 200 million francs (a ransom from the city of Paris) and all the costs of the subsequent occupation of northern France.[27]

It is of course true that such profits—including "reparations," to use the twentieth-century term designed to attach blame as well as hardship to the losers—have more usually been less than the costs of the war that secured them (not to mention the effort of collecting them). About a third of Roman revenue in the time of the Emperor Augustus came from tributes from Egypt, Syria, Gaul and Spain; but the cost of maintaining the Roman army at that time consumed roughly half the total revenue.[28] Between 1548 and 1598 the income from Spain's American conquests amounted to 121 million ducats, between 12 and 24 per cent of all Castilian revenues. But in the same period the annual costs of war waged by Spain outside its own territory rose by a factor of at least four. The fighting in the Netherlands alone consumed some 218 million ducats a year.[29] In the War of the Spanish Succession, contributions from occupied territory covered not much more than two-fifths of the total costs of the French army.[30] Even the profits of France's revolutionary and Napoleonic wars were ultimately consumed by the high costs of her defeat between 1812 and 1815. According to one recent estimate, the indemnity and other costs imposed on France by the victorious Allies after Waterloo—around 1.8 billion francs—amounted to around a fifth of French annual GDP.[31] Large though this sum was, it represented a small fraction of the costs France's enemies had incurred in the preceding two decades of war. The equivalent in sterling terms (£78 million) was only slightly more than the amount Britain had paid to her continental allies in subsidies between 1793 and 1815 (£66 million).[32]

As for the reparations imposed after twentieth-century victories, these have come nowhere near covering the costs of war. The indemnity levied by Germany on Russia under the terms of the Treaty of Brest-Litovsk in 1918 was around $1.4 billion; a huge sum, but only a fraction of the total cost of the war to Germany, which was around $20 billion.[33] The victorious Allies finally made up their minds to demand a total of $31 billion as reparations from Germany in the London Ultimatum of 1921, though realists like Keynes only expected around $12 billion to be forthcoming. Even that lower figure was equivalent to more than 80 per cent of German GDP.[34] But again this was a small fraction of the victors' total war expenditures, which amounted to at least $58 billion. And of course in neither of these two cases was the full amount of the indemnity ever received by the victorious side. The Germans ended up paying no more than $4.5 billion in all between 1919 and 1932, when payments were frozen. (Under the Young Plan, they were supposed to continue until 1988.) This was rather less than they themselves managed to borrow from the United States and never repay—a reflection as much of German guile in feigning impecuniousness as of Allied lack of resolve.[35]

Yet the experience of the inter-war period did nothing to dissuade Germany, Japan and Italy from attempting territorial and financial predations again in the 1930s and 1940s. The Japanese occupation of Manchuria and the later German occupation of most of continental Europe were among the most ruthlessly exploitative in all history. As a proportion of German GNP, the revenues extorted from occupied territory rose from 3 per cent to a peak of 16 per cent in 1943.[36] Once again, this was manifestly far less than the cost to the German economy of waging war. The Allies had failed to collect the spoils of war after 1918 by being too lenient. By being too harsh, however, the Germans shrank the very economies they sought to mulct. On the other hand, leading Nazis (Göring in particular) accumulated immense private fortunes from plundering the regime's internal and external foes. Even a war that ultimately ends in defeat can make sense to the élites of a dictatorship who want a short but merry life. To put it differently: the dictator's time-horizon is shorter than that of a constitutional regime. If ever men discounted the future heavily, it was those who spoke of a "thousand-year Reich."

One lesson the Western powers drew from the failure of reparations in the 1920s was to aim lower in 1945: the total amount demanded from the defeated Axis powers was just $7 billion. This should be compared with a figure for total US war expenditure of $275 billion, to say nothing of Britain's $91 billion.[37] And of course the Americans thought it prudent to assist both Western Europe (including West Germany) and Japan with post-war economic reconstruction: Marshall Aid remains a rare example of "reverse reparations." The Russians tried to recoup some of their war costs by first skinning and then milking their zone of occupation in Germany; once skinned, however, the cow did not yield much milk.[38]

For democracies, then, the lesson of history seems clear: war does not pay. The economic costs of war are always likely to outweigh the benefits of subsequent reparations. Indeed, if the objective of post-war policy is to conciliate—or indeed to democratize—the vanquished state, it is advisable to subsidize rather than to penalize. But an autocratic ruler might not draw the same conclusion. The costs of annexing Kuwait turned out to be very high; but that did not stop Saddam Hussein from trying. Like the dictators of the 1930s and 1940s, the Iraqi leader has no qualms about passing the costs of his failed adventures on to his people, so long as he and his cronies are not materially worse off. And indeed they are not; since, unlike Hitler and Mussolini, Saddam Hussein has not been toppled from power.

THE CHANCE OF VICTORY

A further reason why non-democratic regimes continue to wage wars is that military outcomes are *not* strictly determined by comparative economic advantage. Economic inferiority can in fact be compensated for by superior strategy, operations and tactics. It can also be compensated for by superior mobilization and morale. What war makes clear is that power is *not* exclusively economic, especially over the short run. War obliges peacetime winners to compete under unfamiliar rules. At least in the early phase of a war, the ability to destroy counts for more than the ability to produce. That is precisely the appeal of war to peacetime losers.

The best-known modern wars have of course been won by the economically superior side. The Revolutionary and Napoleonic wars, the Crimean War, the American Civil War, the First World War, the Second World War and the Korean War were all won by the side with the bigger share of total word output. And to that list must be added more recent wars: the Falklands War, the Gulf War and the Kosovo War. All these outcomes would seem to confirm Kennedy's hypothesis in *The Great Powers*. Yet there are significant exceptions to the rule: think only of how Vietnam humiliated France, America and China; and how Russia came to grief in Afghanistan.

For most of the eighteenth century Britain appears to have had a smaller economy than that of its principal foe France. In 1788, according to modern estimates, French GNP was more than double British; the French population nearly three times larger.[39] Yet despite being economically inferior, Britain was able to mobilize more men and ships at lower relative cost than her rival.[40] Thanks in large part to the superiority of British fiscal institutions, the ratio of British to French warships rose from 1.3:1 in 1780 to 3.5:1 in 1810.[41]

There are nineteenth-century examples too. In 1866 the Austrian-led German Confederation had nearly double the number of men under arms than

Prussia and her sole ally Mecklenburg, more than double the population and spent four times as much on defence. Still Prussia won. That victory has sometimes been attributed to economic factors: Prussia's superior railways or higher iron and steel production. The reality is that these played a minimal role in the battle of Königgrätz. In 1870 too, France had the advantage over Germany in terms of military personnel, population and military expenditures. Yet France lost. In the Russo-Japanese War, Russia enjoyed a massive economic advantage: double the amount of military expenditure, treble the population, nearly four times the energy consumption, nine and a half times the military personnel and thirty-two times the iron and steel production. Japan won.[42]

Nor should we forget the enormous achievements in destruction and conquest of the German-led coalitions in the two world wars. Of course, Germany and her allies lost in the end. Nevertheless, the extent of the destruction they were able to wreak serves as a salutary reminder that economic disadvantage can be compensated for by military capability and efficiency in mobilization. It is fortunate indeed that victory in war does not go to the side that inflicts the highest number of casualties: for in both wars the "net body count" went heavily against the Allied side, despite the fact that the Allies enjoyed overwhelming economic superiority.

At the beginning of the First World War, the differential between the Entente Powers and the Central Powers in terms of GNP was at least 60 per cent. In terms of Kennedy's measure of "industrial potential," the ratio of advantage to the Entente was around 1.5 to one. In terms of population, the ratio of advantage was a massive 4.5 to one. Moreover, Germany's net national product contracted by around a quarter during the war, while the economies of Britain and Italy achieved real growth of the order of 10 per cent between 1914 and 1917, and Russian output rose 20 per cent in the three years to 1916. Though the index of industrial output for Britain shows a fall of the order of 13 per cent, for Germany the figure is 31 per cent. German steel output fell by 14 per cent; in Britain it rose by 25 per cent. German grain production slumped by nearly half between 1914 and 1918; in Britain it rose. This was partly due to the impact of the British naval blockade and interference with German trade with neutrals, which reduced German imports (including those of fertilizers) by more than the German U-boats could cut British imports. The Germans also lost a large part of their merchant marine and overseas investments. Lack of access to external finance and the relative weakness of the internal capital market led to a greater reliance on monetizing short-term government debt and a larger monetary expansion than in Britain. By these measures, it could be said, the defeat of the Central Powers was economically inevitable.

Yet the First World War was not a foregone conclusion. Germany and her allies managed to kill 35 per cent more enemy soldiers than they lost of their own men: a "net body count" of approximately 1.4 million. Their military superiority was sufficient to defeat Serbia (in 1915), Romania (in 1916), Russia (in 1917) and very nearly Italy too. The French army was brought to the point of mutiny in 1917; and the British were forced to fall back on the Americans for economic and ultimately military support. This was in large part due to German military superiority, which was only slowly and painfully eroded; but it was also due to a relatively successful response to the organizational challenges of total war on the home front. The Germans allocated labour more efficiently than their enemies. Britain allowed vital skilled workers to volunteer for front-line duty and did not bring as many women into the workforce as the Germans. The Germans also managed to discipline labour better: wages did not rise ahead of output and fewer days were lost to strike action. Finally, it seems clear that the imperial regime—despite the shortcomings of the Kaiser himself—retained legitimacy in the eyes of a majority of its subjects until remarkably late in the war. It was only in August 1918, when it was clear that Germany could no longer win the war, that the morale of the German army began to crumble, a shift manifest in the tenfold increase in the number of prisoners taken by the British. And it was not for another three months that the domestic situation, so often stressed by historians as the key area of German weakness, slid into revolution.[43]

The Second World War witnessed an even more impressive attempt to transcend economic disadvantage by means of mobilization. Although the combined GNP of what became the Allied powers in 1939 exceeded those of the future Axis powers by some 40 per cent, while the Allies' population was 170 per larger, the Axis powers were able to achieve far greater territorial expansion than the Central Powers had achieved in the First World War; to kill many more soldiers and civilians of enemy states; and to resist the military alliance against them for longer. This can only partly be explained in economic terms. While it is true that the German economy grew during the war years rather than contracted as it had after 1914, this was more than compensated for by the growth of the American economy.[44] By any measure of armaments production, the Axis was comprehensively outproduced, by ratios ranging from around 3 to 1 (rifles and machine guns) to more than 5 to 1 (mortars and major naval vessels).[45] As in the First World War, German war finance relied more than British on monetizing short-term debt, with consequent inflationary pressure (cash in circulation grew by a factor of 2.6 in Britain during the war, compared with a sevenfold increase in Germany).[46] The only reason the official German cost-of-living index had risen by less than the British by 1944 was the harsh enforcement of price controls.

Nevertheless, the Axis powers managed to kill nearly two and a half times more of the other side's armed forces than they lost themselves: a net body count of over eight million. If civilian fatalities are included, the extent of Axis murderousness is even more astounding: the civilian death toll on the Allied side was more than eight times higher than on the Axis side. The total Allied death toll was five times higher: a net body count of nearly 38 million.[47] Moreover, as Richard Overy has observed: "No rational man in early 1942 would have guessed at the eventual outcome of the war."[48] For by that date the Axis powers were, thanks to their conquests, on "more or less equal terms" in terms of overall pre-war GNP—and only at a slight disadvantage in terms of population (a differential of about 20 per cent in the Allies' favour, though the Allies were less able to mobilize men on the periphery of their territory).[49] True, the Allies controlled much more of the earth's surface (the territorial ratio was still more than six to one). But on the decisive Eastern Front the Germans achieved an economic superiority over the Soviets in 1941 and 1942. Nor was there a significant technological gap at this stage in the war.[50]

The principal strength of the Axis (Italy apart) was military: the ability to mobilize high proportions of men and material *earlier* than their enemies and then take full strategic advantage of operational and tactical superiority. Storm-troop tactics; more effective co-ordination of infantry, artillery, tanks and air forces in offensives; the defence in depth; greater flexibility of the chain of command: these were just the most obvious respects in which Germany (and to a lesser extent Japanese) troops were able to outfight economically superior opponents in the initial phases of the European and Asian wars. Nor was it only fighting men who were mobilized. More women entered the German and Japanese workforce during the war than in Britain and America (in 1944, 51 and 42 per cent, respectively, compared with 31 and 30).[51] It was a hallmark of the improved efficiency of Hitler's war economy compared with Hindenburg's that Albert Speer was able—despite the disruptive effects of British and American bombing—to raise German real GDP by 1944 to a level 25 per cent higher than in 1938. Moreover, the popular legitimacy of the Third Reich appears to have been more durable than that of the Second Reich, though debate continues as to how far Germans fought on in 1944–5 because of coercion rather than propaganda (or spontaneous zeal). The drastic increase in the use of the death penalty in the years after 1941—some 11,000 executions were ordered by the civilian courts, and 20,000 by the military courts—suggests that coercion became increasingly important after the failure to defeat the Soviet Union, though a high percentage of those executed within the Reich in this period were in fact foreign slave labourers, not "ordinary Germans."[52]

The military performance of the totalitarian regimes in the Second World War provides sobering evidence of what can be achieved by all-out economic, military and cultural mobilization. The fact that it took another totalitarian regime to defeat the Third Reich in the crucial East European theatre speaks for itself. True, the Soviets would have found a war against Nazi Germany harder to win by 1945 without the British and American air and land contribution in Western Europe. But it is worth remembering that American economic aid to the Soviet Union amounted to just 5.6 per cent of Soviet net material product between 1942 and 1945.[53] In purely economic terms, the two dictatorships were quite evenly matched; indeed, in terms of GDP, the Soviet Union fought back to victory from a 20 per cent disadvantage in 1942.

In war, in other words, autocratic regimes appear to enjoy an advantage over liberal democracies which in the short run can significantly reduce, if not altogether eliminate, any economic disadvantage. They seem able to impose greater sacrifices on both their civilian and military populations. Ultimately, the resource gap was too great—and strategy too flawed—for Germany to win either world war; but that should not detract from the way ruthless mobilization narrowed that gap and made victory at least conceivable.

A DEMOCRATIC PEACE?

From all this it is tempting to infer that economic liberalism by itself may not be enough to abolish war; democratization may be just as necessary, since in theory democratic states are less likely to go to war than autocratic states. This argument also dates back to the Enlightenment. According to Kant, "if . . . the consent of the citizens [of a republic] is required to decide whether or not war should be declared, it is very natural that they will have great hesitation." This is because war "would mean calling down on themselves all the miseries of war, such as doing the fighting themselves, supplying the costs of the war from their own resources, painfully making good the ensuing devastation, and . . . having to take upon themselves a burden of debts which will embitter peace itself and which can never be paid off on account of the constant threat of new wars." Such calculations do not concern an autocrat, however, "for the head of state is not a fellow citizen, but the owner of the state, and war will not force him to make the slightest sacrifice so far as his banquets, hunts, pleasure palaces and courts are concerned."[54] True, Kant took care to emphasize that his argument applied to republics, not to democracies.[55] But modern researchers have tended to blur the distinction. In other words, democracies are "constrained by representation."[56]

There is no doubt that there is a close correlation between democracy and defence/GDP ratios: less democratic states tend to spend significantly more on the military.[57] It is also true that, when the unit of analysis is the "dyad" or pair of countries, war—or indeed the threat of war—is less likely to occur between two democratic states than between a democracy and an autocracy.[58] On this basis, "if all states should in the future become democratic, there would be little war."[59] However, when countries are studied individually, democracies emerge as just as likely to become involved in war as autocracies. There is also some evidence that pairs of autocracies will tend to avoid war with one another, much as pairs of democracies do.[60] Most problematic of all for the "democratic peace" theory is the evidence that countries at an early stage of democratization seem exceptionally prone to involvement in wars.[61] One possible explanation for this is that democratization seems to be associated with political fissiparity, as we saw in the previous chapter. A last—and perhaps fatal—difficulty for the "democratic peace" thesis is the absence of any correlation between democratization, as quantified in Chapter 12 (Figure 40), and the actual incidence of war, as quantified in Chapter 13 (Figure 44).

THE BENEFITS OF MILITARISM

There is a final reason why military aggression is unlikely to die out: namely, that high military spending is not necessarily as economically detrimental as Kennedy suggests. Empirical evidence in support of his view is in truth rather scanty.

In a footnote, Kennedy gives a more precise definition of what he means by "excessive" military spending. "The historical record," he states, "suggests that if a particular nation is allocating *over the long term* more than 10 per cent (and in some cases—when it is structurally weak—more than 5 per cent) of GNP to armaments, that is likely to limit is growth rate."[62] Great Britain, however, became the "first industrial nation" at a time when its expenditure on defence was above that threshold: between 1760 and 1810 it averaged 11 per cent of national income.[63] More paradoxically, as Kennedy himself admits, British economic and strategic decline first manifested itself at a time when British defence spending was relatively low. Indeed, his castigation of British strategy in the first half of the twentieth century is strangely contradictory. On the one hand, he is critical of inter-war governments for spending too little on defence while "controlling one-quarter of the globe but with only 9 to 10 per cent of its manufacturing strength and 'war potential.'"[64] On the other, he repeatedly attacks what he calls "the British way of war," meaning reliance in a European war on "colonial operations, maritime blockade, and raids upon the enemy's coasts" as opposed to a "continental commitment" of troops. "The raiding strategy seemed cheaper . . . but it usually had negligible effects and occasionally ended in disaster . . . The provision of a continental army was more expensive in terms of men and money, but . . . was also more likely to assist in the preservation of the European balance."[65] It is not clear from this what Kennedy thinks Britain should have done: while some governments are damned if they spend too much on defence, others are damned for spending too little.

Moreover, it is not without significance that the biggest American boom of the twentieth century (in terms of real GNP growth) occurred not in the much-vaunted Clinton era, but during the Second World War. The average annual growth rate of the US economy between 1942 and 1945 was 7.7 per cent, exactly two percentage points higher than for the period 1995–8. It is also striking that American defence expenditure exceeded 5 per cent of GNP in every year from 1942 until 1990 except the years 1948 and 1976–9 (though it remained well below Kennedy's 10 per cent maximum for a structurally strong state). Taking the longest possible view, there appears to be no long-run statistical correlation—negative or positive—between defence expenditure as a percentage of GDP and real growth for either Britain and the United States.[66] If anything, the relationship is very slightly positive in the American case. Nor is there any correlation when time-lags of five or ten years are introduced.

Finally, a cross-country survey of average defence budgets in relation to average growth for the years 1990–1997 reveals only the slightest negative correlation between the two. Admittedly, only four out of the 59 countries in the sample spent more than 5 per cent of GDP on defence; one experienced negative growth (Russia), and two of the four had less than average growth. Israel, however, spent 9.7 per cent of GDP on defence—a fraction below Kennedy's threshold—but enjoyed growth of 5.8 per cent, more than twice the global average.[67]

After the collapse of the Soviet Union, Kennedy modified his position; but only slightly. The issue, he argued in *Preparing for the Twenty-first Century* (1993), was not "whether high defence spending causes economic slow-down," but rather how the economy was structured. "If [an] economy is growing briskly," he argued, "possesses a flourishing manufacturing base, is at the forefront of new technologies, invests heavily in R&D, is in balance . . . on its current accounts, and is not an international debtor, then it is far better *structured* to allocate 3 or 6 or even 9 per cent of its GNP to defence than if it lacks those advantages." Kennedy conceded that the United States was by no means weak on all these scores, but added that "the single most important fact" was the slowing of the US growth rate since the 1950s and 1960s. An eye-catching figure contrasted average annual growth of over 4 per cent in the 1960s with a miserable –0.5 per cent in 1991.[68] However, an updating of the data shows that average annual growth of GDP in the 1990s was 3.3 per cent: higher than in both the 1970s (3.2 per cent) and the 1980s (2.8 per cent).[69]

Nevertheless, the hypothesis remains an attractive one that the *Soviet* economy ultimately crumbled under the weight of excessive defence expenditure in the 1980s. Superficially at least, it seems plausible that it was the Soviet Union which was suffering from Kennedy's "overstretch," not the United States. As we saw in Chapter 1, estimates of defence spending as a proportion of GNP for the Soviet Union in the mid-1980s were as high as 16 per cent, at a time when the equivalent American figure was just 6 per cent. It has even been argued that the increase in American defence expenditures under Ronald Reagan led to the West's ultimate victory in the Cold War by pushing the Soviet Union over the threshold of sustainable defence expenditure. If so, then Reagan's policy has paid a tremendous dividend: though to call it a "peace dividend" is a misnomer, for it was the hawks not the doves who won it. A simple calculation suffices to illustrate the point. Between 1981 and 1989, under Presidents Reagan and Bush, the annual American defence budget averaged $378 billion (adjusting for inflation): $100 billion a year higher than under President Carter. It was this increase which aroused so much anxiety among Reagan's critics and the prophets of national decline. In the 1990s, however, real spending on defence fell back to just $270 billion (the 1998 figure), largely as a result of the collapse of the Warsaw Pact and the Soviet Union. If the Pentagon's conspicuous consumption contributed anything towards the Soviet regime's external and internal crisis, then the real cost of Reagan's policy was rather lower than was claimed in the 1980s. In fact, the change of policy has cost Americans around $70 billion a year, or slightly less than 1 per cent of GNP.[70] This was not much to pay for the defeat of what was in many ways an "evil empire," just as Reagan said.

Then again, there are those who would maintain that the Soviet Union collapsed because of its own internal contradictions, not because of Reagan's defence spending. Certainly, the Strategic Defence Initiative does not seem to have played as big a part in it as Reagan himself was led to believe.[71] The reality was that a planned economy had been the right model for waging a full-scale conventional war against the Germans in Eastern Europe, but the wrong model for sustaining an arms race with the remote United States. The Soviets might conceivably have won a hot war once they had established superiority in warheads.[72] In its war with Nazi Germany, the regime had already proved its ability to withstand millions of civilian as well as military casualties; and in the event of a hot war, it would have been much less susceptible than its American opponent to popular pressure for peace. Mass civilian death would have been a new experience for Americans, but not for Russians. However, the decision not to risk nuclear war forced the Soviets to compete in an open-ended arms race. In this, the advantage lay not with the side capable of achieving the maximum possible military mobilization in the short run—the key to victory in a hot war—but with the side capable of paying for its armaments without stifling civilian consumption and living standards *in the long run*.

From 1950 until around 1974, the Soviet Union enjoyed real GNP growth rates comparable with those of the United States; indeed in the late 1950s and late 1960s they may even have been higher. But from the mid-1970s Soviet growth lagged behind. As we have seen, high absolute levels of defence expenditure became steadily less and less burdensome to the United States as growth increased in the 1980s. But the Soviet defence burden rose inexorably because the arms race accelerated while the planned economy stagnated. To put it simply, between 1980 and 1989 the United States was able to increase defence spending in real terms by around 50 per cent; but per capita consumption in the same period rose by more than 20 per cent. The equivalent figures for the Soviet Union were 15 per cent for real defence spending and barely 5 per cent for per capita consumption. Why was this? Partly it was because in the Soviet system there could be no spin-offs from military research and development, because there was no technology transfer to the private sector; indeed, there was hardly any private sector at all. When Mikhail Gorbachev gambled on economic "restructuring" in the hope of closing the economic and technological gap between East and West, he unwittingly caused the output of the planned economy to collapse; and the political "transparency" introduced at the same time merely revealed that the system had lost popular legitimacy. In that sense, Reagan's defence budgets were a symptom of American superiority, not a cause of the Soviet collapse. This suggests that high levels of military expenditure are not economically damaging *per se*. Under the right circumstances, rising public expenditure on the technology of defence and destruction can co-exist with rising consumption: the magic combination of guns plus butter—or, to be precise, missiles plus Big Macs.

But there is also a fiscal explanation for the divergence of the two systems, so different from the convergence predicted by so many contemporary commentators. To revert to the theme developed in Chapter 4, a crucial advantage enjoyed by the United States was the ability to finance increased arms spending by selling bonds to the public. The big rise in the federal debt under Reagan may have worried the prophets of overstretch; but as a way of paying for increased military spending, borrowing has the benefit of "tax smoothing" and hence minimizes economic distortions. What Kennedy overlooked was the ease with which the United States financed its increasing debt burden. At its peak in 1991, US net government interest payments amounted to a trivial 2.2 per cent of GDP. By contrast, after the suspension of domestic bond sales in 1957, the Soviets relied on much more distortionary forms of finance to cover their rising defence budget (such as credits to state enterprises and forced loans from ordinary savers), and these almost certainly played a part in the economy's declining productiveness. When Moscow belatedly turned to the international capital markets under Gorbachev, it had to pay a substantial risk premium (though it was not high enough, as the lenders later discovered to their cost). A good parallel can be drawn here with Britain's victory over *ancien régime* France in the eighteenth century. In each case, the state with the most developed bond market had the deeper pockets and hence could sustain its military effort at a relatively lower economic cost.[73]

THE PRECAUTIONARY MOTIVE

Of course, a true cost-benefit analysis of defence spending must go beyond simply adding up the burden represented by the military budget and offsetting the value of any positive spin-offs from R&D. For to estimate the economic value of a given defence policy it is necessary to compare actual costs with the potential costs of doing less or more. As so often in historical analysis, only a "counterfactual" approach will get us close to a sufficient answer. As comparisons have been made in the past between the *Pax Britannica* and the *Pax Americana*, the United Kingdom and the United States will be the focus of what follows.

Was the British Empire "a waste of money," as strict liberals at the time and since have argued? It seems unlikely. No doubt it is true that, in theory, "the benefits from imperial trading blocs were sub-optimal solutions compared to open international trade;"[74] but in practice "open international trade" has not been naturally occurring. It has been asserted that after around 1846—though not apparently before—Britain could have withdrawn from Empire with impunity, and reaped a "decolonization dividend" in the form of a 25 per cent tax cut.[75] Yet the challenges to British hegemony from protectionist rivals were in many ways greater in the late nineteenth and early twentieth century than in any previous period. Abandoning formal control over Britain's colonies would almost certainly have led to higher tariffs being erected against British exports in their markets, and perhaps other forms of trade discrimination. The evidence for this need not be purely hypothetical: it is manifest in the highly protectionist policies adopted by the United States and India after they secured independence, as well as in the protectionist policies adopted by Britain's imperial rivals France, Germany and Russia between 1878 and 1914. Britain's military budget before the First World War can therefore be seen as a remarkably low insurance premium against international protectionism.[76] And the economic benefit of enforcing free trade could have been as high as 6.5 per cent of GNP.[77] (Another way of looking at the problem is to consider the benefits Britain derived from the Empire when the world became even more protectionist in the 1930s: in that decade the share of British exports going to the Commonwealth and colonies rose from 44.4 to 47.6 per cent; the share of her imports coming from there rose from 30.2 per cent to 39 per cent.[78]) In any case, the burden of defending the Empire before 1914 was relatively low (see Chapter 1): as a proportion of net national product, the British defence budget was just 3.2 per cent in 1913, less than that of Russia, France, Italy and Germany.[79]

On the other hand, it is far from certain that the cost of the First World War to Britain was justified in view of the relatively limited threat posed to British interests by German aggression on the continent in 1914. The crucial defect of British policy in the decade before the First World War was that it identified a serious German threat to the continental status quo but made no serious attempt to prepare to check that threat by the only viable means: the creation of a comparably large land army. By going to war before that army was ready, Britain condemned herself to four extremely expensive years of learning "on the job" how to fight a modern land war.[80] The earlier adoption of conscription—which was ruled out not by its cost, which was affordable, but by liberal ideology—might well have deterred the Germans from risking war in 1914.[81]

By contrast, the costs of British involvement in the Second World War need to be compared with the hypothetical costs of either defeat by, or compromise with, Nazi Germany. Given what we know of Hitler's plans for global domination, it is highly unlikely that Britain would have been better off seeking peace in 1939 or 1940.[82] On the other hand, it seems plausible that an earlier and more bellicose reaction to Hitler's demands for Czech territory in 1938 might have been a better strategy than the eleventh-hour guarantees to Poland and the other East European countries issued in 1939 after the partition of Czechoslovakia. None of the arguments advanced by Chamberlain's defenders succeeds in showing that appeasement was the only policy available to the government. Least persuasive of all are the arguments that higher spending on defence would have destabilized the economy, creating labour shortages and other problems. The dangers of a mild upturn in inflation in 1937–8 were infinitesimal compared with the dangers of complete isolation in the event of a Nazi victory on the continent in 1939–40. It was the most false of economies to "play for time" against Hitler in 1938: between Munich and the outbreak of war, Germany's position was strengthened no less than Britain's, and in some respects (such as the conclusion of the Nazi–Soviet Pact) more so.

British foreign policy in the twentieth century was therefore punctuated by a sequence of grave failures of deterrence. Neither in the 1900s nor in the 1930s did Britain succeed in convincing Germany and her allies that the risks of a war against Britain were excessive. In other words, the root cause of Britain's problems was *under*stretch: the failure to spend enough to deter a potential aggressor, which led inexorably to the need for far more expensive full-scale war just a few years later. (Something similar happened, albeit on a much smaller scale, with respect to the Falkland Islands prior to an Argentine invasion.) It is at least arguable that Britain would have declined less rapidly in the twentieth century if successive governments had been willing to spend more on deterring potential enemies. Only after the debilitating costs of two world wars did defence cuts and decolonization become imperative.

Does the British experience of strategic vulnerability through understretch have any relevance to the United States today? There are of course fundamental differences between the two powers, a number of which were pointed out in Chapter 9. Britain was a capital exporter; America is a capital importer. Britain "sent forth the best she bred;" America sucks in immigrants.

Plainly, it is highly unlikely that any state would contemplate a direct attack on the United States in the foreseeable future, though a terrorist campaign against American cities is quite easy to imagine. Even after big defence cuts, the United States is still the world's only superpower, with an unrivalled financial and military-technological capability. Its defence budget is fourteen times that of China and twenty-two times that of Russia. The real issue, however, is whether or not any state is capable of attacking one of America's *allies*—or indeed of using violence anywhere in the world where American interests are deemed to be at stake. In this context, it is significant that while the United States, Europe and the countries of the former Soviet Union have been disarming since the mid-1980s, other parts of the world have been rearming. According to the Stockholm International Peace Research Institute, arms exports to north-east Asia and the Middle East have risen significantly since 1994. Some Asian powers now possess a nuclear capability (China, India and Pakistan); while Iraq continues to resist international efforts to curb its chemical and biological weapons program. The Pentagon estimates that at least twenty countries possess either short- or medium-range ballistic missiles.[83]

The shifting military balance is most easily illustrated by comparing military budgets over the past decade (see Table 23). The difference between East and West illustrated in the table is worth pondering. In North America, Europe and the former Soviet Union, there have been dramatic cuts in real expenditure since 1989: the US budget is down by a third, Britain's by a quarter, and Russia's by more than 90 per cent. Among American countries, including the smaller ones not shown in the table, only Mexico and Brazil have increased their military spending; in Europe, only Finland, Greece and Turkey. But in the Middle East, every state except Egypt (and Oman) has increased spending, in the case of Iran by as much as 70 per cent. And the trend is even more pronounced in Asia, where every major power has cranked up its military budget: by 70 per cent in China, by more than 100 per cent in Singapore.

Table 23. Military expenditure of the world's principal powers (in US $millions, at constant 1995 prices and exchange rates)

	1989	1998	% change
Americas			
US	373,618	251,836	−32.6
Canada	10,965	6,999	−36.2
Brazil	9,220	13,125	+42.4
Europe			
France	52,099	45,978	−11.7
Germany	53,840	38,878	−27.8
Greece	5,001	6,211	+24.2
Italy	22,846	22,809	−0.2
Netherlands	9,907	7,859	−20.7
Russia	240,000	11,200	−95.3
Spain	10,164	8,241	−18.9
Sweden	5,345	5,337	−0.1
Turkey	4,552	7,920	+74.0
UK	42,645	32,320	−24.2
Asia			
China	9,900	16,900	+70.7
Japan	47,409	51,285	+8.2
South Korea	11,253	15,042	+33.7
Taiwan	8,886	10,620	+19.5
Australia	7,320	8,299	+13.4
India	7,756	9,842	+26.9
Middle East			
Israel	7,515	8,540	+13.6
Saudi Arabia	14,912	17,142	+15.0

Source: *SIPRI Yearbook, 1998* (showing only countries with budgets over $5 billion and for which figures are available).

This is not to imply that increased defence spending *necessarily* increases the risk of war. If two potential adversaries both increase their military budgets, the increases may simply cancel each other out. The point is merely that the rush to disarm which has been evident since 1989 in most NATO and former Warsaw Pact countries has not happened in Asia. Moreover, the table shows only the world's biggest military spenders. When the same calculation is done for smaller states, some important regional divergences emerge. In Africa, Algeria, Botswana, Burundi and Uganda have all substantially increased their defence spending in real terms, while Ethiopia, South Africa and Zimbabwe are among the biggest cutters of spending. In Latin America, while Brazil and Mexico have increased spending, Chile and Argentina have cut by comparable amounts. And it is worth remembering that reliable figures are simply not available for the most notorious "rogue states:" Libya, Iraq, Serbia and North Korea.

COSTING KOSOVO

These differentials in military expenditure would signify less if they had not occurred at a time when the scope of US foreign policy has been widening. But as we have seen, the idea that the United States and her allies have the right to intervene militarily in the internal affairs of a country to protect the rights of persecuted minorities implies a radical extension of the American role as "global policeman." Is this a role the United States can afford to play?

One way to begin answering that question is to work out what it has cost since 1999 to get the Serbs out of Kosovo and the Albanians back in. The answer is in fact not much. According to estimates by Jane's defence analysts, Operation Allied Force—which involved flying 36,000 air sorties, dropping 25,000 bombs and assembling a land force numbering close to 50,000 men— cost NATO £4.8 billion, or £62 million a day. However, this was only the first item on the bill. To arrive at the true cost of the war, it is necessary to add in three further items: the costs of relief to refugees from Kosovo, which ran at around £6 million a week in the immediate aftermath of the war (making around £24 million in all, given the unforeseen speed of the refugees' return); the costs of reconstructing the province, which the European Union estimated at £2.5 billion;[84] and the costs of occupying it with a 50,000-strong army for the foreseeable future, around £10–£15 million a year for Britain alone. £4.8 million of that figure is the UK's contribution to the international mission in Kosovo (UMIK), the total budget for which is £77 million.[85] Assuming that a force will have to stay in Kosovo for at least five years, that brings the total cost of the war to £7.7 billion. This is far less than the cost of Operation Desert Storm, which came to £63 billion in all—though admittedly that war was effectively paid for by rich non-combatants like Saudi Arabia and Japan, who had an interest in getting Iraq out of Kuwait. Financially as well as strategically, the 1999 war represented a return to the era of low-cost gunboat diplomacy.

But what was achieved for that £7.7 billion? According to NATO estimates released in September 1999, there were direct hits on some 93 tanks, 153 armoured personnel carriers, 339 other military vehicles and 389 artillery pieces and mortars.[86] Some journalists who witnessed the Serbian withdrawal estimated that this was little more than a third of their forces. On the other hand, not a single NATO serviceman was killed by enemy action. Two US helicopter pilots died in a training accident, and three foolish GIs got themselves captured, but otherwise this was probably the safest army in history—safer, in fact, than some American high schools. By comparison, NATO claimed that the Yugoslav army lost 5,000 men and that a further 10,000 were wounded. Those figures were guesses, but even if they were treble the true body count, NATO was still ahead. Indeed, NATO won even if the official Serbian figure of 576 killed was correct. The main defect of the air campaign, however, was that it was extended to civilian targets. According to the Economist Intelligence Unit, the NATO bombardment may have killed as many as 1,500 civilians, mostly Serbs, not including a substantial number who were killed or maimed after the war was over by cluster bombs which had failed to explode on impact. We do not yet know for sure how many Kosovan Albanians were killed by the Serbs: one estimate by the International Crime Tribunal's forensic expert suggests a total of around 2,500. But however high the figure, the number of civilians killed by NATO was unjustifiably close to it.

What constrained the United States and her allies from using ground forces directly against the Serb army and special forces instead of bombing civilians? Patently, it was not the financial cost, which could easily have been afforded. What the war over Kosovo revealed—or, rather, what it confirmed—is that American power is not inhibited by the expense of military intervention, but by public adversion to the human cost.

British Foreign Secretaries before 1914 often claimed that their room for manoeuvre was circumscribed by "public opinion;" but in practice this usually meant little more than the post-prandial sentiments of the denizens of gentlemen's clubs. The wider public, in the modern sense of the adult population, had only limited influence; and was in any case as often agitated by jingoism as by pacifism. Even today—partly because of the thirty years of Irish terrorism, partly because of victory in the Falklands War—the British electorate is not averse to military action, even when casualties are sustained. The Russian populace has also shown itself willing to tolerate at least some military casualties in its war against Chechnya, provided Russian forces are seen to be winning. By contrast, and in large part due to the bitter memories of Vietnam, many Americans today seem unwilling to expend *any* American lives in foreign wars, no matter how noble the cause. As President Clinton put it to his press spokesman George Stephanopoulos in 1993, at the height of the crisis in Somalia: "Right now the average American doesn't see our interest threatened to the point where we should sacrifice one American."[87] "We look after our own people," was his public response to the news that three GIs had been captured by the Serbs in Kosovo.[88] Few politicians during the war in Kosovo were as frank about what a ground war in the Balkans would have meant as the Vietnam veteran and Republican Senator John McCain; privately, however, most politicians shared his fears, picturing planeloads of bodybags and collapsing poll ratings. For a twenty-first-century democracy, it appears, any military casualties are unacceptable. High altitude bombing of Serb civilians was a strategy adopted to minimize the risks to American servicemen.[89]

Partly for this reason, the American strategy in Kosovo was a bluff. It was not just the air campaign that persuaded the Serbs to pull out of the province. Nor was it only the Russians' decision to end their early diplomatic support for the Milošević government. A key factor was the steady build-up of NATO troops around Kosovo; for without the possibility of a ground invasion after the bombing it seems unlikely that the Serbs would have withdrawn; and without those forces there could certainly be no credible talk of a NATO protectorate after the Serbian withdrawal. Yet if Milošević had decided not to withdraw his forces, it is hard to believe that President Clinton would have authorized an invasion which would certainly have cost some American lives. Even as it was, public support for further bombing had slipped below 50 per cent by the last week of the operation.[90]

Nor is it possible to describe the outcome of the Kosovo war as an unequivocal victory for NATO. Under the terms of the "military technical agreement" that ended the war, the Serbs improved on the Rambouillet proposals which had been the original *casus belli*. The UN Security Council was given ultimate control of the international force in Kosovo; the plan for a referendum in the province after three years was dropped; the Kosovo Liberation Army was excluded from the negotiations—unlike at Rambouillet—and was supposed to be disarmed.[91] True, Milošević probably hoped for more from Russia's equivocal support. It may well be that, in agreeing to withdraw his forces, he was banking on the Russians gaining control of north-east Kosovo, allowing that to become a Serb enclave.[92] Yet the fact remains that, a year and a half after the air strikes, the future status of Kosovo was still uncertain, despite Milošević's fall from power; while Saddam Hussein was still in power a decade after the Gulf War. This suggests that the policy of "surgical" inter-ventions with over-hasty "exit strategies" is directed at symptoms, rather than the diseases that cause them.

THE CASE FOR STRETCHING

The question has frequently been asked and deserves repetition: would it not be desirable for the United States to depose tyrants like Saddam and impose democratic government on their countries? The idea of invading a country, deposing its dictators and imposing free elections at gunpoint is generally dismissed as incompatible with American "values." A common argument is that the United States could never engage in the kind of overt imperial rule practised by Britain in the nineteenth century. Yet it is often forgotten that this was precisely what was done in Germany and in Japan at the end of the Second World War, and with great and lasting success. The historian Charles Maier has argued persuasively that American policy after 1945 *was* a form of imperialism, not different in essence from the European imperialisms of the nineteenth century, based as it was on domestic political consensus, mas-tery of new communications technology and the export of a particular polit-ical economic model which he calls corporatism.[93] With commendable can-dour, Maier argues that

we [the US] relied on something "very like" an empire in the postwar period, that it provided an undergirding of "peace and prosperity," and that we shall need some equivalent territorial ordering to emerge successfully from current turmoil. . . . Civil society and markets alone did not assure the stabilization of Western democratic soci-eties after 1945. Nor did self-sufficient nation-states.[94]

There is an obvious link between this argument about post-war stability and Charles Kindleberger's thesis that the inter-war disaster was due in large part to the failure of the United States to pick up the hegemonic mantle relin-quished by Britain.[95] In a similar vein, Robert Gilpin has maintained that Western economies only flourished after 1945 because they were underwrit-ten by American military power. In Gilpin's view, US hegemony in the West has been weakening since the end of the Cold War as rival power-blocs (such as the EU or the Asia-Pacific Economic Cooperation forum) have grown more self-confident.[96] Maier's fear is simply that a *laissez-faire* approach to the post-Cold War world will not deliver enduring stability.

The evidence of American disengagement from the informal imperialism of the post-war world is hard to miss. Consider the fact that the United States spends just 0.1 per cent of GDP on overseas development aid; or the fact that the plans are well advanced to develop a National Missile Defence system, in breach of the 1972 Anti-Ballistic Missiles Treaty. These are the symptoms of a deep-rooted insularity which is the very reverse of what the world needs from its wealthiest power.

Far from retreating like some giant snail behind an electronic shell, the United States should be devoting a larger percentage of its vast resources to making the world safe for capitalism and democracy. This book has tried to show that, like free trade, these are not naturally occurring, but require strong institutional foundations of law and order. The proper role of an imperial America is to establish these institutions where they are lacking, if necessary—as in Germany and Japan in 1945—by military force. There is no economic argument against such a policy, since it would not be prohibitively costly. Even if the Kennedy thesis is right, imposing democracy on the world's rogue states would not push the US defence budget much above 5 per cent of GDP. There is also an economic argument for doing so, as establishing the rule of law in countries like Iraq would pay a long-run dividend as their trade revived and expanded.

The reasons this will not happen are threefold: an ideological embarrassment about being seen to wield imperial power; an exaggerated notion of what Russia and China would do in response; and a pusillanimous fear of military casualties.[97] Perhaps that is the greatest disappointment facing the world in the twenty-first century: that the leaders of the one state with the economic resources to make the world a better place lack the guts to do it.

Conclusion

Those two essential questions of history: (1) What is power? (2) What
force produces the movement of nations?

Tolstoy, War and Peace[1]

In the majestic concluding chapter of *War and Peace*, Tolstoy scorned the
attempts not only of popular historians, memoir-writers and biographers,
but also of Hegelian idealists, to explain the world-shaking events of 1812.
The role of divine providence, the role of chance, the role of great men, the
role of ideas—all these he dismissed as insufficient to explain the Napoleonic
invasion of Russia and its ultimate failure. Historians, he argued, "ought to
be studying not the manifestations of power but the causes which create
power . . . If the purpose of history is the description of the flux of humanity and of peoples, the first question to be answered . . . will be: What is the
power that moves nations?"[2]

In physics, power is measured only in watts; in history, however, it is measured in many different units. Stalin asked of the Pope: "How many divisions has he?" It certainly seemed true in the 1940s that the Pope's spiritual
power, devoid as it had become of territorial power in the course of the nineteenth century, was as nothing compared with the vast military power at
Stalin's disposal—and indeed at the disposal of all the major combatants of
the Second World War. In 1944 there were more than 12 million men in the
Red Army, around a fifth of the entire Soviet workforce. Of course, the impotence of Pope Pius XII—indeed his systematic appeasement of fascism
throughout Europe[3]—was not solely due to his lack of divisions. It also
reflected his ideological sympathy with a superficially conservative movement which he believed would defend the Church against Communism. Nevertheless, the situation of the Vatican during the Second World War was
something like the epitome of material impotence. Territorially minute and

defended by a handful of pantomime pikemen, it was like a caricature of an ex-power, shrunk to the point of irrelevance.

Yet events less than half a century later in Poland revealed that the Holy See retained a kind of power which, under the right circumstances, was superior to that of the Red Army. What happened in Poland during the 1980s revealed that the Pope's power was in fact more durable than that of Stalin's successors, the would-be Popes of Marxism-Leninism. For there is no question that the visit of John Paul II to his native land in 1979 was one of the critical events in the collapse of Communist power there. Ultimately, the spiritual authority of John Paul II over millions of Catholics transcended their fear of the Red Army, with all its divisions.

Tolstoy's question was: "What is the power that *moves* nations?" Substitute the word "mobilize" and the question is perhaps easier to answer. Clearly, it is something more than purchasing power. Economic resources are important, of course, but they are not the sole determinant of power. A state's means of destruction consist of more than the output of its steel industry. As we have seen, a state can defeat an economically superior foe if it has better strategic, operational and tactical ability. Nor is the effectiveness of military mobilization sufficient. We also need to take into account a state's financial sophistication: its ability to appropriate resources from taxpayers and to borrow from investors. And in major conflicts a state must also be able to mobilize civilians optimally. The right balance must be struck between the different sectors of the economy in order to maximize war-making resources without undermining domestic well-being. The quality of bureaucratic organization in both the state and the private sector can therefore be as important as the quality of military organization.

This book has emphasized the importance of four institutions as the bases of financial strength: a tax-collecting bureaucracy; a representative parliament; a national debt; and a central bank. These were what I called the "square of power" in the Introduction. Sections One and Two of the book suggested that Britain was the first power to develop these, in the eighteenth century; but that they were subsequently adopted by all Western powers, including the United States. War was the driving force behind institutional innovation. It was the unpredictable fluctuations in military expenditure that forced states to develop elastic sources of revenue. In the realm of taxation, it was impossible to rely exclusively on indirect taxation. However, to secure adequate revenue from direct taxation, representative assemblies were advantageous. Even more important was a salaried bureaucracy: such an institution proved itself markedly superior (i.e. less costly) to the system of tax farming used in *ancien regime* France.

But tax alone was not enough. To smooth out the costs of wars—to spread the expense into the years of peace—a system of sustainable government borrowing was necessary. Public debts of the sort which began in medieval Italy were the answer. As Chapter 4 suggested, it was not the absolute or even the relative size of a country's debt that mattered so much as the cost of present (and future) debt service in relation to revenue from taxation. A state like Hanoverian Britain could cope with a very large national debt provided the interest on the debt was kept down. Chapters 5 and 6 considered reasons for differentials in such interest rates, showing how not only past experience but also fears of future defaults and inflations tended to push up a country's bond yields and hence the cost of new borrowing. In the absence of modern financial indicators, investors tended to infer the risk of default or currency depreciation from political events like wars and revolutions. There was also a form of "feedback," in that rising yields could increase the likelihood of political crises, by reducing a state's fiscal room for maneuver.

The key to understanding how well these institutions function is to recognize the wide range of social outcomes they can deliver; this was the subject of Chapter 7. The Venn diagram below (Figure 45) gives one example of a state in which the electorate has been expanded to its maximum (universal suffrage), most but not all voters are taxpayers (meaning direct tax payers), there is a relatively large category of pensioners (which includes the recipients of all transfers, including debt interest) and a relatively small group of government employees (including military personnel as well as civil servants). But this is only one of an infinite number of different combinations. If one were to draw an analogous model of the old Soviet system, for example, the circle of voters would be tiny (in effect, the Politburo), but the circle of government employees immense. It would probably be wrong to think in terms of one unique optimal balance between the four categories; however, it is not difficult to think of examples of unsustainable imbalances—for example, a situation in which the number of taxpayers is small relative to the number of pensioners and government employees.

In democratic systems, when the circle of voters is the largest of the four, it has long been tempting for politicians to use financial institutions to enhance their own chances of re-election. Chapter 8 showed the way calculations about tax rates, government employment (especially the public sector wage bill), increased borrowing, interest rates and inflation came to be dominated by the pursuit of popularity. Yet this "political business cycle" was relatively short-lived, not least because voters did not behave in the Pavlovian way predicted by the simple "feelgood" theory. In Britain, for example, the 1980s saw a gradual breakdown of the supposedly deterministic relationships between leading economic indicators and government popularity.

Democratic governments today are more likely to seek re-election through propaganda—creating the perception of prosperity—than through prosperity itself. But this too has financial implications. With dwindling memberships and rising expenditures on electioneering, political parties are today in a perilously weakened state, stigmatized if they rely too much on wealthy donors, yet corrupted in another sense if they became dependent on state funding. This is one of the ways in which the relationship between capitalism and democracy could be disharmonious.

The fourth and final section of the book extrapolated the "square of power" model to the global level. In many ways, the globalization of Anglo-American financial institutions and the liberalization of trade since the 1980s signal a return to the pre-1914 world. The periods before and after the age of total war have much in common. However, there are differences. There is less mobility of labour than in the nineteenth century, for instance, and this is one reason why financial globalization is leading to less convergence of incomes around the world than was the case a century ago. International capital mobility can lead to bubbles in some asset markets while others languish: here too, in the distribution of capital between stock markets, there is polarization. Nor has the world today evolved a system of international monetary "architecture" comparable with the gold standard after *circa* 1870. Indeed, the experiment with a single European currency seems to swim against a tide of monetary fragmentation. Chapter 11 suggested that EMU is also likely to create conflicts of interest between the member states because of the differing generational imbalances in their fiscal systems, which remain the domain of national governments.

Does economic globalization imply the globalization of democracy? The answer offered in Chapter 12 was skeptical, since both economic growth and political democratization seem to be dependent more on the existence of education, the rule of law and financial stability than on one another. Moreover, democratization has tended to be associated with the fragmentation of multi-ethnic states. Chapter 13 suggested that the political fragmentation which has characterized the past half century does not necessarily have positive economic implications. At the same time, there is little reason to take seriously the idea that supra-national institutions will be more powerful in the twenty-first century than they were in the twentieth. In purely financial terms, institutions like the United Nations and the International Monetary Fund are in no stronger a position than their inter-war precursors.

The final chapter argued that the biggest difference between the past and the present is the absence of an authentic global hegemon—that is to say an imperial power. As a capital-importing democracy which has enjoyed a handsome "peace dividend" since the end of the Cold War, the United States lacks the will to play the policing role played a century ago by the United Kingdom, despite the fact that it manifestly has the economic means to do so. Yet the British experience illustrates strikingly the dangers of "under-stretch." It was not the excessive cost of empire that undermined British power; but failure to prepare adequately for the defence of that empire. The two states which mounted the greatest challenges to Britain's power in the twentieth century, Germany and Japan, were not her equals in institutional terms. In both world wars, Germany's financial structure proved unable to sustain the military projects her leaders undertook, collapsing on two occasions into hyperinflation. Nevertheless, her military performance shows how much damage a regime based on authoritarian mobilization can inflict on ill-prepared democratic states. This is not to say that the United States will face anything like so serious a challenge in the near future; but rather to argue for a precautionary assertion of American power to impose democracy and the market economy on "rogue" states while the going is good.

What is power? Ultimately, of course, it is impossible to give a purely materialistic answer to Tolstoy's question. The legitimacy of a state in the eyes of its citizens is not determined by the rate of income tax, the franchise, the interest rate or inflation rate, any more than it is determined by the butter ration. The institutional model I have tried to construct is simply the framework within which people individually and collectively make up their minds. No matter how efficient the tax system, no matter how representative the parliament, no matter how liquid the bond market and no matter how well managed the currency, in the end the legitimacy of a state is bound up with such intangibles as tradition (the memory of past benefits), charisma (the appeal of present leaders), popular belief (faith in future rewards, material or spiritual) and propaganda (the state's use of available media to bolster all these). Though Carlyle feared that modernity would turn all human relations into economic relations, the true *homo economicus*—constantly aiming to maximize his utility with every transaction—remains a rarity, and to most of us rather a monstrous one. Every day, men and women subordinate their

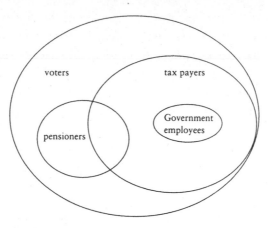

Figure 45: Circles of interest

economic self-interest to some other motive, be it the urge to play, to idle, to copulate or to wreck.

In that sense, the cash nexus is no more than one link in the long and tangled chain of human motivation. The true end of *War and Peace*, after all, is not the Second Epilogue, but the First. In the Second, Tolstoy philosophizes around in circles, and ultimately fails to answer his own question about power, drifting off instead into a labored argument about the illusory nature of free will. In the First Epilogue, however, we see Pierre and Natasha, anti-hero and heroine, united at last in domestic happiness. True, Pierre still has his dreams. But the striking thing about his latest idea—"to give a new direction to the whole of Russian society and to the whole world"—is its naïvety:

You see, I don't say that we ought to oppose this and that. We may be mistaken. What I say is: "Join hands, you who love the right, and let there be but one banner—that of active virtue." . . . My whole idea is that if vicious people are united and constitute a power, then honest folk must do the same. Now that's simple enough.[4]

A higher reality is symbolized by Natasha, hurrying off to feed their son; and by his nephew's dream about his lost but idolized father, Prince Andrei. "Oh, Father, Father! Yes, I will do something with which even he would be satisfied . . ." Of such stuff is composed the inner power that moves men.

Yet the peace Pierre and his family have attained is the product of war, the protracted and well-nigh global conflict unleashed by the French Revolution.

And to understand what it was that mobilized the *Grande Armée*—what got it to the gates of Moscow, but what ultimately forced it to retrace its steps in ignominy—we must look beyond the Russian winter or the Emperor's blunders. Inglorious though it may seem, the key to Napoleon's defeat lies in the fundamental institutional weaknesses of the Imperial regime.

Until we understand the mechanics of power—in this case, the reliance of the Napoleonic regime on extortion from occupied territory, its undemocratic character, its shallow bond market and its crudely mercantilist monetary policy—we cannot begin to make sense of the outcome. In that sense, the cash nexus provides not a sufficient explanation of the modern world, but a necessary one.

Appendices

A. THE BIGGEST WARS IN HISTORY

War	Dates	Duration (years)	Number of major powers involved	Battlefield deaths	Deaths per annum	War dead as a percentage of world population
Second World War	1939–45	6.0	7	19,131,683	3,188,614	0.80
First World War	1914–18	4.3	8	9,450,000	2,197,674	0.54
Thirty Years War	1618–48	30.0	6	2,071,000	69,033	0.44
Napoleonic Wars	1803–15	12.0	6	1,869,000	155,750	0.23
War of the Spanish Succession	1701–13	12.0	5	1,251,000	104,250	0.21
Seven Years War	1755–63	8.0	6	992,000	124,000	0.16
War of the League of Augsburg	1688–97	9.0	5	680,000	75,556	0.11
French Revolutionary Wars	1792–1802	10.0	6	663,000	66,300	0.08
Dutch War of Louis XIV	1672–78	6.0	6	342,000	57,000	0.07
Ottoman War	1682–99	17.0	2	384,000	22,588	0.06
War of the Austrian Succession	1739–48	9.0	6	359,000	39,889	0.06
Korean War	1950–53	3.1	4	954,960	308,052	0.04

Source: Levy, *War*, table 4.1. I have added together his data for the Thirty Years War, which he subdivided in three. I have also amended his totals for battlefield deaths for the world wars, which were too low. World population figures used in calculating the final column are the lower estimates from the table produced by the US Census Department (http://www.census.gov/ipc/www/worldhis.html).

B. MULTIPLE REGRESSION OF BRITISH GOVERNMENT POPULARITY AND ECONOMIC INDICATORS

(a) Adjusted R^2, 1951–1964 to 1997–2000

Government	Adjusted R^2
1951–64	0.17
1964–70	0.43
1970–4	0.23
1974–9	0.34
1979–92	0.38
1992–7	0.60
1997–2000	0.37

(b) Detailed regression breakdown, 1951–1964 to 1997–2000

		B	Significant?
1951–64	Unemployment	−4.83	Y
	RPI	−0.52	Y
	Base rates	−0.89	Y
1964–70	Unemployment	−9.59	Y
	RPI	−0.44	N
	Base rates	−4.32	Y
1970–74	Unemployment	−4.75	Y
	RPI	−1.54	Y
	Base Rates	−0.61	N
1974–9	Unemployment	−5.35	Y
	RPI	−0.33	N
	Base rates	−0.61	N
1979–92	Unemployment	0.19	N
	RPI	0.18	N
	Base rates	−2.57	Y
1992–7	Unemployment	0.49	N
	RPI	−8.65	N
	Base rates	8.36	Y

(continued)

1(b) Detailed regression breakdown, 1951–1964 to 1997–2000 (cont).

		B	Significant?
997–2000	Unemployment	5.02	Y
	RPI	3.12	N
	Base rates	−2.47	N

Sources: Butler and Butler, *British Political Facts*; Central Statistical Office, *Monthly Digest of Statistics*; HMSO, *Ministry of Labour Gazette*; Central Statistical Office, *Retail Prices 1914–1990*. Recent data are from the following websites: Bank of England, HM Treasury, statistics.gov.uk, except for the opinion poll data, which are from the Gallup Organisation (as published in the *Daily Telegraph*).

Notes: The indicators used in the analysis are as follows: government lead: percentage of respondents who would vote for governing party if an election were held tomorrow less percentage who would vote for principal Opposition party.

RPI: retail price index, percentage change over the previous year. Unemployment figures (defined from January 1971 as the claimant count) are given without seasonal adjustment. Base rates: Bank of England base rate at end of month.

B statistic: A one-unit rise in the variable correlates with a B per cent increase or decrease in government popularity.

Significance: Y: less than 5 per cent chance that the relationship is random; N: more than 5 per cent chance that the relationship is random.

C. THE GLOBAL BOND MARKET, JUNE 1999

Region	$bn.	%	Sector	$bn.	%
(a) Domestic					
Developing countries and Eastern Europe	1,352	5	Corporate	3,892	13
Other developed countries	2,572	9	Financial sector	7,831	27
Japan	5,228	18	Public sector	17,645	60
Eurozone	5,602	19			
US	14,607	50			
TOTAL	29,368	100	Total	29,368	100
(b) International					
International institutions	367	8			
Developing countries and Eastern Europe	393	8	Corporate	1,126	24
Other developed countries	1,302	28	Financial	2,205	47
Eurozone	1,494	32	Public	1,360	29
US	1,063	23			
Offshore centres	68	1			
TOTAL	4,691	100	Total	4,691	100
(a) plus *(b)*					
Developing countries and Eastern Europe	1,745	5	Corporate	5,018	15
Other developed countries	2,965	9	Financial	10,036	29
Eurozone	7,096	21	Public	19,005	56
US	15,670	46			
TOTAL	34,059	100	Total	34,059	100

Sources: Financial Times, 28 January 2000; Bank for International Settlements, *Annual Report 1999,* table VII.4.

D. PUBLIC DEBT BURDENS IN 1887–1888

	Nominal debt / revenue	Adjusted net debt/ revenue	Nominal debt / exports	Adjusted net debt/ exports
United Kingdom	7.9	4.4	2.5	1.4
British Asia	2.3	—	1.7	—
British Australasia	6.3	—	3.4	—
British Africa	5.0	—	2.0	—
British Atlantic and South America	1.2		0.3	
British North America	7.2	—	2.7	—
British West Indies	1.6	—	0.4	—
Gibraltar	0.3	—	—	—
Total colonial	3.6	—	2.2	—
British Empire	5.4	—	2.4	—
Austria-Hungary*	6.7	6.5	6.9	6.7
Belgium	6.7	1.7	0.9	0.2
Denmark	3.7	—	1.2	—
France	8.2	6.6	8.6	6.9
German Reich	0.7	—	—	—
German states**	4.3	—	—	—
German Reich + states	3.1	—	1.9	—
Greece	7.4	7.4	8.2	8.2
Italy	6.3	5.6	10.3	9.2
Montenegro	2.0	—	0.5	—
Netherlands	9.3	4.6	1.1	0.6
Portugal	16.0	10.3	21.5	13.8
Romania	5.4	—	3.1	—
Serbia	4.6	—	5.2	—
Spain	7.4	6.0	9.1	7.3
Sweden	2.9	0.7	1.0	0.2
Norway	2.4	0.9	1.0	0.4
Switzerland***	0.6	—	0.1	—
Russia	6.9	6.3	7.3	6.6
Bulgaria + East Rumelia	0.9	—	0.9	—
Turkey	8.7	1.7	12.6	2.5

(continued)

D. *Public Debt Burdens in 1887–8 (see p. 000) (cont).*

	Nominal debt / revenue	Adjusted net debt/ revenue	Nominal debt / exports	Adjusted net debt/ exports
Egypt	11.6	7.3	10.5	6.6
China****	0.2	—	0.2	
Japan	4.0	4.7	6.2	7.4
Argentina	7.6	8.0	5.1	5.4
Brazil	7.5	6.7	5.2	4.6
Chile	2.5	1.6	1.7	1.1
Mexico	7.0	4.6	4.6	3.0
Peru	15.6	—	31.3	—
United States	3.1	—	—	—
US + states	—	—	2.0	1.7

*No allowance made in adjusted debt for Austro-Hungarian income tax on foreign bondholders.

**Figure for revenue only more major states.

***No figures for cantonal revenue; cantonal debt was £14 million.

****No figure for internal debt.

Note: Mexico and Peru were in default, and Austria-Hungary, Russia, Italy, Japan, Argentina and Brazil had depreciated paper currency "estimated to entail a 5 per cent burden on these countries." Turkey's reduced debt calculated as yielding 1 per cent.

Source: Nash, *Fenn's Compendium*, pp. x–iv.

E. ECONOMIC AND SOCIAL INDICATORS AND THE INTER-WAR CRISIS OF DEMOCRACY, 1919–1938

	Number of years democracy lasted after 1918	Urban population (percentage of total population	Army (percentage of total population	School-children (percentage of total population)	Percentage decline in GNP during Depressions, peak to trough
Democracies					
Belgium	20	11.7	1.1	12.1	
Denmark	20	17.5	0.4	13.9	−4.5
Finland	20	6.5	0.9	11.8	−6.5
France	20	15.3	1.6	11.8	−18.1
Ireland	20	13.9	0.3	17.8	0
Netherlands	20	26.0	0.2	15.5	−12.5
Norway	20	9.1	0.2	14.7	
Sweden	20	13.7	0.6	11.3	−14.6
Switzerland	20	16.6		13.8	−5.8
United Kingdom	20	39.7	0.9	13.2	−5.7
Czechoslovakia	19	9.1	1.0	14.4	−19.2
"Dictatorships"					
Austria	16	32.1	0.4	12.9	−22.5
Estonia	16	12.4	1.4		
Latvia	16	19.7	1.3		
Germany	14	33.1	0.5	12.8	−22.6
Romania	12	5.6	1.1	12.3	−10.3
Yugoslavia	10	3.5	1.1	8.7	−11.9
Lithuania	8	1.7	1.2		
Portugal	8	12.1	0.6	6.1	
Italy	6	16.2	1.3	12.0	−6.8
Poland	5	9.5	1.0	12.8	
Spain	5	14.4	1.0	9.8	−4.4
Albania	5	0.0	0.9		
Bulgaria	5	4.2	0.4	14.8	−9.2
Hungary	0	14.5	0.4	10.9	−11.5

Notes

Introduction

1. Marx and Engels, *Communist Manifesto*, p. 82.
2. Berlin, "Disraeli and Marx," p. 283.
3. Carlyle, *Writings*, p. 277. For the full quotations see epigraphs at the front of this book.
4. Ibid., p. 199. On the genesis of the idea of the "cash nexus," see Heffer, *Moral Desperado*, pp. 95, 130, 169.
5. Millington, *Wagner*, pp. 223 f.
6. Holroyd, *Shaw*, vol. ii, pp. 11–13, quoting Shaw's *The Perfect Wagnerite* (1899).
7. Marx, *Capital*, p. 928.
8. Ibid., p. 929.
9. Fontane, *Stechlin*, p. 77.
10. Maupassant, *Bel-Ami*, esp. p. 324.
11. Wheen, *Marx*, p. 268. Cf. ibid., p. 249 for evidence that the socialist leader Ferdinand Lassalle did the same.
12. See Blackbourn and Eley, *Peculiarities of German History*.
13. See Kehr, *Primat der Innenpolitik*, passim.
14. Hobsbawm, *Age of Extremes*, pp. 558–85.
15. As requested by the author, I am providing here the full source: © J. Bradford DeLong, The Shape of Twentieth Century Economic History, *NBER Working Paper*, 7569 (Feb. 2000), pp. 27 f.
16. Ibid., pp. 3, 8.
17. Ibid., pp. 12 f.
18. Ibid., p. 17.
19. Lipset, "Social Requisites of Democracy," pp. 75–85.
20. Barro, "Determinants of Economic Growth," p. 1.
21. Friedman, "Other Times, Other Places," pp. 2, 29. See also pp. 54, 86.
22. Joll, *Europe since 1870*, p. 357.
23. Norpoth, "Economy," p. 317.

24. Kennedy, *Rise and Fall of the Great Powers*, p. 567.

25. Ibid., pp. 696 f.

26. For a sceptical view see Almond, "1989 without Gorbachev."

27. Fukuyama, *Great Disruption*, p. 282.

28. For a useful introduction, see Haigh, *Taking Chances*.

29. Pinker, *How the Mind Works*, p. 395.

30. Bernstein, *Against the Gods*, pp. 272 ff.

31. Spurling, *La Grande Thérèse*, p. 89.

32. Dawkins, *Selfish Gene*.

33. Freud, *Civilization, War and Death*.

34. Weber, *Protestant Ethic*.

35. Offer, "Between the Gift and the Market."

36. See on this point Neal, "Shocking View of Economic History," p. 332.

37. Dostoevsky, *Notes from Underground*, pp. 105–20.

38. See esp. North, *Institutions*.

39. Carlyle, "On History," p. 95.

40. Ferguson, "Introduction: Towards a Chaotic Theory of the Past." Cf. Shermer, "Exorcising Laplace's Demon."

41. *Thoughts on the Late Transactions Respecting Falkland's Islands* (1771), quoted in Black, "Foreign and Defence Polices," p. 290.

Chapter 1

1. Bonney, "Introduction," pp. 2 ff.

2. Goldsmith, *Premodern Financial Systems*, p. 33.

3. Quoted in Parker, "Emergence of Modern Finance," p. 527.

4. Quoted in Luard, *War in International Society*, p. 240.

5. Ibid., p. 239.

6. Ibid., p. 248.

7. See e.g. "One of the few constancies in history is that the scale of commitment on military spending has always risen": Mathias, *First Industrial Nation*, p. 44. In Paul Kennedy's words: "The cost of a sixteenth century war could be measured in millions of pounds; by the late seventeenth century, it had risen to *tens* of millions of pounds; and at the close of the Napoleonic War the outgoings of the major combatants occasionally reached a hundred million pounds *a year*": Kennedy, *Rise and Fall of the Great Powers*, p. 99.

8. Sorokin, *Social and Cultural Dynamics*, vol. iii.

9. Wright, *Study of War*.

10. Richardson, *Statistics of Deadly Quarrels*.

11. Luard, *War in International Society*, appendix.

12. Correlates of War database, www.umich.edu/~cowproj. The database provides figures for total population, urban population, iron and steel production, energy consumption, military personnel and military expenditures. Earlier versions of the Cor-

relates of War data can be found in Singer and Small, *Wages of War* and *Resort to Arms*.

13. Levy, *War*. Levy's definition of which states were "great powers" is rather subjective, but his analysis is nevertheless useful.

14. Luard, *War in International Society*. Adding all the wars listed in Luard's appendix gives a figure of 1,021, but his own sub-totals in the main text imply a different total for reasons which are unclear.

15. Levy, *War*, pp. 97–9.

16. Wallensteen and Sollenberg, "Armed Conflict."

17. Sollenberg, Wallensteen and Jato, "Major Armed Conflicts." Cf. *Financial Times*, 15 June 2000.

18. See Brogan, *World Conflicts*, appendix 1.

19. See e.g. Hinsley, *Power and the Pursuit of Peace*, pp. 278 f.

20. Levy, *War*, p. 139. Cf. pp. 129–31.

21. Calculated from Luard, *War in International Society*, appendix.

22. The Ottoman Empire comes sixth (33), followed by Russia (28), Italy (meaning any Italian state: 22) and Germany (meaning any German state: 18).

23. Bond, *Victorian Military Campaigns*, pp. 309–11.

24. "Only one war of the post-Vienna period has lasted longer than seven years, whereas in the pre-Vienna period there were nearly twenty wars of this duration": see Levy, *War*, pp. 116–29. Cf. Luard, *War in International Society*, p. 47.

25. "In the Seven Years War . . . there were 17 belligerents and 111 battles . . . The numbers in the First World War were 38 and 615": Hinsley, *Power and the Pursuit of Peace*, pp. 278 f.

26. Luard, *War in International Society*, pp. 54 f. Luard identifies 30 "Wars of National Independence" (though only 28 appear in his appendix), of which 20 were suppressed. He also identifies eighteen cases of "External Intervention in Civil War in Europe," though the intention behind such interventions varied. In seven cases, intervention was on the side of the rebels, compared with ten when it was in support of the government. In all, nine liberal revolutions were suppressed.

27. Ibid., pp. 52–61.

28. Figures from Kennedy, *Rise and Fall of the Great Powers*, p. 71, 128; McNeill, *Pursuit of Power*, p. 107; Mann, *Sources of Social Power*, vol. ii, p. 393, tables A1, A4.

29. McNeill, *Pursuit of Power*, pp. 79 ff.

30. Körner, "Expenditure," p. 408.

31. McNeill, *Pursuit of Power*, pp. 120–43.

32. Ibid., pp. 161 f.

33. Ibid., pp. 178 ff.

34. Ibid., pp. 228 ff., 273 n.

35. Ibid., p. 350.

36. Ibid., pp. 357 ff.

37. Ibid., pp. 367–72.

38. Kaldor, *Baroque Arsenal*, quoted in Kennedy, *Rise and Fall of the Great Powers*, p. 570.

39. Kennedy, *Rise and Fall of the Great Powers*, pp. 570 f.

40. Ibid., p. 623.

41. Ibid., pp. 674 f.

42. Ibid., p. 572.

43. These figures are arrived at by deflating nominal defence spending by the consumer price index (CPI), and dividing that figure by the size of the armed forces. Of course, the CPI is not the ideal deflator for the defence budget, so the figures are necessarily very approximate. However, the long-run trend is clear enough.

44. Overy, *Times Atlas of the Twentieth Century*, pp. 102–5; Harrison, "Economics of World War II: An Overview," pp. 3 f., 7 f., and "Soviet Union," p. 291.

45. Calculated from figures in Winter, *Great War*, p. 75.

46. Calculated from figures in Timechart Company, *Timechart of Military History*, pp. 112–27; Perrett (ed.), *Battle Book*.

47. Erickson, "Red Army Battlefield Performance," p. 245. Cf. Beevor, *Stalingrad*.

48. *Daily Telegraph*, 15 March 2000; 13 April 2000.

49. Fieldhouse, "Nuclear Weapon Developments."

50. On the basis of the 1993 Federal Budget Request: IISS, *Military Balance, 1992–1993*, p. 17.

51. Ibid., p. 218.

52. Creveld, *Supplying War*, pp. 233 f.

53. Quoted in Nef, *War and Human Progress*, p. 366.

54. Creveld, *Supplying War*, p. 200.

55. Ibid. pp. 216–30 and n.23.

56. Overy, *Why the Allies Won*, p. 319.

57. McNeill, *Pursuit of Power*, pp. 225 ff.

58. Kubicek, "British Expansion, Empire and Technological Change," pp. 254, 258.

59. Ibid., p. 261.

60. Burroughs, "Defence and Imperial Disunity," p. 336.

61. At Omdurman in 1898 Kitchener's army, equipped with 55 machine guns, killed 11,000 dervishes at a cost of 48 British troops lost. Contrary to popular belief—encouraged by Hilaire Belloc's famous lines ("Whatever happens, we have got / The Maxim Gun, and they have not")—the Sudanese did have machine guns, but only two: Kubicek, "British Expansion, Empire and Technological Change," p. 265.

62. *Wall Street Journal*, 19 April 1999.

63. HMS *Dreadnought* cost the equivalent of 0.12 per cent of Britain's 1906 GDP; a B-2 cost 0.02 per cent of 1998 US GDP.

64. Goldsmith, *Premodern Financial Systems*, pp. 22, 31 f.

65. Ibid., pp. 48, 51.

66. Ibid., p. 79.

67. Körner, "Expenditure," pp. 402 ff.

68. Ibid., pp. 416 f.

69. Goldsmith, *Premodern Financial Systems*, p. 193.

70. Hart, "Seventeenth Century," p. 282; Capra, "Finances of the Austrian Monarchy," pp. 295–7.

71. O'Brien, *Power with Profit*, pp. 34 f.

72. Mann, *Sources of Social Power*, vol. i, p. 373, except for Britain, O'Brien, *Power with Profit*, pp. 34 f.

73. Mann, *Sources of Social Power*, vol. ii, p. 373.

74. Ibid.

75. Calculated from the figures in Mitchell and Deane, *Abstract of British Historical Statistics*, pp. 396–8.

76. Figures taken from Bankers Trust Company, *French Public Finance;* Apostol, Bernatzky and Michelson, *Russian Public Finances*.

77. Calculated from the figures in Flora *et al.*, *State, Economy and Society*, vol. i, pp. 345–449.

78. Kennedy, *Rise and Fall of the Great Powers*, p. 403.

79. Calculated from the figures in Mitchell and Jones, *Second Abstract of British Historical Statistics*, pp. 160 f.

80. For a review of the figures, see Abelshauser, "Germany," table 4.4 and pp. 133–8. Cf. Overy, *War and Economy*, p. 203. Figures for the Reich budget can be found in James, *German Slump*, table XXXV.

81. Petzina, Abelshauser and Faust (eds.), *Sozialgeschichtliches Arbeitsbuch*, vol. iii, p. 149; Hansemeyer and Caesar, "Kriegswirtschaft und Inflation," p. 400.

82. Kennedy, *Rise and Fall of the Great Powers*, p. 388.

83. Defence accounted for a larger proportion of central government expenditure in Germany in the 1960s, but only because much non-military expenditure was carried out at the regional rather than the federal level. Cf. the figures in Flora *et al.*, *State, Economy and Society*, vol. i, pp. 345–449.

84. Hogwood, *Trends in British Public Policy*, p. 45.

85. Goldsmith, *Premodern Financial Systems*, pp. 145, 164 ff.

86. O'Brien, *Power with Profit*, p. 35. It should be emphasized that estimates for national income or national product even for the later twentieth century must be treated with caution, as the margins for error remain large even in the best national statistics. Eighteenth- and nineteenth-century estimates used in this chapter and elsewhere are often little more than educated guesses. Here and elsewhere percentages which use historic national product data as the numerator carry a statistical "health warning."

87. Calculated from figures in Bonney, "Struggle for Great Power Status," p. 345.

88. See Ferguson, *Pity of War*, pp. 105–18.

89. Kennedy, *Rise and Fall of the Great Powers*, p. 644.

90. IISS, *Military Balance 1992–1993*, p. 218.

91. *Financial Times*, 15 June 2000.

92. Omer Bartov, *Hitler's Army*, quoted in Calder (ed.), *Wars*, p. 340.

93. Pennington, "Offensive Women," p. 253.
94. Beevor, *Stalingrad*.
95. Overy, *Battle*.

Chapter 2

1. Benjamin Franklin to Jean-Baptiste le Roy, 13 November 1789.
2. Capra, "Finances of the Austrian Monarchy," p. 306.
3. Goldsmith, *Premodern Financial Systems*, pp. 32 f.
4. Ibid., pp. 49 f., 53 ff.
5. Hocquet, "City-State and Market Economy," pp. 87 f.; Körner, "Public Credit," p. 515.
6. Henneman, "France in the Middle Ages," p. 116.
7. Gelabert, "Fiscal Burden," p. 542.
8. Schremmer, "Taxation and Public Finance," p. 365.
9. Ibid.
10. Isenmann, "Medieval and Renaissance Theories of State Finance," p. 42.
11. Gelabert, "Fiscal Burden," p. 547; Goldsmith, *Premodern Financial Systems*, p. 192.
12. Hobson, *National Wealth*, p. 19.
13. Hart, "Seventeenth Century," p. 284; Bonney, "Revenues," p. 448.
14. Ibid., p. 451.
15. Schremmer, "Taxation and Public Finance," p. 456.
16. Ibid, p. 460.
17. Bonney, "Struggle for Great Power Status," p. 329.
18. Ferguson, *World's Banker*, ch. 2.
19. Gatrell, *Government, Industry and Rearmament*, p. 140.
20. Calculated for the period 1801–1914 from the figures in Mitchell and Deane, *Abstract of British Historical Statistics*, pp. 392–5.
21. Schremmer, "Taxation and Public Finance," p. 402.
22. Gatrell, *Government, Industry and Rearmament*, p. 140.
23. Bonney, "Revenues," p. 490.
24. *Statistical Abstract of the United States 1999*, table 503.
25. Pryce-Jones, *War That Never Was*, pp. 78 f.
26. Paddags, "German Railways," p. 9, 22 f., 28.
27. Calculated from figures in Webb, *Hyperinflation and Stabilization in Weimer Germany*, pp. 33, 37.
28. Duncan and Hobson, *Saturn's Children*, p. 40.
29. Horne, *Macmillan*, p. 627.
30. Crafts, *Conservative Government's Economic Record*, p. 29. See in general, Yergin and Stanislaw, *Commanding Heights*, esp. pp. 114 ff.
31. Goldsmith, *Premodern Financial Systems*, pp. 32 f.
32. Ibid., pp. 49 f., 53 ff.
33. Ormrod, "England in the Middle Ages," p. 32.
34. Ibid., pp. 40 ff.

35. Hilton, *Corn, Cash and Commerce*, passim.

36. Rogowski, *Commerce and Coalitions*, esp. pp. 21–60.

37. O'Rourke and Williamson, *Globalization and History*, pp. 98 f., 114 f. Cf. Weiss and Hobson, *States and Economic Development*, p. 124.

38. Brown, "Episodes in the Public Debt History," p. 234.

39. James, "Ende der Globalisierung," p. 76.

40. James, *Globalization and its Sins*, p. 104.

41. James, "Ende der Globalisierung," p. 69.

42. James, *Globalization and its Sins*, p. 124.

43. Skidelsky, *John Maynard Keyner*, vol. ii, pp. 476–80.

44. Research by Jeffrey Sachs and Andrew Warner conclusively demonstrates that open economies grew six and a half times faster than closed economies in the 1970s and 1980s: *Prospect*, May 2000.

45. Goldsmith, *Premodern Financial Systems*, pp. 32 f.

46. Ibid., pp. 49 f.

47. Henneman, "France in the Middle Ages," p. 112; White, "Failure to Modernise," p. 9.

48. Goldsmith, *Premodern Financial Systems*, pp. 164 f.

49. Kennedy, *Rise and Fall of the Great Powers*, pp. 54 ff.

50. Hellie, "Russia," p. 502.

51. O'Brien and Hunt, "England," pp. 61 ff.

52. Bonney, "Revenues," p. 490.

53. O'Brien and Hunt, "England," pp. 74 ff.

54. Buxton, *Finance and Politics*, vol. i, 1 ff.

55. Quoted in Ibid., p. 19.

56. Compare O'Brien, *Power with Profit*; Kennedy, *Rise and Fall of the Great Powers*, pp. 102 f.; and Gelabert, "Fiscal Burden," pp. 572 ff.

57. Bonney, "Revenues," p. 498.

58. See Morrissey and Steinmo, "Influence of Party Competition," pp. 199 f.

59. Isenmann, "Medieval and Renaissance Theories of State Finance," pp. 47 f.

60. Schulze, "Sixteenth Century," pp. 274 f.

61. Bonney, "Revenues," p. 489.

62. Ibid., pp. 433, 435.

63. White, "France and the Failure to Modernize," p. 13; Kennedy, *Rise and Fall of the Great Powers*, p. 75.

64. Hart, "Seventeenth Century," pp. 289 f.

65. Ibid., p. 51.

66. O'Brien and Hunt, "England," pp. 74 ff.

67. Rudé, *Crowd in History*, pp. 38 ff.

68. Hentschel, *Wirtschaft und Wirtschaftspolitik*, pp. 164 ff.

69. Schremmer, "Taxation and Public Finance," p. 402.

70. Shy, "American Colonies," pp. 312 f.; Conway, "Britain and the Revolutionary Crisis," pp. 327 f. The taxes were projected to raise just £110,000, of which £50,000 would have come from the West Indies: Clark, "British America," p. 153.

71. Chennells, Dilnot and Roback, "Survey of the UK Tax System," p. 2.

72. INSEE website.

73. Chennells, Dilnot and Roback, "Survey of the UK Tax System," pp. 7, 22, 25.

74. Kay and King, *British Tax System*, p. 129.

75. The figures in 1979 were: diesel, 49 per cent; cigarettes, 70 per cent; spirits, 77 per cent; wine, 47 per cent; and beer, 34 per cent: Chennells, Dilnot and Roback, "Survey of the UK Tax System," p. 8.

76. Duncan and Hobson, *Saturn's Children*, p. 120

77. HMSO, *Social Trends 1995*, table 5.15.

78. Hogwood, *Trends in British Public Policy*, p. 106.

79. *Statistical Abstract of the United States 1999*, table 503; Chennells, Dilnot and Roback, "Survey of the UK Tax System," p. 2.

80. Hogwood, *Trends in British Public Policy*, p. 107.

81. Seldon, *Dilemma of Democracy*, pp. 76–86.

82. Bonney, "Revenues," pp. 472 ff., and "France, 1494–1815," p. 130.

83. Hellie, "Russia," pp. 496 f.

84. Goldsmith, *Premodern Financial Systems*, pp. 32 f.

85. Ibid., pp. 60 ff.

86. Ormrod, "England in the Middle Ages," p. 21; Ormrod and Barta, "Feudal Structure," pp. 58 f.

87. Ormrod, "England in the Middle Ages," p. 29; Henneman, "France in the Middle Ages," p. 104.

88. Goldsmith, *Premodern Financial Systems*, p. 91.

89. Ibid., pp. 123 ff.

90. Ibid., p. 117.

91. Bonney, "Early Modern Theories of State Finance," p. 204.

92. Goldsmith, *Premodern Financial Systems*, p. 226.

93. Bonney, "Revenues," pp. 475 ff.

94. O'Brien and Hunt, "England," p. 61 ff.

95. Bonney, "Revenues," p. 483.

96. Bonney, "France, 1494–1815," pp. 158 f.

97. Bonney, "Revenues," pp. 479 ff.

98. Schremmer, "Taxation and Public Finance," p. 381.

99. Goldsmith, *Premodern Financial Systems*, pp. 49 f. 53 ff.

100. Smith, *Wealth of Nations*, bk. V, ch. 3. The other canons were that taxes should be certain (i.e. predictable), convenient to pay and cheap to collect.

101. "La contribution commune . . . doit être également répartie entre tous les citoyens en raison de leurs facultés."

102. Goldsmith, *Premodern Financial Systems*, pp. 60 ff.

103. Ormrod, "England in the Middle Ages," p. 30.

104. Hocquet, "City-State and Market Economy," pp. 87 f.

105. Bonney, "France, 1494–1815," p. 130, "Struggle for Great Power Status," pp.

321 ff., "Revenues," pp. 479 ff. For Vauban's scheme to replace all French taxes with a ten per cent income tax see Braudel, *Civilization and Capitalism*, vol. iii, p. 308.
106. O'Brien and Hunt, "England," p. 86.
107. Ibid., p. 89.
108. Duncan and Hobson, *Saturn's Children*, p. 112.
109. Inland Revenue, "Brief History," p. 2.
110. Ormrod, "England in the Middle Ages," p. 46; Gelabert, "Fiscal Burden," p. 50.
111. Buxton, *Finance and Politics*, pp. 43 ff.
112. Matthew, "Mid-Victorian Budgets."
113. Henneman, "France in the Middle Ages," pp. 116 ff.; White, "France and the Failure to Modernize," p. 8.
114. Gelabert, "Fiscal Burden," pp. 554 f.
115. Bonney, "Revenues," p. 433.
116. Doyle, *Origins of the French Revolution*, pp. 46, 98.
117. Balderston, "War Finance," p. 236.
118. Witt, "Tax Policies."
119. Duncan and Hobson, *Saturn's Children*, p. 100.
120. Bonney, "Revenues," pp. 478 ff.
121. Henneman, "France in the Middle Ages," p. 115.
122. Bonney, "Revenues," p. 485.
123. Ibid.; Bonney, "France, 1494–1815," p. 164.
124. Matthew, "Mid-Victorian Budgets."
125. Murray, "Battered and Shattered."
126. Bonney, "Revenues," pp. 479 ff.
127. Duncan and Hobson, *Saturn's Children*, pp. 107 f.
128. Hogwood, *Trends in British Public Policy*, p. 70. The biggest allowances in 1990 were capital allowances, mortgage interest relief and the married man's allowance, the first two of which were increased under Margaret Thatcher: ibid., p. 71, 84.
129. Schremmer, "Taxation and Public Finance," p. 348.
130. Brown, "Episodes in the Public Debt History," p. 236.
131. Inland Revenue, "Brief History," p. 7.
132. Hogwood, *Trends in British Public Policy*, p. 97.
133. According to Engen and Skinner, a reduction of 2.5 per cent in the average tax rate would raise the growth rate by about 0.2 per cent through effects in capital accumulation and technological change: Engen and Skinner, "Taxation and Economic Growth."
134. Duncan and Hobson, *Saturn's Children*, pp. 88 f.
135. *Social Trends 1991*, table 5.12.
136. Bonney, "Revenues," p. 502; O'Brien and Hunt, "England," pp. 61 ff.
137. Buxton, *Finance and Politics*, vol. i, pp. 39–42.
138. Maloney, "Gladstone," pp 40 f.
139. Figures from Flora *et al.*, *State, Economy and Society*, vol. i, p. 339.

140. Schremmer, "Taxation and Public Finance," p. 402.
141. Bonney, "France, 1494–1815," p. 165.
142. Schremmer, "Taxation and Public Finance," p. 402 (calculated from ordinary and extraordinary revenue)
143. Ibid., p. 390.
144. Burns, *Complete Letters*, p. 214.
145. Burns, *Poems and Songs*, pp. 168f., 602f.
146. Ibid., p. 523. "We'll make our malt and we'll brew our drink, / We'll laugh, sing and rejoice, man; / And many loud thanks to the big black devil, / That danced away with the Exciseman."
147. Fowler, *Burns*, pp. 142 f.
148. Burns, *Complete Letters*, pp. 435–8.

Chapter 3

1. Montesquieu, *Spirit of Laws*, part II, chs. 12, 13. Cf. Bonney, "Early Modern Theories of State Finance," p. 192.
2. Butterfield, *Whig Interpretation, passim*.
3. Wagner, *Die Ordnung des Österreichischen Staatshaushalts* (Vienna, 1863), cit. James, "Ende der Globalisierung," p. 74.
4. Schumpeter, "Crisis of the Tax State."
5. Goldsmith, *Premodern Financial Systems*, pp. 32 f.
6. Quoted in Gelabert, "Fiscal Burden," p. 545.
7. Ormrod, "West European Monarchies," p. 143.
8. Ormrod, "England in the Middle Ages," pp. 20, 29.
9. Goldsmith, *Premodern Financial Systems*, pp. 171ff.
10. Quoted in Gelabert, "Fiscal Burden," p. 539.
11. North and Weingast, "Constitutions and Commitment," pp. 810–14.
12. Sharpe, *Personal Rule of Charles I*, pp. 105–30; Adamson, "England without Cromwell," pp. 120–122.
13. North and Weingast, "Constitutions and Commitment," pp. 815 f.
14. Ormrod, "England in the Middle Ages," p. 20.
15. Henneman, "France in the Middle Ages," p. 107. The name of the French currency *franc* ("free") originated with the coins used to pay the ransom.
16. Bosher, *French Finances*, p. 3.
17. Bonney, "France, 1494–1815," p. 131; Doyle, *Origins of the French Revolution*, p. 49.
18. Ibid., pp. 99–114.
19. Finer, *History of Government*, vol. iii, pp. 1490 f.
20. Shy, "American Colonies," p. 313.
21. Winch, "Political Economy," p. 15.
22. See Clark, "British America," esp. pp. 150–59.
23. Conway, "Britain and the Revolutionary Crisis," pp. 332, 335.
24. Hoffman and Norberg (eds.), *Fiscal Crises*, p. 306.

25. See in general Mann, *Sources of Social Power*, vol. ii.

26. Quoted in O'Brien and Hunt, "England," pp. 61 ff.

27. Filipczak-Kocur, "Poland-Lithuania," *passim*.

28. Bonney, "Struggle for Great Power Status," pp. 347 f.

29. Buxton, *Finance and Politics*, vol. i, pp. 12–15.

30. Inland Revenue, "Brief History," p. 1.

31. Matthew, "Mid-Victorian Budgets."

32. Maloney, "Gladstone," p. 33.

33. Figures in Mitchell and Deane, *Abstract of British Historical Statistics*, pp. 392–5, 427–9.

34. McNeill, *Pursuit of Power*, p. 275 n.

35. Quoted in Ibid., p. 270 n.

36. Clarke, "Keynes, Buchanan and the Balanced-Budget Doctrine," p. 76.

37. Ibid.

38. Peacock and Wiseman, *Public Expenditure in the United Kingdom*, p. 67.

39. Calculated from figures in Butler and Butler, *British Political Facts*, pp. 213–19; Jamieson, *British Economy*, p.145

40. Hogwood, *Trends in British Public Policy*, p. 98.

41. Crafts, *Conservative Government's Economic Record*, pp. 23 ff.; Jamieson, *British Economy*, pp. 146 ff., 158 The total tax burden including national insurance was reduced from a peak of 40 per cent of GDP in 1981 to a low of 33.8 per cent in 1994, though the figure had been 35.5 per cent in 1979, and by 1995 it had once again risen above that level. On the other hand, the proportion of total tax accounted for by indirect taxation rose from 33 per cent to 41 per cent between 1985 and 1995; income tax now accounts for around 26 per cent of the total.

42. Flora *et al.*, *State, Economy and Society*, vol. i, p. 112.

43. Ibid., vol. i, p. 126.

44. Goldsmith, *Premodern Financial Systems*, pp. 123 ff.

45. Ibid., pp. 94–107.

46. Compare Elton, *Tudor Revolution in Government*, and Williams, *Tudor Regime*.

47. O'Brien and Hunt, "England," pp. 61 ff.

48. Bosher, *French Finances*, p. 8.

49. Winch, "Political Economy," pp. 9 ff. Cf. Mathias and O'Brien, "Taxation in Great Britain and France," pp. 606 f.

50. White, "France and the Failure to Modernize," pp. 18 f.

51. Schama, *Citizens*, p. 73.

52. Schulze, "Sixteenth Century," p. 272.

53. Carruthers, *City of Capital*, p. 111.

54. White, "France and the Failure to Modernize," p. 26.

55. Hart, "Seventeenth Century," p. 292; Bonney, "France, 1494–1815," pp. 131 ff., 152 f.

56. O'Brien and Hunt, "England," p. 74.

57. Bonney, "Revenues," pp. 442 f.

58. O'Brien and Hunt, "England," p. 57.

59. Weiss and Hobson, *States and Economic Development*, p. 45.

60. Brewer, *Sinews of Power*, p. 66.

61. Bosher, *French Finances*, esp. pp. 303–18.

62. Wallerstein, *Modern World-System*, vol. iii, p. 82 n.

63. Schama, *Citizens*, pp. 73, 76 f.

64. Gerth and Mills (eds.), *From Max Weber*, p. 244.

65. Kafka, *Castle*, pp. 244 f.

66. Canetti, *Torch in My Ear*, pp. 245 f.

67. See in general Caplan, *Government Without Administration*.

68. Trevor-Roper (ed.), *Hitler's Table Talk*, pp. 237 ff.

69. Figures from Flora *et al.*, *State, Economy and Society*, vol. i, pp. 210–42.

70. Duncan and Hobson, *Saturn's Children*, p. 53.

71. Wages and salaries as a proportion of federal, state and local expenditure: *Statistical Abstract of the United States 1999*, table 503.

72. Hogwood, *Trends in British Public Policy*, p. 50

73. Goldsmith, *Premodern Financial Systems*, pp. 60 ff.

74. Braudel, *Civilization and Capitalism*, vol. iii, p. 310.

75. Goldsmith, *Premodern Financial Systems*, p. 226.

76. Morineau's figures, quoted in Gelabert, "Fiscal Burden," p. 560 n. But see Braudel, *Civilization and Capitalism*, vol. iii, pp. 312 f.

77. Hellie, "Russia," pp. 496 f.

78. Goldsmith, *Premodern Financial Systems*, pp. 171 ff.

79. Bonney, "Early Modern Theories of State Finance," pp. 181 f.

80. O'Brien, *Power with Profit*.

81. Bonney, 'Struggle for Great Power Status,' pp. 336 f., 345 and fig. 337. France's annual revenue was about 1.4 times Britain's; 2.4 times Spain's; 3.5 times Austria's; 3.8 times Holland's; and 6.5 times Prussia''s. Cf. Mathias and O'Brien, "Taxation in Great Britain and France."

82. White, "France and the Failure to Modernize," p. 4.

83. See tables 2.1, 2.2, 2.3, 2.5 and 2.6 in Hogwood, *Trends in British Public Policy*, pp. 40–43.

84. *Statistical Abstract of the United States*, p. 339.

85. OECD, *Economic Outlook*, 65 (1999), annex table 28.

86. Kennedy, *Rise and Fall of the Great Powers*, p. 67.

87. Goldsmith, *Premodern Financial Systems*, p. 117.

88. Harris, "Political Thought and the Welfare State," p. 43.

89. Green, "Friendly Societies."

90. Whiteside, "Private Provision and Public Welfare," p. 34.

91. Thane, "Working Class," p. 106.

92. Ibid., p. 111.

93. I am grateful to Edward Lipman for his unpublished researches on this subject.

94. Although it was worth just five shillings, half a million "very poor, very old" people claimed it: Thane, "Working Class," p. 108.

95. Whiteside, "Private Provision and Public Welfare," pp. 29 f., 41.

96. Hogwood, *Trends in British Public Policy*, p. 38.

97. Hentschel, *Wirtschaft und Wirtschaftspolitik*, p. 150.

98. Butler and Butler, *British Political Facts*, pp. 332 f.

99. See in general Abelshauser (ed.), *Weimarer Republik*.

100. Abelshauser, "Germany," p. 127. Cf. Overy, *War and Economy in the Third Reich*.

101. Burleigh, *Third Reich*, pp. 219–51.

102. Chennells, Dilnot and Roback, "Survey of the UK Tax System," p. 21.

103. Crafts, *Conservative Government's Economic Record*, p. 23.

104. Kay and King, *British Tax System*, pp. 23, 196; Hogwood, *Trends in British Public Policy*, p. 102.

105. Ibid., pp. 101–3.

106. Ibid., p. 49. Cf. David Smith, "Treasury Relaxes its Grip," *Sunday Times*, 23 January 2000.

107. British health spending as a percentage of GDP was 6.8 per cent in 2000, compared with a weighted continental average of 9 per cent. The equivalent figure for the US and Canada is around 10 per cent: Seldon, *Dilemma of Democracy*, p. 52.

108. Figures from Mitchell and Deane, *Abstract of British Historical Statistics*, pp. 396–9; HM Treasury, *Financial Statement and Budget Report, 1999*.

109. Bonney, "Introduction," p. 18.

110. Duncan and Hobson, *Saturn's Children*, p. 59.

111. Dowrick, "Estimating the Impact of Government Consumption on Growth."

Chapter 4

1. Kennedy, *Rise and Fall of the Great Powers*, p. 681 and n.

2. *Financial Times*, 5–6 February 2000. In fact, Clinton was referring to all US debt *held by the public*, excluding the federal government account and the debt held by the Federal Reserve system. The difference is of the order of two trillion dollars.

3. "In the Red: A History of Debt 2000 BC–2000 AD," exhibition at the Ashmolean Museum, Oxford, January–April 2000.

4. Goldsmith, *Premodern Financial Systems*, p. 79.

5. Parker, "Emergence of Modern Finance," pp. 540–545.

6. The *monti* were originally charitable institutions which lent money to the poor at low interest: ibid., p. 534.

7. Hocquet, "Venice," p. 395, and "City-State and Market Economy," pp. 87–91; Parker, "Emergence of Modern Finance," p. 571.

8. Goldsmith, *Premodern Financial Systems*, pp. 157 ff., 164 f., 167 ff.

9. Partner, "Papacy," p. 369.

10. Hocquet, "City-State and Market Economy," pp. 91 f.; Parker, "Emergence of Modern Finance," p. 567. Importantly, the Church did not regard annuities as usurious.

11. Körner, "Public Credit," pp. 507 ff.

12. Muto, "Spanish System," pp. 246–9.

13. Parker, "Emergence of Modern Finance," p. 564.

14. Ormrod, "England in the Middle Ages," p. 37.

15. Ormrod, "West European Monarchies," pp. 122 ff.

16. Bosher, *French Finances*, p. 6; Körner, "Public Credit," p. 521; Schulze, "Sixteenth Century," p. 272; Parker, "Emergence of Modern Finance," p. 568; Hamilton, "Origin and Growth of the National Debt in Western Europe," p. 119; Velde and Weir, "Financial Market and Government Debt Policy in France," p. 7.

17. Bosher, *French Finances*, p. 23.

18. Muto, "Spanish System," pp. 246–9.

19. Neal, *Rise of Financial Capitalism*, pp. 1 ff.

20. Parker, "Emergence of Modern Finance," pp. 549, 571.

21. Capie, Goodhart and Schnadt, "Development of Central Banking," p. 7.

22. Crouzet, "Politics and Banking," pp. 27 f.

23. Ibid., p. 28. Cf. Bosher, *French Finances*, pp. 257 ff. Custine denounced the "fiscal agents" of the old regime as "bloodsuckers on the body politic . . .with fortunes made by the sweat and blood of the people": ibid., p. 262.

24. Crouzet, "Politics and Banking," pp. 36 ff.; Körner, "Public Credit," p. 530.

25. Crouzet, "Politics and Banking," p. 45.

26. Neal, "How It All Began," pp. 6–10.

27. North and Weingast, "Constitutions and Commitment," pp. 819–28.

28. Parker, "Emergence of Modern Finance," p. 581.

29. Neal, *Rise of Financial Capitalism*, pp. 1–43, 117.

30. Körner, "Public Credit," p. 536.

31. Calculated from figures in Mitchell and Deane, *Abstract of British Historical Statistics*, pp. 402 f.

32. Bordo and White, "Tale of Two Currencies."

33. Michie, *London Stock Exchange*, pp. 15–36.

34. Parker, "Emergence of Modern Finance," p. 575.

35. Ibid., p. 576.

36. See Bosher, *French Finances*, pp. 12–16.

37. Neal, "How It All Began," pp. 26–33.

38. Parker, "Emergence of Modern Finance," pp. 584 f.

39. Mirowski, "Rise (and Retreat) of a Market ," p. 569.

40. Parker, "Emergence of Modern Finance," p. 587.

41. Kindleberger, *Financial History*, pp. 59 ff.

42. Neal, "How It All Began," pp. 33 f.

43. Doyle, *Origins of the French Revolution*, p. 50.

44. Bonney, "France, 1494–1815," pp. 131 ff., 152 f.

45. Velde and Weir, "Financial Market and Government Debt Policy in France," pp. 3, 28–36. Cf. Wallerstein, *Modern World-System*, vol. iii, p. 84 n.

46. Doyle, *Origins of the French Revolution*, p. 48.

47. Ibid., p. 114.

48. White, "Making the French Pay," pp. 30 f.

49. Syrett and Cooke (eds.), *Papers of Alexander Hamilton*, vol. ii, pp. 244–45. I am grateful to Professor Richard Sylla for this reference.

50. Sylla, "US Financial System," *passim*. See also Brown, "Episodes in the Public Debt History," pp. 230–7.

51. Capie, Goodhart and Schnadt, "Development of Central Banking," p. 6.

52. Ibid., p. 68.

53. See in general, Cameron (ed.), *Banking*.

54. Parker, "Emergence of Modern Finance," pp. 565 f.

55. See Ferguson, *World's Banker*, passim.

56. In 1924 only around 12 per cent of the internal British national debt was held by small savers through savings banks and the Post Office, compared with 10 per cent held by banks other than the Bank of England, and five per cent held by insurance companies: Morgan, *Studies in British Financial Policy*, p. 136.

57. Quoted in Hynes, *War Imagined*, p. 432.

58. Ferguson, *Pity of War*, p. 225.

59. Feldman, *Great Disorder*, p. 48.

60. Ferguson, *Pity of War*, p. 325.

61. For evidence of waning public enthusiasm for new German War Loans, see Holtfrerich, *German Inflation*, p. 117. The worsening under-subscription suggests that the government was over-pricing the new bonds.

62. Goodhart, "Monetary Policy," p. 8.

63. Morgan, *Studies in British Financial Policy*, p. 140 and table 107. Cf. Bankers Trust Company, *English Public Finance*, p. 30.

64. Bankers Trust Company, *French Public Finance*, pp. 138 f.; Balderston, "War Finance," p. 227; Hardach, *First World War*, pp. 167 ff. Cf. Ferguson, *Pity of War*, ch. 11.

65. Goodhart, "Monetary Policy," p. 12.

66. Makinen and Woodward, "Funding Crises." The authors argue that the cause of the crises was a failure on the part of the authorities to raise the interest rates on treasury bills in line with market rates.

67. Alesina, "End of Large Public Debts," p. 49.

68. Broadberry and Howlett, "United Kingdom," p. 50.

69. Goodhart, "Monetary Policy," p. 8. The floating debt was larger in 1945/6 than in 1918/19 (27 per cent of the total debt compared with 19 per cent); on the other hand, the external debt had been much higher after the First World War (17 per cent of total debt, compared with less than 2 per cent). The term structure of the funded debt differed only slightly.

70. Rockoff, "United States," p. 108. Broad money growth was slightly higher in the US than in Britain: relative to 1938, M3 increased by a factor of 2.6, compared with a British figure of just 2.1. In the Soviet Union, too, the money stock rose by a factor of less than three between 1940 and 1945: Harrison, "Soviet Union," p. 277.

71. Hansemeyer, "Kriegswirtschaft," p. 417; Hara, "Japan," p. 258; Mitchell, *European Historical Statistics*, p. 359.

72. Goodhart, "Monetary Policy," pp. 13–32.

73. Calculated from the unpublished statistical annex of Goodhart, "Monetary Policy."

74. Kennedy, *Rise and Fall of the Great Powers*, pp. 103 ff.

75. Bonney, "Struggle for Great Power Status," pp. 368 f.

76. Doyle, *Origins of the French Revolution*, p. 43.

77. Bonney, "Struggle for Great Power Status," pp. 347 f., 351.

78. Ibid., pp. 341 f.

79. Hinsley, *Power and the Pursuit of Peace*, pp. 62 ff.

80. Clarke, "Keynes, Buchanan and the Balanced-Budget Doctrine," p. 66.

81. Brown, "Episodes in the Public Debt History," table 8.7.

82. Calculated from sources to table 2.

83. A calculation of the deficit as "net increase in debt" produces a much smaller figure of 1.5 per cent.

84. Cf. the figures in Broadberry and Howlett, "United Kingdom," p. 51; Zamagni, "Italy," p. 199; Harrison, "Soviet Union," p. 275; Hansemeyer, "Kriegswirtschaft," p. 400; Abelshauser, "Germany," p. 158; and Brown, "Episodes in the Public Debt History," pp. 249f. (net increase in the debt/GNP ratio).

85. Clarke, "Keynes, Buchanan and the Balanced-Budget Doctrine," p. 67 and table 4.1.

86. Ibid.

87. Congdon, "Keynesian Revolution," pp. 90 ff. As Samuel Brittan memorably put it: "[Conservative] Chancellors [between 1951 and 1964] behaved like simple Pavlovian dogs responding to two main stimuli: one was a 'run on the reserves' and the other was '500,000 unemployed.'"

88. Buchanan and Wagner, *Democracy in Deficit*; Buchanan, Wagner and Burton, *Consequences of Mr Keynes*.

89. Congdon, "Keynesian Revolution," p. 99; Sargent, "Stopping Moderate Inflations," p. 144.

90. Goldsmith, *Premodern Financial Systems*, p. 107.

91. Ibid., pp. 214 ff.

92. Braudel, *Civilization and Capitalism*, vol. iii, p. 307.

93. Goldsmith, *Premodern Financial Systems*, p. 194.

94. Körner, "Swiss Confederation," pp. 337, 348 ff.

95. Barro, "Government Spending," p. 239 n., arrives at a lower figure, peaking at 185 per cent, by adjusting for the fact that in the period up to 1815 large amounts of debt were issued at a discount to yield 5 per cent but were counted in the reported debt total as though issued at par; but for the sake of consistency and in conformity with modern conventions I have used the official debt figure.

96. Stockmar, *Memoirs*, vol. i, p. 44.

97. Bonney, "Struggle for Great Power Status," p. 345.

98. Bosher, *French Finances*, pp. 23 f., 255 f. Braudel, *Civilization and Capitalism*, vol. iii, p. 307. For earlier figures c.1715 see White, "France and the Failure to Modernise," p. 27.

99. Brown, "Episodes in the Public Debt History."

100. Calculated from OECD figures.

101. *Financial Times*, 21 July 2000.

102. Dickens, *David Copperfield*, p. 170.

103. Quoted in Eltis, "Debts, Deficits," p. 117; cf. Winch, "Political Economy," pp. 13 ff.

104. Quoted in Eltis, "Debts, Deficits," pp. 117 f.

105. Smith, *Wealth of Nations*, bk. II, ch. 3. Marx took the opposite view.

106. Quoted in Winch, "Political Economy," p. 18.

107. Quoted in Anderson, "Loans versus Taxes," p. 314.

108. Quoted in Maloney, "Gladstone," p. 30.

109. Anderson, "Loans versus Taxes," p. 325.

110. Hamilton, "Origin and Growth of the National Debt in Western Europe," p. 129.

111. Quoted in Winch, "Political Economy," p. 14; cf. Bonney, "Introduction," p. 14.

112. Quoted in Winch, "Political Economy," p. 20.

113. Quoted in Sylla, "US Financial System," p. 255.

114. See the summary of the various theories in Cavaco-Silva, "Economic Effects," pp. 16–23.

115. Gale, "Efficient Design."

116. See most recently Neal, "How It All Began," pp. 19–25.

117. Quoted in Hamilton, "Origin and Growth of the National Debt in Western Europe," p. 121.

118. Barro, "Determination of Public Debt." Cf. Barro, *Macroeconomics*, pp. 373, 377. The idea is often referred to as "Ricardian equivalence theorem," though Ricardo only raises the issue casually in his *Funding System* (1820) and dismisses it elsewhere as unrealistic. The theory nevertheless has come to bear his name. Cf. Eltis, "Debts, Deficits," p. 121; Barro, "Reflections," p. 49.

119. Barro, "Are Government Bonds Net Wealth?," p. 1095.

120. Barro, "Government Spending," p. 237.

121. Quoted in Anderson, "Loans versus Taxes," pp. 317, 326.

122. The term "sinking fund" dates back to 1717, when legislation was introduced creating sinking funds for specific Bank of England, South Sea and other loans. These were consolidated into a single fund in 1718. The principle was that each year a payment should be made out of current revenue to reduce the debt in question.

123. Clarke, "Keynes, Buchanan and the Balanced-Budget Doctrine," pp. 66ff.

124. Congdon, "Keynesian Revolution," pp. 100 ff. On this basis, Congdon argues that there was a "slightly more" Keynesian era of fiscal policy between 1949 and 1974, when fiscal policy was counter-cyclical in 15 of 26 years, and a slightly less Keynesian era between 1975 to 1994, when policy was counter-cyclical in only 10 out of 20 years.

125. See esp. Kotlikoff, *Generational Accounting*, and "From Deficit Delusion to the Fiscal Balance Rule."

126. See Cardarelli, Sefton and Kotlikoff, "Generational Accounting in the UK," p. 22.

127. Kotlikoff and Leibfritz, "International Comparison of Generational Accounts."

128. Kennedy, *Rise and Fall of the Great Powers*, p. 69.

129. Ibid., p. 73.

130. Körner, "Expenditure," pp. 402 ff.

131. Partner, "Papacy," p. 369.

132. Capra, "Finances of the Austrian Monarchy," p. 297 ff.

133. Hocquet, "City-State and Market Economy," pp. 91 ff.

134. Gelabert, "Castile," pp. 208 ff. Cf. Parker, "Emergence of Modern Finance," p. 570.

135. Hart, "United Provinces," pp. 311 f. See also Kennedy, *Rise and Fall of the Great Powers*, pp. 100 f. for the argument that the Dutch system discouraged entrepreneurship and pushed up labour costs.

136. Bonney, "France, 1494–1815," p. 148; Bonney, "Struggle for Great Power Status," p. 347; Doyle, *Origins of the French Revolution*, p. 43; White, "France and the Failure to Modernize," p. 26.

137. Calculated from figures in Mitchell and Deane, *Abstract of British Historical Statistics*, pp. 386–91. Cf. Bonney, "Struggle for Great Power Status," p. 345; Kennedy, *Rise and Fall of the Great Powers*, p. 109.

Chapter 5

1. Goethe, *Faust*, Part Two, Act I, pp. 70 ff.

2. Ferguson, *Paper and Iron*, p. 87.

3. Ibid., p. 430.

4. Feldman, *Great Disorder*, p. 27.

5. Goethe, *Faust*, Part Two, Act I, pp. 72 f.

6. Ibid., Act IV, p. 222.

7. ONS, quoted in *Daily Telegraph*, 11 June 1999.

8. Brown, "Episodes in the Public Debt History," p. 231.

9. Ibid.

10. Alesina, "End of Large Public Debts," p. 36.

11. Eichengreen, "Capital Levy."

12. Ferguson, *Paper and Iron*, pp. 276 f.

13. Ormrod, "West European Monarchies," pp. 112 ff.

14. Henneman, "France in the Middle Ages," p. 108.

15. A true bankruptcy was the case of the Swiss Count Michel of Gruyäre, who lost his lands as a result in 1555.

16. In 1557, 1560, 1575, 1596, 1607, 1627, 1647, 1652, 1662, 1665, 1692, 1693, 1695 and 1696.

17. Körner, "Public Credit," pp. 520, 524 f.; Muto, "Spanish System," pp. 246–9; Gelabert, "Castile," pp. 208 ff. See also Hart, "Seventeenth Century," pp. 268 f.; Parker, "Emergence of Modern Finance," pp. 568 f.

18. Bonney, "France, 1494–1815," pp. 131 ff.

19. Velde and Weir, "Financial Market and Government Debt," p. 8.

20. Ibid., pp. 8 f.

21. White, "France and the Failure to Modernize," pp. 24 f.

22. Quoted in Eltis, "Debts, Deficits," p. 117.

23. Parker, "Emergence of Modern Finance," p. 579.

24. Brown, "Episodes in the Public Debt History," pp. 232 f.

25. Körner, "Public Credit," pp. 525, 527.

26. Hart, "United Provinces," p. 313.

27. Buxton, *Finance and Politics*, vol. i, pp. 30 n, 34, 64, 116, 125 n, 127 f.; vol. ii, pp. 307 f. Cf. Kindleberger, *Financial History*, pp. 166 ff., 221.

28. Capie, Mills and Wood, "Debt Management." I am grateful to professor Forrest Capie for his assistance on this point.

29. Ibid., p. 1116.

30. Ferguson, *World's Banker*, ch. 4.

31. Alesina, "End of Large Public Debts," p. 64.

32. Williams (ed.), *Money*, pp. 16 ff.

33. Goldsmith, *Premodern Financial Systems*, pp. 36 f.

34. White, "France and the Failure to Modernize," p. 20.

35. Bonney, "Revenues," p. 467. Cf. Henneman, "France in the Middle Ages," p. 105 f.

36. Goldsmith, *Premodern Financial Systems*, p. 178.

37. Bonney, "France, 1494–1815," p. 142.

38. Isenmann, "Medieval and Renaissance Theories of State Finance," p. 36.

39. Williams, *Tudor Regime*, pp. 67 f.

40. Bonney, "Early Modern Theories of State Finance," p. 167.

41. Neal, "How It All Began," p. 7; Goldsmith, *Premodern Financial Systems*, pp. 211 f.

42. Quin, "Gold, Silver and the Glorious Revolution."

43. Kindleberger, *Financial History*, pp. 59 ff.; Cooper, "Gold Standard," p. 3; Quin, "Gold, Silver and the Glorious Revolution," p. 489. This was not the only way in which the Dutch and British systems diverged. The Bank of England did not develop the near-monopoly on domestic and international payments enjoyed by its counterpart in Amsterdam.

44. Bordo and Kydland, "Gold Standard as a Commitment Mechanism," p. 71.

45. Sylla, "US Financial System," p. 252. The 1690 Massachusetts bills of credit were the first Western paper currency; the Bank of England's printed non-interest-bearing banknotes came later. The Bank of Stockholm had anticipated the innovation but had folded in 1663, just seven years after opening its doors: Körner, "Public Credit," p. 531.

46. White, "France and the Failure to Modernize," p. 21.

47. Bonney, "Revenues," p. 470; Körner, "Public Credit," p. 535.

48. Crouzet, "Politics and Banking," p. 28.

49. Hellie, "Russia," p. 500.

50. Gelabert, "Castile," p. 233.

51. Bonney, "Struggle for Great Power Status," pp. 361 f.

52. This pejorative phrase referred not only to venal offices, but also the outstanding debts to tax farmers, office-holders and the clergy, as well as the feudal dues which the National Assembly had abolished.

53. Bosher, *French Finances*, p. 275.

54. Crouzet, "Politics and Banking," pp. 23, 33.

55. Bonney, "Struggle for Great Power Status," p. 383.

56. Crouzet, "Politics and Banking," p. 47.

57. Bonney, "Struggle for Great Power Status," pp. 364, 368; Bonney, "Revenues," p. 464.

58. Thompson (ed.), *Napoleon's Letters*, p. 215.

59. Bordo and White, "Tale of Two Currencies."

60. Only about 10 per cent of the Confederacy's expenditures were covered by taxes; some $2 billion was borrowed, most of it by money creation: Brown, "Episodes in the Public Debt History," p. 233.

61. Brandt, "Public Finances of Neo-absolutism in Austria," p. 100.

62. Good, *Economic Rise of the Habsburg Empire*, tables 12, 29.

63. Bordo and Rockoff, "Good Housekeeping," p. 327. For a good overview, Bordo, "Gold as a Commitment Mechanism," table 1.

64. Flandreau, Le Cacheux and Zumer, "Stability Without a Pact," pp. 146 f.

65. Canetti, *Torch in My Ear*, pp. 51 f.

66. Ferguson, *Paper and Iron*, p. 432.

67. "Kennst du das Land, wo die Devisen blühn, / in dunkler Nacht die Nepplokale glühn? Ein eis'ger Wind vom nahen Abgrund weht—/ wo tief die Mark und hoch der Dollar steht": quoted in Rowley, *Hyperinflation*, p. 182.

68. For the classic definition of a rate of inflation of 50 per cent per month or more, see Cagan, "Monetary Dynamics."

69. Calculated from NBER series 04073.

70. Sargent, "Ends of Four Big Inflations." See also id., "Stopping Moderate Inflations."

71. Ferguson, *Pity of War*, p. 422.

72. The motto on the medal read: "*Geld gab ich zu Wehr; Eisen nehme ich zu Ehre.*"

73. Alesina, "End of Large Public Debts," p. 49.

74. Capie, "Conditions in which Very Rapid Inflation has Occured," pp. 138 f. Capie suggests a link between hyperinflation and "civil war or revolution or at a minimum serious social unrest:" p. 144.

75. Broadberry and Howlett, "United Kingdom," p. 50.

76. The classic monetarist account is Friedman and Schwartz, *Monetary Trends*.

77. Correlation coefficients between the inflation rate and monetary growth rates:

Indicator	Coefficient	Period
Broad money growth	0.62	1871–1997
Narrow money growth	0.51	1871–1997

78. Though the theoretical argument for such a role had been made as early as 1802 by Henry Thornton: see Capie, "Lender of Last Resort," p. 14.

79. See Bordo, "Traditional Approach," pp. 27–67.

80. That is, the rate at which the Bank discounted commercial bills, which were the commonest credit instrument in the nineteenth-century City. This rate was usually referred to as "Bank rate."

81. The 1844 "Act to regulate the Issue of Bank Notes, and for Giving to the Governor and Company of the Bank of England certain Privileges for a limited Period" (7 & 8 Vict. c. 32) divided the Bank into Issue and Banking Departments: Clapham, *Bank of England*, vol. ii, pp. 183 f.

82. The reserve was that part of the Bank's gold which was not needed to cover the difference between the notes outside the Bank and the statutory fiduciary issue.

83. Palgrave, *Bank Rate*, p. 218.

84. Eichengreen, *Golden Fetters*, p. 65. See also id., "Gold Standard since Alec Ford," p. 66.

85. Sayers, *Bank of England*, vol. i, p. 29.

86. Palgrave, *Bank Rate*, p. 218.

87. Bagehot, *Lombard Street*, pp 56 f.

88. Between January 1880 and July 1914 Bank rate fell below the market discount rate in only ten months (May 1893, August and September and December 1899, April and December 1900, September and October 1906, September 1910 and August 1912). This was in marked contrast to the years 1845–7, 1857, 1865 and 1867–71, when Bank rate had tended to be below the market rate: Palgrave, *Bank Rate*, table 4. Significantly, the frequency of changes in Bank rate declined from its peak of 109 times in the 1870s to 65 times in the 1880s, 62 times in the 1890s and just 48 times between 1900 and 1909.

89. Capie, "Lender of Last Resort," pp. 4–6.

90. Ferguson, *World's Banker*, appendix 3.

91. Capie, Goodhart and Schnadt, "Development of Central Banking," p. 13.

92. Palgrave, *Bank Rate*, p. 104.

93. Clapham, quoted in Sayers, *Bank of England*, vol. i, p. 9. Between 1880 and 1913 the ratio of the monetary gold stock to the monetary base was just 17 per cent. It was higher in 1922–39 (27 per cent), 1948–58 (34 per cent) and 1959–71 (22 per cent), and only slightly lower in the post-gold period 1972–90: Bordo and Schwartz, "Changing Relationship," table 2, p. 39.

94. Sayers, *Bank of England*, vol. i, pp. 38 ff. Cf. Drummond, *Gold Standard*, pp. 21 f.; Capie, Goodhart and Schnadt, "Development of Central Banking," p. 13.

95. Dutton, "Bank of England," p. 191.

96. Pippenger, "Bank of England Operations," pp. 216 f.

97. Capie, "Lender of Last Resort," pp. 8 f. Cf. Schwartz, "Real and Pseudo-financial Crises."

98. Indeed, the term "lender of last resort" was coined by Francis Baring as early as

1797, though Capie traces it back to the French *dernier resort*, meaning the ultimate legal authority: Capie, "Lender of Last Resort," p. 17.

99. There is a parallel here with the rescue of Long Term Capital Management in New York in 1998. For a full discussion of the Barings Crisis, see Ferguson, *World's Banker*, ch. 27.

100. Capie, Goodhart and Schnadt, "Development of Central Banking," pp. 16 f. See also Capie, "Lender of Last Resort," pp. 11 f.

101. The distinction which is frequently drawn between bailing out one institution, and providing liquidity to the financial system as a whole, is somewhat artificial. As Bagehot recognized, the failure of one big institution would be very likely to cause a general liquidity crisis: Capie, "Lender of Last Resort," pp. 16, 18.

102. Bordo and Schwartz, "Changing Relationship," pp. 11, 36.

103. Borchardt, "Währung und Wirtschaft," p. 17.

104. Bordo and Schwartz, "Monetary Policy Regimes," p. 26.

105. Capie, Goodhart and Schnadt, "Development of Central Banking," p. 53.

106. James, *Globalization and its Sins*, p. 37.

107. Holtfrerich, "Reichsbankpolitik."

108. On Schacht see esp. James, *Reichsbank*.

109. See in general Eichengreen, *Golden Fetters*.

110. The classic account is Friedman and Schwartz, *Monetary History*. For a critical assessment see Romer and Romer, "Does Monetary Policy Matter?," pp. 32–5. Cf. Bordo and Schwartz, "Monetary Policy Regimes," pp. 30 ff., 44, 64 f.

111. Bordo and Schwartz, "Monetary Policy Regimes," p. 45.

112. Capie, Goodhart and Schnadt, "Development of Central Banking," pp. 22 f.

113. The Federal Reserve is owned by the member banks of the System; only 10 per cent of the Greek central bank's shares and 25 per cent of its Turkish counterpart's are in state hands. The Swiss central bank is majority-owned by the cantons: Capie, Goodhart and Schnadt, "Development of Central Banking," p. 56.

114. Ibid., p. 54.

115. Ibid., pp. 25 f.

116. Romer and Romer, "Does Monetary Policy Matter?"

117. Between 1963 and 1974 the average annual federal deficit was just 0.6 per cent of GDP: Masson and Mussa, "Long-term Tendencies."

118. Feldstein, "Costs and Benefits."

119. Solow and Taylor, *Inflation, Unemployment and Monetary Policy*.

120. Bruno and Easterly, "Inflation Crises and Long-run Growth," esp. pp. 4–6, 20–22; Sarel, "Non-linear Effects of Inflation."

121. Briault, "Costs of Inflation."

122. Bordo and Schwartz, "Monetary Policy Regimes," p. 56.

123. Millard, "Examination of the Monetary Transmission Mechanism." Cf. Lawson, *View from No. 11*.

124. *Economist*, 25 September 1999.

125. See e.g. Luttwak, *Turbo-Capitalism*, pp. 191–6.

126. Capie, Goodhart and Schnadt, "Development of Central Banking," p. 6; King, "Challenges for Monetary Policy," p. 1.

127. Marsh, *Bundesbank*.

128. Independence is defined by Capie, Goodhart and Schnadt, "Development of Central Banking," p. 50, as "the right to change the key operational instrument without consultation or challenge from government."

129. See e.g. Cukierman *et al.*, "Central Bank Independence"; Alesina and Summers, "Central Bank Independence."

130. Wood, "Central Bank Independence," pp. 10 f.

131. For a critique of this reform, see Gowland, "Banking on Change."

132. Posen, "Why Central Bank Independence Does Not Cause Low Inflation."

133. King, "Challenges for Monetary Policy," pp. 29 f. For evidence of the European Central Bank's concern on this score, see its *Report on Electronic Money*, August 1998. I am grateful to Martin Thomas for this reference.

134. Friedman, "Future of Monetary Policy."

135. Capie, Goodhart and Schnadt, "Development of Central Banking," p. 35.

136. These are Charles Goodhart's arguments, as summarized in *The Economist*, 22 July 2000.

137. Capie, Goodhart and Schnadt, "Development of Central Banking," pp. 85–91.

Chapter 6

1. Homer and Sylla, *Interest Rates*, pp. 118–21.

2. Shakespeare, *Merchant of Venice*, Act I, scene 3.

3. Benjamin and Kochin, "War, Prices and Interest Rates."

4. Correlation coefficients between the yield on consols and other monetary and financial indicators:

Indicator	Coefficient	Period
Broad money growth	0.59	1872–1997
Narrow money growth	0.32	1872–1997
Inflation	0.39	1727–1997
Debt interest	0.14	1727–1997
Financial Surplus	-0.09	1727–1997
Primary Surplus	-0.04	1727–1997
Debt/GNP ratio	-0.23	1727–1997
Real rate of growth	-0.03	1831–1997

5. Barro, "Government Spending," p. 228. As we shall see, these two factors are more historically plausible explanations for yield fluctuations. Note that with inflation close to zero over the long run nominal consol yields can be regarded as more or less the same as real interest rates. Regressions of annual yield data against debt/GDP ratios for six countries in the period 1880–1913 also produce mainly negative or

spurious results: Ferguson and Batley, "Event Risk." Only the French data bear out the relationship we would expect, namely a positive relationship between debt and yield levels, although this is not evident at a significant level.

6. See e.g. Charles Davenant's *Discourses on the Public Revenues and on the Trade of England* (1698): Bonney, "Early Modern Theories of State Finance," pp. 181 f.

7. Only Argentina had an extremely strong (0.98) positive correlation between the debt burden and bond yields: I am grateful to Richard Batley for his assistance on this point.

8. Figures from OECD.

9. Bordo and Dewald, "Historical Bond Market Inflation Credibility."

10. Keynes, *General Theory*, pp. 167 f.

11. Musgrave and Musgrave, *Public Finance in Theory and Practice*, pp. 544–64; Buckle and Thompson, *UK Financial System*, pp. 180–99.

12. Masson and Mussa, "Long-Term Tendencies," p. 28.

13. Ibid., pp. 28 f. The question then becomes which falls further in response to a fiscal tightening: the real interest rate or growth. Cf. Eltis, "Debts, Deficits," pp. 126–9.

14. In fact, there are two quite different real interest rates: the *ex ante* rate, which is the difference between the nominal rate of interest and the expected rate of inflation (usually inferred from survey evidence); and the *ex post* rate, the nominal rate less the actual inflation rate: Mishkin, "Real Rate of Interest," p. 152. Perhaps not surprisingly, negative real interest rates are more frequent *ex post* than *ex ante*: King, "Challenges for Monetary Policy," pp. 8 f.

15. Alesina, "End of Large Public Debts," p. 57.

16. Tanzi and Lutz, "Interest Rates," pp. 233 ff. But cf. Dornbusch, "Debt and Monetary Policy," p. 18.

17. Shigehara, "Commentary," p. 87 n.

18. See Barro and Sala-i-Martin, "World Real Interest Rates."

19. Brown, "Episodes," table 8.8.

20. Goodhart, "Monetary Policy," p. 5.

21. Sargent and Wallace, "Unpleasant Monetarist Arithmetic." See also Woodford, "Control of the Public Debt"; Taylor, "Monetary Policy Implications."

22. King, "Commentary," pp. 176 f.; Dornbusch, "Debt and Monetary Policy," p. 14. A further complication is that if bondholders are numerous, higher interest rates may boost their incomes and hence have a perverse expansionary effect: Taylor, "Monetary Policy Implications."

23. Sargent, "Stopping Moderate Inflations," p. 121.

24. Barro, "Optimal Funding Policy," p. 77; Alesina, "End of Large Public Debts."

25. Goodhart, "Monetary Policy," p. 43.

26. *Statistical Abstract of the United States 2000*, table 552.

27. *Financial Times*, 13 October 1999.

28. Brown and Easton, "Weak-form Efficiency," p. 61.

29. Körner, "Public Credit," p. 515.

30. Goldsmith, *Premodern Financial Systems*, p. 170.

31. Körner, "Public Credit," p. 520. However, it is worth noting that the *asientos* were short-term debt instruments. By comparison, Naples long-term *juros* tended to pay more like 10 per cent; while yields on Spanish *juros* fell from 10 to 5 per cent in the course of the sixteenth century.

32. Hart, "United Provinces," pp. 311 ff.; Parker, "Emergence of Modern Finance," p. 573.

33. Körner, "Public Credit," p. 523.

34. Velde and Weir, "Financial Market and Government Debt Policy in France," p. 23.

35. The phrase is James Riley's, quoted in Velde and Weir, "Financial Market and Government Debt Policy in France," p. 37.

36. White, "France and the Failure to Modernize," pp. 31 f.

37. Velde and Weir, "Financial Market and Government Debt Policy in France," pp. 20f. See also p. 23.

38. Ibid., pp. 18, 28. There was no differential in private rates of return. See also White, "Failure to Modernize."

39. Kennedy, *Rise and Fall of the Great Powers*, pp. 103 ff.

40. Quoted in Bonney, "France, 1494–1815," p. 136; id., "Early Modern Theories of State Finance," p. 204.

41. North and Weingast, "Constitutions and Commitment."

42. Wells and Wills, "Revolution, Restoration and Debt Repudiation."

43. Velde and Weir, "Financial Market and Government Debt Policy in France," p. 25.

44. Ibid., p. 37. The authors argue, ingeniously, that Louis XVI could have avoided the revolution by opting for default.

45. Bordo and White, "Tale of Two Currencies," p. 371.

46. White, "Making the French Pay," pp. 11 f.

47. See Balderston, *German Economic Crisis*, pp. 250–265.

48. Borchardt, "Gewicht der Inflationsangst"; Schulz, "Inflationstrauma." See most recently Voth, "True Cost of Inflation."

49. Abelshauser, "Germany," pp. 139 ff. The Metallurgische Forschungsgesellschaft mbH (Mefo) issued bills to pay the major arms concerns for contracts which were in fact from the government. By 1937/8 they had reached a circulation of 12 billion reichsmarks.

50. Alesina, "End of Large Public Debts," p. 62. A somewhat similar role to that of the German Mefo was played by the Italian Consorzio Sovvenzioni su Valori Industriali during the Second World War: Zamagni, "Italy," p. 200.

51. Eichengreen, "Discussion," pp. 83 f.

52. I have not calculated annual averages for short-term interest rates, though this could also be done. For annual averages or means of monthly short-term interest rates from 1824 until 1938, see Mitchell and Deane, *Abstract of British Historical Statistics*, p. 460. Figures for the period before 1824 would not be illuminating because there was a usury ceiling of 5 per cent from 1714 until 1833, though this ceased to be an effective constraint from around 1817.

53. The famous cartoon by James Gillray was published on 22 May 1797.

54. Millard, "Examination of the Monetary Transmission Mechanism."

55. The largest monthly percentage increases/decreases in the yield on consols, 1754–1998:

Rises		Falls	
Nov. 1792	14.76	Sept.1977	-17.84
March 1778	14.73	Oct. 1801	-13.76
March 1803	14.49	June 1919	-13.65
June 1974	12.88	March 1979	-12.32
March 1814	12.15	Aug. 1762	-12.24

56. The source for this and the following calculations is NBER series 11021.

57. Gilbert, *Twentieth Century*, vol. i, p. 690

58. German public sector yields for the period 1928–35 are taken from E. Wagemann, *Konjunkturstatistisches Jahrbuch* (1936), p. 113. I am grateful to Dr Joachim Voth for supplying this series.

59. Frey and Kucher, "History as Reflected in Capital Markets," esp. pp. 478 f.

60. Capie, Goodhart and Schnadt, "Development of Central Banking," p. 30. All calculations from the series for "Long-Term U.S. Government Securities; Including Flower Bonds, Board of Governors," Federal Reserve Bank of St Louis website.

61. Calculated from data in *The Economist*.

62. Ibid., 31 March 1848.

63. Ibid., 17 November 1854.

64. Ibid., 29 April 1859.

65. Lipman, "The City and the 'People's Budget'," pp. 68ff. The "bid-ask spread" is the spread between prices sought by sellers of bonds and the prices buyers are willing to pay.

Chapter 7

1. Cobbett, *Rural Rides*, p. 121.

2. Zola, *L'Assommoir*, pp. 24–7.

3. Kaelble, *Industrialisation and Social Inequality*, table 1.5.

4. Feinstein, "Pessimism Perpetuated," appendix.

5. Rubinstein, "British Millionaires," pp. 207–9.

6. See in general Cannadine, *Class in Britain*.

7. Heine, "Lutetia," in *Sämtliche Schriften*, vol. v, pp. 448 ff.

8. Körner, "Public Credit," p. 510.

9. Heffer, *Carlyle*, pp. 263 f.

10. Hocquet, "City-State and Market Economy," pp. 87–91.

11. Goldsmith, *Premodern Financial Systems*, pp. 167 ff.

12. Ormrod, "England in the Middle Ages," p. 136.

13. Schultz and Weingast, "Democratic Advantage," pp. 11, 24 f.

14. Körner, "Public Credit," p. 529.

15. Bosher, *French Finances*, pp. 262, 265.

16. Hamilton, "Origin and Growth of the National Debt in Western Europe," p. 121.

17. North and Weingast, "Constitutions and Commitment."

18. Cobbett, *Rural Rides*, p. 150.

19. Ibid., pp. 117, 38, 183; 66; 160; 47; 34, 53.

20. Ibid., p. 92.

21. Ibid., p. 117.

22. Marx, *Capital*, bk. I, ch. 31.

23. Heine, "Ludwig Börne" in *Sämtliche Schriften*, vol. iv, p. 28.

24. Pulzer, *Rise of Political Anti-Semitism*, pp. 43 ff.

25. Lane and Rupp (eds.), *Nazi Ideology before 1933*, pp. 31 f.

26. On the political background, see Hilton, *Corn, Cash and Commerce*.

27. I am grateful to J. F. Wright of Trinity College, Oxford, for providing me with his figures, based on his research in the Bank of England archives.

28. See Ch. 2. On the US, see Brown, "Episodes in the Public Debt History," p. 235.

29. Gallarotti, *Anatomy*.

30. Eichengreen, *Golden Fetters*, ch. 1.

31. Gladstone's purchases of Ottoman loans secured on the Egyptian tribute to Turkey—which yielded a handsome profit following the British occupation of Egypt which he himself ordered—were typical of the age: see ch. 9.

32. Buxton, *Finance and Politics*, vol. i, p. 30.

33. Lipman, "The City and the 'People's Budget.'" The events of 1830 and 1909–10 are explored in more detail in Ferguson, *World's Banker*, chs. 8 and 29.

34. Bordo and Rockoff, "Good Housekeeping," pp. 319 f.

35. Flandreau, Le Cacheux and Zumer, "Stability Without a Pact?"

36. Maier, *Recasting Bourgeois Europe*. See also id., "Politics of Inflation."

37. Alesina, "End of Large Public Debts," pp. 38 f.

38. Ibid., p. 40.

39. For an illuminating discussion see Maier, "Interest Representation," pp. 247–60.

40. McKibbin, "Class and Conventional Wisdom."

41. Keynes, *Tract on Monetary Reform*, pp. 3, 29, 36.

42. Graham, *Exchange, Prices and Production*, esp. pp. 289, 318–21, 324.

43. Holtfrerich, *German Inflation*, pp. 271–8.

44. Feldman, *Great Disorder*, pp. 46 f., 816–19.

45. Wormell, *Management of the National Debt*, p. 662.

46. Morgan, *Studies in British Financial Policy*, p. 135.

47. Ibid., p. 136.

48. Balderston, "War Finance," p. 236.

49. Bordo and Rockoff, "Adherence to the Gold Standard."

50. Keynes, *Economic Consequences*, pp. 220–233.

51. Keynes, *Tract on Monetary Reform*, pp. 3, 29.

52. See Feldman, *Great Disorder*, passim; Ferguson, *Paper and Iron*, pp. 419–33.

53. Keynes, *How to Pay for the War*, pp. 57–74.

54. Cf. Dornbusch, "Debt and Monetary Policy," pp. 11, 15. Dornbusch puts the average real yield on consols between 1946 and 1980 at just 0.48 per cent.

55. *Social Trends 1995*, table 5.9.

56. Benefits include contributory as well as non-contributory cash payments, education, health care, housing subsidies, travel subsidies and school meals. Taxes include income tax, national insurance, local taxes and indirect taxes.

57. I am grateful to Martin Wolf of the *Financial Times* for this quotation.

58. Duncan and Hobson, *Saturn's Children*, p. 77; cf. pp. 50, 52, 67.

59. Micklethwait and Wooldridge, *Future Perfect*, p. 151.

60. See Goodin *et al.*, *Real World of Welfare Capitalism*; Atkinson, *Economic Consequences*.

61. See e.g. Freeman, "Single Peaked vs. Diversified Capitalism."

62. *Social Trends 1995*, table 5.12.

63. Jamieson, *British Economy*, p. 182.

64. Figures from Bank of England website. Cf. Goodhart, "Monetary Policy," p. 43, table 8.

65. Ibid., pp. 41 f.

66. *The Economist*, 10 January 1998.

67. Boskin, "Federal Deficits," p. 78. Other assumptions necessary for the "Ricardian" model are that households are rational, that capital markets are perfect, that future income and tax shares are known, that taxes are lump sum and that the transaction costs for issuing and redeeming bonds are zero: Velthoven, Verbon and Van Winden, "Political Economy," pp. 9 ff.

68. Musgrave, "Public Debt," p. 144.

69. Broadway and Wildasin, "Long Term Debt Strategy," p. 64.

70. The following section draws heavily on Ferguson and Kotlikoff, "Degeneration of EMU."

71. It is assumed that each successive generation's lifetime net tax payment (their generational account) is x percent larger than that of the previous generation, where x is the economy's growth rate of real wages per hour. Future rates of population growth and economic growth are based on official projections.

72. Barro, *Macroeconomics*, p. 383.

73. Kotlikoff and Raffelheuschen, "Generational Accounting," also offer figures showing the necessary cuts in government purchases (as opposed to transfers).

74. Anyone who doubts this should consider that, if policy remains unchanged, the share of the federal budget which is consumed by social security spending is set to rise from just over a fifth (20.8 per cent) to only slightly less than a third (32.4 per cent) by 2030.

75. Deutsche Bundesbank, "Opinion," tables 3 and 4.

76. Cardarelli, Sefton and Kotlikoff "Generational Accounting in the UK."

77. Peterson, "Grey Dawn."

78. *The Economist*, 10 June 2000.

79. Ibid., 4 March 2000.

80. According to Kotlikoff and Raffelheuschen, "Generational Accounting," Thailand could—and indeed should—more than double government transfers in order to achieve generational balance. Alternatively, it could cut all taxes by 25 per cent, or virtually abolish income tax altogether.

81. Broadway and Wildasin, "Long Term Debt Strategy," p. 39.

82. Tabellini, "Politics of Intergenerational Redistribution," p. 70.

83. Daykin, "Funding the Future," pp. 22 f.

84. Stein, "Mounting Debts," pp. 32–5.

85. Lawson, *View from No. 11*, p. 37.

86. Butler, *British General Elections*, pp. 69 f.

87. Jones and Kavanagh, *British Politics Today*, p. 90.

88. Coxall and Robins, *Contemporary British Politics*, p. 156.

89. Butler and Kavanagh, *British General Election*, pp. 81, 108, 236.

90. McMorrow and Roeger, "Economic Consequences of Ageing Populations," p. 66.

91. Jeremy Harding, "The Uninvited," London Review of Books, 3 February 2000, p. 3.

92. Stephan Thernstrom, "Plenty of Room for All," *Times Literary Supplement*, 26 May 2000.

93. *The Economist*, 8 July 2000.

94. James, *Globalization and its Sins*, p. 195.

95. Ibid. esp. p. 168. See also O'Rourke and Williamson, *Globalization and History*.

Chapter 8

1. Trollope, *Can You Forgive Her*, ch. XII.

2. Trollope, *Phineas Finn*, p. 49.

3. Mullen, *Trollope*, p. 514.

4. Hanham, *Elections and Party Management*, pp. 265 f., 277.

5. Trollope, *The Prime Minister*, pp. 285–98, and *The Duke's Children*, pp. 84–92.

6. See e.g. *Financial Times*, 11 Feb. 1999.

7. Norpoth, "Economy," p. 299.

8. Hanham, *Elections and Party Management*, p. 228 f.

9. Blake, *Disraeli*, p. 719.

10. Hennessy, *Never Again*, p. 427.

11. Horne, *Macmillan*, pp. 64 f. It is often forgotten that Macmillan went on to warn of the danger of inflation: "the problem of rising prices."

12. Ibid., p. 336.

13. Lewis-Beck, *Economics and Elections*, p. 13

14. Castle, *Diaries*, p. 631.

15. Ibid., p. 342.

16. Thatcher, *Downing Street Years*, p. 153.

17. Ibid., p. 560, 567.

18. Lawson, *View from No. 11*, p. 694. See also Tebbit, *Upwardly Mobile*, p. 161,

200 ff., 254; Fowler, *Ministers Decide*, pp. 282 f.; Baker, *Turbulent Years*, pp. 269, 277.

19. Ridley, *Style of Government*, p. 221. See also pp. 21, 86, 196.

20. King *et al.*, *New Labour Triumphs*, p. 228. Cf. Peter Kellner, "Major's Farewell to Feelgood Factor," *Observer*, 30 March 1997.

21. *You Can Only Be Sure With the Conservatives: The Conservative Manifesto 1997*, p. 7.

22. Saatchi, "Happiness Can't Buy Money," p. 13.

23. *The Times*, 24 April 1997.

24. *Today* programme, BBC Radio 4, 21 Feb. 1999.

25. *Financial Times*, 10 April 1997.

26. Will Hutton, *Observer*, 30 March 1997.

27. See Butler and Kavanagh, *British General Election*, p. 303. Cf. David Butler, "The Spinner's Web," *Times Literary Supplement*, 15 Jan. 1999.

28. Saatchi, "Happiness Can't Buy Money," p. 14.

29. Castle, *Diaries*, p. 93

30. The indicator used was the Bank of England base rate or Minimum Lending Rate at end of month.

31. Downs, *Economic Theory*, pp. 20, 28.

32. Nordhaus, "Political Business Cycle."

33. Tufte, *Political Control*, p. 12.

34. Brittan, "Excessive Expectations," p. 251.

35. Jay, *General Hypothesis,* p. 31.

36. Hibbs, "Political Parties," fig. 8, p. 1482. In fact, the difference between the two parties was remarkably low: 0.6 per cent. If the same calculation had been done ten years later, the difference would have been far higher.

37. For a development of the Hibbs thesis, see Alesina and Sachs, "Political Parties and the Business Cycle."

38. Clarke and Whiteley, "Perceptions of Macroeconomic Performance," p. 114.

39. See esp. Persson and Svensson, "Stubborn Conservative"; Alesina, "Political Economy of the Budget Surplus." It should be emphasized that Alesina's "rational partisan theory" only really works for relatively polarised two-party systems.

40. Alesina and Roubini, "Political Cycles"; Alesina, Cohen and Roubini, "Macroeconomic Policy."

41. Norpoth, "Economy," p. 317.

42. For an introduction to these complexities, see Frey and Schneider, "Recent Research."

43. Norpoth, "Economy," p. 303.

44. Lewis-Beck, *Economics and Elections*.

45. Paldam, "How Robust is the Vote Function?," esp. p. 24.

46. Powell and Whittan, "Cross-national Analysis of Economic Voting," p. 407. They studied in nineteen industrial democracies from 1969 to 1988.

47. Kramer, "Short-term Fluctuations in US Voting Behavior." See also Stigler, "General Economic Conditions."

48. Fair, "Effect of Economic Events." See also his "1992 Update."

49. Partly on the basis of GDP figures from the fourth quarter of the pre-election year through the first quarter of election year Michael Lewis-Beck forecast that Gore would win 56.2 per cent of the two-party vote: *Washington Post*, 26 May 2000. Fair's model predicted a far closer result: www.fairmodel.econ.yale.edu.

50. Goodhart and Bhansali, "Political Economy," pp. 61 ff. In their regressions, total R^2 was 0.38 for the whole period 1947–68, but rose to 0.81 for the period 1961–8.

51. Clarke and Whiteley, "Perceptions of Macroeconomic Performance," p. 110. Allowing for a lag of four months, they find that a 1 per cent rise in unemployment was associated with a 3.9 per cent fall in popularity, and an equal rise in inflation was associated with a 1.1 per cent fall in popularity.

52. Norpoth, *Confidence Regained*.

53. Kirchgässner, "Economic Conditions."

54. Lafay, "Political Dyarchy," p. 131.

55. For evidence of the sophistication of American voters on this issue even in the early 1960s, see Katona, *Psychological Economics*, pp. 339 f.

56. Johnston *et al.*, *Letting the People Decide*, p. 222.

57. Studlar, McAllister and Ascui, "Privatisation."

58. Alt, *Politics of Economic Decline*, pp. 49–55, 127.

59. Fiorina, *Retrospective Voting*, pp. 21–30.

60. Sniderman and Brody, "Coping"; Kiewiet and Kinder, "Economic Discontent"; Kiewiet, *Macroeconomics and Micropolitics*, esp. tables 5.4 and 6.2, pp. 64f., 89. See also Feldman, "Economic Self-Interest."

61. Feldman and Conley, "Explaining Explanations," table 1, p. 190.

62. Kramer, "Ecological Fallacy"; Markus, "Personal and National Economic Conditions," table 1, p. 146, and p. 148.

63. On this basis, Thomas Holbrook predicted in May 2000 that Gore would win 59.6 percent of the two-party vote: *Washington Post*, 26 May 2000.

64. Alt, *Politics of Economic Decline*, pp. 14–20; Clarke, Stewart and Zuk, "Politics, Economics and Party Popularity," table 5, p. 133. See also on the US Fiorina, *Retrospective Voting*, p. 41; Kiewiet, *Macroeconomics and Micropolitics*, tables 4.1 and 4.2, pp. 43ff. See also Powell and Whitten, "Cross-national Analysis of Economic Voting," p. 405; Anderson, *Blaming the Government*.

65. Mischler, Hoskin and Fitzgerald, "British Parties," pp. 222 ff.

66. Norpoth, *Confidence Regained*, table 5.4, p. 74, table 9.1, p. 180.

67. Särlik and Crewe, *Decade of Dealignment*, pp. 83, 87.

68. Franklin, *Decline of Class Voting*, fig. 4.6, p. 95; table 6.5, p. 147; fig. 7.2, p. 171; also Norris, *Electoral Change*, p. 141.

69. See e.g. (for the US) Key, *Responsible Electorate*, table 3.1, p. 35; Weatherford, "Economic Conditions," fig. 2, p. 926; Fiorina, "Elections and the Economy," pp. 28–32; Lanoue, *From Camelot*, table 5.3, p. 81. In general, see Evans (ed.), *End of Class Politics?*

70. See e.g. Bloom and Price, "Voter Response"; Lau, "Two Explanations"; Lanoue, *From Camelot*, p. 80, and table 6.1, p. 95. But see Fiorina and Shepsle, "Negative Voting."

71. Butler and Stokes, *Political Change*, pp. 402 ff. Cf. on the US, Key, *Responsible Electorate*.

72. Horne, *Macmillan*, p. 336.

73. Kramer, "Short-term Fluctuations in US Voting Behavior." Cf. Clarke and Stewart, "Prospections."

74. See also Fiorina, *Retrospective Voting*; Kiewiet and Rivers, "Retrospective Voting."

75. For US presidential elections, MacKuen, Erikson and Stimson, "Peasants or Bankers?" See also for the Senate and Congress, Kuklinski and West, "Economic Expectations."

76. Sanders, "Why the Conservatives Won—Again." For a sceptical view on expectations in the British context see Alt, "Ambiguous Intervention."

77. Norpoth, *Confidence Regained*, table 5.7, p. 80.

78. Nadeau, Niemi and Amato, "Prospective and Comparative."

79. Downs, *Economic Theory*, pp. 39–42; Lewis-Beck, *Economics and Elections*, esp. pp. 49, 60, 72. However, Conover, Feldman and Knight, show that projections about the future are based as much on personal assumptions as on past events: "Personal Underpinning of Economic Forecasts."

80. Saatchi, "Happiness Can't Buy Money," p. 13.

81. Haller and Norpoth, "Good Times."

82. Alesina and Rosenthal, "Partisan Cycles," p. 393. See also Alesina and Sachs, "Political Parties and the Business Cycle" and Chappel and Keech, "Explaining Aggregate Evaluations."

83. Saatchi, "Happiness Can't Buy Money," p. 13.

84. Ferguson, "Introduction."

85. Norpoth, "Guns and Butter," table 1, p. 951, and table 3, p. 956

86. Sanders, "Government Popularity;" and "Why the Conservatives Won—Again;" Price and Sanders, "Economic Competence;" Sanders, "Conservative Incompetence."

87. Sanders's equation for the period 1979–1997 is as follows:

Convote = $6.82 + 0.83$ Convotet$_{-1}$ + 0.09 Aggeconexp$_t$ -0.33Tax$_t$ + 9.2Falklands$_{May82}$ + 5.40Falklands$_{June82}$ -4.91Currency92-1.44 Blair

where "Convote" is the Conservative vote in the current month, the constant is the base figure for Conservative support, "Convotet$_{-1}$" is Conservative support in the previous month, "Aggeconexp$_t$" is the balance of positive over negative household financial expectations, "Tax$_t$" is the change in tax index, "Falklands$_{May, June\ 82}$" is the increase in Conservative support due to the Falklands War, "Currency$_{92}$" is the decrease in Conservative support due to the ERM crisis of September 1992 and "Blair" is the impact of Tony Blair's leadership on voters" perceptions of Labour.

88. The argument is developed in Frank, *Luxury Fever*.

89. Scitovsky, *Joyless Economy*, esp. pp. 133–145.

90. See Erikson and Uusitalo, "Scandinavian Approach," p. 197. See also Sen, "Capability and Well-being," p. 38; Pinker, *How the Mind Works*, p. 392 f.

91. Diener *et al.*, "Subjective Well-being," p. 214.

92. Tobin and Nordhaus, "Is Growth Obsolete?"; Eisner, "Extended Accounts."

93. Franklin, "Electoral Participation," p. 227.

94. Budge *et al.*, *New British Politics*, pp. 364 f.

95. Turnout for European elections in 1999 (1994 figure in brackets):

Total EU	49 (57)
Britain	23 (37)
Germany	45 (60)
Finland	30 (60)
Netherlands	30 (36)
Denmark	49 (53)
Italy	71 (80)

96. Webb, "Party Organizational Change in Britain," p. 128.

97. Farrell, "Ireland," p. 216.

98. King *et al*, *New Labour Triumphs*, p. 222.

99. Mair, "Party Systems," p. 106.

100. Noelle-Naumann and Köcher (eds), *Allensbacher Jahrbuch*, pp. 783 f.

101. Ibid., p. 822.

102. Ibid., p. 825.

103. Ibid., p. 889.

104. Ibid., p. 834.

105. *Le Monde*, 18 November 1999.

106. Speech to the Democratic National Convention, 18 August 1956.

107. *Guardian*, 30 July 1997.

108. *Financial Times*, 28 April 1999

109. Ibid., 8 July 1999.

110. Ibid., 14 July 1999.

111. washingtonpost.com, 15 September 1997.

112. Hanham, *Elections and Party Management*, pp. 249 ff.

113. Kingdom, *Government and Politics*, p. 322.

114. Farrell, "Ireland," pp. 222, 234.

115. Koole, "Vulnerability of the Modern Cadre Party," p. 297.

116. *Financial Times*, 15–16 May 1999; *The Economist*, 31 July 1999; *Prospect*, March 2000, p. 37.

117. Katz, "Party Organizations," pp. 129 f.

118. *Statistical Abstract of the United States 1999*, tables 492, 493, 496, 497, 498, 499.

119. washingtonpost.com, 15 September 1997.

120. All figures calculated from data in *Statistical Abstract for the United States 1999*.

121. Centre for Responsive Politics, www.opensecrets.org.

122. Butler and Butler, *British Political Facts*, pp. 132.

123. Budge *et al.*, *New British Politics*, p. 385.

124. Müller, "Development of Austrian Party Organizations," pp. 64 ff.

125. Bille, "Denmark," p. 137.

126. Koole, "Vulnerability of the Modern Cadre Party," p. 287.

127. Svåsand, "Norwegian Party Organizations," pp. 313 f.

128. *Guardian*, June 23 1998.

129. Pierre and Widfeldt, "Party Organizations in Sweden," p. 341.

130. Katz, "Party Organizations and Finance," p. 114.

131. Deschouwer, "Decline of Consociationalism," p. 102.

132. Coxall and Robins, *Contemporary British Politics*, p. 130.

133. Müller, "Development of Austrian Party Organizations," pp. 64 ff.

134. Poguntke, "Parties in a Legalistic Culture," p. 197.

135. Farrell, "Ireland," pp. 222, 234.

136. Webb, "Party Organizational Change," p. 117.

137. Coxall and Robins, *Contemporary British Politics*, p. 130.

138. "Known company donations to UK political parties," *Labour Research*.

139. Kingdom, *Government and Politics*, p. 324.

140. *The Times*, 13 July 1999; *Independent*, 16 July 1999 and 24 Nov. 1999.

141. Kingdom, *Government and Politics*, p. 325.

142. Bogdanor, *Power and the People*, p. 150.

143. Kingdom, *Government and Politics*, p. 327.

144. Coxall and Robins, *Contemporary British Politics*, p. 117.

145. Hanham, *Elections and Party Management*, pp. 369–84.

146. Centre for Responsive Politics, "Money in Politics Alert," 18 Oct. 1999, www.opensecrets.org/alerts/v5.

147. *The Economist*, 31 July 1999.

148. Gibbon, *Decline and Fall of the Roman Empire*, vol. i, p. 805.

149. King *et al.*, *New Labour Triumphs*, p. 37.

150. Müller, "Development of Austrian Party Organizations," p. 52.

151. *Le Monde*, 18 November 1999.

152. Matthew, *Gladstone*, pp. 14 n., 135 f., 375 f. Matthew's figures are not quite consistent.

153. Cf. Leigh and Vulliamy, *Sleaze*.

154. Butler and Butler, *British Political Facts*, p. 203.

155. Pollard and Adonis, *Class Act*, pp. 115 f.

156. Harding, Leigh and Palliser, *The Liar*.

157. *Independent on Sunday*, 30 November 1997.

158. Bogdanor, *Power and the People*, p. 155. See also Pinto-Duschinsky, *British Political Finance*, pp. 40 f., 55.

159. *Guardian*, 8 July 1997, 9 July 1998, 13 July 1998. One of them, ironically, had previously co-written a book with Peter Mandelson in which they denounced as "one of the most corrupting principles in public life today . . . the idea that there is nothing objectionable about a public figure pursuing a dubious private commercial interest as long as it is declared."

160. *Daily Telegraph*, 17 November 1997; *The Times*, 14 November 1997; *Independent*, 27 November 1997.

161. See for example the "Seven Principles of Public Life" enunciated by the Nolan Committee.
162. Johnston and Pattie, "Great Britain," pp. 139–40.
163. Pinto-Duschinsky, *British Political Finance*, pp. 248–9.
164. Ewing, *Money, Politics and Law*, pp. 69–81.
165. Ibid., pp. 107–16.
166. Katz and Kolodny, "Party Organization as an Empty Vessel," pp. 32 ff.
167. Herrnson, "High Finance of American Politics," pp. 17–40.
168. Mair, "Party Organizations," p. 10.
169. Webb, "Party Organizational Change in Britain," p. 123.
170. Ewing, *Funding of Political Parties in Britain*, pp. 73–4.
171. Mutch, "Evolution of Campaign Finance Regulation," pp. 61–8; Gunlicks (ed.), *Campaign and Party Finance*, p. 6
172. Farrell, "Ireland," p. 235.
173. Koole, "Vulnerability of the Modern Cadre Party," p. 289.
174. Poguntke, "Parties in a Legalistic Culture," p. 194.
175. Drysch, "New French System."
176. Bille, "Denmark," p. 146.
177. Müller, "Development of Austrian Party Organizations," p. 55.
178. Bardi and Morlino, "Italy," p. 259.
179. Svåsand, "Change and Adaptation," p. 321.
180. *The Economist*, 31 July 1999.
181. Bardi and Morlino, "Italy," p. 260.
182. *Independent*, 9 December 1999. See also *The Economist*, 29 Jan. 2000.
183. Giddens, *Runaway World*, p. 77.
184. *Prospect*, April 2000, p. 53.
185. Vincent, *Formation of the Liberal Party*.

Chapter 9

1. Wolfe, *Bonfire of the Vanities*, p. 12.
2. *Financial Times*, 4 February 1998.
3. That is, by 0.35 per cent (one percentage point = 100 basis points).
4. *Financial Times*, 4 February 1998. Cf. Roberts, *Inside International Finance*, p. 36.
5. See Lewis, *Liar's Poker*.
6. *The Economist*, 17 January 1998, p. 115.
7. Bank for International Settlements, *Annual Report 1999*, table VI.5.
8. Ibid., table VII.2.
9. Ibid., table VI.3.
10. Ibid., table VII.5.
11. All figures from Federal Reserve Bank of St Louis.
12. See for example Friedman, *Lexus*, passim.
13. Wharburton, *Debt and Delusion*, pp. 142–59, esp. p. 159.

14. See Girault, *Emprunts russes*.

15. Kynaston, *City of London*, vol. ii, pp. 271 f.

16. Warburg, *Aufzeichnungen*, p. 19.

17. Drazen, "Towards a Political-Economic Theory."

18. Körner, "Public Credit," pp. 507–21; Ormrod, "West European Monarchies," pp. 123 f.

19. Goldsmith, *Premodern Financial Systems*, pp. 157 ff., 167 ff.

20. Neal, *Rise of Financial Capitalism*, pp. 1–43.

21. Muto, "Spanish System," pp. 246–9.

22. Goldsmith, *Premodern Financial Systems*, p. 194.

23. Neal, *Rise of Financial Capitalism*, pp. 62–88.

24. Ibid., pp. 147 f., 211; Wright, "Contribution," pp. 658, 667. The figure for 3 per cent consols was as high as 20 per cent.

25. Ferguson, *World's Banker*, ch. 1.

26. Körner, "Public Credit," pp. 533 f.

27. Kennedy, *Rise and Fall of the Great Powers*, p. 127.

28. Bonney, "Struggle for Great Power Status," p. 382.

29. Ibid., pp. 364 f.

30. Neal, *Rise of Financial Capitalism*, pp. 180–90.

31. Ibid., pp. 190–222.

32. Ferguson, *World's Banker*, p. 104.

33. Sylla, "US Financial System," pp. 259 ff.

34. Bosher, *French Finances*, p. 316.

35. Bonney, "Struggle for Great Power Status," pp. 364 f.

36. Ibid., pp. 351 ff.

37. Chapman, "Establishment of the Rothschilds," p. 20.

38. For details see Ferguson, *World's Banker*, pp. 131–4.

39. Rothschild Archive, London, XI/109/10/3/4, undated documents relating to Prussian loan proposal, *c.* Dec. 1817.

40. This may have been because parliamentary institutions, and therefore their guarantees, were perceived as less ephemeral than monarchs or dynasties, though that was only ever true in the British case. I am grateful to William Goetzmann for this point.

41. Klein, "30-Million-Anleihe," p. 582.

42. Thielen, *Hardenberg*, p. 358.

43. Quoted in Ferguson, *World's Banker*, p. 133.

44. Disraeli, *Coningsby*, pp. 213 f.

45. Quoted in Ferguson, *World's Banker*, p. 226.

46. Prawer, *Heine's Jewish Comedy*, pp. 146 f.

47. Dawson, *First Latin American Debt Crisis*. It was nineteenth-century practice to quote prices in percentages, rather than yields.

48. Bordo and Eichengreen, "International Economic Environment," p. 4.

49. Lewis, *Liar's Poker*, p. 59.

50. Jardin and Tudesq, *Restoration*, pp. 68 f.

51. Bordo and White, "A Tale of Two Currencies."

52. The data are drawn from the weekly London *Economist*, first published in 1843. Yields are unadjusted, calculated by dividing the coupon by the quoted price, which takes no account of (*a*) the tendency for prices to fluctuate depending on the imminence of the quarterly or half-yearly interest payment and (*b*) the differing maturities of bonds. For perpetual debt instruments like French rentes this is a legitimate procedure; for more or less perpetual bonds like consols, this only leads to a distortion in the period after 1888, when yields were inflated by the possibility that consols would be redeemed (see Harley, "Goschen's Conversion"; Klovland, "Pitfalls"). The distortion for long-term bonds like the Austrian Metalliques and Russian 1822s does not prevent accurate computation of yield fluctuations within each series, though calculations of spreads between the different bonds would be affected.

53. Ferguson, *World's Banker*, p. 491.

54. Flandreau, "The Bank, the States and the Market," p. 29.

55. Rothschild Archive, London, XI/109J/J/30, James and Salomon, Paris, to Nathan, London, 10 October 1830.

56. Rothschild Archive, London, XI/109J/J/30, James, Paris, to Salomon, Vienna, 24 November 1830. The French convention was to specify the annual rente due on a bond but not its nominal capital.

57. Rothschild Archive, London, XI/109J/J/30, James and Salomon, Paris, to Nathan, London, 9 August 1830.

58. Rothschild Archive, London, XI/109/71/4, Nat, Paris, to his brothers, London, undated, *c.* April 1849.

59. Castellane, *Journal*, vol. v, p. 240.

60. In fact, James's bearish prognosis proved erroneous until the outbreak of war with Germany, as Figure 26 shows.

61. Royal Archives, Windsor Castle, Y67/6, Leopold, Wiesbaden, to Victoria, 19 September 1840.

62. Monypenny and Buckle, *Disraeli*, vol. iv, p. 225.

63. Roberts, *Salisbury*, p. 53.

64. Taylor, *Struggle*, p. 156.

65. Pflanze, *Bismarck*, vol. ii, p. 81.

66. Stern, *Gold and Iron*, p. 311 n.

67. Einaudi, "Money and Politics," pp. 50, 52.

68. Feis, *Europe*.

69. Edelstein, *Overseas Investment*, pp. 24 ff., 48, 313 ff. Cf. *Financial Times*, 6 May 1997: gross direct plus portfolio investment in the period 1990–5 was just under 12 per cent of GDP.

70. Kindleberger, *Financial History*, p. 225.

71. O'Rourke and Williamson, *Globalization and History*, p. 208.

72. Pollard, "Capital Exports," pp. 491 f.

73. Edelstein, *Overseas Investment*, pp. 24 ff., 48, 313 ff.

74. O'Rourke and Williamson, *Globalization and History*, p. 230.

75. Edelstein, *Overseas Investment*.

76. O'Rourke and Williamson, *Globalization and History*, p. 227. Cf. Davis and

Huttenback, *Mammon and the Pursuit of Empire*, pp. 81–117; Pollard, "Capital Exports," p. 507.

77. O'Rourke and Williamson, *Globalization and History*, p. 231.

78. Davis and Huttenback, *Mammon and the Pursuit of Empire*, p. 107.

79. Crafts, "Globalization and Growth," p. 28. Cf. Bordo, Eichengreen and Irwin, "Globalisation Today," p. 30.

80. Nash, *Fenn's Compendium*, p. 5.

81. See Shaw, "Ottoman Expenditures," pp. 374 ff.; Issawi, *Economic History of the Middle East*, pp. 94–106; Hershlas, *Introduction to the Modern Economic History*, pp. 53–66; Owen, *Middle East*, p. 106.

82. See Crouchley, *Economic Development*, pp. 274–8; Issawi, *Economic History of the Middle East*, pp. 439–45; Hershlas, *Introduction to the Modern Economic History*, pp. 99–122.

83. For details see Ferguson, *World's Banker*, ch. 25.

84. Crouchley, *Economic Development*, p. 276.

85. Hershlas, *Introduction to the Modern Economic History*, pp. 104 f.

86. Issawi, *Economic History of the Middle East*, pp. 439–45; Hershlas, *Introduction to the Modern Economic History*, pp. 113–22.

87. Crouchley, *Economic Development*, pp. 274 ff.

88. Lindert and Morton, "How Sovereign Debt Has Worked."

89. Rothschild, *"You Have It, Madam,"* pp. 46, 49. Unfortunately, it was not until 1979 that the British government sold the shares, by which time they had fallen in value to £22 million—in real terms rather less than their original purchase price.

90. Blake, *Disraeli*, p. 586.

91. Shaw, "Ottoman Expenditures," pp. 374 ff.

92. Homer and Sylla, *Interest Rates*, pp. 216–73, 291 f., 312–317.

93. Bayoumi, "Saving-Investment Correlations"; Zevin, "World Financial Markets"; Taylor, "International Capital Mobility." Cf. O'Rourke and Williamson, *Globalization and History*, pp. 215 f.

94. Neal, "Integration of International Capital Markets."

95. Michie, "Invisible Stabilizer," pp. 10–14.

96. O'Rourke and Williamson, *Globalization and History*, p. 220.

97. Flandreau, Le Cacheux and Zumer, "Stability without a Pact," pp. 128, 145.

98. Ibid., p. 147 n.

99. Flandreau, "Caveat Emptor," pp. 23–31, fig. 4.

100. Correlation coefficients of bond yields against fiscal indicators, 1880–1913:

	Britain	France	Germany	Russia	US	Italy	Spain
Debt/GDP	-0.09	0.26	-0.42	0.77	0.77		-0.40
Deficit/revenue	-0.22	0.80	-0.70	0.28		0.10	0.07

Source: Batley and Ferguson, "Event Risk."

101. The following table gives comparable British statistics since 1980:

	Debt/ revenue	Deficit/ revenue (%)
1980	1.2	13.6
1985	1.2	7.2
1990	1.0	12.4
1995	1.4	14.8

Source: The Economist.

102. By 1913 Russia was by far the biggest gross external debtor in the world, accounting for something in the region of a third of the world total of foreign public debt: Lindert and Morton, "How Sovereign Debt Has Worked," table 1.

103. Flandreau, "Caveat Emptor," fig. 5.

104. Bordo and Rockoff, "Good Housekeeping," p. 337.

105. Ibid., p. 346.

106. Bloch, Is War Now Impossible?, p. xlv.

107. Lindert and Morton, "How Sovereign Debt Has Worked," pp. 3, 20–24.

108. Lewis, Liar's Poker, p. 197.

109. Angell, Great Illusion, p. 209.

110. Albertini, Origins of the War, vol. ii, p. 214.

111. Geiss, July 1914, document 57.

112. See Ferguson, Pity of War, ch. 11.

113. Apostol, Beruatzky and Michelson, Russian Public Finances, pp. 320–322.

114. Hardach, First World War, p. 148.

115. Calculated from figures in Morgan, Studies in British Financial Policy, pp. 317, 320 f.

116. Taylor, "International Capital Mobility," p. 5.

117. Bordo and Rockoff, "Adherence to the Gold Standard," table 1.

118. Ibid., pp. 19 f.

119. Schuker, "American 'Reparations'."

120. Lindert and Morton, "How Sovereign Debt Has Worked," p. 5.

121. Feinstein and Watson, "Private International Capital Flows"; James, Globalization and its Sins, p. 50.

122. Fearon, Origins and Nature of the Great Slump.

123. Ritschl, "Sustainability of High Public Debt."

124. Lindert and Morton, "How Sovereign Debt Has Worked," p. 6.

125. To be precise: in June 1933 Germany imposed a moratorium on all foreign debt repayments except interest and amortisation on 1924 Dawes loan and interest payments on 1930 Young Loan: James, Globalisation and its Sins, p. 140.

126. James, "Ende der Globalisierung," p. 71; James, Globalization and its Sins, pp. 48, 145.

127. Zevin, "World Financial Markets," p. 47; The Economist, World in Figures, pp. 38, 52.

128. Taylor, "International Capital Mobility," p. 3; Eichengreen and Hausmann, "Exchange Rates and Financial Fragility," p. 27.

129. Obstfeld and Tayor, "Great Depression as a Watershed," p. 359; James, "Ende der Globalisierung," p. 63. See also Taylor, "International Capital Mobility," p. 5 and table 1.

130. O'Rourke and Williamson, *Globalization and History*, p. 30.

131. Ibid., pp. 35 f., 98 f.

132. Ibid., p. 11.

133. Micklethwait and Wooldridge, *Future Perfect*, p. 51.

134. O'Rourke and Williamson, *Globalization and History*, p. 119.

135. Ibid., p. 122.

136. Fischer, Krengel and Wietog (eds.), *Sozialgeschichtliches Arbeitsbuch*, pp. 34 f.

137. O'Rourke and Williamson, *Globalization and History*, pp. 119, 155.

138. Ibid., pp. 225, 240-25.

139. Micklethwait and Wooldridge, *Future Perfect*.

140. Giddens, *Runaway World*.

141. Micklethwait and Wooldridge, *Future Perfect*, p. 257.

142. Most technological innovation (measured in terms of US patents taken out in 1997) originates in a tiny élite of five countries. Just 10 per cent of the world's population lives in those countries; yet they account for 87 per cent of all new patents in 1997 and around two-fifths of world GDP. Yet 85 per cent of the world's people can be classified as non-innovators: between them they took out a mere 0.7 per cent of new patents: Jeffrey Sachs, "A New Map of the World," *The Economist*, 24 June 2000.

143. See e.g. O'Rourke and Williamson, *Globalization and History*, chs. 6, 10; Crafts, "Globalization and Growth," pp. 50–52; James, "Ende der Globalisierung," p. 78.

144. See esp. Bordo, Eichengreen and Irwin, "Globalization Today."

145. Ibid., p. 10; Crafts, "Globalization and Growth," p. 25.

146. Friedman, *Lexus*, p. 112.

147. Ibid., p. 167.

Chapter 10

1. A first draft of this was presented at the Royal Institute for International Affairs Workshop on Financial Crisis, 23 March 1999. I would like to thank Dr Brigitte Granville of the RIIA for her comments.

2. Dickens, *Our Mutual Friend*, p. 118

3. *Financial Times*, 17 March 1999.

4. I was one of them.

5. *Financial Times*, 16 March 1999.

6. *Financial Times*, 22–23 April 2000.

7. *Sunday Telegraph*, 21 March 1999, citing article by James Glassman and Kevin Hassett in the *Wall Street Journal*.

8. Goetzmann and Jorion, "A Century of Global Stock Markets," esp table 1.

9. Siegel, *Stocks for the Long Run.*

10. Shiller, *Irrational Exuberance*, pp. 17–43.

11. Gordon, "US Economic Growth." See also Jeff Madrick, "How New is the New Economy?," *New York Review of* Books, 23 September 1999. *The Economist*, 10 June 2000; 17 June 2000.

12. See R.W. Johnson, "Reading the Markets," *Prospect*, October 1999.

13. Bond and Adams, *Barclays Equity-Gilt Study*, pp. 39–50.

14. Shiller, *Irrational Exuberance*, p. 67.

15. Calculated from data provided by Global Financial Data.

16. Bond and Adams, *Barclays Equity-Gilt Study*, p. 63.

17. Calculated from data provided by Global Financial Data.

18. Bond and Adams, *Barclays Equity-Gilt Study*, p. 6.

19. See *Financial Times*, 22 December 1999; 3 January 2000; 6 January 2000; *The Economist*, 25 March 2000. The American earnings yield/bond yield ratio reached a nadir of 0.5 in December 1999, compared with an average figure for the 1970s of 1.14

20. Smithers and Wright, *Valuing Wall Street.*

21. *Financial Times*, 13 May 1999; 19 April 2000. See also Jeff Madrick, "All Too Human," *New York Review of Books*, 10 August 2000.

22. *Financial Times*, 8 April 2000.

23. Perkins and Perkins, *Internet Bubble.*

24. *Sunday Telegraph*, 23 January 2000.

25. Bond and Adams, *Barclays Equity-Gilt Study*, pp. 48ff.

26. Ibid., p. 63.

27. *Financial Times*, 19 April 2000.

28. Every share of every company listed on the New York Stock Exchange now changes hands once a year, compared with once in every three years in 1981: *The Economist*, 25 March 2000.

29. The market fell by 22.6 per cent. In fact, the index appears to have fallen by slightly more on 12 December 1914.

30. Davidson and Rees Mogg, *Great Reckoning.*

31. See James, *Globalization and Its Sins.*

32. *The Economist*, 25 September 1999; 22 April 2000; *Financial Times*, 27 March 2000. See also Wynne Godley, "What If They Start Saving Again?," *London Review of Books*, 6 July 2000.

33. "The Federal Reserve," Greenspan declared, "consistent with its responsibilities as the nation's central bank, affirms its readiness to serve as a source of liquidity to support the [by implication, international] economic and financial system:" quoted in *Prospect*, November 1999.

34. Ibid.

35. See Goodhart and Hofman, "Monetary Policy Adjustments;" *id.*, "Monetary Policy and Asset Prices;" Goodhart, "Price Stability and Financial Fragility."

36. Bernanke and Gertler, "Monetary Policy and Asset Price Volatility;" Vickers, "Monetary Policy and Asset Prices."

37. Voth, "With a Bang, Not A Whimper;" *id.*, "Tale of Five Bubbles."

38. Kindleberger, *Manias*, pp. 204–211.

39. Schwartz, "Real and Pseudo-Financial Crises."

40. Bordo, "Financial Crises," p. 226.

41. Mishkin, "Asymmetric Information."

42. Goodhart and Delargy, "Financial Crises."

43. Bond and Adams, *Barclays Equity-Gilt Study*, pp. 116, 125.

44. Capie *et al.*, "Development," p. 16.

45. Bordo, "Financial Crises," p. 191.

46. Shiller, *Irrational Exuberance*, pp. 75–82; Fair, "Events that Shook the Market." Cf. Cutler, Poterba and Summers, "What Moves Stock Prices?"

47. Parker, "Emergence," p. 554.

48. Baskin and Miranti, *History of Corporate Finance*, p. 97.

49. Ibid., p. 96.

50. See Garber, "Famous First Bubbles." Garber argues that the "tulip mania" was not wholly irrational because the bubonic plague shifted the demand curve for tulips and the Mosaic virus shifted the supply curve by shortening the lifespan of tulip bulbs.

51. Parker, "Emergence," pp. 556 f.

52. Velde and Weir, "Financial Market," p. 10.

53. Baskin and Miranti, *History of Corporate Finance*, p. 98.

54. Michie, "London and New York Stock Exchanges."

55. See Mirowski, "Rise (and Retreat) of a Market."

56. See Michie, *London Stock Exchange*, pp. 88 f., 175, 184, 320, 322, 360 f., 419, 421, 440, 473, 521 f., 589 f.

57. The definitive account is Murphy, *John Law*. Cf. the more colourful Gleeson, *Millionaire*.

58. Officer holders and rentiers were offered reimbursement in bank notes, which they could then use to buy either shares in the Compagnie (paying a 4 per cent annual dividend) or 3 per cent rentes. However, former holders of government debt were not given priority but had to pay market price. Neal, *Financial Capitalism*, p. 74.

59. Ibid., p. 75.

60. Ibid., p. 69.

61. Baskin and Miranti, *History of Corporate Finance*, p. 105.

62. Neal, *Financial Capitalism*, p. 92.

63. Ibid., pp. 94–6.

64. Chancellor, *Devil Take the Hindmost*, pp. 62–4.

65. Neal, *Financial Capitalism*, p. 98.

66. Ibid., pp.78 ff.

67. 5 new companies were formed in January 1720, 23 in February, 27 in April, 19 in May and 87 in June. In all 190 were founded. Only four survived the crash: Chancellor, *Devil Take the Hindmost*, pp. 70 f.

68. Neal, *Financial Capitalism*, p. 109.

69. Ibid., p. 101.

70. *The Economist*, 18 March 2000. See also *Financial Times*, 5–6 February 2000.

71. Bond and Adams, *Barclays Equity-Gilt Study*, pp. 51–62.
72. *The Times*, 24 August 1999.
73. Chancellor, *Devil Take the Hindmost*, pp. 69, 88.
74. Wheen, *Marx*, p. 268.
75. Ibid., p. 249.
76. Ibid., p. 268.
77. The phrase was used by David Smith in the *Sunday Times*, 2 May 1999.

Chapter 11

1. Fleming, *Goldfinger*, pp. 51–59. As a scion of the Fleming banking dynasty, the author was not wholly ignorant of these matters.
2. Readers may find it helpful to bear in mind the troy measures conventionally used in the gold market: 1 ounce is equal to 31.10348 grams; 1 tonne is equal to 1,000,000 grams, therefore 32,150.7 ounces.
3. At June 2000 prices, the gold reserves of the Eurozone were substantially higher than those of the US ($115 bn to $75 bn). Germany, France, Switzerland and Italy all have gold reserves of around $20–$30 billion; compared with just $5.6 billion in Britain: *The Economist*, 17 June 2000.
4. Roth, "View from Switzerland."
5. See in general Ware, "IMF and Gold."
6. See Bordo and Schwartz, "Changing Relationship," pp. 21 f.
7. *Financial Times*, 28 September 1999.
8. Calculated from figures in McCaffrey and Lamarque, "Gold."
9. Harmston, "Gold as a Store of Value," p. 29.
10. Green, *World of Gold*, pp. 357–62.
11. Harmston, "Gold as a Store of Value," p. 5.
12. ONS, quoted in *Daily Telegraph*, 11 June 1999.
13. Harmston, "Gold as a Store of Value," p. 5.
14. But see Bordo and Schwartz, "Changing Relationship," p. 27.
15. Harmston, "Gold as a Store of Value," pp. 10, 18, 54.
16. I am grateful to Henry Gillett of the Bank of England for this information.
17. Harmston, "Gold as a Store of Value," p. 38
18. Ibid., pp. 41–5.
19. 2 July 1819 was the date of "Peel's Act," committing Britain to return to gold at the exchange rate prior to suspension on 26 February 1797.
20. The Bretton Woods Articles Agreement was signed in July 1944 and began working with limited convertibility outside the United States in 1946. The system did not become fully operational until 1959.
21. Obstfeld, "International Currency Experience." A simple measure of purchasing power parity is *The Economist*'s "Big Mac" index, based on comparing the prices of the standard McDonald's hamburger. By this measure, most Asian, Latin American and East European currencies were undervalued against the dollar at the time of writing: *The Economist*, 29 April 2000.

22. See for an accessible account Krugman, *Return of Depression Economics*. Of course, it can be argued that the Asian crisis was a consequence of trying to maintain pegged exchange rates.

23. Rockoff, "Wizard of Oz." I am grateful to professors Charles Goodhart and Forrest Capie for this reference.

24. Yeager, "Fluctuating Exchange Rates."

25. Cooper, "Gold Standard," p. 4; Bordo and Kydland, "Gold Standard as a Commitment Mechanism," pp. 72–5.

26. Eichengreen and Flandreau "Geography of the Gold Standard," table 2.

27. Drummond, *Gold Standard*, p. 12. These naturally varied according to the costs of shipping, mint charges and interest rates.

28. Ford, *Gold Standard*.

29. McCloskey and Zecher, "How the Gold Standard Worked."

30. Bloomfield, *Monetary Policy*.

31. Bordo and Schwartz, "Changing Relationship," p. 15.

32. Cooper, "Gold Standard," p. 9.

33. Barsky, "Fisher Hypothesis"; Bordo and Kydland, "Gold Standard as a Commitment Mechanism," pp. 80–83.

34. Bordo, "Classical Gold Standard," pp. 152, 167.

35. Bordo cites the following figures for Britain:

	1870–1913	1919–1938	1946–1979
Average inflation	-0.7	-4.6	5.6
Average unemployment	4.3	13.3	2.5

Source: Bordo, "Classical Gold Standard," p. 168 and table 5.1.

36. Bordo, "Gold as a Commitment Mechanism," p. 21. Subtracting Bordo's figures for inflation (in Table 19) from his figures for long-term rates suggests that real rates were at their lowest under Bretton Woods.

37. Flandreau, *L'Or du monde*. See also the same author's "Règles de la pratique," "French Crime of 1873" and "Essay on the Emergence."

38. It cannot be without significance that nearly all the best economists of the period, including Marshall and Wicksell, advocated reform of the gold standard.

39. Bordo and Schwartz, "Monetary Policy Regimes," pp. 18, 72.

40. Green, "Central Bank Gold Reserves." I am grateful to Jill Leyland, Economics and Statistics Consultancy, for this reference.

41. Vilar, *History of Gold*, pp. 319 ff.

42. Cooper, "Gold Standard," p. 14. For the argument that prospectors and producers responded to a rising purchasing power of gold see e.g. Bordo, "Classical Gold Standard," p. 166.

43. Cooper, "Gold Standard," p. 18.

44. Ford, *Gold Standard*, p. 25. For a critique of the notion that international monetary systems depend on one country's hegemony, see Eichengreen, "Hegemonic Stability Theories."

45. Eichengreen, *Golden Fetters*, p. 73.

46. Capie, Goodhart and Schnadt, "Development of Central Banking," p. 11.

47. Bordo and Kydland, "Gold Standard as a Commitment Mechanism," p. 56; Bordo and Rockoff, "Good Housekeeping," p. 321; Bordo and Schwartz, "Monetary Policy Regimes," p. 10.

48. Bordo, "Gold as a Commitment Mechanism," p. 7.

49. Bordo and Kydland, "Gold Standard as a Commitment Mechanism," pp. 68, 77.

50. See Bordo and Schwartz, "Monetary Policy Regimes," p. 11.

51. Bordo and Rockoff, "Good Housekeeping," pp. 327, 347 f.

52. Bordo and Rockoff, "Adherence to the Gold Standard," p. 28. "Canada paid 5.53 per cent when off gold and 4.65 per cent when on gold; Australia paid 6.9 and 5.17; Chile 8.05 and 6.75; Denmark 6.93 and 4.8; Italy 7.8 and 6.25."

53. Bordo and Schwartz, "Monetary Policy Regimes," pp. 71 f.; Bordo and Jonung, "Return to the Convertibility Principle"; Bordo and Dewald, "Historical Bond Market Inflation Credibility."

54. Eichengreen and Hausmann, "Exchange Rates and Financial Fragility," p. 35.

55. Mundell, "Prospects for the International Monetary System," p. 31.

56. Bordo and Schwartz, "Monetary Policy Regimes," p. 62.

57. See Obstfeld, "International Currency Experience."

58. Keynes, *Tract on Monetary Reform*, p. 138.

59. The definition of this term is a matter of taste. Schwartz argues from the monetarist perspective that only banking crises precipitated by a "public . . . scramble for high powered-money" qualify: Schwartz, "Real and Pseudo-financial Crises," p. 11. For a more precise definition and a detailed empirical survey see Bordo, "Financial Crises," pp. 190 f. Following in the footsteps of Irving Fisher, Minsky developed the idea of crises as the results of cyclical collisions between indebtedness and interest rates. The more highly geared an economy, the more likely that a rise in the interest rate will spark of debt deflation: see esp. Minsky, "Systematic Fragility." The Minsky–Fisher approach is predominant in Kindleberger, *Manias, Panics and Crashes*.

60. Goodhart and Delargy, "Financial Crises."

61. Bordo and Eichengreen, "International Economic Environment," passim; Bordo, Eichengreen and Irwin, "Globalization Today," pp. 47–56.

62. See Bayoumi, Eichengreen and Taylor, "Introduction," pp. 7 f., 11 f. for a summary of the literature on this point.

63. Eichengreen and Hausmann, "Exchange Rates and Financial Fragility," p. 28.

64. Bordo and Eichengreen, "International Economic Environment," p. 15. See also Wood, "Great Crashes in History."

65. Friedman and Schwartz, *Monetary History*.

66. A violation of the rules of the game of which France was also guilty: Eichengreen, "Gold-Exchange Standard."

67. Only China, Spain, Turkey and the Soviet Union were not: Bordo and Schwartz, "Changing Relationship," p. 18; Bordo and Rockoff, "Adherence to the Gold Standard," p. 14.

68. Eichengreen, *Golden Fetters*. Cf. Eichengreen and Sachs, "Exchange Rates and Economic Recovery."

69. For an outstanding survey see Bordo, "Bretton Woods."

70. Bordo and Schwartz, "Changing Relationship," p. 19; Bordo, "Gold as a Commitment Mechanism," p. 17; Bordo and Schwartz, "Monetary Policy Regimes," p. 19.

71. Bordo, "Bretton Woods," p. 83. See, however, the comment by Cooper in the same volume, p. 106. Cf. Zevin, "World Financial Markets," pp. 56–68.

72. Bordo and Schwartz, "Changing Relationship," pp. 24 f.

73. Krugman, *Return of Depression Economics*, pp. 96 ff.

74. McKinnon and Pill, "International Overborrowing;" Eichengreen and Hausmann, "Exchange Rates and Financial Fragility," pp. 20 f.

75. The argument that this should be the IMF's role has been advanced in a report for the US Congress by Allan Meltzer (*The Economist*, 19 March 2000). Capie argues that there can be no such thing as an international lender of last resort, in that in the absence of world money no institution can provide liquidity to the international financial markets as a whole, only bail-outs on a country-by-country basis with the attendant danger of moral hazard: Capie, "International Lender of Last Resort." For a sceptical view see on the benefits of bailouts see Bordo and Schwartz, "Measuring Real Economic Effects from Bailouts."

76. McKinnon, "East Asian Dollar Standard."

77. Cooper, "Monetary System for the Future."

78. Eltis, "Creation and Destruction of the Euro."

79. See Bergsten, "America and Europe," pp. 20, 22, 26, 27.

80. The following draws on Ferguson and Kotlikoff, "Degeneration of EMU." I am indebted to Laurence Kotlikoff for his comments.

81. Buiter, "Alice in Euroland."

82. Bordo and Jonung, "Future of EMU," p. 27.

83. Panic, *European Monetary Union*.

84. Hitherto both were linked to the French franc, so that in effect they became a part of the Euro zone in 1999: see Fielding and Shields, "Franc Zone."

85. Flandreau, "The Bank, the States and the Market."

86. Schubert, "Dissolution;" Bordes, *Austrian Crown*, pp. 40–45.

87. Einaudi, "Money and Politics," ch. 3.

88. Einaudi, "Monetary Unions."

89. Ibid., p. 353. It remained in formal existence until the withdrawal of Switzerland in 1926; it fell apart the next year: Cohen, "Beyond EMU," p. 191.

90. Ferguson and Kotlikoff, "Degeneration of EMU."

91. See the critiques in Cohen, "Beyond EMU"; Feldstein, "Political Economy;" Obstfeld, "EMU: Ready or Not?"; Lal, "EMU and Globalisation."

92. Neal, "Shocking View of Economic History," pp. 327 f.

93. Deutsche Bundesbank, "Opinion."

94. In fact, Eichengreen and Wyplosz show the opposite to be the case in Europe: "Stability Pact," p. 91.

95. Bovenberg, Kremers and Masson, "Economic and Monetary Union," p. 141; Winckler, Hochreiter and Brandner, "Deficits, Debt and European Monetary Union," p. 265; Hagen, "Discussion," p. 278.

96. Goodhart, "Two Concepts of Money," pp. 408 ff.

97. Defined, it appears, as keeping inflation between zero and 2 per cent per annum.

98. King, "Commentary"; Winckler, Hochreiter and Brandner, "Deficits, Debt and European Monetary Union," p. 273.

99. Bovenberg, Kremers and Masson, "Economic and Monetary Union," pp. 142 ff.; Sims, "Precarious Fiscal Foundations," p. 15.

100. See e.g. Bordo and Jonung, "Future of EMU," p. 30; Berthold, Fehn and Thode, "Real Wage Rigidities."

101. Eichengreen and Wyplosz, "Stability Pact," p. 103.

Chapter 12

1. Tocqueville, *Democracy*, vol. i, pp. 3, 7.

2. Fukuyama, "End of History?"; and *End of History and the Last Man*.

3. Hegel, "Philosophical History of the World," pp. 26–30, 33–141.

4. Sheehan, *German History*, p. 212.

5. Fukuyama, "Capitalism and Democracy," pp. 106ff.

6. Fukuyama, *Great Disruption*, p. 282.

7. Olson, *Power and Prosperity*, pp. 8 f.

8. Ibid., p. 17.

9. Ibid., pp. 187, 192 f. Cf. *idem, Rise and Decline*; *idem*, "Big Bills Left on the Sidewalk," esp. pp. 19 f.

10. North, *Institutions*, p. 51; but see also *ibid.*, pp. 109 f.

11. Sen, *Development as Freedom*, pp. 51 f., 150 ff.

12. Shin, "Democratization," pp. 156 f.

13. Shleifer and DeLong, "Princes and Merchants."

14. Shleifer, "Government in Transition."

15. Przeworksi, "Neoliberal Fallacy," p. 51.

16. Butterfield, *Whig Interpretation*. Cf. Clark, *English Society*, a bold working out of the anti-Whig position.

17. Thomas Babington Macaulay's *History of England* (1848, 1855) is usually identified as the classic Whig text.

18. Tocqueville, *Democracy*, vol. i, pp. 8, 12.

19. Ibid., vol. ii, p. 324.

20. Ibid., vol. ii, p. 336.

21. Tocqueville, *Old Regime*, pp. 219 f.

22. Jardin, *Tocqueville*, pp. 427–61.

23. Przeworski, "Neoliberal Fallacy," pp. 52 f.

24. Institute for Democracy and Electoral Assistance, *Annual Report 1998*, p. xi.

25. Ward *et al.*, "Spatial and Temporal Diffusion," p. 3.
26. Starr, "Democratic Dominoes," p. 356.
27. Modelski and Perry, "Democratization in Long Perspective," p. 23.
28. Herodotus, *Histories*, pp. 238–41 (Book III, 82).
29. Schumpeter, *Capitalism, Socialism and Democracy*, p. 302.
30. Hayek, *Road to Serfdom*.
31. See e.g. Bollen, "Issues"; *idem*, "Liberal Democracy."
32. According to the Freedom House's own definition: "A country grants its citizens political rights when it permits them to form political parties that represent a significant range of voter choice and whose leaders can openly compete for and be elected to positions of power in government. A country upholds its citizens' civil liberties when it respects and protects their religious, ethnic, economic, linguistic, and other rights, including gender and family rights, personal freedoms, and freedoms of the press, belief, and association."
33. Karatnycky, "Decline of Illiberal Democracy," p. 112.
34. The fact that these were Nigeria, Indonesia and Sierra Leone shows how ephemeral, if not wholly illusory, such progress can be.
35. Zakaria, "The Rise of Illiberal Democracy."
36. "The Freedom House roster of electoral democracies is based on a stringent standard requiring that all elected national authority must be the product of free and fair electoral processes": neither Mexico nor Malaysia qualify.
37. Karatnycky, "Decline of Illiberal Democracy," pp. 116 f.
38. LeDuc, and Niemi (eds), *Comparing Democracies*, tables 1.1–1.7.
39. Blais and Massicotte, "Electoral Systems," p. 67.
40. John Vincent, "All That Matters is What Tony Wants," *London Review of Books*, 16 March 2000, p. 11. The House of Lords has always been appointed by the Crown: the main change introduced by the Blair Government has been the abolition of the hereditary principle which allowed those elevated to the peerage to pass on their title and seat in the Lords to their male heirs.
41. Lipset, "Social Requisites of Democracy," p. 87.
42. Shin, "Democratization," p. 159. Cf. Przeworski *et al.*, "What Makes Democracies Endure?," p. 45.
43. Shin, "Democratization," p. 160.
44. Grilli, Mascandiero and Tabellini, "Political and Monetary Institutions," p. 356.
45. Giddens, *Runaway World*, p. 63.
46. Lipset, "Social Requisites of Democracy Revisited," pp. 8 f.
47. "The average of the democracy indicator in sub-Saharan Africa peaked at 0.58 in 1960 (26 countries), then (for 43 countries) fell to low points of 0.19 in 1977 and 0.18 in 1989 before rising to 0.38 in 1994": Barro, "Determinants of Economic Growth," p. 36.
48. For details of the three versions of the Polity dataset, see Gurr, "Persistence and Change in Political Systems"; Gurr, Jaggers and Moore, "Transformation of the Western State"; Jaggers and Gurr, "Tracking Democracy's Third Wave"; Gleditsch and Ward, "Double Take."
49. Huntington, *Third Wave*, pp. 17–21.

50. For a sample of over a hundred countries, Gastil's democracy index (modified by Barro to range from 0.00 for no democracy to 1.00 for complete democracy) shows a peak in the mean of the index at 0.66 in 1960, a low point of 0.44 in 1975, followed by a rise to 0.58 in 1994: Barro, "Determinants of Economic Growth," p. 35. Cf. Gastil, *Freedom in the World*.

51. Modelski and Perry, "Democratization in Long Perspective," p. 25 n.

52. Though overtly xenophobic in its opposition to immigration, the Freedom Party had an undoubted democratic mandate. The further irony of a German Chancellor lecturing Italians that they would suffer the same fate if the National Alliance should enter a coalition requires no comment (interview with Gerhard Schröder, *Corriere della Sera*, 17 February 2000).

53. *The Economist, World in Figures*, pp. 38 f.

54. Karatnycky, "Decline of Illiberal Democracy," p. 123. According to another Freedom House study of post-Communist countries, "consolidated democracies and market economies averaged a growth rate of 4.7 per cent in 1997; transitional polities and economies registered an average growth rate of 1.4 per cent; and consolidated autocracies and statist economies in the region averaged close to a 3 per cent drop in GDP."

55. Lipset, "Social Requisites of Democracy," pp. 75–85.

56. Ibid., p. 103.

57. Lipset, "Social Requisites of Democracy Revisited," pp. 8 f.; pp; Lipset, Seong and Torres, "Comparative Analysis," pp. 165–71.

58. Bollen and Jackman, "Political Democracy."

59. Przeworski *et al.*, "What Makes Democracies Endure?," pp. 41, 49.

60. Barro, "Determinants of Economic Growth," p. 1.

61. Friedman, "Other Times, Other Places," pp. 2, 29. See also pp. 54, 86.

62. Lipset, "Social Requisites of Democracy Revisited," p. 16.

63. Ibid., p. 17. But see Przeworski *et al.*, "What Makes Democracies Endure?," p. 42, for a contrary view.

64. Muller, "Democracy, Economic Development and Income Inequality," and "Economic Determinants of Democracy." See also Muller and Seligson, "Civic Culture and Democracy"; Przeworski *et al.*, "What Makes Democracies Endure?"

65. The correlation was between average annual growth in real GDP and the average Freedom House political freedom ranking (ranging from 1, the most politically free, to 7, the least). The correlation coefficient for the sample as a whole was 0.18.

66. Broadberry, "How did the United States and Germany Overtake Britain?"

67. Przeworski *et al.*, "What Makes Democracies Endure?," p. 42.

68. Joll, *Europe since 1870*, p. 357.

69. See Schiel, "Pillars of Democracy." I am grateful to Juliane Schiel for her assistance with this point.

70. Gasiorowski, "Economic Crisis and Political Regime Change," pp. 883 f., 892.

71. Calculated from figures in Rummel, *Lethal Politics* and Mitchell, *European Historical Statistics*.

72. Easterly and Fischer, "Soviet Economic Decline."

73. Przeworski notes that of twenty investigations he reviewed, eight found that

democracy was better for growth than authoritarianism, eight found the opposite, and four found no difference. Przeworski, "Neo-liberal Fallacy," p. 52.

74. Landes, *Wealth and Poverty*, pp. 217 f.

75. Barro, "Determinants of Economic Growth," p. 32.

76. Schwarz, "Democracy and Market-oriented Reform."

77. Alesina and Rodrik, "Distributive Policies."

78. Barro, "Determinants of Economic Growth," p. 37.

79. Ibid., pp. 2 f. Emphasis added.

80. Eichengreen, *Golden Fetters*, pp. 9, 25, 92–7. To be precise, Eichengreen applies Lipset's idea that proportional representation will lead to unstable government, especially when the electorate is polarized. "Cross-cutting cleavages"—for example when religious and economic divisions are not congruent—will tend to reduce this problem; hence, for example, the relative stability of Holland in the period. Cf. Lipset, "Social Requisites of Democracy," pp. 91 f.

81. Barro, "Determinants of Economic Growth," p. 34.

82. Alesina *et al.*, "Political Instability," pp. 21 f.

83. *Hansard*, 11 November 1947, col. 206.

84. Weber, *Protestant Ethic*, pp. 112, 154.

85. Ibid, p. 24.

86. Weber saw "rational conduct on the basis of the idea of the calling" as "one of the fundamental elements of the spirit of modern capitalism": ibid., p. 180. But elsewhere he acknowledged the irrational character of "Christian asceticism:" "The ideal type of the capitalistic entrepreneur . . . gets nothing out of his wealth for himself, except the irrational sense of having done his job well." The "man exists for the sake of his business, instead of the reverse," which "from the view-point of personal happiness" was "irrational": pp. 70 f. Even more problematic is Weber's scathing sideswipe at the Jews, who posed the most obvious exception to his argument: "The Jews stood on the side of the politically and speculatively oriented adventurous capitalism; their ethos was . . . that of pariah-capitalism. But Puritanism carried the ethos of the rational organisation of capital and labour": p. 166. Weber was also mysteriously blind to the success of Catholic entrepreneurs in France, Belgium and elsewhere.

87. See e.g. Lal, *Unintended Consequences*.

88. Landes, *Wealth and Poverty*, passim. See also Sacks, *Morals and Markets*.

89. Huntington, *Clash of Civilizations*.

90. Lipset, Seong and Torres, "Comparative Analysis," pp. 165–71. See also Bollen, "Political Democracy;" Bollen and Jackman, "Political Democracy."

91. Lipset, Seong and Torres, "Comparative Analysis."

92. See e.g. Soto, *Mystery of Capital*.

93. North, *Institutions*, esp. pp. 96–103, 113 f., 127 f., 139 f.

94. See most recently, Phillips, *Cousins' Wars*.

Chapter 13

1. Rezzori, *Snows of Yesteryear*, pp. 65 f.

2. Ibid., pp. 283, 285.

3. Burleigh, *Third Reich*, p. 620.

4. Sombart, *Die Juden und das Wirtschaftsleben*.

5. Mazower, *Dark Continent*, pp. 51–63 and table 1.

6. Schiel, "Pillars of Democracy," citing Otto Junghahn, *Minorities in Europe* (New York, 1932), pp. 114–19.

7. Ash, *History of the Present*, p. 373.

8. See Davies, *The Isles*. For a critique see Clark, "Protestantism."

9. Hobsbawm, *Age of Capital*, p. 107.

10. Hinsley, *Power and the Pursuit of Peace*, pp. 33 f.

11. Ibid., p. 46.

12. Quoted in Knock, *To End All Wars*, p. 35.

13. Ibid., p. 77.

14. Ibid., p. 113.

15. Ibid., pp. 143 ff.

16. Ibid., p. 152.

17. Keylor, "International Diplomacy," p. 492.

18. Gilbert, *First World War*, pp. 528, 530.

19. Goldstein, "Great Britain: The Home Front," p. 151.

20. Quoted in Fink, "Minorities Question," p. 258.

21. Mazower, *Dark Continent*, p. 61.

22. Petzina, Abelshauser and Faust, (eds), *Sozialgeschichtliches Arbeitsbuch*, vol. iii, p. 23.

23. Overy, *Times Atlas of the Twentieth* Century, p. 51.

24. Rummel, *Statistics of Democide*, appendix, table 16A.1, and *Democide: Nazi Genocide*, tables 1.1 and 1.3.

25. Rummel, *Lethal Politics*, tables 1.3 and 1.B. Cf. Conquest, *Great Terror*, pp. 484–9, and *Nation Killers*, pp. 64, 111; Martin, "Origins of Soviet Ethnic Cleansing," p. 851. I am grateful to Erik Brynhildsbakken for his assistance on this point.

26. Chesnoff, *Pack of Thieves*, p. 283.

27. Rubinstein, "Entrepreneurial Minorities."

28. Mazower, *Dark Continent*, table 1.

29. Cook and Paxton (eds.), *European Political Facts*. Cf. *The Economist*, 3 January 1998.

30. Alesina and Wacziarg, "Openness," p. 4; Alesina, Spolaore and Wacziarg, "Economic Integration," pp. 1, 23.

31. *The Economist*, 3 January 1998.

32. Hobsbawm, *Nations and Nationalism*, p. 175.

33. Alesina and Spolaore, "Number and Size of Nations."

34. Alesina and Wacziarg, "Openness," *passim*.

35. Alesina and Spolaore, "International Conflict," *passim*.

36. Ibid., p. 18.

37. Gourevitch, *We Wish to Inform You*. The catalyst for the slaughter was the assassination of the (Hutu) president Juvenal Habyarimana following his peace agreement with the (Tutsi-led) Rwandan Patriotic Front.

38. Collier and Hoeffler, "Economic Causes of Civil War," pp. 568 ff. Their research on modern Africa stresses ethnic polarization—when there are two groups, one in the majority—rather than ethnic heterogeneity—multiple groups—as a source of conflict.

39. Alesina, Spolaore and Wacziarg, "Economic Integration," p. 26.

40. One obvious defect is that World Bank increasingly does business that could be done by the private sector: 70 per cent of its non-concessional lending over the past seven years went to eleven big countries which had full access to world capital markets (among them China, Argentina, Mexico and Brazil): *The Economist*, 18 March 2000.

41. James, *Globalization and its Sins*, pp. 42–9.

42. Hobsbawm, *Nations and Nationalism*, p. 174.

43. *Prospect*, April 2000. Cf. Simon Jenkins, "The Power of NGOs," *Institute of United States Studies: Lanesborough Lunch*, 5 April 2000.

44. *Hutchinson Almanac 2000*, p. 345.

45. *The Economist*, 19 December 1998; OECD, *Economic Outlook*, 65 (June 1999), p. 252.

46. Hinsley, *Power and the Pursuit of Peace*, p. 315.

47. Shawcross, *Deliver Us From Evil*.

48. Caplan, "Humanitarian Intervention," pp. 25 f.

49. Ibid., pp. 26 f.

Chapter 14

1. From "The White Man's Burden." To avoid offending modern sensibilities, this might be amended to read: "The Rich Person's Burden."

2. Kennedy, *Rise and Fall of the Great Powers*, pp. xvi, xxvi.

3. Ibid., p. 567. See also p. 254.

4. Ibid., pp. xvi, xxvi.

5. Ibid., pp. 696 f.

6. Ibid., pp. 573 f.

7. Ibid., p. 668. This page is also remarkable for the statement: "The present state of Mexican–United States relations . . . makes the Polish 'crisis' for the USSR seem small by comparison."

8. Ibid., p. 689.

9. Ibid., pp. 665 ff.

10. O'Brien, "Imperialism and the Rise and Decline."

11. Olson, *Rise and Decline*.

12. Ibid., p. 236.

13. See the discussion in Kindleberger, *World Economic Primacy*, pp. 46–53.

14. Quoted in Nef, *War and Human Progress*, p. 342.

15. Ibid., p. 333.

16. Smith, *Wealth of Nations*, bk. III, ch. 4.

17. Nef, *War and Human Progress*, pp. 341 f.

18. Angell, *Great Illusion*, p. 295.

19. Friedman, *Lexus*, pp. 248–75.

20. Luard, *War in International Society*, pp. 239 f.

21. Ibid., pp. 80 f.

22. Bonney, "Struggle for Great Power Status," pp. 351 ff.

23. Ibid., p. 357. Cf. Kennedy, *Rise and Fall of the Great Powers*, p. 172.

24. Towle, "Nineteenth-century Indemnities."

25. Ibid. I am grateful to Dr Philip Towle for providing this and other figures for nineteenth-century indemnities.

26. Ferguson, *World's Banker*, pp. 666 ff. Statistics for Prussian military expenditure are from *Jahrbuch für die Statistik des Preussischen Staats* (1869), pp. 372–443, 466–545.

27. White, "Making the French Pay," p. 23. Figures for the 1870 Prussian defence budget are taken from the Correlates of War database.

28. Goldsmith, *Premodern Financial Systems*, pp. 48–51.

29. Muto, "Spanish System," pp. 248 f.; Gelabert, "Fiscal Burden," p. 564 and n.

30. Bonney, "Revenues"

31. White, "Making the French Pay," esp. pp. 21 ff. Cf. Kindleberger, *Financial History*, pp. 219 ff.

32. Bonney, "Struggle for Great Power Status," p. 382. Cf. Buxton, *Finance and Politics*, vol. i, p. 6.

33. Hardach, *First World War*, p. 153.

34. White, "Making the French Pay," p. 23. For a full discussion of the issue see Ferguson, "Balance of Payments Question."

35. See Schuker, "American 'Reparations'."

36. Calculated from figures in Abelshauser, "Germany," p. 143.

37. Calculated from figures in the Correlates of War database.

38. Naimark, *Russians in Germany*.

39. Bonney, "Struggle for Great Power Status," p. 345; White, "France and the Failure to Modernize," p. 5.

40. O'Brien, "Inseparable Connections."

41. Duffy, "World-Wide War."

42. Statistics from the Correlates of War database.

43. Ferguson, *Pity of War*, passim.

44. Harrison, "Overview," p. 10.

45. Ibid., p. 17.

46. Mitchell, *European Historical Statistics*, p. 360.

47. Harrison, "Overview," p. 3.

48. Overy, *Why the Allies Won*, p. 15.

49. Harrison, "Overview," p. 6. Note: these figures exclude China from the Allies.

50. Ibid., p. 26.

51. Broadberry and Howlett, "United Kingdom," p. 55; Rockoff, "United States," p. 101; Abelshauser, "Germany," p. 162; Hara, "Japan," p. 254.

52. Johnson, *Nazi Terror*, pp. 315 f.

53. Harrison, "Soviet Union."

54. Quoted in Doyle, "Liberalism and World Politics," p. 1160.

55. Gates, Knutsen and Moses, "Democracy and Peace," p. 6.

56. Doyle, "Liberalism and World Politics," p. 1162.

57. Calculated from available figures in latest SIPRI and Freedom House surveys.

58. Russett, "Counterfactuals about War," pp. 181.

59. Ibid., p. 185.

60. Maoz and Abdolali, "Regime Types"; Dixon, "Democracy."

61. Ward and Gleditsch, "Democratizing for Peace."

62. Kennedy, *Rise and Fall of the Great Powers*, p. 799 n.

63. O'Brien, *Power with Profit*, pp. 34 f.

64. Kennedy, *Rise and Fall of the Great Powers*, pp. 407, 413.

65. Ibid., pp. 127, 159.

66. Correlation coefficients for defence spending as a percentage of GDP/GDP as against real GDP/GNP growth are as follows: UK 1850–1997: 0.001; US 1890–1998: 0.06; UK 1961–97:—0.03; US 1961–98: 0.07. The closest positive or negative correlation possible is plus or minus 1.00.

67. Defence spending as a proportion of GDP figures calculated from SIPRI's annual totals; average growth figures from *The Economist*. The correlation coefficient for the 59 countries in the sample was –0.05.

68. See Kennedy, *Preparing for the Twenty-first Century*, pp. 293 ff.

69. Author's calculations based on real GDP figures from Federal Reserve Bank of St Louis.

70. If President Carter had miraculously secured three terms in office, and had been succeeded by Bill Clinton, total defence expenditures (assuming unchanged policy) would have been $6.1 trillion from 1977 to 1998. Actual expenditures amounted to $7.4 trillion. The annual cost is the difference spread over the entire period from Ronald Reagan's period in office to 1998, i.e. including both the investment in the Strategic Defence Initiative and other Reagan-era arms spending, and the post-1989 "peace dividend."

71. FitzGerald, *Way Out There*.

72. As late as 1992, after a 22 per cent reduction in the number of superpower warheads, the total yield of the Soviet strategic nuclear arsenal was more than 4 million kilotons, compared with a figure of just over 1 million for the US. Fieldhouse, "Nuclear Weapons Developments," pp. 74–119. It is worth remarking that destructive capability of the Soviet strategic nuclear arsenal was substantially greater than that of the US by a factor of almost four. The possibility cannot be discounted that the Soviets were *over*-armed.

73. Schultz and Weingast, "Democratic Advantage," pp. 30–40.

74. O'Brien and Prados de la Escosura, "Balance Sheets."

75. O'Brien, "Imperialism and the Rise and Decline," pp. 56, 65f., 75.

76. Offer, "British Empire." Cf. Offer, "Costs and Benefits."

77. Edelstein, "Imperialism: Cost and Benefit," p. 205. Admittedly, this is based on a worst-case scenario in which, in the absence of imperial control between 1870 and 1913, trade to the Dominions would have been reduced by 30 per cent and trade with

the other colonies by 75 per cent. In a more benign counterfactual, in which tariffs would have risen but trade would have remained the same, the cost would have been more like 1.6–3.8 per cent of GNP.

78. James, *Globalization and its Sins*, p. 145.

79. Hobson, "Military-extraction Gap and the Wary Titan."

80. Ferguson, *Pity of War*, passim.

81. Hobson, "Military-extraction Gap and the Wary Titan."

82. As hinted in Charmley, *Churchill*.

83. *The Economist*, 3 June 2000.

84. *Financial Times*, 13 July 1999.

85. House of Commons, Foreign Affairs Select Committee, 1 October 1999.

86. *Financial Times*, 17 September 1999.

87. Mark Danner, "Kosovo: The Meaning of Victory," *New York Review of Books*, 15 July 1999.

88. Timothy Garton Ash, "Kosovo and Beyond," *New York Review of Books*, 24 June 1999.

89. Brittan, "Ethical Foreign Policy," p. 10.

90. Ignatieff, *Virtual War*, p. 193.

91. *Financial Times*, 14 June 1999.

92. Zbigniew Brzezinski, "Why Milosevic Cracked," *Prospect*, November 1999, pp. 10 f.

93. Maier, "Empires or Nationals," esp. p. 27 (where he suggests the more clumsy Atlantic system of imperial coordination").

94. Ibid., pp. 33, 35.

95. Kindleberger, *World in Depression*.

96. Gilpin, *Challenge of Global Capitalism*.

97. Ignatieff, *Virtual War*, p. 209.

Conclusion

1. Tolstoy, *War and Peace*, vol. ii, p. 1425.

2. Ibid., p. 1404.

3. Cornwell, *Hitler's Pope*.

4. Tolstoy, *War and Peace*, vol. II, First Epilogue, ch. xvi.

Bibliography

Abelshauser, Werner (ed.), *Die Weimarer Republik als Wohlfahrtsstaat: Zum Ver-hältnis von Wirtschafts- und Sozialpolitik in der Industriegesellschaft* [*Viertel-jahrsschrift für Sozial- und Wirtschaftsgeschichte*, Beiheft 81] (1987).

———, "Germany: Guns, Butter and Economic Miracles," in Mark Harrison (ed.), *The Economics of World War II: Six Great Powers in International Comparison* (Cambridge, 1998), 122–76.

Adamson, John, "England without Cromwell: What if Charles I had avoided the Civil War?," in Niall Ferguson (ed.), *Virtual History: Alternatives and Counter-factuals* (London, 1997), 91–124.

Albertini, Luigi, *The Origins of the War*, 3 vols. (Oxford, 1953).

Alesina, Alberto, "The End of Large Public Debts," in F. Giavazzi and L. Spaventa (eds.), *High Public Debt: The Italian Experience* (Cambridge, 1988), 34–79.

———, "The Political Economy of the Budget Surplus in the U.S.," *NBER Working Paper*, 7496, (2000).

———, and Sachs, Jeffrey, Political Parties and the Business Cycle in the United States, 1948–1984," *Journal of Money, Credit and Banking*, 20, 1 (Feb. 1988), 63–82.

——— and Rosenthal, Howard, "Partisan Cycles in Congressional Elections and the Macroeconomy," *American Political Science Review*, 83, 2 (June 1989), 373–98.

——— and Roubini, Nouriel, "Political Cycles in OECD Economies," *NBER Working Paper*, 3478 (October 1990).

———, Cohen, Gerald D. and Roubini, Nouriel, "Macroeconomic Policy and Elections in OECD Democracies," *NBER Working Paper*, 3830 (1991).

——— and Rodrik, D., "Distributive Policies and Economic Growth," *NBER Working Paper*, 3668 (1991).

———, Oezler, Sule, Roubini, Nouriel, and Zwagel, Phillip, "Political Instability and Economic Growth," *NBER Working Paper*, 4173 (1992).

——— and Summers, Lawrence H., "Central Bank Independence and Macroeco-nomic Performance: Some Comparative Evidence," *Journal of Money, Credit and Banking*, 25, 2 (May 1993), 151–62.

——— and Perotti, Roberti, "The Political Economy of Budget Deficits," *NBER Working Paper*, 4637 (1994).

────── and Spolaore, Enrico, "On the Number and Size of Nations," *NBER Working Paper*, 5050 (1995).

────── and ──────, "International Conflict, Defence Spending and the Size of Countries," *NBER Working Paper*, 5694 (1996).

────── and Wacziarg, Romain, "Openness, Country Size and the Government," *NBER Working Paper*, 6024 (1997).

──────, Spolaore, Enrico, and Wacziarg, Romain, "Economic Integration and Political Disintegration," *NBER Working Paper*, 6163 (1997).

Almond, Mark, "1989 Without Gorbachev: What if Communism had not Collapsed?," in Niall Ferguson (ed.,), *Virtual History: Alternatives and Counterfactuals* (London, 1997), 392–415.

Alt, James E., *The Politics of Economic Decline* (Cambridge, 1979).

──────, "Ambiguous Intervention: The Role of Government Action in Public Evaluation of the Economy," in Helmut Norpoth, Michael S. Lewis-Beck and Jean-Dominique Lafay (eds.) *Economics and Politics: The Calculus of Support* (Ann Arbor, 1991), 239–63.

Anderson, Christopher, *Blaming the Government: Citizens and the Economy in Five European Democracies* (Armonk, NY, 1995).

Anderson, Olive, "Loans versus Taxes: British Financial Policy in the Crimean War," *Economic History Review* (1963), 314–27.

Andic, Suphan and Veverka, Jindrich, "The Growth of Government Expenditure in Germany since the Unification," *Finanzarchiv* (1964), 171–278.

Angell, Norman, *The Great Illusion* (London, 1913).

Apostol, P. N., Bernatzky, M. W., and Michelson, A. M., *Russian Public Finances during the War* (New Haven, 1928).

Ash, Timothy Garton, *The History of the Present* (London, 1999).

Atkinson, A. B., *The Economic Consequences of Rolling Back the Welfare State* (Cambridge, Mass., 1999).

Auerbach, Alan J. and Kotlikoff, Laurence J., *Macroeconomics: An Integrated Approach* (2nd edn., Cambridge, Mass., 1998).

──────, ────── and Leibfritz, Willi (eds.), *Generational Accounting Around the World* (Chicago, 1999).

──────, Gokhale, Jagadeesh, and Kotlikoff, Laurence J., "Generational Accounts: A Meaningful Alternative to Deficit Accounting," in D. Bradford (ed.), *Tax Policy and the Economy*, 5 (Cambridge, Mass., 1991), 55–110.

──────, ──────, ──────, "Generational Accounting: A Meaningful Way to Assess Generational Policy," *Journal of Economic Perspectives* (Winter 1994), 73–94.

Aughey, A. and Norton, P., *Conservatives and Conservatism* (London, 1981).

Bagehot, Walter, *Lombard Street: A Description of the Money Market* (London, 1873).

Baker, Kenneth, *The Turbulent Years: My Life in Politics* (London, 1993).

Balderston, Theo, "War Finance and Inflation in Britain and Germany, 1914–1918," *Economic History Review* (1989), 222–44.

———, *The German Economic Crisis, 1923–1932* (Berlin, 1993).

Bankers Trust Company, *French Public Finance* (New York, 1920).

———, *English Public Finance* (New York, 1920).

Bardi, Luciano, and Morlino, Leonardo, "Italy: Tracing the Roots of the Great Transformation," in Richard S. Katz and Peter Mair (eds.), *How Parties Organize: Change and Adaptation in Party Organizations in Western Democracies* (Thousand Oaks, Calif., 1994), 24.

Barro, Robert J., "Are Government Bonds Net Wealth?," *Journal of Political Economy*, (1974), 1095–1118.

———, "On the Determination of the Public Debt," *Journal of Political Economy*, 87, 5 (1979), 940–71.

———, *Macroeconomics* (2nd edn., New York, 1987).

———, "Government Spending, Interest Rates, Prices and Budget Deficits in the United Kingdom, 1730–1918," *Journal of Monetary Economics* (1987), 221–47.

———, "Reflections on Ricardian Equivalence," in John Maloney (ed.), *Debt and Deficits: An Historical Perspective* (Cheltenham, 1998), 47–59.

———, "Optimal Funding Policy," in G. Calvo and M. King (eds.), *The Debt Burden and its Consequences for Monetary Policy* (London, 1998), 69–80.

———, "Determinants of Economic Growth: A Cross-Country Empirical Study," *NBER Working Paper*, 5698 (August 1996).

——— and Sala-i-Martin, Xavier, "World Real Interest Rates," in *NBER Macroeconomics Annual 1990* (Cambridge, Mass., 1990), 15–59.

Barsky, R. B., "The Fisher Hypothesis and the Forecastability and Persistence of Inflation," *Journal of Monetary Economics*, 19, 1 (1987), 3–24.

Baskin, Jonathan and Paul J. Miranti, J., *A History of Corporate Finance* (Cambridge, 1997).

Batley, Richard, and Ferguson, Niall, "Event Risk and the International Bond Market in the Era of the Classical Gold Standard," unpublished paper (1999).

Baumol, W., "Enterpreneurship in Economic Theory," *American Economic Review*, 58 (1968), 64–71.

Bayoumi, Tamim, "Saving-Investment Correlations: Immobile Capital, Goverment Policy or Endogenous Behaviour," *IMF Working Paper*, 89/66 (1990).

———, Goldstein, Morris, and Woglom, Geoffrey, "Do Credit Markets Discipline Sovereign Borrowers? Evidence from the US States," *Journal of Money, Credit and Banking* (1995), 1046–59.

———, Eichengreen, Barry, and Taylor, Mark P., "Introduction," in Tamim Bayoumi, Barry Eichengreen and Mark P. Taylor (eds.), *Modern Perspectives on the Gold Standard* (Cambridge, 1996), 3–16.

Beevor, Anthony, *Stalingrad* (London, 1999).

Bellucci, Paolo, "Italian Economic Voting: A Deviant Case or Making a Case for a Better Theory?" in Helmut Norpoth, Michael S. Lewis-Beck and Jean-Dominique Lafay (eds.), *Economics and Politics: The Calculus of Support* (Ann Arbor, 1991), 63–80.

Benn, Tony, *Out of the Wilderness: Diaries 1963–7* (London, 1987).

———, *Conflicts of Interest: Diaries, 1977–80* (London, 1990).

Benjamin, D. K., and Kochin, L. A., "War, Prices and Interest Rates: A Martial Solution to Gibson's Paradox," in Michael D. Bordo and Anna J. Schwartz (eds.), *A Retrospective on the Classical Gold Standard* (Chicago/London, 1984), 587–604.

Bergsten, C. Fred, "America and Europe: Clash of the Titans," *Foreign Affairs* (March/April 1999), 20–34.

Berlin, Isaiah, "Benjamin Disraeli and Karl Marx" in id., *Against the Current: Essays in the History of Ideas*, ed. Henry Hardy (Oxford, 1981), 252–86.

Bernanke, Ben and Mark, Gertler, "Monetary Policy and Asset Price Volatility," paper presented at the Federal Reserve Bank of Kansas City conference on "New Challenges for Monetary Policy," Jackson Hole, Wyoming (August 1999).

Bernstein, Peter L., *Against the Gods: The Remarkable Story of Risk* (New York, 1996).

Berthold, Norbert, Fehn, Rainer, and Thode, Eric, "Real Wage Rigidities, Fiscal Policy, and the Stability of EMU in the Transition Phase," *IMF Working Paper*, 99/83 (June 1999).

Bille, Lars, "Denmark: The Decline of the Membership Party," in Richard S. Katz and Peter Mair (eds.), *How Parties Organize: Change and Adaptation in Party Organizations in Western Democracies* (Thousand Oaks, Calif., 1994), 134–57.

Black, Jeremy, "Foreign and Defence Policies: The Challenge of Europe," in Keith Sutherland (ed.), *The Rape of the Constitution* (London, 2000) 285–90.

Blackbourn, David, and Eley, Geoff, *The Peculiarities of German History: Bourgeois Society and Politics in Nineteenth-century Germany* (Oxford, 1984).

Blais, André, and Massicotte, Louis, "Electoral Systems," in Lawrence LeDuc and Richard G. Niemi (eds.), *Comparing Democracies: Elections and Voting in Global Perspective* (Thousand Oaks, Calif., 1996), 49–82.

Blake, Robert, *Disraeli* (London, 1966).

———, *The Conservative Party from Peel to Major* (London, 1997).

Bloch, Ivan S., *Is War Now Impossible? Being an Abridgment of "The War of the Future in its Technical, Economic and Political Relations"* (London, 1899).

Bloom, Howard S., and Price, H. Douglas, "Voter Response to Short-Run Economic Conditions: The Asymmetric Effect of Prosperity and Recession," *American Political Science Review*, 69 (1975) 1240–1254.

Bloomfield, Arthur Irving, *Monetary Policy under the International Gold Standard, 1880–1914* (New York, 1959).

———, *Short-term Capital Movements under the Pre-1914 Gold Standard* (Princeton, 1963).

Bogdanor, Vernon, *Power and the People: A Guide to Constitutional Reform* (London, 1997).

Bollen, K. A., "Political Democracy and the Timing of Development," *American Sociological Review*, 44 (1979), 572–87.

———, "Issues in the Comparative Measurement of Political Democracy." *American Sociological Review*, 45 (1980), 370–390.

———, "Liberal Democracy: Validity and Method Factors in Cross-National Measures," *American Journal of Political Science*, 37 (1993), 1207–30.

────── and Jackman, R., "Political Democracy and the Size and Distribution of Income," *American Sociological Review*, 50 (1985) 438–457.

Bond, Brian, *Victorian Military Campaigns* (London, 1967).

Bond, Tim and Kevin Adams, *Barclays Equity-Gilt Study 2000* (45th edn., London, 2000).

Bonney, Richard (ed.), *Economic Systems and State Finance* (Oxford, 1995).

──────, "Introduction," in id. (ed.), *Economic Systems and State Finance* (Oxford, 1995), 1–18.

──────, "Early Modern Theories of State Finance," in id. (ed.), *Economic Systems and State Finance* (Oxford, 1995), 163–229.

──────, "The Eighteenth Century, II: The Struggle for Great Power Status and the End of the Old Fiscal Regime," in id. (ed.), *Economic Systems and State Finance* (Oxford, 1995), 315–90.

──────, "Revenues," in id. (ed.), *Economic Systems and State Finance* (Oxford, 1995), 423–505.

──────, (ed.), *The Rise of the Fiscal State in Europe, c.1200–1815* (Oxford, 1999).

──────, "France, 1494–1815," in id. (ed.), *The Rise of the Fiscal State in Europe, c.1200–1815* (Oxford, 1999), 123–76.

Borchardt, Knut, "Währung und Wirtschaft," in Deutsche Bundesbank (ed.), *Währung und Wirtschaft in Deutschland, 1876–1975* (Frankfurt am Main, 1976), 1–53.

──────, "Das Gewicht der Inflationsangst in den wirtschaftspolitischen Entscheidungsprozessen während der Weltwirtschaftskrise," in Gerald D. Feldman and E. Müller-Luckner (eds.), *Die Nachwirkungen der Inflation auf die deutsche Geschichte, 1924–1933* (Munich, 1985), 233–60.

Bordes, W. de, *The Austrian Crown: Its Depreciation and Stabilisation* (London, 1924).

Bordo, Michael D., "The Gold Standard: The Traditional Approach," in Michael D. Bordo and Anna J. Schwartz (eds.), *A Retrospective on the Classical Gold Standard* (Chicago/London, 1984), 23–113.

──────, "Financial Crises, Banking Crises, Stock Market Crashes and the Money Supply: Some International Evidence, 1870–1933," in F. Capie and G. E. Wood (eds.), *Financial Crises and the World Banking System* (London, 1986), 190–248.

──────, "The Bretton Woods International Monetary System: A Historical Overview," in Michael D. Bordo and Barry Eichengreen (eds.), *A Retrospective on the Bretton Woods System: Lessons for International Monetary Reform* (Chicago/London, 1993), 3–98.

──────, "Gold as a Commitment Mechanism: Past, Present and Future," *World Gold Council Research Study*, 11 (n.d. [1994]).

──────, "The Classical Gold Standard: Some Lessons for Today," *Federal Reserve Bank of St Louis Review*, 63, 5 (1981), repr. in id. *The Gold Standard and Related Regimes* (Cambridge, 1999), 149–78.

────── and Kydland, Finn E., "The Gold Standard as a Commitment Mechanism," in Tamim Bayoumi, Barry Eichengreen and Mark P. Taylor (eds.), *Modern Perspectives on the Gold Standard* (Cambridge, 1996), 55–100.

—— and White, Eugene N., "A Tale of Two Currencies: British and French Finance during the Napoleonic War," *Journal of Economic History,* 51 (1991), 303–16.

—— and Rockoff, Hugh, "The Gold Standard as a 'Good Housekeeping Seal of Approval'" in Michael D. Bordo *The Gold Standard and Related Regimes* (Cambridge, 1999), 318–66.

—— and ——, "Was Adherence to the Gold Standard a 'Good Housekeeping Seal of Approval' during the Interwar Period?," *NBER Working Paper,* 7186 (June 1999).

—— and Schwartz, Anna J., "The Changing Relationship between Gold and the Money Supply," *World Gold Council Research Study,* 4 (n.d. [1993]).

—— and ——, "The Operation of the Specie Standard: Evidence for Core and Peripheral Countries," in Barry Eichengreen and Jorge Braga de Macedo (eds.), *Historical Perspectives on the Gold Standard: Portugal and the World* (London, 1996).

—— and ——, "Monetary Policy Regimes and Economic Performance: The Historical Record," *NBER Working Paper,* 6201 (Sept. 1997).

—— and ——, "Measuring Real Economic Effects of Bailouts: Historical Perspectives on How Countries in Financial Distress have Fared With and Without Bailouts," paper presented at the Carnegie Rochester Conference on Public Policy, (19–20 Nov. 1999).

—— and Jonung, Lars, "Return to the Convertibility Principle? Monetary and Fiscal Regimes in Historical Perspective," paper presented at the International Economic Association conference in Trento, Italy (Sept. 1997).

—— and ——, "The Future of EMU: What Does the History of Monetary Unions Tell Us?, paper presented at City University Business School and American Express Conference on Monetary Unions (29 Apr. 1999).

——, Eichengreen, Barry, and Irwin, Douglas A., "Is Globalisation Today Really Different Than Globalization a Hundred Years Ago," *NBER Working Paper,* 7195 (June 1999).

—— and Dewald, William G., "Historical Bond Market Inflation Credibility," paper presented at the Annual Western Economic Association Conference, San Diego (8 July 1999).

—— and Eichengreen, Barry, "Is Our International Economic Environment Unusually Crisis Prone?," paper presented at the Reserve Bank of Australia Conference on Private Capital Flows, Sydney (9–10 Aug. 1999).

Bosher, J. F., *French Finances, 1770–1795* (Cambridge, 1970).

Boskin, Michael J., "Concepts and Measures of Federal Deficits and their Impact on Economic Activity," in Kenneth J. Arrow and Michael J. Boskin (eds.), *The Economics of Public Debt* (London, 1988), pp. 77–109.

Bovenberg, Lans, Kremers, Jeroen and Masson, Paul, "Economic and Monetary Union in Europe and Constraints on National Budgetary Policies," in Ben van Velthoven, Harrie Verbon and Frans van Winden (eds.), *The Political Economy of Government Debt,* (Amsterdam/New York/Tokyo, 1993), 137–55.

Bowley, A. L., Schwartz, G. I., and Smith, K. C., *A New Index of Prices of Securities*, London & Cambridge Economic Service, Special Memorandum No. 33 (London, 1931).

Brandt, Harm-Heinrich, "Public Finances of Neo-absolutism in Austria in the 1850s: Integration and Modernisation," in Peter-Christian Witt (ed.), *Wealth and Taxation in Central Europe* (Leamington Spa/Hamburg/New York, 1987), 81–109.

Braudel, Fernand, *Civilization and Capitalism, 15th–18th Century*, vol. iii: *The Perspective of the World*, trans. Siân Reynolds (London, 1984).

Braun, H.-J., *The German Economy in the Twentieth Century: The German Reich and the Federal Republic* (London/New York, 1990).

Bresciani-Turroni, C., *The Economics of Inflation: A Study of Currency Depreciation in Post-War Germany* (London, 1937).

Brewer, John, *The Sinews of Power: War, Money and the English State, 1688–1783* (London, 1989).

Briault, Clive, "The Costs of Inflation," *Bank of England Quarterly Bulletin* (Feb, 1995), 33–45.

Brittan, Samuel, "The Politics of Excessive Expectations" in id. (ed.), *The Economic Consequences of Democracy* (2nd edn., Aldershot, 1988).

———, "An Ethical Foreign Policy?," The Hinton Lecture of the National Council for Voluntary Organisations (24 Nov. 1999).

Broadberry, Stephen N., "How did the United States and Germany Overtake Britain? A Sectoral Analysis of Comparative Productivity Levels, 1870–1990," *Journal of Economic History* (1998), 375–407.

——— and Howlett, Peter, "The United Kingdom: "Victory at All Costs" ATH," in Mark Harrison (ed.), *The Economics of World War II: Six Great Powers in International Comparison* (Cambridge, 1998), 43–80.

Broadway, Robin, and Wildasin, David, "Long Term Debt Strategy: A Survey," in Ben van, Velthoven, Harrie Verbon and Frans van Winden (eds.), *The Political Economy of Government Debt* (Amsterdam/New York/Tokyo, 1993), 37–68.

Brogan, Patrick, *World Conflicts* (London, 1998).

Brown, E. Cary, "Episodes in the Public Debt History of the United States," in Rudiger Dornbusch and Mario Draghi (eds.), *Public Debt Management: Theory and History* (Cambridge, 1990), 229–54.

Brown, Robert L., and Easton, Stephen A., "Weak-form Efficiency in the Nineteenth Century: A Study of Daily Prices in the London Market for 3 per cent Consols, 1821–1860," *Economica*, 56 (1989), 61–70.

Bruno, Michael, and Easterly, William, "Inflation Crises and Long-run Growth," *NBER Working Paper*, 5209 (Aug. 1995).

Buchan, James, *Frozen Desire: An Inquiry on the Meaning of Money* (London, 1997).

Buchanan, James M., and Wagner, Richard E., *Democracy in Deficit: The Political Legacy of Lord Keynes* (New York / London, 1977).

———, ——— and Burton, John, *The Consequences of Mr Keynes* (London, 1978).

Buckle, Mike, and Thompson, John, *The UK Financial System: Theory and Practice* (Manchester, 1995).

Budge, Ian, Crewe, Ivor, McKay, David, and Newton, Ken, *The New British Politics* (Harlow, 1998).

Buiter, Willhelm H., "Generational Accounts, Aggregate Saving and Intergenerational Distribution," *Economica*, 64 (1997), 605–26.

——, "Alice in Euroland," *Journal of Common Market Studies* (1999).

Burleigh, Michael, *The Third Reich: A New History* (London, 2000).

Burns, Robert, *Complete Poems and Songs*, ed. James Kinsley (Oxford, 1971).

——, *The Complete Letters*, ed. James Mackay, 2nd edn. (Ayr, 1990).

Burroughs, Peter, "Defence and Imperial Disunity," in Andrew Porter (ed.), *The Oxford History of the British Empire* (Oxford/New York, 1999), 320–45.

Butler, David, *British General Elections since 1945*, 2nd edn. (London, 1995).

—— and Butler, Gareth, *British Political Facts, 1900–1994* (London, 1994).

—— and Stokes, Donald, *Political Change in Britain: Forces Shaping Electoral Change* (London, 1969).

—— and Kavanagh, Dennis, *The British General Election of 1997* (London, 1997).

Butterfield, Herbert, *The Whig Interpretation of History* (London, 1931).

Buxton, Sydney Charles, *Finance and Politics: An Historical Study, 1783–1885*, 2 vols. (London, 1888).

Cagan, P., "The Monetary Dynamics of Hyperinflation," in Milton Friedman (ed.), *Studies in the Quantity Theory of Money* (Chicago, 1956), 25–117.

Cain, P. J., and Hopkins, A. G., *British Imperialism: Innovation and Expansion, 1688–1914* (London, 1993).

Cairncross, Alec, "The Managed Economy," in id. (ed.), *The Managed Economy* (Oxford, 1970), 3–22.

Calder, Angus (ed.), *Wars* (London, 1999).

Cameron, Rondo (ed.), *Banking in the Early Stages of Industrialisation* (New York/Oxford, 1967).

Canetti, Elias, *The Torch in My Ear*, trans. Joachim Neugroschel (London, 1982).

Cannadine, David, *Class in Britain* (New Haven/London, 1998).

Capie, Forrest, "Conditions in which Very Rapid Inflation has Occurred," *Carnegie-Rochester Conference Series on Public Policy*, 24(1986), 115–68.

——, "The Evolution of the Lender of Last Resort: The Bank of England," unpublished draft paper (July 2000).

—— and Webber, Alan, *A Monetary History of the United Kingdom, 1870–1982*, vol. i: *Data, Sources, Methods* (London, 1985).

——, Mills, Terry C., and Wood, Geoffrey E., "Debt Management and Interest Rates: The British Stock Conversion of 1932," *Applied Economics*, 18 (1986), 1111–26.

—— and Wood, Geoffrey E., "Money Demand and Supply under the Gold Standard: The United Kingdom, 1870–1914," in Tamim Bayoumi, Barry Eichengreen and Mark P. Taylor (eds.), *Modern Perspectives on the Gold Standard* (Cambridge, 1996), 261–83.

————, "Can there be an International Lender of Last Resort?," unpublished paper (Oct. 1998).

————, Charles Goodhart, and Schnadt, Norbert, "The Development of Central Banking," in Forrest Capie, Charles Goodhart, Stanley Fischer and Norbert Schnadt (eds.), *The Future of Central Banking: The Tercentenary Symposium of the Bank of England* (Cambridge, 1994), 1–97.

Caplan, Jane, *Government Without Administration: State and Civil Service in Weimar and Nazi Germany* (Oxford, 1988).

Caplan, Richard, "Humanitarian Intervention: Which Way Forward?," *Ethics and International Affairs*, 14 (2000), 23–38.

Capra, Carlo, "The Eighteenth Century, I: The Finances of the Austrian Monarchy and the Italian States," in Richard Bonney (ed.), *Economic Systems and State Finance* (Oxford, 1995), 295–314.

Cardarelli, Roberto, Sefton, James, and Kotlikoff, Laurence J., "Generational Accounting in the UK," Unpublished paper (Nov. 1998).

Carlyle, Thomas, *Selected Writings*, ed. Alan Shelston (Harmondsworth, 1971).

————, "On History" [1830] in Fritz Stern (ed.), *The Varieties of History from Voltaire to the Present* (London, 1970), 90–107.

Carreras, A., *Industrializacion Espanola: Estudios de historia cuantitiva* (Florence, 1995).

Carruthers, Bruce G., *City of Capital: Politics and Markets in the English Financial Revolution* (Princeton, 1996).

Castellane, Conte de, *Journal du Maréchal Castellane, 1804–1862,* 5 vols. (Paris, 1896–1930).

Castle, Barbara, *The Castle Diaries, 1964–1976* (London, 1990).

Cavaco-Silva, Anibal A., *Economic Effects of Public Debt* (London, 1977).

Cecco, M. de, *Money and Empire: The International Gold Standard, 1890–1914* (Oxford, 1973).

Central Statistical Office, *Monthly Digest of Statistics* (London, various issues from 1957).

————, *Retail Prices 1914–1990* (London, 1991).

————, *Social Trends* (London, various issues from 1991).

Chancellor, Edward, *Devil Take the Hindmost: A History of Financial Speculation* (London, 1999).

Chapman, Stanley, "The Establishment of the Rothschilds as Bankers," *Transactions of the Jewish Historical Society of England* (1982–6), 177–93.

Chappel, Henry W. Jr., and Keech, William R., "Explaining Aggregate Evaluations of Economic Performance," in Helmut Norpoth, Michael S. Lewis-Beck, and Jean-Dominique Lafay (eds.) *Economics and Politics: The Calculus of Support* (Ann Arbor, 1991), 207–20.

Charmley, John, *Churchill: The End of Glory, A Political Biography* (London, 1993).

Chennells, L., Dilnot, A., and Roback, N., "A Survey of the UK Tax System," Institute for Fiscal Studies website (2000).

Chesnoff, Richard Z., *Pack of Thieves: How Hitler and Europe Plundered the Jews and Committed the Greatest Theft in History* (London, 1999).

Clapham, John Harold, *An Economic History of Modern England*, vol. ii: *1850–1886* (Cambridge, 1932).

——, *The Bank of England: A History*, 2 vols. (Cambridge, 1944).

Clark, J. C. D., "British America: What If There Had Been no American Revolution?," in Niall Ferguson (ed.), *Virtual History: Alternatives and Counterfactuals* (London, 1997), 125–74.

——, *English Society, 1660–1832*, 2nd edn. (Cambridge, 2000).

——, "Protestantism, Nationalism and National Identity, 1660–1832," *Historical Journal*, 43, 1 (2000), 249–76.

Clarke, Harold D., and Stewart, Marianne C., "Prospections, Retrospections and Rationality: The "Bankers" Model of Presidential Approval Reconsidered," *American Journal of Political Science*, 38 (1994), 1104–23.

——, —— and Zuk, Gary, "Politics, Economics, and Party Popularity in Britain, 1979–1983," *Electoral Studies*, 5 (1986) 123–41.

——, and Whiteley, Paul, "Perceptions of Macroeconomic Performance, Government Support and Conservative Party Strategy in Britain, 1983–1987," *European Journal of Political Research*, 18 (1990) 97–120.

Clarke, Peter, *Hope and Glory: Britain 1900–1990* (London, 1996).

——, "Keynes, Buchanan and the Balanced Budget Doctrine," in J. Maloney (ed.), *Debt and Deficits: An Historical Perspective* (Cheltenham, 1998), 60–83.

Coase, R. H., "The Nature of the Firm," *Economica*, 4 (1937), 386–405.

Cobbett, William, *Rural Rides* (London, 1985 [1830]).

Cohen, B. J., "Beyond EMU: The Problem of Sustainability," *Economics and Politics*, 5 (1993), 187–202.

Collier, Paul, and Hoeffler, Anke, "On Economic Causes of Civil War," *Oxford Economic Papers*, 50 (1998), 563–73.

Congdon, Tim, "Did Britain have a Keynesian Revolution? Fiscal Policy since 1941," in J. Maloney (ed.), *Debt and Deficits: An Historical Perspective* (Cheltenham, 1998), 84–115.

Conover, Pamela Johnston, Feldman, Stanley, and Knight, Kathleen, "The Personal Underpinning of Economic Forecasts," *American Journal of Political Science*, 31 (1987), 559–83.

Conquest, Robert, *The Great Terror: A Reassessment* (London, 1992).

——, *The Nation Killers* (London, 1970).

Conway, Stephen, "Britain and the Revolutionary Crisis, 1763–1791," in P. J. Marshall (ed.), *The Oxford History of the British Empire*, vol. ii: *The Eighteenth Century* (Oxford/New York, 1998), 325–46.

Cook, Chris, and Paxton, John (eds.), *European Political Facts, 1900–1996* (London, 1998).

Cooper, Richard N., "The Gold Standard: Historical Facts and Future Prospects," *Brookings Papers on Economic Activity*, 1 (1982), 1–56.

——, "A Monetary System for the Future," in id., *The International Monetary System* (Cambridge, Mass., 1987), 259–78.

Cornwell, John, *Hitler's Pope: The Secret History of Pius XII* (London, 1999).

Coxall, Bill, and Robins, Lynton, *Contemporary British Politics*, 3rd edn. (Basingstoke, 1998).

Coyle, D., *The Weightless World* (Oxford, 1997).

Crafts, Nicholas, "The Conservative Government's Economic Record: An End of Term Report," *IEA Occasional Paper*, 104 (1998), 9–42.

——, "Globalization and Growth in the Twentieth Century," *IMF Working Paper*, 00/44 (Mar. 2000).

Craig, F. W. S. (ed.), *British Electoral Facts, 1832–1987* (Dartmouth, 1988).

Creveld, Martin van, *Supplying War: Logistics from Wallenstein to Patton* (Cambridge, 1977).

Crewe, Ivor, and King, Anthony, *SDP: The Birth, Life and Death of the Social Democratic Party* (Oxford, 1995).

Crouchley, A. E., *The Economic Development of Modern Egypt* (London, 1938).

Crouzet, François, "Politics and Banking in Revolutionary and Napoleonic France," in Richard Sylla, Richard Tilly and Gabriel Tortella (eds.), *The States, the Financial System and Economic Modernization* (Cambridge, 1999), 20–52.

Cukierman, Alex, Kalaitzidakis, Pantellis, Summers, Lawrence H., and Webb, Steven B., "Central Bank Independence, Growth, Investment and Real Interest Rates," *Carnegie-Rochester Conference Series on Public Policy*, 39 (1993), 95–140.

Cutler, David, James Poterba and Lawrence Summers, "What Moves Stock Prices?" *Journal of Portfolio Management*, 15, 3 (1989), 4–12.

Cyert, R. M., *The Economic Theory of Organisation and the Firm* (London, 1988).

Davidson, James Dale and William Rees-Mogg, *The Great Reckoning: How the World will Change in the Depression of the 1990s* (London, 1992).

Davies, Norman, *The Isles* (London, 1999).

Davis, Lance E., and Huttenback, R. A., *Mammon and the Pursuit of Empire: The Political Economy of British Imperialism, 1860–1912* (Cambridge, 1986).

Dawkins, Richard, *The Selfish Gene* (Oxford, 1989).

Dawson, Frank Griffith, *The First Latin American Debt Crisis* (London, 1990).

Daykin, Christopher, "Funding the Future? Problems in Pension Reform," *Politeia*, Policy Series, 9 (1998).

DeLong, J. Bradford, "The Shape of Twentieth Century Economic History," *NBER Working Paper*, 7569 (Feb. 2000).

——, "Cornucopia: The Pace of Economic Growth in the Twentieth Century," *NBER Working Paper*, 7602 (Mar. 2000).

Deschouwer, Kris, "The Decline of Consociationalism and the Reluctant Modernization of Belgian Mass Parties," in Richard S. Katz and Peter Mair (eds.), *How Parties Organize: Change and Adaptation in Party Organizations in Western Democracies* (Thousand Oaks, Calif., 1994), 80–108.

Deutsche Bundesbank, "Opinion of the Central Bank Council concerning Convergence in the European Union in view of Stage Three of Economic and Monetary Union," 26 March 1998.

Dickens, Charles, *David Copperfield*, ed. Jeremy Tambling (London, 1996 [1850]).

Diener, Ed, Sandvik, Ed, Seidlitz, Larry, and Deiner, Marissa, "The Relation Between

Income and Subjective Well-being: Relative or Absolute?," *Social Indicators Research*, 28 (1993), 195–223.

Disraeli, Benjamin, *Coningsby, or The New Generation* (London, 1881 edn.).

Dixon, William J., "Democracy and the Peaceful Settlement of International Conflict," *American Political Science Review*, 88, 1 (1994), 14–32.

Dornbusch, Rudiger, "Debt and Monetary Policy: The Policy Issues," in G. Calvo and M. King (eds.), *The Debt Burden and its Consequences for Monetary Policy* (London, 1998), 3–27.

—— and Draghi, Mario, "Introduction," in Dornbusch and Draghi (eds.), *Public Debt Management*, 1–13.

—— and Draghi, M. (eds.), *Public Debt Management: Theory and History* (Cambridge, 1990).

Dostoevsky, Fyodor, *Notes from Underground*, trans. Andrew R. MacAndrew (London, 1980).

Downs, Anthony, *An Economic Theory of Democracy* (New York, 1957).

Dowrick, S., "Estimating the Impact of Government Consumption on Growth: Growth Accounting and Endogenous Growth Models," in S. Durlauf, J. Helliwell and B. Raj (eds.), *Long Run Economic Growth* (Heidelberg, 1996), 163–84.

Doyle, Michael W., "Liberalism and World Politics," *American Political Science Review*, 80, 4 (1986), 1151–67.

Doyle, William, *Origins of the French Revolution* (Oxford, 1980).

Drazen, Allan, "Towards a Political-Economic Theory of Domestic Debt," in G. Calvo and M. King (eds.), *The Debt Burden and its Consequences for Monetary Policy* (London, 1998), pp. 159–176.

Drummond, Ian M., *The Gold Standard and the International Monetary System, 1900–1939* (Basingstoke, 1987).

Drysch, T., "The New French System of Political Finance," in A. B. Gunlicks (ed.), *Campaign and Party Finance in North America and Western Europe* (Boulder, Col., 1993), 155–78.

Duffy, Michael, "World-Wide War and British Expansion," in P. J. Marshall (ed.), *The Oxford History of the British Empire*, vol. ii: *The Eighteenth Century* (Oxford/New York, 1998), 184–207.

Duncan, Alan and Hobson, Dominic, *Saturn's Children: How the State Devours Liberty, Prosperity and Virtue* (London, 1995).

Dutton, John, "The Bank of England and the Rules of the Game under the International Gold Standard: New Evidence," in Michael D. Bordo and Anna J. Schwartz (eds.), *A Retrospective on the Classical Gold Standard* (Chicago/London, 1984) 173–202.

Easterly, William, and Fischer, Stanley, "The Soviet Economic Decline: Historical and Republican Data," *NBER Working Paper*, 4735 (May 1994).

Economist, The, *Economic Statistics, 1900–1983* (London, 1981).

Economist, The, *The Pocket World in Figures: 2000 Edition* (London, 1999).

Edelstein, Michael, *Overseas Investment in the Age of High Imperialism: The United Kingdom, 1850–1914* (New York, 1982).

———, "Imperialism: Cost and Benefit," in Roderick Floud and Donald McCloskey (eds.), *The Economic History of Britain since 1700*, 2nd edn., vol. ii (Cambridge, 1994), 173–216.

Eichengreen, Barry, "Conducting the International Orchestra: Bank of England Leadership under the Classical Gold Standard," *Journal of International Money and Finance*, 45, 2 (1987), 5–29.

———, "Discussion," in F. Giavazzi, and L. Spaventa (eds.), *High Public Debt: the Italian Experience* (Cambridge, 1988), 80–84.

———, "The Capital Levy in Theory and Practice," in Rudiger Dornbusch and Mario Draghi (eds.), *Public Debt Management: Theory and History* (Cambridge, 1990), 191–216.

———, "The Gold-Exchange Standard and the Great Depression," in id., *Elusive Stability: Essays in the History of International Finance, 1919–1939* (Cambridge, 1990), 239–70.

———, "Hegemonic Stability Theories and the International Monetary System," in id., *Elusive Stability: Essays in the History of International Finance, 1919–1939* (Cambridge, 1990), 271–311.

———, *Golden Fetters: The Gold Standard and the Great Depression, 1919–1939* (New York/Oxford, 1992).

———, "The Gold Standard since Alec Ford," in S. N. Broadberry and N. F. R. Crafts (eds.), *Britain in the International Economy* (Cambridge, 1992), 49–79.

———, "Déjà Vu All Over Again: Lessons from the Gold Standard for European Monetary Unification," in Tamim Bayoumi, Barry Eichengreen and Mark P. Taylor (eds.), *Modern Perspectives on the Gold Standard* (Cambridge, 1996), 365–87.

——— and Sachs, Jeffrey, "Exchange Rates and Economic Recovery in the 1930s," in Barry Eichengreen, *Elusive Stability: Essays in the History of International Finance, 1919–1939* (Cambridge, 1990), 215–38.

——— and Flandreau, Marc, "The Geography of the Gold Standard," *International Macroeconomics*, Centre for Economic Policy Research Discussion Paper Series, 1050 (Oct. 1994).

——— and ——— (eds.), *The Gold Standard in Theory and History* (London, 1997).

——— and Wyplosz, Charles, "The Stability Pact: More than a Minor Nuisance?," *Economic Policy*, 26 (1998), 67–113.

——— and Hausmann, Richardo, "Exchange Rates and Financial Fragility," paper presented at the Federal Reserve Bank of Kansas City's Conference on Issues in Monetary Policy, Jackson Hole, Wyoming, (27–29 Aug. 1999).

Einaudi, Luca, "Monetary Unions and Free Riders: The Case of the Latin Monetary Union (1865–78)," *Rivista di Storia Economica*, 3, 8 (1997), 327–61.

———, "Money and Politics: European Monetary Union and the International Gold Standard (1865–1873)," unpublished Ph.D. thesis (Cambridge University, 1998).

Eisner, Robert, "Extended Accounts for National Income and Product," *Journal of Economic Literature*, 26, 4 (1988), 1611–1684.

Eltis, Walter, "The Creation and Destruction of the Euro," *Centre for Policy Studies, Policy Study* 155 (Aug. 1997).

———, "Debt, Deficits and Default," in John Maloney (ed.), *Debts and Deficits: An Historical Perspective* (Cheltenham, 1998), 116–32.

Elton, Geoffrey, *The Tudor Revolution in Government* (Cambridge, 1953).

Engen, E. M., and Skinner, J., "Taxation and Economic Growth," *NBER Working Paper*, 5826 (1996).

Erickson, John, "Red Army Battlefield Performance, 1941–45: The System and the Soldier," in Paul Addison (ed.), *Time to Kill: The Soldier's Experience of War in the West 1939–1945* (London, 1997), 233–48.

Erikson, Robert and Uusitalo, Hannu, "The Scandanavian Approach to Welfare Research," in Robert Erikson, Erik Hansen, Stein Renger (eds.), *The Scandanavian Model: Welfare States and Welfare Research* (London, 1987), 177–93.

Evans, Geoffrey (ed.), *The End of Class Politics? Class Voting in Comparative Perspective* (Oxford, 2000).

Ewing, K. D., *The Funding of Political Parties in Britain* (Cambridge, 1987).

Ewing, K. D., *Money, Politics and Law: A Study of Electroal Campaign Finance Reform in Canada* (Oxford, 1992).

Fair, Ray C., "The Effect of Economic Events on Votes for President," *Review of Economics and Statistics*, 60 (1978) 159–73.

Fair, Ray C., "The Effect of Economic Events on Votes for President: 1992 Update," *Political Behavioral* (June 1996), 119–39.

———, "Events that Shook the Market," unpublished paper, Cowles Foundation and International Center for Finance, Yale (August 2000).

Farrell, David M., "Ireland: Centralization, Professionalization and Competitive Pressures," in Richard S. Katz and Peter Mair (eds.), *How Parties Organize: Change and Adaptation in Party Organizations in Western Democracies* (Thousand Oaks, Calif., 1994), 216–41.

Fearon, Peter, *The Origins and Nature of the Great Slump, 192–1932* (London, 1979).

Feinstein, Charles, *National Income, Expenditure and Output of the United Kingdom, 1855–1965* (Cambridge, 1972).

———, "Pessimism Perpetuated: Real Wages and the Standard of Living in Britain during and after the Industrial Revolution," *Journal of Economic History*, 58, 3 (1998), 627–58.

——— and Watson, Catherine, "Private International Capital Flows in the Inter-War Period," in Charles H. Feinstein (ed.), *Banking, Currency and Finance in Europe between the Wars* (Oxford, 1995).

Feis, Herbert, *Europe, the World's Banker, 1870–1914* (New York, 1930).

Feldman, G. D., *The Great Disorder: Politics, Economics and Society in the German Inflation* (New York/Oxford, 1993).

Feldman, Stanley, "Economic Self-Interest and Political Behaviour," *American Journal of Political Science*, 26 (1982) 446–66.

——— and Conley, Patricia, "Explaining Explanations of Changing Economic Con-

ditions." in Helmut Norpoth, Michael S. Lewis-Beck and Jean-Dominique Lafay (eds.), *Economics and Politics: The Calculus of Support* (Ann Arbor, 1991),
185–205.

Feldstein, Martin, "The Political Economy of the European Economic and Monetary
Union: Political Sources of an Economic Liability," *Journal of Economic Perspectives*, 11 (1997), 23–42.

———, "The Costs and Benefits of Going from Low Inflation to Price Stability,"
NBER Working Paper, 5469 (1997).

Ferguson, Niall, "Public Finance and National Security: The Domestic Origins of the
First World War Revisited," *Past and Present*, 142 (1994), 141–68.

———, *Paper and Iron: Hamburg Business and German Politics, 1897–1927* (Cambridge, 1995).

———, "Keynes and the German Inflation," *English Historical Review*, 110, 436
(1995), 368–91.

———, "Introduction: Towards a "Chaotic" Theory of the Past" in id. (ed.) *Virtual
History: Alternatives and Counterfactuals* (London, 1997).

———, *The World's Banker: The History of the House of Rothschild* (London,
1998).

———, "The Balance of Payments Question: Versailles and After," in Manfred F. Boemeke, Gerald D. Feldman and Elisabeth Glaser (eds.), *The Treaty of Versailles: A
Reassessment after 75 Years* (Cambridge, 1998), 401–40.

———, *The Pity of War* (London, 1998).

——— and Kotlikoff, Laurence J., "The Degeneration of EMU," *Foreign Affairs*, 79,
2 (Mar./Apr. 2000), 110–21.

Fetter, F. W., *Development of British Monetary Orthodoxy, 1797–1875* (Cambridge,
Mass., 1965).

Feuchtwanger, E. J., *Disraeli, Democracy and the Tory Party* (Oxford, 1968).

Fieldhouse, Richard, "Nuclear Weapons Developments and Unilateral Reduction
Initiatives," *SIPRI Yearbook: World Armaments and Disarmament* (1992),
65–84.

Fielding, David, and Shields, Kalvinder, "Is the Franc Zone an Optimal Currency
Area?," unpublished paper, Department of Economics, University of Leicester
(Oct. 1999).

Fielding, S., *Labour: Decline and Renewal* (Manchester, 1995).

Filipczak-Kocur, Anna, "Poland-Lithuania before Partition," in Richard Bonney (ed.), *The Rise of the Fiscal State in Europe, c.1200–1815* (Oxford, 1999),
443–79.

Finer, S. E., *The History of Government*, vol. iii: *Empires, Monarchies and the Modern State* (Oxford, 1997).

Fink, Carol, "The Minorities Question at the Paris Peace Conference: The Polish
Minority Treaty, June 28, 1919," in Manfred F. Boemeke, Gerald D. Feldman and
Elisabeth Glaser (eds.), *The Treaty of Versailles: A Reassessment after 75 Years*
(Cambridge, 1998), 249–74.

Fiorina, Morris, *Retrospective Voting in American National Elections* (New Haven, 1981).

——, "Elections and the Economy in the 1980s: Short- and Long-Term Effects," in A. Alesina and G. Carliner (eds.) *Politics and Economics in the Eighties* (Chicago, 1991), 17–40.

—— and Shepsle, Kenneth, "Is Negative Voting an Artifact?" *American Journal of Political Science*, 33 (1989) 423–39.

Fischer, W., Krengel, J., and Wietog, J. (eds.), *Sozialgeschichtliches Arbeitsbuch: Materialien zur Statistik des Deutschen Bundes 1815–1870* (Munich, 1982).

FitzGerald, Frances, *Way Out There in the Blue: Reagan, Star Wars and the End of the Cold War* (New York, 2000).

Flandreau, Marc, *L'Or du monde: La France et la stabilité du système monétaire international, 1848–1873* (Paris, 1995).

——, "An Essay on the Emergence of the International Gold Standard, 1870–80," *International Macroeconomics*, Centre for Economic Policy Research Discussion Paper Series, 1210 (1995).

——, "Les Règles de la Pratique: La Banque de France, le marché des métaux précieux et la naissance de l'étalon-or 1848–1876," *Annales: Histoire, Sciences Sociales*, 4 (1996), 849–72.

——, "The French Crime of 1873: An Essay on the Emergence of the International Gold Standard, 1870–1880," *Journal of Economic History*, 56, 4 (1996), 862–97.

——, "Central Bank Cooperation in Historical Perspective: A Sceptical View," *Economic History Review*, 50, 4 (1997), 735–63.

——, "The Bank, the States and the Market: An Austro-Hungarian Tale for EMU, 1867–1914," paper presented at City University Business School and American Express Conference on Monetary Unions, 29 April 1999.

Flandreau, Marc, "Caveat Emptor: Coping with Sovereign Risk under the International Gold Standard, 1873–1913," paper presented at the Bank of England, 23 February 1999.

——, "Public Debts under the International Gold Standard, 1880–1914," Working Paper of the Centre François Simiand at the École Normale Supérieure, Paris (forthcoming).

——, Le Cacheux, J., and Zumer, F., "Stability Without a Pact? Lessons from the European Gold Standard, 1880–1914," *Economic Policy*, 26 (1997), 115–62.

Fleming, Ian, *Goldfinger* (London, 1989 [1959]).

Flora, P. *et al.*, *State, Economy and Society in Western Europe, 1815–1975: A Data Handbook in Two Volumes* (Frankfurt, 1983).

Fontane, Theodor, *Der Stechlin* (Stuttgart, 1978 [1899]).

Ford, Alec George, *The Gold Standard, 1880–1914: Britain and Argentina* (Oxford, 1962).

Foreman-Peck, James, "The 1856 Companies Act and the Birth and Death of Firms," in Philippe Tobart and Michael Moss (eds.), *The Birth and Death of Companies: A Historical Perspective* (Park Ridge, NJ, 1980), 33–46.

Foster, R. F., *Lord Randolph Churchill* (Oxford, 1981).

Fowler, Norman, *Ministers Decide: A Memoir of the Thatcher Years* (London, 1991).

Fowler, Richard Hindle, *Robert Burns* (London, 1988).

Frank, Robert H., *Luxury Fever: Why Money Fails to Satisfy in an Era of Success* (London, 2000).

Franklin, M., *The Decline of Class Voting in Britain* (Oxford, 1985).

Franklin, Mark N., "Electoral Participation," in Lawrence LeDuc and Richard G. Niemi (eds.), *Comparing Democracies: Elections and Voting in Global Perpsective* (Thousand Oaks, Calif., 1996), 216–35.

Freeman, Richard B., "Single Peaked vs. Diversified Capitalism: The Relation Between Economic Institutions And Outcomes," *NBER Working Paper*, 7556 (2000).

Freud, Sigmund, *Civilization, War and Death*, ed. John Rickman (London, 1939).

Frey, Bruno S., and Marcel Kucher, "History as Reflected in Capital Markets: The Case of World War II," *Journal of Economic History*, 60, 2 (2000), 468–96.

Frey, Bruno S., and Schneider, F., "Recent Research on Empirical Politico-economic Models," in Douglas A. Hibbs Jr., and Heino Fassbender (eds.) *Contemporary Political Economy* (Amsterdam, 1981), 11–27.

Friedman, Benjamin, "Other Times, Other Places: The European Democracies," draft manuscript (Cambridge, Mass., 1997).

———, "The Future of Monetary Policy: The Central Bank as an Army with Only a Signal Corps," paper presented at Conference on Social Science and the Future, Oxford, (July 1999).

Friedman, Milton, and Schwartz, Anna J., *A Monetary History of the United States, 1867–1960* (Princeton, 1963).

——— and ———, *Monetary Trends in the United States and the United Kingdom: Their Relation to Income, Prices and Interest Rates, 1867–1975* (Chicago, 1982).

Friedman, Thomas, *The Lexus and the Olive Tree* (London, 1999).

Fukuyama, Francis, "The End of History?," *National Interest*, 16 (1989), 3–18.

———, *The End of History and the Last Man* (New York, 1992).

———, "Capitalism and Democracy: The Missing Link," *Journal of Democracy*, 3 (1992) 100–110.

———, *The Great Disruption: Human Nature and the Reconstitution of Social Order* (London, 1999).

Galbraith, J. K., *The Affluent Society* (London, 1958).

———, *The New Industrial State* (London, 1967).

Gale, Douglas, "The Efficient Design of Public Debt," in Rudiger Dornbusch and Mario Draghi (eds.), *Public Debt Management: Theory and History* (Cambridge, 1990), 14–46.

Gall, Lothar, *Bismarck: The White Revolutionary*, 2 vols. (London, 1986).

Gallarotti, Givlio M., *The Anatomy of an International Monetary Regime: The Classical Gold Standard, 1880–1914* (New York, 1995).

Garber, Peter M., *Famous First Bubbles* (Boston, Mass., 2000).

Gash, Norman, *Politics in the Age of Peel: A Study in the Technique of Parliamentary Representation* (London, 1973).

Gasiorowski, M. J., "Economic Crisis and Political Regime Change: An Event History Analysis," *American Political Science Review*, 89 (1995), 882–97.

Gastil, Raymond D., *et al.*, *Freedom in the World* (Westport, Conn., various years).

Gates, Scott, Knutsen, Torbjorn L., and Moses, Jonathon W., "Democracy and Peace: A More Skeptical View," *Journal of Peace Research*, 33, 1 (1996), 1–10.

Gatrell, P., *Government, Industry and Rearmament, 1900–1914: The Last Argument of Tsarism* (Cambridge, 1994).

Gayer, A. D., Rostow, W. W., and Schwartz, Anna J., *The Growth and Fluctuation of the British Economy, 1790–1850*, 2 vols. (Oxford, 1953).

Geiss, Immanuel, *July 1914: The Outbreak of the First World War—Selected Documents* (London, 1967).

Gelabert, Juan, "The Fiscal Burden," in Richard Bonney (ed.), *Economic Systems and State Finance* (Oxford, 1995), 539–76.

———, "Castile, 1504–1808," in Richard Bonney (ed.), *The Rise of the Fiscal State in Europe, c.1200–1815* (Oxford, 1999), 201–41.

Gerloff, Wilhelm, "Der Staatshaushalt und das Finanzsystem Deutschlands, 1820–1927," in id. (ed.), *Handbuch der Finanzwissenschaft*, vol. iii (Tübingen, 1929), 4–69.

Gerth, H. H., and Wright Mills., C. (eds.), *From Max Weber: Essays in Sociology* (London, 1970).

Giddens, Anthony, *Runaway World: How Globalization is Reshaping Our Lives* (London, 1999).

Gilbert, Martin, *The First World War* (London, 1994).

———, *The Twentieth Century*, vol. i: *1900–1933* (London, 1997).

Gilpin, Robert, *The Political Economy of International Relations* (Princeton, 1987).

Gilpin, Robert, *The Challenge of Global Capitalism: The World Economy in the 21st Century* (Princeton, 2000).

Gleeson, Janet, *Millionaire: The Philanderer, Gambler and Duelist who Invented Modern Finance* (New York, 1999).

Gleditsch, Kristian S., and Ward, Michael D., "Double Take: A Re-examination of Democracy and Autocracy in Modern Polities." *Journal of Conflict Resolution*, 41 (1997), 361–82.

——— and ———, "Democratisation and War in the Context of Time and Space," Paper presented at the Annual Conference of the American Political Science Association (1997).

Girault, René, *Emprunts russes et investissements français en Russie* (Paris, 1973).

Goethe, Johann Wolfgang von, *Faust*, Parts One and Two, trans. Philip Wayne (London, 1959).

Goetzmann, William N., and Jorion, Philippe, "A Century of Global Stock Markets," Yale School Management draft paper (Dec. 1996).

——— and Ibbotson, Roger G., "An Emerging Market: The NYSE from 1815 to 1871," Yale School of Management draft paper (16 Dec. 1994).

Goldsmith, Raymond, *Premodern Financial Systems* (Cambridge, 1987).

Goldstein, E., "Great Britain: The Home Front," in Manfred F. Boemeke, Gerald D.

Feldman and Elisabeth Glaser (eds.), *The Treaty of Versailles: A Reassessment after 75 Years* (Cambridge, 1998), 147–66.

Good, D. F. *The Economic Rise of the Habsburg Empire, 1750–1914* (Berkeley, 1984).

Goodhart, Charles, "Price Stability and Financial Fragility," in . . . pp. 439–97.

―――― and Boris Hofmann, "Monetary Policy Adjustments with Asset Price Fluctuations," unpublished paper.

―――― and ――――, "Monetary Policy and Assets Prices," unpublished paper, Financial Markets Group, London School of Economics (1999).

Goodhart, Charles A. E., *The Business of Banking, 1891–1914* (London, 1972).

――――, "Monetary Policy and Debt Management in the UK: Some Historical Viewpoints," unpublished paper (1998).

――――, "The Two Concepts of Money: Implications for the Analysis of Optimal Currency Areas," *European Journal of Political Economy* (1998), 407–32.

――――, and Bhansali, R. J., "Political Economy," *Political Studies*, 18, 1 (1970).

―――― and Delargy, P. J. R., "Financial Crises: Plus ça change, plus c'est la même chose," *International Finance*, 1, 2 (1998), 261–87.

Goodin, Robert E., Headey, Bruce, Muffels, Ruud, and Dirven, Henk-Jan, *The Real Worlds of Welfare Capitalism* (Cambridge, 1999).

Gordon, Robert, "US Economic Growth since 1870: One Big Wave?," *American Economic Review* (May 1999).

Gould, Philip, *The Unfinished Revolution: How the Modernisers Saved the Labour Party* (London, 1998).

Gourevitch, Philip, *We Wish to Inform You that Tomorrow We Will Be Killed with Our Families: Stories from Rwanda* (London, 1999).

Gowland, David, "Banking on Change: Independence, Regulation and the Bank of England," *Politeia*, Police Series, 6 (1997).

Graham, F. D., *Exchange, Prices and Production in Hyperinflation Germany, 1920–1923* (Princeton, 1930).

Green, David G., "The Friendly Societies and Adam–Smith Liberalism," in David Gladstone (ed.), *Before Beveridge: Welfare before the Welfare State* (London, 1999), 18–25.

Green, E. H. H., *The Crisis of Conservatism: The Politics, Economics and Ideology of the British Conservative Party, 1880–1914* (London, 1995).

Green, Timothy S., *The New World of Gold* (London, 1981).

――――, "Central Bank Gold Reserves," unpublished paper (1999).

Gregory, P. R., *Russian National Income, 1885–1913* (Cambridge, 1982).

Grilli, Vittorio, Masciandaro, Donato, and Tabellini, Guido, "Political and Monetary Institutions and Public Financial Policies in the Industrial Countries," *Economic Policy* (1991), 339–92.

Gunlicks, A. B. (ed.), *Campaign and Party Finance in North America and Western Europe* (Boulder, Colo., 1993).

Gunter, Barrie, and Furnham, Adrian, *Consumer Profiles: An Introduction to Psychographics* (London, 1992).

Gurr, Ted Robert, "Persistence and Change in Political Systems, 1800–1971," *American Political Science Review*, 74, (1974), 1482–1504.

——, Jaggers, Keith, and Moore, Will H., "The Transformation of the Western State: The Growth of Democracy, Autocracy, and State Power since 1800," *Studies in Comparative International Development*, 25 (1990), 73–108.

Gwyn, W. B., *Democracy and the Cost of Politics in Britain* (London, 1962).

Hagen, Jürgen von, "Discussion of Winckler, Hochreiter and Brandner's Paper," in G. Calvo and M. King (eds.), *The Debt Burden and its Consequences for Monetary Policy* (London, 1998), 277–82.

Haigh, John, *Taking Chances: Winning with Probability* (Oxford, 1999).

Haller, H. Brandon, and Norpoth, Helmut, "Let the Good Times Roll: The Economic Expectations of American Voters," *American Journal of Political Science*, 38 (1994), 625–50.

Hamilton, Earl J., "Origin and Growth of the National Debt in Western Europe," *American Economic Review*, 37, 2 (1947), 118–30.

Hanham, H. J., *Elections and Party Management: Politics in the Time of Disraeli and Gladstone* (Hassocks, Sussex, 1978).

Hansemeyer, K.-H., and Caesar, R., "Kriegswirtschaft und Inflation, 1936–1948," in Deutsche Bundesbank (ed.), *Währung und Wirtschaft in Deutschland, 1876–1975* (Frankfurt am Main, 1976), 361–429.

Hara, Akira, "Japan: Guns Before Rice," in Mark Harrison (ed.), *The Economics of World War II: Six Great Powers in International Comparison* (Cambridge, 1998), 224–67.

Hardach, Gerd, *The First World War, 1914–1918* (Harmondsworth, 1987).

Harding, L., Leigh, D., and Palliser, D., *The Liar: The Fall of Jonathan Aitken* (Harmondsworth, 1997).

Harley, C. K., "Goschen's Conversion of the National Debt and the Yield on Consols," *Economic History Review* (1976), 101–6.

Harmston, Stephen, "Gold as a Store of Value," *World Gold Council Research Study*, 22 (Nov. 1998).

Harris, Jose, "Political Thought and the Welfare State 1870–1940: An Intellectual Framework for British Social Policy," in David Gladstone (ed.), *Before Beveridge: Welfare before the Welfare State* (London, 1999), 43–63.

Harrison, Mark, "The Economics of World War II: An Overview," in id. (ed.), *The Economics of World War II: Six Great Powers in International Comparison* (Cambridge, 1998), 1–42.

——, "The Soviet Union: The Defeated Victor," in id. (ed.), *The Economics of World War II: Six Great Powers in International Comparison* (Cambridge, 1998), 268–301.

Hart, Marjolein 't, "The Emergence and Consolidation of the "Tax State," II: The Seventeenth Century," in Richard Bonney (ed.), *Economic Systems and State Finance* (Oxford, 1995), 281–93.

——, "The United Provinces 1579–1806," in Richard Bonney (ed.), *The Rise of the Fiscal State in Europe, c.1200–1815* (Oxford, 1999), 309–25.

Hawtrey, R. G., *The Gold Standard in Theory and Practice*, 5th edn. (London/New York/Toronto, 1947).

Hayek, F. A., *The Road to Serfdom* (London, 1971 [1944]).

Heffer, Simon, *Moral Desperado: A Life of Thomas Carlyle* (London, 1996).

Hegel, G. W. F., "Second Draft: The Philosophical History of the World" [1830], in id., *Lectures on the Philosophy of World History* (Cambridge, 1975), 25–151.

Heine, Heinrich, *Sämtliche Schriften*, vols. iv and v (Munich, 1971).

Hellie, Richard, "Russia, 1200–1815," in Richard Bonney (ed.), *The Rise of the Fiscal State in Europe, c.1200–1815* (Oxford, 1999), 481–505.

Henneman, John Bell, Jr., "France in the Middle Ages," in Richard Bonney (ed.), *The Rise of the Fiscal State in Europe, c.1200–1815* (Oxford, 1999), 101–22.

Hennessy, Peter, *Never Again: Britain 1945–51* (London, 1992).

Hentschel, V., *Wirtschaft und Wirtschaftspolitik im wilhelminischen Deutschland: Organisierter Kapitalismus und Interventionsstaat?* (Stuttgart, 1978).

Herodotus, *The Histories*, trans. Aubrey de Sélincourt (Harmondsworth, 1972).

Herrnson, P. S., "The High Finance of American Politics: Campaign Spending and Reform in Federal Elections," in A. B. Gunlicks (ed.), *Campaign and Party Finance in North America and Western Europe* (Boulder, Colo., 1993), 17–40.

Hershlas, Z. Y., *Introduction to the Modern Economic History of the Middle East* (Leiden, 1964).

Hibbs, Douglas A., Jr., "Political Parties and Macroeconomic Policy," *American Political Science Review*, 71 (1977), 1467–87.

Hilton, Boyd, *Corn, Cash and Commerce: The Economic Policies of Tory Governments, 1815–1830* (Oxford, 1977).

Hinsley, F. H., *Power and the Pursuit of Peace: Theory and Practice in the History of the Relations between States* (Cambridge, 1963).

HMSO, *Ministry of Labour Gazette*, 53–65 (London, 1945–57).

HMSO, *Social Trends* (London, various years).

Hobsbawm, E. J., *The Age of Capital: 1848–1875* (London, 1985).

———, *Nations and Nationalism since 1780: Programme, Myth, Reality* (Cambridge, 1990).

———, "Custom, Wage and Work-load in 19th Century Industry," in id. (ed.), *Labouring Men: Studies in the History of Labour* (London, 1964), 344–70.

———, *The Age of Extremes: The Short Twentieth Century 1914–1991* (London, 1994).

Hobson, Dominic, *The National Wealth* (London, 1999).

Hobson, J. A., *Imperialism: A Study* (London, 1988 [1902]).

Hobson, J. M., "The Military-extraction Gap and the Wary Titan: The Fiscal Sociology of British Defence Policy, 1870–1913," *Journal of European Economic History*, 22 (1993), 461–506.

Hocquet, Jean-Claude, "City-State and Market Economy," in Richard Bonney (ed.), *Economic Systems and State Finance* (Oxford, 1995), 81–100.

———, "Venice," in Richard Bonney (ed.), *The Rise of the Fiscal State in Europe, c.1200–1815* (Oxford, 1999), 381–415.

Hoffman, P. T., and Norberg, K. (eds.), *Fiscal Crises, Liberty and Representative Government, 1450–1789* (Stanford, Calif., 1994).

Hoffmann, W. G., Grumbach, F. and H. Hesse, *Das Wachstum der deutschen Wirtschaft seit der Mitte des 19. Jahrhunderts* (Berlin, 1965).

Hogwood, Brian W., *Trends in British Public Policy: Do Governments Make Any Difference?* (Buckingham/Philadelphia, 1992).

Holroyd, Michael, *Bernard Shaw*, vol. ii: *The Pursuit of Power* (London, 1989).

Holtfrerich, Carl-Ludwig, "Reichsbankpolitik 1918–1923 zwischen Zahlungsbilanz und Quantitätstheorie," *Zeitschrift für Wirtschafts- und Sozialwissenschaft*, 13 (1977), 193–214.

———, *The German Inflation, 1914–1923* (Berlin/New York, 1986).

Homer, Sidney, and Sylla, Richard, *A History of Interest Rates*, 3nd edn. (New Brunswick, NJ, 1996).

Horne, Alistair, *Macmillan, 1957–1986* (London, 1989).

Hughes, C., and Wintour, P., *Labour Rebuilt: The New Model Party* (London, 1990).

Huntington, Samuel P., *The Third Wave: Democratization in the Late Twentieth Century* (Norman, Okla., 1991).

———, *The Clash of Civilisations and the Remaking of World Order* (London, 1999).

Hutchinson Almanac 2000 (Oxford, 1999).

Hynes, Samuel, *A War Imagined: The First World War and English Culture* (London, 1990).

Ignatieff, Michael, *Virtual War: Kosovo and Beyond* (London, 2000).

Ingham, G., *Capitalism Divided? The City and Industry in British Social Development* (London, 1984).

Ingle, S., "Party Organisation," in D. MacIver (ed.) *The Liberal Democrats* (London, 1996), 113–34.

Inland Revenue, "A Brief History of Income Tax," Inland Revenue website (2000).

International Institute of Strategic Studies, *The Military Balance* (London, various years).

Isenmann, Eberhard, "Medieval and Renaissance Theories of State Finance, in Richard Bonney (ed.), *Economic Systems and State Finance* (Oxford, 1995), 21–52.

Issawi, C., *Economic History of the Middle East, 1800–1914* (Chicago, 1966).

Jaggers, Keith, and Gurr, Ted Robert, "Transitions to Democracy: Tracking Democracy's Third Wave with the Polity III Data." *Journal of Peace Research*, 32 (1995), 469–82.

James, Harold, *The German Slump: Politics and Economics, 1924–1936* (Oxford, 1986).

James, Harold, *The Reichsbank and Public Finance in Germany 1924–1933: A Study of the Politics of Economics during the Great Depression* (Frankfurt, 1985).

———, "Das Ende der Globalisierung? Lehren aus der Weltwirtschaftskrise," *Jahrbuch des Historischen Kollegs* (1999), 61–89.

———, *Globalization and its Sins: Lessons from Previous Collapses and Crashes* (forthcoming).

Jamieson, Bill, *An Illustrated Guide to the British Economy* (London, 1998).

Jardin, André and Tudesq, André-Jean, *Restoration and Reaction, 1815–1848* (Cambridge, 1983).

Jay, Peter, *A General Hypothesis of Employment, Inflation and Politics* (London, 1976).

Jardin, André, *Tocqueville: A Biography*, trans. Lydia Davis with Robert Hemenway (London, 1988).

Jeffrys, K., *Retreat from New Jerusalem: British Politics, 1951–64* (London, 1997).

Johnson, Eric, *The Nazi Terror: Gestapo, Jews and Ordinary Germans* (London, 2000).

Johnston, R. J., and Pattie, C. J., "Great Britain: 20th Century Parties operating under 19th Century Regulations," in A. B. Gunlicks (ed.), *Campaign and Party Finance in North America and Western Europe* (Boulder, Colo., 1993), to come.

Johnston, Richard, Blais, André, Brady, Henry E. and Crête, Jean, *Letting the People Decide: Dynamics of a Canadian Election* (Stanford, 1992).

Joll, James, *Europe since 1870: An International History* (2nd edn., London, 1976).

Jones, Bill, and Kavanagh, Dennis, *British Politics Today*, 6th edn. (Manchester, 1998).

Kaelble, Hartmut, *Industrialisation and Social Inequality in 19th-Century Europe*, trans. Bruce Little (Leamington Spa/Heidelberg, 1986).

Kafka, Franz, *The Castle*, trans. J. A. Underwood (London, 1997).

Kaldor, Mary, *The Baroque Arsenal* (London, 1982).

Karatnycky, Adrian, "The Decline of Illiberal Democracy," *Journal of Democracy*, 10, 1 (1999), 102–125.

Katona, George, *Psychological Economics* (New York, 1975).

Katz, Richard S., "Party Organizations and Finance," in Lawrence LeDuc and Richard G. Niemi (eds.), *Comparing Democracies: Elections and Voting in Global Perspective* (Thousand Oaks, Calif., 1996), 107.

——— and Kolodny, Robin, "Party Organization as an Empty Vessel: Parties in American Politics," in Richard S. Katz and Peter Mair (eds.), *How Parties Organize: Change and Adaptation in Party Organizations in Western Democracies* (Thousand Oaks, Calif., 1994), 23–50.

Kay, J. A., and King, M. A., *The British Tax System*, 5th edn. (Oxford, 1990).

Kehr, Eckart, *Der Primat der Innenpolitik: Gesammelte Aufsätze zur preußisch-deutschen Sozialgeschichte im 19. und 20. Jahrhundert*, ed. Hans-Ulrich Wehler (Berlin, 1970).

Kennedy, Paul M., *The Rise and Fall of the Great Powers: Economic Change and Military Conflict from 1500 to 2000* (London, 1988).

———, *Preparing for the Twenty-first Century* (London, 1993).

——— and O'Brien, P. K., "Debate: The Costs and Benefits of British Imperialism, 1846–1914," *Past and Present*, 125 (1989), 186–99.

Key, V. O., Jr., *The Responsible Electorate* (Cambridge, Mass., 1966).

Keylor, W. R., "Versailles and International Diplomacy" in Manfred F. Boemeke, Gerald D. Feldman and Elisabeth Glaser (eds.), *The Treaty of Versailles: A Reassessment after 75 Years* (Cambridge, 1998), 469–505.

Keynes, J. M., *The Economic Consequences of the Peace* (London, 1919).

——, *A Tract on Monetary Reform* (London, 1923), repr. in *Collected Writings*, vol. iv (Cambridge, 1971).

Keynes, John Maynard, *The General Theory of Employment, Interest and Money* (Cambridge, 1973 [1936]).

——, *How to Pay for the War* (London, 1940).

Kiewiet, D. Roderick, *Macroeconomics and Micropolitics* (Chicago, 1983).

—— and Kinder, Donald R., "Economic Discontent and Political Behavior: The Role of Personal Grievances and Collective Economic Judgements in Congressional Voting," *American Journal of Political Science*, 23 (1979), 495–527.

—— and Rivers, Douglas, "A Retrospective on Retrospective Voting," in Heinz Eulau and Michael Lewis-Beck (eds.) *Economic Conditions and Electoral Outcomes* (New York, 1985), to come.

Kindleberger, Charles P., *A Financial History of Western Europe* (London, 1984).

Kindleberger, Charles P., *The World in Depression, 1929–1939* (Harmondsworth, 1987).

——, *Manias, Panics and Crashes: A History of Financial Crises*, 3rd edn. (New York/Chichester/Brisbane/Toronto/Singapore, 1996).

——, *World Economic Primacy, 1500–1900* (New York/Oxford, 1996).

King, Anthony, *et al.*, *New Labour Triumphs: Britain at the Polls* (Chatham, NJ, 1998).

King, Mervyn, "Commentary: Monetary Policy Implications of Greater Fiscal Discipline," in Federal Reserve Bank of Kansas City, *Budget Deficits and Debt: Issues and Options* (Kansas, 1995), 171–9.

——, "Challenges for Monetary Policy: New and Old," paper presented at the Federal Reserve Bank of Kansas City's Conference on Issues in Monetary Policy, Jackson Hole, Wyoming (27–9 Aug. 1999).

Kingdom, John, *Government and Politics in Britain: An Introduction* (London, 1999).

Kirchgässner, Gebhard, "Economic Conditions and the Popularity of West German Parties: Before and After the 1982 Government Change," in Helmut Norpoth, Michael S. Lewis-Beck, and Jean-Dominique Lafay (eds.) *Economics and Politics: The Calculus of Support* (Ann Arbor, 1991), 103–22.

Klein, Ernst, "Preussens 30-Million-Anleihe in London vom 31. März 1818," *Zeitschrift für Geschichtwissenschaft* (1956), 568–86.

Klovland, Jan Tore, "Pitfalls in the Estimation of the Yield on British Consols, 1850–1914," *Journal of Economic History*, 54 (1994), 1–33.

Knock, Thomas J., *To End All Wars: Woodrow Wilson and the Quest for a New World Order* (New York/Oxford, 1992).

Koole, Ruud A., "The Vulnerability of the Modern Cadre Party in the Netherlands," in Richard S. Katz and Peter Mair (eds.), *How Parties Organize: Change and Adaptation in Party Organizations in Western Democracies* (Thousand Oaks, Calif., 1994), 278–303.

Körner, Martin, "Expenditure," in Richard Bonney (ed.), *Economic Systems and State Finance* (Oxford, 1995), 393–422.

——, "Public Credit," in Richard Bonney (ed.), *Economic Systems and State Finance* (Oxford, 1995), 507–38.

——, "The Swiss Confederation," in Richard Bonney (ed.), *The Rise of the Fiscal State in Europe, c.1200–1815* (Oxford, 1999), 327–57.

Kotlikoff, Laurence J., *Generational Accounting* (New York, 1992).

——, "From Deficit Delusion to the Fiscal Balance Rule: Looking for an Economically Meaningful Way to Assess Fiscal Policy," *Journal of Economics*, Suppl. 7 (1993), 17–41.

—— and Leibfritz, Willli, "An International Comparison of Generational Accounts," *NBER Working Paper*, 644 (March 1998)

—— and Raffelheuschen, Bernd, "Generational Accounting Round the Globe," unpublished paper (1999).

Kramer, Gerald H., "Short-term Fluctuations in US Voting Behavior," *American Political Science Review*, 65 (1971), 131–43.

——, "The Ecological Fallacy Revisited: Aggregate- Versus Individual-level Findings on Economic and Elections and Sociotropic Voting," *American Political Science Review*, 77 (1983) 92–111.

Krugman, Paul, *The Return of Depression Economics* (London, 1999).

Kubicek, Robert, "British Expansion, Empire and Technological Change," in Andrew Porter (ed.), *The Oxford History of the British Empire* (Oxford/New York, 1999), 247–69.

Kuklinski, James and West, Darrel, "Economic Expectations and Voting Behavior in the United States Senate and House Elections," *American Political Science Review*, 75 (1981) 436–47.

Kynaston, David, *The City of London*, vol. i: *A World of its Own, 1815–90* (London, 1994).

——, *The City of London*, vol. ii: *Golden Years, 1890–1914* (London, 1996).

Lafay, Jean-Dominique, "Political Dyarchy and Popularity Functions: Lessons From the 1986 French Experience," in Helmut Norpoth, Michael S. Lewis-Beck and Jean-Dominique Lafay (eds.) *Economics and Politics: The Calculus of Support* (Ann Arbor, 1991), 123–39.

Lal, Deepak, *Unintended Consequences: The Impact of Factor Endowments, Culture and Politics on Long-Run Economic Performance* (Cambridge, Mass., 1999).

——, "EMU and Globalisation," *Politeia* (1999).

Landes, David S., *The Wealth and Poverty of Nations* (London, 1998).

Lane, Barbara Miller, and Rupp, Leila J., *Nazi Ideology before 1933: A Documentation* (Manchester, 1978).

Lanoue, David, *From Camelot to the Teflon President: Economics and Presidential Popularity* (Westport, Conn., 1988).

Lau, Richard R., "Two Explanations for Negativity Effects in Political Behavior," *American Journal of Political Science*, 29 (1985) 119–38.

Lawson, Nigel, *The View from No. 11: Memoirs of a Tory Radical* (London, 1992).

LeDuc, Lawrence, and Niemi, Richard G. (eds.), *Comparing Democracies: Elections and Voting in Global Perspective* (Thousand Oaks, Calif., 1996).

Leigh, D. and Vulliamy, E., *Sleaze: The Corruption of Parliament* (London, 1997).

Lethbridge, E., "National Income and Product," in M. C. Kaser, and E. A. Radice (eds.), *The Economic History of Eastern Europe, 1919–1975*, vol. i (Oxford, 1986), 533–97.

Levy, Jack S., *War in the Modern Great Power System* (Lexington, Ky., 1983).

Lévy-Leboyer, M., and Bourgignon, F., L'véconomie française au XIXe siècle: Analyse macro-économique (Paris, 1985).

Lewis, Michael, *Liar's Poker* (London, 1989).

Lewis-Beck, Michael S., *Economics and Elections: The Major Western Democracies* (Ann Arbor, 1988).

Lindert, Peter H., and Morton, Peter J., "How Sovereign Debt Has Worked," University of California–Davis Institute of Governmental Affairs Working Paper (Aug. 1997).

Lipman, Edward, "The City and the 'People's Budget'," unpublished MS (1995).

Lipset, Seymour Martin, "Some Social Requisites of Democracy: Economic Development and Political Legitimacy," *American Political Science Review*, 53 (1959), 69–105.

———, "The Social Requisites of Democracy Revisited," *American Sociological Review*, 59 (1994), 1–22.

———, Seong, K.-R. and Torres, J. C., "A Comparative Analysis of the Social Requisites of Democracy," *International Social Science Journal*, 16 (1993), 155–75.

Luard, Evan, *War in International Society: A Study in International Sociology* (New Haven/London, 1987).

Luttwak, Edward, *Turbo-Capitalism: Winners and Losers in the Global Economy* (London, 1998).

McCaffrey, Helen, and Lamarque, William, "Gold: A Trojan Horse in Central Bank Reserves?," N. M. Rothschild & Sons internal memorandum (May 1999).

McCloskey, Donald N., and Zecher, J. Richard, "How the Gold Standard Worked, 1880–1913," in J. A. Frenkel and H. G. Johnson (eds.), *The Monetary Approach to the Balance of Payments* (Toronto, 1976), 357–85.

MacDougall, D., *Don and Mandarin: Memoirs of an Economist* (London, 1987).

McKenzie, R. T., *British Political Parties: The Distribution of Power within the Conservative and Labour parties* (London, 1978).

McKibbin, Ross, "Class and Conventional Wisdom: The Conservative Party and the "Public" in Inter-war Britain," in id., *The Ideologies of Class: Social Relations in Britain, 1880–1950* (Oxford, 1990), 259–93.

McKinnon, Ronald, "The East Asian Dollar Standard: Life after Death?," EDI World Bank Workshop on "Rethinking the Asian Miracle" (1999).

McKinnon, Ronald I., and Pill, Huw, "International Overborrowing: A Decomposition of Credit and Currency Risks," *World Development*, 26, 7 (1998), 1267–82.

MacKuen, Michael B., Erikson, Robert S., and Stimson, James A., "Peasants or

Bankers?" The American Electorate and the US Economy," *American Political Science Review*, 86 (1992) 597–611.

McMorrow, K., and Roeger, W., "The Economic Consequences of Ageing Populations," *European Commission Directorate-General for Economic and Financial Affairs Economic Papers*, 138 (Nov. 1999).

McNeill, William H., *The Pursuit of Power: Technology, Armed Force and Society since A.D. 1000* (Oxford, 1982).

Maddison, Angus, *Dynamic Forces in Capitalist Development: A Long-run Comparative View* (Oxford, 1991).

Maier, Charles S., *Recasting Bourgeois Europe: Stabilisation in France, Germany and Italy in the Decade after World War I* (Princeton, 1975).

——, "The Politics of Inflation in the Twentieth Century," in id., *In Search of Stability: Explorations in Historical Political Economy* (Cambridge, 1987), 187–224.

——, Fictitious Bonds . . . of Wealth and Law:" On the Theory and Practice of Interest Representation," in id., *In Search of Stability: Explorations in Historical Political Economy* (Cambridge, 1987), 225–60.

——, "Empires or Nations? 1918, 1945, 1989 . . . ," in Carl Levy and Mark Roseman (eds.), *1918–1945–1989* (Cambridge, forthcoming), n.p.

Mair, Peter, "Party Organizations: From Civil Society to the State," in Richard S. Katz and Peter Mair (eds.), *How Parties Organize: Change and Adaptation in Party Organizations in Western Democracies* (Thousand Oaks, Calif., 1994), 1–22.

Mair, Peter, "Party Systems and Structures of Competition," in Lawrence LeDuc and Richard G. Niemi (eds.), *Comparing Democracies: Elections and Voting in Global Perspective* (Thousand Oaks, Calif., 1996), 83–106.

Makinen, Gail E., and Woodward, G. Thomas, "Funding Crises in the Aftermath of World War I," in Rudiger Dornbusch and Mario Draghi (eds.), *Public Debt Management: Theory and History* (Cambridge, 1990), 153–83.

Maloney, John, "Gladstone and Sound Victorian Finance," in id. (ed.), *Debt and Deficits: An Historical Perspective* (Cheltenham, 1998), 116–31.

Mann, Michael, *The Sources of Social Power*, vol. ii: *The Rise of Classes and Nation-States, 1760–1914* (Cambridge, 1993).

Maoz, Zeev, and Abdolali, Nasrin, "Regime Types and International Conflict, 1816–1976," *Journal of Conflict Resolution*, 33, 1 (1989), 3–35.

Markus, Gregory B., "The Impact of Personal and National Economic Conditions on the Presidential Vote: A Pooled Cross-Sectional Analysis," *American Journal of Political Science*, 32 (1988), 137–54.

Marsh, David, *The Bundesbank: The Bank that Rules Europe* (London, 1992).

Marsh, Peter T., *Joseph Chamberlain: Entrepreneur in Politics* (New Haven/London, 1994).

Martin, Terry, "Origins of Soviet Ethnic Cleansing," *Journal of Modern History*, 70 (1998), 813–61.

Marx, Karl, *Capital*, vol. i (London, 1976 [1867]).

—— and Engels, Friedrich, *The Communist Manifesto*, with an introduction and notes by A. J. P. Taylor (London, 1985).

Masson, Paul, and Mussa, Michael, "Long-Term Tendencies in Budget Deficits and Debt," in Federal Reserve Bank of Kansas City, *Budget Deficits and Debt: Issues and Options* (Kansas, 1995), 5–55.

Mathias, Peter, *The First Industrial Nation: An Economic History of Britain, 1700–1914* (London, 1969).

——— and O'Brien, Patrick K., "Taxation in Great Britain and France, 1715–1810: A Comparison of the Social and Economic Incidence of Taxes Collected for the Central Governments," *Journal of European Economic History* (1976), 601–50.

Matthew, H. C. G., "Disraeli, Gladstone and the Politics of Mid-Victorian Budgets," *Historical Journal* (1979), 615–43.

———, *Gladstone, 1875–1898* (Oxford, 1995).

Maupassant, Guy de, *Bel-Ami* trans. Douglas Parmée, (London, 1975 [1885]).

Mazower, Mark, *Dark Continent: Europe's Twentieth Century* (London, 1998).

Michie, Ranald, "The London and New York Stock Exchanges, 1850–1914," *Journal of Economic History*, XLVI, 1 (March 1986), 171–87.

Michie, Ranald C., "The Invisible Stabiliser: Asset Arbitrage and the International Monetary System since 1700," *Financial History Review*, 15 (1998), 5–26.

———, *The London Stock Exchange: A History* (Oxford, 1999).

Micklethwait, John, and Wooldridge, Adrian, *A Future Perfect: The Challenge and Hidden Promise of Globalisation* (London, 2000).

Millard, Stephen, "An Examination of the Monetary Transmission Mechanism in the United Kingdom," *Bank of England Working Paper* (n.d.).

Millington, Barry, *Wagner* (New York, 1987).

Mills, T. C., and Woods, G. E., "Money and Interest Rates in Britain from 1870 to 1913," in S. N. Broadberry and N. F. R. Crafts (eds.), *Britain in the International Economy* (Cambridge, 1992), 199–217.

Milward, Alan, with the assistance of George Brennan and Frederico Romero, *The European Rescue of the Nation-State* (London, 1992).

Minkin, L. *The Labour Party Conference: A Study in the Politics of Intra-party Democracy* (London, 1978).

Minsky, H. P., "A Theory of Systematic Fragility," in E. J. Altman and A. W. Sametz (eds.), *Financial Crises: Institutions and Markets in a Fragile Environment* (New York, 1977), 138–52.

Mirowski, Philip, "The Rise (and Retreat) of a Market: English Joint Stock Shares in the Eighteenth Century," *Journal of Economic History*, 41, 3 (1981), 559–77.

Mischler, William, Hoskin, Marilyn, and Fitzgerald, Roy, "British Parties in the Balance: A Time Series Analysis of Long-Term Trends in Labour and Conservative Support," *British Journal of Political Science*, 19 (1989) 211–36.

Mishkin, Frederic S., "The Real Rate of Interest: An Empirical Investigation," *The Costs and Consequences of Inflation: Carnegie-Rochester Conference Series on Public Policy* (1981), 151–200.

———, "Asymmetric Information and Financial Crises: A Historical Perspective," in R. Glenn Hubbard (ed.), *Financial Markets and Financial Crises* (Chicago/London, 1991), 69–108.

—— and Deane, P., *Abstract of British Historical Statistics* (Cambridge, 1962, repr. 1976).

—— and Jones, H. G., *Second Abstract of British Historical Statistics* (Cambridge, 1971).

Mitchell, B. R., *European Historical Statistics, 1750–1975* (London, 1981).

——, *International Historical Statistics: The Americas, 1750–1993* (London, 1998).

Modelski, George and Perry, Gardner III, "Democratisation in Long Perspective" *Technological Forecasting and Social Change*, 39 (1991), 23–34.

Montesquieu, Baron de, *The Spirit of Laws*, trans. Thomas Nugent (New York/London, 1949 [1748]).

Monypenny, W. F., and Buckle, G. E., *The Life of Benjamin Disraeli, Earl of Beaconsfield*, 6 vols. (London, 1910–20).

Morgan, E. V., *Studies in British Financial Policy, 1914–1925* (London, 1952).

—— and Thomas, W. A., *The Stock Exchange* (London, 1962).

Morrisey, O., and Steinmo, S., "The Influence of Party Competition on Post-war UK Tax Rates," *Policy and Politics*, 15 (1987), 195–206.

Mullen, Richard, *Anthony Trollope: A Victorian and his World* (London, 1990).

Muller, E. N., "Democracy, Economic Development, and Income Inequality," *American Sociological Review*, 53 (1988), 50–68.

——, "Economic Determinants of Democracy," *American Sociological Review*, 60 (1995), 966–82.

—— and Seligson, M. A., "Civic Culture and Democracy: The Question of Causal Relationships," *American Political Science Review*, 88 (1994), 635–52.

Müller, Wolfgang C., "The Development of Austrian Party Organizations in the Postwar Period," in Richard S. Katz and Peter Mair (eds.), *How Parties Organize: Change and Adaptation in Party Organizations in Western Democracies* (Thousand Oaks, Calif., 1994), 51–79.

Mundell, Robert, "Prospects for the International Monetary System," *World Gold Council Research Study* (n.d. [1994]).

Murray, B. K., *The People's Budget, 1909/10: Lloyd George and Liberal Politics* (Oxford, 1980).

——, Battered and Shattered:" Lloyd George and the 1914 Budget Fiasco," *Albion* (1991), 483–507.

Murphy, Antoine E., *John Law: Economic Theorist and Policy-Maker* (Oxford, 1997).

Musgrave, Richard A., "Public Debt and Intergeneration Equity," in Kenneth J. Arrow and Michael J. Boskin (eds.), *The Economics of Public Debt* (London, 1988), 133–46.

Musgrave, Richard A. and Musgrave, Peggy B., *Public Finance in Theory and Practice* (New York, 1989).

Mutch, R. E., "The Evolution of Campaign Finance Regulation in the United States and Canada," in F. L. Seidle (ed.), *Comparative Issues in Party and Election Finance* (Toronto, 1991), to come.

Muto, Giovanni, "The Spanish System: Centre and Periphery," in Richard Bonney (ed.), *Economic Systems and State Finance* (Oxford, 1995), 231–59.

Nadeau, Richard, Niemi, Richard G., and Amato, Timothy, "Prospective and Comparative or Retrospective and Individual? Party Leaders and Party Support in Great Britain," *British Journal of Political Science*, 26 (1996) 345–58.

Naimark, Norman, *The Russians in Germany: A History of the Soviet Zone of Occupation, 1945–1949* (Cambridge, Mass., 1995).

Nash, Robert Lucas, *Fenn's Compendium of the English and Foreign Funds, Debts and Revenue of All Nations, Together with Statistics Relating to National Resources & Liabilities, Imports, Exports, Population, Area, Railway Guarantees, Municipal Finance & Indebtedness, Banks of All Nations and All Descriptions of Government, Provincial, and Corporate Securities held and dealt in by Investors at Home and Abroad; The Laws and Regulations of the Stock Exchange, &c.,* 14th edn. (London, 1889).

Neal, Larry, "Integration of International Capital Markets: Quantitative Evidence from the Eighteenth to Twentieth Centuries," *Journal of Economic History* (1985), 219–26.

———, *The Rise of Financial Capitalism: International Capital Markets in the Age of Reason* (Cambridge, 1990).

———, "How It All Began: The Monetary and Financial Architecture of Europe during the First Global Capital Markets, 1648–1815," paper presented at the Conference on the History of Global Finance, Yale School of Management (15 Oct. 1999).

———, "A Shocking View of Economic History," *Journal of Economic History*, 60, 2 (2000), 317–34.

Nef, John U., *War and Human Progress: An Essay on the Rise of Industrial Civilization* (Cambridge, Mass., 1950).

Noelle-Neumann, Elisabeth and Köcher, Renate (eds.), *Allensbacher Jahrbuch der Demoskopie* (Munich, 1997).

Nordhaus, William, "The Political Business Cycle," *Review of Economic Studies*, 42 (Apr. 1975), 169–90.

Norpoth, Helmut, "Guns and Butter and Government Popularity in Britain," *American Political Science Review*, 81 (1987) 949–59.

———, *Confidence Regained: Economics, Mrs Thatcher, and the British Voter* (Ann Arbor, 1992).

Norporth, Helmut, "The Economy," in Lawrence LeDuc and Richard G. Niemi (eds.), *Comparing Democracies: Elections and Voting in Global Perspective* (Thousand Oaks, Calif., 1996), 299–318.

Norris, P., *Electoral Change in Britain* (Oxford, 1997).

North, Douglass C., *Institutions, Institutional Change, and Economic Performance* (New York, 1990).

——— and Weingast, Barry R., "Constitutions and Commitment: The Evolution of Institutions Governing Public Choice in Seventeenth-Century England," *Journal of Economic History*, 49, 4 (1989), 803–32.

Nove, Alec, *An Economic History of the USSR, 1917–1991*, 3rd edn. (London, 1992).

O'Brien, Patrick K., "The Costs and Benefits of British Imperialism, 1846–1914," *Past and Present*, 120 (1988), 163–200.

———, *Power with Profit: The State and the Economy, 1688–1815*, University of London inaugural lecture (London, 1991).

———, "Inseparable Connections: Trade, Economy, Fiscal State, and the Expansion of Empire, 1688–1815," in P. J. Marshall (ed.), *The Oxford History of the British Empire*, vol. ii: *The Eighteenth Century* (Oxford/New York, 1998), 53–77.

———, "Imperialism and the Rise and Decline of the British Economy, 1688–1989," *New Left Review*, 238 (1999), 48–80.

———, and Hunt, Philip A., "The Rise of a Fiscal State in England, 1485–1815," *Historical Research* (1993), 129–76.

——— and ———, "England, 1485–1815," in Richard Bonney (ed.), *The Rise of the Fiscal State in Europe, c.1200–1815* (Oxford, 1999), 53–100.

——— and Prados de la Escosura, Leandro, "Balance Sheets for the Acquisition, Retention and Loss of European Empires Overseas," Universidad Carlos III de Madrid Depto. de Historia Económica e Instituciones Working Paper (Dec. 1998).

Obstfeld, Maurice, "International Currency Experience: New Lessons and Lessons Relearned," paper presented at the 25th anniversary meeting of the Brookings Panel on Economic Activity, (6–7 Apr. 1995).

———, "EMU: Ready, or Not?," *NBER Working Paper*, (1998).

——— and Taylor, Alan M., "The Great Depression as a Watershed: International Capital Mobility over the Long Run," in Michael D. Bordo, Claudia Goldin and Eugene N. White (eds.), *The Defining Moment: The Great Depression and the American Economy in the Twentieth Century* (Chicago, 1998), 353–402.

Offer, Avner, *The First World War: An Agrarian Interpretation* (Oxford, 1989).

———, "The British Empire, 1870–1914: A Waste of Money?," *Economic History Review* (1993), 215–38.

———, "Costs and Benefits, Prosperity and Security, 1870–1914," in Andrew Porter (ed.), *The Oxford History of the Nineteenth Century*, vol. iii: *The Nineteenth Century* (Oxford/New York, 1999), 690–711.

———, "Between the Gift and the Market: The Economy of Regard," *Economic History Review*, 50 (1997), 450–76.

O'Leary, C., *The Elimination of Corrupt Practices in British Elections, 1868–1911* (Oxford, 1962).

Olson, Mancur, *The Rise and Decline of Nations: Economic Growth, Stagflation and Social Rigidities* (New Haven/London, 1982).

———, "Big Bills Left on the Sidewalk: Why Some Nations Are Rich, and Others Poor," *Journal of Economic Perspectives*, 10, 2 (1996), 3–24.

———, *Power and Prosperity: Outgrowing Communist and Capitalist Dictatorships* (New York, 2000).

Ormrod, W. M., "The West European Monarchies in the Later Middle Ages," in Richard Bonney (ed.), *Economic Systems and State Finance* (Oxford, 1995), 123–60.

———, "England in the Middle Ages," in Richard Bonney (ed.), *The Rise of the Fiscal State in Europe, c.1200–1815* (Oxford, 1999), 19–52.

——— and Barta, János, "The Feudal Structure and the Beginnings of State Finance," in Richard Bonney (ed.), *Economic Systems and State Finance* (Oxford, 1995), 53–79.

O'Rourke, Kevin H., and Williamson, Jeffrey G., *Globalization and History: The Evolution of a Nineteenth-Century Atlantic Economy* (Cambridge, Mass./London, 1999).

Overy, Richard, *War and Economy in the Third Reich* (Oxford, 1994).

———, *Why the Allies Won* (London, 1995).

———, (ed.), *The Times Atlas of the Twentieth Century* (London, 1996).

———, *Russia's War* (London, 1997).

———, *The Battle* (London, 2000).

Owen, R., *The Middle East and the World Economy, 1800–1914* (London, 1981).

Paddags, Norbert, "The German Railways—The Economic and Political Feasibility of Fiscal Reforms during the Inflation of the early 1920s," *University of Oxford Discussion Papers in Economic and Social History*, 13 (1997).

Paldam, Martin, "How Robust is the Vote Function? A Study of Seventeen Nations Over Four Decades," in Helmut Norpoth, Michael S. Lewis-Beck and Jean-Dominique Lafay (eds.) *Economics and Politics: The Calculus of Support* (Ann Arbor, 1991), 9–31.

Palgrave, R. H. Inglis, *Bank Rate and the Money Market in England, France, Germany, Holland and Belgium, 1844(1900* (New York, 1968 [1903]).

Panic, M., *European Monetary Union: Lessons from the Classical Gold Standard* (London, 1992).

Parker, Geoffrey, "The Emergence of Modern Finance in Europe, 1500–1730," in C. M. Cipolla (ed.), *The Fontana History of Europe*, vol. ii: *The Sixteenth and Seventeenth Centuries* (London, 1974), 527–94.

Partner, Peter, "The Papacy and the Papal States," in Richard Bonney (ed.), *The Rise of the Fiscal State in Europe, c.1200–1815* (Oxford, 1999), 359–80.

Peacock, Alan Turner, and Wiseman, Jack, *The Growth of Public Expenditure in the United Kingdom*, NBER Publication, 72 (Princeton, 1961).

Pennington, Reina, "Offensive Women: Women in Combat in the Red Army," in Paul Addison (ed.), *Time to Kill: The Soldier's Experience of War in the West 1939–1945* (London, 1997), 249–62.

Perkin, Harold, *The Rise of Professional Society: England since 1880* (London, 1989).

Perkins, Anthony B. and Michael C. Perkins, *The Internet Bubble: Inside the Overvalued World of High-Tech Stocks and What You Need to Know to Avoid the Coming Shakeout* (London, 2000).

Perrett, Byran (ed.), *The Battle Book: Crucial Conflicts in History from 1469 BC to the Present* (London, 1992).

Persson, T., and Svensson, L. E. O., "Why a Stubborn Conservative Would Run a Deficit: Policy with Time-Inconsistent Preferences," *Quarterly Journal of Economics*, 104 (1989), 325–45.

Peterson, Peter G., "Grey Dawn: The Global Aging Crisis," *Foreign Affairs*, (Jan./Feb. 1999), 42–55.

Petzina, D., Abelshauser, W., and Faust, A. (eds.), *Sozialgeschichtliches Arbeitsbuch*, vol. iii: *Materialien zur Statistik des Deutschen Reiches, 1914–1945* (Munich, 1978).

Pflanze, Otto, *Bismarck and the Development of Germany*, vol. ii: *The Period of Consolidation, 1871–1880* (Princeton, 1990).

Phillips, Kevin P., *The Cousins' Wars: Religion, Politics, and the Triumph of Anglo-America* (New York, 1999).

Pierre, Jon, and Widfeldt, Anders, "Party Organizations in Sweden: Colossuses with Feet of Clay or Flexible Pillars of Government," in Richard S. Katz and Peter Mair (eds.), *How Parties Organize: Change and Adaptation in Party Organizations in Western Democracies* (Thousand Oaks, Calif., 1994), 332–56.

Pinker, Steven, *How the Mind Works* (London, 1998).

Pinto-Duschinsky, Michael, *British Political Finance, 1830–1980* (Washington, 1981).

——, "Trends in British Party Funding 1983–1987," *Parliamentary Affair*, 4-2, 2 (1989), 197–212.

Pippenger, J., "Bank of England Operations, 1893–1913," in M. Bordo and A. Schwartz (eds.), *A Retrospective on the Classical Gold Standard* (Chicago, 1984) 203–32.

Poguntke, Thomas, "Parties in a Legalistic Culture: The Case of Germany," in Richard S. Katz and Peter Mair (eds.), *How Parties Organize: Change and Adaptation in Party Organization in Western Democracies* (Thousand Oaks, Calif., 1994), 185–215.

Pollard, Sidney, "Capital Exports, 1870–1914: Harmful or Beneficial?," *Economic History Review* (1985), 489–514.

Pollard, Stephen, and Adonis, Andrew, *A Class Act: The Myth of Britain's Classless Society* (London, 1997).

Posen, A., "Why Central Bank Independence Does Not Cause Low Inflation: There is No Institutional Fix," in R. O'Brien (ed.), *Finance and the International Economy*, vol. vii (Oxford, 1993), 4–65.

Poulsen, Bjorn, "Kingdoms of the Periphery of Europe: The Case of Medieval and Early Modern Scandinavia," in Richard Bonney (ed.), *Economic Systems and State Finance* (Oxford, 1995), 101–22.

Powell, G. Bingham Jr., and Whitten, Guy D., "A Cross-national Analysis of Economic Voting: Taking Account of the Political Context," *American Journal of Political Science*, 37 (1993) 391–414.

Prawer, S. S., *Heine's Jewish Comedy: A Study of his Portraits of Jews and Judaism* (Oxford, 1983).

Price, Simon, and Sanders, David, "Economic Competence, Rational Expectations and Government Popularity in Post-war Britain," *Occasional Papers of the ESRC Research Centre on Microsocial Change*, 4 (1991).

Pryce-Jones, David, *The War That Never Was* (London, 1995).

Przeworski, Adam "The Neo-liberal Fallacy," *Journal of Democracy*, 3 (1992), 45–59.

———, Alvarez, M., Cheibub, J. A. and Limongi, F., "What Makes Democracies Endure?" *Journal of Democracy*, 3 (1996), 39–55.

Pugh, Martin, *The Making of Modern British Politics, 1867–1939* (Oxford, 1982).

Pulzer, Peter, *The Rise of Political Anti-Semitism in Germany and Austria* (London, 1964).

Quin, Stephen, "Gold, Silver and the Glorious Revolution," *Economic History Review*, 49, 3 (1996), 473–90.

Raffelhüschen, Bernd, "Aging, Fiscal Policy and Social Insurances: A European Perspective," mimeo, Albert-Ludwigs-University of Freiburg, Germany and University of Bergen, Norway (1998).

Ramsden, J. *The Age of Churchill and Eden 1940–1957* (London, 1995).

———, *The Winds of Change: From Macmillan to Heath 1957–1975* (London, 1996).

Rasmussen, J., *Retrenchment and Revival: A Study of the Contemporary Liberal Party* (Tucson, Ariz., 1964).

Rezzori, Gregor von, *The Snows of Yesteryear: Portraits for an Autobiography* (London, 1991).

Richardson, L. F., *Statistics of Deadly Quarrels* (Pittsburgh, 1960).

Ricketts, M. *The Economics of Business Enterprise: New Approaches to the Firm* (Hassocks, Sussex, 1987).

Ridley, Nicholas, *"My Style of Government:" The Thatcher Years* (London, 1991).

Ritschl, Albrecht, "Sustainability of High Public Debt: What the Historical Record Shows," Centre for Economic Policy Research Discussion Paper (Feb. 1996).

Roberts, Andrew, *Salisbury: Victorian Titan* (London, 1999).

Roberts, J. "Structure and Organisation," Clarendon Lectures, Oxford, 29, 30 April 1997.

Roberts, Richard, *Inside International Finance: A Citizen's Guide to the World's Financial Markets, Institutions and Key Players* (London, 1998).

Rockoff, Hugh, "The Wizard of Oz as Monetary Allegory," *Journal of Political Economy* (1990), 739–60.

———, "The United States: From Ploughshares to Swords," in Mark Harrison (ed.), *The Economics of World War II: Six Great Powers in International Comparison* (Cambridge, 1998), 81–121.

Rodger, N. A. M., "Sea Power and Empire," in P. J. Marshall (ed.), *The Oxford History of the British Empire*, vol. ii: *The Eighteenth Century* (Oxford/New York, 1998), 169–83.

Roesler, K., *Die Finanzpolitik des Deutschen Reiches im Ersten Weltkrieg* (Berlin, 1967).

Rogowski, Ronald, *Commerce and Coalitions: How Trade Affects Domestic Political Alignments* (Princeton, 1989).

Romer, David, and Romer, Chris, "Does Monetary Policy Matter? A New Test in the Spirit of Friedman and Schwartz," *NBER Working Paper*, 2966 (1989).

Rosenbaum, M., *From Soapbox to Soundbite: Party Political Campaigning in Britain since 1945* (London, 1997).

Roth, Jean-Pierre, "A View from Switzerland in the Run Up to the Demonetisation of Gold," paper presented at the *Financial Times* World Gold Conference (14 June 1999), 3.1–3.5.

Rothschild, Lord [Victor], *"You Have It, Madam:" The Purchase, in 1875, of Suez Canal Shares by Disraeli and Baron Lionel de Rothschild* (London, 1980).

Rowley, Eric E., *Hyperinflation in Germany: Perceptions of a Process* (Aldershot, 1994).

Rubinstein, W. D., "British Millionaires, 1809–1989," *Bulletin of the Institute of Historical Research* (1974), 203–23.

———, "Jewish Participation in National Economic Elites, 1860–1939, and Anti-Semitism: An International Comparison," paper presented at the Australian Association for Jewish Studies Conference, Sydney 1997.

———, "Entrepreneurial Minorities: A Typology," unpublished paper.

Rudé, George, *The Crowd in History: A Study of Popular Disturbances in France and England, 1730–1848*, 3rd edn. (London, 1995).

Rummel, R. J., *Lethal Politics: Soviet Democide and Mass Murder since 1917* (New Brunswick, NJ, 1990).

———, *Democide: Nazi Genocide and Mass Murder* (New Brunswick, New Jersey, 1992).

———, *Statistics of Democide: Genocide and Mass Murder Since 1900* (New Brunswick, NJ, 1997).

Rush, M. *The Selection of Parliamentary Candidates* (London, 1969).

Russett, Bruce, "Counterfactuals about War and Its Absence," in Philip E. Tetlock and Aaron Belkin (eds.), *Counterfactual Thought Experiments in World Politics: Logical, Methodological and Psychological Perspectives* (Princeton, 1996), 171–86.

Rytlewski, Ralf (ed.), *Die Bundesrepublik in Zahlen: Ein sozialgeschichtliches Arbeitsbuch* (Munich, 1987).

Saatchi, Maurice, "Happiness Can't Buy Money," *Centre for Policy Studies Autumn Lecture* (1999).

Sacks, Jonathan, *Morals and Markets* (London, 1999).

Sanders, David, "Government Popularity and the Next Election," *Political Quarterly*, 62 (1991) 235–61.

———, "Why the Conservatives Won—Again," in Anthony King (ed.) *Britain at the Polls 1992* (Chatham, NJ, 1993), 171–222.

———, "Conservative Incompetence, Labour Responsibility and the Feelgood Factor: Why the Economy failed to Save the Tories in 1997," paper presented to Political Studies Conference on Elections, Public Opinion and Parties, Essex University, 26–28 September 1997.

Sarel, Michael, "Non-Linear Effects of Inflation on Economic Growth," *IMF Working Paper*, 95/56 (1995).

Sargent, Thomas J., "The Ends of Four Big Inflations," in Thomas J. Sargent, *Rational Expectations and Inflation* (New York, 1993), 43–116.

——, "Stopping Moderate Inflations: The Methods of Poincaré and Thatcher," in Thomas J. Sargent, *Rational Expectations and Inflation* (New York, 1993), 117–72.

—— and Wallace, Neil, "Some Unpleasant Monetarist Arithmetic," in Thomas J. Sargent, *Rational Expectations and Inflation* (New York, 1993), 173–210.

Särlvik, Bo, and Crewe, Ivor, *Decade of Dealignment* (Cambridge, 1983).

Sayers, Richard Sidney, *Bank of England Operations, 1890–1914* (London, 1936).

——, "The Bank in the Gold Market, 1890–1914," in R. S. Sayers and T. S. Ashton (eds.), *Papers in English Monetary History* (Oxford, 1953), 132–50.

——, *The Bank of England, 1891–1944*, 3 vols. (Cambridge, 1976).

Scammell, M., *Designer Politics: How Elections are Won* (Macmillan, London, 1995).

Schama, Simon, *Citizens: A Chronicle of the French Revolution* (London, 1989).

Schiel, Juliane, "Pillars of Democracy: A Study of the Democratisation Process in Europe after the First World War" (Oxford undergraduate thesis, 2000).

Schmitz, C. J., *The Growth of Big Business in the United States and Western Europe, 1850–1939* (London, 1993).

Schremmer, D. E., "Taxation and Public Finance: Britain, France and Germany," in Peter Mathias and Sidney Pollard (eds.), *The Cambridge Economic History of Europe,* vol. viii: *The Industrial Economies: the Development of Economic and Social Policies* (Cambridge, 1989), 315–494.

Schubert, Aurel, "The Dissolution of the Austro-Hungarian Currency Union," *European Association of Banking History Journal* (1999), unpag.

Schuker, S. "American "Reparations" to Germany, 1919–1933," in G. D. Feldman and E. Müller-Luckner (eds.), *Die Nachwirkungen der Inflation auf die deutsche Geschichte, 1924–1933* (Munich, 1985), 335–84.

Schultz, Kenneth A., and Weingast, Barry R., "The Democratic Advantage: The Institutional Sources of State Power in International Competition," *Hoover Institution on War, Revolution and Peace Essays in Public Policy,* 67 (1996).

Schulz, G., "Inflationstrauma, Finanzpolitik und Krisenbekämpfung in den Jahren der Wirtschaftskrise, 1930–33," in G. D. Feldman and E. Müller-Luckner (eds.), *Nachwirkungen der Inflatian auf die deutsche Geschichte, 1924–19,* 261–96 (Munich, 1985).

Schulze, Winfried, "The Emergence and Consolidation of the "Tax State," I: The Sixteenth Century," in Richard Bonney (ed.), *Economic Systems and State Finance* (Oxford, 1995), 261–80.

Schumpeter, Joseph A., *Capitalism, Socialism and Democracy* (London, 1987 [1943]).

——, "The Crisis of the Tax State," *International Economic Papers* (1954), 5–38, trans. of "Die Krise des Steuerstaates," *Zeitfragen aus dem Gebiet der Soziologie,* 4 (1918), 1–71.

Schwartz, Anna J., "Real and Pseudo-financial Crises," in F. Capie and G. E. Wood (eds.), *Financial Crises and the World Banking System* (London, 1986).

Schwarz, Gerhard, "Democracy and Market-oriented Reform—A Love-Hate Relationship?," *Economic Education Bulletin,* 32, 5 (1992), to come.

Scitovsky, T., *The Joyless Economy: An Inquiry into Human Satisfaction and Consumer Dissatisfaction* (Oxford, 1976).

Seldon, Arthur, *The Dilemma of Democracy: The Political Economics of Over-Government* (London, 1998).

Sen, Amartya, "Capability and Well-being," in Martha Nussbaum and Amartya Sen (eds.), *The Quality of Life* (Oxford, 1993), 30–53.

———, *Development as Freedom* (Oxford, 1999).

Seyd, P., and Whiteley, P., *Labour's Grass Roots: The Politics of Party Membership* (Oxford, 1992).

Sharpe, Kevin M., *The Personal Rule of Charles I* (New Haven/London, 1992).

Shaw, S. J., "Ottoman Expenditures and Budgets in the late Nineteenth and Twentieth Centuries," *International Journal of Middle East Studies* (1978), 373–8.

Shawcross, William, *Deliver Us From Evil: Peacekeepers, Warlords and a World of Endless Conflict* (London, 2000).

Sheehan, James J., *German History, 1770–1866* (Oxford, 1989).

Shermer, Michael, "Exorcising Laplace's Demon: Chaos and Antichaos, History and Metahistory," *History and Theory: Studies in the Philosophy of History*, 34, 1 (1995), 59–83.

Shigehara, Kumiharu, "Commentary: Long-Term Tendencies in Budget Deficits and Debt," in Federal Reserve Bank of Kansas City, *Budget Deficits and Debt: Issues and Options* (Kansas, 1995), 57–87.

Shiller, Robert J., *Irrational Exuberance* (Princeton, 2000).

Shin, Doh Chull, "On the Third Wave of Democratization: A Synthesis and Evaluation of Recent Theory and Research," *World Politics*, 47 (1994), 135–70.

Shleifer, Andrei, "Government in Transition," in Andrei Shleifer, and Robert W. Vishny (eds.), *The Grabbing Hand: Government Pathologies and Their Cures* (Cambridge, Mass./London, 1998), 227–53.

——— and DeLong, J. Bradford, "Princes and Merchants: European City Growth before the Industrial Revolution," in Andrei Shleifer and Robert W. Vishny (eds.), *The Grabbing Hand: Government Pathologies and Their Cures* (Cambridge, Mass./London, 1998), 19–52.

Shy, John, "The American Colonies in War and Revolution," in P. J. Marshall (ed.), *The Oxford History of the British Empire*, vol. ii: *The Eighteenth Century* (Oxford/New York, 1998), 300–24.

Siegel, Jeremy J., *Stocks for the Long Run* (New York, 2000).

———, *John Maynard Keynes*, vol. ii: *The Economist as Saviour, 1920–1937* (London, 1992).

Simon, C. A. "Alternative Visions of Rationality," in P. K. Moser (ed.), *Rationality in Action: Contemporary Approaches* (Cambridge, 1990), 189–204.

Sims, C. A., "The Precarious Fiscal Foundations of EMU," *DNB Staff Reports*, (1999).

Singer, J. David and Small, Melvin, *The Wages of War, 1816–1965* (Mich., 1972).

———, *Resort to Arms* (Beverly Hills, Calif., 1982).

Siverson, Randolph M., and Starr, Harvey, "Opportunity, Willingess and the Diffusion of War," *American Political Science Review*, 84, 1 (1990), 47–67.

Skidelsky, Robert, *John Maynard Keynes*, vol. I: *Hopes Betrayed, 1883–1920* (London, 1983).

Smith, Adam, *An Inquiry into the Nature and Causes of the Wealth of Nations* (London, 1982 [1776]).

Smith, K. C. and G. F. Horne, *An Index Number of Securities, 1867–1914*, London & Cambridge Economic Service, Special Memorandum, 37 (London, 1934).

Smithers, Andrew and Stephen Wright, *Valuing Wall Street: Protecting Wealth in Turbulent Markets* (London, 2000).

Sniderman, Paul M., and Brody, Richard A., "Coping: The Ethic of Self-Reliance," *American Journal of Political Science*, 21 (1977) 501–22.

Sollenberg, Margareta, Wallensteen, Peter, and Jato, Andrés, "Major Armed Conflicts," *SIPRI Yearbook 1999: Armaments, Disarmament and International Security* (1999).

Solow, Robert, "Welfare: The Cheapest Country," *New York Review of Books* (23 Mar. 2000), 20–3.

—— and Taylor, John B., *Inflation, Unemployment and Monetary Policy: The Alvin Hansen Symposium on Public Policy* (Cambridge, Mass., 1999).

Sombart, Werner, *Die Juden und das Wirtschaftsleben* (Leipzig, 1911).

Sorokin, P. A., *Social and Cultural Dynamics*, 4 vols. (New York, 1937–41).

Soto, Hernando de, *The Mystery of Capital: Why Capitalism Triumphs in the West and Fails Everywhere Else* (London, 2000).

Spalding, William F., *Tate's Modern Cambist, Centenary Edition: A Manual of the World's Monetary Systems, the Foreign Exchanges &c.*, 28th edn. (London, 1929).

Spurling, Hilary, *La Grande Thérése: The Greatest Swindle of the Century* (London, 1999).

Starr, H., "Democratic Dominoes: Diffusion Approaches to the Spread of Democracy." *Journal of Conflict Resolution*, 35 (1991), 356–81.

Statistical Abstract of the United States 1999: The National Data Book, 119th edition (1999).

Statistisches Bundesamt, *Statistisches Jahrbuch 1997* (Bonn, 1997).

Stein, Gabriel, "Mounting Debts: The Coming European Pension Crisis," *Politeia*, Policy Series, 4, (1997).

Stern, Fritz, *Gold and Iron: Bismarck, Bleichröder and the Building of the German Empire* (Harmondsworth, 1987).

Stevenson, Robert Louis, "Will O' the Mill," in Charles Neider (ed.), *The Complete Short Stories of Robert Louis Stevenson* (New York, 1998), 255–85.

Stigler, George, "General Economic Conditions and National Elections," *American Economic Review*, 62 (1973) 540–52.

——, *A Theory of Price*, 4th edn., (Macmillan, London, 1987).

Stockmar, Baron E. von, *Memoirs of Baron Stockmar*, 2 vols. (London, 1872).

Studlar, Donley T., McAllister, Ian, and Ascui, Alvaro, "Privatisation and the British Electorate: Microeconomic Policies, Macroeconomic Evaluations and Party Support," *American Journal of Political Science*, 34 (1990) 1077–1101.

Sussman, Nathan, and Yafeh, Yishay, "Institutions, Reforms and Country Risk: Lessons from Japanese Government Debt in the Meiji Era," *Journal of Economic History*, 60, 2 (2000), 442–67.

Svåsand, Lars, "Change and Adaptation in Norwegian Party Organizations," in Richard S. Katz and Peter Mair (eds.), *How Parties Organize: Change and Adaptation in Party Organizations in Western Democracies* (Thousand Oaks, Calif., 1994), 304–31.

Sylla, Richard, "Shaping the US Financial System, 1690–1913: The Dominant Role of Public Finance," in Richard Sylla, Richard Tilly and Gabriel Tortella (eds.), *The States, the Financial System and Economic Modernization* (Cambridge, 1999), 249–70.

Syrett, Harold C., and Cooke, Jacob E. (eds.) *The Papers of Alexander Hamilton*, 27 vols. (New York, 1961–87).

Tabellini, Guido, "The Politics of Intergenerational Redistribution," in Ben van Velthoven, Harrie Verbon and Frans van Winden (eds.), *The Political Economy of Government Debt* (Amsterdam/New York/Tokyo, 1993), 69–86.

Tanzi, Vito, and Lutz, Mark S., "Interest Rates and Government Debt: Are the Linkages Global Rather than National," in Ben van, Velthoven, Harrie Verbon and Frans van Winden (eds.), *The Political Economy of Government Debt* (Amsterdam/New York/Tokyo, 1993), 233–53.

Taylor, Alan M., "International Capital Mobility in History: The Saving-Investment Relationship," *NBER Working Paper*, 5743 (Sept. 1996).

Taylor, A. J. P., *The Struggle for Mastery in Europe, 1848–1918* (Oxford, 1954).

Taylor, John B., "Monetary Policy Implications of Greater Fiscal Discipline," in Federal Reserve Bank of Kansas City, *Budget Deficits and Debt: Issues and Options* (Kansas, 1995), 151–79.

Tebbit, Norman, *Upwardly Mobile: An Autobiography* (London, 1988).

Thane, Pat, "The Working Class and State 'Welfare' in Britain, 1880–1914," in David Gladstone (ed.), *Before Beveridge: Welfare before the Welfare State* (London, 1999), 86–112.

Thatcher, Margaret, *The Downing Street Years* (London, 1993).

Thielen, Peter Gerrit, *Karl August von Hardenberg, 1750–1822* (Cologne/Berlin, 1967).

Thompson, J. M., *Napoleon's Letters* (London, 1998).

Timechart Company, *The Timechart of Military History* (Rickmansworth, 1999).

Tobin, James and Nordhaus, William, "Is Growth Obsolete?" in *Essays in Economics: Theory and Policy* (Cambridge, Mass., 1982), 360–450.

Tocqueville, Alexis de, *Democracy in America*, the Henry Reeve text, as revised by Francis Bowen, now further corrected and edited . . . by Phillips Bradley, 2 vols. (New York, 1945 [1835, 1840]).

———, *The Old Regime and the French Revolution*, transl. Stuart Gilbert (Garden City, NY, 1955 [1856]).

Tolstoy, L. N., *War and Peace*, trans. Rosemary Edmonds, 2 vols. (Harmondsworth, 1978).

Towle, Philip, "Nineteenth-century Indemnities," unpublished paper (Cambridge, 1999).

Trevor-Roper, H. R. (ed.), *Hitler's Table Talk: His Private Conversations*, trans. Norman Cameron and R. H. Stevens, 3rd edn. (London, 2000).

Trollope, Anthony, *Can You Forgive Her?* (Oxford, 1999 [1864]).

———, *Phineas Finn, The Irish Member* (London, 1985 [1869]).

———, *The Prime Minister* (London, 1994 [1875–6]).

———, *The Duke's Children* (London, 1995 [1880]).

Tufte, Edward R., *Political Control of the Economy* (Princeton, 1978).

Vanhanen, T., *The Process of Democratization: A Comparative Study of 147 States, 1980–1988* (New York, 1990).

Velde, François R., and Weir, David R., "The Financial Market and Government Debt Policy in France, 1746–1793," *Journal of Economic History* (1992), 1–39.

Velthoven, Ben van, Harrie Verbon and Frans van Winden, "The Political Economy of Government Debt: A Survey," in Ben van Velthoven, Harrie Verbon and Frans van Winden (eds.), *The Political Economy of Government Debt* (North-Holland/Amsterdam/New York/Tokyo, 1993), 3–36.

Vickers, John, "Monetary Policy and Asset Prices," lecture at the Monetary, Macro and Finance Group 31st Annual Conference (September 1999).

Vilar, Pierre, *A History of Gold and Money, 1450–1920* (London, 1976).

Vincent, J. R., *The Formation of the British Liberal Party, 1857–1868* (2nd edn., Hassocks, Sussex, 1976).

Voth, Hans-Joachin, "A Tale of Five Bubbles—Asset Price Inflation and Central Ban Policy in Historical Perspective," unpublished paper, Centre for History and Economics, Cambridge (2000).

———, "With A Bang Not a Whimper: Pricking Germany's 'Stockmarket Bubble' in 1927 and the Slide into Depression," unpublished paper, Centre for History and Economics, Cambridge (2000).

Voth, Joachim, "The True Cost of Inflation: Expectations and Policy Options During Germany's Great Slump," *Working Paper of the Economics Department of the Universitat Pompeu Fabra* (Sept. 1999).

Wagner, Richard, *Mein Leben* (Munich, 1969).

Wallensteen, Peter, and Sollenberg, Margareta, "Armed Conflict and Regional Conflict Complexes, 1989–97," *Journal of Peace Research* (1998), 621–34.

Wallerstein, Immanuel, *The Modern World-System*, vol. iii: *The Second Era of Great Expansion of the Capitalist World-Economy, 1730–1840s* (San Diego, Calif., 1989).

Warburg, Max M., *Aus meinen Aufzeichnungen* (privately printed, 1952).

Ward, Michael D. *et al.*, "The Spatial and Temporal Diffusion of Democracy, 1946–1994," paper presented at the 37th Annual Conference of the International Studies Association (Nov. 1997).

——— and Gleditsch, Kristian, "Democratising for Peace," *American Political Science Review*, 92, 1 (1998), 51–61.

Ware, Dick, "The IMF and Gold," *World Gold Council Research Study*, 20 (July 1998).

Weatherford, Stephen M., "Economic Conditions and Electoral Outcomes: Class Differences in the Political Response to Recession," *American Journal of Political Science*, 22 (1978), 917–38.

Webb, Paul D., "Party Organizational Change in Britain: The Iron Law of Centralization?," in Richard S. Katz and Peter Mair (eds.) *How Parties Organize: Change and Adaptation in Party Organizations in Western Democracies* (Thousand Oaks, Calif., 1994),

Webb, Stephen B., *Hyperinflation and Stabilization in Weimar Germany* (New York/Oxford, 1989).

Weber, Max, *The Protestant Ethic and the Spirit of Capitalism*, trans. Talcott Parsons (London, 1991).

Weiss, Linda, and Hobson, John M., *States and Economic Development: A Comparative Historical Analysis* (Cambridge, 1995).

Wells, John, and Wills, Douglas, "Revolution, Restoration and Debt Repudiation: The Jacobite Threat to England's Institutions and Growth," *Journal of Economic History*, 60, 2 (2000), 418–41.

Wharburton, Peter, *Debt and Delusion: Central Bank Politics that Threaten Economic Disaster* (London, 1999).

Wheen, Francis, *Karl Marx* (London, 1999).

White, Eugene N., "Was there a Solution to the *Ancien Régime*'s Financial Dilemma?," *Journal of Economic History*, 49 (1989), 545–68.

———, "The French Revolution and the Politics of Government Finance, 1770–1815," *Journal of Economic History*, 55 (1995), 227–55.

———, "France and the Failure to Modernize Macroeconomic Institutions," paper presented at the 12th International Economic History Congress, Madrid, (Aug. 1998).

———, "Making the French Pay: The Costs and Consequences of the Napoleonic Reparations," *NBER Working Paper* 7438 (Dec. 1999).

Whiteside, Noel, "Private Provision and Public Welfare: Health Insurance between the Wars," in David Gladstone (ed.), *Before Beveridge: Welfare before the Welfare State* (London, 1999), 26–42.

Williams, Jonathan (ed.), with Joe Cribb and Elizabeth Errington, *Money: A History* (London, 1997).

Williams, Penry, *The Tudor Regime* (Oxford, 1979).

Wilson, J. F., *British Business History, 1720–1994* (Manchester, 1995).

Wilson, Jack, Sylla, Richard, and Jones, Charles P., "Financial Market Volatility: Panics Under the National Banking System before 1914, and Volatility in the Long Run, 1830–1988," in Eugene N. White (ed.), *Crashes and Panics: A Historical Perspective* (Homewood, 1990), to come.

Winch, D., "The Political Economy of Public Finance in the "Long" Eighteenth Century," in J. Maloney (ed.), *Debts and Deficits: An Historical Perspective* (Cheltenham, 1998), 8–26.

Winckler, Georg, Hochreiter, Eduard and Brandner, Peter, "Deficits, Debt and European Monetary Union: Some Unpleasant Fiscal Arithmetic," in G. Calvo and M.

King (eds.), *The Debt Burden and its Consequences for Monetary Policy* (London, 1998), 254–76.

Winter, J. M., *The Great War and the British People* (London, 1985).

Witt, Peter-Christian, "Finanzpolitik und sozialer Wandel in Krieg und Inflation 1918–1924, in H. Mommsen, D. Petzina and B. Weisbrod (eds.), *Industrielles System und Politische Entwicklung in der Weimarer Republik*, 2 vols. (Düsseldorf, 1977), 395–425.

———, "Tax Policies, Tax Assessment and Inflation: Towards a Sociology of Public Finances in the German Inflation, 1914 to 1923," in id. (ed.), *Wealth and Taxation in Central Europe: The History and Sociology of Public Finance* (Leamington Spa/Hamburg/New York, 1987), 137–160.

Wolfe, Tom, *The Bonfire of the Vanities* (London, 1988).

Wood, Geoffrey, "Great Crashes in History: Have They Lessons for Today?," paper presented at the conference on financial crises, Somerville College, Oxford (9–10 July 1999).

———, "Central Bank Independence: Historical Evidence and the Recent British Experience," paper presented at Conference on Central Bank Independence: The Economic Foundations, Stockholm University (Dec. 1999).

Woodford, Michael, "Control of the Public Debt: A Requirement for Price Stability?," in G. Calvo and M. King (eds.), *The Debt Burdens and its Consequences for Monetary Policy* (London, 1998), 117–???.

Wormell, Jeremy, *The Management of the National Debt of the UK, 1900–1932* (Oxford, 2000).

Wright, J. F., "The Contribution of Overseas Savings to the Funded National Debt of Great Britain, 1750–1815," *Economic History Review*, 50, 4 (1997), 657–74.

Wright, Quincy, *A Study of War* (Chicago, 1942).

Yeager, L. B., "Fluctuating Exchange Rates in the 19th Century: The Experiences of Russia and Austria," in R. Mundell and A. Swoboda (eds.), *Monetary Problems of the International Economy* (Chicago, 1969).

Yergin, Daniel, and Stanislaw, Joseph, *The Commanding Heights: The Battle between Government and the Marketplace that is Remaking the Modern World* (New York, 1999).

Zakaria, Fareed, "The Rise of Illiberal Democracy," *Foreign Affairs*, 76, 6 (1997), 23–43.

Zamagni, Vera, "Italy: How to Lose the War and Win the Peace," in Mark Harrison (ed.), *The Economics of World War II: Six Great Powers in International Comparison* (Cambridge, 1998), 177–223.

Zevin, R. B., "Are World Financial Markets More Open? If So, Why and With What Effects?," in T. Banuri and J. Schor (eds.), *Financial Openness and National Autonomy* (Oxford, 1992), 43–83.

Ziegler, Dieter, *Das Korsett der "Alten Dame:" Die Geschäftspolitik der Bank of England, 1844–1913* (Frankfurt am Main, 1990).

Zola, Émile, *L'Assommoir*, trans. Leonard Tancock (Harmondsworth, 1970 [1876]).

Index